ROUTLEDGE HANDBOOK OF
ENVIRONMENTAL POLICY IN CHINA

T0320260

During the last few decades, China has accomplished unprecedented economic growth and has emerged as the second largest economy in the world. This 'economic miracle' has led hundreds of millions of people out of poverty, but has also come at a high cost. Environmental degradation and the impact of environmental pollution on health are nowadays issues of the greatest concern for the Chinese public and the government.

The *Routledge Handbook of Environmental Policy in China* focuses on the environmental challenges of China's rapidly growing economy and provides a comprehensive overview of the policies developed to address the environmental crisis. Leading international scholars and practitioners examine China's environmental governance efforts from an interdisciplinary perspective. Divided into five parts, the handbook covers the following key issues:

- **Part I:** Development of Environmental Policy in China – Actors and Institutions
- **Part II:** Key Issues and Strategies for Solution
- **Part III:** Policy Instruments and Enforcement
- **Part IV:** Related Policy Fields – Conflicts and Synergies
- **Part V:** China's Environmental Policy in the International Context.

This comprehensive handbook will be an invaluable resource to students and scholars of environmental policy and politics, development studies, Chinese studies, geography and international relations.

Eva Sternfeld is currently visiting professor at the Institute for East Asian Studies at Freie Universität Berlin, Germany. Previously she was director of the Center for Cultural Studies on Science and Technology in China at Technische Universität Berlin and for eight years worked as foreign expert at the Center for Environmental Education and Communication (CEEC) of the Chinese Ministry for Environmental Protection in Beijing, China.

"Understanding China's environmental challenges is critical to understanding China. This handbook offers a comprehensive guide, both to the gravity of the air, water, soil, bio-diversity and other crises, and to the current policy initiatives that seek to address them. Essential reading on a subject of global importance."

– Isabel Hilton, Founder and CEO, www.chinadialogue.net, UK

"The *Routledge Handbook of Environmental Policy in China* brings together a collection of experts from around the world. Their essays delve into the evolution of the state of the environment in China today as well as the country's role in global environmental policy. This book is more than just a great handbook – it is a significant scholarly work as well as a solid reference volume."

– Richard Louis Edmonds, Former Editor of The China Quarterly, *France*

"For anyone who wants to be brought up-to-date on the dramatic environmental, climate, and sustainability policies and programs in China, the initiatives of Chinese leadership to create an ecological civilization and the progress and challenges in program implementation, this book is a must read. This is an excellent collection of contributions addressing China's increasingly ambitious environmental agenda."

– Miranda Schreurs, Professor of Environment and Climate Policy,
Bavarian School of Public Policy at the Technical University of Munich, Germany

ROUTLEDGE HANDBOOK OF ENVIRONMENTAL POLICY IN CHINA

Edited by Eva Sternfeld

LONDON AND NEW YORK

First published 2017
by Routledge

2 Park Square, Milton Park, Abingdon, Oxfordshire OX14 4RN

52 Vanderbilt Avenue, New York, NY 10017

Routledge is an imprint of the Taylor & Francis Group, an informa business

First issued in paperback 2019

British Library Cataloguing-in-Publication Data
A catalogue record for this book is available from the British Library

Library of Congress Cataloging-in-Publication Data
Names: Sternfeld, Eva, editor.
Title: Routledge handbook of environmental policy in China / edited by Eva Sternfeld.
Other titles: Handbook of environmental policy in China
Description: Abingdon, Oxon ; New York, NY : Routledge, 2017. | Includes bibliographical references.
Identifiers: LCCN 2016046508| ISBN 9781138831117 (hb) | ISBN 9781315736761 (ebook)
Subjects: LCSH: Environmental policy--China. | Environmental protection--China. | China--Environmental conditions. | Economic development--Environmental aspects--China. | China--Politics and government--2002-
Classification: LCC GE190.C6 R68 2017 | DDC 363.7/05610951--dc23
LC record available at https://lccn.loc.gov/2016046508

ISBN: 978-1-138-83111-7 (hbk)
ISBN: 978-0-367-27709-3 (pbk)

Typeset in Bembo
by Saxon Graphics Ltd, Derby

CONTENTS

PART II
Key issues and strategies for solution   **69**

PART III
Policy instruments and enforcement   **191**

FIGURES

TABLES

NOTES ON CONTRIBUTORS

Anna L. Ahlers is Associate Professor of Modern Chinese Society and Politics at the University of Oslo. Trained in Sinology and Political Science, her research interests include the administrative system and local governance in China, as well as the comparative analysis of value patterns and inclusion formulas in authoritarian regimes.

Mariachiara Alberton has a PhD in Law and Economics and is Senior Researcher in Environmental Law at the European Academy (EURAC), Bolzano/Bozen (Italy). She has published monographs and edited books and articles on international and EU environmental law and climate change. She is the legal consultant/team leader of several EU-funded projects.

Julian Barg is a research scholar at the Peking University HSBC Business School Center for Green Economy, where he is in charge of international cooperation as a general secretary. Currently pursuing a Master's in Management, his research focuses on sustainability and cooperation in business.

Bettina Bluemling is an Assistant Professor at the Copernicus Institute of Sustainable Development at Utrecht University, the Netherlands. Her research focuses on different modes of environmental governance in rural China.

Cao Guozhi is a research assistant and PhD candidate at the Environmental Risk and Damage Assessment Center, Chinese Academy for Environmental Planning, MEP, with two books and over twenty peer-reviewed papers published.

Chris Coggins (Geography/Asian Studies, Bard College at Simon's Rock) specializes in rural China, political ecology, biodiversity, and nature conservation. He is co-editor (with Emily Yeh) of *Mapping Shangrila: Contested Landscapes of the Sino-Tibetan Borderlands* (2014), and author of *The Tiger and the Pangolin: Nature, Culture, and Conservation in China* (2003).

Sam Geall is a research fellow at the University of Sussex, Executive Editor of chinadialogue. net and Associate Fellow at Chatham House. He edited *China and the Environment: The Green*

Revolution (2013). He was formerly Departmental Lecturer in Human Geography of China at the University of Oxford.

Olivia Gippner is a Dahrendorf postdoctoral fellow at the London School of Economics and Political Science. She specializes in EU–China climate relations and Chinese bureaucratic politics. Her studies on the 2°C temperature target in China and the framing of climate policy were published in Energy Policy and International Environmental Agreements.

Mette Halskov Hansen is Professor of Modern Chinese Society and Politics at the University of Oslo. Her interest in how people's ways of living connect to larger political processes has led to a number of research projects and publications regarding minority identity and education, colonization of border areas, processes of individualization and, most recently, the human dimensions of air pollution in China.

Heike Hartmann is an Associate Professor in the Department of Geography, Geology, and the Environment at Slippery Rock University of Pennsylvania and a lecturer in the Department of Geosciences at the University of Tübingen. She carries out research at the intersection of climatology and hydrology.

Gørild Heggelund, PhD, Senior Research Fellow and China Representative, Fridtjof Nansen Institute (FNI), has carried out research on China's environmental, energy and climate change policy for three decades. From 2009–2014 she was Senior Climate Change Advisor at UNDP China. Gørild has lived and worked in China for many years and is fluent in Chinese, having studied at Peking University.

Jennifer Holdaway is a Senior Research Fellow at the School of Interdisciplinary Area Studies of the University of Oxford. Since 2008 she has been co-Director of the Forum on Health, Environment and Development (FORHEAD), which has pioneered an interdisciplinary approach to understanding environmental health problems associated with China's rapid industrialization and urbanization.

Hu Tao is China Program Director of WWF US and serves as chairman of the Board for the Professional Association for China's Environment (PACE). He was a senior fellow and senior associate at World Resources Institute (WRI). Prior to joining WRI, he was the Senior Environmental Economist of Policy Research Center of the Ministry of Environmental Protection (MEP), China. He also served as the Senior Program Coordinator of UN–China Climate Change Partnership Framework Program (CCPF) during 2009–2010 and served as a member of Lead Expert Group China Council for International Cooperation on Environment and Development (CCICED) during 2001–2007.

Huang Haifeng obtained his PhD at Humboldt University Berlin and studied at the School of Economics of Peking University and at the Johns Hopkins University-Nanjing University Center for Chinese and American Studies. Professor Huang is a full-time Professor and Assistant Dean at Peking University HSBC Business School, and is in charge of Peking University PHBS Center for Green Economy. He is a senior member of the supervisory committee of the Ministry of Land and Resources (2010–2020), and the Chair of Academic Committee in Asia Education Forum.

Jia Qian is a research assistant at the Environmental Risk and Damage Assessment Center, Chinese Academy for Environmental Planning, MEP, with eight peer-reviewed papers published.

Jia Shaofeng is Director of the Department of Water Resources, Institute of Geographic Sciences and Natural Resources Research, Chinese Academy of Sciences. His research focuses on water resources assessment under changing environment, water resources planning, water resources economics, water resources institutions and governance. He is author of more than 150 papers and six books.

Thomas R. Johnson is a lecturer at the Department of Politics, University of Sheffield. Previously he worked as assistant professor in the Department of Public Policy at City University of Hong Kong. His research focuses on Chinese politics and society. He is especially interested in how people in China respond to pollution and in the interplay between regulation and contentious politics.

Genia Kostka is Professor of Chinese Politics at the Free University of Berlin and Fellow at the Hertie School of Governance. Her research and teaching interests are in energy and climate change governance, public policy and political economy, with a regional focus on China. In addition to her extensive academic writing, she regularly consults for international organizations, such as the Asian Development Bank, AusAID, OECD, Oxfam and the World Bank.

Joanna I. Lewis is Associate Professor of Science, Technology and International Affairs at Georgetown University's Edmund A. Walsh School of Foreign Service and Faculty Affiliate in the China Energy Group at the US Department of Energy's Lawrence Berkeley National Laboratory. She has conducted research in China for over fifteen years.

Li Na is a Lecturer at the Law School, Yunnan University, China. Her research focuses on regulation and compliance studies in comparative perspective.

Liu Wenling got her doctoral degree of Environmental Sociology from Wageningen University in 2013 and is now working as an assistant professor at the Center for Energy and Environmental Policy, Beijing Institute of Technology. Her research mainly focuses on household (energy) consumption behaviour and the effectiveness of environmental policy.

Arthur P.J. Mol is Rector Magnificus/Vice-President at Wageningen University & Research, the Netherlands, and Professor in environmental policy at the same institution. He has held visiting professorships at Renmin University and Tsinghua University (China), Chiba University (Japan) and National University of Malaysia (Malaysia). He lectured and published widely on environmental governance, globalization, ecological modernization, South East and East Asia, sustainable production and consumption, and sustainable and smart cities.

Scott Moore is a political scientist specializing in water and environmental politics, especially in China. At the time of writing he is serving as a Council on Foreign Relations International Affairs Fellow.

Rebecca Nadin is the Head of Risk & Resilience at the Overseas Development Institute (ODI), UK. She has more than 14 years' government and consultancy experience in China and Asia.

James E. Nickum, an institutional economist, was a member of the 1974 US Water Resources Delegation to China, and has investigated various aspects of China's water governance ever since. Now busily retired, he lives in Tokyo. He has been Editor-in-Chief of *Water International* since 2007.

Andreas Oberheitmann is Professor at the Sino-German School of Business and Technology of FOM University of Applied Sciences in Essen, Germany. Between 2007 and 2013 he was International Director of the Research Center for International Environmental Policy at the School of Environment of Tsinghua University in Beijing. The focus of his research is environmental policy, especially climate change policy.

Jarmila Ptackova studied Chinese and Central Asian Studies at the Humboldt University in Berlin, where she also obtained her PhD in Tibetan Studies. For several years she has focused on the social and economic changes in ethnic minority areas of western China. She worked as a researcher and lecturer at Leipzig University and at Humboldt University. Currently she is affiliated with the Oriental Institute of the Czech Academy of Sciences in Prague.

Qin Tianbao is Luojia Professor of Law, Director of Research Institute of Environmental Law (RIEL) and Associate Dean for the School of Law, Professor of China Institute of Boundary and Ocean Studies and the European Studies Centre, Wuhan University. He is also co-Chief Editor of *Chinese Journal of Environmental Law*.

Patrick Schroeder is a research fellow at the Institute of Development Studies, University of Sussex. His research is concerned with the transition to a circular economy within the context of sustainable consumption and production (SCP) systems. He previously worked in EU–China development cooperation programmes, including the SWITCH-Asia Programme, and for the German Corporation for International Cooperation (GIZ/CIM).

Yvan Schulz is a PhD candidate in Anthropology at the University of Neuchâtel, a visiting researcher at the University of Oxford and an associate researcher at Sun Yat-sen University. His research focuses on discarded electronics in China and analyses the so-called 'formalization' of recycling.

Judith Shapiro directs the Master's in Natural Resources and Sustainable Development at American University's School of International Service in Washington, DC. She was one of the first Americans to live in China after US–China relations were normalized in 1979. She is the author, co-author or editor of seven books, including *China's Environmental Challenges* (Polity 2012, 2016), *Mao's War against Nature* (Cambridge 2001) and *Son of the Revolution* (with Liang Heng, Knopf 1983).

Sheng Chunhong obtained her PhD from the Environmental Policy Research Center of Free University of Berlin. Her research focus includes green development, energy and environmental policy, and corporate social responsibility in China.

Song Peng is a Lecturer at the School of Public Affairs, and the Center for Population Resource Environment Economics and Management, Chongqing University, China. He is a member of Chinese Society for Environmental Economics (CSEE) and a member of the Professional Association for China's Environment (PACE). His research fields of interest are environmental economics and policy, trade and the environment, strategic environmental assessment and environmental planning and management.

Susanne Stein is a researcher at the Institute for Eastern European History and Area Studies, University of Tübingen, and a centre associate at the University Center for International Studies, University of Pittsburgh. Her current research focuses on the environmental history of China's northern drylands from the 1950s to the present.

Eva Sternfeld is a visiting professor at the Institute for East Asian Studies at Freie Universität Berlin. Her research focuses on China's environmental history, resource economy and environmental governance. Previously she was director of the Center for Cultural Studies on Science and Technology in China at Technische Universität Berlin and worked for eight years as a foreign expert at the Center for Environmental Education and Communication (CEEC) of the Chinese Ministry for Environmental Protection in Beijing.

Benjamin Steuer is a PhD candidate at the University of Vienna (Austria). His thesis centres on the Chinese circular economy, specifically urban waste management. Employing an approach of the Old Institutional Economics, Steuer aims to analyse the interactive dynamics between formal and informal institutions in the circular economy context.

Paul Hugo Suding is a German energy and development economist with over forty years of work experience in academics, consulting and international cooperation. He holds a diploma in Business Administration and a doctorate in Economics, and has published extensively. He has worked at the Cologne Institute of Energy Economics, ENERWA and ELSUD consulting, was programme director for GIZ in Burundi, China and Egypt, and seconded to OLADE, REN21 and to the Inter-American Development Bank.

Benjamin van Rooij is the John S. and Marilyn Long Professor of US–China Business and Law. His research focuses on implementation of law, with a focus on China in comparative perspective.

Wang Can is Professor at the Environmental Systems Analysis Division, School of Environment, Tsinghua University. He works in multi-disciplinary assessment of climate and environment policies and economics, covering the topics of carbon tax, emissions trading, low carbon transition, water–energy nexus, etc.

Wang Qiliang is the Professor of Law School, Yunnan University, China. His research focuses on implementation of law, legal anthropology and sociology studies in China.

Yang Weishan is a research assistant and PhD candidate at the Environmental Risk and Damage Assessment Center, Chinese Academy for Environmental Planning, MEP, who is researching environmental performance assessment, environmental and economic accounting and environmental data analysis, with ten peer-reviewed papers and five co-edited books published.

Yu Fang is Senior Researcher at the Environmental Risk and Damage Assessment Center of the Chinese Academy for Environmental Planning, MEP, and is mainly engaged in the study of environmental risk management, environmental damage assessment, environmental and economic accounting, and environmental and health effect. Yu Fang is author of two books and over sixty peer-reviewed papers.

Zhang Meng is a PhD student at the Centre for Environmental and Energy Law, Ghent University.

Zhang Xuehua is Professor of Environmental Policy and Resource Management at the Institute of New Energy and Low-carbon Technology, Sichuan University. Her research focuses on environmental policy implementation and compliance, agricultural sustainability and waste management.

Zhu Qiaoqiao is Lecturer of Finance in the College of Business and Economics, Australia National University. His research, besides financial market issues, focuses on how laws and regulations affect economic activities, especially in emerging markets.

Zhu Wenying is a research assistant and PhD candidate at the Environmental Risk and Damage Assessment Center, Chinese Academy for Environmental Planning, MEP.

ABBREVIATIONS

3 Rs	reduce, reuse, and recycle
10 YFP	10 Year Framework Plan (on Sustainable Consumption)
ACCC	Adapting to Climate Change in China
AMSC	American Superconductor
APAP	Action Plan on Prevention and Control of Air Pollution
APEC	Asian Pacific Economic Cooperation
APPCL	Air Pollution Prevention and Control Law
AQI	air quality index
AQSIQ	General Administration of Quality Supervision, Inspection and Quarantine
ASEAN	Association of Southeast Asian Nations
BAU	business-as-usual
BIPV	building-integrated photovoltaic
BOD	biochemical oxygen demand
BOT	build, operate and transfer
BSAP	Biodiversity Conservation Strategy and Action Plan
CAFTA	China ASEAN Free Trade Agreement
CASE	China Association for Scientific Exploration
CASS	Chinese Academy of Social Sciences
CBRC	China Banking Regulatory Commission
CCICED	China Council on International Cooperation and Development
CCP	Chinese Communist Party
CCS	Carbon Capture and Storage
CCTV	China Central Television
CDC	Chinese Centre for Disease Control and Prevention
CDE	carbon dioxide equivalent
CDM	Clean Development Mechanism
CE	circular economy
CE3-GEM	China Energy–Economy–Environmental General Equilibrium Model
CEC	China Environmental United Certification Center
CECP	China Energy Conservation Program

CEERHAPS	Chinese Environmental Exposure-Related Human Activity Patterns Survey
CEES	China Ecological Economic Society
CEL	China Energy Label
CELC	China Energy Label Center
CEPL	Circular Economy Promotion Law
CER	certified emission reduction
CFDA	China Food and Drug Administration
CIRC	China Insurance Regulatory Commission
C-J-K FTA	China–Japan–South Korea Free Trade Agreement
CMA	China Meteorological Administration
CNOOC	China National Offshore Oil Corporation
CNPC	China National Petroleum Corporation
CO_2	carbon dioxide
COD	chemical oxygen demand
COSC	Counsellors' Office at the State Council
CPC	Communist Party of China
CPPCC	Chinese People's Political Consultative Conference
CPPL	Cleaner Production Promotion Law
CQC	China Quality Certification Center
CSC	China Scholarship Council
CSR	corporate social responsibility
CSRC	China Securities Regulatory Commission
CTE	Committee on Trade and Environment
DALYs	disability-adjusted life years
DEDs	discarded electrical and electronic devices
DG CLIMA	Directorate-General for Climate Action
DRC	(Provincial) Development and Reform Commission
ECP	energy conservation products
EDC	Environmental Development Center
EEA	Environmental examination and approval
EGP	EU–China Environmental Governance Programme
EIA	environmental impact assessment
EIARTR	environmental impact assessment restriction targeting region
EIP	eco-industrial park
EIP	electronic information product
EIR	environmental impact report
ELITE cities	eco and low-carbon indicator tool for evaluating cities
ELP	eco labelling products
ENGO	environmental non-governmental organization
EPA	Environmental Protection Agency (US)
EPB	Environmental Protection Bureau
EPI	environmental performance index
EPL	Environmental Protection Law
EPR	extended producer responsibility
ETR	export tax rebate
ETS	emissions trading scheme/system
EU	European Union
EU DG	EU Directorate General

EU ETSEU	emissions trading scheme/system
FAO	Food and Agricultural Organization of the United Nations
FCL	Firearms Control Law
FDI	foreign direct investment
FNR	Fifth National Report on Implementation of the Convention on Biological Biodiversity
FON	Friends of Nature
FORHEAD	Forum on Health, Environment and Development
FTA	free trade agreement
ft asl	feet above sea level
FYP	Five-Year Plan
GDP	gross domestic product
GEA	governmental environmental audit
GHG	greenhouse gases
GIZ	German Agency for International Cooperation
GLF	Great Leap Foward
GMD	Guomindang (KMT Kuomintang, Chinese Nationalist Party)
GONGO	Government-organized non-governmental organization
GPP	Green Public Procurement
GPS	global positioning system
GRI	Global Reporting Initiative
GSCM	green supply chain management
HHP	highly hazardous pesticides (HHP)
HP	Hewlett-Packard
ICAP	International Carbon Action Partnership
ICBC	Industrial and Commercial Bank of China
IDNDP	UN International Decade for Natural Disaster Prevention
IMF	International Monetary Fund
INDC	Intended national determined contribution
IP	intellectual property
IPE	Institute of Public and Environmental Affairs
IPO	initial public offering
IRC	Insurance Regulation Committee
ISB	Insurance Supervision Bureau
ISO	International Organization for Standardization
IUCN	International Union for the Conservation of Nature
Jing-Jin-Ji	Beijing, Tianjin and Hebei region
KFP	(Six) Key Forestry Projects
Kt	kiloton (1,000 tons)
kW	kilowatt
kWh	kilowatt-hour
Lao PDR	Lao People's Democratic Republic
LCR	local content requirement
LNG	liquefied natural gas
LVRT	low-voltage ride through
m	metre
MAB	UNESCO Man and the Biosphere Programme

MAPCEIP	Measures for Administration on Pollution Control of Electronic Information Products
MEA	multilateral environmental agreements
MEP	Ministry of Environmental Protection
MIIT	Ministry of Industry and Information Technology
MOA	Ministry of Agriculture
MOF	Ministry of Finance
MOFCOM	Ministry of Commerce
MOH	Ministry of Health
MOHURD	Ministry of Housing and Urban-Rural Development
MOLR	Ministry of Land and Resources
MOST	Ministry of Science and Technology
MoU	Memorandum of Understanding
MRV	measurement, reporting and verification
MSW	municipal solid waste
MW	megawatt
MWR	Ministry of Water Resources
NAFTA	North American Free Trade Agreement
NAS	National Adaptation Strategy
NCCPC	National Congress of Chinese Communist Party
NDC	nationally determined contribution
NDRC	National Development and Reform Commission
NEA	National Energy Administration
NEC	National Energy Commission
NEPA	National Environmental Protection Agency
NFPP	Natural Forest Protection Plan
NGO	non-governmental organization
ngTEQ/m^3	nanogram of toxic equivalent per cubic metre
NIMBY	'not in my back yard'
NKEFA	National Key Ecological Function Areas
NPC	National People's Congress
NPPCC	National (Chinese) People's Political Consultative Conference
NRL	Nature Reserve Law
NSAP	National Sector Adaptation Plan
OBOR	One Belt One Road
OECD	Organisation for Economic Co-operation and Development
OFDI	overseas foreign direct investment
OfN	'old for new' take-back scheme
OGIR	Open Government Information Regulations of the People's Republic of China
OLS	ordinary least squares
PAH	polycyclic aromatic hydrocarbon
PAP	Provincial Adaptation Plan
PBB	polybrominated biphenyls
PBDE	polybrominated diphenyl ethers
PBOC	People's Bank of China
PCF	phosphorous carbon fluorine
pes	primary energy intensity
PES	payment for ecosystem services

pfo	perflourooctanoate
PITI	Pollution Information and Transparency Index
PLA	People's Liberation Army
$PM_{2.5}$, PM_{10}	particulate matter
POP	product of population
POPs	persistent organic pollutants
PRC	People's Republic of China
PRCEE	Policy Research Centre for Environment and Economy
PRTR	Pollution Release and Transfer Registry
PV	photovoltaics
PX	paraxylene
R&D	research and development
REACH	registration, evaluation, authorization and restriction of chemicals
RMB	renminbi
RoHS	Restriction of Hazardous Substances
RTA	regional trade agreement
S&T	science and technology
SAC	Standardization Administration of China
SASAC	State-owned Assets and Administration Commission
SC	State Council
SCP	sustainable consumption and production
SDG	Sustainable Development Goals
SDPC	State Development Planning Commission
SEA	strategic environmental assessment
SEPA	State Environmental Protection Administration
SERC	State Electricity Regulatory Commission
SETC	State Economic and Trade Commission
SFA	State Forest Administration
SIA	sustainability impact assessment
SLCP	Sloping Lands Conversion Program
SME	small and medium enterprises
SNWDP	South-to-North Water Diversion Project (*Nanshui Beidiao*)
SO_2	sulphur dioxide
SOA	State Oceanic Administration
SOE	state-owned enterprise
SPC	State Power Corporation
SPF	Strategic Programme Fund
SPP	Sustainable Public Procurement
SSC CC	South–South Cooperation Climate Change Programme
SSE	Shanghai Stock Exchange
STAACC	Scientific and Technological Action for Addressing Climate Change
SWEPPL	Solid Waste Environmental Pollution Prevention Law
SWRMS	strictest water resources management system
SZSE	Shenzhen Stock Exchange
tce	tons of coal equivalent
TNC	The Nature Conservancy
TQEM	total quality environmental management
TRAFFIC	The Wildlife Trade Monitoring Network (international NGO)

TRI	Toxics Release Inventory
TRL	Three Red Lines
TVE	Township and Village Enterprises
TWh	terrawatt-hour
UK	United Kingdom
UNCCD	UN Convention to Combat Desertification
UNCED	United Nations Conference on Environment and Development
UNCHE	United Nations Conference on Human Environment
UNCOD	UN Conference on Desertification
UNCTAD	United Nations Conference on Trade and Development
UNDP	UN Development Programme
UNEP	United Nations Environment Programme
UNESCO	United Nations Educational, Scientific and Cultural Organization
UNFCCC	United Nations Framework Convention on Climate Change
USD	Unites States Dollar
WEEE	waste electrical and electronic equipment
WEEE PCS	WEEE Pollution Control Standard
WEEE TPPP	WEEE Technical Pollution Prevention Policy
WEFZ	water environmental functional zones
WFZ	water function zones
WHO	World Health Organization
Wp	watt peak
WPL	Wildlife Protection Law
WRI	World Resources Institute
WSB	Water Services Bureau
WTE	waste-to-energy
WTO	World Trade Organization
WWF	World Wide Fund for Nature
XJPCC	Xinjiang Production and Construction Corps

1

INTRODUCTION

Eva Sternfeld

We must not give up eating for fear of choking, nor refrain from building our own industry for fear of pollution and damage to the environment.
Statement by Tang Ke, leader of the Chinese delegation at UNCHE Stockholm, 1972.
(China's Stand on the Question of the Human Environment 1972, 5)

We will resolutely declare war against pollution as we declared war against poverty.
Premier Li Keqiang at the annual People's Congress meeting in March 2014
(Reuters 2014)

Nearly 45 years have passed since the first UN Conference on the Human Environment (UNCHE) in Stockholm 1972. The Chinese delegation, as mentioned in the above quotation, used the international stage to denounce capitalist industrialized countries for causing worldwide environmental degradation and to insist on the developing countries' right to industrial development. However, it is also widely acknowledged that the Stockholm conference provided the impulse for the development of China's domestic environmental policies.

Today, the world looks rather different. During the last few decades, China has accomplished unprecedented economic growth and has emerged as the second largest economy in the world. The 'economic miracle' has led hundreds of millions of people out of poverty, but has also come at a high cost. Environmental degradation and the impact of environmental pollution on health are nowadays issues of the greatest concern for the Chinese public and the government. In 2014, the Ministry of Environmental Protection (MEP) noted 471 incidents that could be designated as 'environmental emergencies' (see Yu et al., chapter 13). In August 2015, the 'Tianjin blast', with the detonation of almost 3,000 tons of toxic materials including ammonium nitrate and sodium cyanide that had been illegally stored in a warehouse in the Tianjin Harbour, killed 173 people and injured a further 800 (*The Guardian* 2015). These incidents are symptoms of an aggravating crisis. Air pollution is related to the premature deaths of as many 1.6 million people in China per year and almost 40 per cent of China's population live in areas where the air that they breathe is regarded as unhealthy all year round, according to international standards (see Ahlers and Hansen, chapter 7). The capital, Beijing, is already infamous for its deteriorating environmental quality. In early 2015, Beijing's mayor, Wang Anshun, declared the city 'unliveable' because of the noxious smog (Kaiman 2015). However, air pollution is not the only ecological peril facing Beijing: the water shortage is also growing more acute. This mega city has, in fact, become greatly dependent on neighbouring provinces for its water supplies. The severe pollution of surface and groundwater is another critical issue (see Nickum, Jia and Moore, chapter 6). In 2014, a nationwide soil survey revealed that approximately 19 per cent of the fields tested were heavily polluted with cadmium, mercury and arsenic (MEP/MLR 2014).

The water and the soil crisis are directly related to the remarkable increase of productivity in the agricultural sector. Intensification comes with serious side-effects for environmental and public health. Not only is the agriculture sector China's leading water consumer and polluter of water bodies. With 14 kg/ha on average more pesticides applied on Chinese agricultural land than in any other country of the world, overuse of agrochemicals is a serious health risk not only for millions of people living in the country but for food safety for the entire population (Bluemling, chapter 9).

China's environmental crisis is a matter of global concern. The country's rapid economic growth has been accompanied by a massive increase in fossil fuel consumption and related emissions (see Oberheitmann and Suding, chapter 19). This level of growth was not foreseen by economists, and the increase in China's emissions substantially outpaced any scenario that had been envisioned in the late 1990s. At that time, when the Kyoto Protocol was being negotiated, the commonly held belief was that China would overtake the United States as the world's leading producer of emissions sometime around 2030 (Frankel 1999), but by 2007, China had already become the world leader in emissions of greenhouse gases. In 2015, China produced 30 per cent of global CO_2 emissions, while China's per capita CO_2 level of 7.6 tonnes was already exceeding the EU28 level of 6.7 tonnes (PBL 2015). As a result, China came under increasing pressure to accept more global responsibility and to play a more active role in the post-Kyoto process (see Heggelund and Nadin, chapter 8). Recent developments, such as the ratification of the Paris Agreement are seen as promising signs that China is taking measures to mitigate climate change impacts. In particular, the rapid development of renewable energies (see Lewis, chapter 20) as well as the announcement that a nationwide carbon emissions trade scheme will be introduced by 2017, are seen as Chinese contributions to global efforts in the area of climate protection.

Recent statements by Chinese officials referring to environmental protection have also sounded a different tone. The government has not only declared 'war on pollution', but is also discussing a value matrix that differs from the pure GDP growth-oriented approach employed in the past:

> The development of ecological civilization is an essential part of the socialist undertaking with Chinese characteristics ... From an overall perspective, however, the development of ecological civilization in China still falls behind economic and social development ... The contradictions between development and population as well as resources and environment are increasingly prominent, which have become a serious bottleneck hindering sustainable economic and social development.
>
> *(CPC 2015)*

The above quotation was taken from a 20-page document entitled 'Opinions on Further Promoting the Development of Eco-Civilisation' that was jointly issued in 2015 by the Central Committee of the Communist Party of China (CPC) and the State Council, to present a road map for the environmental policies of the current 13th Five-Year Plan (FYP). The catalogue of environmental policies that it contains include binding targets for reducing emissions, 'red line' limits on the consumption of natural resources, and the implementation of market mechanisms to establish ecological values, a water rights market and compensation for ecological services. It is anticipated that China will introduce a nationwide trading market for carbon emissions by 2017. In addition, the document issues calls to

> include targets for resource consumption, environmental damage and ecological benefits in the system of comprehensive assessment on economic and social development, significantly raise the weight of these targets, ... and to abandon the concept of regarding economic growth as the only criterion in government performance assessment.
>
> *(CPC 2015)*

In other words, the efforts to introduce a 'Green GDP', which failed in 2007, might see a revival.

Furthermore, the evaluation system for the promotion of cadres was reformed in 2013 and environmental performance (measurable by several indicators, such as air and water quality) has been added to the list of criteria (see Kostka, chapter 3). The 'Opinions on Further Promoting the Development of Eco-Civilisation' even stipulate the 'lifetime accountability of cadres' for environmental damage (CPC 2015).

Remarkable efforts have been made to improve the environmental legislation and the enforcement of these laws. Since 2013, an *Action Plan for Preventing and Combating Air Pollution*, a *Water Action Plan* and, most recently, a *Soil Protection Action Plan* with measurable and binding targets, have been enacted. The MEP, for many years regarded as a toothless tiger, has experienced a radical reshuffle. Towards the end of January 2015, Chen Jining, a scholar trained in environmental engineering and former president of the prestigious Qinghua University, was appointed as the new minister. In early 2016, the ministry's divisions were restructured in order to implement, more efficiently, the policies related to the three action plans mentioned above (Li 2016).

The road map for China's future environmental policies is ambitious, but the country's practical capability to implement them still needs to be proven. This handbook helps to assess the accomplishments as well as the deficiencies of a fragmented authoritarian system. The contributions presented in this handbook offer detailed accounts of the ways in which policies in China are developed, showing how governmental and non-governmental actors are able to respond to the challenges of environmental change. To cover the wide range of issues related to this complex topic, this handbook brings together the work of an interdisciplinary group of international scholars who each have a special field of expertise.

The volume is structured in five parts. Part I explains the development and current status of the environmental policies in China, and introduces the relevant actors and institutions. Part II (Key issues and strategies for solution) provides first-hand details of the latest research on environmental challenges and policies related to water management, air pollution, climate change, rural environmental protection, biodiversity, soil conservation and afforestation, disaster risk management and environmental health. Part III discusses policy instruments and their enforcement. Part IV looks at the environmental impact of related fields, such as energy policies and urban development. Finally, Part V examines China's environmental policies in an international context, for example, sustainable production and international trade as well as international cooperation on climate protection policies.

Development and status of current environmental policy

In recent years, the Chinese authorities have made remarkable efforts to complete and improve the legal framework for environmental protection. In their contribution, Qin and Zhang (chapter 2) trace the development of China's environmental legislation from its early beginnings in the 1970s to the recent revision of the *Environmental Protection Law*. The new *Environmental Protection Law*, which came into effect in 2015, is the second revision of this law since the first provisional law was enacted in 1979. Since then, China has issued a number of national laws aimed at pollution prevention and control, as well as laws, regulations and technical standards related to resource protection. The *Environmental Protection Law* was formally enacted in 1989, but it has taken 25 years and four readings to revise and adapt it to the challenges of rapid modernization. Remarkable amendments have been added to the earlier version of the law, for example, the new chapter 5, which addresses the participation and the rights of civil society in ensuring environmental protection. In addition, the new law provides the MEP with more power and tools, such as the authority to order the restriction and suspension of production, the seizure of property and the right to deny environmental impact assessment (EIA) procedures in ecologically fragile regions. Qin and Zhang also take a close look at several complementary measures that have been introduced by the MEP to regulate the implementation of the new *Environmental Protection Law*.

They show, that law reforms have been remarkable. However, it is widely agreed that institutional structure and capacity are still lagging behind and there are serious deficits when it comes to enforcement at the local level. Kostka (chapter 3) examines the obvious gaps between ambitious national level policy-making and inefficient local policy implementation. She puts forward an analytical framework for identifying the shortcomings in environmental planning, political and economic incentives, public participation, and financial, technical and political capacity. As mentioned previously, recent FYPs have included measurable targets for environmental protection and quality, and this has led to environmental protection issues gaining an enhanced profile on local policy-making agendas. As Kostka argues, however, there have been some undesirable effects, for example, the targets of an FYP might not accurately reflect the actual environmental problems at the local level, or targets might be so rigidly set that they are impossible to fulfil. The recent reforms to the annual cadre evaluation system for local politicians and managers of state-owned enterprises (SOE) also included some environmental quality indicators, the plan being that an excellent environmental performance should result in promotion or, in the case of mismanagement, in redeployment. Nevertheless, as Kostka points out, the cadre evaluation system still has its limitations. Due to their relatively short terms of office (three to four years on average) and frequent rotation, cadres prefer to undertake the implementation of measures that yield fast visible results rather than long-term environmental protection efforts. Despite the amendments to the evaluation system, more value is usually placed on meeting economic targets than on meeting environmental targets. It is therefore understandable that politicians are interested in bolstering local government budgets by selling land-use rights even when they know that this can lead to the loss of agricultural land and green space. The limited opportunities for non-state actors are identified as another reason for the failure of environmental policies at the local level. For example, although small and middle-sized companies account for more than 40 per cent of total energy consumption, small private companies have long been excluded from official policies for improving energy efficiency and reducing emissions. The media and environmental NGOs are playing an increasingly important role as environmental watchdogs, but their impact is still limited to certain topics and fields of participation.

The widening arena for non-state advocacy groups and their impact on environmental policy is examined in two contributions: Shapiro (chapter 4) describes how the strategies of China's civil environmental movement have developed along with the reform process from simple symbolic actions, such as tree-planting and garbage collection, to more creative tactics, such as using the mass media and social media for networking, whistleblowing, information-sharing and undercover investigation. In addition, the amendments to the environmental legislation opened new doors for public participation and information. In Western literature, however, the impact of environmental NGOs and environmental activists as advocacy groups for the promotion of environmental policies is possibly overrated. Huang, Sheng and Barg (chapter 5) argue that, in most cases, the political influence of these groups has been limited to local environmental events and has only had little, if any, impact on national policies. They identify international advisory institutions, such as the China Council for International Cooperation on Environment and Development (CCICED), national think-tanks and professional associations, including the China Renewable Energy Industry Association, as influential advocacy groups that have helped to put green economy concepts such as low carbon economy and circular economy on the agenda of the Xi Administration's 'new normal' development strategy.

Key issues

Water

The availability and quality of water are decisive factors in China's ecological stability. Access to water is crucial for food security and although agriculture is still by far the largest water user, the rapid urbanization process has greatly intensified the competition between agricultural and urban-industrial users. A recent national water census revealed that about three-quarters of China's available water resources are being consumed and that, in some areas, for example the North China Plain, these resources are being used at unsustainable levels, leading to declining groundwater tables. This dramatic data resulted in the enactment of the most ambitious *Water Pollution Prevention and Control Action Plan* (known as the 'Water Ten Plan') in 2015 and efforts to strictly implement the 'Three Red Lines', setting caps on total water consumption and establishing mandatory goals for water efficiency and water quality to be achieved by 2020 and 2030. Observance of the 'Three Red Lines' is also to be included as one of the performance evaluation indicators for the promotion of local officials. In their contribution, Nickum, Jia and Moore (chapter 6) discuss the advantages as well as the limitations of this resource-oriented policy. China has been struggling for many years to reform its highly fragmented water institutions (known as the 'nine dragons ruling the water'). Past policy efforts aimed at basin-wide integrated water management, at integrating supply, drainage and waste water management in urban areas under one authority, and at controlling water demand and quality by employing economic instruments, such as water resources fees and waste water charges, were largely toothless due to the lack of procedures at the local level and inadequate public participation. Against this background, Nickum et al. identify certain barriers to the effective implementation of the 'Three Red Lines', such as the unreliability of water use projections, the lack of advanced monitoring technology, the limited number of pollutants as indicators, and the dangers of misreporting.

Air

The most striking and noticeable symptom of China's environmental crisis is probably the severe air pollution in major Chinese cities. Public perception of this issue is a very new phenomenon and has much to do with the greater transparency and accessibility of air quality data. According to Ahlers and Hansen (chapter 7), until about 2013, the majority of the Chinese public did not even know the word for 'noxious smog', and tended to refer to it as 'haze'. Data on fine particulate pollution ($PM_{2.5}$) was not made available to the public until the American Embassy in Beijing began to publish daily $PM_{2.5}$ data on their website in 2011. Today, hourly updated data on air quality is available everywhere in China and even children are aware that $PM_{2.5}$ is an air pollutant and a health risk. The public debate on air pollution gained traction when the documentary *Under the Dome* produced by the prominent TV anchor woman, Chai Jing, was viewed by several hundred million viewers in a matter of days. Air pollution in major Chinese cities does not only damage their reputation as tourist destinations, but also seriously reduces the quality of life of the inhabitants. In 2013, the government responded with an ambitious *Action Plan on Prevention and Control of Air Pollution* (APAP), referring to China's three most industrialized and urbanized regions, the Beijing–Tianjin–Hebei area, the Yangzi River Delta and the Pearl River Delta. For each of these three regions, detailed implementation rules were issued, which include binding targets for emissions and the reduction of coal consumption as well as radical industrial restructuring. Ahlers and Hansen's case study of Hangzhou provides clear evidence that this Action Plan strengthened the position of local Environmental Protection Bureaux (EPBs) and promoted public participation by involving companies, schools, NGOs and local residents.

Climate

China is the world's leader in greenhouse gas emissions and, at the same time, is also extremely vulnerable to the impact of climate change and natural hazards such as floods and droughts. In recent years, China has undertaken remarkable policy efforts to address climate change. Heggelund and Nadin (chapter 8) trace the development of China's domestic climate policies from when the topic first appeared on the international agenda. In the early 1990s, climate change in China was viewed as a purely scientific issue and was mainly perceived as falling into the area of competence of the National Meteorological Administration. This changed after 1998, when the State Planning Commission and, later, its successor, the National Development and Reform Commission (NDRC), became the lead agencies in charge of climate change policies. The NDRC is striving to synergize climate change policies and programmes that target energy security and energy efficiency. The first road map for China's domestic climate policy was outlined in the National Climate Programme in 2007. The 12th FYP (2011–2015) included, for the first time, climate policy as a key principle for sustainable development. This plan is widely recognized as marking a turning point in Chinese domestic climate policies because it set binding targets for carbon intensity and introduced carbon emissions trading for selected pilot regions. The 13th FYP (2016–2020) continues and strengthens these policies, which include the anticipated nationwide introduction of an emissions trading scheme (ETS). The economic slowdown since 2013, labelled as the 'new normal' by the Xi Administration, is seen as providing an opportunity to achieve more sustainable and climate-friendly growth. China has also started to pay greater attention to adaptation issues, with most of the research focusing on the biophysical impact of climate change on agriculture and grasslands. In 2013, the *National Adaptation Strategy* was released by the NDRC, but most provincial and sector adaptation plans have not yet been completed. Heggelund and Nadin also show that adaptation is a complex issue that needs to be linked with other policy areas, such as social security reform, disaster risk reduction and poverty alleviation.

Biodiversity and nature protection

China is one of the most biologically diverse countries in the world, covering a vast territory with a wide range of landforms and climate zones. In many parts of the country, however, industrial development and rapid urbanization have resulted in a critical loss of natural habitats and loss of biodiversity. Chris Coggins (chapter 10) investigates China's nature conservation efforts and the related policies starting from the 1950s, when the first nature protection reserve was established. Today, China features 2,671 nature reserves and protected areas covering almost 10 per cent of China's territory. It is important to note that the larger nature reserves are all located in the western provinces of Tibet, Qinghai and Xinjing, where this development had an impact on the lives of several hundred thousand people who suddenly found themselves living in a nature protection zone with specific restrictions on economic activities, such as hunting and gathering wild plants. So far, the effects of biological conservation and environmental justice on indigenous people have often been unsatisfactory, as shown in Jarmila Ptackova's (chapter 16) case study on the ecological resettlement (*shengtai yimin*) programme for the Three Rivers' Headwater Nature Reserve in Qinghai Province. The nature reserve to protect the headwaters of the Yellow River, Yangtze and Mekong covers an area of almost 400,000 square kilometres. Between 2004 and 2010, approximately 55,000 herders were resettled and subsequently banned from grazing in their former pastures. According to the findings of Ptackova's field research, the resettlement of the herders, which was also aimed at poverty alleviation, was far from successful in either ecological or socio-economic terms.

Land degradation and land-use strategies

The northern and north-western dryland regions of China are confronted with the accelerating degradation of arable land, including salinization, soil erosion, dust storms and desertification. Stein and Hartmann (chapter 11) review the historical development of land-use practices as well as water and forest management in the region and the impact of these activities on the natural environment. In the Chinese scientific literature, the problems of land degradation are often attributed to poorly managed land reclamation campaigns, especially those of the 1950s and 1960s. More recent studies have also investigated the impact of climate change. Since the late 1970s, the Chinese government has undertaken large-scale ecological restoration programmes, such as the Three-North Shelterbelt Project, the Six Key Forestry Projects and the Sloping Lands Conversion Program. In addition, large-scale engineering projects, such as long distance water transfers mark the significant efforts made by the government to improve the adverse natural conditions that prevail in Northern China. However, the long-term effectiveness and sustainability of these interventionist approaches still need to be examined.

Environment and human health

The reports concerning 'cancer villages' along polluted rivers, the reduced life expectancy of citizens living in smoggy northern Chinese cities and food poisoned by agrochemicals are alarming. The social cost of the impact of environmental pollution on human health is tremendous. Jennifer Holdaway (chapter 12) shows that due to resource constraints, disparities in the pace of regional development and changes in production and consumption, China is being confronted with a multiplicity of simultaneously emerging environmental health issues. She argues that there is no linear relationship between GDP growth, industrialization and effects on human health, but that there is a myriad of differing, complex causes. Environmental health, as a cross-sectoral issue, demands the integrated and coordinated efforts of the economic sectors (industry, energy, agriculture) and the environmental protection and health authorities. Holdaway provides a comprehensive overview of the evolution of policies addressing environmental health, and also shows that, due to the recent increase in public pressure, the authorities in the relevant sectors have been paying greater attention to environmental health aspects. These are addressed, for example, by the *Environment and Health Plan for the 12th Five-Year Plan* period, by the more recent action plans for addressing air, water and soil pollution, and by the *National Plan for Sustainable Agriculture (2015–2030)*. However, as Holdaway points out, considerably greater efforts will be required to prevent a regional split which could result in poorer regions and communities bearing a disproportionate burden of the costs of environmental pollution and the related health issues.

Policy instruments and enforcement

The underlying issue of environmental justice caused by the regional divide between poorer, less developed regions and richer coastal regions in the types and levels of environmental pollution and the related costs are one of the central themes of Van Rooij et al. (chapter 14), who investigate the regional variations in environmental law enforcement. Their findings provide evidence that environmental laws tend to be enforced more strictly in coastal regions and larger cities than in remote areas in central and western provinces. There are several reasons for these differences, including the various levels of commitment of local governments, the capabilities of local environmental authorities and the pressure that is applied by local communities. It has become obvious that in less developed regions, local governments often try to prevent EPBs from taking action against industries, because these are of economic importance to the region. It has also been observed that in wealthier regions, the population is more sensitive to environmental issues and more willing to put pressure on their local governments to enforce environmental laws, while in regions where one single industrial enterprise is the sole provider of jobs, people are generally more reluctant to complain about environmental pollution. The authors warn of a potential split between the wealthier coastal and municipal areas and the less developed regions of China in terms of environmental law enforcement.

It is widely agreed that market-based instruments have now become more important in the implementation of environmental policies. Arthur Mol (chapter 15) examines China's efforts to introduce environmental standards for financial institutions. The introduction of green standards for granting credit, for stock markets and insurance companies has been pushed forward by government authorities. During the last few years, Chinese banks have certainly rejected a considerable number of loan requests on the grounds that environmental standards had not been fulfilled or that an EIA had not been carried out. Due to the lack of pressure from local governments, however, the implementation of the *Green Credit Guidelines*, introduced in 2012, remains weak. On the other hand, loans to the 'green economy sector' have increased considerably, especially in the case of loans for renewable energy projects. A further green finance instrument has also been introduced in the form of environmental pollution liability insurance, which is aimed at compensating pollution victims and mitigating pollution risks by conducting an environmental examination of the insurance holder. In 2012, 14 cities and provinces launched pilot insurance plans but, in practice, the dissemination of pollution insurance has been very slow, for a number of reasons.

Transparency of information and public participation are important preconditions for the implementation of environmental policy. The *Environmental Impact Assessment Law* in 2002 was the first environmental law of the People's Republic of China that included a vague paragraph referring to these issues, but this law only really started to be applied in 2006, after the MEP issued the *Temporary Methods of Public Participation in Environmental Impact Assessment*. The *Environmental Impact Assessment Law* has also gained more ground since 2015, when the corresponding paragraphs were included in the new *Environmental Protection Law*. Mariachiara Alberton's contribution (chapter 17) provides an overview of the instruments related to public participation in EIA and looks at the practical implementation of these instruments at the local level in Yunnan and Shandong provinces. This chapter is based on interviews with stakeholders, such as officials of EPBs, Municipal Bureaus of Complaints, and NGOs. The analysis reveals that despite national provisions at the local level, public participation and access to information are still quite limited because the definition of the scope and the forms of public participation remains vague. In the cases examined by Alberton, the public had only been informed about planned projects at a very late stage and the time-slot was too brief to allow full consideration of the issues involved. In addition, the details of the EIA procedures were not made clear to the public and therefore lacked transparency.

In chapter 18, Sam Geall considers the role played by the Chinese media and the scope of their information brokerage for increasing environmental awareness and promoting public participation in environmental governance. He shows that for the promotion of public participation UN organizations played a role. The right to access environmental information was agreed upon in 1992 at the United Nations Conference on Environment and Development (UNCED) in Rio and was specified in the 2010 UNEP *Guidelines for the Development of National Legislation on Access to Information, Public Participation and Access to Justice in Environmental Matters* (the 'Bali Guidelines'), which were signed by China. A number of Chinese environmental regulations and government documents include clauses that refer to environmental information, including the 2015 *Environmental Protection Law* and the Central Committee document on building an 'Ecological Civilisation'. Although the wording of these provisions is in line with international norms, Geall notes that they are often neither effectively nor consistently implemented. Government authorities very often reject requests for information by referring to clauses that exempt from information disclosure projects that are regarded as being important for national security or social stability. China has come a long way since the Maoist era, when the official media was so tightly controlled that major disasters could be concealed, such as a dam collapse in 1975 with approximately 170,000 casualties, up to the present day when activists are able to access and spread information through the mass media and social media. Nonetheless, as Geall points out, despite the progress made since the Maoist era, transparency and public participation are still contested areas.

Related policy fields – conflicts and synergies

The dramatic increase in fossil fuel consumption in recent decades is one of the main causes of the deteriorating environmental quality and the increase in greenhouse gas emissions. Oberheitmann and Suding (chapter 19) investigate the underlying reasons for the growing energy demands and the related environmental issues. Economic growth and rapid urbanization are identified as the major challenges in assessments of the environmental impact of energy usage. Their analysis shows that from the 1990s onwards until very recently, the decoupling of economic development, energy consumption and energy-related emissions has gradually been taking place, but that the turning point, known as the 'Environmental Kuznets Curve', when an improvement in the environmental situation can be expected, has not yet been reached.

One important policy that would help China to reach this turning point would include setting targets to reduce coal consumption and to increase the share of renewable energy resources in the energy mix. Joanna Lewis (chapter 20) provides an insight into China's green innovation strategy and the country's aspirations to become not only internationally competitive in the green technology and clean energy sector, but to become an innovator and a global leader in this field. Starting with the 12th FYP, China has made great efforts to replace and modernize the coal-based industry. Since 2012, China has been the global leader in clean energy investment, partly due to policies that have protected and favoured local companies. By this means, China has advanced to become the world's leading manufacturer of renewable energy technology. This development has prompted serious trade disputes with the US and Europe. In recent years, due to incentives offered by the government, there has been rapid development in installed energy capacities within China. In 2013, China overtook Germany as the leading country in installing additional photovoltaic (PV) capacities. According to Lewis, despite the remarkable developments in this sector and the steady increase in R&D spending on renewables and clean energy, China is still lagging behind global leaders in innovation in clean energy technologies. The lack of clarity and transparency of intellectual property rights are still a barrier to innovation, and represent a risk for both the nascent industry and international cooperation.

Rapid urbanization and the growing improvements in the living standards of the urban classes appear to be significant factors in the sharp increase in greenhouse gas (GHG) emissions. Consequently, the cities have become a major focus of China's climate mitigation policies. Liu Wenling and Wang Can (chapter 21) explore concepts related to low carbon urban development. Since the 12th FYP, China has started implementing pilot demonstration programmes in five provinces and more than 30 cities. In this way, China has become a laboratory for all kinds of strategies related to low carbon urban development. In addition to programmes supported by the Chinese government, a number of programmes have been initiated in cooperation with foreign donor agencies and international NGOs, such as the World Wide Fund for Nature (WWF). By 2012, all cities at prefectural level (374 in total) were already announcing that they had implemented a form of low carbon or eco-city development strategy. Among these, several cities stand out for their successful and innovative strategies. The city of Zhenjiang in Jiangsu Province, for example, has set a peak target for CO_2 emissions and plans to reach the peak by 2019. A number of cities have also followed the example of Zhenjiang and have set CO_2 emission peaks that should be reached between 2019 and 2025 (at least five years ahead of the intended national determined contribution (INDC) that was announced at COP 21 in Paris in 2015). However, Wang and Liu's research has revealed that there are still implementation gaps and that there is a long way to go before such emission peaks become actuality. Recent evaluations have shown that emissions per unit GDP as well as per capita in a number of 'low carbon' cities are still higher than China's national average and higher by far than the per capita emissions in other major international cities, such as Paris, Tokyo and Berlin.

Municipal solid waste (MSW) management is related to multiple environmental issues such as air pollution, GHG emissions, and surface and groundwater pollution and is therefore an important issue that needs to be addressed by low carbon and eco-city strategies. Along with rapid urbanization, China has also advanced to become the world's leading generator of MSW. The following contributions by Johnson (chapter 22) and by Schulz and Steuer (chapter 23) highlight the complex socio-economic and environmental challenges posed by the ever-increasing quantities of waste and the increasing amounts of non-degradable and harmful substances that it contains. Johnson takes a look at the efforts made by cities to cope with these growing amounts of waste. All over China, there are obviously huge differences in the levels and content of MSW, depending on the economic status and institutional capacity of the cities. Although a relatively well-developed national legal framework for waste management is in place, the implementation costs often represent a serious financial burden for municipal governments. In 2009, according to an assessment by the World Bank, approximately half of the MSW was disposed of in suburban areas without being treated. In recent years, however, the funding problem has been solved, to some extent, by introducing waste management fees. A considerable number of treatment facilities have also started operating and, according to more recent estimates, about 86 per cent of MSW is currently being collected. Up to now, the authorities have still been tending to focus on end-of-pipe solutions while, despite the huge informal waste collection and recycling sector, recycling rates are still astonishingly low. Until the early 2000s, the authorities preferred to use landfill sites to dispose of MSW, but this trend has changed in recent years. While the amounts of waste are rising, the land that is available in suburban areas is limited and often too expensive to be used as a landfill site; as a result, more and more Chinese municipal governments are investing in waste incineration plants. The 12th FYP is also known as China's 'Great Leap Forward' in waste generation. By the end of 2015, China had approximately 300 incineration plants with the capacity to treat about one-third of its MSW. Waste incineration could become a profitable business, as waste-to-energy generators take advantage of subsidized feed-in-tariffs for renewable energies. However, the construction of incineration plants has also given rise to numerous protests and demonstrations by citizens living near the facilities. Opponents are particularly concerned about the impact of dioxin emissions on health. Not only are Chinese standards for dioxin emissions less strict than EU standards, those who are opposed to the use of these incinerators also become suspicious if the operators avoid the investment in expensive filters that often cost more than the entire facility. According to Johnson, China is still suffering from the lack of efficient equipment and the personnel to monitor dioxin emissions.

Any reforms to the waste management system also need to take into account the huge informal sector of waste pickers, sellers and recyclers. This aspect is discussed by Schulz and Steuer (chapter 23) who look at the recycling of discarded electrical and electronic devices. Since 'e-waste' contains considerable amounts of raw materials, recycling makes economic sense and also, if done properly, ecological sense. China has often been in the headlines, however, for recycling imported e-waste in primitive workshops in what are known as 'garbage villages', where the waste is disassembled and the valuable materials it contains are recovered. One of the most infamous locations for this practice is the town of Guiyu in Guangdong. Schulz and Steuer analyse the dominant discourse on this issue that calls for the closing down of informal e-waste recycling businesses and the introduction of a 'formal' recycling system. A full regulatory system, the *Waste of Electrical and Electronic Equipment Directive* (known as the China WEEE) and the *Restriction of Hazardous Substances* (RoHS), largely inspired from EU standards, came into force between 2008 and 2012, but Schulz and Steuer show that this legal framework has yet to revolutionise the field. The infamous town of Guiyu, for example, still continues to function as a major base for informal e-waste recycling in China, at least until 2016. In the case of Guiyu, the local population has little incentive to give up this business because they do not have an alternative source of income. The local EPB faced difficulties in monitoring and curtailing pollution caused by the recycling business due to a lack of resources.

Schulz and Steuer also look at the informal actors who engage in collection, refurbishment and resale of electrical and electronic equipment. In China, there is still a big market for second-hand spare parts. They show that policies adopted from other parts of the world, such as the take-back scheme known as 'old for new', are not appropriate in a country where large second-hand repair markets still exist.

China's environmental policy in an international context

It is estimated that up to 20 per cent of China's emissions can be traced back to export-oriented production. In their case study, Hu and Song (chapter 24) assess the amount of emissions caused by export-oriented industries and calculate the emissions involved in China's trade with the lower Mekong countries. Hu and Song predict that export-related emissions will decrease in the foreseeable future, but that China's trade-related emissions will not achieve a balance before 2030. This is because of the specific structure of China's export sector, which is heavily dependent on energy and resource-intensive goods, whereas the export trade in services is still underdeveloped. Hu and Song suggest that the system of export taxes for energy and resource-intensive goods could be optimized by imposing export taxes not only on iron and steel, but also in the long term on leather, paper and chemical products. Their findings show how China's and the global environmental trade balance could be improved and how a 'post-fast development era' or 'new normal era' could translate into a green trade policy.

In the next contribution, Patrick Schroeder (chapter 25) presents his research on the impacts on Chinese industries of policy and legal initiatives that have been adopted in the context of the *UN 10 Year Framework Plan for Sustainable Consumption and Production*. He shows that EU directives, such as RoHS, had a serious impact on China's export-oriented electronic sector and also provides evidence that leading Chinese manufacturers are well aware of the existing international and domestic legislation for implementing green supply chain management. They are interested in branding their products 'eco-friendly' to improve their international competitiveness. In addition, multinational companies that are engaging in green supply management have helped to improve the environmental performance of Chinese suppliers. One important step in promoting sustainable production was the adoption of the *Circular Economy Promotion Law,* which encourages manufacturers to produce goods that can easily be recycled, reused or remanufactured. On the consumption side, product labelling, for example, the China Environmental Label, serves as an important strategy for enhancing consumers' awareness of environmentally-friendly products.

As mentioned earlier, EU environmental legislation has played an important role in shaping China's modern environmental policies. Gippner (chapter 26) takes the case of emission trading policies as an example, and follows the ETS policy process from EU agenda-setting to policy adoption in China. She argues that current Chinese pilot programmes are based on EU ETS amongst others and that they have been established through constant consultation with DG CLIMA as well as by the capacity-building support provided by the EU. In addition, since 2003, China has been closely cooperating with the UK to explore market-based approaches, such as a 'green tax'. The Chinese decision to adopt the EU ETS was surprising, given the fact that the EU system is experiencing a serious credit crisis. The initial results in China have shown that some pilot projects have over-allocated emissions allowances and are now facing problems that are similar to those experienced in EU countries. Several of Gippner's interviewees argued that the introduction of a carbon tax might have been more appropriate for the conditions in China. The Ministry of Finance, however, which put forward the proposal for the carbon tax seems to have lost its fight against the NDRC, the main decision-making body involved in the development of China's climate diplomacy and low carbon policies.

Conclusion

This handbook provides an idea of the broad scope and variety of the issues and the challenges involved in environmental and climate governance which have emerged as China has risen to become the world's second largest economy. At the time of writing this introduction, China seems to be positioned at a crossroads: on the one hand, the severe environmental crisis is increasingly becoming an issue involved with social instability. Chinese citizens calling for a healthy environment have never before taken such a decisive and resolute position. On the other hand, the recent 'new normal' downturn has had a positive impact on environmental quality. Since 2014, for the first time in this century, indications have emerged that a decline in emissions is taking place, not only due to the economic slowdown but also as a result of the stricter enforcement of environmental policies and the promotion of renewable energies. This development offers a glimmer of hope that the measures being undertaken globally to protect the climate will meet with success.

Acknowledgements

My sincere thanks go to all the contributors for sharing the results of their research. I would further like to express my gratitude to the editorial board, Arthur Mol, James Nickum, Qin Tianbao aand Miranda Schreurs, for their support and valuable advice.

References

China's Stand on the Question of Human Environment, 1972. *Peking Review* 24, 5–8.
Communist Party of China (CPC) Central Committee and State Council, 2015. Opinions of the CPC Central Committee and the State Council on further Promoting the Development of Ecological Civilisation. http://environmental-partnership.org/wp-content/uploads/download-folder/Eco-Guidelines_rev_Eng.pdf (accessed 6 August 2016).
Frankel, Jeffrey, 1999. Greenhouse Gas Emissions. *Brookings Policy Series* http://www.brookings.edu/research/papers/1999/06/energy-frankel (accessed 5 August 2016).
The Guardian, 2015. Tianjin Explosion: China Sets Final Death Toll to 173, Ending Search for Survivors. *The Guardian* 12 September 2015. https://www.theguardian.com/world/2015/sep/12/tianjin-explosion-china-sets-final-death-toll-at-173-ending-search-for-survivors (accessed 2 August 2016).
Kaiman, Jonathan, 2015. Beijing Smog Makes City Unliveable, Says Mayor. *The Guardian* 28 January 2015. http://www.theguardian.com/world/2015/jan/28/beijing-smog-unliveable-mayor-wang-anshun-china (accessed 24 February 2015).
Li Jing, 2016. China's Environment Ministry Unveils Restructuring Plan Aimed at Making it More Effective. http://www.scmp.com/news/china/policies-politics/article/1920423/chinas-environment-ministry-unveils-restructuring-plan (accessed 5 August 2016).
MEP/MLR, 2014. (Ministry for Environmental Protection/Ministry of Land Resources): Quanguo Turang Wuran Zhuangkuang Diaocha Baogao (Investigation Report on the Status of Nationwide Soil Pollution). http://www.mep.gov.cn/gkml/hbb/qt/201404/W020140417558995804588.pdf (accessed 3 August 2016).
PBL Netherland Environment Assessment Agency, 2015. Trends in Global CO_2 Emissions. http://edgar.jrc.ec.europa.eu/news_docs/jrc-2015-trends-in-global-co2-emissions-2015-report-98184.pdf (accessed 5 August 2016).
Reuters, 2014. China to 'Declare War' on Pollution, Premier Says. http://www.reuters.com/article/us-china-parliament-pollution-idUSBREA2405W20140305 (accessed 2 August 2016).

PART I

Development of environmental policy in China – actors and institutions

2

DEVELOPMENT OF CHINA'S ENVIRONMENTAL LEGISLATION

Qin Tianbao and Zhang Meng

Introduction

To see a world in a grain of sand
And a heaven in a wild flower

William Blake's romantic poem provides a vivid description of the world in which human beings live, discover and develop. All the species of flora and fauna are the essential elements and the crucial foundation for human life. For thousands of years, the interactions between the environment and human beings have been perceived as an important part of human history and the development of society. We sometimes refer to the environment as a monster that we have to fight and sometimes as a resource that we have to exploit, but more recently, we have started to see the environment as a friend that we have to protect and live with in harmony, since we have finally realized that the road towards sustainable development is the only one that really offers us a future on this planet.

Anyone currently interested in environmental issues must eventually examine China's circumstances and rapidly growing 'Green Law Movement'. China's attitude to environmental issues is derived from its own distinctive cultural and historical features. Like many other ancient civilizations, China demonstrated considerable understanding of the need to achieve an ecological balance, developing a strong tradition rooted in the efforts of people centuries ago to survive and prosper in agrarian and pastoral societies. For millennia, in ancient China, the dominant environmental philosophy, *Tian Ren Gan Ying*, recognized the correlation and interaction between the natural environment and human activities (Wiener 2008). According to this ideology, extreme weather conditions and other dislocations in the natural order were understood as portents of misgovernment demonstrating the mismanagement of the balance. Unfortunately, the rise of an industrial and urbanized society in the nineteenth and especially the twenty centuries has significantly undermined this approach. Like many developing countries in the twenty-first century, China is now confronted with a fundamental challenge in pursuing continuous economic development while avoiding the accompanying environmental degradation (Deal 2007).

As the most populous and most rapidly developing country in the world, China faces environmental challenges on an unprecedented scale and timeframe. Since the late 1970s, China's economy has developed rapidly and continuously. During that 40-year process, many environmental problems that haunted the now developed countries at different stages of their centuries-long industrialization have occurred in China all at the same time. As a result, the conflict between the environment and development is becoming ever more acute and prominent. The relative shortage of resources, a fragile ecological environment and insufficient environmental capacity are becoming critical problems that hinder China's development. In order to supply the world with inexpensive products, many environmentally toxic enterprises have been established in China, thus heavily polluting local environments (Wen 2009). A dramatically increased demand for energy and natural resources of all kinds, including water and land, has accompanied the country's rapid economic development. Resources have been depleted, triggering a range of secondary impacts in the form of desertification, flooding and biodiversity loss (Orts 2003). The water resources of China have been affected by both severe water shortages and severe water pollution, but an increasing population and rapid economic growth as well as lax environmental supervision have increased the demand for water as well as levels of pollution. China has responded with various measures, such as building new water infrastructure elements and increasing regulation as well as exploring a number of possible technological solutions. Nevertheless, water usage by coal-fired power stations is leading to the drying-up of Northern China (Liu 2013). As a similar example, conventional air pollution has become so serious in China that it has been blamed for the deaths of 400,000 to 750,000 people per year and accounts for about 5.78 per cent of Chinese GDP (World Bank and State Environmental Protection Administration 2007). Recently the smoggy haze in China's capital city, Beijing, was reported as the worst air pollution in recent memory (Langfitt 2013). Pollution levels in the major cities of China are among the highest on Earth.

China is not an exception of course, in facing severe environmental problems. Indeed, as Miller et al. (2006, 3) have noted: 'The domain of environmental law and policy extends to any place where the earth is modified by human action.' Despite the concern being voiced not only in developing countries that are considered to be prominent players in the current game, but also in the broader international community, Chinese efforts play an important role in the global trend of improving the environment through legal tools. Since legislation can provide for sound environmental management and governance, particularly when it comes to modern environmental problems, legal tools have gradually attained greater importance to become a considerable factor in the political, economic and social transformation of the country. China has been working with great determination in recent years to develop, implement and enforce a solid environmental legal framework. Nevertheless, Chinese officials have faced critical challenges when trying to implement the laws, clarify the roles of their national and provincial governments, and strengthen the operation of the legal system (US Environmental Protection Agency 2008). While explosive economic and industrial growth have led to significant environmental degradation, China is currently in the process of developing more stringent legal controls (McElwee 2011).

Historical development of China's environmental legislation

China's environmental legislation is not merely a fashionable new movement in a legal framework. It should rather be perceived as a social experiment, focused on addressing environmental problems by triggering broad societal reform that will affect people's everyday lives by modifying their ways of thinking and behaviour. The aim is to achieve economic and social prosperity in the context of sustainable development.

Table 2.1 Historical development of China's environmental legislation

Period	Time	Milestone
'The early stage'	1949–1978	1972 United Nations Conference on the Human Environment
'The emerging stage'	1978–1989	1979 Environmental Protection Law (for trial)
		1978 & 1982 Constitution
'The maturity stage'	1989–2015	1989 Environmental Protection Law
		1992 United Nations Conference on Environment and Development
		2014 Environmental Protection Law

Source: Author.

Over the millennia of dynastic Chinese history, the dominant legal tradition has been based on the philosophy of Confucianism, a system of human governance that places the emphasis on moral education and social harmony (Bosworth and Yang 2000, 455). This ideological foundation contrasts radically with the western system of 'legalism'. However, the rise of an industrial and urbanized society in recent times has substantially challenged the traditional Confucian approach and demonstrated the need for adaptation. Thus, China's environmental legislation has evolved slowly, developing over three periods that commenced with the establishing of the People's Republic in 1949 (Beyer 2006).

Early stage of China's environmental legislation (1949–1978)

The first historical period of China's environmental legislation, from the establishment of the People's Republic of China in 1949 until the 1970s, may be regarded as the 'Blank or Preliminary Period'. First of all, an entirely new political, economic and legal order had to be set up without delay. Subsequently, the decade from 1966 to 1977 witnessed the ruin of entire social systems and social chaos nationwide by the 'Cultural Revolution'. Consequently, throughout this period, hardly any advances were made in the field of environmental legislation; only a few environmental interests were addressed, such as the regulation of mineral resources and factory safety, including provisions for the prevention of water pollution and for waste disposal (Bachner 1996).

Although measures for the protection of the environment were not included in the government's working plan at the time, the first United Nations Conference on the Human Environment (UNCHE) in 1972 spurred important developments in China's early environmental legislation. During that year, Chinese representatives attending the conference were made aware of the serious environmental problems that had emerged around the world, and they realized that the problems in China were at least equally serious as those facing other nations, if not more severe. After signing the 1972 *Stockholm Declaration on the Human Environment*, the Chinese central government convened the First National Conference on Environmental Protection the following year and, in 1974, the Chinese authorities established the Environmental Protection Leadership Group. This led to the formulation of the first environmental protection regulations, such as the *Provisional Standards for the Emission of Three Industrial Wastes* (wastewater, waste gas, solid waste), the *Provisional Standards for Emmissions* (defining environmental quality), the *Provisional Regulations on Pollution Prevention of Coastal Waters*. In effect, the 1972 UNCHE provided the ideological basis for the development of China's environmental legislation and pushed the Chinese government to rethink the environmental issues and the interaction between human activities and the ecosystem.

The emerging stage of China's environmental legislation (1978-1989)

China's modernization drive was launched in the late 1970s under the following conditions: the country had a large population base, the per-capita average consumption of natural resources was low, and economic development as well as scientific and technological levels remained quite backward. Since the 1970s, China has experienced not only continuous population growth and economic development, but also a steady increase in the population's consumption levels, which has ratcheted up the pressure on resources that were already in rather short supply, and on the fragile environment. The choices along the road to development have, historically, created issues of paramount importance for the survival and posterity of the Chinese people.

In 1978, after the Third Plenary Session of the 11th Central Committee of the Chinese Communist Party (CCP), China made a policy shift towards 'reform and opening up'. The Central Committee also decided to learn from the lessons and experiences of the past ten years by placing the emphasis on the construction of democracy and rule of law. From this point onward, legislation in China, including environmental laws, experienced important development. As a sign of significant progress, the concept of 'environmental protection' was introduced for the first time in the Constitutional Law of 1978. Environmental protection became a fundamental duty of the state, while the prevention of pollution and the protection of natural resources became the main realm of environmental law. On this foundation, considerable environmental legislation in China was officially introduced. Since 1979, for example, based on clauses pertaining to the *Constitutional Law*, the provisional *Environmental Protection Law* has addressed the environmental situation in China. This new trial law took foreign experiences into consideration by including regulations on the competences of various authorities, including their tasks and scope, and by embedding the 'polluter pays' principle and other legal regimes, such as environmental impact assessments, emission charges, environmental standards, and so on. Since the early 1980s, environmental legislation has expanded, starting with the new Constitution of 1982 and the *Marine Environmental Protection Law* of the same year, to include the *Water Pollution Prevention and Control Law* and the *Forest Law* in 1984, followed by the *Grassland Law* in 1985, and the *Air Pollution Prevention and Control Law* in 1987 (Beyer 2006).

The maturity stage of China's environmental legislation (from 1989 to the present)

This period has witnessed rapid, vigorous and significant progress in China's environmental legislation as a result of the growing awareness of environmental issues, which coincided with China's remarkable miracle of achieving economic prosperity and improvements in the standard of living. During this stage, China's environmental legislation has been characterized by systematization that will ultimately develop into an independent sector. The improvements and reforms of this period are, in essence, the real development of a body of modern environmental legislation in China that began with the 1989 *Environmental Protection Law*. As the most important milestone in the development of China's environmental legislation, the 1989 *Environmental Protection Law* contained significant and varied institutional innovations that launched Chinese environmental law into a new era. After this significant turning point, the way was paved for China to enact further environmental protection legislation, make progress in the fields of both pollution control and natural conservation, and to form a sound framework of environmental legislation.

Since the beginning of the 1990s, the international community has made important steps in finding ways to resolve problems related to the environment and development. The United

Nations Conference on Environment and Development (UNCED), held in June 1992, made sustainable development the common strategy for all development in the future, to the wide acclaim of governments of all countries represented at the conference. In August 1992, shortly after the conference, the Chinese government put forward ten major measures to enhance the balance of the environment and development, clearly adopting the road towards sustainable development as the logical choice for China. Based on the principles of sustainable development introduced after the 1992 UNCED, China undertook new efforts to strengthen its environmental laws and to bring them into closer compliance (Qin 2015). Since then, sustainable development has become the guideline and basic principle of all environmental legislation in China.

Moreover, during this period, China has regarded resource conservation and environmental protection as two basic state policies, and has continuously worked to strengthen legislation in these two areas. China has enacted nine laws concerning environmental protection, including the *Environmental Protection Law*, the *Law on Environmental Impact Assessment*, the *Law on the Prevention and Control of Atmospheric Pollution*, the *Law on the Prevention and Control of Water Pollution*, the *Law on the Prevention and Control of Environmental Noise Pollution*, the *Law on the Prevention and Control of Environmental Pollution by Solid Waste* and the *Law on the Prevention and Control of Radioactive Pollution*, as well as seventeen laws concerning resource conservation and protection (see Table 2.2), such as the *Renewable Energy Law*, the *Energy Conservation Law*, the *Land Administration Law*, the *Water Law*, the *Forest Law*, the *Grassland Law*, the *Mineral Resources Law*, the *Coal Law*, the *Electric Power Law* and the *Clean Production Promotion Law* (The State Council Information Office 2011).

In addition, the state has also promulgated over 50 administrative regulations, more than 660 local and sectoral regulations as well as government rules, and over 800 national standards related to environmental and resource protection. It has established and improved legal systems by setting up regimes for environmental impact assessment, synchronous project design, construction and completion of safety and sanitation facilities, pollution discharge declaration and registration, pollution discharge fees, elimination or control of pollution within a prescribed period of time, control of levels of pollution and pollution discharge permission, and legal systems concerning the planning, ownership, permission, paid use and energy conservation assessment of natural resources. At the same time, China is interested in international cooperation regarding resource conservation and environmental protection. It has acceded to or joined over

Table 2.2 Nature resource and energy legislation

Law	Time	Official Chinese Translation
Renewable Energy Law	Enacted in 2006, amended in 2009	中华人民共和国可再生能源法
Energy Conservation Law	Enacted in 1998, amended in 2007	中华人民共和国节约能源法
Land Administration Law	Enacted in 1987 amended in 2004	中华人民共和国土地管理法
Water Law	Enacted in 2002	中华人民共和国水法
Mineral Resources Law	Enacted in 1986 amended in 1996	中华人民共和国矿产资源法
Coal Law	Enacted in 1996 amended in 2013	中华人民共和国煤炭法
Electric Power Law	Enacted in 1996 amended in 2015	中华人民共和国电力法
Clean Production Promotion Law	Enacted in 2003	中华人民共和国清洁生产促进法

30 international conventions on environmental and resource protection, including the *United Nations Framework Convention on Climate Change*, the *Kyoto Protocol on Global Warming*, the *United Nations Convention on Biological Diversity* and the *United Nations Convention to Combat Desertification*. It is important to recognize that China has actively worked to meet its obligations under each of these conventions.

Furthermore, in the second decade of the twenty-first century, Chinese society and the Chinese economy entered a new epoch of enforcement. Increasing pollution and environmental deterioration resulting from the unsustainable approach to economic growth of the previous periods prompted new changes to environmental legislation. On 24 April 2014, the Chinese authority approved an amendment to the National *Environmental Protection Law* for the first time in 25 years. The amended *Environmental Protection Law*, which came into effect in January 2015, allows government environmental authorities to enforce much stricter penalties, seize the property of illegal polluters, and take stronger measures to crack down on environmental violations. Thus the 2014 Environmental Protection Law can be regarded as a new chapter of enforcement in the history of China's environmental legislation.

Framework of China's environmental legislation

During the last few decades, China has created a well-established framework of environmental legislation that takes the *Constitution of the People's Republic of China* as the foundation and the *Environmental Protection Law of the People's Republic of China* as the main body while incorporating two departmental branches of legislation: one to prevent and control pollution and the other to conserve nature and biodiversity.

At the same time, China has promulgated laws and regulations related to environmental protection (State Council Information Office 2011), while continuously improving the statutes concerning the environment by formulating strict law enforcement procedures and increasing the intensity of law enforcement in order to ensure the effective implementation of the environmental laws and regulations.

For example, to prevent negative impacts on the environment in the course of a construction project, the state has enacted the *Law on Environmental Impact Assessment*. The state has enacted laws targeting specific areas of environmental protection, such as those concerned with the prevention and control of water pollution, the marine environment, atmospheric pollution, environmental noise pollution, environmental pollution by solid waste, and radioactive pollution, among others. In addition, the State Council has formulated the *Regulations on the Administration of Environmental Protection of Project Construction, Regulations on the Safe Management of Hazardous Chemicals, Regulations on the Collection and Use of Pollutant Discharge Fees, Measures on the Administration of Permits for Operations Involving Hazardous Waste*, and other administrative regulations. To bolster the state regulations, the local people's congresses, according to the specific local conditions in their respective areas, have drawn up a large number of additional local regulations on environmental protection. In effect, China had established a system of nationwide environmental protection standards, and had implemented over 1,300 national environmental protection standards by the end of 2010.

Environmental protection in the Constitution

In China's legislation framework, the Constitution is the core. The present Constitution, on the basis of the 1954 Constitution, was adopted at the Fifth Session of the Fifth National

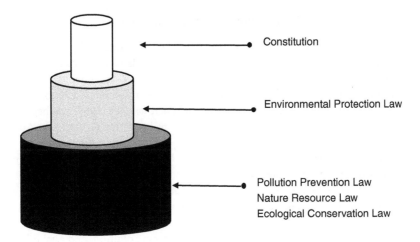

Constitution

Environmental Protection Law

Pollution Prevention Law
Nature Resource Law
Ecological Conservation Law

Figure 2.1 Framework of China's environmental legislation

Source: Author.

People's Congress (NPC) in 1982 after public discussion. As the fundamental law of the state, the Constitution has supreme legal authority.

The concept of 'environmental protection' had been introduced earlier, but in the 1982 Constitution, environmental protection became the fundamental duty of the state with pollution prevention and natural resources protection becoming the main realms of environmental law. Article 26 clearly asserts: 'the state protects and improves the living environment and the ecological environment, and prevents and remedies pollution and other public hazards'. Article 9 also states that 'the state ensures the rational use of natural resources and protects rare animals and plants; the appropriation or damage of natural resources by any organization or individual by whatever means is prohibited' (Constitution of the PRC). In this way, the Constitution clearly establishes the basic framework for China's environmental law, providing the top-level guidelines for environmental legislation and a legal basis for environmental protection.

In 2011, the Chinese government officially announced that the Chinese socialist system of laws should be interpreted as the organic integration of the laws related to the Constitution, that is, the civil and commercial laws, administrative laws, economic laws, social laws, criminal laws, litigation and non-litigation procedural laws, and other legal branches. This interpretation maintains the Constitution on top, these branches of law as the main body, and the administrative and local regulations as major components (State Council Information Office 2011). Unfortunately, according to this official announcement, environmental law is not regarded as an individual branch of China's legal framework. As a result, the announcement triggered a vigorous debate on what the role of environmental legislation in China should be and whether environmental rights should be regarded as constitutional rights. In the opinion of some scholars, elevating environmental rights to the level of the Constitution has been a trend for environmental protection legislation in various countries (Cai 2012). However, contrary to this point of view, other scholars have argued that if environmental rights are considered to be a kind of human right, the 2004 amendment to the 1982 Constitution has already addressed the issue since this requires the state to respect and protect citizens' human rights. In this way, the Constitution need not expressly confirm the environmental rights (Qin 2013).

Environmental Protection Law

The overall framework for China's environmental legislation is stipulated in the *Environmental Protection Law*, which was passed provisionally in 1979, amended and enacted in an advanced form in 1989, and then passed in its latest final form in 2014. In order to cope with the challenges arising from increasingly severe pollution and environmental deterioration, a new round of discussions to amend the *PRC Environmental Protection Law* (1989) was begun in 2011 with the aim of incorporating the results into the current legislative plan. On 24 April 2014, after three years of waiting and several reviews, the Chinese authority approved the first amendment to the National Environmental Protection Law in 25 years. The new *Environmental Protection Law*, a significant milestone, has already been in effect since January 2015.

The *Environmental Protection Law* covers a broad spectrum of environmental issues, ranging from protection against pollutants and control of pollutants to the protection of wildlife, and provides basic principles for both preventive and rehabilitative measures. The regulatory measures of this law address water, air, solid waste and noise pollution, and establish a system for environmental management, monitoring, liability and enforcement (Beyer 2006). Specifically, this law established and improved legal systems by setting up general requirements for environmental impact assessment, synchronous project design, construction and completion of safety and sanitation facilities, pollution discharge declaration and registration, a pollution discharge fee scheme, elimination or control of pollution within a prescribed period of time, control of levels of pollution and pollution discharge permission, and legal systems concerning the planning, ownership, permission, paid use and energy conservation assessment of natural resources (Law of PRC on Environmental Protection). At the same time, the law also stipulates the scope of the duties and obligations of environmental management authorities.

Without doubt, the *Environmental Protection Law of the People's Republic of China* is the cardinal law for environmental protection in China, laying down the basic principles for the coordinated development of economic construction, social development and environmental protection, while stipulating that governments at all levels, all organizations and all individuals have the right and duty to protect the environment.

Pollution prevention and control legislation

Since environmental pollution, especially related to water and air, causes more serious problems than China's other environmental challenges, the environmental legislation focuses more attention on pollution prevention. This is the focal point of the current environmental protection strategy, and the legislation seeks to control the environmental pollutions effectively and to prevent even worse problems from arising.

China has become the world's second-largest economy, but decades of breakneck economic growth have left many of its rivers polluted and its cities perennially shrouded in smog (Kaiman 2014). Indeed, water and air pollution clearly manifest the effects of the last 30 years of industrialization in China. Of the many potentially dangerous pollutants, water and air pollution tend to trigger public crises, arousing great concern at both international and national levels. Various factors have contributed to China's pollution crises in these areas, although perhaps most significant is the increasing consumption of fuel triggered by rapid economic development and out-of-date technologies. Thus, the guidelines within China's anti-pollution legislation regarding air and water pollution are undergoing major changes. The changes involve a number of shifts: from attempting to control only the resulting pollution to establishing control of the origin and the whole process of pollution as well; from regulating only the concentration of the pollutants to regulating both the concentration and total amount of pollutants; from controlling the source point of pollution to ensuring the comprehensive control of river valleys or entire regions, and from simply addressing the pollution problem of one corporation to adjusting the entire industrial structure by promoting clean production and developing a cyclical economy.

As a necessary requirement for these controls, China has enacted laws establishing specific targets to limit pollution. The most significant among these are focused on the prevention and control of water pollution, the marine environment, atmospheric pollution, environmental noise pollution, environmental pollution by solid waste, and radioactive pollutions. The State Council has issued the *Regulations on the Safe Management of Hazardous Chemicals, Regulations on the Collection and Use of Pollutant Discharge Fees, Measures on the Administration of Permits for Operations Involving Hazardous Waste*, and other administrative regulations concerning pollution prevention and control. For instance, the *Air Pollution Prevention and Control Law* (2000) and *The Administration Regulations of Ozone Depleting Substances* (2010) have played a key role in limiting air pollution in China. Originally, the legislation focused on air pollution in workplaces, but over the years, laws have been passed that expand into many aspects of this field. For example, in 2015, after a lengthy period of waiting and debate, the Air Pollution Prevention and Control Law was amended by the NPC standing committee in order to address the new challenges arising from air pollution and to fight the serious smog affecting Chinese cities. Similarly, in the field of water pollution prevention and control, the most important legislation in China addressing water pollution is the Water Pollution Prevention and Control Law. First adopted in 1984, the law was amended in 1996 and 2008 to include comprehensive measures to prevent and control water pollution. Nevertheless, several problems continue to exist, including a lack of coordination between the Ministry of Environmental Protection and the Ministry of Water Resources Management as well as the government's failure to act in the countryside and a lack of public participation.

Table 2.3 Pollution prevention and control legislation

Law	Time	Official Chinese Translation
Air Pollution Prevention and Control Law	Enacted in 2000, amended in 2015	中华人民共和国大气污染防治法
Water Pollution Prevention and Control Law	Enacted in 1984, amended in 2008	中华人民共和国水污染防治法
The Administration Regulations of Ozone Depleting Substances	Enacted in 2010	消耗臭氧层物质管理条例
Solid Waste Pollution Prevention and Control Law	Enacted in 1995, amended in 2013	中华人民共和国固体废物污染环境防治法
Environmental Noise Pollution Prevention and Control Law	Enacted in 1996	中华人民共和国环境噪声污染防治法
Radioactive Pollution Prevention and Control Law	Enacted in 2003	中华人民共和国放射性污染防治法
Environmental Impact Assessment Law	Enacted in 2003	中华人民共和国环境影响评价法

Source: Author.

Nature and biodiversity conservation legislation

China is one of the twelve countries with the richest biodiversity in the world. Due to its vast land area, China has various and complicated types of ecosystems, with abundant plant and animal resources. The number of higher plant species in China ranks third in the world, while the total number of vertebrate species in China accounts for 13.7 per cent of the world's total. Nevertheless, China is also one of the countries facing serious threats to biodiversity. Biodiversity loss can lead to serious consequences, such as worsening health problems, higher food risks, increasing vulnerabilities and fewer development opportunities. Biodiversity conservation is therefore strategically important for China's long-term socio-economic development, and the well-being of present and future generations as evidenced in the attempt to build an ecological civilization in China by implementing initiatives such as Beautiful China (MEP 2014e).

In recent years, the Chinese government has established a legal system for the conservation of nature and biodiversity by formulating or amending over 50 related laws and regulations (see Table 2.4). Related laws include *Island Conservation Law* (2010), *Forest Law* (enacted in 1984, amended in 1998), *Wild Fauna Protection Law* (enacted in 1998, amended in 2004), *Marine Environment Protection Law* (1999), *Fisheries Law* (enacted in 1986, last amended in 2013), *Seed Law* (enacted in 2000, amended in 2004) and *Animal Epidemic Prevention Law* (enacted in 1997, amended in 2007). Related regulations include the *Regulation on Nature Reserves* (1994), *Regulation on Wild Plant Conservation* (1996), *Regulation on Protection of New Plant Varieties* (1997), *Regulation on Administration of Import and Export of Endangered Wild Animals and Plants* (2006), *Regulation on Scenic Spots and Historical Sites* (2006), *Regulation on Biosafety Management in Pathogenic Micro-organism Laboratories* (2006) and *Regulation on Protection of New Plant Varieties* (2013). These laws and regulations constitute the legal frameworks for nature conservation and the sustainable use of biodiversity in China.

Table 2.4 Nature and biodiversity conservation legislation

Law	Time	Official Chinese Translation
Wild Fauna Protection Law	Enacted in 1998, amended in 2004	中华人民共和国野生动物保护法
Forest Law	Enacted in 1984, amended in 1998	中华人民共和国森林法
Island Conservation Law	Enacted in 2010	中华人民共和国海岛保护法
Fisheries Law	Enacted in 1986, amended in 2013	中华人民共和国渔业法
Animal Epidemic Prevention Law	Enacted in 1997, amended in 2007	中华人民共和国动物防疫法
Regulation on Nature Reserves	Enacted in 1994	中华人民共和国自然保护区条例
Regulation on Wild Plant Conservation	Enacted in 1996	中华人民共和国野生植物保护条例
Regulation on Administration of Import and Export of Endangered Wild Animals and Plants	Enacted in 2006	中华人民共和国濒危野生动植物进出口管理条例

Source: Author.

Nevertheless, China needs to do much more in the context of biodiversity conservation. The next few years will be a key period for biodiversity conservation in China. China needs greater determination, more effective measures and more resources to fundamentally reverse the trend of biodiversity loss. In the future, priority should be given to the revision and updating of existing laws such as the *Environmental Protection Law*, the *Wild Animal Protection Law*, the *Wild Plant Protection Regulation* and the *Regulation on Nature Reserves*. Furthermore, new laws and regulations focused on wetland protection, invasive alien species control, the management of genetic resources and the biosafety management of genetically modified trees must also be formulated and implemented.

Local environmental legislation in China

With such a vast landmass, China faces complex environmental conditions and unbalanced development in different regions. To guarantee the uniformity of the state's legal system while adapting to the varied environmental problems arising in different regions, the Constitution and legislative framework both prescribe that, in addition to the NPC and the Standing Committee, the people's congresses and the standing committees of the provinces, autonomous regions and municipalities directly under the central government may enact local environmental regulations, provided that such regulations do not contradict the Constitution or the national environmental legislation. Similarly, the people's congresses of the ethnic autonomous areas have the power to enact autonomous environmental regulations and separate environmental regulations on the basis of the environmental conditions of the local ethnic group's territory (Legislation Law 2015).

Unfortunately, this approach leaves some grey areas in the local environmental protection systems, exposing local governments to scissor-like pressure: pressure from above, through the national environmental legislation and pressure from below, from the local interest groups. As a result, local authorities are more often interested in local economic growth than in environmental protection.

New trend in China's environmental legislation: 2014 *Environmental Protection Law*

The 2014 *Environmental Protection Law* provided environmental protection authorities with many new supervisory powers and tools. Measures, such as continuous daily fines, the seizure and distrainment of property, restricted production and production suspension for rectification made the new law a sharp tool for promoting changes in behaviour to protect the environment. However, since the continuous daily fines, seizure and distrainment of property and other measures were all brand new, and the environmental protection authorities at all levels had generally had little experience in legal practice, these provisions of the *Environmental Protection Law* remained significant in principle only. It was imperative that China should issue supplementary implementation measures to standardize the items of each provision, such as the scope of application and the implementation procedures and supervision methods with a view to truly turning these new regulatory instruments into powerful weapons for China's environmental protection departments to crack down on violations. Only through practical and consistent implementation with the full force of the law will polluters be prompted to conscientiously fulfil their obligations as the main actors most directly responsible for environmental protection.

Thus, in order to implement the newly revised Environmental Protection Law and ensure the utilization of the supervisory powers and tools entrusted to environmental protection departments by the new law, the Ministry of Environmental Protection (MEP) issued four supplementary measures on 19 December 2014 including the *Measures of the Competent Environmental Protection Department on Enforcement of Continuous Daily Fines*, the *Measures of the Competent Environmental Protection Department on Restricted Production and Production Suspension for Rectification*, the *Measures on Sharing Environmental Information by Enterprises and Public Institutions* and the *Measures of the Competent Environmental Protection Department on Seizure and Distrainment of Property*.

Continuous daily fines

The *Measures of the Competent Environmental Protection Department on Enforcement of Continuous Daily Fines* consist in 22 articles in four chapters. Elaborating on Article 59 of the new *Environment Protection Law* on imposing continuous daily fines on 'illegal pollutant discharge' and 'refusal to correct', the measures specify the categories of violations subject to this fine, standardize the procedures for its being imposed, clarify the contents and forms of the orders for corrections, set the criteria for identifying conduct that amounts to refusing to stop the illegal discharge of pollutants, provide the calculation method for a continuous daily fine, and identify the complementarity of the continuous daily fine system and other environmental protection systems (MEP 2014a).

Seizure and distrainment of property

The *Measures of the Competent Environmental Protection Department on Seizure and Distrainment of Property* consist of 25 articles in four chapters that are mainly designed to address the problem of frontline law enforcement officials who lack the knowledge and courage to carry out the seizure and distrainment of property. To promote the practical implementation of the provision that environmental departments 'may seal up and detain the facilities and equipment causing pollutant discharge' in cases of actual 'illegal pollutant discharge' or cases that are 'causing or having the potential to cause severe pollution' as specified in Article 25 of the new environmental law, the measures identify and clarify the definition, applicable scope, object and implementation procedure, as well as the oversight and inspection of seizure and distrainment (MEP 2014b). At the same time, while regulating the exercise of power, these measures can substantially reduce the enforcement risk caused by the misuse or abuse of seizure and distrainment of property.

Restricted production and production suspension for rectification

The *Measures of the Competent Environmental Protection Department on Restricted Production and Production Suspension for Rectification* consist of 22 articles in four chapters that focus on the application of Article 60 of the new law. According to these articles, measures such as 'restricted production', 'production suspension for rectification' and 'closure or shutdown' may be applied to the offence of discharging pollutants 'in excess of emission standards or in excess of the total emission quota'. In particular, these measures aim to identify and define the applicable circumstances of 'restricted production', 'suspended production for rectification' and 'applying for government approval for operation shutdown' in order to refine implementation procedures for restricting production and suspending operation to rectify as consequences, and to strengthen supervision of enforcement of these measures (MEP 2014c).

Sharing environmental information by enterprises and public institutions

Finally, the eighteen articles containing the *Measures on Sharing Environmental Information by Enterprises and Public Institutions* aim to meet the basic needs of the public for environmental information about corporate enterprises, while taking the information disclosure capabilities of corporate enterprises into account. It combines principles with feasibility to focus on addressing such issues as 'who should disclose information', 'what information should be disclosed', 'how to disclose information' and 'how to supervise information disclosure', thus providing guidelines for the scope, content, approach and supervision of information disclosure (MEP 2014d).

To better serve and guide local officials in the effective implementation of the new environmental law, these four supplementary measures define the statutory duties and boundaries of responsibility of the environmental protection departments while highlighting the fact that the polluter is the major party directly responsible for environmental protection. For example, the most prominent features of the *Measures of the Competent Environmental Protection Department on Enforcement of Continuous Daily Fines* and the *Measures of the Competent Environmental Protection Department on Restricted Production and Production Suspension for Rectification* follow the legislative spirit of the new *Environmental Protection Law* by making the polluter the main party responsible for stopping any illegal pollutant discharge and conducting rectification, insisting on the polluter's self-discipline as the foundation for implementing the ordered correction, ensuring that restricted production and suspended production are used for rectification, and holding the polluter responsible for any environmental behaviour and damages. Once a polluter is ordered to limit production or suspend operations, a rectification plan must be filed, self-monitoring of the rectification process must be carried out, and responsibility for rectifying the situation must be accepted. In the same way, the polluter's responsibilities as the main party in the environmental protection system are underscored in the process of releasing the corporate entity from restrictions. Lifting the provisions that restrict and suspend production to allow for rectification no longer require the verification and acceptance procedures of an environmental protection department, but is now dependent on the decision and plan of the polluter. This encourages the polluter to take the initiative in the rectification process. The polluter is required to take full responsibility for the results of the rectification, thus strengthening the self-discipline of the polluter.

Concluding remarks

Is China a superhero intent on saving the world economy or a monster focused on damaging the global environment? As a developing country with the largest population in the world, China has wrought a stunning miracle of economic development. However, this rapid economic growth, like a double-edged sword, has given rise to severe environmental problems, such as climate change, water pollution and resource exhaustion among others. Moreover, these environmental challenges will in turn lead to new political, economic and social problems. Although the Rio Conference is now 20 years old, sustainable development is still a hot topic of discussion and a crucial issue in China. Currently, the country is facing a grave ecological situation and must undertake the arduous task of addressing the environmental problems. Widespread, persistent smog has continued to afflict many parts of China in recent years, arousing public concern and underlining the need to switch from the current model of extensive development to a green, environment-friendly economy. China's environmental legislation has evolved slowly and developed over the last few decades, marking remarkable achievements in the context of a legal framework for environmental protection. However, China still has a long way to go on the road towards achieving the goals that underlie the environmental legislation.

References

Bachner, B., 1996. Regulating Pollution in the People's Republic of China: An Analysis of the Enforcement of Environmental Law, *Colorado Journal of International Environmental Law and Policy* 7, 373–408.

Beyer, S., 2006. Environmental Law and Policy in the People's Republic of China, *Chinese Journal of International Law* 5 (1), 185–211.

Bosworth, D. and Yang D., 2000. Intellectual Property Law, Technology Flow and Licensing Opportunities in the People's Republic of China, *International Business Review* 9, 453–477.

Cai S., 2012. Huanjing Yu Ziyuan Baohu Fa (Environment and Nature Resource Protection Law) Beijing: Higher Education Press (only available in Chinese).

Constitution of the People's Republic of China, 1982. Available at http://english.gov.cn/archive/laws_regulations/2014/08/23/content_281474982987458.htm (accessed 20 December 2016).

Deal, C., 2007. Climate Change, Technology Transfer: Opportunities in the Developing World, ASME WISE Intern, p. 2.

Environmental Protection Law of the People's Republic of China, 2014. Available at www.npc.gov.cn/npc/xinwen/2014-04/25/content_1861279.htm (accessed 12 December 2015).

Kaiman, J. 2014. China Strengthens Environmental Laws, Chinese Legal Database, 25 April 2014.

Langfitt, F., 2013. China's Air Pollution: Is the Government Willing to Act?, WBUR News 24 May. Available at http://wbur.org/npr/186246634/Chinas-air-pollution-is-the-government-willing-to-act (accessed 2 February 2016).

Legislation Law of the People's Republic of China, 2015. Available at www.gov.cn/zhengce/2015-03/18/content_2834713.htm (accessed 12 February 2016).

Liu C., 2013. Water Demands of Coal-Fired Power Drying Up Northern China, *Scientific American* 25 March. Available at http://scientificamerican.com/article/water-demands-of-coal-fired-power-drying-up-northern-china/ (accessed 10 February 2016).

McElwee, C., 2011. *Environmental Law in China: Mitigating Risk and Ensuring Compliance.* New York: Oxford University Press.

MEP (Ministry of Environmental Protection of China), 2014a. *Measures of the Competent Environmental Protection Department on Enforcement of Continuous Daily Fines.*

MEP (Ministry of Environmental Protection of China), 2014b. *Measures of the Competent Environmental Protection Department on Seizure and Confiscation of Property.*

MEP (Ministry of Environmental Protection of China), 2014c. *Measures of the Competent Environmental Protection Department on Restricted Production and Production Suspension for Rectification.*

MEP (Ministry of Environmental Protection of China), 2014d. *Measures on Sharing Environmental Information by Enterprises and Public Institutions.*

MEP (Ministry of Environmental Protection of China), 2014e. *China's Fifth National Report on the Implementation of the Convention on Biological Diversity.* Available at https://www.cbd.int/doc/world/cn/cn-nr-05-en.pdf (accessed 20 December 2016).

Miller, A.; Leape, J.; Schroeder, C. and Percival, R., 2006. *Environmental Regulations: Law, Science, and Policy*, New York: Aspen.

Orts, E.W., 2003. Environmental Law with Chinese Characteristics, *William & Mary Bill of Rights Journal* 11 (2). Available at http://scholarship.law.wm.edu/wmborj/vol11/iss2/3 (accessed 22 November 2016).

Qin T. (ed), 2013. *Huanjingfa: Zhidu, Lilu he Anli* (Environmental Law: Systems, Theories and Cases), Wuhan, China: Wuhan University Press.

Qin T., 2015. *Research Handbook on Chinese Environmental Law*, Cheltenham, UK and Northampton, MA, USA: Edward Elgar.

State Council Information Office of the People's Republic of China, 2011. *White paper: The Socialist System of Laws with Chinese Characteristics.* Available at http://www.gov.cn/jrzg/2011-10/27/content_1979498.htm (accessed 12 November 2015).

U.S. Environmental Protection Agency, 2008. *China Environmental Law Initiative.* Available at http://www.ncbi.nlm.nih.gov/pmc/articles/PMC2516562/ (accessed 11 January 2016).

Wen, J., 2009. Climate Change and China: Technology, Market and Beyond. Report for Focus on the Global South, Occasional Paper 6. Available at http://focusweb.org/sites/www.focusweb.org/files/occ6.pdf (accessed 22 November 2016).

Wiener, J., 2008. Climate Change Policy and Policy Change in China, *UCLA Law Review* 55, 1805–26.

World Bank and State Environmental Protection Administration PRC, 2007. *Costs of pollution in China.* Washington DC: World Bank and State Environmental Protection Administration.

3

CHINA'S LOCAL ENVIRONMENTAL POLITICS

Genia Kostka

Introduction

China's national leaders have recently made a priority of changing lanes from a pollution-intensive, growth-at-any-cost model to a resource-efficient and sustainable one. There is strong reasoning behind this shift in emphasis: China's leaders see political risks in the rising tide of domestic environmental protests and they worry about energy and resource security. Beijing's determination to steer China toward greater resource efficiency and lower carbon emissions is beyond dispute. Yet creating green and liveable cities remains an uphill battle for national policymakers. The immense challenges of rapid urbanization are one aspect of the problem. An estimated 300 million people will be added to Chinese cities by 2030 (OECD 2009), adding further pressure to cities that already struggle with serious air and water pollution. Central–local relations are another source of difficulty since Beijing's green agenda also does not always find willing followers at lower levels. Indeed, many of Beijing's low-carbon and green initiatives are implemented only selectively across China, when sub-national leaders take the lead.

The objective of this chapter is to identify barriers to a more comprehensive implementation of environmental policies at the city level and suggest ways to reduce or remove them. The research focuses particularly on the reasons for the gap between national plans and local policy outcomes. While environmental goals and policies at the national level are quite ambitious and comprehensive, it is insufficient and inconsistent implementation at the local level that holds back significant improvements in urban environmental quality. By analysing local institutional obstacles and by highlighting best-practice examples, this chapter outlines possible options that can be used at the national and local levels to close the local 'environmental implementation gap'. These findings contribute to the ongoing debate regarding how China can switch to a greener urban growth path and emphasize the need to create additional incentives and increase local implementation capacities.

Analytical framework

While national policymakers have started impressive efforts to switch to a more green and low carbon growth path, many elements of Beijing's green agenda fall to local governments for

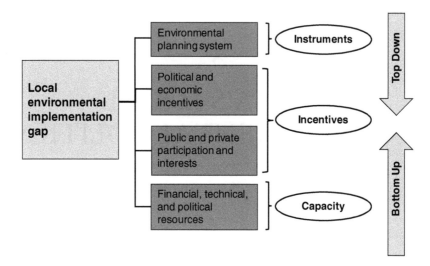

Figure 3.1 Institutional barriers to explain the local environmental implementation gap

Source: Author; adapted from Kostka 2014.

delivery. Despite numerous incentives for local cadres to abide by Beijing's directives woven into the cadre management system and provision of additional resources for green projects, a substantial environmental policy implementation gap exists.

Figure 3.1 offers an analytical framework, which aims to explain the main institutional challenges for the persisting environmental implementation gap at the local level. To better understand how institutional barriers affect local environmental policy outcomes, the following pages analyse the principal aspects: shortcomings in China's planning system and policy instruments; weak economic and political incentives for local implementers; low levels of public participation and private sector involvement; and insufficient implementation capacities of local agencies in charge of policy implementation.

Policy instruments and shortcomings in China's green planning system[1]

China has employed a mix of top-down command and control methods and market-based mechanisms to propel the switch to a resource-efficient and low carbon growth path. Since 1972, the central government has very noticeably deployed more and more administrative instruments to enhance compliance with national environmental rules and standards. In the last four decades, more than 28 environmental and resource laws, 150 national administrative environmental regulations, 1,300 national environmental standards, and 200 departmental administrative regulations have been issued (Chang 2008 quoted in He et al. 2012, 31 and Qin and Zhang chapter 2 this volume).

More recently, China has also experimented with a variety of market-based instruments to supplement existing command and control tools, including piloting a dozen sub-national voluntary emission cap-and-trade schemes, rolling out a three-tiered electricity pricing system, promoting energy service companies and introducing numerous payment for ecosystem services to improve water, air, forest, and soil management (Jotzo and Löschel 2014; Kostka and Shin 2013; Liang and Mol 2013; Shin 2013). Yet the majority of these market-based instruments have not scaled up to nationwide programmes due to the lack of market preconditions and excessive state intervention in emission trading formats, allocation methods, and pricing approaches (Lo 2013; Shin 2013). With market-based instruments still in their infancy, China's environmental governance system continues to rely primarily on top-down command and control instruments.

Among the many different command and control instruments, setting binding environmental targets has become the key environmental management tool in China. Environmental targets are incorporated into the target responsibility system (*mubiao zeren zhi*), wherein the central government sets a national target for a policy or programme and then assigns specific targets for particular areas. Central leaders' priorities are communicated by differentiating between 'soft', expected (*yuqixing*), and 'hard', literally restricted (*yueshuxing*) binding environmental targets in the national FYPs. The majority of these 'hard' binding targets have been accorded 'veto power' (*yipiao foujue*) status, meaning that, if these targets are not met, all other achievements of a local leader will be rendered null and void. This is a powerful incentive in the context of stiff competition between local cadres for promotion to upper-level positions.

Although environmental targets had been incorporated into national FYPs as of the late 1990s, they were accorded fairly low priority in the context of the overriding emphasis on national economic growth and the 'soft' nature of these targets (Wang 2013). In 2006, at the beginning of the 11th FYP, central planners in Beijing upgraded a number of environmental targets from 'expected' to 'binding' status. Binding environmental targets were thereafter written into local leading cadres' annual responsibility contracts and became an important criteria in cadre promotion decisions. The intent was to incentivize officials at each layer of government administration to fulfil Beijing's environmental mandates (Heberer and Senz 2011; Ran 2013). In addition, the scope of binding environmental targets widened from the original three binding environmental targets in the 11th FYP to a total of nine binding targets in the 12th FYP. These targets touch on air quality (sulphur dioxide and nitrogen oxide), water quality (chemical oxygen demand and ammonium), energy efficiency, carbon efficiency, the production/use of non-fossil fuels, water consumption intensity, and forest coverage. By adding new environmental targets to the two most recent national FYPs, and making them binding, Beijing has added teeth to its green growth ambitions.

The heavy reliance on binding environmental targets reflects Chinese leaders' pragmatic judgements about how best to fit new policies to existing implementation structures. Indeed, the target-based approach has delivered on intended policy outcomes in the past. Two notable examples are the family planning targets used to implement China's one-child policy and investment growth targets that set limits on local investment growth in order to curb China's inflation (Huang 1996). Environmental targets are, however, unlike family planning and investment targets, in several important ways. For example, in comparison to family planning, allocating environmental targets can be a much more contentious political process since environmental targets frequently impose high costs on local businesses and local employment. In addition, the implementation of environmental targets is often characterized by a time lag such that costs are incurred in the short term but benefits only materialize in the long term. This is problematic since the realization of such policies is out of sync with the rhythms of the cadre rotation system with the result that local cadres are strongly incentivized to undertake initiatives which yield results in the short term. With respect to the matter of target verification, local deviation from the one-child policy is relatively easy to detect, whereas non-compliance with energy intensity targets is not as readily apparent since measurement standards for energy efficiency are complicated and outcomes are not visible (Rietbergen and Blok 2010). Given these distinctive characteristics of environmental targets, a critical analysis of leaders' responses to top-down targets helps to generate a realistic picture of what binding environmental targets can and cannot achieve.

The heavy reliance on a target-based implementation approach has so far yielded a number of *desirable* results. First, environmental issues have moved quickly onto the policy agenda of many city mayors and Party secretaries. Second, the target-based system allows for some flexibility in factoring in local circumstances. Environmental targets can be allocated either through a 'one-size-fits-all' or a 'differentiated' approach. In Jiangsu, for instance, all municipalities received a uniform forest coverage target of 20 per cent, while forest coverage targets in Shandong and Hunan were differentiated for municipalities. In addition to the question of how to allocate targets to subordinate governments and enterprises, local governments are also given flexibility as to *when* to implement binding targets during the five-year planning period. For instance, in one county in Hunan, leaders set the same annual energy intensity targets of minus 3.43 per cent per year over the entire planning period, while in the neighbouring county, energy intensity targets started high with minus 5 per cent for the first year and declined to minus 3.5 per cent over time. Leaders selected this descending method since they believed that there would be less and less room to achieve additional energy savings.

Another desirable or intended aspect of the system is that frequent reporting on environmental target fulfilment strengthens the Party's performance legitimacy. At the end of the 11th FYP, frequent announcements on environmental targets communicated to the Chinese public that the central government is doing everything possible to realize announced goals. For example, when, during the last months leading up to the end of the 11th FYP, it became clear that China was not on track to meet its national energy intensity target of 20 per cent, former Chinese Premier Wen Jiabao publicly called for local officials to use an 'iron hand' when implementing the energy intensity targets. Such announcements communicate to the Chinese public that the central government takes the implementation of environmental policies very seriously and if targets are not met, it is likely because of policy shirking by local governments. Therefore, authoritarian regimes can exploit binding environmental targets to enhance trust in central authorities and enhance the appearance of effective governance, thus ultimately furthering the Party's legitimacy.

While the introduction of binding environmental targets has, to date, resulted in a number of positive outcomes, the target system also generates multiple *undesirable* (and often unanticipated) results. Heavy reliance on binding environmental targets can also be problematic as allocated targets can be inappropriate to local circumstances and units of protection, unscientific, rigid, arbitrarily inflated as they get passed down the administrative hierarchy, and difficult to verify (Kostka 2016).

Inappropriate to local circumstances and units of protection

First, picking nine binding environmental targets in the 12th FYP also means neglecting other important environmental targets and issues, such as binding targets for particulate matter 2.5 ($PM_{2.5}$) or water efficiency in the agricultural sector. As binding environmental targets cascade downward through the administrative hierarchy, targets set by upper-level governments might not fully represent local conditions or local environmental priorities. As a result, the most urgent local environmental protection challenges might be untouched by the target system. For example, heavy non-ferrous mining industries in Chenzhou municipality (Hunan) caused severe pollution in multiple counties over the last two decades. Yet because there was no binding target addressing non-ferrous metal pollution until the most current 12th FYP, the most pressing local pollution issue was not tackled until recently (Kostka 2016). Moreover, targets can be inappropriate since targets are usually distributed based on administrative boundaries, which do not necessarily match the unit of protection. Lakes, rivers or wetlands are complete ecosystems that should be managed as single entities rather than parcelled out to different administrative units (for more detailed case studies, see Kostka (2014)).

Unscientific targets

As targets get distributed at each level, bureaucrats need to make decisions as to how to share the burden of implementation. Yet, this decision-making process requires a constant flow of high quality information in order to identify the 'right' target level for subordinate governments and enterprises. In the absence of such information, the use of one-size-fits-all targets can distribute the implementation burden very unequally between different reporting units. For example, within the same municipality in Hunan, one EPB reported that air pollution targets were 'easy' to achieve while two neighbouring counties felt they were 'difficult'. Such scenarios can generate resentment and supply incentives for heavily-burdened localities to misreport data on difficult targets. With many local governments lacking in the technical know-how and resources needed to decide on differentiated targets, they are often not allocated in the most optimal way.

Rigid targets

Targets also remain rigid. For example, one urban district in Hunan failed to meet its 11th FYP energy intensity target because a large-sized, central state-owned power enterprise moved into the district. District leaders escaped punishment only because the municipality still managed to meet its overall target despite the shortfall in the district.

Inflated targets

Moreover, as binding environmental targets get passed down to lower tiers of government and bureaus, sometimes unattainable targets are allocated to subordinate governments. Provincial and municipal government officials often inflate environmental targets when passing them down the administrative hierarchy in order to allow for slippage as they anticipate that some environmental projects and efforts will fail or that the results will be questioned by national inspection teams. For example, in one municipality in Shanxi, energy intensity targets among counties generally ranged from 27 to 30 per cent, despite a municipal overall target of only 25 per cent (Kostka and Hobbs 2012). Receiving unattainable targets demotivates local leaders in charge of implementation and, in extreme cases, can trigger non-cooperation by local leaders.

Verification difficulties

In addition, because targets differ widely in terms of their ease of measurability, verifiability, and the extent to which they are tied to vital economic and social issues, the effectiveness and efficiency of binding environmental targets can vary widely. For example, forest coverage targets are easier to measure and verify due to existing GPS technologies, while energy intensity is more difficult to measure and verify since there are multiple ways to calculate energy and GDP data and no sophisticated technical equipment exists to monitor performance. Some localities measured energy intensity per GDP or per value added in large-scale (*guimo yi shang*) enterprises. This measure can be problematic because GDP data for the service sector is often not reliable, especially when it gets down to county-level data.

Political and economic incentives for local policy implementers

As described in the analytical framework, besides the green planning system, the incentives provided to local actors via the cadre management system play a crucial steering function in local policy implementation. One can differentiate between political incentives, meaning political awards local bureaucrats can expect, and economic incentives, referring to the economic payoffs different actions are likely to produce for both political leaders and private actors.

Political incentives for local governments

Political incentives play a central role in motivating local cadres to fulfil national green mandates and targets. Like other mandatory targets, binding environmental targets have been linked with the annual cadre promotion and evaluation system. Outstanding performances in the annual cadre evaluation are rewarded through promotions (in rank or position), additional wage or bonus payments, or other material benefits, including administrative benefits (e.g., free transport, entertainment, training, and travel), and other allowances for cadres (e.g., subsidized housing, health care, and opportunities for further education). If local leaders fail to meet binding targets, they can face punishments through, for example, denial of promotion and formal censure, such as redeployment to a remote region or, in rare cases, expulsion from office. Local leaders (e.g., the Party secretary and mayor of a province, municipality, or county) also sign individual responsibility contracts that include specific annual energy or emission reduction requirements for their locality. The signing of personal responsibility contracts helps to ensure that government officials at each layer of government administration are motivated to at least partially fulfil upper-level government directives.

Managers of state-owned enterprises (SOEs) are also embedded within the same system of annual cadre evaluation, meaning that they are more easily incentivized to comply with environmental standards than managers of private enterprises (Kostka and Hobbs 2012; Harrison and Kostka 2014). SOE managers who fall short of their annual goals can be excluded from year-end bonuses and be subject to other political punishments. Managers of certain large SOEs who significantly increase energy efficiency and reduce emissions may yield political benefits including promotions. SOEs have a reputation for shirking regulations and getting away with worse environmental practices (Lo and Tang 2006, 204), but the above example suggests that the government can sometimes effectively leverage links to SOE managers to achieve environmental gains. Informants also reported that SOEs are more easily regulated because local government officials have better information access to them as compared to private enterprises.

Shortcomings of the cadre incentive system

In spite of political and economic incentives woven into the cadre management system, the incentive system does not always work effectively. Leading cadres' pressures for target fulfilment can lead to short-term maximization behaviour instead of long-term innovative environmental management. Many of the environmental and energy intensity targets in the 11th FYP were implemented at the eleventh hour and implementation measures did not yield lasting change. In some localities, binding energy intensity targets were fulfilled at the very end of the planning period using extreme and sometimes socially harmful measures. These included cutting electricity to hospitals, homes and rural villages. Local governments also temporarily shut down energy-intensive companies for a given period of time only to allow the same enterprises to later reopen, a method known as 'sleeping management' (*xiumian guanli*) (Kostka and Hobbs 2012). These low quality implementation approaches ensured that leading cadres met their energy intensity target outlined in their individual responsibility contracts but effectively put off the difficult matter of economic restructuring (Eaton and Kostka 2014). In contrast, after the completion of the 11th FYP targets in 2010, many localities went back to 'business as usual' and, at the beginning of the 12th FYP in 2011, they thought of creative ways of easing their new burden. For example, they worked to attract outside companies in the hopes of boosting local growth as a means of manipulating the energy intensity ratio since energy intensity = energy consumed/GDP.

The existing cadre incentive system is also somewhat problematic as tensions between environmental and economic targets result from the different weights allocated to targets in the cadre evaluation forms (*kaohebiao*). Generally, economic targets significantly outweigh social and environmental targets. For example, in one county in Shanxi province, government officials could obtain a maximum of 28 points for meeting economic targets in the 2011 evaluation forms, while just 14 points were allocated to resources and environment targets (Eaton and Kostka 2013).

Overall, it is clear that environmental targets, while substantially more important now than previously, compete for space on the crowded agenda of local officials. In these circumstances, most local officials have adopted the attitude of doing the very minimum required.[2] One official in a county in Shandong said: 'It is like a constraint maximization problem (youyue shue de jidahua): We try to maximize GDP and fiscal income, but we meet only the bare minimum of environmental standards. This is of course not always efficient for the environment'.[3] A leading EPB official further reflects: 'Environmental and energy targets are binding targets but they are not our ultimate targets. No leader will be promoted because of their better achievements in environmental protection and energy savings. GDP growth is still the target that we work hardest to achieve'.[4] This attitude explains why all the three municipalities and six counties visited during fieldwork in 2012 set an annual GDP growth rate between 12 to 17 per cent in the local 12th FYP, twice as high as the national 12th FYP growth rate of 7 per cent. A local EPB official notes 'in theory, all local departments should together decide about local GDP growth rates, but in practice it is finally decided by the local Development and Reform Commission (DRC), while the EPB does not have much say in this'.[5] When asked why they selected such high growth targets, local DRC officials often replied that national or provincial figures are 'average' figures and some regions will have higher growth and some regions will have lower growth.[6] Naturally, no locality wants to 'sacrifice' their economic development and have average or below-average growth. In addition, promotion-seeking cadres will look for projects with high 'political accomplishment value' to impress their superiors but these actions can lead to less optimal outcomes for the locality in the long term (Eaton and Kostka 2014).[7]

Cadre rotation system and local leaders' short time horizon

Implementation of environmental targets is made harder through the institutionalized cadre rotation system that switches leading cadres to a new position or locality every three to four years (Eaton and Kostka 2014). Available data suggest that leading local cadres do not stay long in their positions.[8] Party secretaries and mayors, the two pillars of a city's leadership group (*lingdao banzi*), are typically whisked off to a new locale well before the recommended five-year term for civil servants and Party cadres in leadership positions.[9] On average, mayors and Party secretaries at county and municipal levels tend to serve between three and four years before moving on to their next assignment (Seckington 2007; Eaton and Kostka 2014). For instance, data on 898 former municipal Party secretaries appointed across China between 1993 and 2011 reveals that the average time in office was 3.8 years, 1.2 years shorter than the recommended tenure time for cadres in leadership positions (Kostka and Yu 2015). Beyond the leadership group, departmental heads with a key role in environmental policy implementation also rotate on average every four years. For instance, the average time served as head of a provincial DRC, the head of a provincial EPB, and the head of a provincial Construction Bureau was 3.6 years, 4.0 years, and 4.6 years, respectively (Kostka 2013).

There are pros and cons of the cadre turnover system and its effects on environmental policy implementation. Frequent post-shuffling among local cadres can help to bridge departmental gulfs, an eternal problem in China's huge and fragmented bureaucracy. Circulating cadres between different administrative levels can also enhance communication across administrative levels and improve cadres' knowledge of upper or lower governments' daily tasks. Job rotations through SOEs can also aid effective environmental governance; cadres with previous work experience in state-owned enterprises can draw from their knowledge of enterprises' decision-making processes and internal politics and thus negotiate more effectively with enterprise managers on implementation of onerous environmental regulations (Eaton and Kostka 2014).

Although cadre rotation has some benefits for environmental policy implementation, there are also significant downsides to the rotation system. Short tenure cycles incentivize cadres to prioritize short-term over long-term gains. For instance, a series of short-staying mayors and Party secretaries in Datong City, Shanxi province, had reputations for extracting rents from local industries while avoiding the painful restructuring Datong urgently needed (Eaton and Kostka 2013). In addition, frequent rotation of leading cadres can be disruptive to local development planning. Newly-posted cadres frequently stop existing initiatives, regardless of their merits, in order to place their own stamp on a locality. Finally, in the space of a three- or four-year tenure, circulating officials spend much of their time simply getting up to speed in their new localities and their limited knowledge of local circumstances can result in suboptimal environmental policy outcomes (Eaton and Kostka 2014). Once leading cadres move on to a new post, they are also no longer held responsible for environmental outcomes of their previous actions. This inability to hold cadres responsible for environmental damage after they leave a post prompted Xi Jinping's call for 'lifetime accountability' for cadres (*South China Morning Post* 2013). In 2015, the State Council approved the inclusion of such a lifetime accountability rule for environmental pollution in the new 'Guidelines of Pushing the Construction of Eco-Civilization' (Lelyveld 2015) and announced a roll out of this policy across China by the end of the decade. Yet, whether such a rule can be effectively enforced remains to be seen because there are serious concerns whether an independent audit system can be established to effectively audit officials' performances (Zhang 2015).

Economic incentives for local governments

Next to personal political incentives, local cadre behaviour is also determined by economic incentives. Local governments increasingly face pressure to enhance local income since local governments are assigned the main responsibilities for delivering public services and infrastructure provision, yet revenues based on tax revenue sharing and intergovernmental fiscal transfers are insufficient to cover these costs (Wu et al. 2013; Wong 2010, 2013a). The revenues received from the sale of land use rights and urban construction projects have become a particularly important source of extra-budgetary income for local governments, but this often has led to urban sprawl and wasteful land use. The revenues received from the sale of land use rights have become the most important source of extra-budgetary income for local governments (Man 2011, 12). The institutional structure of the land transfer process also enables local governments to make significant profits. The compensation required for requisitioned agricultural land, based on the administrative formula, is usually much lower than the conveyance fees governments receive from private developments (Lichtenberg and Ding 2009, 58). Estimates and anecdotal evidence suggest conveyance fees are approximately 10 to 20 times the value of compensations (Tian and Ma 2009, 603; Lichtenberg and Ding 2009, 58). In addition, prior to the transfer, the price for the land sale is often intentionally driven up by increasing values through infrastructure construction such as investments in highways, metro stations, or even airports (Wei and Zhao 2009, 1034). Given these economic incentives, city expansion *'always pays off, whether people end up living there or not'* (Kaufman 2012, 43). At its most extreme, these economic incentives can lead to the emergence of ghost cities such as Kangbashi New Area in Ordos City in Inner Mongolia.

In summary, insufficient political incentives and severe budget constraints at the local level disincentivize local cadres to faithfully implement national environmental mandates. As a result, cadres quite rationally invest the majority of time and funds in projects that produce tangible evidence of economic growth within their own tenure.

Limits on public and private participation

Another barrier at the local level is the limited opportunities that exist for participation of local non-state actors to improve environmental management. In the following, this problem is referred to as the 'participation gap'. Participation in China's environmental policy-making has traditionally been structured and institutionalized within the state and party systems, for instance, through the Chinese People's Political Consultative Conference (CPPCC) at various levels. These mechanisms of participation – characterized by restricted opportunities for participation and limited access to decision makers – continue to define Chinese environmental policy-making (Kostka and Mol 2013). Environmental guidelines and measures are initiated, driven, and executed by the government. As discussed in the following, local government officials from the EPB and other government agencies interact with and respond to pressures from industry, public, non-governmental organizations and the mass media.

Vested interests of the business sector

Despite the central government's push for tighter environmental regulations and restrictions, industry has various means of countering costly environmental measures. Many larger companies at the local level – especially central- or provincial-level state-owned oil and power companies – have continued to prioritize profit-making over fulfilling environmental standards at the local level (Eaton and Kostka 2017). For instance, state-owned power companies are reported to violate government regulations on emissions from coal-burning plants and regularly ignore guidelines to upgrade coal-burning electricity plants (Wong 2013b; Eaton and Kostka 2015). China's oil companies have also held up an improvement in diesel fuel for years.

Moreover, in cities where only a small number of companies contribute to the major share of tax revenue or employment, these few companies wield great bargaining power, making it particularly difficult for local government officials to enforce unwelcome environmental regulation on them. Finally, enforcing compliance from private enterprises and SMEs has proven to be difficult for local governments. For example, under the recent Top-10,000 Energy-Consuming Enterprises Program, large energy-intensive enterprises have started to undertake substantial efficiency improvements, but the programme needs to broaden its scope beyond targeting larger, predominantly state-owned, enterprises. For instance, China's industrial SME sector – which is largely privately owned – accounts for 41 per cent of the total energy consumption, followed by non-industrial enterprises (29 per cent) and large industrial enterprises (17 per cent) (IFC 2012, 20). As such, the SME sector is not unimportant in terms of overall energy usage and emissions (Kostka et al. 2013).

Limited role of public and media

The public has numerous ways to participate in local environmental governance, but the scope and effectiveness of these practices have their limits.[10] As early as the 1970s, China set up a complaint system (the so-called *letters and visits system*) to assist in government accountability and in setting priorities in the field of environmental pollution mitigation. Urban citizens also increasingly use social media like *Weibo* and online chat rooms to exchange opinions and alert fellow citizens to local environmental problems. Although there are clear indications that these complaint systems do have an impact on priority setting and control and enforcement activities of local environmental officials (Kostka and Mol 2013), such bottom-up pressure still plays only a very minimal role.

Public hearings form a more institutionalized arrangement for participation in China's environmental policy-making. The best-known example concerns local public hearings in the Environmental Impact Assessment (EIA) procedure, as formalized in the 2002 EIA law and its implementation measures. Yet, such a legal obligation to organize consultation with citizens does not mean that they always take place – and in a meaningful way (for EIA procedures and public participation see also chapter 18).

Citizens also put pressure on local governments to enforce pollution standards by exposing local polluters through the media. The media is influential in shaping both public and government officials' perceptions of environmental issues, but particular attention is placed on issues that have immediate implications for citizens' lives. For instance, the media heavily covers $PM_{2.5}$ pollution issues but pays much less attention to less visible pollution issues such as heavy metal pollution. Media reports also tend to focus more on specific events (e.g., a new polluting enterprise moving to a particular region) than they do on pollution problems that develop gradually. As a result, local government agencies increasingly feel pressure to immediately respond to media reports and might sideline other equally pressing but less publicly reported environmental problems (Lora-Wainright 2013). Sometimes local government agencies also rely on local media to put pressure on other local government agencies or local enterprises. For instance, in Lanzhou, the local EPB criticized central SOEs in their jurisdiction for non-compliance with emissions guidelines in the local media, adding pressure to the leading government officials to finally take punitive action (Eaton and Kostka 2017). Organized protests in cities have also recently helped to oust polluting factories and, in some cases, have succeeded in putting a stop to polluting projects and closing down polluting enterprises.

Limited role of local NGOs

Over the last few years, NGOs working on environmental issues have considerably increased in number but their influence is limited as they are not integrated in policy formulation processes and play a 'supplementary role' at best. While reliable official numbers do not exist, estimates suggest that there are currently approximately 1,000 registered environmental non-governmental organizations (ENGOs), as well as a similar number of unregistered ENGOs. The majority are quite small and are not directly engaged in environmental policy-making and implementation, but instead focus on awareness-raising, education, study, and research. A number of those ENGOs engaged in policy advocacy are spin-offs of governmental organizations and institutes and are often referred to as government organized NGOs (GONGOs). Through closed networks with policymakers and their expert knowledge, these GONGOs articulate environmental interests and bring them into state institutions and decision-making processes. In doing so, GONGOs play a role in bridging the gap between NGOs and civil society, on the one hand, and the state on the other, but they are sometimes criticized for having achieved a place at the table at the expense of taking a softer stand on environmental issues than independent ENGOs. Increasingly, we see also independent ENGOs being incorporated into environmental policy-making and implementation processes, by sharing their knowledge with government agencies, writing petitions, using media outlets, discussing policy alternatives with officials and providing legal assistance to pollution victims. Several studies have detailed how such ENGOs explore the boundaries of what is allowed in contemporary China in terms of NGO engagement, policy involvement and protest (Hildebrandt 2011; Wu 2013). Often local governments are not very enthusiastic about ENGOs playing these watchdog roles.

Capacity constraints

State capacity is of key importance to the enforcement of environmental policies at the local level as well as the effective use of environmental policy instruments (Schwartz 2003). Local governments work under certain political, technical, or financial capacity constraints that influence environmental policy outcomes.

Political capacity: fragmented and weak environmental bureaucracies

Political capacity constraints can result from coordination difficulties due to the following three factors. First, the implementation and enforcement of environmental mandates at the local level is partly hindered by the fragmented and ambiguous allocation of environmental responsibilities. Usually, numerous government agencies are responsible for the implementation of a single environmental issue but sometimes without a clear division of labour, which in practice ultimately leads to a lack of accountability (Ran 2013). For example, more than five departments have a role to play in energy efficiency implementation at sub-national levels: the local DRC, the Economic Commission, the Construction Department, the Transportation Department and the EPB.

Second, implementing agencies also face multiple and sometimes conflicting goals within an organization (for a comprehensive table of conflicting priorities, see Ran 2013). For example, the local DRC is in charge of multiple functions; its main interest lies in economic overseeing planning and investment management, while at the same time it is also responsible for overseeing energy efficiency and climate change issues. In many cases, the DRC's industrial and economic policy goals trump its environmental mandates.

Third, the implementation capacity of local departments in charge of environmental mandates is further constrained by their low bureaucratic status and rank within the local political hierarchy. Local agencies in charge of enforcing China's binding environmental targets vary in their political status within the locality. For example, as the agency in charge of energy efficiency issues, the local DRC holds a wider net of bureaucratic links and access to finance than, for instance, the EPB. The EPB, on the other hand, has the authority to impose 'regional investment restrictions', an enforcement practice that can restrict the environmental approvals of all new projects. By contrast, local Water and Resource Bureaus do not have the same range of enforcement tools available to enforce water consumption targets (Kostka 2014).

The importance of providing local bureaucracies with an adequate independent status to enforce environmental policies can be illustrated with the example of local EPBs. Although the total number of employees working in local EPBs increased from 105,900 in 1998 to 166,800 in 2005 (Li and Higgins 2013, 412), EPB officials frequently complained that they have only limited enforcement authority. For example, government officials in SOEs are often senior in rank to directors of local EPBs, making it difficult for local EPBs to assert bureaucratic authority to compel compliance to minimum environmental standards (Ma and Ortolano 2000). EPB officials frequently mentioned the 'central SOE problem' and noted that nothing could be done to prevent central SOEs (*yangqi*) from polluting their localities except bringing this problem to the attention of their superiors at the next administrative level (Eaton and Kostka 2017).

Moreover, leadership appointments of local EPBs are subject to the preferences of local Party secretaries and mayors as well as leaders in the local organization departments and Party committees. Together, they have control over who gets appointed as a local EPB director. Among all 31 provincial EPB directors, only one-quarter of appointed directors were promoted within the ranks of the EPB bureaucracy, while the remaining came from other government or Party positions (Kostka 2013). When selecting bureaucrats for promotion to EPB head, local leaders will balance considerations on the need for economic development, the complexity of environmental pollution, required implementation practices, as well as their own political career concerns (Kostka 2013). For example, while Shanxi, a province under heavy external pressure to improve air pollution in 2006, selected a candidate with the skills and credentials to effectively implement air pollution targets to head the provincial EPB, the still-developing Inner Mongolia appointed a candidate with the experience needed to balance economic growth and environmental protection concerns. The power to select local EPB directors gives local authorities significant scope to influence the local path of environmental policy enforcement. Given these appointment procedures, EPB directors might feel sometimes more beholden to local leaders than to their duty to pursue environmental protection goals.

Technical capacity: lack of equipment and know-how

Technical capacity constraints can further hinder the implementation of national environmental mandates. Two pertinent technical constraints commonly cited in the literature are a lack of technical equipment and insufficiently trained local staff (Mol and Carter 2006).

First, the verification of environmental outcomes, a key component of effective environmental management, is a difficulty faced in many localities due to a shortage of advanced monitoring equipment. The available technologies and forms of monitoring systems differ for the verification of environmental targets. For energy intensity targets, there is no purpose-built monitoring equipment in place and reported data relies on self-reported figures from enterprises. For the verification of forest targets, recent GPS technologies make it somewhat easier to independently confirm reported forest coverage rates as these latest technologies can serve as 'the central state's eyes in the sky' (Shue 2012, 24; Interview 9 May 2012). For COD and SO_2 targets, real-time monitors are usually installed in larger companies. This monitoring equipment is reported to be not very technically advanced, unreliable and too few in number (Kostka 2014). Overall, the COD and SO_2 data collected from monitors can only serve as a reference (*can kao*) and many counties continue to rely more strongly on monthly or quarterly inspection visits to larger companies (Interview 10 May 2012). Although it is very taxing in terms of staffing requirements and time consumption, sending frequent inspection teams is seen to be quite necessary. For example, inspection teams sent from the national Ministry of Environmental Protection to the provinces sometimes rejected 30 to 50 per cent of claimed SO_2 reductions by some provinces

(Schreifels et al. 2012). Heavy reliance on inspection visits gives local officials a certain amount of discretion when it comes to verifying targets, including the decision about which enterprises to inspect or on which day to visit a lake to test its water quality.

In addition, the environmental bureaucracy is also in chronic need of well-trained staff to strictly monitor the accuracy of reported figures and targets. Such skills are needed, for example, in deciding which method is appropriate to the estimation of energy intensity levels, defined as energy consumption per unit of GDP. Interviewees working in local EPBs frequently admitted that sector-specific technical knowledge is needed to be able to critically check enterprises' self-reported energy consumption reports. The lack of formal and informal training of EPB staff in environmental sciences is also visible among the top leaders in the EPB bureaucracy. Among all 31 provincial EPB heads as of 2010, only one director has undergone university training in environmental sciences and only one-quarter were promoted to their leadership position from within the EPB (Kostka 2013).

In summary, the combination of shortages in advanced technical equipment and officials' limited technological know-how leaves ample room for business managers to play the 'game about numbers' with the local environmental bureaucracy (Ran 2013).

Financial capacity: insufficient funding

At the national level, China has increased funding for environmental protection and is planning major future investments over the next decade. According to the *China Daily* (2013), the total government spending on environmental protection in 2011 was 419 billion RMB, or about 0.9 per cent of GDP. Although this figure is a significant step up from previous years, it is still below the 2–4 per cent of GDP that is estimated as necessary to tackling environmental damage. Further investments are planned at the national level. For instance, the MEP budgeted a further 200 billion RMB for cleanup projects and 350 billion RMB for more than 13,300 projects to control emissions and reduce $PM_{2.5}$ levels between 2011 and 2020.

Despite the significant increase in funding from Beijing, most of these environmental funds are assigned for specific programmes and projects managed by different central ministries. Local branches of the EPB tend to be seriously underfunded as their responsibilities and tasks have multiplied over the past decade. For example, the allocated budget for local EPBs visited during fieldwork ranged from 0.5 to 2.5 per cent of local GDP. Typically, more advanced localities in coastal provinces spend proportionally more on environmental protection than less advanced localities in central and western provinces. The financial capacity of local EPBs is further constrained by fiscal and administrative interdependence between the local EPB and other local government agencies and leaders. As the de facto first-in-charge, local Party secretaries and mayors have substantial influence over local EPBs through the allocation of resources. From their leadership positions, they can exercise influence over the comprehensive budget set by the local finance bureau, which includes the annual budget for local EPBs. This makes EPBs dependent on local finance bureaus for their funding needs; thus, EPB officials often worry that their budgets are dependent on the good graces of local leaders.

To overcome funding shortages, local EPBs can apply for project funding and staff expansion from the municipal, provincial, and national government, but these funding applications are often lengthy and require sustained effort by the local leadership over several years (Lo and Tang 2006; Kostka 2014). Limited financial capacity can lead to shortages of needed inspection vehicles, up-to-date testing equipment and skilled staff. For instance, a single city air-monitoring station costs on average approximately 200,000 RMB, and a city would need multiple stations for effective pollution control. Most EPB leaders interviewed admitted that they could control air and water pollution better if they had multiple air-monitoring stations and monitoring equipment. In summary, local EPB leaders receive mixed signals: they are asked to fully implement binding environmental targets but these demands by upper-level governments are not always matched with a corresponding increase in financial resources.

Conclusion

This chapter identified barriers to a more comprehensive implementation of environmental policies at the city level in China and suggests an analytical framework to analyse these barriers. Key institutional barriers at the local level include shortcomings in the current environmental planning system, insufficient political and economic incentives provided to local implementers, limits to public and private participation, as well as financial, technical, and political capacity constraints of local implementing agencies.

In particular, the analysis showed that reliance on a target-based implementation system as the main environmental management instrument has yielded mixed results. Although environmental issues have moved quickly onto the policy agenda of local governments over the past decade, the target system itself produces multiple unanticipated and undesirable results. As binding environmental targets cascade downward through the administrative hierarchy, targets can become inappropriate, rigid, and are routinely inflated. Binding environmental targets also aggravate cyclical behaviours among cadres, and pressures for target fulfilment can result in eleventh-hour, short-sighted actions. In addition, because targets differ widely in terms of their ease of measurability, verifiability, and the extent to which they are linked with economic and social issues, the effectiveness and efficiency of binding targets can vary among environmental issues.

Weak political and economic incentives for local policymakers further help to explain why there is often insufficient motivation for effective environmental governance at the local level in China. Environmental targets, while substantially more important now than previously, compete for space on the crowded agenda of local officials. In these circumstances, many local officials have adopted the attitude of doing the very minimum required to implement green targets while most attention continues to be placed on maximizing GDP growth rate and fiscal income. Among local leaders, the attitude prevails that 'no leader will be promoted because of their better achievements in environmental protection and energy savings'.

In addition, the failure to implement environmental policy at the local level is also shaped by the preferences of powerful public and private interests. Large local businesses typically put the bottom line above the public interest and can use their considerable leverage vis-à-vis local governments to shirk on costly regulations. Moreover, the participation of NGOs and the public often remains ad hoc and limited in scope, especially in non-coastal, low profile cities. Current participation of non-state actors at the level of *designing* and *formulating* policies and practices are particularly rare.

At the most basic level, environmental policy implementation at the local level is also constrained by the political, technical, and financial capacities of implementing agencies. Political capacity constraints can result from coordination difficulties due to a fragmented environmental bureaucracy, conflicting priorities *within* implementing agencies, and low bureaucratic status and authority granted to environmental bureaucracies. The main pertinent technical constraints include the lack of advanced technical equipment and insufficiently trained local staff. Finally, greening growth demands by upper-level governments are also not always matched with a corresponding increase in financial resources, providing mixed signals to local leaders.

Numerous recent innovations and experiments provide a better understanding of how to address existing institutional barriers in China.[11] First, Chinese planners and local governments have recently begun to address some of the unanticipated and undesirable consequences of China's target-based green planning system. For instance, there are increasing efforts to improve environmental governance across provincial borders to ensure complete ecosystems are protected. There are also efforts under way to improve target allocation, implementation, and verification processes. For instance, in order to avoid cyclical implementation behaviour among cadres observed at the end of the 11th FYP period, in the 12th FYP more emphasis has been placed on achievement of annual targets instead of accumulated five-year targets. In addition, some sub-national governments devised additional incentives to motivate local policymakers and enterprises to pursue green goals. For example, Shanxi started a competition among the most polluted municipalities and offered price rewards to those localities that first got themselves off the national list of 'most polluted cities'. Finally, efforts are under way to address local governments' political, technical, and financial capacity constraints that influence environmental policy outcomes. For instance, to prevent central SOEs (*yangqi*) from polluting localities, the State Owned Assets Supervision and Administration Commission (SASAC) has included energy savings in the annual performance evaluation of SOEs. In addition, increased environmental NGO activism, public hearings, and improved information disclosure, also contribute to enhance local environmental policy implementation, and sometimes even policy-making (Kostka and Mol 2013). These findings contribute to the ongoing debate regarding how China can switch to a greener urban growth path, and particular emphasis is needed in the coming years to create additional incentives and increase local implementation capacities.

Notes

1 This section draws on Kostka (2016).
2 The next three paragraphs draw on Kostka (2014).
3 Personal Interview 8 May 2012.
4 Personal Interview 14 May 2012.
5 Personal Interview 23 May 2012.
6 Personal Interview 23 May 2012.
7 It is also important to stress that not all cadres are responsive to political incentives outlined in the cadre evaluation system. A recent study based on 898 local Party secretaries' biographies shows that county-level cadres face only a slim possibility of being promoted upwards to the municipal government (Kostka and Yu 2015). The study suggests that the importance of political incentives in the cadre evaluation system might be overestimated.
8 This section draws on Eaton and Kostka (2013, 2014).
9 The five-year tenure limit is, in reality, a firm recommendation rather than a hard and fast rule. A 1999 CCP Organization Department document set ten years as the absolute limit for cadres in leading positions but rules stating that cadres change positions at five-year intervals is phrased in the language of 'should' (*yinggai*) rather than 'must' (*bixu*). This flexibility explains why some cadres have tenures longer than five years.
10 This section draws on Kostka and Mol (2013).
11 For a more detailed list, see Kostka (2014).

References

China Daily, 2013. Fixing the Environment is in Our Hands. http://usa.chinadaily.com.cn/weekly/2013-04/26/content_16451383.htm (Accessed on 29 June 2015).

Eaton, S. B. and Kostka, G., 2013. Does Cadre Turnover Help or Hinder China's Green Rise? Evidence from Shanxi Province. In: Ren B. Q. and Shou S. S., 2013. *Chinese Environmental Policy: Dynamics, Challenges, and Prospects in a Changing Society*, Palgrave Macmillan, London, 83–111.

Eaton, S. B. and Kostka, G., 2014. Authoritarian Environmentalism Undermined? Local Leaders' Time Horizons and Environmental Policy Implementation. *The China Quarterly* 218, 359–380.

Eaton, S. and Kostka, G. 2017. Central Protectionism in China: The 'Central SOE Problem' in Environmental Governance. *The China Quarterly* 231, forthcoming September 2017.

Harrison, T. and Kostka, G., 2014. Balancing Priorities, Aligning Interests: Developing Mitigation Capacity in China and India. *Comparative Political Studies* 47 (3/4), 450–480.

He G. Z., He L. Y. Mol, A. P. J. and Beckers, T., 2012. Changes and Challenges: China's Environmental Management in Transition. *Environmental Development* 3, 5–38.

Heberer, T. and Senz, A., 2011. Streamlining Local Behaviour Through Communication, Incentives and Control: A Case Study of Local Environmental Policies in China. *Journal of Current Chinese Affairs* 40 (3), 77–112.

Hildebrandt, T., 2011. The Political Economy of Social Organization Registration in China. *The China Quarterly* 208, 970–989.

Huang, Y., 1996. Central-Local Relations in China During the Reform Era: The Economic and Institutional Dimensions. *World Development* 24 (4), 655–672.

International Finance Corporation (IFC), 2012. Study on the Potential of Sustainable Energy Financing for Small and Medium Enterprises in China, October 2012, Online Report: http://www.ifc.org/wps/wcm/connect/39ecf5004ff94de2acc8ff23ff966f85/China+SME+Report+for+web.pdf?MOD=AJPERES (Accessed 4 August 2015).

Jotzo, F. and Löschel, A., 2014. Emissions Trading in China: Emerging Experiences and International Lessons. *Energy Policy* 75, 3–8.

Kaufman, B. J., 2012. Drivers and Barriers for Sustainable Urban Form: The Case of China, Unpublished Master's Thesis, Frankfurt School of Finance and Management.

Kostka, G., 2013. Environmental Protection Bureau Leadership at the Provincial Level in China: Examining Diverging Career Backgrounds and Appointment Patterns. *Journal of Environmental Policy and Planning* 15 (1), 41–63.

Kostka, G., 2014. Barriers to the Implementation of Environmental Policies at the Local Level in China, *World Bank Policy Research Working Paper*.

Kostka, G., 2016. Command Without Control: The Case of China's Environmental Target System. *Regulation & Governance* 10, 58–74.

Kostka, G. and Hobbs, W., 2012. Local Energy Efficiency Policy Implementation in China: Bridging the Gap between National Priorities and Local Interests. *The China Quarterly* 211, 765–785.

Kostka, G. and Mol, A. P. J., 2013. Implementation and Participation in China's Local Environmental Politics: Challenges and Innovations. *Journal of Environmental Policy & Planning* 15 (1), 3–16.

Kostka, G. and Shin K., 2013. Energy Conservation Through Energy Service Companies: Empirical Analysis from China. *Energy Policy* 52, 748–759.

Kostka, G. and Yu X., 2015. Municipal Party Secretaries' Career Backgrounds: Tight Links to the Province and Limited County Level Experience. *Modern China* 41 (5), 467–505.

Kostka, G., Moslener, U. and Andreas, J., 2013. Barriers to Increasing Energy Efficiency: Evidence from Small- and Medium-sized Enterprises in China. *Journal of Cleaner Production* 57, 59–68.

Lelyveld, M., 2015. China's Officials Feel Pollution Pressure, http://www.rfa.org/english/commentaries/energy_watch/officials-feel-pollution-pressure-05262015111624.html, (Accessed 4 August 2015).

Li W. and Higgins, P., 2013. Controlling Local Environmental Performance: An Analysis of Three National Environmental Management Programs in the Context of Regional Disparities in China. *Journal of Contemporary China* 22 (81), 409–427.

Liang, D. and Mol, A. P. J., 2013. Political Modernisation in China's Forest Governance? Payment Schemes for Forest Ecological Services in Liaoning. *Journal of Environmental Policy and Planning* 15 (1), 65–88.

Lichtenberg, E. and Ding C. (2009). Local Officials as Land Developers: Urban Spatial Expansion in China. *Journal of Urban Economic*, 66, 57–64.

Lo A. L., 2013. Carbon Trading in a Socialist Market Economy: Can China Make a Difference? *Ecological Economics* 87, 72–74.

Lo W. H. C. and Tang S. Y., 2006. Institutional Reform, Economic Changes, and Local Environmental Management in China: The Case of Guangdong Province. *Environmental Politics* 15 (2), 190–210.

Lora-Wainwright, A., 2013. Introduction: Dying for Development: Pollution, Illness and the Limits of Citizens' Agency in China. *The China Quarterly* 214, 243–254.

Ma X. Y. and Ortolano, L., 2000. *Environmental Regulation in China: Institutions, Enforcement, and Compliance*. Rowman & Littlefield, Lanham, MD, USA.

Man, J. Y. (2011). Local Public Finance in China: An Overview. In J. Y. Man & Y.-H. Hong (eds), *China's Local Public Finance in Transition*. Cambridge, MA: Lincoln Institute of Land Policy, 3–17.

Mol, A. P. J. and Carter, N. T., 2006. China's Environmental Governance in Transition. *Environmental Politics* 15 (2), 149–170.

OECD, 2009. Urban Trends and Policy in China. Authored by Lamia Kamal-Chaoui, Edward Leman, Zhang Rufei, *OECD Regional Development Working Papers* 2009/1.

Ran R., 2013. Perverse Incentive Structure and Policy Implementation Gap in China's Local Environmental Politics. *Journal of Environmental Policy and Planning* 15 (1), 17–39.

Rietbergen, M. G. and Blok, K., 2010. Setting SMART Targets for Industrial Energy Use and Industrial Energy Efficiency. *Energy Policy* 38, 4339–4354.

Schreifels, J., Fu Y. and Wilson, E., 2012. Sulfur Dioxide Control in China: Policy Evolution during the 10th and 11th Five-Year Plans and Lessons for the Future. *Energy Policy* 28, 779–789.

Schwartz, J., 2003. The Impact of State Capacity on Enforcement of Environmental Policies: The Case of China. *The Journal of Environment & Development* 12 (1), 50–81.

Seckington, I., 2007. County Leadership in China: A Baseline Survey. *Nottingham China Policy Institute*. Discussion Paper 17.

Shin S., 2013. China's Failure of Policy Innovation: The Case of Sulphur Dioxide Emission Trading. *Environmental Politics* 22 (6), 918–934.

Shue V., 2012. Governing by Design: A Strategic Plan to Re-Engineer the Chinese Nation-Space, Paper Presented at the Conference on 'Power in the Making: Governing and Being Governed in Contemporary China', Oxford.

South China Morning Post, 2013. Xi Warns Officials They'll Be Held Responsible for Pollution 'for Life'. http://www.scmp.com/news/china/article/1245558/xi-jinping-warns-officials-theyll-be-held-responsible-pollution-life (Accessed 21 December 2016).

Tian L. and Ma W., 2009. Government Intervention in City Development of China: A Tool of Land Supply. *Land Use Policy*, 26 (3), 599–609.

Wang A. L., 2013. The Search for Sustainable Legitimacy: Environmental Law and Bureaucracy in China. *Harvard Environmental Law Review* 37, 367–440.

Wei, Y. and Zhao M., 2009. Urban Spill Over Vs. Local Urban Sprawl: Entangling Land-Use Regulations in the Urban Growth of China's Megacities. *Land Use Policy*, 26 (4), 1031–1045.

Wong C., 2010. Fiscal Reform: Paying for the Harmonious Society. *China Economic Quarterly* 14 (2), 20–25.

Wong C., 2013a. Paying for Urbanization: Challenges for China's Municipal Finance in the 21st Century. In: Bahl R. J. Linn and Wetzel D. eds. 2013. *Metropolitan Government Finances in Developing Countries*. Lincoln Institute for Land Policy, Cambridge, MA.

Wong C., 2013b. As Pollution Worsens in China, Solutions Succumb to Infighting, *The New York Times*, Asia Pacific. http://www.nytimes.com/2013/03/22/world/asia/as-chinas-environmental-woes-worsen-infighting-emerges-as-biggest-obstacle.html?pagewanted=all&_r=0 (Accessed 19 June 2015).

Wu F., 2013. Environmental Activism in Provincial China. *Journal of Environmental Policy and Planning* 15 (1) 89–108.

Wu J., Deng Y. H., Huang J., Morck R. and Yeung B., 2013. Incentives and Outcomes: China's Environmental Policy. NBER Working Paper No. 18754, February 2013.

Zhang C., 2015. China Trials Environmental Audits to Hold Officials to Account. China Dialogue Articles. https://www.chinadialogue.net/article/show/single/en/7990-China-trials-environmental-audits-to-hold-officials-to-account (Accessed 4 August 2015).

4

THE EVOLVING TACTICS OF CHINA'S GREEN MOVEMENT[1]

Judith Shapiro

Since their emergence in the mid-1990s, Chinese environmental advocacy groups have creatively and courageously expanded their range of political tools and techniques. Meanwhile, ordinary citizens protesting pollution and industrial accidents and resisting planned factories, mines, dams, high-speed rail lines and other development projects are being swept into activism. The combination might best be understood as an environmental movement with Chinese characteristics.

The maturation of Chinese environmental activism has been spurred by modern factors such as the globalization of environmental civil society, Chinese non-governmental organizations' mastery of sophisticated international tools and relationships, and the proliferation of social media. But indigenous factors also shape the movement, including the Confucian tradition of appealing to a higher authority for redress of wrongs, and a cleverness, cultivated over decades, in circumventing the restrictions of authoritarian rule.

At the same time, even as the central government highlights 'ecological civilization' as a core national goal and vows to crack down on corruption, the bolder, more impatient and confrontational landscape of activism and resistance has brought increasing government scrutiny to environmental organizing and protests – leaving the movement's prospects unclear.

Fouled nest

Chinese citizens are fed up with dwelling in a life-threatening toxic soup. Intense pollution now extends over much of the developed eastern part of the country, as well as the rapidly growing cities of the hinterland. Five hundred million Chinese lack access to safe drinking water. Only 1 per cent of urban dwellers breathe air acceptable by the standards of the European Union (Li et al. 2014). Those in the elite who can afford it send their families abroad, while the less privileged seethe at the government's inability to curb corrupt practices that foul the Chinese nest.

Increasingly, middle class Chinese are asking whether their country's vaunted development success is an improvement over the harsh lives that they knew during the Mao years. Yes, many urban Chinese now have cars, flush toilets, fashionable clothing and cell phones, in addition to personal freedoms that would have been unimaginable only a few decades ago. But they are also afraid to breathe the air, drink the water and eat the food.

They wear face masks in public to protect themselves from smog. They are terrified of getting cancer from water contaminated by heavy metals that they are unable to taste or smell. They suspect their vegetables are tainted with pesticides and chemical fertilizers – so on small plots of land or on balconies, city dwellers now grow their own vegetables in a sort of urban peasant renaissance. In rural areas, farmers, minorities and the poor are increasingly suffering the impacts of pollution foisted on them by more politically powerful urban areas.

China's environmental challenges may be the single most powerful determinant of whether the government can maintain its fragile legitimacy and stability. Yet the Chinese leadership is caught between a Scylla and Charybdis of bad choices. Officials must continue to raise living standards – by making China the manufacturing hub of the planet – while at the same time addressing citizens' fury at the government's apparent inability to curb the pollution choking the country. The Communist Party, already insecure about its status, is vulnerable to social unrest over environmental issues.

Yet the state it runs with an authoritarian hand is nonetheless weak in implementation and enforcement of environmental laws. This is a result not only of widespread corruption, but also of bureaucratic structural ambiguity. Responsibilities for governance are fractured, overlapping, or in conflict across agencies and geographic areas, and perverse incentives reward astronomical economic growth over environmental protection and pollution mitigation. Unfortunately, the same decentralization that unleashed China's entrepreneurial passions beginning in the early 1980s has resulted in a lack of central government control over the mid-level, regional bureaucrats charged with enforcing environmental laws.

The salaries of low-ranking environmental officials often depend on a steady diet of pollution fines. Accordingly, they censure rather than close factories for violations, while local governments are often loath to cite, curtail or even inspect the industries on which they rely to fill their tax coffers. Indeed, government officials themselves own some of the nation's dirtiest township and village enterprises.

The central state's response to widespread pollution has been to put more stringent environmental laws on the books – and to try to give them sharper teeth – while also sporadically cracking down on isolated cases of corruption. These efforts seem ineffectual, given the breadth and depth of the problem.

Toxic challenges

The implications of government failure have become increasingly obvious. In March 2013, more than 16,000 dead, diseased pigs were fished from the river that supplies Shanghai with drinking water. In recent months there have also been major spills of cadmium, aniline and other toxics, and cadmium has been widely detected in rice grown in south China. Air pollution in Beijing, which citizens expected would be largely resolved with the 'blue skies' 2008 Summer Olympic Games, in January 2013 was so 'crazy bad' (in the words of a US Embassy official) that it defied measurement on any monitoring device (Watts 2010). Winter 2016–2017 was equally bad. Some urban apartment dwellers are afraid to allow their children to go outside to play.

Even dairy products are seen as unsafe, due to melamine adulteration and chemical residue scandals of recent years. Mainland Chinese demand for imported milk powder and infant formula has overwhelmed the supply in Hong Kong. The Hong Kong government has restricted exports, placing a limit of two cans per person leaving the territory, which has caused tensions at border checkpoints and led to a thriving black market.

Environmental protests and 'mass incidents' break out regularly, in opposition to planned factories and landfills, in protest against chronic effluent discharge into waterways, in anger at chemical spills and leachate from land spills. Objections to proposed paraxylene petrochemical plants have sparked widespread uprisings in Xiamen, Dalian, Ningbo and, most recently, Kunming. Other protests have centred on lithium battery factories, and planned high-speed rail lines that would cut through neighbourhoods. From Sichuan and Yunnan in the interior to Jiangsu and the Yangtze delta, major demonstrations over mines, factories and industrial pollution have involved thousands of people and led to clashes with police.

Hope may be found in the seriousness with which some senior officials in the central government, particularly within the Ministry of Environmental Protection and government planning agencies, regard the problem. During the recent leadership transition – which saw Xi Jinping replace Hu Jintao as president of the nation – a top leader described the air pollution as depressing. Pilot projects have been launched throughout the country, with 'green' awards for more sustainable cities, efforts to shift leadership incentives away from unfettered economic growth and toward 'sustainable development', and experiments with carbon trading and cleaner coal-fired power plants that limit both climate change-inducing carbon emissions and ground-level smog.

Some cities have pushed innovations such as bicycle sharing and green building standards. China has become a world leader in the production and use of solar and wind technologies, albeit not without international trade controversies. Western NGOs including the Natural Resources Defense Council and the World Resources Institute are welcomed in China for their efforts to share best practices in green building and sustainable transport.

Enter the activists

However, China's greatest prospect for change may lie in its environmental civil society. Officially registered groups number in the thousands; a count of unofficial groups would yield many more (Chen 2006). Some government bureaucracies, such as the comparatively weak Ministry of Environmental Protection, are looking to civil society to strengthen their hand against polluters who find tacit support in more powerful trade, energy, and construction ministries. Indeed, without top environmental officials' assent, the NGOs could not exist.

The past few decades have brought a dramatic evolution of environmental activism, from the use of the simplest and most cautious techniques to the aggressive harnessing of global civil society to appeal directly to consumers, and even using the threat of international law to pressure multinational corporations to 'green' their supply chains. Activists' political tools have progressed from simple tree planting and recycling pioneered in the mid-1990s to a sophisticated panoply of tactics, including those practised by the international NGOs that have trained increasing numbers of Chinese activists.

Many of the tactics used today would have been unimaginable a few decades ago. An abbreviated list includes information politics, intergroup networking, bearing witness, accountability politics, symbolic politics (naming and shaming), undercover investigations, transparency politics, supply chain analysis, blogging, online and in-person petitioning, and the use of the courts to bring class action and public interest lawsuits. This list, detailed below, expands on Margaret Keck and Kathryn Sikkink's typology of the ways in which advocacy groups 'matter' in international affairs (Keck and Sikkink 1998).

The activists' strategies, many of which overlap and are used in concert, reflect both the importance of new social media and the shifting constraints under which civil society must operate in an authoritarian state.

Information politics

Information sharing is the simplest way in which citizens' groups exert pressure. In China, early NGOs publicized basic environmental knowledge, translated environmental classics like Rachel Carson's *Silent Spring*, filmed television nature programmes aimed at instilling environmental literacy among children, and generally exerted the utmost care not to threaten the state. Their inoffensive activities included tree planting and recycling campaigns, accompanied by efforts to educate people about ecosystems and pollution.

Networking

The first Chinese environmental campaign to involve multiple groups (including environmental clubs organized under university Communist Youth Leagues) was an effort to save the Tibetan antelope (*Panthalops hodgsonii*), an endangered species poached for its fine belly hair. Smugglers generally take the furs to India, where they are woven into luxury shawls called *shahtoosh*. During the 1990s, groups from different parts of China linked together via the internet to coordinate a public information drive, often on college campuses. They painted 'antelope cars' to bring their message into remote areas.

Perhaps because the poaching occurs on the Tibetan Plateau, far from centres of power, the government allowed the campaign. It was the first to involve large numbers of Chinese young people, and it established the environment as an issue area in which political organizing space was relatively open, in contrast to human rights, democracy, religious freedom and other more sensitive topics.

Bearing witness

Also in the early days of the Chinese environmental movement, a young couple – Shi Lihong (formerly of *China Daily*) and Xi Zhinong (a wildlife photographer) – pioneered the technique of recording events occurring in remote areas and bringing them through the media to the public's attention. Xi's photographs of the lovely Yunnan snub-nosed monkey (*Rhinopithecus bieti*) have become icons of the Chinese environmental movement. The Beijing couple's relocation, with their newborn child, to a remote mountainous area so as to monitor and film the illegal logging of the highly endangered monkeys' habitat drew the attention of national and international media and inspired a generation.

Shi has since used other film techniques, innovative in China, to fight dams in Yunnan. For example, she and other activists arranged for villagers in areas slated for inundation to travel to areas that had already been flooded, where they spoke to displaced villagers living in harsh conditions. Shi recorded the conversations and then showed her film to those who could not make the trip. The film became a powerful mobilizing tool, as shown in a 2011 documentary, *Waking the Green Tiger*, by Canadian filmmaker Gary Marcuse (2011). The thirteen dams postponed as a result of these efforts remain off the table, although hotly contested Chinese-funded dams are being built downstream across the border in Myanmar.

Accountability politics

The use of accountability politics, in which citizens' groups publicly hold governments and corporations accountable for their legal obligations or other promises, has expanded in China in the past decade. Chinese environmental laws have become more explicit and publicity about corporate malfeasance has become easier to spread.

A classic example of accountability politics is the effort by the NGO TRAFFIC to help the Chinese government enforce the Convention on International Trade in Endangered Species, which China signed and ratified in 1981. From a Hong Kong office, TRAFFIC monitors the trade in endangered species. It pays particular attention to the Chinese market for tiger bones and rhinoceros horns as ingredients in traditional Chinese medicine, as well as shark fins and certain species of turtle prized as delicacies with medicinal properties. This group seeks to hold the Chinese government accountable to its commitments under the endangered species convention by publicizing illegal behaviour, while also working with government agencies to help identify violations.

Accountability politics is also an important technique in civil society battles against hydropower projects, chemical plants, oil refineries, and mines. For example, citizen activists routinely criticize companies for failing to conduct legally required environmental impact assessments before construction, or for failing to publicize the results. Activists hold up the impact assessment law as a standard that has not been met. Accountability politics comes into play, too, when a corporation falls short of its promises of environmental and social responsibility.

Naming and shaming

The innovative technique of 'naming and shaming' – one that often blends information, accountability leverage, and symbolic politics – is commonly used by international NGOs, but is a surprising tool in an authoritarian country. The practice consists of aggressively pressuring companies to change their polluting ways. Unlike the traditional civil society focus on changing the ways of the state, however, this technique uses social media and modern marketing to go directly to the consumer, both within China and overseas, leveraging global civil society and stronger NGOs overseas to attack a brand and threaten a corporation's bottom line.

In recent years, Chinese citizens' groups have started to adopt the street theatre 'actions' and shock advertising techniques pioneered by Greenpeace International, with powerful effect. For example, in a 2005 campaign to embarrass Hewlett-Packard into manufacturing electronics products using fewer toxics and more easily recycled materials, Greenpeace-East Asia activists stood in front of HP's Beijing offices dressed in hazmat suits emblazoned with the message 'HP=Harmful Product'. Photographs of the protest went viral and HP eventually promised to phase out some of the worst chemicals (a promise that has only partially been kept).

Weeping pandas

In May 2013, Greenpeace began to protest the Sichuan government's redrawing of a panda reserve's boundaries so as to permit the construction of a phosphate fertilizer mine. This campaign also went viral, featuring photos of an activist in a panda suit standing before a desecrated landscape with paws over its weeping eyes.

But the most famous example of naming and shaming is Greenpeace-East Asia's campaign to rid the Yangtze and Pearl rivers of chemical dumping by the textile industry. In 2011 the group produced a detailed investigative report, 'Dirty Laundry', based on samples that it gathered secretly to avoid harassment by factory or government officials, and then had tested in top scientific laboratories in Europe (Greenpeace 2011). The group followed the report with a public 'Detox' campaign, in which the 'X' in Detox was written as the Chinese character for water, which it resembles.

Greenpeace named and shamed the companies involved, beginning with the sportswear manufacturers Nike, Adidas and Li Ning (a Chinese firm). When the companies promised to phase out toxic chemicals in their supply chains, Greenpeace shifted attention to some of the top brands in the fast-fashion industry. Zara, Victoria's Secret, Benetton and Mango quickly promised to detox by 2020. Some 19 major brands, including H&M, Esprit, Benetton, Victoria's Secret and Levi's made commitments, subsequently monitored by Greenpeace via a virtual 'catwalk' (Greenpeace 2014). The campaign involved demonstrations in front of retail stores throughout the world, as activists sought to educate shoppers and imperil corporations' brand image and profits.

Undercover investigations

There is a long Chinese tradition of appealing to a higher authority for redress of wrongs, traceable to a Confucian system in which those with higher status have an obligation to take care of those below them. As a result, petitioning higher authorities to come 'down' to a locality to investigate and correct an injustice is a long-standing cultural practice – the petitioner often makes a journey to seek a personal audience with the powerful official and present a document detailing the grievance. It is often the victim's first resort, rather than taking a tort to a court of law.

In addition to high officials and well-known advocacy groups like Greenpeace, individual Chinese journalists often feel a special obligation to respond to petitions. Disenfranchised citizens and pollution victims frequently bring their complaints to the media. Top environmental officials have supported investigations over the years, creating a huge wave of environmentally themed stories in the press.

Liu Jianqiang, formerly of the hard-hitting (and often censored) Guangdong newspaper *Southern Weekend*, investigated a planned dam in Yunnan's Tiger Leaping Gorge in response to a local citizen activist's appeal for help. Liu's coverage ultimately led to the suspension of the dam in December 2007 (Liu 2013). But perhaps the most famous environmental activist with a journalist's background is Ma Jun, the founder of the Institute of Public and Environmental Affairs (IPE) and the Chinese pioneer of what we may call transparency politics.

Transparency politics

Unlike information politics, transparency politics actively uncovers suppressed data and uses the internet and other electronic media to empower the public with information. For example, in 2009 the journalist Deng Fei published an online map of China's 'cancer villages', which are found in almost every province (Deng 2010). Their high levels of cancer are associated with the presence of factories, often those making goods for export. It was not until the spring of 2013 that the government acknowledged that the phenomenon of cancer villages existed. Today, water pollution data are readily available online, thanks to the efforts of Ma Jun's Institute of Public and Environmental Affairs (IPE 2014).

Twitter tempest

Air pollution data, too, are finally being released – after a very public struggle in Beijing, where results from the US Embassy's air pollution monitors, publicly reported via Twitter, were routinely showing higher pollution levels than those reported by the Chinese government. This happened in part because the Americans measured the far more dangerous smaller particulates, measuring less than 2.5 microns, which lodge in the lungs and have long-term negative health impacts. After a public outcry in 2011, online petitions (one spearheaded by a real estate tycoon, Pan Shiyi), and rogue private air monitoring efforts, the Chinese government agreed to monitor the smaller particles and release the data beginning in 2012. It is now possible to find accurate, current air pollution information for Beijing and many Chinese cities.

Supply chain analysis

A final technique pioneered by Ma involves scrutinizing the global political economy of supply chains – uncovering levels of contractors and subcontractors and demanding that multinational corporations take responsibility for the environmental performance of their suppliers, both direct and indirect. Collecting official government pollution data on various business entities into a searchable database, Ma's environmental institute provides a basis for researching the suppliers of major corporations. In addition, through its network of 41 participating NGOs, the institute uncovers violations and contacts the companies to demand that they change their behaviour and compensate those affected.

The case of Apple provides a recent example of aggressive supply chain analysis. While Walmart and many other companies had started cooperating with Ma to monitor their suppliers, Apple was slow to respond. Five NGOs collaborated on a 2010 investigative report that included information on workers at the Apple supplier Foxconn who died from exposure to chemicals used to clean touchscreens (Friends of Nature et al. 2011).

A naming and shaming campaign – dubbed 'Poison Apple' – led to regular talks in California and Beijing between the Institute of Public and Environmental Affairs and Apple officials. Apple eventually agreed to a jointly monitored environmental and labour audit by an external firm, and extended the investigation from the huge, Taiwanese-owned Foxconn to other, smaller electronics suppliers. Ma's background at the *South China Morning Post*, his postgraduate studies at Berkeley, and his sophistication in the ways of international business enabled him to pioneer such campaign techniques in China.

Internet activism

An increasingly significant arena for Chinese environmental civil society activism is the internet, via digital information centres such as Chinadialogue (chinadialogue.net) and the China Digital Times (chinadigitaltimes.net), as well as through micro-blogging on Sina Weibo (the oft-censored Chinese hybrid of Facebook and Twitter, with 100 million posts per day). Some micro-bloggers have followers numbering in the many thousands, so the opinion-shaping influence of loose online coalitions of like-minded individuals can be significant.

'Taking a walk'

Moreover, citizens have learned to use social media to circumvent government filters and censorship, as when the phrases 'taking a walk' and 'going sightseeing' were used in several cities to coordinate public protests. One of the better-known Weibo posts was a February 2013 message by Zhejiang eyeglasses entrepreneur Jin Zengmin, whose sister died young of cancer. Jin offered 200,000 RMB (about US$32,000) to a top local environmental official if he would swim in the shoe factory-polluted waters of Rui'an, near Shanghai, for 20 minutes. The official refused and the challenge went viral, becoming a powerful example of the internet's potential as a tool to pressure local agencies to do their jobs.

Online petitioning has also become a critical form of social mobilization. Internet petitions to clean up Beijing's air have included demands for greater information transparency and the distribution of free face masks. In an international echo of the tradition of appealing to powerful figures, in May 2013 a Chengdu resident opposing an oil refinery posted a petition on the US White House website. When the petition received several thousand signatures, police visited the resident and told her to take it down (which she could not do).

Lawsuits

Compared to Western NGOs, Chinese civil society groups lag in their use of the courts as a channel for environmental activism, but there have been dramatic developments in this area since the passage of new environmental protection laws in January 2015. These laws empower Chinese environmental NGOs to bring public interest lawsuits, and an Environmental Public Interest Law network has rapidly sprung up to address this opportunity. Formerly, only Wang Canfa's Center for Legal Assistance to Pollution Victims, which was in operation beginning in 1998 and has handled more than 100 cases, helped those who were directly harmed. Now, with the public interest lawsuit regulations, special environmental courts have been set up and groups like Friends of Nature are bringing suits against polluters in the interest of affected communities. The Ministry of Environmental Protection is often co-plaintiff but it is sometimes also defendant. The first punitive awards are being made, and even in cases where local officials are complicit in the pollution as owners of offending corporations, important court victories are being won. This is not an easy road, however; in 2016 ENGO's lost a lawsuit in Intermediate People's Court in Jiangsu's Changzhou city, where they sued polluting factories that left soil so toxic that hundreds of teenagers became ill when a school moved onto the site. The decision that exonerates the factories is being appealed, and additional lawsuits are being brought against companies that were contracted to remediate the soil.

Unanswered questions

The tools and techniques available to Chinese environmental groups and citizens have evolved dramatically since the mid-1990s. However, the best efforts of Chinese citizens to speak out against pollution and to curb the corrupt practices that have so profoundly destroyed the environment have thus far yielded only limited success. Moreover, pollution increasingly is being shifted to poor rural areas, to the Chinese interior hinterlands, and to developing countries overseas, where more vulnerable populations are less able to resist powerful economic interests.

Despite the extraordinary advances in activism – and in light of them – key questions remain. Will an emboldened environmental movement succeed in mitigating China's environmental degradation? Can it muster enough power against a heavy-handed state that is afraid of its own citizens and a corrupt business elite drunk on economic growth? Can the pent-up consumption needs of more than a billion Chinese be reconciled with sustainable development? Will a globalized world continue to shift its pollution to Chinese manufacturers? Will China's increasingly muscular middle class simply drive polluting enterprises out of urban areas, with assistance from an insecure authoritarian state primarily interested in defusing environmental protest rather than finding an innovative path out of our global conundrum?

We must ask whether the environmental movement, both in China and around the globe, can address these questions today, rather than simply postponing a reckoning with the limits of the planet's resources. The answers will determine the well-being not only of one-fifth of the world's population, but of the entire planet.

Finally, a special note for this volume: China's citizen activists have continued to flourish since this essay was first published, most dramatically with the release in February 2015 of Chai Jing's anti-pollution documentary, 'Under the Dome', which had millions of viewers during the few days it was widely available with the support of the new head of the Ministry of Environmental Protection and the *People's Daily*. That a single influential and well-connected individual had the resources and celebrity to produce such a film speaks volumes about the transformation of the landscape of environmental activism. Yet the film's rapid suppression, and the stricter control of NGOs under the Xi Jinping Administration (both domestic and international), illustrates how difficult a road lies ahead. In my view, China's environmental activists will continue to adapt new tactics, even as the Chinese government takes ever-more dramatic steps to ameliorate and shift toxic activities, if only to counter citizen disillusionment with a Party that has allowed the country to become so badly befouled.

Note

1 Reprinted, with permission, from September 2013 *Current History*.

References

Chen J., 2006. NGO Community in China: Expanding Linkages with Transnational Civil Society and their Democratic Implications, *China Perspectives* 68, 29–40.
Deng F., 2010. China's Cancer Villages. Available at https://maps.google.com/maps/u/0/ms?msa=0&msid=207156850501906471306.0004da7c080a323c331b3&dg=feature (accessed 3 October 2014).
Friends of Nature, Institute of Public and Environmental Affairs (IPE) and Green Beagle, 2011. The Other Side of Apple, *IT Investigative Report (Phase IV)* 1–35. Available at http://ipe.org.cn/Upload/Report-IT-V-Apple-I-EN.pdf (accessed 1 November 2014).
Greenpeace, 2011. Dirty Laundry: Unraveling the Corporate Connections to Toxic Water Pollution in China. Available at http://www.greenpeace.org/international/en/publications/reports/Dirty-Laundry (accessed 1 November 2014).
Greenpeace, 2014. Detox Catwalk. Available at http://www.greenpeace.org/international/en/campaigns/toxics/water/detox/Detox-Catwalk/#pvh (accessed 3 October 2014).
Institute of Public and Environmental Affairs (IPE), 2014. China Water Pollution Map, China Air Pollution Map, China Solid Waste Pollution Map. Available at http://www.ipe.org.cn (chinese) and http://wwwen.ipe.org.cn (English) (accessed 27 November 2016).
Keck, M. and Sikkink, K., 1998. *Activists beyond Borders: Advocacy Networks in International Politics*, Cornell University Press New York
Li L., Qian J., Ou C.-Q., Zhou Y.-X., Guo C. and Guo Y., 2014. Spatial and Temporal Analysis of Air Pollution Index and its Timescale-Dependent Relationship with Meteorological Factors in Guangzhou, China, 2001-2011, *Environmental Pollution* 190, 75–81.
Liu J., 2013. Defending Leaping Tiger Gorge. In: Geall, S., 2013. *China and the Environment: The Green Revolution*, New York: Zed Books, 203–35.
Marcuse, G., 2011. *Waking the Green Tiger: The Rise of China's Green Movement*. Documentary film, 78 minutes. Face to Face Media. Canada.
Watts, J., 2010. Twitter Gaffe: US Embassy Announces 'Crazy Bad' Beijing Air Pollution. Available at http://www.theguardian.com/environment/blog/2010/nov/19/crazy-bad-beijing-air-pollution (accessed 3 October 2014).

5

ADVOCACY COALITIONS OF GREEN ECONOMY AND THEIR INFLUENCE ON GOVERNMENT POLICY IN CHINA

Huang Haifeng, Sheng Chunhong and Julian Barg

Introduction

The PRC central leaders seemingly made a U-turn on their attitudes about the relationship between economic development and environmental protection during the last two decades: up until the mid-2000s economic development took by far the highest priority of all political targets. While laws on environmental protection existed, there was not just a failure in implementation, but in fact environmental protection did just take a very low position in the bureaucratic system (Wang 2013, 388). Scientists could barely get officials ears when bringing forwards concerns about the environment. The Chinese central government is endeavouring to add more green elements in its economic development. Green development has been firmly put in place in the 18th National Congress of Chinese Communist Party's report in 2012 (Hu 2012). The 13th Five-Year Plan emphasized repeatedly the necessary transition of the development mode towards green development, and the tenth section focuses particularly on how to improve environment protection, promote resource conservation, and provide ecological products to the people (Xinhua 2016).

The United Nations Environment Programme (UNEP) defines

> a green economy as one that results in improved human well-being and social equity, while significantly reducing environmental risks and ecological scarcities. In its simplest expression, a green economy can be thought of as one which is low-carbon, resource efficient and socially inclusive.
>
> *(UNEP 2011)*

The term green economy was first used by a group of leading environmental economists in Great Britain, namely David Pearce, Anil Markandya and Edward Barbier, who published a book entitled *Blueprint for a Green Economy* in 1989 (Pearce et al. 1989). A large body of literature from both international and domestic academia exists to help us to understand China's green economy in the form of environmental and energy policies, and the relationship between green economy and brown economy (Lu and Zhang 2005; Zhu 2012; UNEP 2014; Weng et al. 2015).

The U-turn on the surface blocks our view of a more gradual development in different subsystems – there is 'an emerging economic dimension' of environmental protection in China (Economy 2006). As Huang and Zhou (2015) state in *The Road of China's Economic Transition 21st Century Green Revolution*, China's leaders are integrating green economy into economic transition from a high-energy and resource-consumption economy model to 'a resource-conservation and environmentally friendly' model, which may have enormous implications not only for China but also other developing countries.

In the context of Chinese politics, green economy refers to the concepts of circular economy, low-carbon economy and ecological economy (Ren 2014). A lot of articles have been written on the green economy sectors, such as green finance, green buildings etc. (DRC and IISD 2014; Zhong and Hong 2014; Weng et al. 2015). Based on them, this chapter explores the actors and powers that have contributed to the policy change towards a green economy in China.

It will introduce the advocacy coalition theory for the analysis of environmental and economic policy change in China. According to Sabatier (1988, 130), an informal policy advocating group is defined as a group of 'people from a variety of positions (elected and agency officials, interest group leaders, researchers) who share a particular belief system – i.e. a set of basic values, causal assumptions, and problem perceptions'.

Scholars pay intensive attention to policy change relating to China's environmental protection, climate change and energy issues. Hofem and Heilmann (2013) argue that transnational actors and domestic policy researchers with international financial support and top level leaders' attention are preferable conditions for realizing policy change in China. Wuebbeke (2013) points out the influence of the 'expert community' in China's policy making process. Scholars commonly recognize experts' and research institutions' impacts on China's policy change and their policy-oriented learning, especially through the international community (Fewsmith 2001; Li 2001; Hofem and Heilmann 2013; Wuebbeke 2013). This chapter explores not only the experts and their policy-oriented learning, but also their impact on government policy change through advisory institutional settings and close relationships with the government leaders in three key sub-policy fields, namely circular, low-carbon and ecological economy. This study emphasizes the multiple identities or roles of experts and focuses on experts who have a strong influence on government policies. Experts could be governmental officials or industrial leaders. Furthermore, through tracing three specific policy changes, this study contributes to understanding the policy making institutional setting, particularly the consultancy institution setting.

Advocates for a shift to green economy?

Green economy has been advocated by the UNEP as 'global green new deal' to divert governmental public investment in transiting to a green economy and changing the financial crisis to opportunity in 2008; subsequently many nations started their own green stimulus package, including China (Nhamo 2011; UNEP 2011). China is shifting its investment more on to green economy sectors and domestic demands than encouraging export as before (Huang and Wu 2015). The Chinese government has invested a large amount of capital in environmentally friendly and green energy technologies (UNEP 2011). The estimated cost for reaching the targets set in the 12th Five-Year Plan for Environmental Protection from 2011 to 2015 are as much as 3.4 trillion RMB (State Council 2011). Yet, since China's environmental problems predominantly stem from the country's excessive use of coal, China has invested a huge amount of capital in clean energy and China is becoming a leading country in clean energy investment in the world (Bloomberg 2015). The rapid development of renewable energy is one key focus of the literature on Chinese green economy (Pan et al. 2011; Liu et al. 2013; Weng et al. 2015). In this regard, through addressing which actors contributed to heaving green economy on to the agenda of the central government, this chapter will complement the other contributions in this handbook.

A large body of literature presents the astonishing development of environmental non-governmental organizations (ENGOs) in China (Knup 1997; Schwartz 2004; Yang 2005; Tang and Zhan 2008). Since the Chinese public's environmental awareness is rising, environmental demonstrations occur more often to urge the government to become greener (Jing 2000; Stalley and Yang 2006; Tong and Lei 2010; Li et al. 2012). However, these protests usually result in forcing local governments to give up certain projects, but hardly lead to fundamental change in governmental policy or challenge the government (Ho 2001). The space is too narrow in the Chinese political system to let the ENGOs participate in political decision making process directly (Ho 2007; Ho and Edmonds 2007). They at least need some connections with CCP, such as through senior officials. This study suggests that more attention should be paid to key experts and governmental officials instead of focusing on the role of ENGOs in pushing for policy change on environmental and climate change issues.

Advocacy coalition theory

Advocacy coalitions are defined as 'people from various governmental and private organizations who share a set of normative and causal beliefs and who often act in concert' (Jenkins-Smith and Sabatier 1994, 180). One important indicator of advocacy coalitions is policy-oriented learning, '[the] relatively enduring alterations of thought or behavioral intentions which result from experience and which are concerned with the attainment (or revision) of policy objectives' (Sabatier 1998). In a globalized world, there is more and more cooperation between China and the international community in environmental protection, climate change and green development, which creates the opportunities for Chinese advocators to learn from international counterparts about green economy policies and practices. For example, China participates in the UNEP programme in green economy (UNEP 2011). The advocacy coalition framework is exceptionally suitable for analogizing China, since it is governed by elites and technocrats, most of whom enjoyed an education in technical sciences, some also abroad (Fewsmith 2001; Li 2001).

Few studies have applied advocacy coalitions in China's environmental studies, this chapter applies an advocacy coalition framework to analyse the green economy policy change in China (Wu 2005; Han et al. 2014). In the advocacy coalitions of China's green economy, the high and senior political actors have played as policy brokers and policy advocate at the same time, on the platform of consultancy institutions (Hofem and Heilmann 2013). In the advocacy coalition of green economy, the Chinese multiparty cooperation institutions are undermined. The common nature of multiparty cooperation is the emphasis of expertise and knowledge. The consultants from the other parties play an important role in providing data from fieldwork, acting as policy consultants, sharing information and knowledge, and generally being able to flexibly participate in the administrative work of different levels of government (Wang 2008; Wu 2013). Other authors point out the role of the experts, senior officials, and their relationships with environmental governance in China, particularly their role as bridges between the governments and the civil society in environmental social movements (Li et al. 2012). The National People's Congress (NPC) and Chinese People's Political Consultative Conference (NPPCC) gain more independency in the field of environment, which means they probably have influence on issues regarding green economy (Xie and Van Der Heijden 2010).

As changes are usually more expected to come from civil society, another sphere of influence that is often underrated are companies and other forms of private professional associations formed by interest groups in green economy. In the renewable energy areas, because of the fast development of wind and solar energy, different associations are founded, whose members typically are businessmen and professionals. The China Renewable Energy Industries Association founded in 2000 is one example (CREIA 2010). Professional associations are a major part of the advocacy coalition for green economy policy in China, since they are devoted to lobbying for this and have close relationships with governmental officials (Foster 2002; Kennedy 2009).

According to Sabatier, policy change is better to have a focus on policy subsystems. Policy subsystems are composed of people coming from different institutions aiming for one policy (Sabatier 1987, 1988). Green economy is separated into different policy subsystems; usually scholars use green sectors to describe green economy, like green financing, green building, electric vehicles etc. (Zhu et al. 2005; Cai et al. 2009; Aizawa and Yang 2010; Weng et al. 2015). This study turns the focus on to specific sectors to circular, low-carbon, and ecological economy as the key policy subsystems of China's green economy, since the three policies are advocated by people from different sectors. The Chinese laws, regulations, programmes and fiscal support regarding green economy are proof that the CCP has changed its belief system about the relationship of environment and economy.

Advocacy of green economy in China

Circular economy

Circular economy, based on similar concepts from Germany and Japan, was adopted as an official policy by the central government in 2002 (Yuan and Moriguichi 2006, 4). The successful implementation in several eco-industrial parks throughout the country resulted in the adoption of a national law in 2008 (Hu 2008). Its core principles are summarized in the slogan 'reduce, reuse and recycle'. Reduce refers to an optimized resource use and cutbacks in resource waste and consumption.

The principle of circularity as described by reuse and recycle is very similar to international concepts. It is most easily understood when juxtaposed with its counterpart, a linear economy. A linear economy is a very simple system: there is an input of resources into the economy on one side, and an output of products and different kinds of waste on the other. A circular economy, in contrast to the former, would be a very complex system, mimicking natural processes. To make the most effective use of the resources which enter the system, whenever possible, waste is fed back into the system to be used as resources by other parts of the economy.

For example, the residue of a food company, instead of being disposed of, could be given to a company that uses organic matter of a similar composition for its production. This example also highlights a special characteristic of the Chinese implementation of the concept: while the main target is still to cut back on the use of resources, circular economy is also advertised as a way for companies to cut costs and improve profits. In this context, it is very important to note that the circular economy concept is not being promoted solely by the Ministry of Environmental Protection (MEP), but that in fact very early on, in 2004, the National Development and Reform Commission (NDRC) was tasked with being the main responsible institution for implementing the concept (Yuan and Moriguichi 2006, 5).

The abovementioned example could without doubt also be used to explain the concept of eco-industries. These two can be more clearly distinguished after the *Circular Economy Promotion Law* had been adopted in 2008. While in the early phase, support for eco-industrial parks highlights had been supported by the environmental authorities as part of the advocacy coalition for green development, the law shows their potential to influence national legislation – though it remains to be seen to what extent the advocacy coalition can transform the national economy to the circular economy concept.

Advocacy coalitions for implementation of circular economy

The implementation of circular economy takes place on different legislative levels, offering a demonstration of an advocacy coalition at work. Firstly, through saving resources and reducing cost of waste disposal, it offers companies a competitive advantage, as well as improving its image or even the chance to gain an international reputation. Secondly, the circularity principal is applied in many eco-industrial projects and parks on the municipal and provincial level (see the section below on ecological economy), by officials hoping to attract businesses, truly wanting to integrate development and ecology or simply to advance their career. Thirdly, the *Circular Economy Promotion Law* proved that the MEP on the national level was able to reach an agreement with other policy makers to take some first steps towards a national circular economy.

Though circular economy was introduced as a national development policy in 2002, the *Circular Economy Promotion Law* was only passed in 2008 and took effect on 1 January 2009. The law itself as a framework is very vague, for example naming the State instead of specific organs as responsible. However, the law still includes a number of major improvements to previous laws:

- The standardization department of the State Council is mandated with issuing a statistics system for circular economy and furthermore standards for resource saving.
- The responsibilities of enterprises and various sections of the government are laid out.
- Fines for violations of the provisions enacted under the framework of this law are set.
- The general administration for promoting circular economy under the State Council is mandated with establishing an assessment index system for circular economy (Circular Economy Promotion Law 2008).

As mentioned above, the law is only a framework, and most of the paragraphs are very vague. Furthermore, the fines do not include jail sentences and limit monetary penalities to only RMB 200,000 for most violations. The law also includes the measure of revoking the licence for non-compliance – a step probably deemed too extreme by most of the governmental bodies in charge. The notion of an assessment index system is promising though. Many different indicator systems for circular economy have already been established in China, and could potentially form a bridge between local eco-economic parks and central government policies.

Low-carbon economy

Low-carbon economy specifically aims at achieving a sustainable low output of carbon and other greenhouse gases, usually measured in their carbon dioxide equivalent (CDE). Thus its rise begun only when the climate change issue began to gain attention in the 1990s. In 2001, the OECD ministers adopted an environmental strategy calling for a decoupling of environmental degradation from economic growth (OECD 2001, 5). In 2003, the UK Department of Trade and Industry published a milestone White Paper titled *Our Energy Future – Creating a Low-carbon Economy* in which low-carbon economy is the major strategy to reduce carbon emissions in developing countries (DTI 2003; Hofem and Heilmann 2013).

A major policy of the low-carbon economy programme are the five provinces and eight cities low-carbon pilot projects launched by the NDRC in 2012 (for more details see chapter 21 this volume by Liu and Wang). A strong motive for low-carbon development in China is a big potential for efficiency improvements. The country's climate mitigation programme is based on efficiency improvements – and energy security as the energy sector can hardly keep up with the economic growth. Especially, the rapid development of renewable energies demonstrates strong governmental support for a low-carbon economy.

Dynamic low-carbon advocacy

Advocates for the development of low-carbon industry can be found in research and advisory institutions, business and civil society. In 2006, the first *National Climate Change Assessment Report* was published as a result of the cooperation between nine ministries and 88 consultants (Schneider 2009). It marks the entry of climate change as an important issue into Chinese politics and led to some research projects about low-carbon economy related to energy politics. At the same time, government-led research and advisory institutions started an exchange on the topic with the international research community and subsequently became supporters of a low-carbon economy.

In April 2007, the China Council for International Cooperation on Environment and Development (CCICED) held a conference titled '2007 Low-carbon Economy and China's Energy and Environment Policies'. This conference drew both on the expertise of international and Chinese leading experts, governmental officials and NGO leaders in climate change and low-carbon economy, for example, officials from EU climate change policy, China's State Council and the World Wide Fund for Nature (WWF) (CCICED 2007). CCICED has played an important role in bringing international policy-oriented learning to the Chinese officials and experts (Hofem and Heilmann 2013).

The Chinese government sets up advisory institutions to provide information for decision making to top leaders, for example, the Counsellors' Office of the State Council (*Guowuyuan Canshishi*) (COSC). COSC is mainly made up of outstanding experts from the so-called eight minor parties or outstanding independent individuals. Several members of the COSC expressed in public their support for a low-carbon economy (Feng 2009; Hu 2010; Nanfang doushibao 2010; De and Hong 2012). Officially, the COSC is only an advisory organ, but their impact should not be underestimated and can be understood through anecdotes. For example, the former director of energy administration of NDRC and a fossil fuel expert, Xu Dingming, who attended the CCICED conference mentioned above, argued in 2008 for the importance of low-carbon economy for energy transition (Wang 2008). As these experts and counsellors serve the Premier and the State Council, their words had a strong impact on Chinese central governmental policies.

The eight minor parties also play a role in China's advisory institutions and influence the CCP's decision making (Wang 2008). Individual minor party members already advocated low-carbon economy as early as 2007/2008 (Kejibu 2007; Wu 2008). In 2010, during the CPPCC, their joint proposal of a low-carbon economy foreshadowed its national adoption in the 12th Five-Year Plan (Lianghui Baogaozu 2010).

The experts and officials of these parties have not only positions in the government, but also on boards of closely related associations, research institutions and NGOs. For example, Wan Gang, the Minister of Science and Technology, an expert on electric vehicles and vice-chair of CPPCC, is a member of a minor party (MOST 2013), as well as Shi Dinghuan, the director of China's Renewable Energy Association (Nanfang doushibao 2010) and Niu

Wenyuan, the director of Sustainable Development Strategy Research Group at China Academy of Science. Shi and Niu are both counsellors at COSC and in this function have direct contact with the top leaders and society (De and Hong 2012). They are the key actors in an advocacy coalition which has strong influence on government policies, though it cannot be denied that they might also follow economic interests dictated by their functions in business or industrial associations.

Renewable energy industry bases are another strong source of support for the advocacy of low-carbon economy. Some local governments become keen supporters of low-carbon economy for their renewable energy industries. For example, in 2010 there were over 100 low-carbon cities, and 100 renewable energy industrial parks have been established (Cai 2010; Meng 2010). For example, Shanghai and Baoding cooperated with WWF from 2005 on low-carbon economy and launched their low-carbon city initiatives in 2008 (WWF-China 2012). The cities have very strong renewable energy manufacturing industrial bases, and the local officials and businessmen have participated in international conferences to learn more about renewable energy since the late 1990s (Xie 2010). Some cities early on built low-carbon demonstration sites, such as Shenzhen's International Low-carbon Eco-city, which was constructed in 2012, and Wuxi's Sino-Swedish low-carbon city, which was constructed in 2010. These cities have taken an innovative stand and a pilot role in low-carbon economy.

Ecological economy

Compared to the circular economy and low-carbon economy, ecological economy has the longest history and is the best developed and best adopted concept in China. The concept of 'ecological civilization' that the CCP eventually adopted in its 17th National Congress is that it characterizes a development step after industrial civilization and a harmony between human and nature (Hu 2007). Ecological economy is interpreted in 'ecological civilization' ideas and policies in China. The Chinese interpretation of 'ecological civilization' as 'Sansheng Gongying', 'production, wealth, and ecology win–win' includes protecting the environment while raising living standards and developing city, countryside and nature (i.e. public parks) (Zhang 2010).

A key project for promoting ecological economy is the setup of so-called ecological red lines (see for example Nickum et al., chapter 6 this volume). Aimed at improving ecological protection work, these red lines are supposed to clarify property and usage rights as well as establish fees for the use of natural resources but, most importantly, they draw red lines around fragile areas and establish warning systems for the environmental carrying capacity of these areas (CCP 2013; CCCCP and State Council 2015). There are ecological pilot projects in 14 provinces, over 150 cities and thousands of townships and villages. Examples of ecological economy include projects such as rehabilitation of the Three River Headwaters (Sanjiangyuan), referring to the headwaters of the Lancang, Yellow and Yangzi rivers (see Ptackova chapter 16 this volume). The idea is to protect a fragile ecosystem and at the same time create new economic opportunities for local people.

The Chinese Ecological Economic Society (CEES) was set up in 1984 under the supervision of the China Academy of Social Science (CASS) and the State Forestry Administration of the People's Republic of China (CEES 2013). The directors of CEES are usually senior CCP or government officials as well as renowned economic experts like, for example, the first director Xu Dixin. CEES gathers Chinese experts in ecological economy and its close relationship with CASS and MOF guarantees that the experts' opinions and policies are very likely to reach the decision makers.

In 1999, the China Association of Scientific Exploration (CASE) organized an exploration to search the headwaters of the Lancang river. The serious ecological degradation, like desertification and deforestation, caught their attention. After finishing exploration, scientists organized by CASE proposed 'Western Development, Protect Three River Headwaters' to China's Forest Administration and the Qianghai Provincial Government. The proposal has been approved by both of them (Gao 2015). Scientists have played a bridging role in bringing local information into the decision making process of the government.

The majority of ecologically fragile areas are located in the western parts of China. How to protect these areas is a key issue in China's ecological economy. It is expected that the idea of ecological red lines will be expanded upon in the next years when China's new 'Silk Road' is developed as laid out in the 'One Belt and One Road' strategy as an economic belt in China's economically underdeveloped and ecologically fragile west (NDRC 2015).

Conclusions

Through the study of circular, low-carbon and ecological economy policy change in China, there are several common findings. First, the key advocators, such as experts, scientists or industrial professionals, have multiple identities with close relationships with the government decision makers, which enables them to push for policy change in green economy. Second, the advisory institutional settings in the Chinese government are important channels for advocates of policy change to let their agenda be heard by government officials. The NPC, CPPCC, CCICED, and COSC all are important platforms for advocates to communicate with government officials; through them, scientists, consultants, and other experts channel their ideas and opinions from the bottom- to the top-level leaders. It should be examined more deeply how much they can influence the CCP's environmental policies.

Third, the dynamic development of associations and research institutions has promoted green development in China. These organizations become a place where people with different backgrounds form advocacy coalitions for green economy. They provide information transfer and coordination. There is also noticeable economic interest in the advocacy for green economy. For example, the green industries associations push for green economy policy change in their interests. The green business interests have strongly affected the green economy policy change, which reflected the mingled environmental protection and green growth consideration in China's green economy.

In the case of the green economy advocates, we can observe an international learning process. These experts participated in conferences with international experts and officials in the green economy. It is important for China to embrace more international cooperation for its green economy development.

References

Aizawa M. and Yang C., 2010. Green credit, green stimulus, green revolution? China's mobilization of banks for environmental cleanup. *The Journal of Environment & Development,* 19(2), 119–144.
Bloomberg New Energy Finance, 2015. Sustainable Energy in America (http://www.bcse.org/wp-content/uploads/2015-Sustainable-Energy-in-America-Factbook.pdf) Accessed 23 July 2015.
Cai S., 2010. Ditan Rang Chengshi Gengjia Mishi. (http://opinion.china.com.cn/opinion_5_8305.html) Accessed 23 April 2016.
Cai W., Wu Y., Zhong Y. and Ren H., 2009. China building energy consumption: situation, challenges and corresponding measures. *Energy Policy,* 37(6), 2054–2059.

CCCCP (Central Committee of CCP) and State Council, 2015. Zhonggong Zhongyang Guowuyuan Guanyu Jiakuai Tuijin Shengtai Wenming Jianshe de Yijian (http://paper.people.com.cn/rmrb/html/2015-05/06/nw.D110000renmrb_20150506_3-01.htm) Accessed 21 July 2015.

CCICED (China Council for International Cooperation on Environment and Development), 2007. Ditan Jingji he Zhongguo Nengyuan yu Huanjing Zhengce Yantaohui Richeng (http://www.cciced.net/ztbd/yzh/2007nyzhy/hyrc_7363/201210/t20121019_239741.html) Accessed 23 July 2015.

CCP (Chinese Communist Party), 2013. Zhonggong Zhongyang Guanyu Quanmian Shenhua Gaige Ruogan Zhongda Wenti de Jueding (http://news.xinhuanet.com/politics/2013-11/15/c_118164235.htm) Accessed 23 July 2015.

CEES (Chinese Ecological Economics Society), 2013. Zhongguo Shengtai Jingjixue Xuehui Jianjie (http://www.cees.org.cn/show.asp?id=25) Accessed 23 July 2015.

Circular Economy Promotion Law of People's Republic of China, 2008. Passed in the 4th meeting of the Standing Committee of the 11th National People's Congress on Aug. 29, 2008 (http://www.fdi.gov.cn/1800000121_39_597_0_7.html) Accessed July 2015.

CREIA (China Renewable Energy Industries Association), 2010. Zhongguo Xunhuan Jingji Xiehui Kezaisheng Nengyuan Zhuanye Weiyuanhui Jianjie (http://www.creia.net/about/) Accessed 19 December 2016.

De N. and Hong L., 2012. Guowuyuan Canshi Niu Wenyuan Tan Zhuanbian Jingji Fangshi he Ditan Jingji. haixiazhisheng (http://www.counsellor.gov.cn/ztbd/fcs/2012-04-16/1363.shtml) Accessed 23 July 2015.

DRC and IISD (The Development Research Center of the State Council and the International Institute for Sustainable Development), 2014. *Greening China's financial system* (https://www.iisd.org/sites/default/files/publications/greening-chinas-financial-system.pdf) Accessed 10 December 2016.

DTI (Department of Trade and Industry), 2003. Our energy future – creating a low-carbon economy (http://webarchive.nationalarchives.gov.uk/+/http:/www.berr.gov.uk/files/file10719.pdf) Accessed August 2015.

Economy, E., 2006. Environmental governance: the emerging economic dimension. *Environmental Politics*, 15(2), 171–189.

Feng, Z., 2009. Ditan Jingji Li Women Haiyou Duoyuan (http://env.people.com.cn/GB/9324694.html) Accessed 23 July 2015.

Fewsmith, J., 2001. *Elite politics in contemporary China*. Routledge, London.

Foster, K. W., 2002. Embedded within state agencies: business associations in Yantai. *The China Journal*, 47, 41–65.

Gao D., 2015. Zhongguo Meng yu Zhongguo Kexue Tanxianmeng: Zhongguo Kexue Tanxian Xiehui Wujie Huiyuan Daibiao Dahui Jianghua (http://blog.sciencenet.cn/blog-1275197-865350.html) Accessed 23 July 2015.

Han H., Swedlow, B. and Unger, D., 2014. Policy advocacy coalitions as causes of policy change in China? Analyzing evidence from contemporary environmental politics. *Journal of Comparative Policy Analysis: Research and Practice*, 16(4), 313–334.

Ho P., 2001. Greening without conflict? Environmentalism, NGOs and civil society in China. *Development and Change*, 32(5), 893–921.

Ho P., 2007. Embedded activism and political change in a semiauthoritarian context. *China Information*, 21(2), 187–209.

Ho P., and Edmonds, R., 2007. *China's embedded activism: opportunities and constraints of a social movement*. Routledge, London.

Hofem, A. and Heilmann, S., 2013. Bringing the low-carbon agenda to China: a study in transnational policy diffusion. *Journal of Current Chinese Affairs*, 1, 199–215.

Hu J., 2007. Hu Jintao zai Zhongguo Gongchandang Dishiqici Quanguo Daibiao Dahuishang de Baogao (http://cpc.people.com.cn/GB/104019/104099/6429414.html) Accessed 23 July 2015.

Hu J., 2008. Zhonghua Renmin Gognheguo Xunhuan Jingji Cujinfa, (http://www.gov.cn/flfg/2008-08/29/content_1084355.htm) Accessed August 2015.

Hu J., 2012. Full text of Hu Jintao's report at 18th Party Congress (http://news.xinhuanet.com/english/special/18cpcnc/2012-11/17/c_131981259.htm) Accessed 23 July 2015.

Hu Q., 2010. Guowuyuan Canshi Liu Yanhua: Ditan Jingji 'Hunyao Futi' (http://hxd.wenming.cn/ysb/2010-09/29/content_169304.htm) Accessed 23 July 2015.

Huang H. and Wu B., 2015. China's economic transition: the 'new normal' is here to stay (http://english. phbs.pku.edu.cn/index.php?m=content&c=index&a=show&catid=591&id=766) Accessed 23 July 2015.

Huang H. and Zhou G., 2015. *The road of China's economic transition: 21st century green revolution.* Kexue Chubanshe, Beijing.

Jenkins-Smith, H., and Sabatier, P., 1994. Evaluating the advocacy coalition framework. *Journal of Public Policy,* 14, 175–203.

Jing, J., 2000. Environmental protests in rural China. In: Perry, E. J., and Selden, M., eds. 2000. *Chinese society: change, conflict and resistance.* Routledge, London, 208–226.

Kennedy, S., 2009. *The business of lobbying in China.* Harvard University Press, Cambridge.

Knup, E., 1997. Environmental NGOs in China: an overview. *China Environment Series,* 1(3), 9–15.

Li C., 2001. *China's leaders: the new generation.* Rowman & Littlefield, Lanham, MD, USA.

Li W., Liu J. and Li D., 2012. Getting their voices heard: three cases of public participation in environmental protection in China. *Journal of Environmental Management,* 98, 65–72.

Lianghui Baogaozu, 2010. Jinnian Zhengxie Yihao Tian Liting Ditanjingji (http://www.ccchina.gov.cn/ Detail.aspx?newsId=29983) Accessed 19 December 2016.

Liu M. M., Henry, M. and Huang H., 2013. *Renewable energy in China: towards a green economy.* Enrich Professional, Hong Kong.

Lu M. and Zhang X., 2005. *Zhongguo Lvse Jingji Yanjiu.* Henan Renmin Chubanshe, Henan.

Meng X., 2010. Difang Zhengfu Rezhong Xinnengyuan Chanye Jidi Huozhe Channeng Guosheng (http://www.ccidnet.com/2010/0804/2141943.shtml) Accessed 23 July 2015.

MOST (Ministry of Science and Technology), 2013. Wan Gang Buzhang Chuxi Xinnengyuan Qiche Zuotanhui (http://www.most.gov.cn/kjbgz/201303/t20130312_100100.htm) Accessed 25 July 2015.

Nanfang doushibao, 2010. Ditan Shidai Niandu Renwu Pingxuan (http://ditan.kdnet.net/2010/reason. php?candidate_no=4) Accessed 24 July 2015.

NDRC (National Development and Reform Commission), 2015. Tuidong Gongjian Sichouzhilu Jingjidai he 21 Shiji Haishang Sichouzhilu de Yuanjing yu Xingdong (http://www.sdpc.gov.cn/ gzdt/201503/t20150328_669091.html) Accessed 23 July 2015.

Nhamo, G., 2011. *Green economy and climate mitigation: topics of relevance to Africa.* African Books Collective, Oxford, UK.

OECD, 2001. Environmental strategy for the first decade of the 21st century (http://www.oecd.org/env/ indicators-modelling-outlooks/1863539.pdf) Accessed 23 July 2015.

Pan J., Ma H. and Zhang Y., 2011. *Green economy and green jobs in China: current status and potentials for 2020.* Worldwatch Institute, Washington.

Pearce, D. W., Markandya, A., and Barbier, E., 1989. *Blueprint for a green economy.* Earthscan, London.

Ren Y., 2014. Lvse Jingji Zhangfang Zhongguomeng Zhongguo Linye Chanye, *Zhongguo Linye Chanye,* 1, 22–24.

Sabatier, P. A., 1987. Knowledge, policy-oriented learning, and policy change an advocacy coalition framework, *Science Communication,* 8(4), 649–692.

Sabatier, P. A., 1988. An advocacy coalition framework of policy change and the role of policy-oriented learning therein. *Policy Sciences* 21(2/3), 129–168.

Sabatier, P. A., 1998. The advocacy coalition framework: revisions and relevance for Europe. *Journal of European Public Policy,* 5, 98–130.

Schneider, S. H., 2009. *Climate change science and policy.* Island Press, Washington.

Schwartz, J., 2004. Environmental NGOs in China: roles and limits. *Pacific Affairs,* 77(1), 28–49.

Stalley, P. and Yang D., 2006. An emerging environmental movement in China? *The China Quarterly,* 186, 333–356.

State Council, 2011. Guojia Huanjing Baohu 'Shierwu' Guihua (http://www.gov.cn/zwgk/2011-12/20/ content_2024895.htm). Accessed 23 July 2015.

Tang S.-Y. and Zhan X., 2008. Civic environmental NGOs, civil society, and democratisation in China. *The Journal of Development Studies,* 44(3), 425–448.

Tong Y. and Lei S., 2010. Large-scale mass incidents and government responses in China. *International Journal of China Studies,* 1(2), 487–508.

UNEP (United Nations Environment Programme), 2011. Toward a green economy: pathways to sustainable and poverty eradication (http://www.ipu.org/splz-e/rio+20/rpt-unep.pdf) Accessed 19 December 2016.

UNEP (United Nations Environment Programme), 2014. *Modelling China's Green Economy: 2010–2050* (http://web.unep.org/greeneconomy/sites/unep.org.greeneconomy/files/2015_05_31_china_t21_june22_final.pdf) Accessed 19 December 2016.

Wang A., 2013. The search for sustainable legitimacy: environmental law and bureaucracy in China. *Harvard Environmental Law Review*, 37(2), 365–440.

Wang S., 2008. Changing models of China's policy agenda setting. *Modern China*, 34(1), 56–87.

Wang Y., 2008. Xu Dingming: 2008 Nian Jixu Fazhan Ditan Jingji. Diyi Caijing Ribao (http://www.in-en.com/article/html/energy-176971.shtml). Accessed 23 July 2015.

Weng X., Dong Z., Wu Q. and Qin Y., 2015. China's pathway to a green economy (http://pubs.iied.org/pdfs/16582IIED.pdf). Accessed 23 July 2015.

Wu B., 2013. *New theory on leadership management science*. Chartridge Books, Oxford, UK.

Wu F., 2005. Double-mobilization: transnational advocacy networks for China's environment and public health (http://drum.lib.umd.edu/bitstream/1903/2970/1/umi-umd-2764.pdf). Accessed 23 July 2015.

Wu X., 2008. Wu Xiaoqing Weiyuan: Dali Fazhan Ditan Jingji Kongzhi Wenshi Qiti Paifang (http://www.gov.cn/gzdt/2008-03/14/content_920392.htm). Accessed 23 July 2015.

Wuebbeke, J., 2013. China's climate change expert community – principles, mechanisms and influence. *Journal of Contemporary China*, 22(82), 712–731.

WWF-China (World Wide Fund for Nature-China), 2012. Low-carbon city initiative (http://en.wwfchina.org/en/what_we_do/climate___energy/mitigation/lcci/). Accessed 23 July 2015.

Xie D., 2010. Yizuo Ditan Chengshi de Dansheng (http://doc.qkzz.net/article/81ac7cb4-a8f1-4aa2-a2e4-82433d7a27fa.htm). Accessed 23 July 2015.

Xie L. and Van Der Heijden, H.-A., 2010. Environmental movements and political opportunities: the case of China. *Social Movement Studies*, 9(1), 51–68.

Xinhua, 2016. Zhonghua Renmin Gongheguo Guomin Jingji He Shehuifazhan Di Shisange Wunian Guihua Gangyao (http://news.xinhuanet.com/politics/2016lh/2016-03/17/c_1118366322_11.htm), Accessed 25 April 2016.

Yang G., 2005. Environmental NGOs and institutional dynamics in China. *The China Quarterly*, 181(1), 44–66.

Yuan Z., Bi, J., and Moriguichi, Y. 2006. The circular economy: a new development strategy in China. *Journal of Industrial Ecology*, 10(1/2), 4–8.

Zhang X., 2010. Chengshi Xiangcun Yewai Yiti Guihua Shengtai Shenghuo Shengchan Sansheng Gongying (http://zhongou.gotoip2.com/zjgd4.html). Accessed 23 July 2015.

Zhong M. and Hong L. 2014. Environmental and industrial policy environment for the development of green finance in China. In: DRC and IISD 2014. *Greening China's financial system* (https://www.iisd.org/sites/default/files/publications/greening-chinas-financial-system.pdf) Accessed 10 December 2016.

Zhu D., 2012. Lvse Jingji Xinlinian Ji Zhongguo Kaizhan Lvse Jingji Yanjiu De Sikao *Zhongguo Renkou Ziyuan Yu Huanjing*, 22(5), 40–47.

Zhu Q., Sarkis, J. and Geng Y., 2005. Green supply chain management in China: pressures, practices and performance. *International Journal of Operations & Production Management*, 25(5), 449–468.

PART II

Key issues and strategies for solution

6

THE THREE RED LINES AND CHINA'S WATER RESOURCES POLICY IN THE TWENTY-FIRST CENTURY

James E. Nickum, Jia Shaofeng and Scott Moore

David Lampton (2014), former long-time President of the National Committee on United States–China Relations, observes that Chinese leaders at both central and local levels have the same 'nightmares' that can keep them awake at night. By far most of these are domestic: (1) the peasantry, population and food; (2) workers and urban-industrial issues, including the environment; (3) economic growth and volatility; and (4) disasters, natural and manmade. They worry not only about the problems themselves but forming and, even more, implementing policies to address them effectively in a 'fragmented authoritarian' state that is far-flung, often gridlocked in a complex matrix (*tiaokuai*) of authority and personal relations (*guanxi*), and that is becoming increasingly pluralistic, divisive and often out of effective control of either the bureaucracy or the rule of law.

Water courses through all these nightmares. Agriculture remains the largest water user, withdrawing twice as much as all other uses combined (Ministry of Water Resources and National Bureau of Statistics 2013) and consuming an even higher proportion. With the growth of cities and industry occupying farmland, there has been a shift in the country's grain basket from the wet but mountainous south to the flat, dry north, and with it a growing reliance on receding groundwater. The demands of a rapidly expanding urban population and industry have added to the burdens on the water supply and in many places have resulted in appropriation of water from the rural areas. In particular, the abundant coal reserves that fuel much of China's rapid economic growth lie in particularly arid parts of the north and northwest that rely heavily on irrigation to produce crops. The poor quality of ambient waters and shallow aquifers due to untreated waste from all sectors is increasingly recognized as a threat to further growth, to the natural environment, and to the legitimacy of the state. The historical scourges of floods and droughts moreover continue to plague China, often worsened by unwise land use.

Water policy in the late twentieth century

Our focus here is on policies adopted in the twenty-first century to address this panoply of water nightmares, centring on the Strictest Water Resources Management System (SWRMS) and the Three Red Lines (TRL) that stem from it. We will describe these in detail later, but since they did not come out of nowhere, we provide here an account of how China's twenty-first-century water management policies evolved out of the hyperactive hydraulic state of the previous half century.

The history of China's water resources management system in that period can be divided roughly into three periods: (1) A project-oriented period with no formal water resources management (1949–1977); (2) A deceleration of construction, with increased focus on efficiency and a more formal system based on command-and-control (1978–1987); and (3) A renewed focus on the water sector, with regularization of management via abstraction permits, the enactment of a *Water Law*, and moves towards quasi-exchanges of water rights (1988–2001).[1]

If you build it, water will come (1949–1977)

In the pre-reform period through 1977, there was an enormous amount of construction of water-related works but no formal system for managing water resources. Although water rights were completely 'socialized' in the hands of the state or collectives by 1956, fragmented management ruled, with the Ministry of Water Resources focused on flood control and interbasin transfer projects, while hydropower, municipal water supply, water transport were managed by other ministries. The biggest water use, irrigation, was in the domain of the Ministry of Agriculture. Because in most places a small share of available water was used and water pollution was not as serious as it subsequently became, there were relatively few conflicts (Jia and Zhang 2011). It must be noted, however, that not all was harmonious, especially for interprovincial waters. A particularly notorious example was the contentious Zhang River that originates in Shanxi Province and forms the border between Hebei and Henan provinces and provides water to the famous hand-crafted Red Flag Canal built in the 1960s (Nickum 1983, 184).

Coasting downhill (1978–1987)

Lampton (2014, 85) notes that the toolkit of Chinese leaders includes both command and market or other bargaining mechanisms. The early reform period after 1978 was one when the state took its foot off the accelerator, especially in agriculture. The result was a severe cutback in funding going to the state water agencies and even more in commitments by local governments and with them a reduction in project construction and maintenance (Lohmar et al. 2003, 9; Wang and Hu 2011, 80). Compounding matters, the end of collective agriculture was accompanied by the elimination of the work point system, possibly one of the more effective complements to command measures for mobilizing farmers to contribute their labour to project construction (Nickum 1978). Non-agricultural demands on water grew with the revitalization of the cities and the spread of industry, including township enterprises. To the extent that there was resort to any of the tools in the kit, administrative (command) measures continued to dominate by default, but with highly fragmented siloed authority – paraphrased as 'nine dragons ruling the water'.

Mixing it up (1987–2001)

From the late 1980s water regained the attention of policy makers, who moved to create a full toolkit for the sector. A formal legal framework was established, centring on the 1988 *Water Law* (*shuifa*) (more a Code in western terms, due to its lack of implementation provisions), identified by Shen (2014, 716) as 'the most important event in the 1980s for the water sector'. The Law called for integrated management of China's water resources, and provided a legal foundation to the collection of water fees and water resource fees, as well as for the subsequent establishment of a water abstraction permit system. The same year, the State Council moved to make the Ministry of Water Resources (MWR) the lead dragon, by bringing under its control groundwater management that had resided in the Ministry of Geology (for non-urban) and the Ministry of Construction (for urban), as well as the latter's urban flood control portfolio.

At the local levels, from provincial-level municipalities to counties, Water Services Bureaux (WSB) integrating water supply and drainage functions were established gradually in much of China following Shenzhen's 1993 initiative (Jia and Zhang 2011). By the year 2004 about 52 per cent of local administrations and 31 per cent of cities had set up WSBs (Nickum and Lee 2006). Problems of coordination have persisted under the bureau umbrella, however, given that the levels of government above the WSBs still operate on a line agency basis; and outside it, notably between the water and environmental authorities in areas such as wastewater discharge (Cosier and Shen 2010, 76–77). Some WSBs in Qinghai Province have changed their names back to Water Resources Bureaux, explicitly reverting to the exclusive administrative chain of the MWR. Many others, especially at the lower levels (prefectures and counties), have simply changed the name to WSB but remain in the water supply silo.

Water policy in the early twenty-first century

Reframing water policy (2001–2008)

In the 1990s, the Yellow River made headlines by not flowing to the sea – in 1997, for most of the year. It was the most dramatic, but far from the only example of 'basin closure'. Shortage was not the only, or even the most damaging, water problem. The major 1998 flood along the Chang Jiang, affecting one of China's economic heartlands, was a further wake-up call that all was not well in the water sector and that dikes and dams, themselves sometimes poorly constructed and with unintended effects on river flow and sedimentation, could not compensate for the loss of storage capacity in lakes due to reclamation. Hence the new millennium saw a decisive policy turn against a sectoral project-oriented approach towards a frame of 'resources-oriented water resources development' (Shen 2014, 720). While investment actually increased significantly, attention turned away from developing new sources (interbasin transfer and rural water supply being significant exceptions) towards greater appreciation for resource management, environmental effects, and demand management, including waste reduction (improved efficiency) as well as greater use of price incentives and market mechanisms. Included among these mechanisms were tentative steps towards water rights trading.

This new perspective was incorporated into the 2002 revision of the *Water Law* which established the right to safe water, and elevated the importance of conservation and pollution control as objectives of water policy (Xie 2009, 28). The revised law also provided a legal base for the river and lake basin management commissions that had already been set up under the MWR.

China's legal framework, sometimes quite well developed, has rarely gone far beyond being just a set of principles, however. A World Bank report attributed the ineffectiveness of China's water laws and regulations to their lack of specific provisions for enforcement and frequent ambiguity in demarcating the authority of different sectors; an excessive reliance on local governments who often have weak enforcement capacity and who resist measures that could result in reductions of the limited tax revenue at their disposal; and inadequate transparency or public participation (Xie 2009, 43–45).

Perhaps in consequence, this period was characterized more by framing and adoption of principles than by taking concrete steps to address China's water stress points in the face of rapid economic growth and structural transformation (Shen 2014, 722). After remaining steady for a long period due primarily to the decline in agricultural uses, total water use began to rise; pollution of ambient waters, both surface and underground, reached alarming levels; and water use efficiency appeared to be well below best-practice levels internationally.

Crucially, the Chinese government came to the conclusion that these water-related challenges stemmed from incomplete central control over local levels of water resource administration. In particular, pervasive local non-compliance with centrally-formulated water resource management policies and inter-jurisdictional conflict over water quality and quantity issues guided Beijing to the conclusion that local authorities had to be more closely supervised, and that it required better tools to compel local compliance with central policy (Moore 2014). This conclusion set the stage for the most recent phase of water resource management in China, characterized by a new-found stringency in both the formulation and implementation of water-related targets.

Getting strict (since 2009)

The approach of a 'strictest system' at national and provincial levels was first adopted as state policy for land use from 2005, when a 'red line' floor of 120 million hectares was set for China's cultivated land (Li 2009).[2] Both Party Secretary Hu Jintao and Premier Wen Jiabao were professionally trained in water-related areas, and Wen was a former chair of the high-level Central Leading Group for Rural Work (Li 2009), so an extension of the approach placing a floor on cultivated area to set a ceiling on the water sector was a natural next step.

At the beginning of 2009, the then chair of the Leading Group, Vice-Premier Hui Liangyu, called for a similar strictest system for water resources management. Minister of Water Resources Chen Lei, another member of the Group, followed up quickly by announcing a 'strictest water resources management system' that would have three 'red lines' as its mandatory goals: to control total withdrawal and use, raise water use efficiency and improve ambient water quality. Chen did not specify targets at this time; these were set subsequently in November 2010 in the *National Comprehensive Water Resources Plan*.

The first National Census in 2010–12 (MWR and State Statistical Bureau 2013), conducted outside the normal and not necessarily reliable annual reporting system, put some relatively definitive numbers on the growing stresses on the water sector. Total water use (measured by withdrawals) in 2011 was 621 km³, only 1.7 per cent above the total reported through the routine statistical system, but with significant differences in use sectors (agricultural use was 8.6 per cent more than reported, the already insignificant amount attributed to environmental use 4.8 per cent less) (Zhang et al. 2013). For some provinces, however, the difference from conventionally reported figures was over 10 per cent.

The total figure in the Census amounted to 74 per cent of the available water resource of 810 km³, with business-as-usual water use projected to rise to 740 km³ in 2030. Locally, especially in northern river basins, water was already oversubscribed, drawing unsustainably on receding groundwater levels. Irrigation use efficiency was estimated at 0.5, meaning that half of the water released or diverted for irrigation actually reached and was used by the crops within the designated command area. In addition, there was a high rate of non-attainment of ambient water quality standards in water function zones established along rivers and in lakes.

The Three Red Lines and Document No. 1

The growing salience of the water sector as being directly related to the country's 'economic, ecological and national security' led to its being featured in the prominent Document No. 1 for 2011. Titled 'Resolution on Accelerating the Development of Water Resources Reform', this document called for a significant step-up in the pace of hydraulic construction, including for flood control, the completion of the eastern and middle routes of the South–North Water Transfer from the Chang Jiang (Yangze River), and the construction of other interbasin link canals. This surge in construction was made possible to some extent by the government's adoption of a massive countercyclical increase in public investment in response to the 2007–2008 global economic crisis. At the same time, Document No. 1 (2011) affirmed the SWRMS as national policy, affirming the specific national TRL targets for the years 2015, 2020 and 2030 that had just been laid out in the National Comprehensive Water Resources Plan (Table 6.1).

The first and most ambitious of the red lines consists of caps on China's water withdrawals at national, provincial, and subprovincial levels, aiming to hold total consumption below the country's estimated total renewable freshwater reserves. The target year of 2030 is when China's population is expected to near a stable or declining level, and the economy to reach a certain level of maturity. The second consists of two quite different indices of water productivity, one for industrial use (measured in m^3 per 10,000 RMB) and the other for irrigation. The third aims at improvement of ambient water quality through increasing the percentage of zoned sections of water bodies that meet certain minimum standards for water quality that apply to the designated purposes of those zones.

All told, the TRL are an extremely ambitious effort to apply the techniques of a top-down planned approach to address China's water problems in a comprehensive manner. According to a MWR official, 'There are no other countries that have set such detailed targets to restrict their own development by limiting usage of water resources' (Wu 2012). As such, the TRL is one of the world's most noteworthy environmental policy initiatives.

Subsequent policy development

Shortly thereafter, a Central Water Resources Work Conference attended by all the top leaders who were in Beijing further showed support for the SWRMS and its TRL across the spectrum of government and Communist Party leadership. The following year, Central Document #3 established 'Four Systems' to implement the TRL. Each of the first three are related to a specific red line. The fourth and arguably most critical placed observance of the red lines in the

Table 6.1 The specific targets of the Three Red Lines

Red Line	2010	2015	2020	2030
1 *total water use*	>600 km^3	<635 km^3	<670 km^3	<700 km^3
2a *industrial water used per 10,000 yuan output* (*2000 prices*)	120 m^3	<94 m^3	65 m^3	<40 m^3
2b *water efficiency of irrigation*	0.50	0.53	0.55	0.60
3 *water function zones meeting COD, AN standards*	48%	>60%	>80%	>95%

Notes: COD = chemical oxygen demand; AN = ammonium nitrate ($N_2H_4O_3$)

Source: State Council Office 2013.

performance evaluation (*kaohe*) criteria for promotion of officials. This gets it the attention of administrators but is a mechanism for managing personnel, not water resources (Shen 2014), and as such may lead to undesirable distortions, as noted later. Also, officials are faced with a large and growing number of performance criteria demanding their attention. If there is a conflict between limiting water use and one of the targets designated as a core task (particularly economic growth or social stability), it is unlikely that the water red line would be observed in practice – on paper is another matter.[3]

How strict is strict? Institutional and informational limitations on TRL

The TRL are significant in that they seek to address simultaneously three often separate domains of water policy: total water use, ambient water quality and efficiency of water use. The core of the red lines, and the one most clearly in the domain of the MWR, is the first, setting a cap on total water use, beginning at the provincial level, and then sub-allocated down to the basic levels. This limit, if effective, could provide the basis for a system of entitlements, or initial rights, that are an essential precondition of establishing a market-based cap-and-trade system of rights transfer (Jia et al. 2012; Garrick 2015; Moore 2015). Focusing on two cases in the United States and one in Australia, Garrick (2015, 80) cautions, however, that even there 'the politics and design of the cap, initial allocation and tradable water rights merit careful analysis of path dependency and inter-temporal trade-offs' due to potential adverse effects on 'flexibility and long-run adaptive efficiency'. Yet, as the history of post-reform land allocation has demonstrated, quotas are not complete entitlements, since they are contingent upon top-down enforcement and are limited in the rights delegated to the user. For such contingent entitlements to be fully effective as a basis for trading it is necessary for the state to also allow market mechanisms and civil society to play an independent role (Shen 2014). In a system where fear of 'disorder' underlies the nightmares of the leaders, this is difficult to achieve.

Another problem is that, as evidenced in the TRL, the SWRMS may not be all that strict. In the case of total water use, the targets are aimed at holding total use below a business-as-usual (BAU) projection. Yet BAU rarely happens. The history of water use projections both worldwide (Gleick 2000) and in China (e.g. Qian et al. 2009, 21) is that they almost invariably overstate future demands as there is a kind of inverted Kuznets curve where those demands peak and decline as economies mature and technologies and habits lead to greater water efficiency. This suggests that instead of representing an ambitious attempt to limit total water use, the TRL may instead codify a loose cap that will not require substantial reductions in water use.

Perhaps the most significant limitations on the TRL are its information requirements. The hydrological cycle is far-flung and complicated, and expensive and difficult to measure directly even with current advances in monitoring technology. This forces reliance on a bureaucratic construction of reality, both in the categories that can be used and in the numbers reported by subordinates who are in turn rewarded or penalized on the basis of their reports (cf Nickum 2003). In the case of the TRL, all categories are problematic to some degree as performance measures.

Total water use, even when measured in the simplest way, in terms of withdrawals, requires formidable measurement capacity, even at macro scales, and is for the most part estimated indirectly using back-of-the-envelope calculations of one sort or another often based on fixed 'norms'. In most cases, water withdrawn is not entirely consumed but returned in part to the usable water cycle. Water withdrawals are therefore an imperfect measure of water consumption, which is the more important one for quantity impact. Actual water use increasingly includes non-conventional sources such as recycled water and brackish or sea water, reducing the burden on water resources in a way not picked up by this red line. Furthermore, experience elsewhere, such as in the Colorado River Basin, has shown that the lack of fit between fixed allocations and wild hydrological swings, leads to conflict and paralysis (Garrick 2015, 102). This problem is addressed in the case of the TRL water use targets through adjustments for dry or wet years at the time of assessment, but this is an ex-post evaluation and probably not as useful to affecting behaviour as a proportional allocation system such as in the Murray–Darling in Australia.

Industrial water use per 10,000 RMB output value reflects pricing and financial policies and, perhaps even more, changes in economic structure, as much as or more than improvements in water use efficiency at the plant or industry level. It is a single factor measure of *economic* efficiency.

Irrigation efficiency is commonly based on measures such as the percentage of total water released at the head of a canal system that is taken up by the crops. This measure is an indicator of *technical* efficiency that supports engineering policies such as improved canal lining to reduce seepage, without consideration of the value of that seepage as a source of recharge for well irrigators. Hence basin use efficiency, which is very difficult to calculate but usually much higher than canal use efficiency, is a more appropriate measure of how much water is actually used, but even it may not be the best indicator (see, e.g. Frederiksen and Allen 2011 and the rejoinder by Gleick et al. 2011). If the goal is to produce 'more crop per drop', the appropriate measure would be water productivity, which incorporates changes in agronomy and agricultural practices as well as water per se. If the goal is to produce more value per drop for the farmers, it would need to incorporate market factors such as the return to cash crops. If the goal is to produce more value for the economy, it would have to consider alternative uses of the water and the benefits of inter-sectoral transfers. Neither efficiency measure addresses the impact of industrial or agricultural use on the environment.

Environmental standard attainment in water function zones requires agreement on what those zones and standards are. Water function zones (WFZ) have been delineated and classified by the MWR in two tiers. There are about 5,000 top tier WFZs, divided into protected zones (*baohuqu*), conservation zones (*baoliuqu*), buffer zones (*huachongqu*), environmental restoration zones (*shengtai huanjing huifuzuqu*) and developmental use zones (*kaifa liyongqu*). The second tier breaks the last of those down into specific types of use, each with its own quality standards, such as potable water, industry, agriculture or recreation. The Ministry of Environment has its own set of water environmental functional zones (WEFZ) with nearly identical classifications to the second tier WFZs, but different in number and coverage. Attainment rates for WFZs are unlikely to coincide with those for WEFZs.

Further, COD and ammonium nitrate are only two of many possible measures of water quality. They were selected in large part on the basis of the capacity for monitoring them. By comparison, the national standards for water quality include 24 parameters. Other 'parameters may be added when monitoring capacity improves' (Shen et al. 2015, 18). In the meantime, a water function zone could attain those two standards but still contain a witches' brew of other pollutants such as phenols, phosphates, persistent organic pollutants (POPs), novel chemicals and hormones or heavy metals. In the original design of the TRL agreed upon by eight ministries, total pollution inflow for a number of pollutants was suggested as the third red line, but this was abandoned as being too difficult to formulate. Also much of the pollutant load entering ambient waters is from non-point sources such as agriculture or highway runoff that are effectively out of the control of either the Ministry of Environment or the Ministry of Water Resources. These gaps in administrative authority suggest the significant informational and institutional challenges that confront implementation of the TRL.

Implementation, both successes and problems

As previously indicated, in addition to the above informational complications, there are at least two significant institutional problems in the design of the TRL. The first, common to organized society anywhere, stems from the use of indicators to evaluate performance. Behaviour then focuses on performing well in terms of those indicators, as they are measured, to the possible neglect of intangibles and other areas that are not included in performance criteria – intensifying 'silo' orientations that already exist due to coordination costs. The second and related problem is that for the most part the system relies on indirect estimates and self-reporting by those who are subject to the reward/penalty system, creating an agency (conflict of interest) problem. 'Misreporting' is pervasive in China (e.g. Serrato et al. 2016).

There is a clear reporting bias in China's water use statistics. In some provinces, totals change perceptibly when personnel in charge of reporting the statistics change. Some provinces reported inflated figures for total water use and industrial water use, and lowered numbers for canal use rate in anticipation of the TRL quotas, under the rubric of making 'technical adjustments'. Reporting bias, which can reach 10–20 per cent at the provincial level, can be as much as 50 per cent at the county level (Jia 2013).

Major policies in China are typically phased in both temporally and spatially, and the TRL and related policies have been no exception. Temporally, the provision of interim targets for the years 2015 and 2020 provide benchmarks, and the national quotas have been decomposed, first to the provincial level, from where they are to be set for prefecture-level jurisdictions and counties.

Spatially, four provinces (Jiangsu, Shandong, Hebei and Zhejiang), three province-level municipalities (Shanghai, Tianjin and Beijing) and three others (Han River Basin, as well as Zhangjiagang and Yongkang cities) were chosen as pilots in 2011 to develop and apply TRL policy before its wider dissemination (Shen et al. 2015, 28). The case of Shandong, the first of the provincial pilots, provides an indication of how these policies were implemented at the provincial level. The provincial government established a broad-reaching, inter-governmental working group with representatives from a wide range of relevant provincial agencies, including the Water Resource Department, Development and Reform Commission, Environmental Protection Agency, Economic and Information Technology Commission, Finance Department, Land and Resources Department, Housing and Urban Construction Department, Agriculture Department, and the Audit Office. The provincial Water Resource Department was made responsible for assigning targets and quotas to local governments within the TRL policy framework, in consultation with the other parties represented in the working group. A Working Group Assessment Office (*sheng jieshui ban*) was also established under the auspices of the working group to prepare annual compliance assessments and to monitor progress in implementation (Shuilibu Bangongting 2014).

The designation of specific monitoring and compliance verification functions for the Assessment Office is significant, because a fundamental element of TRL policy implementation has been the inclusion of mechanisms to ensure that the policy is taken seriously by local governments, and that its provisions are adhered to. In an early sign of the importance attached to compliance, the initial TRL policy document contained three stipulations that have the intent of making it very difficult for local officials to avoid implementation of and compliance with the TRL policy framework. First, the document directed that officials above county level, and therefore more closely monitored by central authorities, were to be responsible for overseeing TRL policy implementation. Second, the central government directive made provincial Water Resource Departments responsible for documenting provincial compliance with the TRL policy, establishing a robust reporting mechanism. Third, and even more significantly, as noted earlier, meeting the TRL targets was made part of the *kaohe* performance metrics that are one of the most important incentives for Chinese officials (Tsui and Wang 2004). As noted previously, however, there are often dozens of these performance indicators, some of which likely have much higher weight in the portfolios of most officials, and others, not only the TRL, which can be manipulated (Landry 2008, 82–86).

Nonetheless, as mentioned, a number of factors militated against the successful implementation of the TRL and threatened to turn the red lines into green lights – i.e., render them ineffective. Three are particularly salient. The first of these is inadequate coordination between ministries, in particular the MWR and the Ministry of Environmental Protection (MEP). The second is the deformation of quantitative targets and the reporting system due to agency problems. The third is the political nature of the setting of quotas. For example, many provinces argued for and received 'technical adjustments' upwards in the original plan figures (Jia 2013).

In Document No. 2 (2013) the State Council set the TRL targets for all provinces, for all three target years (2015, 2020 and 2030) for total water use and water function zone quality attainment, and for 2015 alone for the two efficiency objectives. The rate of increase in water use allowed over the amount reported for 2010 varied considerably, with relatively water-abundant provinces such as Guangdong agreeing to lower caps, anticipating a continued decline in use with changes in economic structure, while some of China's most highly water stressed places, notably Shaanxi, Tianjin, Shanxi, Henan, Shandong and Hebei, were allowed higher than average increases in their quotas. Greater austerity in relatively water-abundant regions allows more lenience to oversubscribed ones. This helps ensure the attainment of red lines at both national and provincial levels, but without imposing a lot of pain, thereby subverting the stated intent of the TRL. The devil had already begun to show in the details.

In January 2014, provincial heads were held accountable for meeting the TRL. The Document No. 1 kicking off the 13th Five-Year-Plan period (2016–20) reiterated the red lines for water and farmland, and it appears that the red-line approach will be applied to other sectors such as forests, grassland, wetlands and oceans as part of a renewed effort to address environmental degradation and create a 'Beautiful China' (Tan 2016).

Discussion

It is quite likely that the TRL is the best that can be done given institutional and political realities, despite the impressive mobilization of support across silos at the central level. They certainly may help guide policy but are very imprecise tools for addressing the range of China's water nightmares. They are particularly weak in addressing environmental problems outside of those that can be measured by COD and ammonium nitrate.

With the issuance of the 'Water Ten Plan' (more formally, the *Water Pollution Prevention and Control Action Plan*) in April 2015, the State Council did take a step towards filling that gap. With similar target dates to the TRL of 2020 and 2030, it uses the existing six-grade water quality standards that, as noted, are based on two dozen parameters, not two. Like the SWRMS, it resulted from a coordination of numerous government ministries and departments. The lead agency, however, is the MEP, not the MWR. Like the TRL, the initial targets of what is promoted as a strict approach to a serious problem are surprisingly lenient, perhaps also reflecting a sense that the business-as-usual future is one of even more severe deterioration (Tan 2015).

Relationship between administrative and market approach

The administrative, target-driven approach of the TRL has many of the characteristics of the planned economy that was abandoned for the most part with the reforms of the 1980s, and as such may seem to be a regression to a command-and-control system with all of its well-known pathologies of informational and motivational distortions and lack of flexibility and efficiency. At the same time, a market or a quasi-market, such as a cap-and-trade system, must be based on a determination of initial entitlements to the resource. The allocation of maximum withdrawal rates, supplemented by the long-existing water abstraction permit system, promises to provide such de facto entitlements. The next step is to allow the exchange of entitlements. Commitment to greater use of water transfers through entitlement exchange has not been supplanted by the TRL (Jia et al. 2012). Nonetheless, implementation failures of the TRL, in particular in effectively allocating verifiable abstraction quotas, also make exchangeable entitlements and other market mechanisms more problematic.

A final word

At the national level, the first-stage targets of the TRL were all met, usually by a wide margin. Industrial water use per 10,000 RMB output fell to 58 m^3 (82 m^3 in 2000 prices), well below the target of 94 m^3; agricultural water use efficiency increased to 0.532 (target: 0.53). Water quality met standards in 67.9 per cent of water function zones (target: >60 per cent). Total water use at 618 km^3 was also comfortably below the 635 km^3 red line and even under the 621 km^3 estimated for the year 2011 in the National Water Census. It was reported that this was an increase above 2014, however, and that water use grew in all major use categories (domestic, industrial, agricultural and even environmental) (State Statistical Bureau 2016). Unfortunately, all these results can be explained as much by rational bureaucratic actors playing numbers games as by any actual change in water parameters or underlying reform to China's water resource management structure.

Notes

1 We call them 'quasi-exchanges' because they are in practice not direct exchanges between users but modifications of state allocations of use and other rights.
2 In 2008, it was combined with another strictest system, with a second red line, on economical land use, and incorporated into the landmark *Resolution of the CCP Central Committee on Some Major Issues in Rural Reform and Development* that aimed at being the most significant land reform in three decades (Li 2009).
3 For core tasks, a 'one strike and you are out' (一票否决) policy obtains, in effect making other targets subsidiary (e.g., Smith 2009, 49).

References

Cosier, M. and Shen, D. J. 2010. Urban water management in China. In: Sun, X. T., Speed, R. and Shen, D. J. eds, 2010. *Water resources management in the People's Republic of China*, Routledge, London and New York, 61–80.

Frederiksen, H. D. and Allen, R. G. 2011. A common basis for analysis, evaluation and comparison of offstream water uses. *Water International* 36(3), 266–282.

Garrick, D. E. 2015. *Water allocation in rivers under pressure: water trading, transaction costs and transboundary governance in the Western US and Australia,* Edward Elgar, Cheltenham, UK and Northampton, MA, USA.

Gleick, P. 2000. Pictures of the future: A review of global water resources projections. In: Gleick, P., *The world's water 2000–2001*. Island Press, Washington DC, 39–61.

Gleick, P. H., Christian-Smith, J. and Cooley, H. Water-use efficiency and productivity: rethinking the basin approach. *Water International* 36(7), 784–798.

Jia S. F., 2013. Ruhe fangzhi 'Santiao Hongxian' bian lv (How to prevent the Three Red Lines from turning green). In: China Water Resources Association Water Resources Committee and Zhengzhou University Water Resources and Environment Institute, eds. *2012 nian nianhui ji xueshu yantaohui lunwenji* (Proceedings of the 2012 annual meeting and symposium) Huanghe Shuili Chubanshe.

Jia S. F. and Zhang J., 2011. Biangezhong de Zhongguo shui ziyuan guanli (China's water resources management in transformation). Zhongguo renkou ziyuan yu huanjing (*China Population, Resources and Environment*) 21(10), 102–106.

Jia S. F.; Zhang L. H.; Cao Y.; Yan H. Y.; Li J. P. and Nickum, J. E., 2012. *Zhongguo shuiquan jinxing shi: Geernu anlie yanjiu* (*When water rights are implemented in China – a case study of Golmud*) Zhongguo Shuili Chubanshe, Beijing

Lampton, D., 2014. *Following the leader: Ruling China from Deng Xiaoping to Xi Jinping* University of California, Berkeley.

Landry, P. F., 2008. *Decentralized authoritarianism in China,* Cambridge University Press, Cambridge, UK.

Li, C. 2009. Hu Jintao's land reform: ambition, ambiguity, and anxiety. *China Leadership Monitor* 27, 1–22.

Lohmar, B.; Wang J. X.; Rozelle, S.; Huang J. K. and Dawe, D., 2003. *China's agricultural water policy reforms: Increasing investment, resolving conflicts, and revising incentives.* United States Department of Agriculture Agriculture Information Bulletin 782.

Ministry of Water Resources and National Bureau of Statistics, PR China, 2013. Diyici quanguo shuili pucha gongbao (Bulletin of first national census of water) issued 26 March Zhongguo shuili (*China Water Resources*) 7, 1–3.

Moore, S. M. 2014. Hydropolitics and inter-jurisdictional relationships in China: the pursuit of localized preferences in a centralized system. *The China Quarterly* 219, 760–780.

Moore, S. M. 2015. The development of water markets in China: progress, peril, and prospects. *Water Policy* 17(2), 253–267.

Nickum, J. E., 1978. Labour accumulation in rural China and its role since the Cultural Revolution. *Cambridge Journal of Economics* 2, 273–286.

Nickum, J. E. 1983. Institutions and China's long-distance water transfer proposals. In: Biswas, A. K.; Zuo D. K.; Nickum, J. E. and Liu C. M., eds. *Long-distance water transfer: A Chinese case study and international experiences.* Tycooly International, Dublin 181–191.

Nickum, J. E., 2003. Irrigated area figures as bureaucratic construction of knowledge: The case of China. *International Journal of Water Resources Development* 19(2), 249–262.

Nickum, J. E. and Lee Y. S. F., 2006. Same longitude, different latitudes: Institutional change in urban water in China, north and south. *Environmental Politics* 15(2), 231–247.

Qian Z. Y.; Chen J. Q. and Feng J., 2009. Cong gongshui guanli dao xushui guanli (From supply management to demand management of water). *Zhongguo shuili (China Water Resources)* 5, 20–23.

Serrato, J. C. S.; Wang X. Y. and Zhang S., 2016. The limits of meritocracy: Screening bureaucrats under imperfect variability. NBER Working Paper No. 21963. National Bureau of Economic Research, Cambridge, MA.

Shen D. J., 2014. Post-1980 water policy in China. *International Journal of Water Resources Development* 30: 4 714–27.

Shen D. J.; Jiang Y. Z. and Sun F., 2015. *China's water resources management challenge: The 'Three Red Lines'* Global Water Partnership Technical Focus Paper, Stockholm.

Shuilibu bangongting (Ministry of Water Resources General Office), 2014. Shandong: yong kaohe rang 'santiaohongxian' ying qilai (Shandong: use assessment to strengthen the 'Three Red Lines'). Shuilibu [Ministry of Water Resources]. January 24. http://www.mwr.gov.cn/ztpd/2011ztbd/2011gzhy/fxgcz/201401/t20140124_547922.html (accessed 18 December 2016).

Smith, G., 2009. Political machinations in a rural county. *The China Journal* 62, 29–59.

State Council Office, 2013. Shixing zui yange shui ziyuan guanli zhidu kaohe banfa (Implementing Methods for Assessing the Strictest Water Management System) (Document 2013[2]). 2 January. http://www.gov.cn/zwgk/2013-01/06/content_2305762.htm (accessed 1 July 2015).

State Statistical Bureau of the People's Republic of China, 2016. 2015 nian guomin jingji he shehui fazhan tongji gongbao (Statistical Bulletin of the national economy and social development for the year 2015). http://www.stats.gov.cn/tjsj/zxfb/201602/t20160229_1323991.html (accessed 4 March 2016).

Tan D., 2015. Water Ten: Comply or else. *China Water Risk* http://chinawaterrisk.org/resources/analysis-reviews/water-ten-comply-or-else/ (accessed 1 July 2015).

Tan D., 2016. Beautiful China 2020: Water & the 13 FYP. *China Water Risk* http://chinawaterrisk.org/resources/analysis-reviews/beautiful-china-2020-water-and-the-13-fyp/ (accessed 19 April 2016).

Wang Y. H. and Hu A. G., 2011. Zhongguo shuili fazhan de jieduan huafen ji zhanlue hanyi (Demarcation and strategic significance of stages of development of China's water control). In: Li G. Y., ed. *2011 Zhongguo shuili fazhan baogao* (China water development report 2011) China Water and Power Press, Beijing, 71–90.

Xie J., 2009. *Addressing China's water scarcity* The World Bank, Washington DC.

Zhang H. T., Gan H., Zhang X. M. and Zhang B. Z., 2013. Jingji shehui yongshui qingkuang diaocha (Survey of the socioeconomic water use situation) *Zhongguo shuili* (China Water Resources) 7, 22–23, 55.

7

AIR POLLUTION

How will China win its self-declared war against it?[1]

Anna L. Ahlers and Mette Halskov Hansen

> The Chinese government is determined to tackle smog and environmental pollution as a whole [...] But the progress we have made still falls far short of the expectation of the people. Last year, I said the Chinese government would declare war against environmental pollution. We're determined to carry forward our efforts until we achieve our goal.
>
> Prime Minister Li Keqiang, March 2015 (cited in Wong and Buckley 2015)

Up until 2013, people in Beijing would normally refer to the frequent haze over the capital as fog (*wu*), and few, if any, were able to predict that within a year's time the largely unknown Chinese term for 'smog' (*wumai*), would be on everybody's lips. Leading up to the 2008 Olympics five years earlier, much international attention was focused on the levels of Beijing's air pollution, and the Chinese government took unprecedented steps to clean the air for the athletes by temporarily shutting down polluting factories and limiting the number of cars on the roads, among other measures (Hsu 2014, 160). However, at that time the Chinese term for smog hardly appeared in journal titles even in specialized academic ones, and few researchers were familiar with the term. This, however, changed dramatically in 2013 when no less than 766 journal and newspaper titles from across the country and various disciplines contained the word *wumai* (Svarverud, n.d.). By 2015, even Chinese children knew that $PM_{2.5}$ had to do with air pollution and was a health hazard. 'It is particles in the air that enter the lungs and are smaller than 2.5 micrometres in diameter, or 1/20 the thinness of a human hair', a children's book explains (Hangzhou City Environmental Protection Center 2012, 18).

The phenomenon of heavy air pollution in China obviously has a much longer history than is indicated by the popular use of the term *wumai*. The Communist government's first five-year plan for industrialization, developed in 1953, was based on the country's abundance of coal resources, and later when the Cultural Revolution ended and Deng Xiaoping launched his new reform policies in 1978, a plethora of new small-scale, inefficient industries and coal-fired power plants sprang up across the country.[2] Within a short period of time, China's rapid industrialization transformed the country's economy and improved most families' standards of living. But by 2009 the country also overtook the United States as the world's largest emitter of greenhouse gases. The air in China's expanding cities, as well as in rural industrial areas, deteriorated. For millions of families, the price of welcomed economic development was increased health problems caused by ambient pollution and persistent household air pollution – the result of using solid fuels for cooking and heating. A large-scale survey conducted in 2011 showed that in more than 9,000 villages in China solid fuels remained the dominant fuel for cooking in more than 47 per cent of the households (Duan et al. 2014, 693).

Air pollution has become the single largest environmental health risk in the world. In 2012 the World Health Organization (WHO) estimated that one in eight of 7 million global deaths resulted from either household or ambient air pollution exposure (2014a). Scholars at Berkeley Earth claim that as many as 1.6 million people die prematurely each year in China due to air pollution, and that 38 per cent of the population live in areas with air regarded as unhealthy by American standards (Rohde and Muller 2015, 1). The ambient air pollution is first of all caused by coal combustion and the substantial increase of vehicles from 16 million in 2000 to more than 93 million in 2011 (Chen et al. 2013, 1959). China accounts for 50 per cent of the world's total coal consumption and produces the largest amount of major air pollutants in the world (Chen et al. 2013, 1959). Nevertheless, as pointed out by leading natural scientists, due to the physical and chemical complexity of the atmosphere there are no quick fixes, neither for the problem of high concentrations of $PM_{2.5}$ in many of China's mega-cities nor for the level of emissions of greenhouse gases that affect the global climate (Wang and Hao 2012; Nielsen and Ho 2013). Local air pollution reduction is essential to prevent major long-term health problems, and as a co-benefit it helps decrease emissions of greenhouse gases that cause climate change (Aunan et al. 2006, 4822). However, scrubbing coal-related pollutants and reducing coal use is not enough in and of itself to curtail CO_2 emissions and diminish the global rise of temperatures (Karplus 2015, 1).

The complexity of the issues of air pollution and climate change not only calls for a strengthening of global cooperation but for coordinated efforts within China nationally. However, it is only in recent years that air pollution has become a matter of *joint* concern on a deep level for government, media, industry and the general population beyond environmental NGOs. The boom of media coverage, culminating in Chai Jing's documentary *Under the Dome* that was streamed more than 300 million times within a week in March 2015,[3] and the numerous environmental apps and weather forecasts that now provide real-time figures on $PM_{2.5}$,[4] testify to what we argue in this chapter is a new era in both the Chinese authorities' and the public's engagement in the topic of air pollution. The Chinese government declared a 'war against air pollution' in 2014 and has now vowed to include the population to a greater extent than before in its endeavour to create an environment that allows for both economic growth and sustainability.

The topic of polluted air can be approached from the perspective of the individual's health, a local community's well-being, a society's general economic development and its future, even national security, and, not least, the perspective of global climate change. It is a complex matter, and governments, as well as scientists and media, face the problem of how to sufficiently understand and explain to the general population how different types of emissions impact each other and what role other factors, such as weather conditions, play in air pollution. Based on our ongoing research of the human dimensions of air pollution in China, we suggest that an unprecedented popular engagement in the problem of air pollution is prompting new forms of interfaces between Chinese political authorities, scientists, public organizations, the general population, and industry. In its fight against air pollution the government has to take into consideration the activities, perceptions, fears and expectations of a wider variety of stakeholders than ever before across divisions of gender, age, class and rural/urban society. The government must negotiate its environmental policies on the ground in order to maintain the support of the population and gain the upper hand in its war against pollution. In the past, the Communist Party's (CCP) legitimacy has largely been based on its continued ability to provide economic growth and social stability. To this now has to be added the need to secure a long-term, ecologically sustainable and healthy society without jeopardizing already hard-won economic gains and the population's improved standard of living.

In this chapter, we first provide an overview of the design and dynamics of China's major national policies regarding air quality control and air pollution prevention, hereafter called 'air policy'. We then briefly zoom in on two concrete examples of interfaces related to control of the industry, and consumption habits and life styles, mainly based on data collected in the province of Zhejiang. We present them here as prototypes of interfaces that manifest themselves in local contexts where different stakeholders take action. We deliberately apply the concept of 'social interface' rather than the more frequently used 'interaction' or 'participation'. The notion of interface better captures the relationship between different actors' worldviews, attitudes, and agency related to air pollution and air policies. It leaves open the possibility that these relations are often not a result of conscious or rational choice but just as much imply spontaneous, and sometimes enforced or involuntary, contacts with unequal levels of 'action'. So for example, the relationship between, on the one hand, a government agency implementing policies that restrict vehicle use and, on the other hand, the population targeted in such a campaign, is not necessarily characterized by 'interaction' or even attempts at 'participation'. Nevertheless, the very meeting or encounter – the social interface – of these parties' different and sometimes conflicting values, perceptions, and interests may be crucial for understanding the relevance and outcome of the policy in question.[5]

National policies facing weak local implementation (1980s–2010s)

In what follows, we concentrate on policies and politics related to air pollution (*kongqi wuran*) as defined in the Chinese context. The type of air pollution that currently receives most attention is *atmospheric particulate pollution*. This is a complex pollution variant in China 'because of the large variations in sources, energy structures, climatic conditions and living habits across the nation'. Atmospheric particulate pollution usually contains 'pollution caused by coal combustion, vehicular emissions and perhaps biomass burning (altogether called "complex air pollution"), plus regional haze' (Fang et al. 2009, 81). Often climate change (*qihou bianhua*) policies, such as 'low-carbon cities' initiatives that target mainly the reduction of carbon dioxide (CO_2) and other greenhouse gas emissions, are treated and approached separately in Chinese central policy making. In general, it seems that atmospheric particulate pollution brings on immediate challenges and effects in terms of visibility and health in the perception of both the Chinese population and the authorities. Arguably, this also has consequences for the current prioritization of dealing with particulate air pollution in the Chinese context rather than climate change on a global scale (see also Karplus 2015).

Although developing a comprehensive air policy has gained steam in China only in recent years, preventing and reducing air pollution is not a new item on the government's agenda.[6] The country's first *Air Pollution Prevention and Control Law* was ratified in 1987 and was of the 'first generation of environmental statutes' that took into account changing political, economic, and social conditions after the launch of 'reform and opening' in 1978 (Alford and Liebman 2001, 711). Strikingly, this law already had in its purview many of the same pollutants, institutions and measures that have since been included in all the law's revisions, as well as in the latest central action plan to save China's air. The articles of the first version already comprised statements about the protection of human and ecological environments, human health, and the promotion of 'socialist modernization'. The law transferred the major responsibility for its implementation and for monitoring air quality to the environmental departments at all levels of government administration and called for the establishment of national environmental standards. It suggested environmental impact assessments for construction projects, banned the use of air pollution-prone disposal of certain materials and substances, and granted prosecutors the right to sanction and fine polluters, even allowing involved parties to seek a ruling of the case in court (Alford and Liebman 2001, 712).

However, in the years following the law's ratification, discussions between central government agencies, instigated by the National Environmental Protection Agency (NEPA),[7] took place, and fierce disagreements arose at all governmental levels over the lack of implementation and consequently the law's effectiveness. The main causes for complaint were the ever-soaring air pollution levels in metropolises, the increasingly grave acid rainfalls throughout China, and the law's inability to address the rapid economic development in China seen, for instance, in the rise of private industry (Alford and Liebman 2001; Fang et al. 2009, 81). The law's amendment in 1995 – not considered fully successful either by its proponents or by environmental experts and activists – tightened the regulations on coal washing, toughened the requirements for desulphurization technologies and unleaded gasoline, enforced control of vehicle exhaust and elimination of substandard automobiles, and called for stricter monitoring of emissions. Further revisions in 2000 called for emission fees and pollution permits, the promotion of renewable energy sources and natural gas, the disclosure of pollution information to the public, and new handles for fining and prosecuting polluters (Central Government of the PRC 2000; Alford and Liebman 2001, 734–735).

All this demonstrates how the PRC had already established a legal basis for air pollution prevention and control decades before the explosion of popular interest in the 2010s. However, in spite of laws and regulations, the skies over China were far from clearing up. On the contrary, the problem became more and more critical and, not least, increasingly visible (Chan and Yao 2008; Fang et al. 2009). What was lacking was an adequate political prioritization, a robust consensus among relevant actors, and effective coordination and implementation of available measures. The earlier air protection legislation met with problems well-known in China's environmental politics. Firstly, legislative procedures at the national level were obstructed and watered-down by stakeholders with conflicting interests. In the case of air pollution, these were the coal, steel, and cement industries, the car industry, gasoline producers, energy companies, and those Chinese provinces that relied heavily on these industries. Secondly, although national environmental laws and regulations generally seemed to be increasingly comprehensive and adequate responses to serious problems, statutory formulation was rather weak (Beyer 2006, 205–207), and the ultimate and necessary implementation on the ground was conducted half-heartedly and ineffectively (Ran 2015, 39–54). For the sake of steering local economic growth and development, local governments, just as they are today, were highly dependent on, and often entwined with, energy-intensive local industries. Collusion between the two led to lax control and frequently resulted in manufactured pollution-monitoring data, the bottom line being that up to this point the post-Mao fixation on economic growth usually outplayed environmentalism (Kostka 2015). Even when air pollution reduction targets in governmental performance evaluations existed, they usually ranked in priority well below other indicators related to economic development, and even birth control. Consequently, they have rarely, if ever, had a significant impact on air quality protection.

In the early 2000s, the Hu Jintao and Wen Jiabao administration's new ideology of 'harmonious society' also brought about a new emphasis on the problems of environmental pollution. Thus, both goals and financial resources for air quality control were significantly boosted with the government's 11th Five-Year Plan (2006–2010). Nevertheless, tangible results still failed to materialize, and around 2008 international inquiries about the safety of athletes competing in the Beijing Olympic Games accelerated (China Daily 2007). This coincided with increased public pressure on the government to release more information about air pollution after the American Embassy in Beijing publicized on its webpage the results of its own air quality tests (Roberts 2015). Worries culminated in the winter of 2012/13 when the pollution readings in Beijing and other northern Chinese cities 'went, quite literally, off the charts' (*The Economist* 2013), and the country's smog problem was finally dubbed an 'airpocalypse' in international media (Wong 2013). The Chinese internet was flooded with angry and concerned posts from citizens all over the country. The severity of the problem and the population's unprecedented reaction left the Chinese authorities with little breathing space. They had to respond – and show that they had responded – more firmly than ever before.

Taking new action: policy shifts in the 2010s

Building on the initiative of its precursor, in 2011 the 12th Five-Year Plan (2011–2015) fortified pledges for a restructured and sustainable growth pattern in China, paying special attention to environmental issues, in particular the challenge of climate change and air pollution (State Council 2011). The recently announced 13th Five-Year Plan (2016–2020) further underlines the ambition to shift emphasis from heavily polluting industry towards stronger third-sector development and more green energy production. It follows up on China's commitment to carbon intensity reduction made in Paris in 2015, and, for the first time ever, includes in particular the binding target to reduce the accumulated annual $PM_{2.5}$ concentration in bigger cities by 18 per cent until 2020 (State Council 2016). In sum, successive five-year plans have increasingly prioritized issues related to pollution, the safeguarding of natural resources, ecological protection, and the rehabilitation or conservation of a healthy living environment. This testifies to the fact that these topics have finally become major goals on the Chinese political agenda.

However, it was mainly with the *Ten Measures for Prevention and Control of Air Pollution* (Xinhua 2013) and the following *Action Plan on Prevention and Control of Air Pollution* (hereafter APAP) (Central Government of the PRC 2013) that the central government sought to reframe air quality protection as a project *involving all members* of Chinese society. The plans placed special emphasis on particulate matter identified as the major culprit in creating urban smog and constituting the most immediate threat to human health (see Table 7.1). Within a few years the terms for particulate matter, $PM_{2.5}$ and PM_{10}, had become household terms, and everybody was now expected to unite in a nationally coordinated attack on pollutants: 'Since we breathe together, we must fight together', the Minister of Environment pleaded (Luo et al. 2013). The APAP explicitly refers to the Beijing–Tianjin–Hebei (*Jing-Jin-Ji*) area, the Yangtze River Delta and the Pearl River Delta, the three most industrialized and urbanized regions of China, as key areas for implementation. For the Jing-Jin-Ji area, detailed implementation measures even include radical industrial restructurings, such as a 25 per cent cut in steel production and a 68 per cent cut of cement production in Hebei province by 2017 (Ministry of Environmental Protection 2013a).

In 2014, the State Council once again passed a revised draft law for air pollution prevention and control, now specifying penalties for 'discharging pollutants without a certificate, over-discharging pollutants and fabricating monitoring data', and, most importantly, providing for a 'coordinated control of pollutants' and 'coordinated regional actions in key areas' (Xinhua 2014). It also included new and much more specific measures to control industrial emission and

Table 7.1 Main APAP goals to be achieved by 2017

Targets	Key measures
Cutting inhalable particulate matter by at least 10 per cent from 2012 level in cities above prefecture level	*Reducing emissions* • eliminate small coal-fired boilers from urban areas • install desulphurization, de-nitration, and dust removal equipment in key sectors
Cutting fine particulate matter by 25 per cent in the Beijing–Tianjin–Hebei region, 20 per cent in the Yangtze River Delta, and 15 per cent in the Pearl River Delta	• control dust from construction sites and transportation • scrap heavily polluting vehicles • restrict driving and the number of licence plates issued • promote public transportation • increase petroleum quality *Structural adjustments*
Keeping the annual average fine particulate level in Beijing at 60 µg/m³	• foster technological innovation • increase supply of renewable energy, nuclear energy and clean coal
Reducing coal consumption to less than 65 per cent of total energy consumption	• set up a special fund to combat air pollution • explore new finance models • increase bank credits • mobilize incentive-based market mechanisms
Cutting emissions from key industries by 30 per cent from the 2012 level Cutting energy consumption per unit of industrial added value creation by 20 per cent from the 2012 level	*Policy and law* • improve policies for energy pricing, subsidies, and export tax rebates for industries with high pollution and high energy consumption • fast-track the revised APPCL • amend the Environmental Protection Law • draft an Environmental Tax Law *Regional measures* • establish regional coordination mechanisms with special focus on the Beijing–Tianjin–Hebei region and the Yangtze River Delta • strictly limit high pollution and high energy consumption projects in sensitive and ecologically fragile areas

Source: Authors; data from Central Government of the PRC 2013

vehicle exhaust (National People's Congress 2014). The law was ratified in August 2015 and took effect from January 2016.

Three aspects of the APAP are worth paying special attention to. First, by way of a central government action plan and all of its associated rhetoric, the management of air quality becomes a crucial political issue that signals binding relevance for implementers at all levels of government. This is perhaps one of the most remarkable qualitative differences that distinguishes the new initiative from the previous merely legal basis for air quality protection. In China, formulating a national political initiative as a campaign, or as an action plan like APAP, testifies to its utmost importance. The APAP sets grand targets for air quality preservation across the country and subscribes key measures for achieving them. It is up to all levels of the political administration to work out detailed implementation plans, taking into account local circumstances. In this way the APAP is not solely a rigorous top-down plan but one that requires local adjustment and action. Leaders of local governments can make a name for themselves if they prove to be especially vigorous in executing national top-priority policies or add innovative features to enhance their local effectiveness. The authorities of Zhejiang province's capital Hangzhou, for instance, take pride in the fact that their emission control indicators and evaluation targets are stricter than those required by central level guidelines, a claim that is backed by observers and local researchers.[8]

Such measures also enhance the careers of local cadres because environmental indicators are increasingly included in the local governments' target responsibility contracts (Heberer and Senz 2011) and were recently given more weight in the leading cadre evaluation system (Ministry of Environmental Protection 2013b). Since 2012, largely following international criteria, an air quality index (AQI) combining measurements of major ambient air pollutants has been used to standardize the monitoring of air pollution in China. Annual target evaluations now use the number of days with an AQI level of 1 ('excellent') or 2 ('good') as a performance indicator.[9] Hangzhou City, for example, in its evaluation of subordinate government levels, allocates full points if 70 per cent of days during a year are classified as excellent or good. Achieving less than 45 per cent means obtaining zero points in this target category.[10] A good showing of economic growth, birth control and social stability are no longer sufficient to secure credits from higher-level authorities, and it is therefore not surprising that a substantial drop in total $PM_{2.5}$ readings in 2014 led to overt gasps of relief in Hangzhou's environmental bureaucracy.

Second, when a topic of national concern is elevated to the status of a campaign, the power balance between different governmental institutions may be affected. This is now happening as a result of the announcement of APAP. The environmental protection bureaus (EPB) that used to hold a notoriously weak position in the departmental hierarchy are gradually being given more steering and coordination powers. In interviews and informal conversations in Zhejiang province with municipal and county government officials in 2014–15, representatives of EPBs univocally described how their coordinating capacities and authority were being strengthened by the new national initiative. The fact that environmental performance can now make or break a leading cadre's career helps the EPBs when, for example, they have to organize the implementation of complex air pollution regulation that involves different government agencies and stakeholders.

Third, the inflation of central government air protection plans and programmes represents to some extent a shift from treating 'the people' as passive bystanders to regarding them as responsible stakeholders. All collective public actors, such as companies, schools, NGOs, and even ordinary residents, are encouraged to join the battle against air pollution. It also means that most sectors of state and society are subjected to a stricter and more authoritative regulation of activity that directly contributes to air pollution. The political turn that now both allows for and requires unprecedented action – even participation – of people in the fight against air pollution results in changing interfaces between key actors.

In the following, we briefly outline two concrete examples of how such interfaces of local administration, science, industry, and the general population evolved in two areas that have top priority in the government's current air policy: the regulation of polluting industries and the campaign to change people's behaviour and attitudes.

Allying against air polluting industries

Until recently, the arguments against a regime of tight environmental control have focused on the country's need for rapid economic growth and the concomitant need for cheap energy (mainly coal) and low costs in the industry (Alford and Liebman 2001, 723). In China's new war against air pollution, one of the weapons entails taking firmer steps against air pollution caused by local industries, state-owned enterprises (SOE), as well as private ones. Tools range from the traditional enforcement of emission controls and monitored facility upgrading (higher chimneys, new fume filters, etc.) to the much more radical shutting down of whole factories and power plants in or near residential areas. Needless to say, implementing such action is very complex – local areas may depend on income from industry, industry provides employment for residents, and cadres need to do well in performance evaluations.

Hangzhou City, the capital of China's richest province, features a well-developed economy with a strong service sector largely based on tourism. It appears to be a good example of a locality that can 'afford' – and even has a special reason – to clean up industrial polluters, and it is attempting to be at the national frontline as a 'low-carbon' and 'green' city (Delman 2014). While Hangzhou may therefore not be particularly representative, many other cities and regions now faced with the binding task of 'expelling' polluting industry from their cores can be expected to implement developments similar to those discussed below.

Local governments have started to adopt strategies of public communication used by NGOs (Xu 2014), most notably seen in their increasing interest in employing new technologies for regulated information disclosure and in seeking public collaboration in identifying pollution sources. In Hangzhou and throughout Zhejiang province, hotlines to EPBs, which have existed for many years, have recently been upgraded. Local authorities must now respond to inquiries and complaints received via telephone or new e-government platforms, although evasive feedback such as 'the case is in progress' is often adequate to meet the new political requirements. Furthermore, as an experiment with new forms of communication and information, the provincial government launched a web-based environmental protection communication project in 2014. In close cooperation with a local information technology SOE and Zhejiang's largest environmental NGO (ENGO) Green Zhejiang (*Lüse Zhejiang*), and seeking the advice of local environmental researchers, the provincial government developed an online platform and an app for smartphones called Love Environmental Protection (*Ai Huanbao*). At much the same time, the same SOE supported Green Zhejiang in developing its own version of an environmental app called Environmental Watch *(Huanjing Guancha)*. Both apps use data from official measuring stations, and include, to different degrees, options for air quality information, including recommendations regarding health, outdoor and indoor activities, and suggestions for how individuals can contribute to improving air quality. Interestingly, they also feature a 'report forum', emphasizing their second function as a kind of monitoring tool. Users can upload information about environmental pollution they witness and support it with photos and geographic coordinates. Users' reports are often channelled to Green Zhejiang for follow-up investigation, to check, for instance, that the report has not been fabricated and that the reporter has a known ID, after which Green Zhejiang may decide whether or not to forward the case to the relevant local authorities. Developing new technologies for communicating with citizens is not confined to the matter of air quality, but air pollution does seem to inform a major part of the activities connected to the apps.

Another trait of this new interface occurs when conflicts arise due to plans to remove coal power plants or other heavily polluting production facilities from residential areas. To some extent, these interfaces are alliances between government, ENGOs, and local inhabitants. SOEs horizontally aligned with the local government and private enterprises are easier to deal with than SOEs managed by a higher level of government, such as a province-managed steel plant within a city. In order to gain leverage and bargaining power vis-à-vis superior authorities and their powerful business interests, local governments sometimes mobilize residents' support in their struggle. They make use of the fact that perceived airborne health risks are one of the factors that trigger massive local NIMBY opposition. Project feasibility assessments are increasingly forced to take this human factor into account, according to local environmental scholars involved in assessment processes in Hangzhou and beyond.

Local governments are evaluated partly on their ability to maintain social stability, and for this reason they increasingly seek to avoid 'importing' new pollution problems into their jurisdictions.[11] They rather seem to prefer a new role of facilitating agent, mediating conflicts between polluting industrial companies and affected residents. In a form of consultation mechanism called Enterprise and Residents' Dialogue (*changqun duihua*), the local EPB in Hangzhou stages regular meetings between enterprises and local residents with the aim to achieve a code of conduct for how to deal with environmental problems, for example, how to diminish pollution, eliminate its source or upgrade filters, but also how to draw a time plan for shutting down entire plants. By discussing the matter publicly, EPBs seek to enhance popular understanding of the complexity of issues at stake and to contain the situation. At the same time, they may manage to play the conflicting parties' demands against each other, thereby creating breathing space for themselves.

Further research is needed to study the consequences of these 'triangular dialogues' in cities that have ambitions to become green. What actually happens after a 'successful' shutdown of an air polluting company? It is a well-known fact that rural inhabitants, including those in rich Zhejiang, complain that many of the more polluting and low-tech industries move out of urban areas into less regulated rural areas as a result of new policies and pressure from the growing urban middle class. The result may be a 'double dose' of air pollution for poorer rural inhabitants: heavy household air pollution due to the burning of solid fuels, and increased ambient air pollution coming from new industrial parks or factories. While city governments seem to express a strong urge to mobilize the power of pollution-affected residents for the sake of bolstering local political performance, our research in rural areas suggests a widespread sense of powerlessness vis-à-vis the local establishment of polluting industries.

Cleaning the air by changing habits and consumption

Our second example of a new interface between local administration, science, industry and the general population relates to APAP's call for all members of society to play their part in the national battle for better air. The plan also requires local governments to address, through direct interventions and education, people's lifestyle and consumption habits.

In sharp contrast to earlier attempts to slowly develop environmental consciousness in future generations the government now tries to prescribe what we would term as 'shock therapy environmentalism' in order to get quicker results. China's new vehicle policies are an example for this: vehicular emission is a major, and maybe even the fastest growing, source of atmospheric particulates in Chinese cities (Fang et al. 2009, 83). Therefore, curbing vehicle use in larger cities is one of the top priorities of the APAP (Central Government of the PRC 2013, see especially 1.2 and 1.3). According to Hangzhou city-level officials interviewed in spring 2015, one-third of urban particulate pollution countrywide is caused by vehicular exhaust. Local environmental experts estimated that around 40 per cent of $PM_{2.5}$-relevant emissions in Hangzhou were caused by vehicular emissions. Already in 1993, SEPA began regulating vehicle use and emissions, but measures under the new APAP framework are considerably more stringent. The central government now encourages outright command-and-control mechanisms: strictly controlling the number of licence plates issued, restricting vehicle use through a rotating ban of certain licence plate numbers each day, and removing old and heavy-polluting vehicles from circulation. Hangzhou City, for example, introduced a lottery/auction system for licence plates in May 2014 to limit the number of newly licensed cars, has implemented a licence-plate-number-based driving-permit system to control traffic in downtown areas during the week, and restricts vehicular access to sightseeing and ecological conservation areas such as the West Lake depending on an odd/even licence-plate number system. Official figures report that the number of small passenger cars registered in Hangzhou within the first year of the new policy was reduced by 44 per cent, with positive effects on traffic congestion and air pollution (Zhejiang News 2015).[12]

But what appear to be simple political measures have become a complex interface upon closer scrutiny. For city leadership and local EPBs, creating vehicle-related policies is risky and has unpredictable effects. They need to be coordinated across numerous agencies, such as the transportation department and the police. The acceptance of these policies by the general public is low or even non-existent. Moreover, when any policy restricting vehicle use is implemented, the public expects improved public transportation and the facilitation of alternative or greener modes of individual motorized transportation, such as e-car rental or car pooling/sharing.

The risk for the government lies in the fact that urban residents may sometimes respond in unpredicted ways when confronted, often overnight, with significant restrictions to their lifestyle choices, mobility and convenience. According to our preliminary observations in Hangzhou, supported by studies in other localities (e.g. Chen and Zhao 2013), the measures themselves are generally accepted because of a widely shared preference for air quality improvement and congestion control. Nevertheless, public disgruntlement prevails when it comes to how these policies are implemented and the inconveniences they bring (Horizon Key 2015). Questions of fairness, social inclusion, and trust in the licensing system arise: are the policies transparent enough? What are the chances of success in auctions and lotteries to get a licence plate?[13] What is the substantial revenue generated used for? Moreover, a part of the population will develop counterstrategies to get around the restrictions, and this results in new tensions. To complicate the matter, significant economic interests are obviously at stake. At a moment's notice, local and regional car dealers in Hangzhou had to adapt to a slight decrease in sales resulting from the new measures and prepare for changing customer behaviour and demands. The domestic and international car industry had to deal with setbacks, but also new opportunities arose for them, for instance, developing cars with air-filtering technologies, receiving subsidies for upgrading electronic car technology, etc. Bicycle and e-car rental companies, despite previous scepticism about them, now flourish in the city of Hangzhou, and the models tested there are now emulated in other Chinese cities (Rogowsky 2013).

The Chinese central government would like to see similar vehicle-related policies implemented beyond the handful of cities where they are already in place. At the same time, the population's often strong reactions towards new car-use policies might help to explain why the 2015 revision of the *Air Pollution Law* does not include a national legislation for car-use restrictions. The revised law therefore continues to encourage 'reasonable' individual solutions according to local conditions (Central Government of the PRC 2015). It remains to be seen – and further studied – how an authoritative approach to restructuring mobility for the sake of air quality preservation plays out on the ground, and with what effects for the environment and for the relationships between governments, the general population and industry.

Conclusion

In mid-June 2015, at the time of writing this article, Beijing had experienced more than a week of unusually good air quality (ranging from 35 to 52 on the $PM_{2.5}$ scale) and visibly blue skies. The city was not hosting any major international event like the Olympic Games (2008) or APEC (2014), when special measures were taken to halt production in factories and reduce the number of vehicles on the streets in order to keep the skies blue. So this time Beijing residents could be heard saying: 'Yes, incredibly good air. That's because Xi Jinping has his birthday this week!' A joke to be sure, but it can be interpreted as an indication of the popular perception of air pollution and the measures taken to improve air quality. Is there at least a certain degree of trust in the ability of Chinese authorities to make a difference, albeit coloured with some scepticism that their efforts are arbitrary and not necessarily undertaken for the common good? Although Beijingers seem not to believe in a breakthrough improvement, they are nonetheless happy for the chance to enjoy a few days of easier breathing without worrying too much about the reasons for the reprieve. Similar responses were seen during the APEC meeting when the term 'APEC blue' became popular, suggesting that the population trusted the government to create blue skies for at least a short period of time. Beijingers can also be sure that the government will do its best to clear the local skies well ahead of all other upcoming major international events hosted by the city.

However, China's air pollution hazard is a complex problem. Multiple factors influence air quality, and finding one linear causation chain for even a single pollutant within this mix of particulates and haze is often difficult. Solutions too need to be complex. It is of course much too early to draw conclusions as to if and when the battle against air pollution can be won, or about the effectiveness of the new government action plans and other activities concerned with air quality protection in China. A reason for some optimism is Greenpeace's (2015) report that found that Beijing and other cities, especially in the coastal regions, saw a slight improvement in air quality over the course of 2014. The report attributed this change to the harsh measures taken in the new initiative, and China can now claim to be doing somewhat better than India. Seeing China's air pollution problem in all its complexity, however, it is difficult to draw a positive conclusion at this stage. Not only do China's cities need bluer skies and the poorest rural areas cleaner energy for cooking and heating, the country also needs to reduce its emissions of greenhouse gases in order to assist the entire world in slowing the acceleration of climate change.

In this process, as we have tried to demonstrate in this chapter, a larger number of stakeholders than ever before in the PRC's history is being drawn into, or actively getting involved in, political action. Triggered by collective experiences of visible air pollution and its implied health risks, Chinese society as a whole is becoming much more conscious of the possible downsides of keeping economic growth cheap. Since the beginning of the decade, some newly configured interfaces between different members of Chinese society are evolving around the outlets of the APAP. It remains to be seen to what extent increased consciousness and willingness to adopt more stringent political measures will translate into new forms of local action that will bring about the necessary long-term change.

Notes

1 The authors wish to thank especially Li Hongtao, Liu Zhaohui, Shen Yongdong, Shi Yao and Qiao Lingling for their help and suggestions. The chapter is based on data collected for the research project *Airborne* (http://www.hf.uio.no/ikos/english/research/projects/air-china/), financially supported by the Norwegian Research Council, the University of Oslo and Zhejiang University.
2 See Wright 2013 about China's coal industry.
3 The film was removed from most of China's popular websites within a week of its release when the government seemingly got anxious about its popularity. It remained on Caixin.com.
4 See, for instance, popular apps such as Moji Weather (www.mojichina.com), AQICN (www.aqicn.com), Bluesky Map http://www.weibo.com/u/5042247906 (previous Pollution Map).
5 This use of 'interface' borrows from Norman Long's analytical use of 'social interfaces' in the field of development studies (2001).
6 For a comprehensive overview of laws and policies, see Lin and Elder (2013).
7 NEPA was the predecessor of SEPA and ultimately the MEP.

8 Interviews with government officials and environmental/climate researchers in Hangzhou City, January and March 2015.
9 An AQI is based on a complicated calculation of the health effects of different air pollutants according to their concentration at either hourly or 24-hourly intervals or as an annual mean exposure. See e.g. Andrews (2014) for a comparison between the AQIs in use in the United States, Europe and China, and a particular comparison of $PM_{2.5}$ values. China orients its latest AQI to the U.S. indicator system, but is much more lenient on many of the crucial thresholds. While an AQI of 50–100 points is labelled 'moderate' in U.S. terms, in China it is still 'good'. $PM_{2.5}$ levels up to 35.5 mg/m^3 are called 'excellent' in China, while even 12.5 mg/m^3 in U.S. terms is only 'moderate'. WHO air quality guidelines are even stricter (WHO 2014b).
10 Interview with the director of Hangzhou's Evaluation Bureau, 11 March 2015.
11 Interviews with government officials and environmental/climate researchers in Hangzhou City, January and March 2015.
12 It is questionable, however, whether, after just one year of implementation, there is any reliable data that corroborates these statements.
13 In the first year of Hangzhou's new car policy, from 1 May 2014 to 30 April 2015, the gratis lottery had an estimated success rate of 0.81–2.20 per cent. Bidding for a licence plate costs as much as 47,785 RMB (Zhejiang News 2015), or about one-third of the price of a 2014 FAW Volkswagen Golf in China.

References

Alford, W. P. and Liebman, B. L., 2001. Clean air, clear processes? Struggle over air pollution law in the People's Republic of China. *Hastings Law Journal*, 53 (3), 703–748.
Andrews, Steven Q., 2014. China's air pollution reporting is misleading. *Chinadialogue*, 27 March. https://www.chinadialogue.net/article/show/single/en/6856-China-s-air-pollution-reporting-is-misleading. Accessed 26 June 2015.
Aunan, K., Fang J. H., Hu, T., Seip, H. M. and Vennemo, H., 2006. Climate change and air quality: measures with co-benefits in China. *Environmental Science & Technology*, 40 (16), 4822–4829.
Beyer, S., 2006. Environmental law and policy in the People's Republic of China. *Chinese Journal of International Law*, 1 (5), 185–211.
Central Government of the People's Republic of China, 2000. Zhongguo renmin gongheguo daqi wuran fangzhi fa (The Air Pollution Prevention and Control Law of the People's Republic of China), enacted on 29 April 2000, effective since 1 September 2000. http://english.mep.gov.cn/SOE/soechina2000/chinese/atmosphericc/daqifa.htm. Accessed 20 December 2016.
Central Government of the People's Republic of China, 2013. Daqi wuran fangzhi xingdong jihua (Action plan on prevention and control of air pollution). http://www.gov.cn/zhengce/content/2013-09/13/content_4561.htm. Accessed 16 March 2015. English summary available at: http://english.mep.gov.cn/News_service/infocus/201309/t20130924_260707.htm. Accessed 16 May 2015.
Central Government of the People's Republic of China, 2015. Zhongguo renmin gongheguo daqi wuran fangzhi fa (The Air Pollution Prevention and Control Law of the People's Republic of China), second amendment of 29 August 2015, to take effect from January 2016. http://news.xinhuanet.com/legal/2015-08/30/c_128180129.htm. Accessed 30 August 2015.
Chan C. K. and Yao X., 2008. Air pollution in mega cities in China. *Atmospheric Environment*, 42, 1–42.
Chen X. and Zhao J. H., 2013. Bidding to drive: car license auction policy in Shanghai and its public acceptance. *Transport Policy*, 27, 39–52.
Chen Z., Wang J., Ma G. and Zhang, Y., 2013. China tackles the health effects of air pollution. *The Lancet*, 382, (9909) 1959–1960.
China Daily 2007. Pollution challenge for Olympics: UN, 26 October. http://www.china.org.cn/english/environment/229719.htm. Accessed 20 May 2015.
Delman, J., 2014. Climate change politics and Hangzhou's 'Green City Making', in *Branding Chinese megacities: policies, practices and positioning*, eds P. O. Berg and E. Björner, Edward Elgar: Cheltenham and Northhampton MA, 249–261.
Duan X., Jiang Y., Wang B., Zhao X., Shen G., Cao S., Huang N., Qian Y., Chen Y. and Wang L., 2014. Household fuel use for cooking and heating in China: results from the First Chinese

Environmental Exposure-Related Human Activity Patterns Survey (CEERHAPS). *Applied Energy,* 136, 692–703.

The Economist (n.s.), 2013. Beijing's air pollution: blackest day. 14 January. http://www.economist.com/blogs/analects/2013/01/beijings-air-pollution. Accessed 10 January 2015.

Fang M., Chan C. K. and Yao X., 2009. Managing air quality in a rapidly developing nation: China. *Atmospheric Environment,* 43, 79–86.

Greenpeace, 2015. New data shows Beijing air pollution improving, but rest of China still suffering. http://www.greenpeace.org/eastasia/press/releases/climate-energy/2015/air-ranking-2015-Q1/. Accessed 21 May 2015.

Hangzhou City Environmental Protection Centre for Information and Education, 2012. Huanbao shenghuo mei yi tian (The everyday environmental life). Hangzhou: Hangzhou City Environmental Protection Bureau.

Heberer, T. and Senz, A., 2011. Streamlining local behaviour through communication, incentives and control: a case study of local environmental policies in China. *Journal of Current Chinese Affairs,* 40 (3), 77–112.

Horizon Key, 2015. Shuzi jieshi 'xianxing buru jianliang' (Numbers show 'limits do not equal reduction'). 13 January. http://www.ctin.ac.cn/yuanchuang/265807.html. Accessed 20 December 2016.

Hsu A., 2014. Seeing through the smog: China's air pollution challenge for East Asia, in *Routledge handbook of environment and society in Asia,* eds. P. G. Harris & G. Lang, London, Routledge, 60–75.

Karplus, V., 2015. Double impact: Why China needs coordinated air quality and climate strategies. Paulson Institute. http://www.paulsoninstitute.org/think-tank/paulson-papers-energy-environment/2015/02/25/double-impact-why-china-needs-coordinated-air-quality-and-climate-strategies/. Accessed 20 June 2015.

Kostka, G., 2015. Command without control: the case of China's environmental target system. *Regulation & Governance,* 1 (10), 58–74.

Lin X. and Elder, M., 2013. Major developments in China's national air pollution policies in the early 12th Five-Year Plan. *IGES Policy Report* No. 2013-02. http://pub.iges.or.jp/modules/envirolib/view.php?docid=4954. Accessed 21 May 2015.

Long, N., 2001. *Development sociology: actor perspectives,* Routledge: London.

Luo S., Wu J. and Gu R., 2013. Huanbao buzhang tan daqi wuran: 'jiran tong huxi jiu yao tong fendou' (The Minister of Environment discusses air pollution: 'since we breathe together, we must fight together'). 15 June 2006. http://news.sohu.com/20130615/n378878788.shtml. Accessed 26 June 2015.

Ministry of Environmental Protection (MEP) of the People's Republic of China, 2013a. Guanyu yinfa 'Jingjinji yu zhoubian diqu luoshi daqi wuran fangzhi xingdong jihua shishi xize' de tongzhi (Notification on the issuance of 'detailed implementation regulations of the action plan for prevention and regulation of air pollution in the Jingjinji [provinces] and adjacent regions'). 17 September. http://www.mep.gov.cn/gkml/hbb/bwj/201309/W020130918412886411956.pdf. Accessed 26 June 2015.

Ministry of Environmental Protection (MEP) of the People's Republic of China 2013b. Zhongzubu yinfa tongzhi gaijin zhengji kaohe gongzuo. Jiada huanjing sunhai deng zhibiao quanzhong (Central Organization Department issues notice on the revision of evaluation work. Increases the weighting of environmental harm as a criterion). 11 December. http://edcmep.org.cn/hjxw/5762.html. Accessed 26 June 2015.

National People's Congress (NPC) of the People's Republic of China, 2014. Daqi wuran fangzhi fa (xiuding cao'an) (Draft revision of 'The Air Pollution Prevention and Control Law of the People's Republic of China'). 29 December. http://www.npc.gov.cn/npc/xinwen/lfgz/flca/2014-12/29/content_1891880.htm. Accessed 21 May 2015.

Nielsen, C. P. and Ho M. S., 2013. Atmospheric environment in China: introduction and research review, in *Clearer skies over China: reconciling air quality, climate, and economic goals,* eds. C. P. Nielsen and M. S Ho, The MIT Press: Cambridge MA & London, 3–59.

Ran R., 2015. *Zhongguo difang huanjing zhengzhi: zhengce yu zhixing zhe jian de jilü* (China's local environmental politics: discrepancies between policies and their implementation), Zhongyang bianyi chubanshe: Beijing.

Roberts, D., 2015. Opinion: how the U.S. embassy tweeted to clear Beijing's air. *Wired.* 3 June. http://www.wired.com/2015/03/opinion-us-embassy-beijing-tweeted-clear-air/. Accessed 19 June 2015.

Rogowsky, M., 2013. Kandi crush: an electric-car vending machine from China could upend the auto industry. *Forbes.* 28 December. http://www.forbes.com/sites/markrogowsky/2013/12/28/kandi-crush-an-electric-car-vending-machine-from-china-could-upend-the-auto-industry/. Accessed 14 June 2015.

Rohde, R. A. and Muller, R. A., 2015. Air pollution in China: mapping of concentrations and sources. *PLOS ONE*, August. http://journals.plos.org/plosone/article?id=10.1371/journal.pone.0135749. Accessed 18 December 2016.

State Council, 2011. *Woguo guomin jingji he shehui fazhan shierwu guihua gangyao* (China's 12th Five-Year-Plan, 2011–2015). http://news.sina.com.cn/c/2011-03-17/055622129864.shtml. Accessed 2 November 2014.

State Council, 2016. *Zhongguo guomin jingji he shehui fazhan shisanwu guihua gangyao* (China's 13th Five-Year-Plan, 2016–2020). http://news.xinhuanet.com/politics/2016lh/2016-03/17/c_1118366322.htm. Accessed 5 April 2016.

Svarverud, R., n.d. A genealogy of Chinese perceptions of 'polluted air', work in progress.

Wang S. and Hao J., 2012. Air quality management in China: issues, challenges and options. *Journal of Environmental Sciences,* 24, (1), 2–13.

Wong E. and Buckley, C., 2015. Chinese premier vows tougher regulation on air pollution. *The New York Times*, 15 March. http://www.nytimes.com/2015/03/16/world/asia/chinese-premier-li-keqiang-vows-tougher-regulation-on-air-pollution.html. Accessed 26 June 2015.

Wong, H., 2013. Year of the smog. *Quartz*. 19 December. http://qz.com/159105/2013-will-be-remembered-as-the-year-that-deadly-suffocating-smog-consumed-china/. Accessed 17 April 2015.

World Health Organization (WHO), 2014a. 7 million premature deaths annually linked to air pollution. *WHO News Release*. 25 March. http://www.who.int/mediacentre/news/releases/2014/air-pollution/en/. Accessed 17 April 2015.

World Health Organization (WHO), 2014b. Ambient (outdoor) quality and health. Fact sheet no 313, March. http://who.int/mediacentre/factsheets/fs313/en/. Accessed 26 June 2015.

Wright, T., 2012. *The political economy of the Chinese coal industry: black gold and blood-stained coal*, Routledge: London.

Xinhua, 2013. Jiedu guowuyuan changwu huiyi daqi wuran fangzhi shi cuoshi (Interpreting the ten measures for air pollution prevention and control by the State Council). 14 June. http://news.xinhuanet.com/politics/2013-06/14/c_116152583.htm. Accessed 21 May 2015.

Xinhua, 2014. China focus: Hangzhou protest tests China's governing capacity. 14 May. http://news.xinhuanet.com/english/china/2014-05/14/c_133334098.htm. Accessed 20 December 2016.

Xu J. H., 2014. Communicating the right to know: social media in the do-it-yourself air quality testing campaign in Chinese cities. *International Journal of Communication*, 8, 1374–1393.

Zhejiang News (Zhejiang xinwen), 2015. *Shenqing yao bu yao jiashi? Hangzhou xianpai zhengce jiang tiaozheng 4 yue 30 ri qian fabu xingui* (Driving license required for applications? New regulations published before Hangzhou's [car] license limitation policy is adjusted on April 30th). 13 March. http://zjnews.zjol.com.cn/system/2015/03/13/020550157.shtml. Accessed 21 May 2015.

8

CLIMATE CHANGE POLICY AND GOVERNANCE[1]

Gørild Heggelund and Rebecca Nadin

Introduction

In 2007, the same year in which China was ranked as the world's largest emitter of greenhouse gases in total terms (Heggelund et al. 2010; PBL 2007), major changes were also taking place in the country's climate policy making and governance (Stensdal 2014). Certainly, over the past couple of decades, China's approach to addressing climate change has evolved from viewing it as a purely scientific concern to a foreign policy issue primarily discussed in international negotiations, to one that is now seen as fundamental to the nation's socio-economic development.

The purpose of any policy is to provide direction and targets, which then form the basis or framework for decision making at international, national or local levels. Targets identified may be in line with the status quo or represent new directions (Nadin et al. 2015). In the context of an already complex socio-economic development environment, the critical question facing China's leaders is how to develop and implement climate policies and enforce related laws, mobilize finance and establish institutional mechanisms to address the challenges of a changing climate. China is facing a number of key challenges in reducing poverty, over-reliance on fossil fuels and maintaining economic growth while ensuring sustainable development. Rapid urbanization, uneven regional economic development, unregulated urban planning and limited per-capita natural resources have created vulnerabilities, such as water vulnerability, and increased exposure to risks of natural hazards like drought or heavy rainstorms. As a result of previous and ongoing socio-economic processes, coupled with climate change, China has already experienced significant impacts on agriculture, water resources, ecosystems and human health.[2] The challenge for China is to address the risks and opportunities presented by climate change while also addressing long-term economic development needs, and in particular the needs of diverse rural and urban vulnerable populations, in more sustainable ways. Comprehensive climate policies are essential to ensure energy security, curb emissions and address increasing frequency and intensity of droughts, floods and extreme weather events (Nadin et al. 2015).

This chapter aims to provide an overview of the rapid developments and evolutions in China's government institutions and domestic climate policy,[3] starting with a brief overview of historic developments and a presentation of the main policy drivers. It does so through the lens of basic national policies, communications and national government policy documents in key sectors like energy and economic development. As awareness of the complexities of climate risks has grown among China's policy makers, approaches to it have shifted from treating it as an issue area to development of mitigation and adaptation-specific policies to an approach designed to unify other policies, programmes and responses.

The evolution and drivers of China's domestic climate policy and governance

Since 2007 climate change has moved up the agenda of the Chinese leadership's policy priorities. Over the past decade there has been a growing awareness of climate risk on key sectors, and increased pressure from G77 countries to take a lead in international negotiations.

In the early 1990s, focus on climate change policy was given limited attention. Climate change was largely viewed as a scientific issue that was discussed in international negotiations (Stensdal 2014). Initially, the China Meteorological Administration (CMA) had been the lead agency in charge of climate change. In 1998, the State Development Planning Commission (since 2003 the National Development and Reform Commission (NDRC)) was given the responsibility of coordinating the country's climate change efforts. This move reflected the shift in thinking of the Chinese government on climate change from a purely scientific issue to one that was inherently linked to the country's economic development policy.

In the years that followed, China's approach towards mainstreaming climate change has been to integrate climate change action into the central economic development framework in response to a number of core drivers such as energy security and water resource management. Climate policy and governance have evolved rapidly in the past decades, as reflected in policy documents such as the Five-Year Plans[4] and other climate strategies, such as the National Climate Programme (2007). There have been a number of internal and external drivers that have influenced the evolution of China's climate policy and development of governance mechanisms. These include the need to manage energy consumption and ensure energy security. Climate change has traditionally been seen through the prism of energy and economic development (Heggelund et al. 2010). In the past few years, the air pollution problem in China has become one of several important drivers for restructuring the energy sector, in addition to issues such as energy security. Likewise, addressing climate risk is starting to emerge at the centre of China's climate policy (see also chapter 7 this volume by Ahlers and Hansen, and chapter 19 by Oberheitmann and Suding).

Mitigation, energy consumption and energy security

Energy has long been a dominant element in the climate change discussions for China. China's domestic climate policy has been linked to its energy policy since the 1990s. Economic growth in China remains fuelled by fossil-based energy and access to energy has been critical for the country's development, poverty alleviation and raised living standards. Growing energy demands, water resource management issues and a changing climate are challenging the country's energy security.

Climate mitigation policy impetus

Energy efficiency remains one of China's top energy and climate change policy agendas (He 2014). Increasing energy efficiency reduces greenhouse gas (GHG) emissions, reduces air pollution and reduces overall energy consumption, which improves China's energy security

(Green and Stern 2015). China's large emissions are mainly caused by its heavy reliance on fossil fuels. Fossil fuel combustion (90 per cent) and cement production (10 per cent) make up China's carbon emissions (Liu 2015). In 2014, the Chinese energy mix constituted coal (66 per cent), oil (17 per cent), hydroelectricity (8 per cent), natural gas (6 per cent), renewables (2 per cent) and nuclear energy (1 per cent) (BP 2015).

It was reported that China's coal consumption growth rate went down in 2014, when China consumed total energy of 4.26 billion tons of standard coal, less than 2.2 per cent increase from the previous year of 4.17 billion tons, the lowest growth rate of the century (National Bureau of Statistics 2014, 2015). The reduction in coal was attributed to an overall economic slowdown, as well as to the decline of energy intensity;[5] in 2014 energy intensity declined 4.8 per cent, the largest decline since 2009 (Cheng and Eikeland 2015).

Chinese energy consumption has mainly consisted of burning coal for industry, heating and electrical purposes. Although coal is a cheap source of energy, it is the main source of local air pollution. As part of its mitigations plans, the Chinese government aims to raise the share of non-fossil fuel in its energy mix to 15 per cent by 2020, up from 10 per cent in 2013, and 20 per cent in 2030 (Green and Stern 2015). In November 2014, the Energy Strategy Development Action Plan (State Council 2014) was issued that aims to cap primary energy consumption at 4.8 billion tons of standard coal equivalent per year by 2020. The annual coal consumption will be held at 4.2 billion tons until 2020. And coal would constitute a maximum share of 62 per cent in that year's primary energy structure down from 64 per cent in 2015[6] (Xinhua 2014a; Cheng and Eikeland 2015). Yet, recent media reports disclosed new data on China's coal consumption based on revised official statistical figures; thus, data will be adjusted and previous forecasts will have to be revised (Buckley 2015).

As a result of these energy concerns and in recognition of the need for mitigation, climate change was introduced as a topic in the 10th Five-Year Plan (FYP) in 2001 (2001–2005). At the time, climate change was still largely perceived through the energy lens, and more effort was given to mitigation efforts with the economic development of the country (Heggelund et al. 2010). The 10th FYP targeted energy saving and energy consumption in high-intensity energy consuming industries. The targets set by the plan were not reached, and the 11th FYP (2006–2010) therefore continued the focus on energy efficiency and energy intensity. One binding target was the energy consumption per unit of GDP (energy intensity) to decrease by 20 per cent by 2011 (Li et al. 2011).

China's response to curb increasing emissions from fossil fuel and to address air pollution have been to set energy efficiency/intensity goals, and carbon intensity goals in its last two FYPs. Yet, these goals have been challenging to reach by administrative methods (in particular the 11th FYP) and China has therefore turned to more market-based approaches such as the carbon market, in line with its deepening of market reform and economic restructuring as decided at the 18th Communist Party Congress in November 2012 (China.org. 2012). China is currently in the process of preparing a national emissions trading scheme (ETS) to begin operation in 2017.[7]

Adaptation began playing a more prominent policy role alongside mitigation and energy efficiency when China adopted its *National Climate Change Programme* in 2007 (NDRC 2007). The purpose of this plan was to outline policies and measures China would adopt towards climate change, and its official stance towards global warming (Dai 2015). The plan placed equal emphasis on adaptation and mitigation and stated that 'climate change and mitigation of greenhouse gas emissions involve many aspects of the social and economic sectors, policies to address climate change and other related ones will only be effective if they are integrated' (NDRC 2007, 25). The strengthened emphasis on the need to integrate mitigation and adaptation illustrated a growing sensitivity towards the complexities of climate change. The climate mitigation strategy was introduced as part of its sustainable development framework to alter its economic growth pattern through development methods such as industrial structure adjustment, renewable energy development and population control (Dai 2015).

Developing and implementing policy requires cooperation and understanding between numerous divergent ministries and agendas. To address this challenge, during the 11th FYP, China established the *Leading Group on Energy Efficiency and Emission Reduction and Addressing Climate Change* in 2007, led by the Chinese Premier. To many observers this demonstrated that climate issues were now being taken seriously at the highest levels of the Chinese government (He 2014). Moreover, China elevated the Climate Change Office in NDRC to department level. The office took the lead in the UN climate change negotiations from that year, a role previously held by the Ministry of Foreign Affairs.

During the 11th FYP, in 2009, before the Climate Conference in Copenhagen, China detailed for the first time its policy goals of reducing its CO_2 emissions per unit of GDP (what is also known as carbon intensity) by 40–45 per cent in 2020 compared with 2005 to curb greenhouse gas emissions (Xinhua 2009; Dai 2015). In addition to the carbon intensity goal, as part of China's pledges to the Copenhagen Accord were the goals to increase the share of non-fossil fuels in primary energy consumption to around 15 per cent and increase its forest areas to 1.3 billion cubic metres by 2020 (NDRC 2010).

China's 12th FYP in 2011 (2011–2015) provided another turning point in the country's history of climate change. The Plan had for the first time integrated climate change action as one of the key principles for national sustainable development. It devoted several sections to climate change and low carbon development and set the goal of establishing a carbon market. Key objectives in the Plan that received much attention were achieving a 16 per cent energy intensity reduction and 17 per cent carbon intensity (CO_2 emission per GDP) based on its 2010 levels (He 2014). Both targets were overachieved at the end of the Plan: an 18.2 per cent reduction in energy intensity and 20 per cent decrease of carbon intensity (PRC 2016). Moreover, the Plan underlined the necessity of integrating climate actions into various key aspects of national economic development (e.g. sustainable development, technology and innovation, transformation of economic model). For the first time in a FYP equal emphasis was placed on mitigation and adaptation.[8] In the 13th FYP (2016–2020) that was approved at the National People's Congress (NPC) in March 2016, the binding goal by 2020 is 15 per cent reduction in energy intensity, and an 18 per cent decline in carbon intensity. The Plan (PRC 2016, chapter 16, 92) states that equal emphasis must be put on adaptation and mitigation, to fulfil the emission reduction commitments, and strengthen capacity building in adaptation.

In 2013, China had an absolute level of 9,524.3 million tons of carbon emissions, i.e. 27.1 per cent of the world's total (BP 2015). Its per-capita emission, 6.99 tons, has exceeded the world's per-capita emission of 4.89 tons. To support domestic climate targets, the State Council approved in September 2014 the issuance of the '*National Plan for Coping with Climate Change*' (2014–2020) to guarantee the reduction of carbon emission intensity by 40 to 45 per cent by 2020 from the 2005 level. This was followed by China's first public commitment to peak its emissions by 2030 at the latest (and possibly before) in 2014. The announcement came as part of an agreement with the United States on combating climate change, announced in Beijing during APEC (The White House 2014). To reach the goal, President Xi pledged that clean energy sources would account for 20 per cent of China's total energy production by 2030. Clean energy would potentially reduce air pollution as well as ease the dependency on coal. China has issued a number of energy and climate related laws in the past decades,[9] but has not yet finalized an overarching climate legislation. A climate change law has been discussed for some time, following the NPC Standing Committee 2009 resolution on actively responding to climate change to focus on strengthening laws and institutions (NPC 2009).[10] Preparations for a climate law were initiated, and a draft climate law was released for public comment in 2012 (CCF 2012). There have been discussions on the climate law for some time, and the State Council issued a notice in 2016 which includes work on the climate change law that is placed on its 'to do' list (State Council Office 2016), though there is no specific date for its issuance.

Sustainable economic development

In recent years there has been an increasing recognition by China's leadership that the country's rapid economic growth has brought about serious environmental degradation and increasing emissions of hazardous pollutants. Yet, neither environment in general nor climate policy in particular has had a priority on a par with economic development, similar to most other countries. At the central level this has somewhat changed, in particular since the 12th FYP. Moreover, in recent years the Chinese leadership has declared 'war on environmental pollution', realizing the high costs for the country (Xinhua 2014b). The same level of awareness does not exist throughout the country, and economic growth still remains the most urgent priority in the provinces, at the expense of other concerns. Thus, implementation of existing policies and enforcement of laws are challenging, though the new Environmental Law in 2015 attempts to address implementation issues by streamlining environmental policy making and authority within the Ministry and its subordinate departments (Reuters 2015). In the past couple of years, the central government has indicated that a growth rate of approximately 7 per cent is acceptable for China. Its GDP growth between 2002 and 2014 reached an average of 7–8 per cent, and IMF predictions project China's average GDP growth to be 6.8 per cent in 2016 (Green and Stern 2015). Premier Li Keqiang confirmed these predictions at the NPC in March when he announced that an annual growth of 6.5 per cent is needed in the 13th FYP period (Xinhua 2016).

Air pollution

Air pollution has become one of the key drivers for climate action in China and one of the strongest incentives for reform in China's energy sector (see chapter 7 by Ahlers and Hansen this volume for more details).[11] Air pollution leads to heavy smog in a majority of Chinese cities. Curbing local air pollution has become a high priority for the Chinese leadership. The Chinese government's action to mitigate some of the air pollution involves changing its energy structure with enhanced use of renewable energy sources and natural gas in electricity generation. The areas that have accumulated the most smog are Beijing, Tianjin and Hebei (Jing-Jin-Ji region) the Yangtze River Delta, and the Pearl River Delta regions.

In an effort to address air pollution, the Chinese government at the central and provincial level has introduced a series of energy saving regulations, emission reduction policies and environmental standards (Zheng et al. 2015). For instance, on 5 December 2012, the Chinese government issued the *12th Five-Year Plan on Air Pollution Prevention and Control in Key Regions*. The purpose of the plan was to address air pollution in major Chinese cities, and the urban projects are expected to require US$55.6 billion in investments (Tao 2014). Moreover, in 2013, the *Airborne Pollution Prevention and Control Action Plan* (2013–2017) was issued, with a funding of US$277 billion over the next five years to improve air quality nationally (see Table 8.1). To alleviate some of the negative impacts of coal burning, natural gas has become a source of energy as a measure for mitigating some of the local air pollution, primarily aimed at the

Table 8.1 Recent policies and laws issued

Revised air quality standards	In 2012, Ministry of Environmental Protection introduced revised air quality standards, including indicators of $PM_{2.5}$ and ozone concentrations to take effect in 2016.
Airborne Pollution Prevention and Control Action Plan (2013–17)	In July 2013, the government announced it would spend 1.7 trillion RMB (US$277 billion) over the next five years to improve air quality nationally. The Airborne Pollution Prevention and Control Action Plan (2013–17) was issued by the State Council in September 2013, focused on improving air quality in the Beijing–Tianjin–Hebei area, the Yangtze River Delta and the Pearl River Delta. Targets include reduction of PM_{10} by 10 per cent compared to 2012 levels for all second-tiered cities, and reductions of $PM_{2.5}$ by 25 per cent, 20 per cent and 15 per cent for the three key regions respectively.

electricity, heating and residential sectors. Air pollution is a window of opportunity to address energy-related climate issues. Another opportunity is through the economic transitions China is currently undergoing, as it develops more secondary and tertiary sectors.

The economic slowdown is presented by the Chinese leadership as the 'new normal' and stresses a sustainable economic growth. This model emphasizes services, reduced inequality, innovation and environmental stability (Green and Stern 2015). Economic development is important for China to ensure social and domestic stability. One approach by the Chinese government has been to integrate its climate policy in the development policy strategies (Li et al. 2011). In addressing climate change this provides an opportunity to compete technologically and commercially with other countries in clean energy sectors (He 2014). The structural changes and reform in China's growth model will include clean energy and reducing energy intensity in China. As such, the energy efficiency objective is a contributing factor to economic growth in China as it enhances productivity (Green and Stern 2015).

Importantly, it is believed that further market reforms could decrease emissions. For instance, a quantitative study examining the impact of marketization and CO_2 emissions discovered that market reform has shown to have positive effect on energy efficiency and CO_2 emissions (Lin and Du 2015). However, future uncertainties concerning China's economic growth and innovation in its industry are issues that will affect how China responds to climate change due to its developmental commitment towards climate change (Hübler et al. 2014).

Managing risk and building resilience

Rapid urbanization and industrial development have created vulnerabilities, such as water vulnerability, and increased exposure to risks of natural disasters. Development has also created new social vulnerabilities. Urban poverty has become more significant since the 1990s, as economic transition, privatization of housing and an ageing population created 'winners and losers' from economic growth (see Table 8.2). Large-scale migration to urban areas has created inequalities in access to housing and social insurance among the urban population. Climate change increases pressure on natural and social resources. The challenge for China is to address the risks and opportunities presented by climate change while also addressing long-term development needs, and in particular the needs of diverse rural and urban vulnerable populations, in more sustainable ways (Nadin et al. 2015).

Table 8.2 Socio-economic factors for China that are components in the 'big climate change picture'

China's Gini coefficient	• 0.473 in 2013 (National Bureau of Statistics) indicating large income disparity in the country
GNI per capita	• US$6,560 in 2013, China is considered (WB) an upper middle-income economy (US$4,086–US$12,615)
Urbanization	• 53.73 per cent of the population are urban dwellers in 2013 compared to 17.9 per cent in 1978. It is expected that urbanization will reach 70 per cent with 1 billion urban dwellers by 2030 (UNDP 2013)
Migrant workers and 'hukou'	• China had around 274 million migrant workers in 2014. It is estimated that the total migrant worker population may reach over 340 million by 2025 (NBS 2015)
	• Majority of migrant workers do not have 'hukou' (household registry) in cities and therefore do not access medical and educational facilities
Ageing society	• 9.4 per cent of China's population has reached the age of 65 and above in 2012. By 2050 the share is predicted to reach 31 per cent of the total population, around 437 million people, roughly the current population of USA and Japan combined

In addition to mitigation policy responses to reduce emissions and address air pollution, managing climate risk has risen rapidly up the political agenda in China, reflecting in part a greater focus on climate change adaptation financing in the international climate change negotiations, as well as the recognition that China is likely to be seriously adversely impacted by climate change. From a policy perspective this means formulating national and provincial adaptation policies to respond to current and future impacts of climate change. Since the 12th FYP this work has increased in significance.

Administratively, China is divided into 31 provinces, autonomous regions and municipalities, which are directly under the control of the Central Government. Each has different demographic characteristics, varying natural resource allocation, topography and climatic conditions ranging from the frigid north to the tropical south. In addition, China's sheer size, vast population and competing development priorities, as well as increasing economic disparity across regions, make uniform policymaking and implementation unrealistic. This is in part because no simple association can be made between socio-economic status or regional economic development and levels of vulnerability or risk.

China's two *National Climate Change Assessment Reports* (NCCC 2006; The Second National Assessment 2011) brought understanding of biophysical risk in core sectors to the fore. Over the past couple of decades China's numerous research institutes and universities have carried out research to understand the impacts of climate change across a range of priority sectors (Wübbeke 2013). Certainly, China's understanding of the biophysical impacts of climate change has increased in recent years and there is also growing awareness of the impacts on socio-economic systems. The Third National Climate Change Assessement (2015) clearly illustrates the severity of the climate impacts China is facing. However, due to the complexity of climate change, current levels of scientific understanding are still insufficient to support comprehensive adaptation planning.

In terms of understanding biophysical impacts Chinese research has historically focused on investigating crop yields and grassland degradation. In contrast there are far fewer studies investigating the macro or micro socio-economic impacts of the biophysical changes, and even fewer studies investing the cost-effectiveness of adaptation policies and options in China. To develop robust climate policies and integrate climate resilience into cross-cutting sectoral policies provincial governments need to understand the socio-economic impacts and the costs of various adaptation options in order to select the most cost-effective and socially feasible policy options. Without such assessments, the provincial governments run the risk of wasting time and money on ineffective approaches. There are studies on backward-looking socio-economic disaster risk for China (e.g. Guan et al. 2015; Vu and Noy 2015), but not many are forward-looking. Such studies are just emerging in other locations as well, and are often on a smaller scale (e.g. urban).

Additionally, developing climate risk management policies is difficult for a number of other reasons, including limited data records; low financial, computational and research capacity for conducting and understanding integrated risk assessments; and the necessity of cross-sector policies and actions that do not sit conveniently within any one government agency or research discipline (Nadin et al. 2015).

China's initial policy response to managing climate risk has been the *National Adaptation Strategy* (NAS), released in November 2013. Its publication demonstrates a more strategic approach to managing climate risk and is the result of more than two years' work by 12 ministries and government agencies including the NDRC (coordination), Ministry of Finance, China Metrological Administration and Ministry of Agriculture.

The NAS builds on and drives forward priority work areas outlined in the 2007 *National Climate Change Programme*. The NAS also complements the *Scientific and Technological Action for Addressing Climate Change Report* (STAACC),[12] jointly issued by 14 ministries and commissions including the Ministry of Science and Technology (MOST).

The primary purpose of the NAS is to provide guidance on priority areas and institutional arrangements to local governments, agencies and authorities on climate adaptation. The priority areas and sectors identified in the NAS include: infrastructure, agriculture, water resources, coastal zones and maritime waters, forests and ecological systems, tourism and other industries and human health. The NAS mandates for the drafting of a Provincial Adaptation Plan (PAP) and identifies pilot provinces and demonstration areas to test and promote effective practices and experiences. Pilot provinces include Shanghai, Guangdong, Hebei, Yunnan, Jilin, Heilongjiang, Inner Mongolia, Jiangxi, Xinjiang, Hainan, Sichuan, Ningxia, Guangxi and Chongqing Municipality (Three Gorges area).

China's ministries and provinces are required to make National Sector Adaptation Plans (NSAP), Urban Adaptation Plans and Provincial Adaptation Plans. It mandates them to align existing policies and institutions to the strategy, develop work mechanisms, funding policies and technical support to safeguard adaptation actions. In theory, this represents the most critical phase of mainstreaming climate change adaptation process in China. However, in practice the degree to which the requirements of the NAS have been implemented is extremely variable among different provinces.

Policies are decided upon at the central level, but inputs from provincial and local levels are central to the decision-making process, and critical to implementation. At the provincial level climate change adaptation is addressed within the existing planning system. The provincial Development and Reform Commissions (DRC) are responsible for the administration and coordination of adaptation measures at the provincial level. Provincial DRCs are responsible for developing adaptation plans and for determining which sectors or issues are a priority in terms of adaptation for that province. These plans are then reported to the provincial government who then decide which options to issue as policy (either on behalf of provincial government or in the name of the DRC) and what to implement. In China, as in many countries, for climate adaptation policy to be effective it needs to be linked to and intersect with a number of other policy areas including social security reform, disaster risk reduction and poverty alleviation. Effective adaptation seldom consists of a single measure; it is dependent upon linking policies

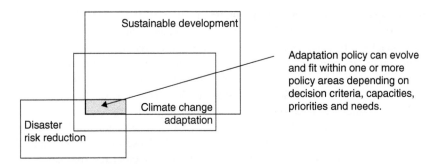

Figure 8.1   Adaptation policy outcomes and objectives may lie along the spectrum of Sustainable
Development, Climate Change Adaptation and Disaster Risk Reduction, depending on the
priorities, needs and capacities of stakeholders identified in the first and subsequent phases of
the adaptation planning process

and actions and building capacity to implement them. In short, adaptation is a process – not an
end goal or discrete action. All of this must be done within socio-economic development and
natural systems, while recognizing the trade-offs and potential benefits between actions
(adaptation dividends) and within existing gaps (deficits). However, it is clearly evident at local
levels that the DRCs do not have a systematic approach to mapping and coordinating policies
across related areas.

Some provinces are further along than others in terms of mainstreaming adaptation into
existing socio-economic planning. For example, Ningxia has addressed climate change within
the existing planning system. The 11th FYP mentioned climate change in relation to disaster
risk as an area to pay attention to. In 2009, the *Ningxia Climate Change Program* was issued
(Ningxia DRC 2009), which listed priorities for adaptation. Climate change is also included in
the 12th FYP, proposing continued scientific assessment of impacts (Ningxia DRC 2011–
2015b) and in some sectoral 12th FYPs, e.g. the *Plan for Ecological Migration and Development*
(Ningxia DRC 2011–2015c), *Plan for Agriculture and Rural Economic Development* (Ningxia DRC
2011–2015a), *Plan for Water Resources* (Ningxia DRC 2011–2015d) and *Meteorology Plan*
(Ningxia DRC 2011–2015b). Ningxia has also issued meteorological and meteorological
disaster regulations, and committed to developing a meteorological disaster prevention plan,
including setting standards for designating meteorological disasters. Inner Mongolia has set up a
provincial Climate Change Leading Group in which 26 provincial departments are represented.
Inner Mongolia Meteorology Bureau has also set up a Climate Centre, which houses an
Ecology and Agriculture Climate Centre. Inner Mongolia University often plays the role of
'think tank' for the provincial DRC. Other provinces such as Jilin are still struggling to fully
understand the nature of climate change adaptation in terms of its scope, roles and relationships
with other planning objectives/priorities.

From international collaboration projects to South–South cooperation

China's participation in the United Nations Framework Convention on Climate Change
(UNFCCC) negotiations and international collaboration have been motivating drivers for
developing a more active domestic climate policy. Following the UNFCCC adoption at the Rio
Earth Summit in 1992, China was one of the parties to the Convention when it went into effect
in 1994, and issued its Agenda 21 as one of the first developing countries.[13] The country later
ratified the Kyoto Protocol on 30 August 2002, though being a developing country it did not

have any emissions reduction commitments under the Protocol.[14] The UN climate negotiations are the preferred arena for reaching global climate agreements, in addition to participating in other multilateral and bilateral collaboration frameworks (Heggelund et al. 2010). China values international cooperation in climate change, both bilateral and multilateral. Recently, China has entered into agreements on climate change with several countries, including the US, India, Brazil and France (Denyer 2015; Goswami 2015; *New York Times* 2015).

China's participation in the UNFCCC has been meaningful for the continued development of domestic climate policies and efforts. The UNFCCC requires individual nation states to report their emissions and approaches to mitigation and adaptation (O'Brien and O'Keefe 2015). In response to the requirements of UNFCCC, China stipulated the *National Climate Change Programme* in 2007. The programme included a variety of climate policies and measures towards climate change, such as the objective of 20 per cent reduction in energy consumption per unit of GDP for the period until 2010 (Wang and Chang 2014). Moreover, China's Intended National Determined Contribution (INDC) submitted to the UNFCCC before COP21 in Paris aims to peak CO_2 emissions around 2030 (or earlier).[15]

In 2004, China began publishing climate change data in *The People's Republic of China Initial National Communications on Climate Change*. This was in accordance with its obligations to the National Committee on Climate Change (UNFCCC) (Dai 2015). The *Second National Communication on Climate Change* was completed in 2012, while the third is being prepared. These were central for the development of a more comprehensive national greenhouse gases (GHG) inventory, the statistical system and the data quality of emissions factors, and optimized the GHG emissions calculation methodology (Gunneng 2012).

The Clean Development Mechanism (CDM), one of the flexible mechanisms under the Kyoto Protocol, is another example of how China has made use of international mechanisms in its domestic policy. CDM provided a good opportunity that corresponded with economic development and energy, key objectives for China. The agencies in charge of these areas also set the agenda in climate policy. In 2005, China introduced *Measures for Operation and Management of CDM* projects in China. China became the major beneficiary of CDM projects with more than half of global projects and about 60 per cent of registered CERs (UNEP et al. n.d.). CDM also led to the establishment of a CDM apparatus to screen and approve the projects, and expertise was developed throughout the country (Heggelund et al. 2010).[16] The majority of the CDM projects were in renewable energies, and in particular wind power developed rapidly through CDM. Moreover, the certified emission reduction (CER) revenue from CDM projects was used to establish a CDM Fund with the purpose to leverage private sector engagement and support policy research and capacity building in addressing climate change in China (Irawan et al. 2012).[17] This was initially China's first mitigation effort and implementation of climate policies towards climate change (Dai 2015).

The carbon market has been promoted as an important policy tool for emission reduction in the international climate negotiations. China has decided to establish a carbon market as proposed in its 12th FYP (2011–2015) to further its emissions reduction efforts and a national Emissions Trading Scheme (ETS) is under preparation. It is regarded as a complementary approach to command-and-control mechanisms (Duan 2015). Seven ETS pilots were established in 2013 and 2014 to provide experience for the national system. The national ETS is set to begin operation in 2017 as announced by President Xi Jinping during his state visit to the US (The White House 2015a).

International cooperation projects such as the Adapting to Climate Change in China project (ACCC), are also working in partnership with NDRC to develop risk-based climate resilience planning approaches. ACCC II is working at two policy levels – national and sub-national – to support the aims of China's NAS, which seeks to build resilience into socio-economic planning and development starting with priority sectors such as agriculture, water, human health and infrastructure, among others. Projects such as ACCC aim to enhance the understanding of climate risk and build resilience in policy making and application. It works with sub-national policy makers to enhance their understanding of climate risk and the trade-offs and benefits of potential resilience policies and solutions.[18]

Over the past decades, China has developed policy measures/approaches, institutional frameworks and technology that could be of relevance to other developing countries. Xie Zhenhua, China's special representative for climate change and chief negotiator[19] (Carbon Pulse 2015) and head of the Chinese delegation to UNFCCC, announced its determination to assist developing countries in four major areas of South–South cooperation at COP 17 in Durban (China.org.cn 2014). The South–South Cooperation Climate Change (SSC CC) Programme was initiated in 2011 in order to provide assistance to other developing states. The SSC CC Programme was officially announced at Rio+20 in 2012 by then Premier Wen Jiabao who pledged RMB 200 million (US$31.7 million '*sannian liangyi*') for a three-year international project to help Small Island States, least developed and African countries to tackle climate change.[20] China's commitment to SSC CC and establishing a South–South Fund has been further cemented and announced at the UN Climate Summit in 2014, followed by Premier Li Keqiang's announcement at a high level meeting (State Council 2015).[21] In September 2015, President Xi Jinping pledged the allocation of RMB 20 billion (US$3.1 billion) to establish the SSC Fund on Climate Change at the UN General Assembly (White House 2015b; Xinhua 2015). The design and the features of the SSC CC Fund are currently being developed.

Concluding comments and the 13th FYP

China's climate policies have developed rapidly over the past decade; policies and actions underscore the political willingness to deal with domestic climate change challenges. Mitigation measures were introduced early through energy policies and administrative measures. In recent years, China is increasingly looking to market mechanisms to deal with its emissions. Moreover, there is growing awareness among China's policy makers of the complexities of climate risks, and the costs of climatic changes to the Chinese economy. Yet, much remains to be done in China. The 13th FYP (2016–2020) has seen a strengthening and continuation of China's commitment to address climate change by key policies in mitigation including strengthened nationally binding targets for energy consumption per unit GDP (energy intensity), carbon emissions per unit GDP (carbon intensity), as well as increased non-fossil energy share. For adaptation and resilience, ministries and provinces will continue to develop and implement National, Sector, Provincial and Urban Adaptation Plans; in this regard, capacity building will be of great importance to strengthen understanding of managing climate risks and building resilience throughout China. In all areas there are still challenges to efficient implementation of policies and enforcement of laws, as capacities and understanding of the climate change challenges vary in the country.

Notes

1 The authors would like to thank Dr Sarah Opitz-Stapleton, Senior Risk Analyst, Plan8 Risk Consulting for valuable comments on the chapter, and Gard Heggelund for helpful research and formatting assistance. Many thanks to the Fridtjof Nansen Institute (FNI) for financial and institutional support to the research.

2 For example, the reliance on coal has also brought about severe air pollution in the country.

3 The chapter does not analyse the rationale of China's diplomatic position within international climate change negotiations as this is outside the scope of this handbook.

4 The Five-Year-Planning (FYP) process is crucial in China's national economic planning, as it lays out the framework and even legislation for socio-economic development over five years. Given the political significance of FYP, the mainstreaming of climate change mitigation and adaptation into the national economic development framework has demonstrated strong political will, as well as integration at the highest possible level. NDRC is the commission in charge of coordinating, compiling and soliciting inputs from the line ministries for the Five Year Plans.

5 Energy intensity is energy consumption per unit of GDP.

6 The China Coal Consumption Cap Plan and Policy Research Project recommends 58 per cent in its recommendations to the 13th Five-Year Plan. China Coal Consumption Cap Plan and Research Report: Recommendations for the 13th Five-Year Plan. Executive Summary (NRDC 2015).

7 Seven ETS pilots were initiated in 2013 (Duan et al 2014; Jotzo and Loschel 2014, IETA and CDC Climate Research 2015), and will provide experience for the national regime.

8 For a translation of the 12th FYP (British Chamber of Commerce in China, 2011).

9 Examples of laws in China are Renewable Energy Law, Energy Conservation Law, Air Pollution Law etc. For more details please see Sabin Center for Climate Change Law, Columbia Law School at http://web.law.columbia.edu/climate-change/resources/climate-change-laws-world/china#Laws on Climate Change

10 Resolution of the Standing Committee of the National People's Congress of China on Actively Responding to Climate Change, adopted at the Tenth Meeting of the Standing Committee of the Eleventh National People's Congress, 27 August 2009 (NPC 2009).

11 China's Renewable energy law went into effect in 2006, and was amended in 2009. Article 1 states that 'The Law is intended to advance the development and use of renewable energy, increase the supply of energy, improve the energy structure, maintain the energy security, protect the environment and realize the economic and social sustainable development' (Lehman et al. 2009). In recent years renewables have had increased importance as an alternative to fossil fuels, due to air pollution.

12 The STAACC outlines broad scientific policies, technologies and measures for addressing climate change including: (1) intensifying funding and support; (2) strengthening the basic work and the related capacity building activities for adaptation to climate change; (3) conducting climate change risk analysis in vulnerable sectors including agriculture, water resources, forestry, natural ecology system, human health, coastal zone; and (4) carrying out research on key technologies and measures for climate change adaptation and adaptation demonstration models in pilot areas.

13 China's National Agenda 21 – White Paper on China's Population, Environment and Development in the 21st Century was approved by the State Council in 1994, and introduced the concept of sustainable development in all sectors, and was a guideline for the formulation of economic and social development plans (UNDESA, 2016).

14 This was announced at the World Summit on Sustainable Development (Earth Summit) in Johannesburg, and was reported in *China Daily*: Zongwei Shao, Nation Approves Kyoto Protocol, *China Daily*, 4 September 2002 (China.org.cn 2002).

15 The objectives in the INDC are reducing CO_2 emissions per unit of GDP (carbon intensity) by 60 to 65 per cent below 2005 levels, and increase the forest stock volume by around 4.5 billion cubic metres over the 2005 level. Moreover, it aims to increase the share of non-fossil fuels in primary energy consumption to around 20 per cent (NDRC 2015).

16 Assistance was provided by international organizations and bilateral and multilateral donors. Projects were carried out by the UNDP, the World Bank, the Asian Development Bank and some bilateral donors.

17 Established jointly by Ministries of Finance, Foreign Affairs and National Development and Reform Commission (NDRC) as an innovative finance mechanism to support National Climate Change Programme and promote international cooperation, the mandate of the Fund is to support China's effort to address climate change and promote social and economic sustainable development. It supports CDM projects in China and collects, manages and utilizes the national share of proceeds from CDM projects. The Fund totalled approximately CNY 10 billion in 2012 (Irawan et al., 2012. http://www.gov.cn/flfg/2010-10/21/content_1727534.htm (in Chinese)).

18 The project is being rolled out in the Provinces of Jiangxi, Guizhou, Jilin, Inner Mongolia and Ningxia, and the city of Qingdao.

19 Xie Zhenhua stepped down as NDRC vice chairman in 2015 as he had reached retirement age. He continued to head the Chinese delegation to COP21 in Paris.

20 In 2011, Xie Zhenhua, Vice Chairman of the National Development and Reform Commission (NDRC) – the key Government institution in charge of climate change – announced four major areas of South-South cooperation at COP17 in Durban. In 2012, at Rio+20, Premier Wen Jiabao pledged 200 million RMB (US\$31.7 million) for a three-year international project to help Small Island States, least developed and other African countries to tackle climate change.

21 Zhang Gaoli announced South South Cooperation at the UN: Zhang Gaoli Attends UN Climate Summit and Delivers Speech (MoFA 2015).

References

BP, 2015. *BP Statistical Review of World Energy*. London: British Petroleum.

British Chamber of Commerce in China, 2011. China's Twelfth Five-Year Plan (2011–2015) the full English version. http://www.britishchamber.cn/content/chinas-twelfth-five-year-plan-2011-2015-full-english-version (accessed 2 May 2016).

Buckley, C., 2015. China Burns Much More Coal Than Reported, Complicating Climate Talks. *The New York Times*, 3 November. http://www.nytimes.com/2015/11/04/world/asia/china-burns-much-more-coal-than-reported-complicating-climate-talks.html?action=click&pgtype=Homepage&version=Moth-Visible&module=inside-nyt-region&region=inside-nyt-region&WT.nav=inside-nyt-region&_r=3 (accessed 3 November 2015).

Carbon Pulse, 2015. China's Xie Zhenhua Makes Climate Comeback http://carbon-pulse.com/2945/ (accessed 25 May 2016).

CCF (China Carbon Forum), 12 November, 2012. China's New Climate Change Law: The Pathway to a Low Carbon Economy? http://www.chinacarbon.info/chinas-new-climate-change-law-the-pathway-to-a-low-carbon-economy/ (accessed 16 May 2016).

Cheng H. and Eikeland, P., 2015. *China's Political Economy of Coal. Drivers and challenges to restructuring China's energy system*, Lysaker, Norway: Fridtjof Nansen Institute (FNI).

China.org.cn, 2002. China Approves Kyoto Protocol, China Daily, 4 September 2002. http://www.china.org.cn/english/China/41661.htm (accessed 17 December 2016).

China.org.cn, 2012. Amendments Reflect CPC's Resolve. http://china.org.cn/china/18th_cpc_congress/2012-11/15/content_27118842.htm (accessed 2 May 2016).

China.org.cn, 2014. China Stresses South–South Cooperation. 2014 UN Climate Change Conference. http://www.china.org.cn/environment/2014-12/09/content_34270037.htm (accessed 11 November 2015).

Dai Y., 2015. Who Drives Climate-Relevant Policy Implementation in China? Brighton, UK: Institute of Development Studies.

Denyer, S., 2015. China Tries to Recast Itself as a Global Leader in Climate-Change Fight. 2 November 2015. *Washington Post*. https://www.washingtonpost.com/news/worldviews/wp/2015/11/02/china-tries-to-recast-itself-as-a-global-leader-in-climate-change-fight/?utm_term=.e17fe43de554 (accessed 17 December 2016).

Duan M., 2015. From Carbon Emissions Trading Pilots to National System: The Road Map for China. *Carbon and Climate Law Review, 9* (3), 231–242.

Duan M., Pang T., & Zhang X., 2014. Review of Carbon Emissions Trading Pilots in China. *Energy & Environment, 25* (3), 527–550.

Goswami, U., 2015. Brazil, South Africa, India and China chalk out plan for climate negotiations. 8 August 2014. *The Economic Times*. http://articles.economictimes.indiatimes.com/2014-08-08/news/52594309_1_green-climate-fund-climate-change-major-economies-forum (accessed 17 December 2016).

Green, F. and Stern, N., 2015. China's 'New Normal': Structural Change, Better Growth, and Peak Emissions. Policy report, Centre for Climate Change Economics and Policy (CCCEP), University of Leeds, 2015.

Guan Y., Zheng F., Zhang P. and Qin C., 2015. Spatial and Temporal Changes Of Meteorological Disasters in China during 1950–2013. *Natural Hazards 75*, 2607–2623.

Gunneng, A., 2012. *Climate Change and Development in China*. Beijing: UNDP China.

He G., 2014. Engaging Emerging Countries: Implications of China's Major Shifts in Climate Policy. In: N. A. Putra and E. Han, eds, *Governments' Responses to Climate Change: Selected Examples From Asia Pacific* . Springer–Verlag Singapour,11–24.

Heggelund, G., S. Andresen and I. Fritzen Buan, 2010. Chinese Climate Policy: Domestic Priorities, Foreign Policy and Emerging Implementation. In K. Harrison and L. McIntosh Sundstrom (eds), *Global Commons, Domestic Decisions*. Cambridge (MA), USA / London, UK: MIT Press, 239–261.

Hübler, M., Voigt, S., and Löschel, A., 2014. Designing an Emissions Trading Scheme for China: An Up-To-Date Climate Policy Assessment. *Energy Policy*, 75, 57–72.

IETA & CDC Climate Research, 2015. China: An Emissions Trading Case Study. March 2015. (http://www.cdcclimat.com/IMG/pdf/china_emissions_trading_case_study_cdc_climat_ieta_march_2015.pdf (accessed 16 December 2016).

Irawan, S., SivSilvia X. F., Li C., Meng X. and Heikens, A., 2012. *Case Study Report: China Clean Development Mechanism Fund*. UNDP/CCDMF Working Paper.

Jotzo, F. and Loschel, A., 2014. Emissions Trading in China: Emerging Experiences and International Lessons. *Energy Policy*, 75, 3–8.

Lehman, Lee and Xu, 2009. Renewable Energy Law of The People's Republic of China (Amended 2009). http://www.lehmanlaw.com/resource-centre/laws-and-regulations/general/renewable-energy-law-of-the-peoples-republic-of-china-amended-2009.html (accessed 2 May, 2016)

Li Y., Yang X., Zhu X., Mulvihill, P. R., Mathews, D. H., and Sun X., 2011. Integrating Climate Change Factors into China's Development Policy: Adaptation Strategies and Mitigation to Environmental Change. *Ecological Complexity, 8*, 294–298.

Lin B. and Du K., 2015. Energy and CO_2 Emissions Performance in China's regional Economies: Do Market-Oriented Reforms Matter? *Energy Policy, 78*, 113–124.

Liu, Z., 2015. *China's Carbon Emission Report 2015*. Cambridge, MA: Harvard Kennedy School of Government.

MoFA (Ministry of Foreign Affairs of the People's Republic of China), 2015. Zhang Gaoli Attends UN Climate Summit and Delivers Speech. http://www.fmprc.gov.cn/mfa_eng/zxxx_662805/t1194544.shtml (accessed 2 May 2016)

Nadin, R., Opitz-Stapleton, S. and Yinlong, X., 2015. *Climate Risk and Resilience in China*. London: Routledge.

National Bureau of Statistics of China, 2014. Statistical Communiqué of the People's Republic of China on the 2013 National Economic and Social Development. http://www.stats.gov.cn/english/PressRelease/201402/t20140224_515103.html (accessed 3 January 2017).

National Bureau of Statistics of China, 2015. Statistical Communiqué of the People's Republic of China on the 2014 National Economic and Social Development. (http://www.stats.gov.cn/english/PressRelease/201502/t20150228_687439.html) (accessed 5 November 2015)

National Climate Change Co-ordination Committee (NCCC), 2006. China's National Assessment Report on Climate Change. Beijing: Science Press.

NDRC (National Development and Reform Commission), 2010. Climate Change Department. Letter to UNFCCC Secretariat. 28 January 2010. https://unfccc.int/files/meetings/cop_15/copenhagen_accord/application/pdf/chinacphaccord_app2.pdf (accessed 17 December).

NDRC (National Development and Reform Commission of China), Department of Climate Change, 2015. China's Intended Nationally Determined Contribution: Enhanced Actions on Climate Change. http://www4.unfccc.int/submissions/INDC/Published%20Documents/China/1/China's%20INDC%20-%20on%2030%20June%202015.pdf (accessed 6 November 2015).

NDRC (National Development and Reform Commission), 2007. China's National Climate Change Programme. Beijing.

Ningxia Development and Reform Commisssion (DRC) 2009. Ningxia Ying Dui Qihou Bianhua Fang'an (Ningxia Climate Adaptation Planning).

Ningxia Development and Reform Commisssion (DRC) 2011–15a. Ningxia Nongye he Nongcun Jingji Fazhan Shierwu Guihua (The Twelfth Economic Development Plan for the Agricultural Sector and Rural Economy of Ningxia).

Ningxia Development and Reform Commisssion (DRC) 2011–15b. Ningxia Shierwu Jingji Shehui Zongti Fazhan Guihua Gangyao (The Outline of the Twelfth Five-Year Social Economic Development Plan of Ningxia).

Ningxia Development and Reform Commisssion (DRC) 2011–15c. Ningxia Shierwu Shengtai Yimin Fazhan Guihua (The Twelfth Five-Year Ecological Migration Development Plan of Ningxia).

Ningxia Development and Reform Commisssion (DRC) 2011–15d. Ningxia Shierwu Shuili Guihua (The Twelfth Five-Year Water Resources Plan of Ning Xia).

NPC (National People's Congress of the People's Republic of China), 2009. Resolution of the Standing Committee of the National People's Congress of China on Actively Responding to Climate Change, adopted at the Tenth Meeting of the Standing Committee of the Eleventh National People's Congress, 27 August 2009. http://www.npc.gov.cn/npc/xinwen/rdyw/wj/2009-08/27/content_1516165.htm (accessed 9 May 2016).

NRDC (National Resource Defense Council), 2015. China Coal Consumption Cap Plan and Policy Research Project. http://www.nrdc.cn/coalcap/index.php/English/index (accessed 2 May 2016).

O'Brien, G. and O'Keefe, P., 2015. Climate Governance and Climate Change and Society. In: U. F. Paleo, ed., *Risk Governance: The Articulation of Hazard, Politics and Ecology*. Dordrecht Heidelberg New York: Springer, 277–293.

PBL, Netherlands Environmental Assessment Agency, 2007. China Now No.1 in CO_2 Emissions: USA in Second Position. http://www.pbl.nl/node/47363 (accessed 4 May 2016).

PRC (People's Republic of China), 2016. Zhonghua renmin hongheguo Guomin jingji he shehui fazhan di shisange wunian guihua gangyao (cao'an) (People's Republic of China outline for 13th FYP (Draft))

Reuters, 2015. China Passes New Pollution Law, Sets Sights on Coal Consumption Cap. 29 August 2015. http://www.reuters.com/article/us-china-pollution-idUSKCN0QY08A20150829 (accessed 2 May 2016).

State Council Office, 2014. Guowuyuan Bangongting Guanyu Yinfa Nengyuan Fazhan Zhanlve (2014–2020) de Tongzhi (announcement by the State Council about Energy Strategy (2014–2020). Beijing.

State Council Office, 2015. Li Keqiang: Zhuoli tuijin tizhi shengji fazhan qianghuaying dui qihuobianhua xingdong(Li Keqing: Strongly Promote the activities against climate change). Beijing.

State Council Office, 2016. Guowuyuan bangongting guanyu yinfa guowuyuan 2016 nian lifagonzuo jihuade tongzhi (State Council Office Notice on issuing legislative work plans for 2016). Beijing.

Stensdal, I., 2014. Chinese Climate-Change Policy, 1988–2013: Moving On Up. *Asian Perspectives, 38*, 111–135.

Tao X., 2014. Problems of Air Pollution Prevention in Key Regions of China. *Science China: Life Sciences, 57* (3), 356–357.

The New York Times, 2015. Climate Goals Pledged by China and the U.S. (http://www.nytimes.com/interactive/2014/11/12/world/asia/climate-goals-pledged-by-us-and-china-2.html?_r=2 (accessed 2 May 2016).

The Second National Assessment of Climate Change Writing Committee, 2011. The Second National Assessment of Climate Change. Beijing: Science Press.

The Third National Assessment of Climate Change Writing Committee, 2015. The Third National Assessment of Climate Change. Beijing: Science Press.

The White House: Office of the Press Secretary, 2014. U.S.-China Joint Announcement on Climate Change. 11 November 2014. https://www.whitehouse.gov/the-press-office/2014/11/11/us-china-joint-announcement-climate-change (accessed 17 December 2016).

The White House: Office of the Press Secretary, 2015a. The United States and China Issue Joint Presidential Statement on Climate Change with New Domestic Policy Commitments and a Common Vision for an Ambitious Global Climate Agreement in Paris. 25 September 2015. (https://www.whitehouse.gov/the-press-office/2015/09/25/fact-sheet-united-states-and-china-issue-joint-presidential-statement) (accessed 2 May 2016).

The White House: Office of the Press Secretary, 2015b. U.S.-China Joint Presidential Statement on Climate Change. (https://www.whitehouse.gov/the-press-office/2015/09/25/us-china-joint-presidential-statement-climate-change) (accessed 5 November 2015).

UNDESA (United Nations Department for Social and Economic Affairs), 2016. Institutional Aspects of Sustainable Development in China http://www.un.org/esa/agenda21/natlinfo/countr/china/inst.htm (accessed 29 June 2016).

UNEP DTU Partnership. Centre on Energy, Climate and Sustainable Development, n.d. http://www.cdmpipeline.org/cdm-projects-region.htm#1 (accessed 2 May 2016).

Vu, T. B. and Noy I., 2015. Regional effects of natural disasters in China: investing in post-disaster recovery. *Natural Hazards, 75*, 111–126.

Wang N. and Chang Y.-C., 2014. The evolution of Low-Carbon Development Strategies in China. *Energy, 68*, 61–70.

Wübbeke, J. 2013. China's Climate Change Expert Community: Principles, Mechanisms and Influence. *Journal of Contemporary China, 22* (82), 37–41.

Xinhua, 2009. China Announces Targets on Carbon Emission Cuts. http://news.xinhuanet.com/english/2009-11/26/content_12544181.htm (accessed 5 November 2015).

Xinhua, 2014a. National Economic and Social Development Bulletin, National Bureau of Statistics http://news.xinhuanet.com/2015-02/26/c_127520244.htm (accessed 2 May 2016).

Xinhua, 2014b. Xinhua Insight: China Declares War Against Pollution. Xinhua News. http://news.xinhuanet.com/english/special/2014-03/05/c_133163557.htm (accessed 3 May 2015).

Xinhua, 2015. China Pledges 3 Billion USD for Developing Countries to Fight Climate Change. http://news.xinhuanet.com/english/2015-09/26/c_134663006.htm (accessed 5 November 2015).

Xinhua, 2016. Full Text: Report on the Work of the Government, March 17 2016 http://news.xinhuanet.com/english/china/2016-03/17/c_135198880_2.htm (accessed 25 May 2016).

Zheng S., Yi H. and Li H., 2015. The Impacts of Provincial Energy and Environmental Policies on Air Pollution Control in China. *Renewable and Sustainable Energy Reviews, 49*, 386–394.

9

ENVIRONMENTAL POLICY AND AGRICULTURE IN CHINA

From regulation through model emulation to regulatory pluralism

Bettina Bluemling

Introduction

Agricultural intensification has been a political programme for decades in China (Marks 2012). Also today, despite a growing population and rising living standards, the Chinese government is convinced that the country's agriculture can maintain a self-sufficient supply in main food crops (Xinhua 2015). Even if in China, 22 per cent of the world population live on only 7 per cent of the world's arable land, in 2010, the country's farmers produced about 95 per cent of the staples consumed (McBeath and McBeath 2010). Agricultural intensification, however, is not only driven by policy, it is also a result of two other major drivers. First, agricultural intensification is a response to changing diets. Figure 9.1 shows the production of the three major crops in China over the period from 2001 to 2011: while paddy rice increased by 13.2 per cent, vegetable production increased by 23.7 per cent and maize production even by 68.9 per cent. This increase in maize production can to some extent be attributed to a rise in meat consumption. Pig production increased by 113.4 per cent over the period from 1989 to 2009 (Bluemling and Hu 2011). From 1990 to 2000, meat consumption almost doubled in China (Kanaly et al. 2010). Diets in China have not only increasingly incorporated meat but also fruits and vegetables. Areas under vegetables and fruits have been expanding annually and now make 22.3 per cent of the total cultivated area (Fan et al. 2015). This increase in area under vegetable and fruit cultivation will put further pressure on the remaining land for grain production. Adding to this, a further driver for agricultural intensification is the decrease in arable land. According to Food and Agricultural Organization of the United Nations (FAO) data, arable land decreased from 0.105 ha/person in 1983 to 0.078 ha/person in 2013, a reduction of 74 per cent (World Bank 2016a), which can be partly attributed to a population increase from 1.01 billion in 1982 to 1.41 billion in 2015 (FAO 2016) and related soaring urbanization and transfer of agricultural land. In conclusion, increased meat consumption, intensification of grain production and a shift to more pesticide and fertilizer intensive cultivations like vegetable and fruit are likely to have their impact on China's rural environment.

This chapter will first review the current state of China's rural environment, then focus on three major drivers for its deterioration, i.e. pesticides, fertilizer and manure, and related policy measures to combat further environmental decline. This part will show how the national

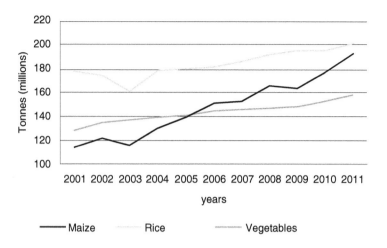

Figure 9.1   Production of three major crops in China 2001–2011 (FAO 2016)

government has been trying to prevent or mitigate environmental deterioration by regulating the pesticide industry as well as farmers' behaviour. Focus hereby is on policy measures taken by the Ministry of Agriculture and related agencies. In rural China, without the cooperation of or initiation by the Ministry of Agriculture, the Ministry of Environmental Protection (MEP) is not likely to have the means to implement environmental policies. Environmental departments often do not exist below the township level and hardly have either the staff or the financial means to monitor policy implementation by small- and medium-scale farmers. Therefore, it is often the Ministry of Agriculture which initiates or monitors the implementation of policies that mitigate or prevent environmental deterioration by agriculture.

The third part of this chapter will then look deeper into the difficulty of implementing national policies, and discuss the former approach of regulation by model emulation. It will explain why this kind of regulation is likely to become less important within the frame of overall regulatory pluralism.

State of the rural environment

During the 50th Munich Security Conference in January 2014, a report presented water scarcity as well as water pollution as the major security risks for China (Earth Security Initiative 2014). Agriculture is a major contributor to this situation. In 1980, agriculture in China abstracted 88.2 per cent of the total water withdrawal by economic sectors (see Figure 9.2). At that time, this was 391 billion cubic metres. About 30 years later, agriculture is still consuming about 392 billion cubic metres; however, in 2013, this made up only 64.5 per cent of the total water used. As can be seen from Figure 9.2, agriculture has been facing increasing competition over water with the industrial sector: the increase in industrial water use quantity in the mid-1990s is mirrored by a decline in water withdrawal for agriculture. However, since the early 2000s, agricultural water use, and total water withdrawal, are again on the rise. The period from 1982 to 2014 witnessed an increase in actually irrigated agricultural area by 42.7 per cent, presumably making up for the loss of water to industrial water use. Impacts from agricultural water use are particularly visible in North China, where the massive extraction of groundwater over a period of several decades has brought about land subsidence and the intrusion of saltwater in coastal areas, leading to deteriorating groundwater quality (COWI 2013).

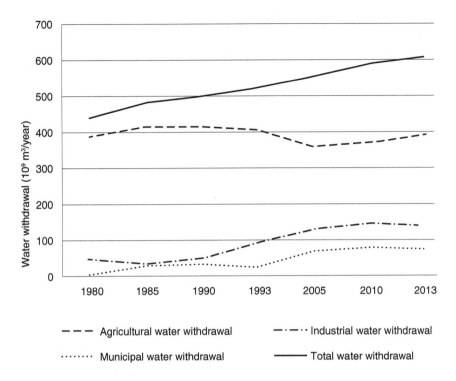

Figure 9.2 Water use across sectors (FAO 2016)

Agriculture and industry not only compete over water use. Both sectors are major water polluters. While this chapter focuses on environmental impacts of agriculture, it should be noted that industrial development has been having severe effects on the rural environment. Some see rural industry, estimated to comprise about 6.4 million township and village factories and a workforce of more than 80 million (Tilt 2010, 39), as 'responsible for up to two-thirds of China's total air- and water-pollution burden' (Tilt 2010, 3). However, according to others, organic pollutants from livestock breeding and overuse of agricultural inputs are the main reasons for groundwater pollution in China (Earth Security Initiative 2014). Sources for water pollution in the countryside can indeed not easily be traced back. Chinese Ministries see water pollution in rural areas as originating from mainly three sources, i.e. agriculture, improper domestic sewage discharge and rural industry (NDRC 2010).

Accumulated effects from these polluters are alarming. According to the 2016 'Groundwater Dynamics Report' of the Groundwater Monitoring Centre, Ministry of Water Resources, 80.1 per cent of shallow groundwater in northern China (i.e. comprising the North China Plain, Shanxi Province, China's North-West and the Jianghan Plain) have water quality of IV or V and are therefore 'unfit for direct human contact' (Groundwater Monitoring Centre 2016). According to the 2014 National Environmental Report (*Zhongguo Huanjing Zhuangkuang Gongbao*) of the Ministry of Environmental Protection (MEP 2014a), 36.9 per cent of the water in 423 major rivers and 62 key lakes (reservoirs) is not suitable for direct human contact. A point worth noting here is that water, which is of quality inferior to industrial use, still is considered suitable for agricultural water use (see Category V, Table 9.1).

As water of rank V is still considered suitable for use in agriculture, questions of its impact on soil and food safety are evident. According to the country's first national survey of soil

Table 9.1 Water quality in national rivers and lakes

Category	Water function	Percentage
I	Can be used for National Nature Protection Areas	3.4
II	Can be used for centralized drinking water supply (1st grade water protection areas), rare aquatic habitats, shrimp production and breeding grounds	30.4
III	Can be used for centralized drinking water supply (2nd grade water protection areas), aquaculture and swimming	29.3
IV	Can be used for industrial water use and for recreational water use without direct human contact	20.9
V	Can be used for agriculture and aquatic landscapes	6.8
Less than V		9.2

Source: China's Ministry of Environmental Protection 2014

pollution, 19.4 per cent of arable land is polluted (MEP 2014b). Pollution originates from industrial plants, their waste, mining operations, agricultural use of chemical fertilizers and pesticides and sewage irrigation (McBeath and McBeath 2010; Zhang 2014). According to McBeath and McBeath (2010, 58), about 7 per cent of China's agricultural land 'has been polluted through improper uses of pesticides and fertilizers, not to mention the number (50,000–120,000) of people who are poisoned each year by pesticides'. The most common cause of food poisoning is indeed reported to be pesticide residues in vegetables (Zhou and Jin 2013). However, not only the safety of agricultural products, but also drinking water safety for the rural population is at risk. 'Every year, 190 million people in China fall ill and 60,000 people die from diseases caused by water pollution' (Tao and Xin 2014, 527). In rural areas, the situation is particularly alarming. By the end of 2010, 42 per cent of the rural population, i.e. over 400 million people, were still using water directly from water sources, with either no or very simple water supply facilities (Liu 2015). The rural population is hence very vulnerable to the eminent pollution in China's countryside.

A further kind of agricultural pollution that has emerged in recent years in China is 'land pollution'. Land pollution is 'the deposition of solid or liquid waste materials on land or underground in a manner that can contaminate the soil and groundwater, threaten public health, and cause unsightly conditions and nuisances' (Nathanson 2016). Land pollution from agriculture comprises pollution by plastic film that are used for mulching and are not collected from the field after the harvest (Liu et al. 2014), and from pesticide packaging that is discarded on the field after pesticide use (Jin et al. 2017). Sixty-two per cent of Chinese farmers randomly dump pesticide packaging into or nearby the fields (Jin et al. 2017). Land pollution can destroy the soil structure and lead to soil degradation, which is a further major environmental problem in China. Soil degradation is the degradation by erosion, desertification, soil salinization, soil impoverishment and pollution (Zhang 2014). In fact, 40 per cent of China's cultivated land is degraded, and 37 per cent of its total land area is eroded (UN News Centre 2010; Zhang 2014). The shrinking of productive arable land is considered a threat to China's food security (UN News Centre 2010), and again agricultural practices are one of the underlying drivers (McBeath and McBeath 2010, 54).

In conclusion, agriculture has been playing a major role in the deterioration of the rural environment, and at the same time is its major victim.

Agricultural policies and their inclusion of the environment

The year 2015 witnessed several initiatives by the Ministry of Agriculture to reduce environmental impact by agriculture in the long term. The most comprehensive plan is the *National Plan for Sustainable Agriculture (2015–2030)* (MoA 2015). It divides the country into three agricultural zones, based also on their environmental conditions to 'host' intensive agriculture. The plan foresees the achievement of a more sustainable agriculture and considers the following to be crucial measures: resource recycling and a soil classification system, improved technology use and research input, increased agricultural water-use efficiency and curbing environmental pollution by reducing chemical fertilizer and pesticide use and manure recycling.

Pesticide policies

From the beginning of the People's Republic, the Chinese government has shown a certain determination to eliminate pests. The 'Four Pests Campaign' that started in 1958 foresaw the eradication of rats, sparrows, flies and mosquitos. Sparrows were part of the campaign as they ate grain seeds. 'Millions of Chinese of all ages' coordinated their 'attacks' against sparrows by destroying nests, breaking eggs, killing nestlings and beating gongs that would not allow sparrows to alight, so that they in the end would die from exhaustion (Shapiro 2001, 87). Soon after a noticeable decline in sparrows, it was recognized that they were indeed 'allies in insect control' (Shapiro 2001, 88). And even if it is hard to estimate how much influence the near extinction of sparrows had on pest control, the campaign is said to have had a lasting effect on the ecological balance in the countryside (Shapiro 2001).

While the enthusiasm with which 'pests' were killed has ceased, some determination persists to make use of pesticides. According to data from the National Bureau of Statistics of China, pesticide use increased by 66.2 per cent in the period from 1995 to 2014 (National Bureau of Statistics of China 2016). More than 14 kg/ha of pesticides are applied on cultivated land in China annually, which is considerably higher than pesticide application in the USA (2.2 kg/ha), France (2.9 kg/ha) or the Netherlands (8.8 kg/ha) (Fan et al. 2015). With the shift to vegetable and fruit production, the average amount of pesticides is likely to increase even further. However, not only the pesticide quantity determines possible hazards to the environment. A variety of pesticides exist, particularly in China, as a country that for some years already is reported to be not only the world's biggest user but also producer and exporter of pesticides (PAN 2010). In 2013, China's pesticide industry had an output of 1.3 million tons 'with about 300 technical products produced by more than 1800 factories' (FAO 2015, 47).

With the detrimental effects of pesticide use having become apparent, Chinese policy-makers have taken measures to combat pesticide overuse. The Chinese government hereby relies on both regulatory measures, and plans and programmes.

Since 2012, all pesticides, whether produced in China or imported, need to be registered (State Council 2011). Reviewing the registration of new pesticides is hence one regulatory measure together with the establishment of Maximum Residue Limits in food for these registered pesticides. Risk assessments are done for dietary risks, as well as for groundwater and surface water (FAO 2015). The hazardousness of pesticides is furthermore determined in international Convention lists of highly hazardous pesticides (HHP) (e.g. the World Health Organization's (WHO) *Recommended Classification of Pesticides by Hazard*). If a pesticide is added to such an international list, its registration in China is reviewed and a decision is made whether to restrict, phase-out or cancel its registration. This decision is taken by the Pesticide Registration and Evaluation Committee based on documented accidents and risk assessment research, but also based on whether Maximum Residue Limits are regularly exceeded or pesticides are misused (FAO 2015).

According to the FAO (2015), 581 HHPs are currently still registered in China, of which 159 either belong to the WHO Class 1 ('extremely hazardous') or Class 0 (pesticides that are believed to be obsolete or discontinued and therefore are not classified) or are not approved in the EU. As of 2010, China banned 46 HHPs (PAN 2015).

Apart from the stricter regulation of pesticides, the *Action Plan for Zero Growth in the Application of Pesticides* that was launched in the frame of the 13th Five-Year Plan forms another more recent attempt to curb pesticide use. The plan foresees that from 2020 on, pesticide use quantities shall not further increase. The major pathways for reducing pesticides are research into technological innovation to reduce pesticide application, e.g. 'green prevention and control technologies' (*lvse fangkong jishu*), but also increasing the use of pesticides of low toxicity and high effectiveness, as well as improved pesticide management (e.g. integrated pest management), in order to reduce pesticide residues, related environmental pollution and production costs. By these means, the current rather low utilization rate of 35 per cent should be increased. The majority of objectives in the *Action Plan* target farmers' behaviour.

Empirical research in China (see Fan et al. 2015; Jin et al. 2015) has shown that farmers' pesticide use behaviour bears chances for improvement. Since the reform and commercialization of the extension system in the late 1980s, agricultural extension has had to be economically self-reliant, which has led to extension officers either starting their own business or being called for other duties so that only about one-third of their work time is spent on agricultural extension (Jin et al. 2015). This situation has led to farmers basically relying on the pesticide-use manual to determine their pesticide use. Jin et al. (2015) show how 66 per cent of their survey's farmers buy pesticides in local family-run shops. To maintain good relations with farmers, owners of such shops recommend high dosages so that they will not be responsible for possible crop loss. As a result, 73.4 per cent of the survey farmers use double the amount recommended on the pesticide manual, 14 per cent use more than double and only 12.6 per cent use the recommended amount. Particularly elder farmers seem to be in need for further training on pesticide use (Fan et al. 2015).

Fertilizer policies

According to Robert B. Marks (2012), by the second half of the eighteenth century already, 'population growth, efficient markets, and state interests were propelling China toward more intensive use of existing natural resources, to conflict over the use of those resources, and toward the limits of empire' (ibid., 251). Therefore, 'the Chinese Communists were to inherit a seriously degraded natural environment' (ibid., 253), and in particular nitrogen was deficient in nearly all of China's cultivated land. By 1949, only two chemical fertilizer plants existed in China, and *some* additional fertilizer plants were built in the 1960s. This all changed with the visit of US president Richard Nixon in 1972, subsequent to which China ordered 'thirteen of the world's largest synthetic ammonia complexes for producing nitrogen-based chemical fertilizer' (ibid., 274). More chemical plants were to follow, and the country developed its own capacity to build chemical fertilizer plants in the 1980s, became self-sufficient in the 1990s and started to export chemical fertilizer by the turn of the millennium.

Nowadays, according to World Bank data (World Bank 2016b) from 2013, 364.4 kilograms of fertilizer per hectare (of arable land) are applied in China, considerably more than in the

---

General objectives and specific targets
Action Plan for Zero Growth in the Application of Fertilizers

General agenda: *Based on the general objective to warrant the country's food security and to guarantee the efficient supply of important agricultural products, the paradigm of "increase the production of manure, fertilizer and organic fertilizer" should rely on scientific and technological progress, as well as on new business entities and professional agro-chemical service organizations. It should focus on a continuous and holistic implementation, accelerate the transition in fertilization methods, further promote "scientific fertilization", spend great efforts on protecting and improving soil quality, increase the use of organic fertilizer, reduce irrational investment in chemical fertilizers, strengthen training, dissemination and fertilizer management, follow the road of "high yield, high efficiency", strengthen high quality environmental protection and sustainable development, promote the increase in food production, farmers' increase in incomes and their environmental safety.*

Objectives and tasks: *By 2020, a first "scientific fertilizer management and technology system" has been set up, the level of scientific fertilization has significantly increased. From 2015 to 2019, the annual growth rate of fertilizer use will be contained within a 1% increase; until 2020, hard work is needed to achieve zero growth in fertilizer use quantity on main agricultural crops.*

1 *The fertilizer structure is further optimized: by 2020, the nutrient structure of nitrogen, phosphorous, potassium and other trace elements tends to be reasonable, and there is rational use of organic fertilizer. The coverage rate of soil testing technology is higher than 90%; 60% of the livestock manure is used on the field, i.e. an increase by 10%; the straw recycling rate achieves 60%, i.e. an increase by 25%.*
2 *Fertilizer application methods are further improved: by 2020, oblivious and excessive fertilizer use is basically kept within limits, traditional ways of applying fertilizer have been changed. Mechanized fertilization accounts for more than 40% of the agricultural area under the main crops, which implies an increase by 10%; integrated water and fertilization technology is distributed on an area of 150 million mu, i.e. an increase by 80 million mu.*
3 *Steady increase in fertilizer utilization rate: from 2015 onwards, the average crop fertilizer utilization rate increases by an average of 1% or more annually, and hard work is needed to achieve a fertilization rate of 40% for the main agricultural crops by 2020.*

Figure 9.3 Agenda, objectives and tasks for fertilizer use until 2020

Source: MoA 2015.

United States (131.9 kg/ha), the Netherlands (231.1 kg/ha), or the United Kingdom (246.6 kg/ha). As can be seen from Figure 9.4, total chemical fertilizer use increased tremendously between 1995 and 2014, i.e. by 66.85 per cent.

Given the politics of self-sufficiency, rising living standards and shrinking per capita area of arable land, fertilizer use is likely to remain high. The most notable effort to curb excessive fertilizer use is the *Action Plan for Zero Growth in the Application of Fertilizers* that was launched in 2015. Figure 9.3 shows the inherent conflicts in fertilizer policies: The 'general agenda' starts out with an emphasis on the nation's food security, and remains with the objective to increase fertilizer production, albeit under conditions of improved production and application. Figure 9.3 also shows how a shift from 'traditional farming' to 'new business entities' is foreseen, which will be further examined in the final section of this chapter.

Manure management

Whereas in 1991, nitrate in the North China Plain mainly originated from inefficient chemical fertilizer use, in 2001, fertilizer along with untreated domestic wastewater and seepage from manure and urine were the major sources (Chen 2010). Ten years later, MEP reports that

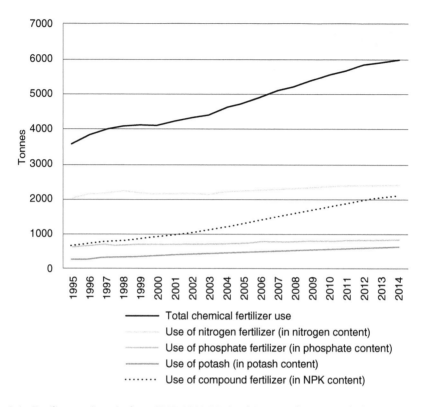

Figure 9.4 Fertilizer use in agriculture 1995–2014 (National Bureau of Statistics of China 2016)

livestock production is responsible for 38 per cent of agricultural nitrogen and 56 per cent of agricultural phosphorous non-point source pollution (Zheng et al. 2014).

As shown in the introduction, livestock production has increased significantly over the last decades. At the same time, a transition in livestock farm scales has taken place that may to some extent have contributed to the increased environmental pollution. Traditionally, pig breeding has taken place on the scale of a farm household, with the manure of a few pigs being used as organic fertilizer on the farmland (Bluemling and Hu 2011). With increased demand for meat, an intensification of livestock breeding has taken place, which was also promoted and institutionalized as part of the New Socialist Countryside (*Xin Nongcun*) programme that was launched in 2006. Nowadays, only 51 per cent of the pig production comes from household-scale farms, 22 per cent from large- and 27 per cent from medium-scale farms (Zheng et al. 2014). Large- and medium-scale livestock production are confronted with limitations in land where to dispose of manure (Zheng et al. 2014). Large-scale farms are monitored by Environmental Protection Bureaus since 2001, based on management measures for pollution control and standards of pollutant discharge (Zheng et al. 2015). This leaves medium-scale farms (with up to 1,000 pigs) as reportedly the laggards in mitigating environmental pollution (Zheng et al. 2014), and an important source for manure pollution in rural China.

In a situation where monitoring of dispersed livestock farms becomes difficult, the Ministry of Agriculture initiated a programme to support the recycling of manure. Chinese agriculture has a certain tradition of taking a system perspective on nutrient use, e.g. in the 'fruit tree and fish pond' agro-ecosystem, the muck from fish is scooped up from the bottom of the fish pond and used to

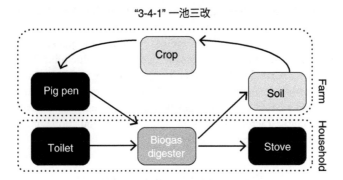

Figure 9.5 Eco-engineering model for livestock emission reduction

Source: Author.

fertilize fruit trees and rice fields (Marks 2012, 249). Also, wet-rice cultivation enhances soil fertility through nutrient recycling (Marks 2012, 115f.). In the case of livestock breeding, a new 'eco-engineering model' (Bluemling and Hu 2011) should resolve emission problems from agriculture by means of creating multiple positive incentives and feedback loops (see Figure 9.5).

In 2003, the Chinese government initiated a large-scale programme in which the construction of biogas digesters with livestock farms was promoted and subsidized. By the end of 2011, 40 million rural households (33 per cent of households suitable for biogas production) had biogas digesters and 80,000 communities had a collective biogas digester (He et al. 2013). Medium-scale livestock farms are in principle required to build a biogas digester in order to guarantee manure waste collection. The biogas can be used for lighting or for heating piglet sheds. In the household systems, manure and excreta are collected in the biogas digester and hence do not drain into and pollute the environment (see Figure 9.5). Households value improved sanitary conditions in both the village and the household even more than the production of biogas (He et al. 2013). After processing in the digester, the sludge can be applied to the field as organic fertilizer. The production of biogas in turn should replace the use of traditional biomass fuels, i.e. of straws and firewood. Traditional biomass stoves emit Particular Matter, which can lead to respiratory diseases. Household members do not have to spend time, or spend less time, on the collection of firewood, as well as for cooking. Farm households can furthermore save money, which they had previously spent on other fuel and chemical fertilizer.

Hence, this eco-engineering model works through integrating different emission streams and converting them into yields. It offers multiple incentives to maintain the system, and in this way provides reason for farmers to adopt it. However, many household biogas digesters have been discontinued (Bluemling 2013). Societal changes due to outmigration, the speediness of the biogas project's implementation (He et al. 2013) and the government's 'infrastructure-focused approach' (Tao and Xin 2014, 527) have had their effect on discontinuation.

Implementation effectiveness

To decrease environmental hazards from agriculture, the government regulates, on one side of the agricultural production chain, agro-chemical industries, and on the other side of the chain, the environmental improvements in the agricultural sector depend crucially on farmers' likelihood to change their behaviour in response to regulation. While the Chinese government has launched various policies to mitigate environmental harm from agriculture, implementation effectiveness has often been low (see e.g. Aarnoudse et al. 2012; Qu et al. 2013; Li et al. 2014). At times, governmental regulation reaches out to only some farmers (see e.g. Zheng et al. 2014; Qu et al. 2013). In other cases, the use of subsidized technology is quickly outpaced by societal developments, as in the case of household biogas digesters (see Bluemling 2013).

In China, as in many Asian developing countries, agriculture is still to a major extent carried out by small-scale producers. As the following section will argue, efforts aiming at modifying their resources use practices have been 'regulating by model emulation'. However, with the diversification of agricultural actors in rural China, this kind of regulation is increasingly replaced by regulatory pluralism (van Rooij et al. 2016).

Regulation by model emulation

As China's rural society has been composed of smallholders for decades, agricultural policy has been regarded not only as a matter of crop or livestock production in a narrow sense, but also as a societal endeavour. This is best expressed in the term '*san nong*', i.e. 'the three rural issues', i.e. agriculture (*nongye*), rural areas (*nongcun*) and farmers (*nongmin*). The meaning of '*san nong*' is that if one targets one of the three rural issues, the other two also need to be addressed. Against this background, it may become clear why policy that is designed to target agriculture often takes a societal approach in China. For example, to increase agricultural water-use efficiency and improve water management, the Chinese Ministry of Water Resources launched the 'water saving society' in 2006. In 2007, the 'ecological civilization' was launched as a national programme, and it is still part of the National Plan for Sustainable Agriculture. In the frame of such plans and programmes, ministries are creating a discourse within which 'models' are established that exemplify the integrative view on the goals to be achieved.

Regulation by model emulation is regulation that is based on emulation as a social process to implement a certain policy. In rural China, signs are common with '示范', i.e. *shifan* on the walls of dwellings, village community centres, companies or schools, for example. *Shifan* can be loosely translated as 'model'. A model is the embodiment of an ideal theme, an 'ideal point of orientation' (Cua 2007). If a county, village, school, company or household has attained certain achievements, it may be awarded the status of a *shifan*. Media will report about, and policy-makers promote the *shifan*, and a sign is put up in a publicly visible place which indicates that this village (or household, company, farm) has performed outstandingly. These promotional activities invite other social entities to emulate, i.e. to learn from and follow, the *shifan*. Model emulation hence is a social process implemented through shared narratives and practices, which are evoked by 'state frames' (Mertha 2009) provided by media and governmental propaganda for the interpretation of the model.

Model emulation is partially rooted in Chinese culture, partially rooted in socialism. Socialist model emulation has not only been employed in China, but also in Cuba and the Soviet Union (Cheng 2009). However, it is also a crucial concept in Confucianism (Tan 2005; Cua 2007; Shen 2008). In China, model emulation is established in Article 42 of the Constitution, which declares that the state 'promotes socialist labour emulation, and commends and rewards model and advanced workers'. Emulation however does not address individuals only. Its regulatory power increases when it involves communities, as in the case of 'village *shifan'*.

A variety of governmental policies have been implemented in agriculture with the help of *shifan* emulation. In 2007, the government enacted the policy of creating an 'eco-civilization' (*shengtai wenming*), in which village *shifan* play a crucial role. Villages can become an 'eco-civilization' *shifan*, i.e. an 'exemplary embodiment' (Shen 2008, 53) of the government's ideal theme. Several criteria must be met. They are not only environmental (e.g. pollution control, conservation of natural resources), but also address energy use (i.e. degree of 'clean energy' use, e.g. biogas), economic development (average net income per capita) and agricultural practices (e.g. low pesticide use). Hence, a village *shifan* does not embody the 'eco-civilization' in a technical way. It furthermore does not necessarily address a particular environmental problem. It is a comprehensive localized societal effort, entailing a diversity of changes within local society towards environmental improvement. An 'eco-civilization' village is a situation that shall be created and reproduced through local interactions within the *gemeinschaft* (see e.g. Lai 2007; Ames 1998), leading to the emergence of norms and rules which are realized in villagers' practices and memorized in villagers' narratives (see Tan 2005). A *gemeinschaft* hence is a basic condition.

Regulation by *shifan* emulation presumes a society that is relatively homogeneous as it can find itself in the models and emulate from them. However, the Chinese countryside has been undergoing major changes: In 2000, the agricultural workforce made up 66.6 per cent of the total labour force, and fifteen years later, only 57.8 per cent of China's workforce worked in agriculture. The 'hollowing out' of the Chinese countryside has led to a loss of social structure by means of which processes of model emulation work. Besides *shifan* emulation, other forms of regulation hence have emerged.

Regulatory pluralism

Responding to the long-term trend of outmigration from the countryside, and the related increase in farmland per farm, the government has promulgated the 'new professional farmer' (*xinxing zhiye nongmin*) as the new target for its agricultural policy. While smallholders have been pursuing agriculture as only one source of income, this new type of farmer is presumed to pursue agriculture as the main source of income, therefore to work more professionally and to have 'scientific and cultural qualities' and management skills that suit modern agricultural production.

While the above definition is a rather idealized view of a new emerging entity in agriculture, it does find resonance. Already the *National Plan for Sustainable Agriculture (2015–2030)*, the *Action Plan for Zero Growth in the Application of Fertilizers* and the *Action Plan for Zero Growth in the Application of Pesticides* stress that they intend to rely on 'new agricultural business entities' (*xinxing nongye jingying zhuti*) to achieve their targets. Empirical research shows that there is a variety of new entities. In the livestock sector, intensive livestock medium-scale and large-scale farms are likely to be 'new entities' (Zheng et al. 2014). For each of them, different policy measures are effective (Zheng et al. 2015).

Not all 'new agro-business entities' are furthermore composed of one single farm. Li et al. (2016) show how in forestry, different kinds of governance modes are created by smallholders, ranging from a few farmers joining together in a 'partnership' to the village taking the role of the rural entrepreneur and farmers participating in the village scheme to varying degrees. Dragon-head enterprises are yet another new kind of farm in rural China which consists of a 'headquarters' and numerous smaller-scale farms as a 'tail' who deliver their agricultural products to the headquarters. Regulation of agricultural production within the 'dragon-head enterprise' varies, but, in principle, dragon-heads regulate through standardization of agricultural inputs and in this way can also reduce environmental impact.

With the development of different 'new agro-business entities', a regulatory pluralism evolves that requires robust institutions to be effective. As Li et al. (2014) show, without such robust formal institutions, the time perspectives of the different actors involved in agro-environmental problems are likely to not bring about those long-term solutions that are required for environmental protection. 'Time perspectives' are 'composite cognitive structures that characterize the way an individual projects, collects, accesses, values, and organizes events that reside in distinct temporal loci' (Hoogstra 2008). Some actors involved in agro-ecological institutional arrangements (farmers, local government staff) focus on annual income revenue (see Li et al. 2014). Other actors (e.g. NGOs, the central government) focus on longer-term agro-environmental improvements. New institutions therefore need to be able to make diverging (time) perspectives converge if environmental deterioration is to be put to a halt.

References

Aarnoudse, E., Bluemling, B., Wester, P. and Qu W., 2012. The Role of Collective Groundwater Institutions in the Implementation of Direct Groundwater Regulation Measures in Minqin County, China. *Hydrogeology Journal*, 20(7), 1213–1221.

Ames, R.T. (ed.), 1998. *Wandering at Ease at the Zhuangzi*. Albany, USA: State University of New York Press.

Bluemling, B., 2013. Synopsis of the Special Issue Section 'The social organization of agricultural biogas production and use', *Energy Policy*, 63, 52–54.

Bluemling, B. and Hu C.S., 2011. Vertical and System Integration Instead of Integrated Water Management? Measures for Mitigating NPSP in Rural China. GroundWater 2011, Conference: Gestion des ressources en eau souterraine. Orléans, France, 14–16 March 2011.

Chen J.Y., 2010. Holistic Assessment of Groundwater Resources and Regional Environmental Problems in the North China Plain. *Environmental Earth Sciences,* 61, 1037–1047.

Cheng Y.H., 2009. *Creating the New Man: From Enlightenment Ideals to Socialist Realities*. Honolulu: University of Hawai'i Press.

COWI, 2013. Groundwater in China. Part 1 – Occurrence and Use. Ministry of the Environment, Nature Agency, June 2013. Kongens Lyngby, Denmark. http://cewp.org/wp-content/uploads/2014/08/Groundwater-in-China_Part-1_Occurrence-and-Use_COWI.pdf (accessed 17 December 2016).

Cua A.S., 2007. Virtues of *junzi*. *Journal of Chinese Philosophy,* 34(Supplement s1), 125–143.

Earth Security Initiative, 2014. *The Earth Security Index 2014.* http://esi.archivestudio.co.uk/index/1533_ESI_RSI_31.pdf (accessed 16 December 2016).

Fan L.; Niu H.; Yang X.; Qin W.; Bento, C.P.M.; Ritsema, C.J. and Geissen, V., 2015. Factors Affecting Farmers' Behaviour in Pesticide Use: Insights from a Field Study in Northern China. *Science of the Total Environment,* 537, 350–358.

FAO (Food and Agriculture Organization of the United Nations), 2015. Progress in Pesticide Risk Assessment and Phasing-Out of Highly Hazardous Pesticides in Asia. Food and Agriculture Organization of the United Nations Regional Office for Asia and the Pacific, RAP Publication 2015/01. Bangkok.

FAO Food and Agriculture Organization of the United Nations, 2016. *Aquastat.* http://www.fao.org/nr/water/aquastat/main/index.stm (accessed 27 July 2016).

Groundwater Monitoring Centre, 2016. Groundwater Dynamics Report. Ministry of Water Resources, Beijing (in Chinese).

He G.Z.; Bluemling, B.; Mol, A.P.J.; Zhang L. and Lu Y.L., 2013. Comparing Centralized and Decentralized Bio-Energy Systems in Rural China. *Energy Policy*, 63, 34–43.

Hoogstra, M.A., 2008. Coping with the Long Term – An Empirical Analysis of Time Perspectives, Time Orientations, and Temporal Uncertainty in Forestry. PhD Thesis, Wageningen University. Wageningen, The Netherlands.

Jin S.; Bluemling, B.; and Mol, A.P.J., 2015. Information, Trust and Pesticide Overuse. *NJAS – Wageningen Journal of Life Sciences* 72–73, 23–32.

Jin S., Bluemling, B. and Mol, A.P.J., 2017. Mitigating Land Pollution through Pesticide Packages – The Case of a Collection Scheme in Rural China. *Journal of Cleaner Production* (under review).

Kanaly, R.A.; Manzanero, L.I.O.; Foley, G.; Panneerselvam, S. and Macer, D., 2010. Energy Flow, Environment and Ethical Implications for Meat Production. Ethics and Climate Change in Asia and the Pacific (ECCAP) Project, Working Group 13 Report. Bangkok: UNESCO.

Lai K.L., 2007. Understanding change: The Interdependent Self in its Environment. *Journal of Chinese Philosophy,* 34(Supplement s1), 81–99.

Li J.; Bluemling, B.; Mol, A.P.J. and Herzfeld, T., 2014. Stagnating Jatropha Biofuel Development in Southwest China – an Institutional Approach. *Sustainability,* 6(6), 3192–3212.

Li J.; Bluemling, B. and Dries, L., 2016. Property Rights Effects on Farmers' Management Investment in Forestry Projects: The Case of Camellia in Jiangxi, China. *Small-scale Forestry* 15, 271–289.

Liu E.K.; He W.Q. and Yan C.R., 2014. 'White Revolution' to 'White Pollution' – Agricultural Plastic Film Mulch in China. *Environmental Research Letters,* 9, 091001.

Liu H., 2015. *China's Long March to Safe Drinking Water.* China Water Risk / chinadialogue, March 2015. http://chinawaterrisk.org/wp-content/uploads/2015/03/Chinas-Long-March-To-Drinking-Water-2015-EN.pdf (accessed 17 December 2016).

McBeath, J. and McBeath, J.H., 2010. Environmental Degradation and Food Security Policies in China. In: Kassiola, J.J.; Guo S. (eds.), *China's Environmental Crisis – Domestic and Global Political Impacts and Responses.* New York: Palgrave MacMillan, 85–119.

Marks, R.B., 2012. *China: its Environment and History.* Plymouth: Rowman & Littlefield.

MEP (Ministry of Environmental Protection), 2014a. National Environmental Report [*Zhongguo Huanjing Zhuangkuang Gongbao*]. Ministry of Environmental Protection of the People's Republic of China.

MEP (Ministry of Environmental Protection), 2014b. Ministry of Environmental Protection and the Ministry of Land Resources Publish a Report on a Nationwide Survey of Soil Pollution [*Huanjing baohu bu he guotu ziyuan bu fabu quanguo turang wuran zhuangkuang diaocha gongbao*]. Ministry of Environmental Protection of the People's Republic of China. http://www.mep.gov.cn/gkml/hbb/qt/201404/t20140417_270670.htm (accessed 20 November 2015).

Mertha, A., 2009. 'Fragmented Authoritarianism 2.0' – Political Pluralization in the Chinese Policy Process. *The China Quarterly,* 200, 995–1012.

MoA (Ministry of Agriculture) *Nongyebu Guanyu Yinfa,* 2015. '*Dao 2020 nian huafei shiyongliang ling zengchang xingdong fang'an' he 'Dao 2020 nian nongyao shiyongliang ling zengchang xingdong fang'an' de tongzhi. Nongyebu Zhongzhiye Guanli* (Ministry of Agriculture about 'Action Plan concerning the zero growth in application of chemical fertilizers by 2020' and 'Action Plan concerning the zero growth in application of pesticides by 2020') http://www.moa.gov.cn/zwllm/tzgg/tz/201503/t20150318_4444765.htm (accessed 26 July 2016).

Nathanson, J.A., 2016. Land Pollution. Encyclopaedia Britannica online, updated 14.03.2016. https://www.britannica.com/science/land-pollution (accessed 26 August 2016).

National Bureau of Statistics of China, 2016. National Data. http://data.stats.gov.cn/easyquery.htm?cn=C01 (accessed 28 July 2016).

NDRC (National Development and Reform Committee), 2010. *National Rural Drinking Water Safety Project (Public Draft). Together with Ministry of Water Resources, Ministry of Health, Ministry of Environmental Protection* (in Chinese). http://www.sdpc.gov.cn/zcfb/zcfbghwb/201402/P020140221360445500781.pdf (accessed 29 July 2016).

PAN (Pesticide Action Network International), 2010. *Communities in Peril: Global Report on Health Impacts of Pesticide Use in Agriculture.* Manila, Philippines: Red Leaf Printing Press.

PAN (Pesticide Action Network International), 2015. *PAN International Consolidated List of Banned Pesticides.* Pesticide Action Network International. http://pan-international.org/pan-international-consolidated-list-of-banned-pesticides/ (accessed 17 December 2016).

Qu W.; Tu Q. and Bluemling, B., 2013. Which factors Are Effective for Farmers' Biogas Use? Evidence from a Large-Scale Survey in China. *Energy Policy,* 63, 26–33.

Shapiro, J., 2001. *Mao's War against Nature – Politics and the Environment in Revolutionary China.* Cambridge: Cambridge University Press.

Shen V. 2008. Antonio Cua's conceptual analysis of Confucian ethics. *Journal of Chinese Philosophy,* 35(1), 43–61.

State Council, 2011. *Guowuyuan fazhi bangongshi guanyu gongbu nongyao guanli tiaoli gongkai zhengqiu yijian de tongzhi.* (Legislative Affairs Office of the State Council announces a public comment notice on the 'Pesticide Management Regulations (draft)'). Legislative Affairs Office of the State Council P.R. China, 20.07.2011. http://www.chinalaw.gov.cn/article/cazjgg/201107/20110700345296.shtml (accessed 26 August 2015).

Tan S.-H., 2005. Imagining Confucius: Paradigmatic characters and virtue ethics. *Journal of Chinese Philosophy,* 32(3), 409–426.

Tao T. and Xin K., 2014. A sustainable plan for China's drinking water. *Nature,* 511, 527–528.

Tilt, B., 2010. *The Struggle for Sustainability in Rural China – Environmental Values and Civil Society*. New York: Columbia University Press.

UN News Centre, 2010. Land Degradation among China's Food Supply Challenges, Says UN Expert. [23 December 2010] UN News Centre, http://www.un.org/apps/news/story.asp?NewsID=37151# (accessed 26 August 2016).

Van Rooij, B.; Stern, R.E. and Fuerst, K., 2016. The Authoritarian Logic of Regulatory Pluralism: Understanding China's New Environmental Actors. *Regulation & Governance*, 10, 3–13.

World Bank, 2016a. *World Development Indicators* http://databank.worldbank.org/data/reports.aspx?Code=CHN&id=556d8fa6&report_name=Popular_countries&populartype=country&ispopular=y# (accessed 27 July 2016).

World Bank 2016b, *Indicators*. http://data.worldbank.org/indicator/ (accessed 28 July 2016).

Xinhua, 2015. Report: China confident of food self-sufficiency. *Xinhua*, 20.04.2015. http://english.gov.cn/news/top_news/2015/04/20/content_281475092700264.htm (accessed 23 March 2016).

Zhang Y., 2014 Soil Quality in China – Policy Implications. Short Term Policy Brief 98, Europe China Research and Advice Network (ECRAN). http://eeas.europa.eu/archives/docs/china/docs/division_ecran/ecran_is121_paper_97_chinese_thinking_on_eu-china_relations_mathieu_duchatel_en.pdf (accessed 16 December 2016).

Zheng C.; Bluemling, B.; Liu Y.; Mol, A.P.J. and Chen J., 2014. Managing Manure from China's Pigs and Poultry: The Influence of Ecological Rationality. *AMBIO*, 43(5), 661–672.

Zheng C.; Liu Y.; Bluemling, B.; Mol, A.P.J. and Chen J., 2015. Environmental Potentials of Policy Instruments to Mitigate Nutrient Emissions in Chinese Livestock Production. *Science of the Total Environment*, 502, 149–156.

Zhou J. and Jin S., 2013. Food safety management in China – A Perspective from Food Quality Control System. Singapore: World Scientific Publishing.

10

CONSERVING CHINA'S BIOLOGICAL DIVERSITY

National plans, transnational projects, local and regional challenges

Chris Coggins

Our hunting chariots so lovely,
Our four steeds so strong,
We climb that high hill
Chasing the herds of game...
Here the beasts congregate,
Doe and stag abound,
We have drawn our bows...
We shoot that little boar,
We fell that great wild ox.
So that we have something to offer, for guest, for stranger,
To go with the heavy wine.

From 'Lucky Day', The Book of Songs
(Minor Odes, 900–800 BCE)[1]

Fallen nuts mark the monkeys' trail,
Dry leaves rustle to the passage of deer.
A plain zither [guqin] – an untrammeled heart –
Hollowly accompanies the clear spring at night.

From 'Early Autumn in the Mountains'
by Wen Tingyun (812–870)[2]

Introduction

As these poems suggest, wild landscapes and their fauna and flora have long figured prominently in Chinese literature, just as they have in painting, music and other artistic traditions. Since at least the Zhou Dynasty (1046–256 BCE), detailed renderings of hunting, plant-gathering and observing the mystery and beauty of nature have given rise to aesthetic norms based on biophilia – a sense of wonder for the living world and the myriad organisms and landscapes that thrive beyond the cities, towns, fields, and fences that have come to define the human domain (Kellert and Wilson 1993). While the first poem describes a royal hunt conducted in chariots on the plains of the Yellow River valley, celebrating the valour of hunters and the bounty of game harvested for a noble feast, the second describes a time when wildlife had grown scarce in the north – the mountain setting lies far from Tang Dynasty (618–906) centres of power. The soft tones of the ancient zither blend with the footfalls of passing deer; the feeding signs of monkeys mark their passage. These images forge a strong connection between civilization (*wenming*) and the human capacity to appreciate the intricate beauty of wild things, a sensibility viewed by the elite as a hallmark of culture (*wenhua*).[3] Centuries before this poem was written, classical Daoist philosophy promoted a worldview in which human activities emerge from the folds of an organically evolving cosmos. The related conception of *tian ren he yi* – humans and nature (or the cosmos) conjoined – has found resonance within modern environmental discourse worldwide, but the history of Chinese civilization is also a history of state formation, warfare, and radical environmental transformation based on the domestication of landscapes and the reconfiguration of ecosystems to meet human demands. This has entailed widespread and intensive ecological disturbance and a radical reduction in the ranges and populations of numerous species of plants and animals. Indeed, as in the case of all complex, socially stratified agrarian civilizations based on centralized power, ecological degradation and resource drawdown have been ubiquitous features of the Chinese imperium since early historical times, and there has always been a significant contradiction between reverence for nature, on the one hand, and the commodification and exploitation of natural resources, on the other.[4] More recently, especially during the Maoist period (1949–1976), natural resource extraction accelerated unmediated by reverence for non-human life forms or the integrity of ecological systems; 'nature' was assessed in terms of immediate instrumental value for industrial economic development and agrarian socialism. China's contemporary nature conservation policies and the daunting challenges of ecosystem restoration must be understood in the context of long-term environmental history, including the latest chapters – the Maoist 'war on nature', the plethora of environmental problems associated with post-reform industrial capitalism, and recent state campaigns to build an 'ecological civilization' (*shengtai wenming*).

This chapter provides an overview of China's terrestrial biodiversity and species loss, with a brief history of people, plants, and wildlife since imperial times; the rise of a national nature conservation system that articulates with global networks of transnational nature conservation; and how the emerging system affects the protection of biodiversity at local and regional levels. Over the last 35 years, despite a plethora of environmental problems, many government agencies and citizens of the PRC have made tremendous strides to protect biodiversity and make nature conservation part of the definition of contemporary Chinese civilization. The rapid movement toward an accountable, reliable, and durable system of nature conservation based on protecting biological diversity marks a sea change in Chinese conceptions of nature – 'biodiversity' is a new term and a recently articulated concept, emerging in Anglophone literature only in the 1980s, and being translated into Mandarin (as *shengwu duoyangxing*) still more recently. As a foundation for understanding and protecting the stunning array of landscapes, ecosystems, habitats and organisms that compose China's biological heritage, biodiversity is generating new ways of understanding the world and what it means to be human, even as it articulates with older forms of reverence for nature. As is true in other countries, biodiversity management is also giving rise to new institutional structures, new policies on resource regulation, and new forms of political conflict and negotiation.

China's biological diversity in geographic perspective

Biodiversity is 'the variability among living organisms from all sources including, *inter alia*, terrestrial, marine and other aquatic ecosystems and the ecological complexes of which they are a part; this includes [genetic] diversity within species, between species, and of ecosystems' (UN 1992, 3; Wilson 2002). Biodiversity is foundational for human survival, providing critical resources for socio-economic development and secure livelihood, including food, medicine, clean water, timber, energy, a variety of industrial products and myriad ecosystem services.

China's high biodiversity is a function of long-term biological adaptation and speciation within a highly diverse range of landforms, climate zones, vegetation types, and ecosystems covering an area slightly larger than the United States. Elevations range from Earth's highest point, the summit of Mount Everest (8,850 m, 29,035 ft asl), to Ayding Lake in the Turpan Depression in Xinjiang (−154 m, −505 ft asl), and China's diversity of landforms increases the diversity of local and regional climate patterns and ecological systems. Chinese scientists have delineated five topographic macro-regions: Eastern China which is subdivided into the Northeast Plain, North China Plain and Southern Hills; Xinjiang–Mongolia; and the Qinghai–Tibet High Plateau. Landforms include snow-capped mountains, deep river valleys, broad basins, high plateaus, rolling plains, terraced hills, sand dunes, craggy karst, volcanic calderas, low-latitude glaciers and myriad variations of each. The land is generally high in the west and descends to the east coast. Mountains, plateaus, and hills comprise close to 70 per cent of the country's land surface. This has been critical for the persistence of China's flora and fauna because most of the country's arable land and human population are found in lowland plains (12 per cent of the land area) and basins (19 per cent), and much of the latter are not arable because they occur in desert zones in the north and northwest (CHEC 2002).

Over the span of evolutionary time, China's complex terrain has not only undergone dramatic changes in geology and climate, but also played host to plants and animals associated with two of the world's eight ecozones – the humid tropical and subtropical Indomalaya Ecozone, which includes South and Southeast Asia, and the temperate and cold Palearctic Ecozone, which is associated with Central Asia, Russia, and Europe. China is a mixing ground for organisms associated with these distinctive biogeographic zones, thus the fauna and flora have formed unusually diverse assemblages. *In situ* evolution and vicariant events[5] have also resulted in high levels of endemism. China's eight major vegetation regions reflect this diversity at a general level (Figure 10.1). The border between the two ecozones in China is known as the Qinling (Mountain)–Huai River Ecotone, an approximate line (and actually a mixing zone itself) that divides the humid tropics and subtropics of the south from temperate, cold, and dry regions further north and west. South of the line lie the tropical monsoonal rain forest and subtropical broadleaved evergreen forest regions, comprising China's Indomalaya Ecozone. North and west of the line lie the Palearctic vegetation regions, which include deciduous forest throughout the North China Plain and parts of the Loess Plateau; mixed conifer and hardwood forest in the northeast; steppe grasslands across Inner Mongolia; highland deserts in northwestern China; and a variety of highland vegetation types across the Qinghai–Tibet Plateau and the Himalayas. These vegetation regions are products of long-term adaptation to China's monsoonal climate, which is associated with a markedly decreasing precipitation gradient from the south and eastern coasts to the western and northern interior zones. The western boundary of the potentially forested regions is roughly defined by a 38 cm (15 inch) isohyet (line of equal precipitation), west of which lies the steppe, highland vegetation and highland desert (CHEC 2002).

This remarkable array of ecoregions accounts to a large degree for China's high species richness despite more than four millennia of intensive land use and environmental transformation.

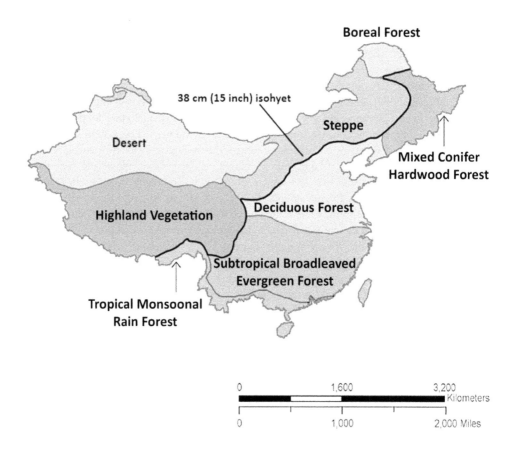

Figure 10.1 The vegetation regions of China. The 38 cm (15 inch) isohyet, or line of equal rainfall, separates the forested regions to the south and east, from the mostly non-forested regions to the north and west. In the latter regions, agriculture requires irrigation and pastoralism has long been the prevalent land-use practice.

Source: P. Tiso, A. Kalischer-Coggins, C. Coggins.

Today China is one of the world's most biologically diverse countries, identified by Conservation International in 1998 as one of the world's 17 megadiversity countries and the eighth most biologically diverse country after Brazil, Indonesia, Colombia, Mexico, Australia, Madagascar, and the Philippines. China has 6,347 species of vertebrates including 3,787 fish, 1,310 bird, 539 mammal, 390 reptile, and 321 amphibian species (Xu et al. 2008).[6] China ranks third in the world for mammals, with 9.8 per cent of the world's total; eighth for birds, with 12.6 per cent; and seventh for both reptiles and amphibians, with 3.4 per cent and 4.3 per cent respectively. In each of these categories, China is the most biodiverse country lying mostly outside of the tropics (Table 10.1). One way to grasp the level of mammalian diversity in China versus North America is to compare species within the order Artiodactyla (even-toed hoofed animals),[7] of which there are 43 species in China and only 15 in North America (encompassing the land areas of Canada, the US, and Mexico). High levels of endemism, represented by such well-known species as the giant panda and the Yangtze River dolphin are another indicator of biodiversity, and about one-sixth of China's mammal species and two-thirds of amphibians are endemic. There are 165 vertebrates in China on the International Union for the Conservation of Nature

Table 10.1 Known plant and vertebrate species in China

	Known Species in China (Vert. – Xu et al. 2008; Plants – Kram et al. 2012)	Critically Endangered Species in China (IUCN Red List)	Per cent Critically Endangered of Species in China	Endangered Species in China (IUCN Red List)	Per cent Endangered of Species in China	Known Species in World (IUCN Red List)	China Per cent of World Species	China World Ranking (Diverse Sources, Includes Endemism)
Mammals	539	13	2.40%	40	7.40%	5,488	9.8%	3rd
Birds	1,310	11	0.84%	16	1.20%	10,425	12.6%	8th
Reptiles	390	12	3.00%	18	4.60%	10,038	3.9%	7th
Amphibians	321	10	3.10%	35	10.90%	7,391	4.3%	7th
Fishes	3,787	9	0.24%	1	0.03%	33,100	11.4%	ND
Total Vertebrates	**6,347**	**55**	**0.87%**	**110**	**1.70%**	**66,469**	**9.5%★**	**5th**
Bryophytes	2,200	ND	ND	ND	ND	16,236	13.6%	ND
Pteridophytes	2,600	ND	ND	ND	ND	12,000	21.7%	ND
Gymnosperms	200	ND	ND	ND	ND	1,052	19%	ND
Angiosperms	25,000	ND	ND	ND	ND	268,000	9.3%	ND
Total Plants	**30,000**	ND	ND	ND	ND	297,288	10.1%	3rd

Source: Xu et al. 2008; Kram et al. 2012; CNBCSAP 2010; IUCN Red List 2015.

(IUCN) Red List of Critically Endangered or Endangered Species, and over 600 additional vertebrates are listed as Vulnerable. China's genetic diversity also includes crop resources such as rice, soybeans, and many species of wild and cultivated fruit trees (MEP 2014).

Biodiversity loss and present threats

During the long history of Chinese civilization, the highest levels of ecological disturbance have occurred in the forest ecoregions east and south of the 38 cm (15 inch) isohyet, each of which has undergone widespread conversion into agricultural zones with relatively high population densities. During the last 5,000 years of the Holocene, extinction and range reduction have been primarily a function of habitat loss and hunting pressure,[8] with a close correlation between the growth and expansion of Chinese civilization starting in the Bronze Age (2600–650 BCE), large-scale deforestation, and the population decline, range reduction and extinction of many vertebrates (Coggins 2003; Elvin 2004; Marks 2012). Responses to the wide array of ecological disturbances have not been uniform across taxa, and Chinese historical sources such as local gazetteers comprise a unique source of data on long-term range reduction among large and medium-sized vertebrates such as tigers, elephants, gibbons, monkeys, peacocks, alligators and dolphins.[9] Historical records also indicate that imperial governments established protected areas in selected forest zones, starting in the Qin and Han dynasties and extending through the Qing (1644–1911). Examples include mountain areas designated as imperial hunting reserves, Buddhist and Daoist temple and monastic grounds, and village common and sacred forests protected by government edicts and local custom (Menzies 1994; Marks 2012; Coggins 2014).

Ecological disturbance accelerated dramatically after the Chinese Communist Party (CCP) came to power, and the environmental impacts of the Maoist period (1949–1976) are well known. The Great Leap Forward (and Backyard Iron Smelting Movement) (1958–1960) and Cultural Revolution (1966–1976) were defined by fierce efforts to transform natural resources, including wild and domestic plants and animals, minerals, and water resources, into forms most useful for industrial development (Shapiro 2001; Coggins 2003; Marks 2012). Degradation of biodiversity was not simply a byproduct of agricultural expansion and industrial pollution, timber resources were exploited without long-term plans for regeneration or sustainable harvests. The Great Leap Forward has become known as 'the First Great Cutting', and the Cultural Revolution as 'the Second Great Cutting'.[10] Radical transformation of traditional perceptions of nature became explicit CCP doctrine, and the famous quasi-military campaigns against 'the Four Pests' (rats, flies, mosquitos and sparrows), beginning in 1958, were supplemented with less well-known anti-predator campaigns such as the 'Kill the Tiger movement' (*da hu yundong*), with its slogan 'Kill the tiger, banish evil' (*dahu chuhai*). Systematic tiger extermination carried out by teams of farmers and soldiers caused the decimation of a population of perhaps 2,000–4,000 in southern China, precipitating their extinction in the wild by the end of the century (Table 10.2) (Coggins 2003). From the 1950s through the early 1980s, numerous species of wild plants and animals were culled by rural residents and sold at state-run Foreign Trade Stations (*waimaozhan*) run by county Foreign Trade Bureaus (*waimaoju*), which purchased pelts, bones, fruits, roots, and other products for sale in urban centres and for international trade. Data from eight provinces in southern and central China show an average of 400 tiger pelts per year from 1951–1955, a figure that fell to less than ten in most provinces by the 1970s (Coggins 2003). While the systematic harvest of wild fauna and flora was guided and encouraged by the state, there were also small but significant efforts to protect nature.

Table 10.2 Modern conservation in China: policies, initiatives, milestones

Year(s)	Policies, Initiatives, Milestones
1950	First National Forestry Conference
1956	Seventh National Forestry Conference
1956	Establishment of Dinghushan Nature Reserve
1957–1965	Establishment of 18 additional nature reserves
1978	Total number of nature reserves: 34
1979	China begins first international conservation partnership, working with WWF (The Worldwide Fund for Nature) on panda conservation in Sichuan
1979–1981	Forestry Law of the PRC ratified (1979)
1979–1980	Changbaishan Biosphere Reserve established (1979)
1987	Total number of nature reserves: 481
1988	Wildlife Protection Law
1992	China signs the United Nations Convention on Biological Diversity (UNCBD) on 11 June
1994	Nature Reserve Law
1996	Firearms Control Law
1997	Total number of nature reserves: 926
1999	Sloping Lands Conversion Program (SLCP) aka 'Grain for Green' implemented
1999–2000	Natural Forest Protection Plan (NFPP), aka the 'logging ban' implemented
2000	TNC (The Nature Conservancy) initiates the Yunnan Great Rivers Project in NW Yunnan
2001	South China tiger determined to be most likely extinct in the wild
2003	Total number of nature reserves: 1,999
2007	Yangtze River dolphin declared 'extinct'; survey results published 2007
2007	Establishment of Pudacuo National Park (Shangrila County, Yunnan)
2007	Total number of nature reserves: 2,500
2009	Establishment of Meili Snow Mountains National Park and Shangrila Yunnan Golden Monkey National Park
2010	Promulgation of China National Biodiversity Conservation Strategy and Action Plan (NBSAP) 2011–2030
2010	State Council launches the National Plan for Major Function Zones
2010	Total number of nature reserves: 2,541 (all administrative levels)
2014	Promulgation of China's Fifth National Report on the Implementation of the Convention on Biological Diversity
2014	Establishment of 21 new national-level nature reserves established, bringing total national reserves to 428
2015	Total number of nature reserves: 2,671 (all administrative levels), 428 national nature reserves, reserves at all levels protecting 14.8% of China's total land area

History of Biodiversity Conservation

1949–1978: Selective conservation amid large-scale ecological disturbance

The First National Forestry Conference was held in 1950 and focused on the formulation of policies to protect forests, implement afforestation, and develop rational systems of timber harvest and utilization (Yang 2001). Biodiversity was not an operative concept; the goal was to afforest roughly 10 per cent of China's land area for watershed protection and timber production, especially on barren hillsides and mountain slopes using fast-growing species. The results were mixed to poor, with a net national forest loss of perhaps 25 per cent by 1962 (Robbins and Harrell 2014).

A critical exception emerged from the Third Meeting of the Number One People's Congress, in April 1956, with the approval of Proposal 12, designating logging ban areas in specific natural forests to protect wild fauna and flora. In the same year, the Seventh National Forestry Conference passed the *Draft Roles of the Natural Forest Logging Ban Areas* (aka nature reserves, *ziran baohuqu*) and the *Draft Plan for Hunting Control*, which led to the establishment of China's first nature reserve in Dinghushan, in Guangdong Province, designed to protect southern subtropical monsoon rain forest (Xu 2005; McBeath and Leng 2006). Biologists played important roles in locating, justifying, and designating reserves, and they often had to do so on strictly pragmatic grounds, as in the case of Letu Subtropical Rain Forest Reserve in Nanjing County Fujian. This former village *fengshui* forest – a type of traditional sacred forest in southern China (Coggins 2003, 2014) – was granted official status as a nature reserve in 1958, when a courageous and adroit biology professor from Xiamen University named He Jing argued that liana species in Letu might have value for latex production (Lin, personal communication 2014). Although the 1956 law stated that 'forestry reserves must be designated in the woodlands and grasslands of all areas … to preserve the original state of fauna and flora in each region' (Li and Zhao 1989, 11–12), only 19 reserves were established over the next ten years. These were not subject to uniform national laws or regulatory codes, and a net loss of habitat combined with uncontrolled hunting and gathering caused radical declines in the populations and ranges of numerous species of fauna and flora (Li and Zhao 1989; Harris 2008).

1979–1996: The rise of a national nature conservation system and initial alliances with global conservation organizations

The beginning of the reform period in 1978–1979 gave rise to deep ideological and structural changes for nature conservation in China, marking the beginning of a 35-year period of exponential growth in the number of protected areas in China with a concomitant reconfiguration of official discourse and practice. In 1979, China entered its first international conservation partnership, working with WWF (The World Wide Fund for Nature) on panda conservation in Sichuan. In the same year, the Ministry of Forestry passed the *Forestry Law of the PRC*, calling for the establishment of nature reserves in places of special ecological value, and held official meetings and symposia with the National Committee of Man and the Biosphere. These were the first meetings held by national government organs to develop a system of protected areas in China, and they established a tripartite zonation system based on the biosphere reserve model, which includes a core area of strict protection, a buffer zone of mixed land use and human settlement, and a transition or cooperation zone. In Chinese reserves, the latter is called an 'experimental zone' (*shiyanqu*), denoting that it can be used for experimental land use or scientific research (Li and Zhao 1989). Within the first eight years of the reform period, the number of nature reserves grew from 34 to 481, a 15-fold increase, and Changbaishan was China's first biosphere reserve to join the international UNESCO Man and the Biosphere Programme (MAB) biosphere reserve system in 1980. In 1986, WWF established a tropical rain forest conservation project in southern Yunnan's Xishuangbanna (Hathaway 2013). At the United Nations Conference on Environment and Development (the Rio 'Earth Summit') in 1992, China was one of the earliest signatories of the United Nations Convention on Biological Diversity (UNCBD) on 11 June. International consultation and cooperation corresponded with the development of national conservation policy. The implementation of the *Wildlife Protection Law* (WPL) in 1988, the *Nature Reserve Law* (NRL) in 1994, and the *Firearms Control*

Law (FCL) in 1996 allowed for unprecedented levels of state control over rural land management, hunting, land use, trade in wild plants and animals, and the politics of nature more broadly. The WPL designated wildlife as state property and classified protected species according to two levels of state protection ('first-level' or 'second-level' based on non-standardized importance values). The NRL delineated a legal structure for a national nature reserve system, including procedures for reserve establishment; differentiation of reserves associated with different administrative levels (national, provincial, prefectural, county/municipal; management regulations pertaining to the tripartite zonation; regulations on land use, research, and captive breeding facilities; and guidelines for law enforcement and punishment of offenders, inter alia). The FCL cleared the way for widespread confiscation of guns used for hunting in all regions (Coggins 2003; Harris 2008; ALII 2015). By 1996, there were 926 nature reserves and within the decade of the nineties the number increased by 93 per cent (Harris 2008). Not only did millions of people find themselves residing within new nature reserves, but they were also subject to prosecution for hunting or gathering the newly designated protected species, many of which they had taken freely for generations (Coggins 2003; Harris 2008; Hathaway 2013).

1997–2016: Maturation of China's national nature conservation system and integration with global conservation networks

From the late 1990s on, central and regional state agencies expanded nature conservation via an increasingly multi-faceted network of reserves and other protected areas, in tandem with sustainable development policies, and in conjunction with international agreements on the protection of biological diversity. In October 2011 the 6th Plenary Session of the 17th Communist Party Congress called for the building of an 'ecological civilization' (*shengtai wenming*). A new national zonation system aimed to conserve and rationalize the management of natural resources nationwide. However, a number of keystone species were found to be extinct in the wild, habitat degradation continued in many regions, and there was a growing awareness among both officials and citizens that efforts to protect biodiversity must be enhanced dramatically if the country was to preserve significant vestiges of its biological heritage.

The *Sloping Lands Conversion Program* (SLCP 1999), the *Natural Forest Protection Program* (NFPP 1999–2000), and the *Yunnan Great Rivers Project* (2000) sponsored by The Nature Conservancy (TNC) exemplify a policy shift toward integrated conservation and development, the involvement of multiple government agencies in regional conservation initiatives, and the important, if limited, and sometimes thwarted, roles of international conservation organizations. The SLCP (aka 'Grain for Green Program'), part of the Great Western Development Strategy, aimed to reduce runoff and soil erosion while increasing forest coverage by converting former crop-growing areas on sloping lands into forest lands. As the world's largest programme of payment for ecosystem services (PES), the SLCP provides farmers with saplings to plant, along with grain and cash subsidies in lieu of income from foregone agricultural production. A secondary goal is to shift farmers into less-intensive agricultural activities (e.g. livestock breeding) and off-farm employment. The SLCP affects the landholdings of some 40–60 million households across 25 provinces, and works in conjunction with the NFPP, aka the 'logging ban', which calls for reducing annual timber harvests in natural forests by 63 per cent and for the afforestation and revegetation of 31 million hectares. The NFPP has included logging bans in the upper reaches of the Yangtze and Yellow rivers, reducing logging in state-owned forests, engaging in reforestation and improved silviculture, and providing alternative employment opportunities for state forest workers. Implemented in 18 provinces and autonomous regions, the NFPP predominantly targets the upper Yangtze and Yellow River watersheds, as well as the northeast and Hainan. The NFPP and SLCP played large roles in raising China's total forest coverage to 21 per cent by 2008 (Robbins and Harrell 2014). These policies also ushered in stronger alliances with international nature conservation organizations such as TNC, which initiated the Yunnan Great Rivers Project in northwest Yunnan. After attempts to integrate local peoples' land-use practices, spiritual landscape values and development priorities into comprehensive regional protected area planning, TNC encountered a host of provincial and prefectural government agencies competing for funds and development opportunities. TNC helped facilitate the establishment of the first national parks in China to meet IUCN standards – Pudacuo National Park in 2007, Meili Snow Mountains National Park in 2009, and Shangrila Yunnan Golden Monkey National Park also in 2009. Due to conflicting agendas among state agencies, however, residents of the new parks were not effectively integrated into land-use planning and management, and TNC's specifications for protection of high levels of biodiversity, low tourist volume and preservation of backcountry sites respecting local peoples' traditions and livelihoods were not implemented (Moseley and Mullen 2014; Zinda 2014).

Further accentuating the severity of biodiversity loss, in 2001 an eight-month field survey in five southern provinces determined that the South China tiger (*Panthera tigris amoyensis*) was extinct in the wild (Figure 10.2) (Tilson et al. 2010). Another population census in 2007,

Figure 10.2 A South China tiger in the captive breeding and retraining centre in the Meihuashan Nature Reserve, in southwest Fujian Province, 2014. The tiger on the left exhibited a severe hip deformity due to inbreeding depression. In 2005 there were 57 individuals in the captive breeding population in China. This population was founded from the descendants of one wild Fujian tigress and five Guizhou tigers, but by 2007 there was genetic evidence of cross-breeding with other subspecies.

Source: Photo by Author.

yielded the same findings for the Yangtze River dolphin (Turvey 2008). In both cases, the Chinese government refused to acknowledge the results, but the rapid establishment of new nature reserves continued apace. From 2000–2004, the total number of reserves increased by 25 per cent, and by 2007 there were 2,500 reserves (Yeh 2013). By 2010, the total number of nature reserves was 2,541, and by that year there were also 208 national scenic areas, 660 national forest parks, and 28 UNESCO Biosphere Reserves (Yeh 2013; Zinda 2014). In 2014, 21 new national level nature reserves were established, bringing the total to 428 (State Council PRC 2014). By 2015, the total number of nature reserves was 2,671 and there were 428 national nature reserves, with reserves at all levels protecting 14.8 per cent of China's total land area.[11] During the second decade of the twenty-first century, the rate of expansion of the nature reserve system began to slow, with 5.1 per cent growth in the last five years. It is important to note that only about 9.8 per cent of China's land area is strictly protected, and if nine super-large national nature reserves (>10,000 sq. km.), in the Tibet Autonomous Region, Qinghai, and Xinjiang were removed, the percentage of strictly protected area would be a mere 2.7 per cent of the land area of China (Guo and Cui 2015). Also of note is the expansion of marine protected areas, which numbered over 240 at different levels, but still accounting for only 3 per cent of the marine areas within China's national boundaries (MEP 2014).

Current national policies, plans, and regulatory frameworks

China's Fifth National Report on the Implementation of the Convention on Biological Diversity

By 2010, the central government raised land use and conservation planning to a new level of specificity and intricacy. The State Council launched the National Plan for Major Function Zones (NPMFZ, *Guojia Zhuti Gongnengqu Guihua*), dividing all land into four major function zones: land for priority development, land for key development, land for limited development, and land prohibited for development. This 'ecological security strategy' conforms with the 12th Five-Year Plan (2011–2015), the *Fifth National Report on the Implementation of the Convention on Biological Diversity* (MEP 2014), referred to here as *FNR*, and the *China National Biodiversity Conservation Strategy and Action Plan 2011–2030* (CNBCSAP 2010), referred to here as BSAP.[12] The first two function zones are conventional economic development zones. The latter two are priority areas for ecological management. There are 35 Priority Regions for Biodiversity Conservation (*Zhongdian Shengtai Gongneng Qu*) – target areas for stricter ecological protection. Within these zones, 25 specific areas are designated as National Key Ecological Function Areas (NKEFAs). NKEFAs lie within limited development zones, while existing nature reserves and other strictly protected areas are in the prohibited development zones (MEP 2014). Each of the 35 priority regions include both 'limited' and 'prohibited' development zones and are distributed fairly evenly across the vegetation regions (Figure 10.1), and the *FNR* (2014) delineated national biodiversity conservation strategy according to short-term (2015), mid-term (2020), and long-term goals (2030) (MEP 2014).

Short-term, mid-term, and long-term goals cited in the Fifth National Report

The primary short-term goals of the *Fifth National Report*, slated to be achieved by 2015, centred on *in situ* conservation objectives, *ex situ* conservation objectives, increasing forest coverage, developing biodiversity monitoring systems, management of genetic and other biological resources, reduction of pollutants, and building a more 'environmentally friendly society' (MEP

2014, 3). *In situ* conservation was to be strengthened and terrestrial protected areas maintained on approximately 15 per cent of the country's land area, protecting 90 per cent of national key protected species and typical ecosystem types primarily through the growing network of nature reserves (*ziran baohuqu*), complemented by scenic spots (*fengjing mingshengqu*), forest parks (*senlin gongyuan*), community-based conservation areas (*ziran baohu xiaoqu*), wild plant protected sites (*nongye yesheng zhiwu baohudian*), wetland parks (*shidi gongyuan*), desert parks (*shamo gongyuan*), geological parks (*dizhi gongyuan*), special marine protected areas (*haiyang tebie baohuqu*) and germplasm conservation areas (*zhongzhi ziyuan baohuqu*) (MEP 2014).

Ex situ conservation was to focus on endangered species in areas where *in situ* conservation was inadequate or whose wild populations were too small to be protected by *in situ* strategies alone. The seven primary components of ex-situ conservation were: (1) botanical gardens and zoos; (2) protection of crop germplasm; (3) protection of forage germplasm (for livestock); (4) protection of livestock genetic resources; (5) protection of forest/tree germplasm resources; (6) protection of non-woody, lower plant, fungal, micro-organism, and wild animal germplasm resources; and (7) protection of marine germplasm resources (MEP 2014). Among the most important *ex-situ* components for protecting wild fauna and flora were the botanical gardens and zoos, which were estimated to number over 200 (with 20,000 plant species) and 240, respectively. There were also an estimated 250 rescue and reproduction centres for wild animals (MEP 2014). Botanical gardens were among the research and collection centres for forest tree germplasm, where genetic material for over 2,000 species, including 120 key (category one or two) tree species, had been analysed. In the Southwestern Germplasm Bank of wild species, seed materials had been archived for 10,096 plant species, as had non-seed *in vitro* reproductive material for 844 plant species, along with active plant materials for 437 species. Similar achievements were cited for marine genetic resources, and marine germplasm banks and research institutes, where geneticists mapped the entire genome of oysters, the first such map for a shellfish species, in 2010 (MEP 2014).

Short-term and mid-term goals for increasing forest coverage, developing biodiversity monitoring systems, management of genetic and other biological resources, and the reduction of pollutants were premised on a number of policies meant to have overlapping and mutually reinforcing effects. Short-term goals of the *FNR* were to increase forest coverage to 21.66 per cent, and by 2020; national forest holdings were to exceed 2.23 million square kilometres, an increase of roughly 10 per cent over 2010 holdings. Mid-term goals for habitat restoration included strategies to decrease and reverse land degradation, including the control of salinized and desertified grasslands through improvements in grassland ecology and pastoral management. Similarly, coastal and near-shore biodiversity protection was to focus on reversing the degradation of near-shore marine habitats and the decline of marine biodiversity, while freshwater aquatic ecosystems were to be gradually restored and the depletion of fishery resources and species populations contained. All of these goals were to rely substantially on the stabilization and improvement of the nature reserve network, improvement of their layouts and management systems, and the development of biodiversity monitoring systems, first, via status surveys and assessments in eight to ten priority areas for biodiversity conservation, and by 2020, in all priority areas for biodiversity conservation. In the same year there should be an early warning system for species loss, systems for managing the import and export of biological resources, and methods for documenting and protecting traditional knowledge and intellectual property rights (MEP 2014). Given the scope of this comprehensive, overlapping, and integrated national strategy for biodiversity conservation, the *FNR* calls for funding amounting to over 2.5 per cent of GDP by 2020, and contributions from science and technology agencies exceeding 60 per cent (MEP 2014). The long-term goal is to have 'effectively protected' biodiversity in China by 2030 (MEP 2014, 3).

Present and future challenges

Crises and critiques

By 1999, with the implementation of the *Natural Forest Protection Plan (NFPP)* and the *Sloping Lands Conversion Program (SLCP)*, the central government had incorporated large-scale nature conservation and ecological tourism into national development policies such as the Great Western Development Strategy. The latter programme was implemented from 2000 onwards with the aim of bringing impoverished regions of western China into closer economic parity with the prosperous eastern provinces (through development of infrastructure, enhanced foreign investment, education, and ecological protection projects), thereby alleviating tensions between the Han and non-Han nationalities (see also chapter 16 this volume on ecological resettlement programmes). This strategy is linked to the broader initiatives of 'harmonious society' (*hexie shehui*), 'the ecological state' (*shengtai liguo*) and 'ecological civilization' (*shengtai wenming*) (Yeh and Coggins 2014). As a result of the logging ban, many Tibetans and other inhabitants of the upper reaches of the Yangtze and Yellow rivers could no longer participate in the timber industry and found themselves without a stable livelihood. Thus the move toward eco-cultural tourism throughout the Sino-Tibetan borderlands and parts of southwest China has become a matter of economic urgency, and indigenous identities, as well as scholarship and activism, have been renegotiated around new understandings of landscapes, indigenous knowledge and national identity (Xu 2000; Yin 2001; Hathaway 2013; Yeh and Coggins 2014). The present phase of nature conservation in China is simultaneously one in which transnational conservation projects have been critically important. Thus the Nature Conservancy's (TNC) Yunnan Great Rivers Project (2000–2008) was largely an attempt to develop a system of nature conservation based on Tibetan, Naxi, and other non-Han peoples' sacred landscapes, indigenous knowledge systems and local resource management practices, with priority given to locations with high biodiversity and lacking previous protection. As noted, the new national parks established in the Diqing Tibetan Autonomous Prefecture, were predominantly top-down, conventional Yellowstone-style parks in which planners and administrators lacked deep concern for local community needs and aspirations. This was in stark contrast to the State Forest Administration's (SFA) early embrace of the biosphere reserve model and TNC participatory models, revealing complex intra-governmental policy conflicts and an emphasis on high-revenue mass tourism (Moseley and Mullen 2014; Zinda 2014).

Given the astonishing speed with which China's nature conservation policies, programmes, and initiatives have developed, the primary social policy challenge is to balance biodiversity conservation and environmental justice. Chinese and foreign conservation biologists note that many of China's protected areas are insufficiently large to serve as adequate habitat for certain species – particularly large mammals like the giant panda, and that because of the zonation system that allows for human activities in the buffer zones, if not by default in the core areas as well, habitat degradation is commonplace even in nature reserves such as Wolong in Sichuan (Liu et al. 2001). Chinese researchers are currently deploying increasingly sophisticated methodologies to assess these problems (Xu et al. 2008, 2009). At the same time, social scientists and some biologists argue that many protected areas and wildlife laws constitute (or are perceived as) enclosures of local peoples' resources, exacerbating ongoing conflicts and often nullifying potential conservation gains (Coggins 2003; Harris 2008; Yeh 2013). Harris (2008, 101) points out that the *1988 Wildlife Protection Law* prohibits killing of endangered wildlife, but fails to establish an infrastructure that can monitor or enforce these strictures. Moreover, it allows virtually no participation of local people in even limited taking of a great number of species that are numerous enough to be sustainably used. Thus it acts principally to alienate people from the wildlife with which they live, providing them little benefit beyond the vague sense of helping to preserve national treasures. Such a blanket prohibition in the absence of accompanying incentive programs tends to encourage movement of existing use patterns out of the mainstream and into the underground economy.

Similarly, Yeh (2013) shows that in implementing large-scale programmes involving payment for ecosystem services, such as the NFPP, the SLCP, and grassland conservation programmes, government agents often blame local people for ecological problems that stem from previous government interventions, especially those involving wetland drainage or pasture degradation. Technocratic 'solutions' to these problems often involve relocation of communities, enclosure and privatization of resources, and environmental injustice against non-Han nationalities that parades as rational resource management. Finally, given the troubling mix of contradictory goals embraced by the state – to provide goods and develop local and regional economies – there may not be a sufficiently strong commitment to prioritize socially just and ecologically effective biodiversity conservation. As Wandesforde-Smith et al. (2014, 93) note, the leadership

> wants to do right by the environment but not at the expense of doing other things it believes are much more important to its legitimacy, like sustaining economic growth, modernizing the economy, alleviating poverty, corralling pastoral people and containing social unrest … the center isn't getting the balance right between competing and even conflicting concerns.

Conclusions

The emerging national system of biodiversity conservation in China is increasingly interwoven with the rights, obligations, and access to resources associated with international treaties and supranational organizations – a realm of increasingly transnational engagement. Given the country's unique biological heritage and unusual history of human–environment interactions spanning several millennia of recorded history, the future preservation of biodiversity worldwide depends on a clearer understanding of the problems and opportunities influencing nature conservation policy and environmental justice in China. With the world's largest human population and many of the world's most endangered species, China provides an index of the challenge of 'ecological civilization' and an indicator of how much collective labour and common understanding must be marshalled in order to realize the venerable ideal of *tian ren he yi*, with all of its contemporary global implications.

Notes

1 Excerpt from Waley (1996, 154–155).
2 Excerpt from Liu and Lo (1975, 246).
3 Both words contain the character for literature (*wen*, 文). Deng Xiaoping promoted the idea of a progression from 'material civilization' (*wuzhi wenming*) in the Maoist period to the 'spiritual civilization' (*jingshen wenming*) of the new party directives on morality and social order. Later political elaborations have included the term 'ecological civilization' (*shengtai wenming*) (Dynon 2008).

4 Even during the Zhou Dynasty, philosophical treatises and historical texts show a remarkable divergence between those that value earth (*di*) and land (*tu*) as commodities and those that view them as sacred embodiments of cosmic vitality or agency (Sommer 2014).

5 These are processes that change the geographic ranges of individual taxa or entire biota, dividing them into separate parts due to the formation of physical or biotic barriers to gene flow or dispersal.

6 Data on China's species richness vary considerably. China's official figures indicate that the number of vertebrate species is 6,445, comprising 13.7 per cent of the world's total (MEP 2014; CNBCSAP 2010). The Nature Conservancy (Kram et al. 2012) has figures of 6,266 and 14.7 per cent respectively. These and similar disparities for specific taxonomic groups are a function of taxonomic reclassification, the discovery of new species, and disagreements on which species are extinct in the wild.

7 The even-toed ungulates include pigs, peccaries, hippopotamuses, camels, chevrotrains, deer, giraffes, pronghorn, antelopes, sheep, goats, and cattle.

8 Holocene climate conditions led to a peak in forest coverage in the North China Plain and Loess Plateau 6,000 years ago, after which widespread, ongoing anthropogenic forest disturbance prevailed (Ren 2007).

9 Much can be learned from the extinction processes of three large vertebrates that were once keystone species in the Chinese fauna – South China tigers (*Panthera tigris tigris*), Asian elephants (*Elaphas maximus*) and the Yangtze River dolphin (Lipotes vexillifer), as well as a number of other medium- and small-bodied vertebrates (Marks 1997, 2010; Zhang 1999; Coggins 2003, 2007; Elvin 2004; Turvey 2008; Turvey et al. 2013).

10 The 'Third Great Cutting' is associated with the post-reform era (1978–1988), when decollectivization and deregulation of many rural economic activities led to a timber boom driven by rural entrepreneurs and government bureaus who harvested timber for sale on the free market.

11 MEP (2014) claims a total of 2,697 reserves by 2013, covering the same land area, with 407 national-level nature reserves, comprising 64.3 per cent of the total area of nature reserves and 9.8 per cent of the country's land area.

12 As a signatory of the *Convention on Biological Diversity* in 1992, China's Ministry of Environmental Protection (*Huanjing Baohubu*) is required to develop and update its national strategy, plan or programme (CNBCSAP 2010). The tenth meeting of the Conference of the Parties held in Japan in October 2010 adopted the *Strategic Plan for Biodiversity* (2011–2020), which identified 2020 Biodiversity Targets.

References

ALII (Asian Legal Information Institute), 2015. Regulations on Nature Reserves. http://www.asianlii. org/cn/legis/cen/laws/ronr333/ (accessed 16 December 2016).

China Handbook Editorial Committee (CHEC), 2002. *Geography of China*. Honolulu: University Press of the Pacific.

CNBCSAP (*China National Biodiversity Conservation Strategy and Action Plan 2011–2030*), 2010. https:// www.cbd.int/doc/world/cn/cn-nbsap-v2-en.pdf (accessed 29 June 2015).

Coggins, C., 2003. *The Tiger and the Pangolin: Nature, Culture, and Conservation in China*. Honolulu: University of Hawaii Press.

Coggins, C., 2014. When the Land is Excellent: Village Feng Shui Forests and the Nature of Linage, Polity and Vitality in Southern China. In: Miller, J., Yu D.S. and van der Veer, P. eds, *Religion and Ecological Sustainability in China*. London and New York: Routledge, 97–126.

Dynon, N., 2008. 'Four Civilizations' and the Evolution of Post-Mao Chinese Socialist Ideology. *The China Journal*, 60, July, 83–109.

Elvin, M., 2004. *The Retreat of the Elephants: An Environmental History of China*. New Haven and London: Yale University Press.

Guo, Z. and Cui G., 2015. Establishment of Nature Reserves in Administrative Regions of Mainland China. *PLoS One*, 10(3): e0119650.

Harris, Richard B., 2008. *Wildlife Conservation in China: Preserving the Habitat of China's Wild West*. Armonk. New York: M.E. Sharpe.

Hathaway, M., 2013. Environmental Winds: Making the Global in Southwest China. Berkeley and Los Angeles: The University of California Press.

IUCN Red List, 2015. Table 1: Numbers of Threatened Species by Major Groups of Organisms (1996–2015). http://cmsdocs.s3.amazonaws.com/summarystats/2015_2_Summary_Stats_Page_Documents/2015_2_RL_Stats_Table_1.pdf (accessed 10 July 2015).

Kellert, S. and Wilson, E.O. eds, 1993. *The Biophilia Hypothesis.* Washington: Island Press.

Kram, M., Bedford, C., Durnin, M., Luo Y., Rokpelnis, K., Roth, B., Smith, N., Wang Y., Yu G., Yu Q. and Zhao X., 2012. *Protecting China's Biodiversity: A Guide to Land Use, Land Tenure, and Land Protection Tools.* Beijing: The Nature Conservancy.

Li W. and Zhao X., 1989. *China's Nature Reserves.* Beijing: Foreign Languages Press.

Li Y., Lu C., Deng O., Chen P., 2015. Ecological Characteristics of China's Key Ecological Function Areas. *Journal of Resources and Ecology,* 6 (6): 427–432.

Lin G., personal communication. 29 July 2014. Nanjing County, Fujian.

Liu, J., Linderman, M., Oyang, Z., An, L., Yang, J. and Zhang, H., 2001. Ecological Degradation in Protected Areas: The Case of Wolong Nature Reserve for Giant Pandas. *Science,* 292, 98–101.

Liu W. and Lo I.Y., 1975. *Sunflower Splendor: Three Thousand Years of Chinese Poetry.* Garden City, New York: Anchor Press/Doubleday.

McBeath, G. and Leng T.K., 2006. *Governance of Biodiversity Conservation in China and Taiwan.* Cheltenham and Northampton: Elgar Publishing.

Marks, R.B., 2012. *China: Its Environment and History.* Lanham: Rowman and Littlefield.

Menzies, N.K., 1994. *Forest and Land Management in Imperial China.* New York: Palgrave Macmillan.

MEP (Ministry of Environmental Protection, China), 2014. *China's Fifth National Report on the Implementation of the Convention on Biological Diversity.* (https://www.cbd.int/doc/world/cn/cn-nr-05-en.pdf) (accessed 29 June 2015).

Moseley, R.K. and Mullen, R.B., 2014. The Nature Conservancy in Shangrila: Transnational Conservation and Its Critiques. In: Yeh, E.T. and Coggins, C. ed., *Mapping Shangrila: Contested Landscapes in the Sino-Tibetan Borderlands.* Seattle: University of Washington Press: 129–152.

Ren, G., 2007. Changes in Forest Cover in China During the Holocene. *Vegetation History and Archaeobotany,* 16, 119–126.

Robbins, A.S.T. and Harrell, S., 2014. Paradoxes and Challenges for China's Forests in the Reform Era. The China Quarterly, Available on CJO 2014 doi: 10.1017/ S0305741014000344.

Shapiro, J., 2001. *Mao's War Against Nature: Politics and the Environment in Revolutionary China.* Cambridge: Cambridge University Press.

State Council PRC., 2014. China Sets Up 21 New National Nature Reserves. December 23, 2014. http://english.gov.cn/policies/latest_releases/2014/12/23/content_281475028455671.htm (accessed 15 July 2015).

Tilson, R., Nyhus, P.J. and Muntifering, J.F., 2010. Yin and Yang of Tiger Conservation in China. *Tigers of the World (Second Edition): The Science, Politics, and Conservation of Panthera tigris.* Amsterdam; Boston: Elsevier/Academic Press.

Turvey, S., 2008. *Witness to Extinction: How We Failed to Save the Yangtze River Dolphin.* Oxford: Oxford University Press.

Turvey, S.T., Tong H., Stuart, A.J., Lister, A.M., 2013. Holocene survival of Late Pleistocene Megafauna in China: A Critical Review of the Evidence. *Quaternary Science Reviews,* 76, 156–166.

UN (United Nations), 1992. *Convention on Biological Diversity.* (https://www.cbd.int/doc/legal/cbd-en.pdf) (accessed 20 January 2016).

Waley, A., 1996. *The Book of Songs: The Ancient Chinese Classic of Poetry.* New York: Grove Press.

Wandesforde-Smith, G., Snyder, K.D. and Hart, L.A., 2014. Biodiversity Conservation and Protected Areas in China: Science, Law and the Obdurate Party-State, *Journal of International Wildlife Law & Policy,* 17 (3), 85–101.

Wilson, E.O., 2002. *The Future of Life.* New York: Alfred A. Knopf.

Xu H., Wu J., Liu Y., Ding H., Zhang M., Wu Y., Xi Q. and Wang L., 2008. Biodiversity Congruence Strategies: A National Test. *BioScience,* 58 (7), 632–639.

Xu H., Tang X., Liu J., Ding H., Wu J., Zhang M., Yang Q., Cai L., Zhao J. and Liu Y., 2009. China's Progress Toward the Significant Reduction of the Rate of Biodiversity Loss. *BioScience,* 59 (10), 843–852.

Xu J. ed., 2000. *Links Between Cultures and Biodiversity: Proceedings of the Cultures and Biodiversity Congress 2000.* Kunming: Yunnan Science and Technology Press.

Xu J., 2005. *Who Drives Conservation in China? A Case study in Protected Areas in Yunnan, Southwest China.* © 2005 Forest Trends. http://www.forest-trends.org/documents/files/doc_1108.pdf (accessed 20 January 2016).

Yang Y., 2001. Impacts and Effectiveness of Logging Bans in Natural Forests: People's Republic of China. In: Durst, P.B., Waggener, T.R., Enters, T. and Cheng T.L. eds, *Forests Out of Bounds: Impacts and effectiveness of logging bans in natural forests in Asia-Pacific.* Bangkok: FAO of the UN Regional Office for Asia and the Pacific: 81–102.

Yeh, E., 2013. The Politics of Conservation in Contemporary Rural China. *Journal of Peasant Studies*, 40 (6), 1165–1188.

Yeh, E.T. and Coggins, C. eds, 2014. *Mapping Shangrila: Contested Landscapes in the Sino-Tibetan Borderlands.* Seattle: University of Washington Press.

Yin S., 2001. *People and Forests: Yunnan Swidden Agriculture in Human-Ecological Perspective.* Trans. Magnus Fiskesjo. Kunming: Yunnan Education Publishing House.

Zhang Y., 1999. *China Zoogeography.* Beijing: Science Press (Chinese).

Zinda, J.A., 2014. Making National Parks in Yunnan: Shifts and Struggles Within the Ecological State. In: Yeh, E.T. and Coggins, C. ed., *Mapping Shangrila: Contested Landscapes in the Sino-Tibetan Borderlands.* Seattle: University of Washington Press, 105–128.

11

LAND DEGRADATION AND LAND-USE STRATEGIES IN CHINA'S NORTHERN REGIONS

Soil conservation, afforestation, water resource management

Susanne Stein and Heike Hartmann

Introduction

During recent decades, north-east China, north China and north-west China, collectively referred to as the country's 'three northern regions' (*sanbei diqu*, Figure 11.1),[1] have become notorious for the degradation of their drylands.[2] This includes serious soil erosion from wind and water, salinisation, shrinking water resources, sand drift and dust storms, extensively covered in the media and scholarship under the catch-all term desertification (*huangmohua*)[3] (Cao 2008, 1827–8; Sun et al. 2014, 154–5). From the late 1970s onwards, scientists and scholars from China and abroad have published numerous case studies, which reveal to what extent these land degradation processes have accelerated since the 1950s. With few exceptions, the greatest share of blame has been allocated to a succession of ill-conceived and poorly managed land-use policies mainly in conjunction with the mass campaigns of the so-called Maoist era, but also increasingly associated with the pursuit of rapid economic growth during the first decades of reform (Smil 1984; Shapiro 2001; Economy 2002; Williams 2002; Jiang 2005; Yeh 2015, 620–3). Climate change is expected to have compounding effects on dryland degradation in the future (Sun et al. 2014).

Since the late 1990s, the CCP leadership and the Chinese government have claimed to be striving towards more sustainable solutions to improve the environmental and socio-economic conditions in the *sanbei* regions within the overlapping frameworks and the respective regional foci of large-scale ecological restoration programmes, long-distance water transfer projects and the Great Western Development strategy (*Xibu da kaifa zhanlüe*).[4] Several of these measures have received widespread international attention and some (re)forestation programmes have been singled out as exemplary and are co-funded by the international community as part of the United Nations' global efforts to combat desertification and alleviate poverty in the world's drylands (Liu 2009, 101; Stein 2015, 343–4). However, as we will show, many officials, scientists and environmental activists question the long-term effectiveness of the approaches applied (Cao et al. 2011; Xu 2011; Mátyás et al. 2014).

This chapter provides an overview of the dominant land-use strategies that have been adopted in China's northern regions since the inception of the PRC in 1949. These strategies have had to meet a trifold challenge: to deal with a semi- to hyper-arid climate with limited surface-water availability, a pressing demand for agricultural surpluses to foster rapid industrialisation and the urgency to cope with the increasing deterioration of the country's dryland ecosystems. We describe the interdependence between conflicting land-use strategies and competing perceptions of land degradation in the *sanbei* regions, emphasising that land degradation as well as its countermeasures should be understood as an aggregate result of socio-environmental processes varying over space and time (Blaikie and Brookfield 1987; Marks 2012, 231–43; Yeh 2015). Accordingly, the chapter is organised into three chronological sections tracing the dynamic interplay between the natural environment, land-use practices, soil, water and forest resources management and environmental change from the 1950s to the present.[5] The regional geographical and historical contexts are summarised first, followed by a review of how the efforts to prevent and mitigate land degradation in different parts of China's northern regions have evolved over the last 65 years in relation and response to shifting political priorities, local experiences, natural hazards, transnational interactions and available technologies. The concluding section of the chapter outlines the recent debates on more sustainable options for land management in the *sanbei* regions.

Geographical and historical contexts

Apart from the rugged topography alternating between plains, mountain ranges, depressions and plateaus, the most conspicuous feature of northern China's physical geography is aridity, gradually increasing from east to west (Figure 11.1). While the easternmost parts up to the Greater Xing'an mountain range are still influenced by the summer monsoon rainfall from the Pacific, the dominant climatic factor in the central northern and north-western regions is continentality. The westerly winds of the middle latitudes supply only very small amounts of moisture to this area as the greatest portion is blocked out by the high mountain ranges to the north (Altay and Tianshan), west (Pamir and Karakorum) and south (Kunlunshan and Nanshan).

Along its northern frontier, China's land cover accordingly transitions from forests and forest steppe in the north-east, sustained by more than 500 mm of annual precipitation into large tracts of grasslands, Gobi (e.g. gravel desert) and sandy deserts further west, with an annual precipitation of 200 mm along the Helan mountains in the Ningxia Autonomous Region to less than 25 mm in the hyper-arid Tarim Basin of southern Xinjiang (Zhao 1994). Only the surrounding mountain ranges show annual precipitation totals in the order of 400 mm and higher (Kundzewicz et al. 2015). Their snow and glacier meltwater feeds several rivers which constitute the major water source for the region's natural ecosystems and human activities (Thevs 2011).[6]

Viewed from a historical perspective, the territorial expansion of the Qing Empire (1644–1911) into Inner Asia[7] left a lasting environmental and socio-economic imprint on this immense stretch of dryland ecosystems (Perdue 2005). Although Qing policy generally sought to segregate China proper (*neidi*) from its northern and western borderlands, in the wake of natural hazards and social dislocations in the core areas, increasing numbers of Han Chinese settlers migrated to the 'outer' forest, steppe and desert regions. Fundamental changes in local livelihood systems ensued, as the 'reluctant pioneers' (Reardon-Anderson 2005) from the inner provinces hardly adapted their land-use patterns to the new environments (Marks 2012, 256–9). In the beginning, land reclamation for agriculture was restricted to comparatively small areas within the reach of China proper and Qing military garrisons (Fletcher 1978a; Zhao 2005). Over the

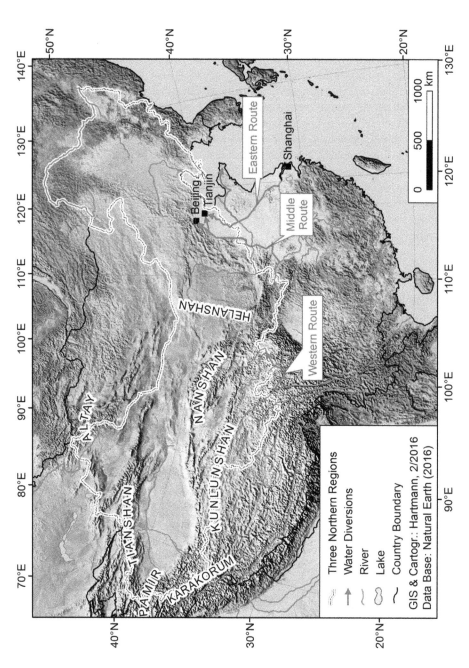

Figure 11.1 China's three northern regions: topography, land cover and water diversions

Source: Author.

course of two centuries, however, forest-, shrub- and grassland systems became increasingly fragmented due to the expansion of irrigated farmland (Vermeer 1998; Squires and Yang 2009, 17, 25–6; Becker and Zmijewski 2014). Among other driving forces, these developments ushered in a gradual decline of nomadic pastoralism and ecological resilience on China's Inner Asian frontiers witnessed and chronicled by Lattimore (1940), Cressey (1934, 252, 268–71) and several other observers during the 1920s and 1930s (Fletcher 1978b; Squires and Yang 2009, 25; Geng and Gao 2012).

According to their reports, the northern margins of China proper were especially characterised by severe environmental degradation at this time (Lowdermilk 1925; Lowdermilk and Li 1930). Eroded and depleted soils resulting from centuries of intensive cultivation and the progressing deforestation and denudation of slopes led to repeated cycles of devastating floods and droughts, earning China the image of being the 'Land of Famine' during the Republican era (Mallory 1926).

While the interrelated dynamics of political and socio-economic crises, warfare, natural hazards, environmental decline and major famines in Late Imperial and Republican China have been dealt with more extensively during recent years (Li L.M. 2007; Janku 2012), much less is known about the environmental legacy of Sun Yat-sen's visionary plan of integrating and modernising China through large-scale infrastructure development. His designs were based on the construction of a comprehensive system of railroads and waterways that would facilitate the (re)distribution of goods and people including the colonisation of Mongolia and Xinjiang (Sun 1919; Sun 1921). Sun's proposal inspired both Chinese and Western contemporaries to draft blueprints for creating a 'second Jiangnan' in China's (far) north-west, largely based on overly enthusiastic assessments of the region's physical properties and the possibilities of modern technology. Fundamental ideas from these publications were instrumental to the Nanjing government during the mid-1930s in its campaign to 'open up the Northwest' (*kaifa Xibei*) for agriculture, ranching, timber exploitation and mining (Li and Cao 2003). Like several other projects of national reconstruction, the ambitious attempts to tap northern China's natural resources and to 'colonise the frontier with migrant farmers' (*yimin zhibian*) did not materialise on a larger scale due to Republican China's political and territorial disintegration (Christiansen 1992; Wang 2008). However, these schemes remained on the political agenda after 1949 with the aim of consolidating state power throughout the northern China regions by way of strategic resettlement, land reclamation and economic development.[8]

Strategies of the past, 1950s–1970s

By 1949, large tracts of Chinese society were 'impoverished along with their environment' (Marks 2012, 263). With water conservancy facilities having fallen into disrepair and natural resources seriously depleted after decades of political strife and (civil) war, agricultural productivity continued to decline. In stark contrast to the bleak material realities of the day, the Communist leadership propagated an appealing vision of general affluence to be attained in the near future through the 'socialist transformation' (*shehuizhuyi gaizao*) of nature, epitomised by large hydro-engineering projects and the 'rational' re-ordering of land- and waterscapes (Liu 1956; Chao 1963). For the northern parts of the country, this 'high modernist' endeavour (Scott 1998, 88–9) implied the creation of high-yielding croplands on hitherto uncultivated 'waste' (*huang*). The systematic agro-industrial conquest of China's Inner Asian drylands would soon eradicate the image of natural hazards, poverty and famine reflexively associated with these environments from a Han Chinese perspective. Consequently, during the period of post-war economic reconstruction (1949–52) and throughout the PRC's first Five-Year Plan (FYP,

1953–7), the *sanbei* regions became the target area for a multitude of agricultural reclamation and hydrological development projects at different levels of the administrative hierarchy, reshaping traditional land-use patterns, landforms and ecosystems on an unprecedented scale (Marks 2012, 271–2).

To begin with, the expansion of agriculture into the northern dryland environments essentially depended on the construction of water storage, irrigation and drainage systems to compensate for scarce and highly variable rainfalls as well as recurrent droughts. From 1950 to 2010, China built 87,873 dams and reservoirs of different sizes throughout the country (Liu et al. 2013). While the relevance of water management had been stressed by the new government from the beginning, the lack of expertise, technical limitations and capital constraints made the building of large multi-purpose dams very difficult, as the failed development of the Yellow River dam and reservoir at Sanmenxia illustrates (Pietz 2015, 130–3, 161–4). Still, the number of dams of varying sizes almost doubled from 1,222 dams in 1949 to 2,301 in 1957 (Liu et al. 2013). On the one hand, regional authorities in many parts of the country were eager to emulate the central government's ultimately hapless efforts of 'controlling the Huai River' (Marks 2012, 299–300; Pietz 2015, 133–9); on the other, China's first FYP stipulated that the irrigated acreage of the People's Republic was to be extended by 4.8 million ha, mainly achieved through the construction of smaller reservoirs and irrigation facilities at the local level (Chao 1963, 13; Pietz 2015, 174–82).

The pattern of Xinjiang's 'military agrarian colonisation' that set in shortly after the establishment of the PRC provides a telling example in this context. Dryland reclamation was expedited by military units from the People's Liberation Army and disbanded Guomindang troops that set up state farms north and south of the Tianshan mountain range. In 1954, their members were reorganised into the paramilitary Xinjiang Production and Construction Corps (XJPCC, *Xinjiang shengchan jianshe bingtuan*) that systematically took control over the headwaters of the region's major rivers. Over the years, the XJPCC built expansive irrigation networks that regularly intersected with strips of land cleared and levelled for the cultivation of grain and cotton. The artificial agro-ecosystems thus created were usually enclosed by a rectangular system of field windbreaks or shelterbelt plantations protecting the crops from sand drift, wind, desiccation and frost (Betke 1994).[9]

Despite asynchronies and conspicuous differences in site conditions, similar approaches of land appropriation and transformation were pursued throughout the *sanbei* regions during the period of rural collectivisation, be it 'grassland improvement' in parts of northern Xinjiang, Ningxia and Inner Mongolia (Jiang 2005), or the gradual transformation of Heilongjiang's 'Great Northern Wilderness' (*Beidahuang*) in the sub-humid Northeast China Plain into the country's 'Great Northern Granary' (*Beidacang*) (Zhao 1994, 157; Shapiro 2001, 165–8).

The different 'tides' of land reclamation and water conservancy campaigns of the 1950s and early 1960s (Pietz 2015) were flanked by desert expeditions, soil and forest surveys, various on-site investigations and field experiments on intercropping, dryland (re)vegetation and sand control mandated by the Chinese Academy of Sciences and its regional branches. Modelled on the examples of contemporary Soviet soil science, forestry and desert research, these scientific activities were geared towards the compilation of a comprehensive inventory of the land, water, forest and mineral resources the outer regions of China provided for the 'socialist construction' (*shehuizhuyi jianshe*) of the country as a whole (Zeng et al. 2015, 4–5).

The PRC's intensified agricultural activities in dryland environments inevitably created new tasks for soil conservation. In addition to water management, responsibility for protecting and improving arable land was likewise delegated to the level of the rural cooperatives and people's communes respectively. By drawing directly on the Soviet experiences of the 'Great Stalin Plan for the Transformation of Nature' (Brain 2011), afforestation became the centrepiece of the measures applied to raise rural production. In addition to planting (traditional) field windbreaks and long strips of trees to protect and stabilise rangelands, riverbanks, irrigation structures and communication lines, Chinese protection forestry was aimed at more ambitious objectives as well. Since 1951, six expansive multi-tiered shelterbelt systems had been 'constructed' in different parts of the country to adjust climate and soil conditions on a regional scale. In the mid-1950s, the government claimed that these so-called 'Green Great Walls' (*lüse Changcheng*) already had measurable effects on water supply, soil moisture, air temperature, wind velocity and precipitation, reportedly leading to much higher yields on formerly marginal lands (Stein 2015, 336–8). In the 'Draft Plan for the National Development of Agriculture between 1956 and 1967', the pre-eminent role of afforestation for soil and water conservancy was re-emphasised and translated into a mass campaign that called for 'Greening the Fatherland' (*lühua zuguo*) within the next twelve years. Wherever possible, trees should be planted 'in a planned way', including all kinds of shelterbelts and windbreaks (*Renmin Ribao*, 1956, 2; Chao 1963, 14–22).

But even though the ecological functions and benefits of forests (and, though to a lesser degree, of shrubs and grasses) were widely propagated during the 1950s, land-use conflicts became more pronounced during the following decades. For a start, the policies of the Great Leap Forward (GLF, 1958–61) pursued very contradictory approaches and goals. They were oriented towards further dryland reclamation and 'desert control' by means of mass mobilisation for large-scale environmental and hydro-engineering projects, such as shelterbelt systems and the Sanmenxia dam; simultaneously, these highly symbolic ventures of transforming China's deserts into pastures, orchards and cropland were constantly counteracted by the economic priorities of rapid industrialisation. As Richardson (1990, 95–8) has concluded from official Chinese forestry statistics released retroactively since 1981, the increasing demand for timber and firewood impinged upon the country's natural and man-made forests alike, including the newly planted shelterbelts in northern China. Trees were logged to a great extent for industrial construction purposes or to fuel the GLF's famous backyard steel furnaces, exposing ever larger tracts of land to wind and water erosion.

Secondly, the 'grain first' policy that was launched in response to the nationwide famine in the wake of the GLF proved to be rather ambivalent in terms of land degradation as well. Conceived by the central government in 1960 as a relief strategy, the campaign actually called for agricultural diversification and an integrated development of farming, forestry, animal husbandry and rural industries. However, the original message was soon cut down to 'take grain as the key link' (*yi liang wei gang*) of the rural economy, irrespective of environmental conditions and local livelihood systems. Consequently, in many parts of the *sanbei* regions, two opposing strategies were employed simultaneously: the implementation of forest protection, soil conservation and rangeland improvement measures coincided with an indiscriminate reclamation of marginal land for agriculture, which inevitably depended on the expansion of irrigation networks and groundwater mining (Ho 2003, 40–54).

The general bias towards grain cultivation became even stronger when the village of Dazhai, located in Shanxi province in the hilly lands surrounding the North China Plain, was canonised by the central government as a national model for rural development in 1964. The Dazhai strategy relied on the full use of local labour power. It propagated a subsistence economy based on local self-sufficiency in grain production (*zili gengsheng*), with surpluses to be delivered to the regional and national supply systems. The model was neither tailored to the terrain of the Dazhai area itself nor was it appropriate for the *sanbei* regions at large. More often than not, though, functionaries were pressured to promote the 'Dazhai spirit' with little regard for local circumstances (Xiao 1996; Shapiro 2001, 95–114; Pietz 2015, 246–8 on water management).

149

Ho (2003) and Jiang (2005) have described the Inner Mongolian village of Wushenzhao, officially acknowledged as the pastoral equivalent of Dazhai (*muqu Dazhai*) in 1965, as one of the more successful examples of adaptation. At first, the preferential development of animal husbandry (*yi mu wei zhu*) effectively minimised pressures to open up new plots of grassland for grain cultivation and expand irrigation districts, but the attempts to counterbalance the agricultural focus of the Dazhai campaign soon came to a standstill again.[10]

During the initial and most intense phase of the Cultural Revolution (1966–76), the natural resources of the northern frontier regions were increasingly subject to random exploitation, as the central administrative apparatus was largely on hiatus and communal autarky became enshrined as one of the fundamental tenets accompanying the construction of a 'Third Front' industrial defence base in the Chinese interior (Naughton 1988; Shapiro 2001, 145–9; Jiang 2005). It was not before the early 1970s that government agencies and research institutions for agriculture, forestry and water management gradually resumed their work (Pietz 2015, 237–8; Zhang 2008, 216–7). Despite repeated efforts to adjust land-use strategies and establish tighter control over the management and consumption of land, forest and water, environmental conditions in the *sanbei* regions continued to deteriorate and gave rise to a widespread sense of ecological and socio-economic crisis at the end of the decade (Cao 2008, 1827).

Changing strategies in the context of China's reform policies, 1978–present

The subsequent trajectory of land-use strategies for China's northern regions had been decisively shaped by the reform policies and institutions emerging under the leadership of Deng Xiaoping (1904–97) since 1978. As the country embarked on its new developmental course, existing concerns about the extent and pace of dryland degradation could be voiced more openly. In November 1978, the *People's Daily* confronted its readers with alarming reports of the environmental situation on the Loess Plateau in the middle reaches of the Yellow River. Scientists explained that the political imperative of grain production had seriously reduced the region's grassland and forest cover. Expansive agricultural land-use had set off a vicious circle of accelerated soil erosion and rural poverty, with living standards in the Shaan Gan Ning border region (including parts of Shaanxi, Gansu, Ningxia and the southern tip of Inner Mongolia) being lower than before or shortly after 'liberation'.[11] Moreover, it was reported that these on-site ecological damages had tangibly impacted the hydrological systems of the Yellow River's downstream areas, both in terms of floods and water scarcity (Tong and Bao 1978). Countless reservoirs and irrigation canals, built with more revolutionary fervour than adequate technical expertise, compounded the environmental problems that resulted from intensified agricultural activities. This included rising water tables, high evaporation rates, salinisation–alkalisation due to inadequate drainage and seepage, and siltation of river beds leading to the reduction of downstream flows (Pietz 2015, 254–7).

Land-use/land cover classification maps derived from aerial photography and the newly available satellite data eventually enabled Chinese earth scientists to lend visibility to the enormous dimensions of land-use change in the *sanbei* regions. From the evidence accumulated by the early 1980s – however incomplete it may seem in retrospect – scholars concluded that the majority of the PRC's earlier dryland 'construction' strategies had led to widespread ecological destruction (Smil 1984; Edmonds 1994).

The surge of discussions on the state of northern China's environment was also fuelled by the increasing number of international scientific encounters and the intensified arid lands research around the globe. Surveyed from the perspective of transnational environmental history, the formation of China's domestic 'desert discourse' (Williams 1997) coincided with a heightened global concern among scientists and political decision-makers about the accelerated deterioration of the world's drylands and its socio-economic consequences. Newly conceptualised as 'desertification', the alarm about dryland degradation had emerged in response to the devastating Sahelian drought-famine of the early 1970s and culminated in the convention of the 1977 UN Conference on Desertification (UNCOD) in Nairobi (Stein and Gestwa 2015, 245–8). The PRC's participation in UNCOD helped to (re-)direct political and public attention as well as increased state funding to the cause of soil and water conservation in China's northern regions (Glantz and Orlovsky 1983, 16) and probably acted as a catalyst for the Chinese State Council's approval to plant a system of forest shelterbelts throughout the three northern regions in 1978 (Li Y. 2007).

Similar to previous projects of landscape transformation, the construction of this recent 'Green Great Wall' has followed the well-established pattern of an environmental mass campaign, including 'voluntary' labour stints and tree-planting competitions organised by 'afforestation shock teams' on the occasion of China's Arbour Day each spring since 12 March, 1979. The 'greening of the fatherland' signified the creation of a 'modernised environment' which would in turn facilitate the implementation of China's four modernisations in agriculture, industry, national defence, science and technology (Stein 2015, 340–1). At the same time, however, decollectivisation, the transfer of land-use rights to the level of individual households and the introduction of market mechanisms were powerful incentives to increase rural productivity. The enhanced economic activities generated new pressures on the limited forest, land and water resources of China's northern regions. The first decade of reform has come to be viewed as one of the most serious episodes of environmental degradation since 1949, including massive deforestation and overgrazing, unsustainable expansion of irrigated cropland into rangelands, over-use of surface and groundwater supplies as well as agro-chemical and industrial pollution of water and soils (Harkness 1998; Liu 2009, 92–3; Squires and Yang 2009; Marks 2012, 287; Yeh 2015, 620–3). Between 1984 and 1991, the Chinese government passed six major environmental laws to counteract this trend (Table 11.1).

These legislative initiatives attested to the rising awareness for the enormous scope of environmental challenges in China's northern regions on the part of the state, but they were not systematically implemented at the regional and local levels (Tao 1993, 52; Delang and Yuan 2015, 21). Instead, the central government adhered to large-scale (ecological) engineering projects, irrespective of previous failures to improve environmental conditions in the *sanbei* regions through dam construction and expansive irrigation, huge shelterbelt systems and mass afforestation (Richardson 1990; Mátyás et al. 2014; Pietz 2015). These approaches to mitigate and reverse land degradation also gained substantial international recognition and funding within the context of the United Nations International Decade for Natural Disaster Prevention (IDNDP, 1990–9) and the enforcement of the UN Convention to Combat Desertification (UNCCD) in 1996.

Table 11.1 Environmental legislation in China, 1984–91

Year	Law Passed
1984	Forest Law
1985	Grassland Law
1986	Law of Land Administration
1988	Water Law
1989	Environmental Protection Law
1991	Law on Water and Soil Conservation

While Chinese environmental policies display an undiminished preference for highly interventionist solutions to this day, scientific discourse has gradually shifted towards the less aggressive concept of 'ecological restoration' (*shengtai huifu*) since the end of the 1990s, prompted by a succession of extreme weather events (indicating climate change) and their socio-economic consequences (Mátyás et al. 2014, 256). In 1993, a 'black dust blizzard' (*heifengbao*) hit north-western China, killing many people and devastating an area of 1.1 million km² (Tao 1993). It was followed by spells of drought in the mid-1990s, a complete dry-up of the Yellow River's lower reaches in 1997 for altogether 226 days, the Yangtze summer flood of 1998 with more than 4,000 people dead and another 18 million displaced (Liu 2009; Delang and Yuan 2015, 20) and an increased frequency and intensity of spring dust storms attributed to desertification that had affected ever larger parts of northern China between 2000 and 2006 (Cao 2008, 1827–8).

This accumulation of ecological disasters not only indicated that the overall environmental situation in China's frontier regions had worsened throughout the reform period and could hardly be offset by localised successes in protection forestry. They also demonstrated the extent to which the prosperity of northern China's densely populated urban-industrial and agricultural core areas along the seaboard depended upon undisturbed dryland systems and forests further north and west. As a response, the central government began to launch a series of five large-scale environmental conservation programmes on a trial basis in 1998, which were eventually reorganised into China's 'Six Key Forestry Projects' (KFP, *liu da linye zhongdian gongcheng*) in 2001, including the various shelterbelt programmes of the last two decades (*Renmin Ribao* 2001; State Forestry Administration 2007).

The KFP agenda comprises the protection and rehabilitation of natural forests and grassland areas, the (re-)conversion of low-yielding farmland to forest and grassland vegetation (Figure 11.2), various measures of desertification control, wildlife conservation, the establishment of nature reserves and the cultivation of timber plantations to compensate for logging bans on China's remaining natural forests (Table 11.2). According to the State Forestry Administration, in 2002, 97 per cent of the PRC's county-level administrative entities were already involved in one or several of these projects concurrently (Delang and Yuan 2015, 22–30).

In line with the stated goals of the PRC's Great Western Development strategy introduced in March 2000, the KFP were designed to balance the country's socio-economic disparities through state-sponsored measures of 'ecological construction' (*shengtai jianshe*) and financial 'compensation for ecological benefits' (*shengtai xiaoyi buchang*) (Economy 2002). Together, they aim at an integrated system of sustainable land management on China's ecological margins to be established by 2050 (Liu et al. 2008).

While the KFP's initial achievements have been widely publicised and acclaimed by the Chinese state and international organisations (Xu 2011; UNCCD, n.d.), a synopsis of the more recent scientific evaluations of the individual projects reveals a tableau of highly ambivalent results. Scientists have particularly questioned the Chinese government's staunch reliance on large-scale afforestation in drylands by emphasising the negative impacts of this 'classic' tool of ecosystem restoration on water resources, biodiversity and soil properties if used without regard for local circumstances (Ma et al. 2013). In areas with an annual precipitation of 250–400 mm, tree plantations have indeed proven useful when appropriate tree species were chosen and auxiliary irrigation was provided. However, these short-term and small-scale successes seem to have been too readily generalised and thus impeded the examination of potentially more sustainable approaches of revegetation (Cao et al. 2010, 2011; Jiang 2010), e.g. the cultivation of local hemp varieties in the Tarim River basin (Thevs 2011).

Due to persisting criticism, increasing water shortages and afforestation failures, China's environmental policies have been adjusted to minimise trade-offs between erosion control and

Table 11.2 China's six key forestry programmes (*Zhongguo liu da linye zhongdian gongcheng*)

Programme	Duration (Pilot Phase)	Area/Scope	Goals
Natural Forest Protection Programme (*tianranlin baohu gongcheng*)	1998–2050 (1998–2000)	nationwide; particular focus on natural forests in the upper Yangtze basin, mid- to upper Yellow River basin, and state forests in north-eastern China and Inner Mongolia	protection of remaining forest resources, logging bans on commercial harvests (Yangtze and Yellow River basins); reduction/adjustment of timber output, forest worker relocation (Northeast and Inner Mongolia); afforestation and reforestation by means of mountain closure, aerial seeding, tree planting (nationwide)
Conversion of Farmland to Forest and Grassland (*tuigeng huanlin huancao gongcheng*) [also referred to as "Sloping Land Conversion Programme" or "Grain for Green Programme"]	1999–2016 (1999)	northern and western China, mid- to upper Yangtze basin	erosion control through (re)forestation/revegetation (natural vegetation restoration)
Beijing Area Desertification Control Programme (*huan Beijing diqu fangsha zhisha gongcheng*)	2000–2010 (2000–2001)	Beijing, Tianjin, Hebei, eastern Inner Mongolia, Shanxi	reduction and prevention of dust weather events in the Beijing–Tianjin metropolitan area; desertification control through land conversion (farmland to forest), grassland protection, development of water conservation facilities and 'ecological relocation'
Key Shelterbelt Development Programmes (*zhongdian fanghulin jianshe gongcheng*) embraces China's major shelterbelt construction programmes	since 1978	three northern regions, mid- to lower Yangtze basin, coastline from Guangxi to Liaoning, Pearl River, Huai River, plains regions, Taihang Mountain, Lake Dongting and Lake Poyang	desertification control, erosion control, river bank reinforcement, shoreline stabilisation
Wildlife Conservation and Nature Reserve Development Programme (*yesheng dongwu baohu ji ziran baohuqu jianshe gongcheng*)	since 2001	nationwide	conservation of wild fauna and flora, enhancement of biodiversity, establishment of nature reserves (forests, drylands, wetlands)
Fast-Growing and High-Yielding Timber Plantation Programme (*zhongdian diqu yi susheng fengchan yongcailin wei zhu de linye chanye jidi jianshe gongcheng*)	since 2001	areas east of the isohyet of 400 mm	areas east of the isohyet of 400 mm

Source: Adapted from Delang and Yuan 2015, 22–30; Liu et al. 2008.

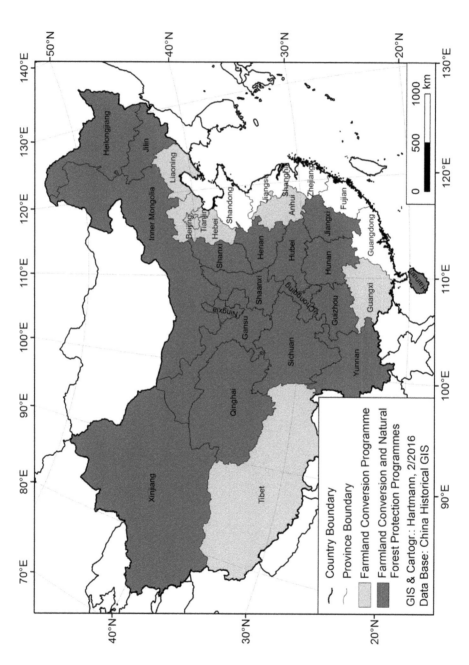

Figure 11.2 Distribution of the farmland conversion and the national forest protection programmes (Liu et al. 2008)

water conservation (Yang et al. 2010). Instead of tree plantations, logging and grazing bans have been enacted to facilitate ecosystem recovery through natural processes. Alongside location-specific attempts to improve water balances, such as integrated water management for the *sanbei* region's major river basins (Liu and Xia 2004), more efficient irrigation methods (e.g. drip irrigation) and water pricing tools, China actively pursues large-scale projects of inter-basin water transfer. Several such projects are currently under way, including the South-to-North Water Diversion Project (SNWDP; *Nanshui Beidiao*), which originated in the early 1950s and was revived during the 1990s (Pietz 2015, 299). Officially launched in 2002, it is the largest water transfer project ever implemented worldwide (Zhang 2009). When completed, about 50 billion m³ of water are planned to be transferred annually from the Yangtze River to North China via three routes (Figure 11.1).

The Eastern Route was finished in 2013 (Chen 2015). Up to 14.8 billion m³ annually can be diverted from the lower reaches of the Yangtze River to the eastern North China Plain and to Tianjin City (He et al. 2010). Since 2014, the Middle Route has been transferring water from the Danjiangkou Reservoir on the Han River to the North China Plain and further north-eastwards to Beijing and Tianjin (He et al. 2010; Xinhua News Agency 2014). The Middle Route will enable the diversion of up to 14 billion m³ annually and is planned to be extended to the Three Gorges Reservoir or the upper middle reaches of the Yangtze River in the future (Office of the SNWDP Commission, n.d.). The Western Route is still in the planning phase. It is intended to transfer water from the source region of the Yangtze River to the source region of the Yellow River to mitigate water shortages in north-western China (He et al. 2010). The implementation of the Western Route is particularly challenging in this high-elevation, cold-climate region with high seismic activity. In total, about 20 billion m³ of water are planned to be transferred annually (Office of the SNWDP Commission, n.d.). Despite increasing concerns about the long-term environmental consequences of the scheme, the SNWDP has been fully supported by the state and is officially portrayed as indispensable for meeting the constantly high water demands in northern and north-western China resulting from irrigation farming, expanding urban-industrial systems as well as long-term climatic changes (Sun et al. 2014, 155–6; Pietz 2015, 299–307).

Conclusion

Looking back on the trajectory of China's land-use strategies for its northern dryland regions over the past six decades, one can observe a continued preference for large-scale engineering solutions, often legitimised by referring to Sun Yat-sen's early twentieth-century 'Programme for National Reconstruction' (Shaanxi shifan daxue 2006). Earlier failures notwithstanding, official Chinese discourse still presents the combination of hydro-engineering and massive afforestation as a panacea – a rationale that has recently been strengthened anew in the context of international debates on global climate change and carbon sequestration. Simultaneously, however, alternative approaches have also been discussed and introduced. While for some areas ecosystem recovery through natural processes seems to be the appropriate solution, in other cases carefully planned interventions to restore the potential natural vegetation were preferred (Ma et al. 2013, 76). Generally speaking, there has been a shift from political to economic solutions, such as the introduction of payments for ecosystem services[12] (Liu et al. 2008). The most renowned examples illustrating this trend are the above-mentioned programmes for Natural Forest Protection and Farmland Conversion (Figure 11.2). Yet, as recent studies of political ecology indicate, future research should also examine whether and to what extent China's state-sponsored conservation programmes have limited local people's access to resources and engendered new forms of land appropriation ('green grabbing') in the name of sustainable land-use strategies (Fairhead, Leach and Scoones 2012; Yeh 2015, 623–5).

Acknowledgements

Susanne Stein acknowledges funding by the German Science Foundation (DFG) within the Collaborative Research Center 923 'Threatened Order – Societies under Stress' and by the Gerda Henkel Foundation. Heike Hartmann acknowledges funding by the German Ministry for Education and Research (BMBF) within the project 'Sustainable Management of River Oases along the Tarim River / China (SuMaRiO)'. We would like to thank James C. Nickum and Johannes Küchler for their helpful comments and suggestions on an earlier draft of this chapter.

Notes

1 The 'three northern regions' is an umbrella term dating back to the early administrative system of regional military divisions (*daqu*) during the first years of the People's Republic of China (PRC). As an administrative unit it encompasses the provinces, municipalities and autonomous regions of north-east China (Dongbei), north China (Huabei) and north-west China (Xibei). In official Chinese rhetoric, these regions are characterised as 'the area over which China's eight great deserts, her four large sandy lands as well as the extensive Gobi and the Loess Plateau are distributed. Within this area, dust storms, drought and water erosion are severe, the environment is very fragile, natural hazards occur frequently, agricultural output is low and fluctuating [...]. The adverse environmental conditions seriously hamper local economic and social development.' (Li 2007, 36).
2 As opposed to the term desert, drylands are usually more broadly defined to include areas ranging from hyper-arid to sub-humid conditions. However, both terms are often used interchangeably. See Middleton 2009, 2–4.
3 On meanings and misconceptions inherent to this often ill-defined term see Thomas and Middleton 1994, 1–16. According to the United Nations Convention to Combat Desertification (UNCCD) adopted in 1994, desertification 'means land degradation in arid, semi-arid and dry sub-humid areas resulting from various factors, including climatic variations and human activities' (http://www.unccd.int/en/about-the-convention/Pages/About-the-Convention.aspx).
4 On the geographical and conceptual intersections of the *sanbei* regions and China's newly defined 'West' (Xibu), see Li Y. 2007, 66–9 and Economy 2002, 2, 4.
5 It has to be noted, though, that much of the available information on this complex topic is surrounded by ambiguity. This not only pertains to the reliability of published data but also to the fragmented information when, why and by whom certain land-use policies have been launched and how they were implemented locally.
6 For a more detailed geographical description of the *sanbei* regions see Chen et al. 2014, 3–14 and Zhao 1985.
7 This includes Manchuria, Mongolia, Inner Mongolia, Xinjiang and Tibet. On the different concepts and implications of the terms Inner Asia, Central Asia and Central Eurasia, see Bulag 2005.
8 As Kirby (2000, 138) has noted, 'Sun's strategies to "develop the vast resources of China ..." [...] would be shared by his Nationalist and Communist successors.'
9 According to Betke (1994, 95–7), many Soviet scientists and advisors were involved in the reclamation process.
10 Despite severe problems with salinity and respectively high fluctuations in acreage, the area of irrigated farmland in Inner Mongolia increased from less than 5 million *mu* in 1950 to approximately 15 million *mu* in the latter half of the 1970s (Pietz 2015, 250).
11 Which was of great symbolic significance as the early Communist base areas were located in this region.
12 In the Millennium Ecosystem Assessment (2005, 40), ecosystem services have been defined as the benefits people obtain from ecosystems.

References

Becker, R.H. and Zmijewski, K.A., 2014. Land Use and Land Cover Change in Dryland East Asia. In: Chen J., Wan S., Henebry, G., Qi J., Gutman, G., Sun G. and Kappas M., eds. 2014. *Dryland East Asia*. Berlin: Higher Education Press/De Gruyter, 61–80.

Betke, D., 1994. Zur politischen Ökologie des sozialistischen Zentralstaats in Innerasien: Ein Beispiel aus Xinjiang, VR China. In: B.G. Fragner and B. Hoffmann, eds. 1994. *Bamberger Mittelasienstudien*. Berlin: Klaus Schwarz Verlag, 81–108.

Blaikie, P. and Brookfield, H., 1987. *Land Degradation and Society*. London: Methuen.

Brain, S., 2011. *Song of the Forest: Russian Forestry and Stalinist Environmentalism, 1905–1953*. Pittsburgh: Pittsburgh University Press.

Bulag, U.E., 2005. Where is East Asia? Central Asian and Inner Asian Perspectives on Regionalism. *The Asia-Pacific Journal*, 3(10), 1–7.

Cao, S., 2008. Why Large-Scale Afforestation Efforts in China Have Failed to Solve the Desertification Problem. *Environmental Science & Technology*, 42(6), 1826–31.

Cao S., Sun G., Zhang Z., Chen L., Feng Q., Fu B. et al., 2011. Greening China Naturally. *Ambio*, 40, 828–31.

Chao, K.-C., 1963. *Agrarian Policies of Mainland China: A Documentary Study (1949–1956)*. Cambridge, Mass.: Harvard University Press.

Chen, J., John, R., Qiao, G., Batkhishig, O., Yuan, W., Zhang, Y. et al., 2014. State and Change of Dryland East Asia (DEA). In: Chen J., Wan S., Henebry, G., Qi J., Gutman, G., Sun G. and Kappas M., eds. *Dryland East Asia*. Berlin: Higher Education Press/De Gruyter, 3–22.

Chen T.-P., 2015. Cities in China's North Resist Tapping Water Piped from South. *Wall Street Journal*, 23 April 2015.

Christiansen, F., 1992. New Land in China, 1900–1937. *Leeds East Asia Papers*, 10, 1–79.

Cressey, G.B., 1934. *China's Geographic Foundations: A Survey of the Land and its People*. New York and London: McGraw-Hill.

Delang, C.O. and Yuan, Z., 2015. *China's Grain for Green Program: A Review of the Largest Ecological Restoration and Rural Development Program in the World*. Heidelberg: Springer.

Economy, E.C., 2002. China's Go West Campaign. Ecological Construction or Ecological Exploitation. *China Environment Series*, 5, 1–10.

Edmonds, R.L., 1994. *Patterns of China's Lost Harmony: A Survey of the Country's Environmental Degradation and Protection*. London: Routledge.

Fairhead, J., Leach, M. and Scoones, I., 2012. Green Grabbing: A New Appropriation of Nature? *The Journal of Peasant Studies*, 39(2), 237–61.

Fletcher, J., 1978a. Ch'ing Inner Asia c. 1800. In: J.K. Fairbank, ed. 1978. *The Cambridge History of China*, 10(1), Cambridge: Cambridge University Press, 35–106.

Fletcher, J., 1978b. The Heyday of the Ch'ing Order in Mongolia, Sinkiang and Tibet. In: J.K. Fairbank, ed. 1978. *The Cambridge History of China*, 10(1), Cambridge: Cambridge University Press, 351–408.

Geng X. and Gao G., 2012. A Case of 'Over-Cropping': Causes and Consequences of Qing Dynasty Approval to Plough and Plant the Inner Mongolian Grasslands. *Nomadic Peoples*, 16(1), 21–35.

Glantz, M.H. and Orlovsky, N.S., 1983. Desertification: A review of the concept. *Desertification Control*, 9, 15–22.

Harkness, J., 1998. Recent Trends in Forestry and Conservation of Biodiversity in China. *The China Quarterly*, 156, 911–34.

He C., He X. and Fu L., 2010. China's South-to-North Water Transfer Project: Is it Needed? *Geography Compass*, 4(9), 1312–23.

Ho P., 2003. Mao's War Against Nature? The Environmental Impact of the Grain-First Campaign in China. *The China Journal*, 50, 37–59.

Janku, A., 2012. From Natural to National Disaster: The Chinese Famine of 1928–1930, in A. Janku, G.J. Schenk and F. Mauelshagen, eds. 2012. *Historical Disasters in Context: Science, Religion, and Politics*. New York: Routledge, 227–60.

Jiang H., 2005. Grassland Management and Views of Nature in China since 1949: Regional policies and local changes in Uxin Ju, Inner Mongolia. *Geoforum*, 36, 641–53.

Jiang H., 2010. Desertification in China: Problems with Policies and Perceptions. In: Kassiola, J.J. and Guo, S., eds. 2010. *China's Environmental Crisis: Domestic and Global Political Impacts and Responses*. New York: Palgrave Macmillan, 13–40.

Kirby, W.C., 2000. Engineering China: Birth of the Developmental State, 1928–1937. In: W. Yeh, ed. 2000. *Becoming Chinese*. Berkeley: University of California Press, 137–60.

Kundzewicz, Z. W., Merz, B., Vorogushyn, S., Hartmann, H., Duethmann, D., Wortmann, M., Huang, S., Su, B., Jiang, T. and Krysanova, V., 2015. Analysis of Changes in Climate and River Discharge with Focus on Seasonal Runoff Predictability in the Aksu River Basin. *Environmental Earth Sciences*, 73(2), 501–16.

Lattimore, O., 1940. *Inner Asian Frontiers of China*. New York: American Geographical Society.

Li L.M., 2007. *Fighting Famine in North China: State, Market, and Environmental Decline, 1690s–1990s*. Stanford: Stanford University Press.

Li Y., 2007. *Lüse Changcheng: Zhongguo de 'Sanbei' fanghulin jianshe gongcheng* (Green Great Wall: China's 'Three North' Shelterbelt Construction Project). Beijing: Lantian chubanshe.

Li Y. and Cao M., 2003. Kang Ri shiqi de guomin zhengfu yu Xibei kaifa (The National Government and North-western Development during the War of Resistance Against Japan). *Kang Ri Zhanzheng Yanjiu*, 3, 51–78.

Liu C. and Xia J., 2004. Water Problems and Hydrological Research in the Yellow River and the Huai and Hai River Basins of China. *Hydrological Processes*, 18(12), 2197–210.

Liu D., 2009. Reforestation after Deforestation. In: K. Abe and J. Nickum, eds. 2009. *Good Earths*. Kyoto/Melbourne: Kyoto University Press/Trans Pacific Press, 90–105.

Liu J., Li S., Ouyang Z., Tam C. and Chen X., 2008. Ecological and Socioeconomic Effects of China's Policies for Ecosystem Services. *Proceedings of the National Academy of Sciences*, 105(28), 9477–82.

Liu J., Zang C., Tian S., Liu J., Yang H., Jia S., You L., Liu B. and Zhang, M., 2013. Water Conservancy Projects in China: Achievements, Challenges and Way Forward. *Global Environmental Change*, 23, 633–43.

Liu T.H., 1956. Changing the Economic Map of China. *China Reconstructs*, 5, 2–6.

Lowdermilk, W.C., 1925. A Forester's Search for Forests in China. *American Forests and Forest Life*, 379, 387–90, 427, 444–6.

Lowdermilk, W.C. and Li T.I., 1930. Forestry in Denuded China. *Annals of the American Academy of Social Science*, 152, 127–41.

Ma H., Lü Y. and Li H., 2013. Complexity of Ecological Restoration in China. *Ecological Engineering* 52, 75–8.

Mallory, W.H., 1926. *China: Land of Famine*. New York: American Geographical Society.

Marks, R.B., 2012. *China: Its Environment and History*. Lanham: Rowman & Littlefield.

Mátyás, C., Sun G. and Zhang Y., 2014. Afforestation and Forests at the Dryland Edges: Lessons Learned and Future Outlooks. In: Chen J., Wan S., Henebry, G., Qi J., Gutman, G., Sun G. and Kappas M. eds., 2014. *Dryland East Asia*. Berlin: Higher Education Press/De Gruyter, 245–63.

Middleton, N.J., 2009. *Deserts: A Very Short Introduction*. Oxford: Oxford University Press.

Millennium Ecosystem Assessment, 2005. *Ecosystems and Human Well-being: Synthesis*. Washington DC: Island Press.

Naughton, B., 1988. The Third Front: Defence Industrialization in the Chinese Interior. *The China Quarterly*, 115, 351–86.

Office of the SNWDP Commission of the State Council (n.d.), South-To-North Water Diversion, http://www.nsbd.gov.cn/zx/english/ (accessed 15 December 2016).

Perdue, P.C., 2005. *China Marches West: The Qing Conquest of Central Eurasia*. Cambridge, MA: Belknap Press.

Pietz, D.A., 2015. *The Yellow River: The Problem of Water in Modern China*. Cambridge, MA: Harvard University Press.

Reardon-Anderson, J., 2005. *Reluctant Pioneers: China's Expansion Northward, 1644–1937*. Stanford: Stanford University Press.

Renmin Ribao, 1956. 1956 nian dao 1967 nian quanguo nongye fazhan gangyao (cao'an) (Draft plan for the national development of agriculture between 1956 and 1967). *Renmin Ribao*, 26 January 1956, 2.

Renmin Ribao, 2001. Guowuyuan pizhun shishi liu da linye zhongdian gongcheng (State Council approved implementation of Six Key Forestry Projects). *Renmin Ribao*, 16 February 2001, 1.

Richardson, S.D., 1990. *Forests and Forestry in China: Changing Patterns of Resource Development*. Washington D.C.: Island Press.

Scott, J.C., 1998. *Seeing Like a State: How Certain Schemes to Improve the Human Condition Have Failed*. New Haven: Yale University Press.

Shaanxi shifan daxue Xibei huanfa zhongxin, ed. 2006. *Xibu kaifa yu shengtai huanjing de kechixu fazhan* (The opening up of the West and the sustainable development of the ecological environment). Xia'an: Sanqin chubanshe.

Shapiro, J., 2001. *Mao's War Against Nature: Politics and the Environment in Revolutionary China*. Cambridge: Cambridge University Press.

Smil, V., 1984. *The Bad Earth: Environmental Degradation in China*. Armonk: M.E. Sharpe.

Squires, V.R. and Yang, Y., 2009. Historical Degradation Episodes in China. In: V.R. Squires et al., eds. 2009. *Rangeland Degradation and Recovery in China's Pastoral Lands*. Wallingford: CABI, 15–29.

State Forestry Administration, 2007, Forestry Development in China, http://www.china.org.cn/e-news/news071204-1.htm (accessed 15 December 2016).

Stein, S., 2015. Coping with the 'World's Biggest Dust Bowl': Towards a History of China's Forest Shelterbelts, 1950s–Present. *Global Environment*, 8(2), 320–48.

Stein, S. and Gestwa, K., 2015. Introduction. *Global Environment*, 8(2), 236–58.

Sun G., Feng X., Xiao J., Shiklomnnov, A., Wang S., Zhang Z., 2014. Impacts of Global Change on Water Resources in Dryland East Asia. In: Chen J., Wan S., Henebry, G., Qi J., Gutman, G., Sun G. and Kappas, M. eds., 2014. *Dryland East Asia*. Berlin: Higher Education Press/De Gruyter, 152–81.

Sun W., 1919. Jianguo fanglüe zhi yi (Programme for National Reconstruction, Part 1). *Jianshe* 1, 1–23.

Sun Y.-S., 1921. *The International Development of China*. New York: Da Capo Press.

Tao S., 1993. Baohu cuiruo shengtai xitong, xuejian shabao zaihai qiangdu (Protect fragile ecosystems, reduce the intensity of sandstorm disasters). *Gansu Qixiang*, 11(3), 49–53.

Thevs, N., 2011. Water Scarcity and Allocation in the Tarim Basin: Decision structures and adaptations on the local level. *Journal of Current Chinese Affairs*, 40(3), 113–37.

Thomas, D.S.G. and Middleton, N.J., 1994. *Desertification: Exploding the Myth*. Chichester: John Wiley & Sons.

Tong D. and Bao T., 1978. Guanyu Xibei huangtu gaoyuan de jianshe fangzhen wenti (On problems concerning the construction policy for the Loess Plateau in the North-west). *Renmin Ribao*, 26 November, 2.

UNCCD, n.d. Stories on Desertification. China Afforestation: Heroes of the Three North Shelterbelt. http://www.unccd.int/en/media-center/Feature-Stories/Pages/China-Afforestation.aspx (accessed 15 December 2016).

Vermeer, E.B., 1998. Population and Ecology along the Frontier in Qing China. In: M. Elvin and T.-J. Liu, eds. 1998. *Sediments of Time: Environment and Society in Chinese History*. Cambridge: Cambridge University Press, 235–79.

Wang Y., 2008. Minguo Xibei kenhuang yu yimin shibian zhi lishi kaoping (Reclaiming Wasteland and Filling up the North-Western Frontier with Migrants in Republican China: A Historical Appraisal). *Nei Menggu nongye daxue xuebao* (Shehui kexue ban), 6, 313–6.

Williams, D.M., 1997. The Desert Discourse of Modern China. *Modern China*, 23, 328–55.

Williams, D.M., 2002. *Beyond Great Walls: Environment, Identity, and Development on the Chinese Grasslands of Inner Mongolia*. Stanford: Stanford University Press.

Xiao K., 1996. 'Zui gao zhishi: Nongye xue Dazhai' de youlai (The Origin of 'The Highest Instruction: In Agriculture Learn from Dazhai'). *Dangdai Zhongguoshi Yanjiu*, 5, 92–3.

Xinhua News Agency, 2014. China opens key section of massive water project. *China Daily*, Dec. 12, 2014. http://www.chinadailyasia.com/nation/2014-12/12/content_15202804.html (accessed 15 December 2016).

Xu J., 2011. China's New Forests Aren't as Green as They Seem. *Nature*, 477, 371.

Yang X., Jia Z. and Ci L. 2010. Assessing Effects of Afforestation Projects in China. *Nature*, 466, 315.

Yeh, E.T., 2015. Political Ecology in and of China. In: R.L. Bryant, ed. 2015. *The International Handbook of Political Ecology*. Cheltenham: Edward Elgar, 2015, 619–32.

Zeng W., Tomppo, E., Healey, S.P., Gadow, K.V., 2015. The National Forest Inventory in China: History – Results – International Context. *Forest Ecosystems* 2 (23), 1–16.

Zhang, L., 2008. Reform of the Forest Sector in China. In: P. Durst et al., eds. 2008. *Reinventing Forestry Agencies: Experiences of Institutional Restructuring in Asia and the Pacific*. FAO: Bangkok, 215–29. http://www.fao.org/docrep/010/ai412e/ai412e00.HTM (accessed 15 December 2016).

Zhang, Q., 2009. The South-to-North Water Transfer Project of China: Environmental Implications and Monitoring Strategy. *Journal of the American Water Resources Association*, 45(5), 1238–47.

Zhao, S., ed. 1985. *Zhongguo ganhan diqu ziran dili* (The Physical Geography of China's Arid Lands). Beijing: Kexue chubanshe.

Zhao, S., 1994. *Geography of China: Environment, Resources, Population, and Development.* New York: John Wiley & Sons.

Zhao, Z., 2005. *Qingdai Xibei shengtai bianqian yanjiu* (Research on ecological changes in the North-West During the Qing Dynasty). Beijing: Renmin chubanshe.

12

BALANCING ENVIRONMENT, HEALTH AND DEVELOPMENT

Evolving policy interactions

Jennifer Holdaway[1]

Introduction

The majority of articles in this volume are concerned with the making and implementation of various aspects of environmental law and policy in China. This chapter is somewhat different in considering the way in which environmental policy intersects with two other crucial policy domains: health and development. It first lays out the rationale for this integrated approach and then analyses the way in which these three policy sectors have interacted over time, highlighting shifting patterns of intersection and dislocation.

Although the social environment is also important for health, in keeping with the focus of this volume, the emphasis here is on risks stemming from the degradation of the physical environment, and in particular from pollution associated with industrialization, urbanization and the intensification of agriculture.

Background: environment and health as a policy domain

Interactions between economic development, environment and health are extremely complex. There is no linear relationship between increases in GDP and health outcomes, and relative as well as absolute wealth has an effect on health. However, especially for poor countries, economic growth, usually pursued through increases in productivity from industrialization and the intensification of agriculture, can bring important benefits for health through increased incomes, better nutrition, improved living conditions and more funding for health and other public services (Biggs et al. 2010). It can also provide more resources for environmental protection. Urbanization is also usually associated with improvements in public health because it facilitates the development of infrastructure and the provision of health and other services (Brady et al. 2007). Yet at the same time, processes of industrialization and urbanization, as well as the higher levels of consumption that generally accompany rising living standards, also generate pollution that is harmful to health in the short term and can cause long-term damage to ecosystems, as well as depleting the natural resources essential for sustaining human life. It is therefore increasingly recognized that environmental protection is crucial to human health and well-being (for example, Forget and Lebel 2001; WHO 2005; Prüss-Üstün and Corvalán 2006).

Nowhere are these tensions starker than in China, where extremely rapid economic growth has gone hand in hand with mounting levels of pollution and rising carbon emissions. However, before turning to China, it is important to highlight some of the generic difficulties of environmental health as a policy domain, which include the high level of scientific complexity and uncertainty; the need for cross-sectoral engagement; and conflicts of interests between different actors and jurisdictions (OECD 2007).

Scientific complexity and uncertainty

Pollution-related health impacts have complex causality and different pollutants have different effects on health, individually and in combination, over different time frames and geographies. For example, air pollution can be composed of numerous different chemicals emitted by a variety of sources from vehicles, power stations and industries to the burning of agricultural stubble. These chemicals have different individual health effects and also interact in the atmosphere to form new compounds that may be more (or less) damaging to health than the individual components. This means that reductions in emissions of individual pollutants also do not always result in linear reductions in health effects. Emissions that are not directly damaging to human health may also have long term indirect effects through climate change or other impacts on the ecosystem: greenhouse gases are the obvious example. Topology, wind patterns and population concentrations will also affect who is exposed to emissions and at what level of intensity (Nielsen and Ho 2013).

Similarly, risks to health through food can result from pollution of the agricultural environment by industrial and household waste as well as agricultural practices including the use of chemical fertilizers and pesticides, veterinary drugs and animal feed containing heavy metals and other chemicals harmful to health. However, it is not always easy to extrapolate simply from pollution levels to specific health impacts. For example, whether or not heavy metals present in soil are absorbed by food crops depends on a combination of factors such as soil acidity and moisture levels; and certain crops and even different crop varietals have a much higher propensity to absorb heavy metals than others. As a result, crops can sometimes be unsafe even when soil meets environmental standards, and, equally, safe food can sometimes be grown in soil that does not (FORHEAD 2014).

Over the long term, general improvements in environmental quality will certainly have benefits for human health, but reducing the health impacts of pollution quickly in specific places requires an understanding of the particular pollutants involved and their interactions with each other and with other relevant characteristics of the physical and social environment. This scientific complexity makes environmental health a very challenging issue for both policy-makers and the public.

The need for cross-sectoral engagement

The fact that pollution often stems from many sources also means that addressing it usually requires a high level of policy coordination. For example, the engagement of the Agriculture and Land Resources ministries is crucial in dealing with heavy metals in food, while air pollution reduction strategies must often involve agencies responsible for transportation, energy, industry and commerce, and agriculture. These different policy streams all have different mandates and goals. In particular, there is a strong tension between agencies responsible for the drivers of environmental health problems (energy, industry, agriculture and transportation) – whose primary goals are usually to increase the supply or added-value of goods and services – and environmental protection and health agencies that play a regulatory role. The scientific complexity of environment and health as an issue domain is an added barrier to coordination, because few officials have cross-disciplinary training and the data-collection systems of different agencies are also often established with different units of analysis and sampling rationales. This makes it hard to conduct integrated monitoring and analysis.

This situation is not unique to China. A 2007 OECD review of environment and health governance noted that policy coordination was extremely hard to achieve, with individual departments working in policy 'silos' and no one agency having overall responsibility (OECD 2007).

Conflicts of interest

Even when there is a strong political commitment at the national level, implementing environment and health policy often involves dealing with deep conflicts of interest between different actors which can occur at multiple scales, have complex geographies and centre on different issues over time. Many conflicts are over responsibility for the health and economic costs caused by pollution and take place between industries and affected individuals or communities, or between different jurisdictions. As environmental protection policies are more strongly enforced, conflict can also occur over the distribution of the costs of reducing pollution, which may not only affect industry profits but also lead to unemployment and loss of government revenue. The relationship between Hebei Province and Beijing, discussed below, illustrates this problem with regard to air pollution.

This tension between improving environmental quality and maintaining the benefits for health of economic growth is evident in the history of many other countries in the world. However, most early industrializing countries did not attempt to implement strict environmental protection or environmental health measures when they were at China's current level of development and urbanization. For example, serious concern with the health impacts of pollution in the US is often dated to the publication of Rachel Carson's *Silent Spring* in 1962, and it was not until the 1970s that environmental protection got into full swing. By this time, the US was a rich country (per-capita GDP in 1970 was US$15,030 (Maddison Project 2013)) that was already de-industrializing. China's per-capita GDP in 2014 was US$7,400 (World Bank 2015), and industry still contributes a significant proportion of GDP: 42.8 per cent in 2014 (ADB 2015). The process is therefore likely to be considerably more difficult.

China's particular environmental health challenges

In considering what is special about China's situation with regard to environment and health, a number of factors stand out. The first is the population to resources ratio. China has a fifth of the world's population but only 7 per cent of its arable land. Water resources are also tight, at only about a third of the global average of 6,200 cubic metres per person (World Bank 2012). This situation encourages intensive agriculture and creates competition for land and water between agricultural, industrial and residential uses (Holdaway 2015). Of course, China's sheer size also matters because even small changes in the production and consumption patterns of such a massive population have global impacts on the climate and on ecosystems.

Second, China is a country of continental scale and as a result there is enormous diversity in its natural environment and in the distribution of natural resources. Eighty per cent of water resources are located in the south; deposits of coal and heavy metals are regionally concentrated; and the topology and climate of the country lend themselves to the cultivation of different crops in different regions (Gale et al. 2002). In interaction, these factors have led different regions to follow very different development pathways (Bramall 2003) which have in turn generated different constellations of environmental health challenges (Holdaway 2013, 2014; Wang et al. 2014). For example, air pollution is generally worse in the north, and acid rain is concentrated in the south, while heavy metal contamination of rice occurs mostly – although not exclusively – in southern provinces where rice cultivation takes place alongside the exploitation of heavy metals (Wu and Li 2015).

Lastly, the rapidity of change in production and consumption activities means that policies, regulatory mechanisms, institutional infrastructure and human resources almost inevitably lag behind what is needed. At the same time, internal diversity and uneven development also mean that China faces environmental health problems associated with different levels and types of development at the same time. These problems often overlap across space and populations, and are in constant flux, as the environmental determinants of health change along with livelihoods and lifestyles. Dealing with this differentiated and shifting landscape of risks is a very significant challenge for policy (Holdaway 2013).

The evolution of environmental health problems and policy responses

Overall, China has seen the evolution of its environmental health problems from those of a poor, largely agricultural and rural society to those associated with industrialization and urbanization. In many ways this represents a classic environmental health risk transition as described by Smith and Ezzati (2005), which in turn is part of a broader health transition from infectious to non-communicable diseases (Cook and Dummer 2004; IHME 2010). However, the factors discussed above mean that China faces a more regionally differentiated and rapidly changing landscape of environmental health risks than most other countries.

Legacies of the Mao era

In 1949, when the Chinese Communist Party came to power, China was a very poor country, with an annual per-capita GDP of only US$60 in 1990 dollars – less than half the average for Asia (Du et al. 2014). Median life expectancy for 1950–1955 was only 44.6 years (UN Population Division 2012). The focus of policy was therefore on meeting basic needs for food and shelter. Health policy prioritized bacteriological and animal-borne diseases through aggressive sanitation and pest-eradication policies referred to as environmental hygiene (*huanjing weisheng*). The positive impact of these policies was bolstered by general improvements in living standards and, later, investment in basic but quite comprehensive medical services provided by state-owned enterprises and rural collectives. Any evaluation of China's performance on health during this period must also consider the tragic policy failures of the *Great Leap Forward*, which resulted in the deaths of more than 30 million people from hunger. However, overall, long-term public investment led to significant improvements in public health, and by 1978 China had impressive health indicators for a country of its level of development: median life expectancy from 1980–1985 was 67.7 years (UNDP 2013), compared with only 56.3 in India (UN Population Division 2012).

Until the late 1970s, environmental impacts on disease could be fairly easily predicted. In general, rural people were more likely than urban residents to be affected by problems related to poverty, including bacterial diseases resulting from the lack of sanitary facilities and access to clean water, endemic diseases caused by the absence or excess of certain elements in the soil or water and respiratory diseases from burning solid fuels for cooking and heating. Zoonoses such as malaria, schistosomiasis and plague were also rife in some areas. These problems were exacerbated by poorer nutrition and inferior access to health services. Urban populations were more likely to be exposed to air pollution from industry and coal burning and to occupational diseases related to industrial work, but they generally had much better sanitation and access to water and health services than people in rural areas (Banister 1998).

In terms of pollution, the main risks were from mining and from industry, which was concentrated around Shanghai and in the North East, as well as in rural areas in which industries were located as part of the *Third Front (sanxian)* policies. The period of the *Great Leap Forward* led to a sudden, but relatively short-lived, increase in pollution as countless factories, smelters and power stations and cement factories were hastily constructed in both cities and rural areas. Major infrastructure projects such as dams also exacerbated risks by concentrating pollution in some areas due to reduced water flow and increasing the risk of accidents in the case of infrastructure collapse, for example in the Huai River Basin (Economy 2004). However, pollution from the transportation and agriculture sectors, which would later become major problems, was not yet serious. Private cars were extremely rare, and increases in agricultural output were largely due to the intensification of traditional practices rather than high levels of inputs, although chemical fertilizers and pesticides were coming into wider use.

This period saw some general guidelines on the conservation of soil and water. A number of environmental incidents in 1972 prompted the formation of a small leading group on the protection of water resources (Economy 2004) and in 1974 an inter-ministerial Environmental Protection Leading Group was set up within the State Council, which acknowledged that pollution 'jeopardizes people's health and industrial and agricultural development' and that China should not 'follow a zigzag path of construction first, control second' (Qu 1999: 219 cited in Economy 2004). But it was not until 1979 that the National People's Congress passed the draft Environmental Protection Law and health impacts were not salient in this legislation. However, although environmental protection policies were limited, overall development and health policies were quite effective in reducing the poverty-related environmental health risks that China faced during this period.

Reform and rapid growth 1978–2002

With reform and opening up, China's economy underwent dramatic structural changes that transformed people's livelihoods and lifestyles. In rural areas, collective agriculture was dismantled and land contracted out to farmers who were permitted to sell their surplus produce on the market. Agricultural output increased and rural incomes rose as the result of greater economic incentives, mechanization, new high-yield seeds, and the greater use of chemical fertilizers and pesticides. Improved productivity also freed up large numbers of rural workers and policy encouraged the establishment of Township and Village Enterprises to absorb them. Other rural people began to migrate to cities as the establishment of Special Economic Zones in coastal areas and the marketization of the urban economy provided work in manufacturing, construction and service industries that brought far higher incomes than farming (Cai and Wang 2010). From 1982 to 2002, agriculture's share of GDP fell by 20 per cent (ADB 2003) and by 2001 the level of urbanization was 37.7 per cent (ADB 2003), up from 19 per cent in 1979[2] (Yeh et al. 2011).

The number of people living in poverty fell dramatically and life expectancy rose, from 66 years in 1978 to 73 in 2002 (World Bank 2015). But rapid industrialization also created serious pollution. The first Report on the State of the Environment issued by the State Environmental Protection Administration (SEPA 1997) stated that in 1996, 'the water of rivers, lakes and reservoirs in China was universally polluted to varying degrees'. By 2002, SEPA reported that only 29 per cent of water in China's seven main river basins was suitable for human use (Grades 1–111) and that particulate concentrations in 66 per cent of cities, home to nearly three-quarters of the population, exceeded the national Grade II standard (SEPA 2003). The rapid growth of cities put pressure on urban infrastructure and services; in 2002, the treatment rate for domestic solid waste was only 54 per cent (SEPA 2003).

This period saw growing attention to environmental issues but progress was slow and uneven. It was not until 1988 that environmental protection became an independent policy stream with the formation of the National Environmental Protection Agency, and in 1989 the first Environmental Protection Law was formally promulgated. At this point there was still little attention to reducing the health impacts of pollution. Nor, indeed, was there much knowledge about them, although scattered evidence was beginning to appear and was reported by the Deputy Director of the Ministry of Health at the Second National Conference on Environmental Protection in 1983–1984 (Otsuka 2016).

The health sector, which has been a champion of environmental health in many other countries, was in no position to push the agenda forward at this time. The focus of health policy during this period continued to be on diseases of poverty and had not yet begun to respond to the rise in non-communicable diseases (Holdaway 2010; Su and Duan 2010). The health system was also in a state of internal crisis. The shift from a planned to a more market-based economy resulted in the dismantling of the collective fiscal base for the provision of healthcare and investment in public health. By 1992 only 10 per cent of rural residents nationally had health insurance, compared with 90 per cent in the 1970s, and in 2001, the percentage of health costs paid out of pocket was 60 per cent (World Bank 2015). In this context, traditional preventive health care was more or less discontinued and the new problems presented by pollution were neglected.

By the 1990s, however, evidence of the health effects of pollution was beginning to mount and concern was growing. Reports of cancer clusters, especially in the Huai River Basin, prompted a large-scale government investigation (Yang and Zhuang 2013). In 1997 a study by the World Bank and SEPA estimated that 178,000 people in major cities suffered premature deaths each year because of pollution, and that indoor air pollution caused 111,000 premature deaths annually, mainly in rural areas (World Bank 1997).

2002–2007: Growing concern and early environmental health policies

In retrospect, the period from 2002–2007 was a transitional one in which addressing the negative side effects of China's extremely rapid economic growth emerged as a policy priority. Concern about mounting inequality, and the growing numbers of people falling into or back into poverty due to the cost of healthcare, was accompanied by growing awareness of the health effects of environmental degradation. Although most policies to address these problems were not rolled out until the 11th Five-Year Plan, many of them were incubated during this 2002–2007 period.

An important first step was the *National Action Plan for Environment and Health 2007–2015*, which was signed by 18 ministries (MOH 2007). This plan for the first time indicated the government's commitment to address environmental health problems, using the term environment and health (*huanjing yu jiankang*) rather than the traditional environmental hygiene (*huanjing weisheng*). It enabled a preliminary review of the state of knowledge on environment and health and of existing management capacity. It also provided for the establishment of parallel offices in the Ministry of Health (MOH) and Ministry of Environmental Protection

(MEP) to provide an organizational structure for coordinating environment and health work (Holdaway 2010).

Environment and health had emerged as a discrete policy domain. But despite this initiative at the central level, during the 11th Five-Year Plan (2006–2007), actual policy activities continued to operate mostly on parallel tracks. Environmental protection policies became more comprehensive in scope and were more strictly enforced, but they still focused on reducing aggregate emissions, and did not prioritize pollutants particularly damaging to health or protecting potentially vulnerable populations. Meanwhile, health-sector policies were undergoing a transition towards a greater focus on non-communicable diseases but appeared to be largely ignoring the contribution to these of pollution, with little targeted monitoring of or responses to pollution-related diseases, especially in rural areas (Fang and Bloom 2010). Coordination of environment and health policy with ministries responsible for industrial development and land use was almost entirely absent, and there was no integrated action at the local level (see Holdaway 2010 for a summary).

2007–present: environment and health to centre stage

Since 2007, the trade-offs between the benefits of economic growth and its negative effects in terms of environmental degradation and related health impacts have become even more painfully apparent. On the one hand, 35 years of rapid growth has raised incomes more than sixfold (UNDP 2010) and brought China to middle-income status. This has had enormous benefits for health. By 2010 life expectancy had risen to an average of 75.5 years and China had seen impressive reductions in infectious diseases and improvements in maternal and child health (IHME 2010).

However, the environmental cost has been high. In 2014, only 16 of 161 Chinese cities monitored met national standards for air quality (MEP 2015) and 29 per cent of water monitored in the major river systems and 39 per cent of that in major lakes was Grade IV or below (unfit for human consumption or most agricultural purposes). More than 60 per cent of groundwater was reported to be of either 'quite bad' or 'extremely bad' quality (MEP 2015). A national soil survey conducted from 2005 to 2013 found that 19 per cent of agricultural land was polluted to some degree, mostly with heavy metal and pesticides (MEP and MOLR 2014). Furthermore, acid rain, over-intensive farming and the heavy use of chemical fertilizers means that soil quality is also degraded in many parts of the country, making heavy metals more mobile. Meanwhile, agriculture itself has also become an important source of greenhouse gases (Garnett and Wilkes 2014) as well as of pollution from chemical fertilizers, pesticides and livestock waste containing heavy metals and other chemicals (FORHEAD 2014). In urban areas, emissions from 154 million cars have become a major new source of pollution (China Daily 2015).

Assessing the environmental burden of disease

Although the health effects of pollution are notoriously hard to measure, a growing number of studies have attempted to capture their extent. A study published in 2007 by the World Bank and SEPA estimated, conservatively, that the economic burden of premature mortality and morbidity associated with air pollution was 157.3 billion RMB in 2003, or 1.16 per cent of GDP, and that about 11 per cent of digestive tract cancers might be attributable to polluted drinking water (World Bank and SEPA, 2007). More recently, the *Global Burden of Disease* study listed outdoor air pollution and indoor air pollution as the fourth and fifth most significant risk factors contributing to the loss of disability-adjusted life years (DALYs) in China (Yang et al. 2013). A major study conducted by the Chinese Centre for Disease Control and Prevention (CDC) found a clear association between water pollution and deaths from digestive tract cancers in the Huai River Valley (Yang and Zhuang 2014). Nutrition and diet studies, which provide the best data on exposure to toxic levels of chemicals through food, show that cadmium, lead and a range of persistent organic pollutants are above safe levels in certain parts of the country (Wu and Li 2015).

The importance of understanding demographic and regional variation in risks is discussed below but clearly environmental degradation is taking a serious toll on health in China. In its Environment and Health Work Plan for the 12th Five-Year Plan, the MEP reported that

> first, complex pollution is serious and widespread, and the population exposed is large; second, the period of exposure is long, exposure levels are high, and it will be difficult to eliminate the health impacts of historically accumulated pollution in a short period of time ... at the same time that traditional environment and health problems caused by inadequate basic sanitation facilities have not been entirely dealt with, risks stemming from rapid industrialization and urbanization are gradually increasing ... it will be hard to resolve these four problems within a short period of time.
>
> *(MEP 2011, author's translation)*

Environment and health policy

Since 2011 there has been a marked increase in the intensity of efforts to address environmental impacts on health. The overarching *Outline of the 12th Five-Year Plan for National Economic and Social Development* referred explicitly to the threat that pollution presents to health and to social stability, and the *Environment and Health Work Plan for the 12th Five-Year-Plan Period 2011–2015* (MEP 2011) stepped up investment in integrated monitoring and risk assessment in key regions, the development of standards and legal statutes, and public education. The MEP introduced location- and sector-specific goals for pollution control and remediation, and heavy-metal pollution received explicit attention for the first time in the State Council's *12th Five-Year Plan for the Comprehensive Control of Heavy Metal Pollution*, which stipulated target regions and industries. Other initiatives included the *Program for Comprehensive Control of the Rural Environment* and the plans of the Land Resources, Agriculture and Transport ministries. Many of these statements remained on a general level, but it was clear that the health impacts of pollution were now on the policy agenda (see Holdaway 2013).

2013 was something of a watershed year for environment and health policy in China, prompted partly by a number of serious incidents. These included the prolonged and very severe air pollution that settled over Beijing in January of that year and the discovery of high levels of cadmium in rice from Hunan on sale in markets in Guangdong. This precipitated a surge of media attention and public concern about the impacts of pollution and health – in particular air pollution and food safety – and has in turn prompted a series of government initiatives that have been dubbed a 'War on Pollution'. This has included national, regional and provincial-level action plans to tackle air pollution and the establishment of a new China Food and Drug Administration (CFDA).

Although the MEP continues to be the most active agency in the sphere of environment and health, the health sector has become more involved, particularly in the area of food safety, where, after a number of reorganizations, it has emerged as the lead agency (FORHEAD 2014). Other policy streams are also now showing signs of a more integrated approach to development. For example, the *National Plan for Sustainable Agriculture (2015–2030)* addresses overuse of pesticides and fertilizers, dealing with waste from livestock and soil pollution (MOA 2015); a new soil pollution law is also being drafted and expected to be passed in 2017. It is also increasingly recognized that addressing environment and health problems – particularly those that involve cross-jurisdictional flows of pollution – requires coordinated regional policies. The integrated plan to address air pollution in the Beijing–Tianjin–Hebei region is an example of this (MEP 2013).

The 'new normal' and its challenges

Since 2007, China has entered a new phase in which both market forces and government policies are changing the nature and distribution of economic activities and associated pollution and health impacts. Several factors have contributed to this 'new normal' (*xin changtai*) (Xinhuanet 2014). They include the global financial crisis, slowing growth and China's desire to reduce its dependence on exports and increase domestic consumption; the government's commitment to reducing rural–urban and interregional inequalities; and mounting public concern about pollution, particularly in affluent parts of the country. The 'new normal' has complex and somewhat contradictory implications for environment and health.

Prior to the international financial crisis, China saw annual growth in GDP that averaged around 10 per cent for more than 30 years. This is no longer the case. In 2014, official statistics put the rate of growth at 7.4 per cent and many international analysts estimate it to be far lower (World Economics 2015). China's economy is not just cooling down, it is also restructuring as the result of government policies that seek to promote a shift to cleaner, higher value production and services; and also to reduce inequalities between rural and urban and coastal and hinterland/ western provinces.

In absolute terms, slower growth – in combination with stricter environmental protection – has potential benefits for environment and health. As demand for energy and other inputs, such as steel and cement, slows and production facilities are upgraded, pollution and carbon emissions should also fall. To the extent that China can make a structural transition to cleaner industries and services, this, too, should contribute to reductions in pollution with benefits for health. However, the 'new normal' also brings new challenges.

Inter/intra-regional tensions

Different parts of the country are very differently positioned in terms of their ability to make this transition. For example, there is a fourfold difference between the per capita GDP of the richest provincial-level city of Tianjin, at 99,607 RMB, and the poorest province of Guizhou at 22,922 RMB (NBS 2014). Their economic structures and levels of human capital are also very different: in 2013, 65 per cent of Guizhou's population was still employed in agriculture, and in 2011, only 12 per cent of the province's population had a high school education or more (NBS 2014). Although China is committed in principle to a 'leapfrog' development strategy, it will be difficult for poor provinces to transition quickly to high value industry and services, and it is not surprising that the expansion of polluting industries such as steel, cement, chemicals and ferrous metals is strong in western China. Avoiding rising emissions and health effects in those areas will be hard.

China's uneven development is generating tensions over environmental regulation even within relatively affluent coastal areas. Depending on wind patterns, as much as a quarter of Beijing's air pollution is estimated to come from outside the city, and recent policy has therefore shifted towards regional planning. But Beijing's per capita GDP in 2013 was more than twice that of the surrounding province of Hebei (NBS 2014), and, while services already account for 80 per cent of Beijing's GDP, industry still accounted for 52 per cent of Hebei's economy in 2013 and services for only 35 per cent (Hebei Bureau of Statistics 2014). Within industry, high-energy and polluting industries including steel and cement contribute a substantial part, while the service industry is dominated by transport, retail, household and other relatively low-value traditional services (HBS 2014). Compared with Beijing, Hebei's human capital base is also much less ready for a transition to a high-value economy: only 15 per cent of the population has a secondary school education and 7.4 per cent has attended university (HBS 2014).

If these interregional and inter-jurisdictional tensions cannot be addressed effectively, there is a risk either that environment and health policies will be impossible to implement or that their economic and social costs will fall disproportionately on poor areas and populations. For this reason, greater consideration is needed not only of the impacts of development policies on the environment and on health, but also of the distributional effects of environmental policies. This is not an argument against stronger environmental regulation, which is clearly essential, but a package of integrated environmental, development and social protection policies will be needed to ensure that it does not place an excessive burden on less developed areas (Holdaway and Wang 2014).

Scientific and administrative capacity gaps

Effective measures to address environment and health problems are further hindered by differences in scientific and administrative capacity gaps; many provinces and lower tier cities have inadequate scientific and enforcement capacity that cannot be rapidly increased. For example, Johnson (chapter 22 this volume) discusses the fact that less-developed cities do not have the capacity to test for dioxin emissions from solid waste disposal and that in 2006 the city of Dalian was able to spend 4.5 times the national average on waste treatment (Chen et al. 2010 cited in Johnson this volume). Similar differences exist between rural and urban jurisdictions. In the area of food safety, for example, Liu and McGuire (2015) found significant differences in investment between rural and urban areas even within the same county.

Managing public expectations, building trust and 'co-governance'

Public opinion has played a major role in driving forward the development of environment and health policies, especially with regard to air pollution and food safety. Government documents regularly cite the growing number of protests related to environmental problems as a reason for taking action (for example, MEP 2011). China's environmental NGOs have also used health concerns as a way to push for stronger environmental protection (see Shapiro chapter 4 this volume and Fürst and Holdaway 2015).

However, there are also risks associated with policy being too heavily influenced by public opinion. The scientific complexity of environment and health means that it is quite difficult for the public, or the media and NGOs, to have a good understanding of the nature and level of risks from different sources, or the costs and benefits associated with different policy options (Fürst and Holdaway 2015). Furthermore, in any policy sphere, privileged social groups – in China, wealthy east-coast urbanites – usually have the strongest voice, which can create pressure for policies biased in their favour (Yang 2010; Liu and McGuire 2015). For example, Beijing's air pollution is indeed bad, but it is far from being the worst in the country. It receives a disproportionate amount of attention and resources because it affects the most privileged city in China (Holdaway and Wang 2014).

Of course these problems are not unique to China, but they are exacerbated here by the lack of good public information as well as evidence of cover-ups and official corruption in relation to some environmental health problems, which have produced a kind of free-floating anxiety. Government can, and is beginning, to play a bigger role in the communication of environmental health risks and new laws allow a greater role for public supervision, for example in the joint governance provisions of the *Food Safety Law* (Wang forthcoming). However, too little reliable information about environmental health risks is available, and as a result, public trust remains low. This is a problem not only for the legitimacy of the government, but also in terms of gaining public support for policy.

Conclusion

Over the last 35 years, China has gone from being a country in which the burden of environment-related disease was largely associated with poverty – inadequate sanitation, indoor air pollution and endemic diseases – to one in which pollution from energy generation, industry, intensive agriculture, transportation and household waste are the major problems. After a slow start, environment and health policy has also shifted its focus, driven at least partly by strong public demand for a healthier environment. Environment and health has moved rapidly up the government's agenda over the last ten years, and now occupies a prominent place not only in the environmental protection stream but also in health, agriculture and other agencies. As part of its larger programme of transitioning to a cleaner economic development pathway, the government has vowed to ensure cleaner air and water, and safer food.

But although progress is already evident on some fronts, particularly in China's wealthier coastal cities, delivering on this promise will not be easy. Environmental impacts on health are complex and addressing them requires the coordination of many policy systems. Both scientific and administrative capacity for this is extremely varied across the country.

More fundamentally, and as the government recognizes, tackling pollution will entail deep changes in China's development strategy in the direction of cleaner industry and more compact and less resource-intensive urbanization. While an industrial transition is already under way in many wealthy coastal areas, it will be more of a challenge for hinterland areas which do not have similar levels of resources or human capital and will find it difficult to shift quickly to cleaner economic development pathways. If conflicts over the cost of pollution are not to be replaced with conflicts over the cost of reducing it, the government will have to walk a careful path in balancing environment, health and development policies in the years to come.

Notes

1   The author is also Co-Director of the Beijing-based interdisciplinary Forum on Health, Environment and Development (www.forhead.org). While the opinions expressed are the author's own, the work and insights of many FORHEAD members have informed the analysis presented here. For more detail, see the notes in the text.

2   An urban area is defined in China's 2000 census as one with more than 1,500 people per km². Since 2000 China has adopted the standard definition of six months' residence (Yeh et al. 2011).

References

Asian Development Bank (ADB), 2003. *Key Indicators of Developing Asian and Pacific Countries, 2003: China*. http://www.adb.org/sites/default/files/publication/27733/prc.pdf (accessed 30 November 2016).

Asian Development Bank (ADB), 2015. *Key Indicators of Developing Asian and Pacific Countries, 2014: China.* http://www.adb.org/sites/default/files/publication/175162/prc.pdf (accessed 30 November 2016).

Banister, J., 1998. Population, public health and the environment in China. *The China Quarterly*, 156, 986–1015.

Biggs, B., King, L., Basu, S. and Stuckler, D., 2010. Is wealthier always healthier? The impact of national income level, inequality and poverty on public health in Latin America. *Social Science and Medicine*, 71, 266–273.

Brady, D., Kaya, Y. and Beckfield, J., 2007. Reassessing the effect of economic growth on well-being in less-developed countries, 198–2003. *Studies in Comparative International Development*, 42(1/2), 1–35.

Bramall, C., 2003. Path dependency and growth in rural China since 1978. *Asian Business & Management*, 2 (3), 301–321.

Cai F. and Wang M., 2010. Growth and structural changes in employment in transition China. *Journal of Comparative Economics*, 38, 71–81.

China Daily, 2015. Car ownership tops 154 million in China in 2014. January http://www.chinadaily.com.cn/business/motoring/2015-01/28/content_19424673.htm (accessed 14 September 2016).

Cook, I. G. and Dummer, T.J.B., 2004. Changing health in China: re-evaluating the epidemiological transition model. *Health Policy*, 67, 329–343.

Du S.F., Wang H.J., Zhang B., Zhai F.Y., and Popkin, B.M., 2014. China in the period of transition from scarcity and extensive undernutrition to emerging nutrition-related non-communicable diseases, 1949–1992. *Obesity Reviews*, 15 (Supp) 1, 8–15.

Economy, E., 2004. *The River Runs Black.* Cornell University Press, Ithaca.

Fang J., and Bloom, G., 2010. China's rural health system and environment-related health risks. *Journal of Contemporary China*, 19 (63), 23–35.

Forget, G., and Lebel, J., 2001. An ecosystem approach to human health. *International Journal of Occupational and Environmental Health*, supplement to 7 (2), 3–38.

Forum on Health, Environment and Development (FORHEAD), 2014. Food Safety in China. http://www.ssrc.org/publications/view/food-safety-in-china-a-mapping-of-problems-governance-and-research/ (accessed 14 September 2016).

Fürst, K. and Holdaway, J., 2015. Environment and health in China: the role of environmental NGOs in policy innovation, in A. Fulda (ed.), *Civil Society Contributions to Policy Innovation in the PR China.* Basingstoke, UK: Palgrave Macmillan, 33–76.

Gale, F., Tuan F, Lohmar, B., Hsu H. and Gilmour, B., 2002. *China's Food and Agriculture: Issues for the 21st Century. Agriculture Information Bulletin* No. (AIB-775).

Garnett, T. and Wilkes, A., 2014. *Appetite for Change: Social, Economic and Environmental Transformations in China's Food System.* Food Climate Research Network, Oxford University. http://www.fcrn.org.uk/sites/default/files/fcrn_china_mapping_study_final_pdf_2014.pdf (accessed 30 November 2016).

Hebei Bureau of Statistics (HBS). 2014. *Hebei Province Statistical Yearbook.*

Holdaway, J., 2010. Environment and health: an emerging interdisciplinary research field. *Journal of Contemporary China*, 19 (63), 1–22.

Holdaway, J., 2013. Environment and health research in China: the state of the field. *The China Quarterly*, 214, 255–282.

Holdaway, J., 2014. Migration, environment and health: towards a more integrated analysis. United Nations Research Institute for Social Development (UNRISD) Working Paper. http://www.unrisd.org/holdaway (accessed 30 November 2016).

Holdaway, J., 2015. Food security, urbanization and rural transformations: the view from China. International Institute for Environment and Development (IIED) Working Paper. http://pubs.iied.org/pdfs/10753IIED.pdf (accessed 30 November 2016).

Holdaway, J. and Wang W., 2014. Stronger enforcement won't be enough to solve China's environment and health problems. *China Dialogue*, April 29. https://www.chinadialogue.net/article/show/single/en/6926-Stronger-enforcement-won-t-be-enough-to-solve-China-s-environment-and-health-problems (accessed 14 September 2016).

Institute for Health Metrics and Evaluation (IHME), 2010. *Global Burden of Disease Country Profiles.* Seattle: Institute for Health Metrics and Evaluation. https://www.healthdata.org/sites/default/files/files/country_profiles/GBD/ihme_gbd_country_report_china.pdf (accessed 15 December 2016).

Liu P. and McGuire, W., 2015. One regulatory state, two regulatory regimes: understanding dual regimes in China's regulatory state building through food safety. *Journal of Contemporary China*, 24(91), 119–136.

Maddison Project, 2013. Analysis from the database. 2013 version. http://www.ggdc.net/maddison/maddison-project/home.htm (accessed 14 September 2014).

Ministry of Agriculture (MOA), 2015. National Sustainable Agriculture Plan 2015–30. May 20. http://www.mof.gov.cn/zhengwuxinxi/zhengcefabu/201505/t20150528_1242763.htm (accessed 14 September 2016).

Ministry of Environmental Protection (MEP), 2011. The 12th Five-Year Plan for the Environmental Health Work of National Environmental Protection. September 21. http://english.mep.gov.cn/Resources/Plans/Special_Fiveyear_Plan/201201/P020120110355818985016.pdf (accessed 15 December 2016).

Ministry of Environmental Protection (MEP), 2013. Jingjinji ji zhoubian diqu luoshi daqi wuran fanzhi xingdong jihu shishi xize (Detailed measures for implementing the pollution control plan in Beijing-Tianjin-Hebei and surrounding areas) http://www.zhb.gov.cn/gkml/hbb/bwj/201309/W020130918412886411956.pdf (accessed 20 November 2016).

Ministry of Environmental Protection (MEP), 2015. State of China's Environment Report 2014. May 19.

Ministry of Environmental Protection and Ministry of Land Resources (MEP and MOLR), 2014. National Soil Survey Report. http://www.sdpc.gov.cn/fzgggz/ncjj/zhdt/201404/t20140418_607888.html (accessed 14 September 2016).

Ministry of Health (MOH), 2007. Guojia huanjing yu jiankang xingdong jihua. (National Action Plan on Environment and Health (2007–2015)). http://www.moh.gov.cn/open/web_edit_file/20071108173502.doc (accessed 30 November 2016).

National Bureau of Statistics, 2014. *China Statistical Yearbook 2014.* http://www.stats.gov.cn/tjsj/ndsj/2014/indexeh.htm (accessed 14 September 2016).

Nielsen, C.P. and Ho, M., 2013. *Clearer Skies over China: Reconciling Air Quality, Climate and Economic Goals.* Cambridge, MA: MIT Press.

OECD, 2007. *Improving co-ordination between environmental and health policies: Final Report.* Rome: Environment Policy Directorate.

Otsuka, K., 2016. Developing environment and health policy in China. *The Journal of Contemporary China Studies,* 5 (1), 27–42.

Prüss-Üstün, A., and Corvalán, C., 2006. *Preventing Disease through Healthy Environments: Towards an Estimate of the Environmental Burden of Disease.* Geneva: WHO.

Smith, K. R. and Ezzati, M., 2005. How environmental health risks change with development: the epidemiologic and environmental risk transitions revisited. *Annual Review of Environment and Resources* 30, 291–333.

State Environmental Protection Administration (SEPA), 1997. 1996 Report on the State of China's Environment. May 22. http://www.mep.gov.cn/hjzl/zghjzkgb/lnzghjzkgb/201605/P020160526549917367367.pdf (accessed 15 December 2016).

State Environmental Protection Agency (SEPA), 2003. Report on the State of the Environment in China 2002. http://english.mep.gov.cn/SOE/soechina2002/index.htm (accessed 14 September 2016).

Su Y. and Duan X., 2010. Zhongguo huanjing yu jiankang gongzuo de xianzhuang, wenti he duice (Current situation, problems and responses in China's environment and health work). In Holdaway, H., Wang W., Zhang S. and Ye J. (eds.), *Huanjing yu jiankang: kuaxueke shijiao (Environment and Health: Cross-disciplinary Perspectives).* Beijing: Social Science Academies Press, 72–98.

United Nations Development Programme (UNDP), 2010. *China and a Sustainable Future: Toward a Low Carbon Economy and Society.* UNDP China Human Development Report 2009/10. China Translation and Publishing Company. http://hdr.undp.org/sites/default/files/chine_2010.pdf (accessed 15 December 2016).

United Nations Development Programme (UNDP), 2013. *Human Development Report 2013 The Rise of the South: Human Progress in a Diverse World.*

United Nations Population Division, 2012. *World Population Prospects: the 2012 Revision.* http://data.un.org/Data.aspx?d=PopDiv&f=variableID%3a68 (accessed 14 September 2016).

Wang W., Yang L., Li H., He Z., et al. (eds.), 2014. *Zhongguo quyu huanjing, jiankang yu fazhan zonghe fenxi.* (Integrated Analysis of Regional Development, Environment and Health in China), Beijing: China Environment Press.

Wang, X., forthcoming. National governance and food safety. Developments in Food Safety Problems and Governance in China. *Journal of Ecology and Resources.*

World Bank, 1997. *Clear Water Blue Skies: China's Environment in the New Century.* Washington, DC: World Bank.

World Bank, 2012. Renewable internal fresh water resources per capita (cubic meters), 2012. http://data. worldbank.org/indicator/ER.H2O.INTR.PC (accessed 14 September 2016).

World Bank, 2015. World Bank Country Data, China. Downloaded from http://data.worldbank.org/ country/china (accessed 14 September 2016).

World Bank and State Environmental Protection Administration, 2007. *The Cost of Pollution in China: Economic Estimates of Physical Damages*. http://siteresources.worldbank.org/INTEAPREGTOP ENVIRONMENT/Resources/China_Cost_of_Pollution.pdf (accessed 30 November 2016).

World Economics, 2015. China Growth Tracker. http://www.worldeconomics.com/Papers/China%20 Growth%20Tracker_cac90741-8882-4311-969e-3ae0e3e2575c.paper. (accessed 3 October 2015).

World Health Organization, 2005. *Ecosystems and Human Well-Being: Health Synthesis: A Report of the Millennium Ecosystem Assessment*. Geneva: World Health Organization.

Wu Y. and Li X. (eds.), 2015. *The Fourth China Total Diet Study*. Beijing: Chemical Industry Press.

Xinhuanet, 2014. Xi's 'new normal' theory. November 9. http://news.xinhuanet.com/english/ china/2014-11/09/c_133776839.htm (accessed 3 October 2016).

Yang G., 2010. Brokering environment and health in China: issue entrepreneurs of the public sphere. *Journal of Contemporary China*, 19(63), 101–118.

Yang G., Wang Y., Zeng Y., Gao G.F., Liang X., Zhou M., Wan X., Yu S., Jiang Y., Naghavi, M., Vos, T., Wang H., Lopez, A.D., Murray C.J., 2013. Rapid health transition in China, 1990–2010: findings from the Global Burden of Disease Study 2010. *Lancet*, 381(9882),1987–2015.

Yeh G., Xu J. and Liu K., 2011. China's post-reform urbanization: Retrospect, policies and trends. International Institute for Environment and Development (IIED) Working Paper. http://pubs.iied. org/pdfs/10593IIED.pdf. (accessed 30 November 2016).

Yang G. and Zhuang D., (eds), 2014. *Atlas of the Huai River Basin Water Environment: Digestive Cancer Mortality*. Beijing: Springer.

13

ENVIRONMENTAL ACCIDENTS AND RISK REDUCTION IN CHINA

Yu Fang, Cao Guozhi, Jia Qian, Zhu Wenying and Yang Weishan

Overview of environmental emergency accidents in China

Types and numbers

During the last decade, in the process of rapid industrialization, China has suffered a series of environmental emergencies that have resulted in damage to the ecosystem, human health, and property. According to the statistical data pertaining to the period between 2001 and 2010, a total of 11,069 accidents occurred which led to environmental pollution and damage resulting in an annual loss of RMB 100 million (ZHTN 2001–2010). Table 13.1 and Figure 13.1 show the total number of environmental emergency accidents and the associated trends observed between 2010 and 2014.

The number of accidents continued to increase between 2010 and 2013; 712 accidents were registered in 2013, an increase of more than 30 per cent compared with 2012. In 2014, the number of accidents dropped significantly to 471. Of these, three were rated as major emergency accidents, 16 as serious emergency accidents, and 452 as minor emergency accidents, accounting for 0.6 per cent, 3.4 per cent, and 96 per cent respectively of the total number of accidents (ZHTN 2015). Table 13.2 lists a few of the typical accidents that have occurred in recent years.

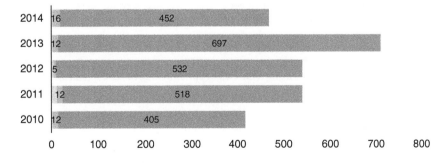

Figure 13.1 Number of environmental emergency accidents in recent years (Data from *ZHTN China Environmental Statistical Yearbook 2010–2015*)

Table 13.1 Number of environmental emergency accidents in recent years

Year		Major	Serious	Minor	Total
2010	Amount	3	12	405	420
	%	0.7	2.86	96.4	100
2011	Amount	12	12	518	542
	%	2.2	2.2	95.6	100
2012	Amount	5	5	532	542
	%	0.9	0.9	98.2	100
2013	Amount	3	12	697	712
	%	0.4	1.7	97.9	100
2014	Amount	3	16	452	471
	%	0.6	3.4	96.0	100

Source: Data from ZHTN China Environmental Statistical Yearbook 2010–2015.

Table 13.2 Typical examples of severe environmental emergency accidents in recent years

	Date	Description	Cause	Impacts
1	2015.8	Hazardous chemical warehouse blast in Tianjin	Illegal storage of hazardous chemicals	165 people died, 8 others were missing, 798 people were injured; surface water, air, soil was polluted; some buildings and cars are damaged
2	2014.8	Qianzhangyan Reservoir pollution	Illegal discharge	Drinking water for 50,000 people affected; estimated economic loss of 3.34 million RMB
3	2013.11	Pipeline explosion accident in Qingdao	Pipeline leakage	62 people died and 136 injured; estimated economic loss of 0.75 billion RMB
4	2012.1	Cadmium pollution accident in Longjiang River in Guangxi Province	Illegal discharge	More than 160 km of Long River and the drinking water of riverside inhabitants affected; aquaculture industry suffered from great loss, and the ecosystem of Long River damaged
5	2011.6	Phenol leakage in Xin'an River	Traffic accident	One person died; water body of Xin'an River was partially polluted, affecting the resident drinking water
6	2010.7	Oil leaking at Xingang Port of Dalian	Improper operation by unloading cargo ship	Leakage of crude oil; pollution occurred in ocean and air

[1] *Source*: News from the State Council. http://www.gov.cn/xinwen/2016-02/05/content_5039785.htm

[2] *Source*: News from MEP. http://www.mep.gov.cn/gkml/hbb/qt/201501/t20150120_294598.htm

[3] *Source*: News from the Central People's Government of the People's Republic of China. http://www.gov.cn/gzdt/2014-01/11/content_2564671.htm

[4] *Source*: Report from CAEP.

[5] *Source*: News from Xinhua net. http://news.xinhuanet.com/2011-06/08/c_121508745.htm

[6] *Source*: News from Sina net. http://finance.sina.com.cn/china/dfjj/20100720/01328323519.shtml

Analysis of environmental emergency accidents

Increasing scale and dimension of environmental risks

China is currently going through a phase of rapid industrialization and urbanization, during which the scale and dimensions of environmental risks have continually been increasing. In the last decade, China's heavy industry experienced rapid development, for example, the total output of the petrochemical industry grew by 8.6 times (ZHTN 2001–2015). In 2014, the total output capacity of heavy industrial sectors amounted to 2.47 billion tons of cement production and over 1 billion tons of crude steel production (ZHTN 2015). At the same time, China has also become the leading emitter of major pollutants. Extensive industrial development has had a serious impact on the regional environment and resources, including health risks related to air, water and soil pollution and ecological degradation. According to an environmental risk and chemicals inspection conducted by the Ministry of Environmental Protection (MEP) in 2009, only about 12 per cent of a total of 46,682 enterprises were located at a distance of less than one kilometre from residential areas and about 10 per cent of these enterprises were located less than one kilometre away from residential areas with a high population density. Roughly 72 per cent of the chemical industrial plants are located along river basins, such as the Yangtze River, the Pearl River, and Taihu Lake (ZHTN 2015). It must be assumed that during the phase of the 13th Five-Year-Plan (FYP) (2016–2020) and even the 14th FYP (2021–2025), the environmental risks posed by inappropriate industrial structures and sites will remain high.

Increasing health issues related to accumulated environmental pollution

In addition to environmental accidents, accumulated environmental pollution has become a hidden danger to public health. For example, recent media reports on heavy metal pollution including the lead poisoning accidents in Wugang (Hunan province) and Fengxiang (Shaanxi province), and cadmium pollution in Liuyang (Hunan province) have raised public concern (HYSYSDZ 2010). A total of 56 environmental health accidents above the medium-serious levels occurred between 2006 and 2010, of which 26 were due to accumulated environmental pollution, which accounted for more than 46 per cent of the total number of accidents (HYSYSDZ 2010). In recent years, the water quality of several river basins and lakes has been affected by an 'algal bloom outbreak', for example, the Taihu Lake (2007–2014) and the Chao Lake (2012, 2013, 2015). These outbreaks have had adverse effects on aquatic organisms and pose a threat to drinking water safety. Accumulated environmental pollution is not only a potential risk and hidden danger for the ecosystem and human health, but also a critical factor in social stability.

Environmental emergency response related to production safety issues

In the course of China's current rapid industrialization and urbanization, investment remains focused on polluting and high-risk industries, for instance, the petrochemical industry, the mining and smelting industry and coal-fired power plants. Production safety issues have become a subject of environmental risk management due to weak environmental awareness, benefits-oriented economic growth, and ageing equipment, especially in enterprises which produce and process hazardous chemicals. In addition, factors such as insufficient environmental investment and unimplemented mechanisms for environmental risk management also play roles in triggering environmental emergency accidents. For example, in 2015, the catastrophic accident involving a fire and an explosion in a dangerous chemicals warehouse in Tianjin and the tailings leakage accident in Gansu, were both caused by inadequate risk management. Both accidents resulted in huge economic losses and had a significant impact on the environment.

Impact of environmental accidents on social stability

With rising economic growth and living standards, individuals have started to pay greater attention to environmental protection and to show greater awareness of environmental pollution and risks. In recent years, a number of public protests have taken place against newly-built waste incineration plants in Guangzhou, Beijing, and Wujiang and against paraxylene, 'PX', chemical manufacturing projects in Xiamen, Dalian, Ningbo, Kunming, Pengzhou and other cities. All these cases are indicators of growing public concern about potential environmental risks and represent a public appeal for environmental rights. The number of environmental petition cases and bills (proposals and suggestions) submitted to the National People's Congress (NPC) and Chinese People's Political Consultative Conference (CPPCC) are increasing year by year. These can be seen as signs of a conflict between the public demand for environmental safety and the inadequate capacities of the environmental emergency response system. According to the China Environmental Statistical Yearbook (ZHTN 2015), appeals and petitions related to environmental pollution and cases of mass protests are growing at an annual rate of 30 per cent, and this trend seems unlikely to change in the near future.

Environmental emergency accidents induced by natural disasters

China has a vast territorial area with complex landscapes, and suffers from a high frequency of natural disasters that often cause severe loss of property. Moreover, China lacks the facilities to conduct early-warning emergency responses. This is a time bomb for tailings and chemical enterprises that pose severe environmental risks and do not have sufficient capacity to implement risk prevention measures or to respond rapidly in emergency situations. In 2013, 39 environmental emergency accidents were caused by natural disasters, accounting for 5.5 per cent of the total number of accidents (ZHTN 2015).

Measures for risk control and management of environmental emergency accidents

The *11th Five-Year Plan for Environmental Protection* represented the beginning of a period when the total emissions of pollutants started to decrease and the quality of the environment gradually improved, but acute environmental incidents still frequently occurred. In the case of specific environmental problems, the *12th Five-Year Plan for Environmental Protection* proposed 'to lower the total amount of emissions, improve environmental quality, and prevent risk' as a guideline. This included the promotion of the strategic transformation of environmental management; the setting up of a management system emphasizing environmental quality; a coordinated approach towards pollution abatement, total emissions reduction, environmental risk control and environmental quality improvement.

Laws and regulations

China has issued laws and a regulations system for environmental risk management based on the Constitutional Law, national laws and ministerial provisions and regulations. Article 47 of the newly revised *Environmental Protection Law* states that in the case of risk control, emergency preparedness, emergency response and recovery efforts for environmental emergencies, governments at all levels as well as the relevant departments, enterprises and institutions shall act in accordance with the *People's Republic of China Emergency Response Law* (2007).

The *Water Pollution Prevention and Control Law* (1984, amended 2008), the *Air Pollution Prevention and Control Law* (2000, amended 2015) and the *Solid Waste Pollution Prevention and Control Law* (1995, amended 2013), among others, mentioned the principle of combining risk prevention and emergency response, preparedness for environmental emergencies in emergency preparedness, emergency response and recovery according to the proposed requirements. The *Water Pollution Prevention and Control Law* includes chapters for dealing with environmental accidents involving water, and the *Air Pollution Prevention and Control Law* (2015) states the rules for dealing with accidents involving atmospheric pollution. China enacted the *Environmental Impact Assessment Law* (2013) to comprehensively lower environmental impacts, control pollution, and protect the ecological environment at its roots. In addition, the *Construction Project Environmental Protection Regulations* (1998) aimed to mitigate the environmental pollution and ecological damage related to construction projects. However, China still lacks unified legislation related to environmental risk prevention.

In the case of an environmental emergency response, the laws and regulations that apply to environmental emergency accidents have become more complex. The *National Environmental Emergency Plan* (2014) was enacted to improve emergency response mechanisms and to manage emergency accidents in a more effective manner. Furthermore, emergency response, accident investigation and classification, and post-accident management were endorsed by a series of regulations, including the revised *Environmental Emergency Response Measures by Ministry of Environmental Protection* (2013), *Information Report Measures of Environmental Emergency* (2011), *Notification Measures of Environmental Emergency* (2010), *Work Procedure Regulations of Environmental Damage Assessment in Emergency Disposal* (2013), and *Investigation and Handling Measures of Environmental Emergency Accidents* (2014).

Emergency plan management

Since the 11th FYP, China has paid increasing attention to developing environmental emergency response mechanisms. In January 2006, the State Council issued 25 specific plans and 80 further plans, including the *National General Plan for Public Emergencies* and the *National Environmental Emergency Plan* (hereafter referred to as the National Plan). In the same year, the State Council issued the *Advice from State Council on the Overall Emergency Management*, which clearly regarded the implementation and improvement of emergency plans as guidelines for emergency management, and called for a comprehensive environmental emergency prevention system to be set up that covers all regions and sectors.

Since the 11th FYP period, China has made progress in establishing an environmental emergency response system that is focused on four stages of risk control and prevention (i.e. prevention, preparation of emergency response, emergency response and post-accident management). Focused on the emergency plan, management system, mechanism and legislation, a key framework has been established, which is also known as 'one plan and three systems'. In the course of nearly a decade, provinces (autonomous regions and municipalities), cities (districts) and counties as well as relevant departments have issued emergency plans for environmental emergencies, and have implemented a relatively comprehensive emergency plan system. Environmental emergency plans, as a starting point for emergency management, have played an important role in implementing an environmental emergency management system.

Table 13.3 Relevant laws and regulations concerning risk management and emergency response

Classification	Laws/Regulations/Codes	Year	Authorities	Contents
Accumulated Risk	Air Pollution Prevention and Control Law	Amended 2015	National People's Congress	Mainly includes regulations about air pollution prevention standards and planning of reaching nation standard within a time limit, supervision and management, prevention and control measures, joint prevention and control of key regional air pollution, response to heavy pollution weather, legal responsibility, and so on.
	Solid Waste Pollution Prevention and Control Law	Amended 2015	National People's Congress	It mainly includes rules about supervision and management of solid waste pollution prevention, regulations about prevention from pollution of industrial solid waste, living garbage and hazardous waste, rules on legal liability and so on.
	Environmental Protection Law	Amended 2014	National People's Congress	It includes 6 chapters: general principles, environment supervision and management, protect and improve environment, prevent and control environmental pollution and other public hazards, legal responsibility and supplementary provisions.
	Water Pollution Prevention and Control Law	Amended 2008	National People's Congress	Mainly includes regulations about water pollution prevention standards and planning, supervision and management, prevention and control measures, protection of drinking water sources and other special water body, response to water pollution accident, legal responsibility, and so on.
	Environmental Impact Assessment Law	2002	National People's Congress	Mainly includes regulations on environmental impact assessment of planning and construction projects, aiming to prevent adverse effects caused by planning and construction projects.
	Noise Pollution Prevention and Control Law	1996	National People's Congress	A law for prevention and control of environmental noise pollution, in order to protect and improve the living environment.

	Document	Year	Issuing Body	Description
Acute Risk	National Environmental Emergency plans	Amended 2014	General Office, State Council	Includes rules on organization command system, monitoring and early warning, information report, emergency response, the late treatment, and emergency assurance.
	Investigation and Handling Measures of Environmental Emergency Accidents	2014	MEP	It is suitable for the cause, property and responsibility investigation of the environmental emergency, including subject and object of investigation, and investigation measures and contents.
	Environmental Emergency Response Measures by Ministry of Environmental Protection	2013	MEP	Rules about response grading, manner, procedures, work content of the working group.
	Work Procedure Regulations of Environmental Damage Assessment in Emergency Disposal	2013	MEP	It rules work procedures of environmental damage assessment in emergency disposal, including the subject, principle, time limit and so on.
	Information Report Measures of Environmental Emergency	2011	MEP	It applies to environmental protection department, and mainly includes rules about procedure, content, manner of information report of environmental emergency.
	Notification Measures of Environmental Emergency	2010	MEP	Emergency office of MEP makes notification about information report of the provinces. This document gives notification form and content.
	Emergency Response Law	2007	National People's Congress	Mainly includes regulations about risk control, emergency preparedness, emergency response and recovery efforts for environmental emergencies.

At present, China's emergency plan management system is close to completion. It consists of a general emergency response plan, specific emergency response plans, emergency response plans for goverments, enterprises and public institutions, and a provisional emergency response plan. The current emergency plans are still at a preliminary stage. Only about half of the provincial environmental protection departments have designed emergency plans for the environmental management system and a specified local environment management emergency plan. In addition, since the development and implementation of the *Temporary Provisions for Environmental Emergency Plan Management* (2010), 25 provinces and municipalities (with the exception of Inner Mongolia, Xinjiang, Tibet, Jiangxi and Hubei) have enacted supporting documents to promote environmental emergency response plans for development, evaluation, recording, training and exercises.

In addition, China has issued the *Temporary Provisions for Environmental Emergency Plan Management* (2010) which provides standards for the preparation, assessment, recording, modification, drills and other procedures that form part of the emergency plans. Further to this, *Instructions for Emergency Plan for Petrochemical Enterprises* (2010) and the *Risk Assessment Guide for Enterprises (Trial)* (2014) have been enacted in order to steadily promote the risk management preparation work in enterprises and institutes. China has also organized and guided the Shanghai World Expo security environment emergency drills, the Chongqing municipal environmental emergency joint exercise, as well as the Yunnan province environmental emergency drills for toxic gases environmental emergencies.

According to a survey conducted by the Center of Environmental Emergency and Accident Investigation of the MEP, by the end of 2013 the provincial environmental emergency plan had reached full coverage, 80 per cent of the plan had been revised; about half of the provincial environmental protection departments had established an emergency plan management system; more than 90 per cent of the environmental protection departments above municipal districts had planned for environmental emergencies; Beijing, Tianjin, Shanxi, Chongqing and county environmental protection departments had reached a preparedness rate of 100 per cent; all localities had strengthened the enterprise management emergency plans, and had actively carried out pilot plans for dealing with corporate environmental emergencies. The business environment emergency plan filing rate of Chongqing had reached 100 per cent; Jiangsu Industrial Park had also implemented environmental emergency plans.

Organization

China's environmental emergency response system is divided into three levels, namely, national, regional and local levels. At the national level, the MEP is in charge of major environmental emergency response guidance, coordination, the daily supervision and management of environmental emergencies. In 2002, the MEP established the Environmental Emergency and Accident Investigation Center, which is responsible for establishing and managing a national environmental pollution and ecological destruction emergency response system. The centre set up an Environmental Emergency Command Group, which is responsible for investigating serious accidents and sudden environmental pollution emergencies as well as ecological damage incidents.

At the regional level, the MEP has set up six regional environmental protection supervision centres for the investigation of major cases of environmental pollution, ecological destruction and supervision in serious environmental emergencies.

At the local level, Beijing Municipal Environmental Protection Bureau, Shanghai Environmental Protection Bureau, Jiangsu Provincial Environmental Protection Bureau,

Guangdong Provincial Environmental Protection Bureau and Dalian Municipal Environmental Protection Bureau have set up environmental emergency centres that are responsible for provincial and municipal environmental emergency response efforts. These emergency response agencies are mainly responsible for accidents, sudden environmental pollution and the investigation of ecological destruction emergencies. Relying on environmental monitoring stations, environmental science research institutes and other institutes, China now has a basic system in place that includes an appropriate personnel structure and funding to protect the environment. At present, about 70 per cent of the environmental authorities at provincial level and 50 per cent at local level have set up management authorities to deal with environmental emergencies, 13 of which are operated at provincial level, and 84 are operated at local level. In particular, Jiangsu, Gansu province and Chongqing, have established a sophisticated emergency management system at both provincial and local levels.

Regulation and guidance

Technical standards can be divided into two areas: risk prevention and control, and emergency response. In terms of risk prevention and control, specific standards are developed for construction projects, key industries, business ventures and chemical industries. The *Technical Standards for Environmental Impact Assessment* (2014) have been enacted to implement the *Environmental Protection Law of the PRC* (2015) as well as the *Environmental Protection Regulations for Construction Projects* (1998), and specify the general principals, methods, content, and requirements of EIAs. In addition, the *Technical Guidelines for Environmental Risk Assessment on Projects* (2004) have been enacted to promote a comprehensive risk management system for construction projects. For high environmental risk industries, such as those that are involved in the production of sulphuric acid, alkalis and crude lead smelting, environmental risk classification methods have been defined to promote the implementation of environmental pollution liability insurance. In order to prevent environmental emergencies, the MEP emergency centre issued the *Guidelines for Risk Assessment of Enterprise Environmental Emergency Accidents (trial)* (2014) and classified enterprises into different levels for an environmental emergency scenario. In addition, the *Environmental Risk Assessment Guidelines for Contaminated Sites* (2014) and the introduction of the *Key Environmental Management of Hazardous Chemicals Environmental Risk Assessment Methods* (2013) further improved the environmental risk evaluation system. Taking the current environmental risk management plan management as the starting point, China unveiled the *Guidelines for Preparation of Emergency Plans for Hazardous Waste Management Units*, the *Guidelines for an Environmental Emergency Response Plan for the Petrochemical Corporation* (2010) and the *Guidelines for the Preparation of Urban Serious Atmospheric Pollution Emergency Plan* (2013) for the purpose of improving the quality of emergency plans for enterprises and institutes.

Emergency response technical standards include emergency response procedures specifications and technical guides for conducting an emergency response, monitoring an emergency and assessing emergency phase damage. In 2006, the State Environmental Protection Administration (the SEPA, later the MEP), issued an *Emergency Response Handbook for Environmental Accidents* (SEPA 2006). In the context of the frequent accidents involving tailings and oil leakages, the MEP commissioned experts to develop the *Environmental Protection Solutions for Tailing Accidents* and *Environmental Emergency Response Techniques and Solutions of Oil Leakage*. The *Monitoring Standard for Emergency Accidents*, enacted in October 2010, provides standards for stationing sampling points, monitoring subjects, site monitoring and laboratory analysis methods, data processing and reporting, monitoring quality control, and other associated requirements. To deal with the calculation of direct economic losses resulting from environmental emergencies,

Table 13.4 Relevant standards and guidance concerning risk management and emergency response

Classification	Laws/Regulations/Codes	Year	Authorities	Contents
Accumulated Risk	Guidelines of industrial enterprise site environment survey assessment and restoration	2014	MEP	Guidelines for environmental site investigation, risk assessment, remediation, environmental supervision of remediation, remediation acceptance and late management.
	Technical guidelines for environmental site investigation	2014	MEP	Guidelines about the general principle and work procedure of environmental site investigation.
	Technical guidelines for environmental site monitoring	2014	MEP	It mainly includes the principle, contents and work procedure of environmental site monitoring.
	Technical guidelines for risk assessment of contaminated sites	2014	MEP	It mainly includes the principle, contents, procedure, methods and technical requirements of risk assessment of contaminated sites.
	Technical guidelines for site soil remediation	2014	MEP	It includes the general principle and work procedure for site soil remediation.

	Name	Year	Organization	Description
Acute Risk	Technical guideline for environmental risk assessment of tailings ponds	2015	MEP	Method for environmental risk assessment of tailings ponds, including risk assessment prepare, risk prediction, grading classification, risk analysis and report compilation.
	Guidelines for environmental risk assessment in Enterprises	2014	MEP	It mainly includes the procedure, contents and grading classification method of environmental risk. It applies to some types of enterprises, and the document gives range of application.
	Technical Specifications for Environmental Damage Assessment in Emergency Disposal	2014	MEP	It provides scientific methodology on Environmental Damage Assessment.
	Guidelines for environmental risk assessment method for environmental risk grading classification of crude lead smelting enterprises	2013	MEP	Method for environmental risk grading classification of crude lead smelting enterprises.
	Guidelines for preparation of urban serious atmospheric pollution contingency plan	2013	MEP	It includes the procedure and main contents for preparation of urban serious atmospheric pollution contingency plan.
	Guidelines for environmental risk assessment method for environmental risk grading classification of sulphuric acid enterprises	2011	MEP, CIRC (China Insurance Regulatory Commission)	Method for environmental risk grading classification of sulphuric acid enterprises.
	Guidelines for environmental risk assessment method for environmental risk grading classification of chlor–alkali enterprises	2010	MEP	Method for environmental risk grading classification of chlor–alkali enterprises.
	Guidelines for preparation of environmental emergency response plan for petro–chemical enterprises	2010	MEP	It includes the procedure and main contents for preparation of environmental emergency response plan for petro–chemical enterprises.
	Technical specification for emergency monitoring in abrupt environmental accidents	2010	MEP	It includes the methods of stationing, sampling, monitoring, analysis, data processing, report writing, and quality control in emergency monitoring.
	Technical guidelines for environmental risk assessment on projects	2004	SEPA, now MEP	It mainly includes the level, procedure, contents and scale of environmental risk assessment on projects.

China issued the *Work Procedure Regulations of Environmental Damage Assessment in Emergency Disposal* (2013) and *Technical Specifications for Environmental Damage Assessment in Emergency Disposal* (2014).

Capacity building

Environmental emergency teams at all levels are gradually improving. The MEP issued a *Management Approach for Environmental Emergency Specialists* in order to invite more than 300 experts from research institutes, enterprises and institutions, universities, the military and industrial associations to establish an environmental emergency expert database. In addition, provincial and municipal environmental emergency centres have set up environmental emergency specialist databases according to the regional characteristics of environmental risk and types of environmental emergencies. For the purpose of establishing emergency rescue teams, China has also explored some emergency rescue models, such as the specialized government rescue staff, the enterprises rescue group and professional rescue companies.

The standardization of environmental emergency response capacity building has gradually been implemented. Several measures and standards have been issued, such as the *Emergency Response Capacity Building Standard of Environmental Protection Authorities* (2010) and the *Measures of Compliance for Examination of Emergency Response Capacity of Environmental Protection Authorities (trial)* (2012), which have been launched at pilot-sites in Suzhou, Liaoning, and Shenyang at provincial and city levels. Emergency materials storage and emergency staff capacity have increased year by year. Through the financial assistance provided by central government and local support, a total of 59 high-capacity emergency monitoring vehicles, which are capable of monitoring water, air, and radiation, have been provided for 27 provinces, three municipalities, and the Production and Construction Corps of Tibet. By this means, a preliminary mobile monitoring network using monitoring vehicles has been established. An information system is being set up. An MEP environmental emergency response management system has been established and is fully operational. A supporting command platform is under construction. The *National Information Platform of Environmental Emergency Supplies* (www.12369.com.cn) has been established to facilitate the collection of emergency supplies and information. In addition, the supplies that are needed in order to respond to minor environmental emergencies are being stored at local facilities and enterprises.

The training of response capacities is reinforced at different levels and takes different needs into consideration. Since various functions and duties are involved in response command and on-site disposal, the training sessions are specifically designed for heads of environmental bureaus at provincial and local levels, and the staff in the environmental emergency management system. The training sessions are aimed at boosting the capabilities of local environmental protection bureaus (EPBs) with regard to on-site reaction and on-site disposal, strengthening the macro decision-making capabilities of heads of provincial EPBs, and improving the response and rescue capabilities of practitioners. Up to now, more than 400 EPB officials at local level and 3,000 emergency management practitioners have attended at least one training session.

Strategies

To further control and manage environmental risk, China should follow the steps described below:

- Revise and perfect the top-level design of national environmental risk control and management.
- Reduce the environmental risk related to industrial layout and structure.
- Clarify the liability of companies.
- Solve the inherited environmental risk problems step-by-step.
- Improve the capacity of environmental risk control and emergency response at local level.
- Emphasize risk communication.
- Strengthen fundamental research on environmental health and ecological risk assessment.
- Enhance the acute environmental risk control measures by introducing other techniques, such as socialized environmental risk management.

Perfecting the top-level design of national environmental risk management and fundamental research

A comprehensive design can be achieved by the following means: collecting risk information by adopting cloud technologies; setting risk control and management objectives; employing effective risk control and management methodologies and techniques; and introducing universal measures of risk control and management as administrative commands and orders and economic instruments. In this way, China will hopefully achieve top-level design in the field of environmental risk control and management. Meanwhile, national environmental risk control and management in key sectors should be further supported by optimizing environmental risk zoning codes; creating an inventory list for contaminated sites; identifying areas of high environmental and health risk; clarifying the pollution levels of older contaminated sites; perfecting the control of chemicals and hazardous waste step-by-step; formulating laws and regulations for risk prevention and emergency response efforts in the case of accidents involving chemicals.

Reducing the environmental risks related to layout and structure

Research on early-warning mechanisms for the environmental carrying capacity of major environmental conservation areas and water bodies (rivers, lakes, and reservoirs) should be strengthened. Comprehensive environmental planning and regional risk assessment should be optimized. Various policy and legal measures should be enforced to manage high-risk projects safely.

Specifically, this line of action should take into consideration the regional geological and natural features, the distribution and layout of environmental sensitive objects, the number of enterprises in key industrial sectors, and the basic capacity of the environmental emergency response system. This approach should also include research on environmental accidents, the setting of technical guidelines for regional environmental risk assessment and regional planning at the local level. At the same time, it is necessary to set limits and standards for the numbers and types of enterprises in the zones where limited construction is tolerated and to increase the distance between the industrial chemical enterprises and environmentally sensitive areas. In this way, high-risk, polluting projects and enterprises located in the protected zones could be phased out, and the environmental risks posed by an inappropriate layout could be reduced.

Clarifying the liability of enterprises

The following measures should be introduced to promote the environmental liability awareness of enterprises: first of all, relevant guidelines and technical standards should be formulated to include technical standards for investigating the environmental dangers posed by key industries, techniques for environmental risk assessment, capacity building standards for responding to environmental emergencies, and guidelines for environmental emergency plans. Secondly, some specific legislation and policies should be enforced, including laws related to environmental liability and damage compensation, policies related to classified credit levels, accounting, auditing, and risk inspection. Moreover, enterprises can be encouraged to accept responsibility for any pollution or damage by means of financial instruments such as 'green credit', an environmental liability fund, mandated environmental liability insurance, and a security deposit for remediation.

Solving the problems of inherited pollution

An investigation should be conducted to assess contaminated sites at national level; compile a list of the contaminated sites; finalize an inventory of contaminated sites; define remediation plans; achieve the dynamic data management of the contaminated sites; create guidelines and methods for the classification of contaminated sites, including priority ranking for remediation; generate a remediation fund for inherited contaminated sites; specify pilot sites for contaminated site remediation; and formulate a supervision framework for historic cases of pollution.

Improving the capacity for environmental risk control and emergency response at local level

The enhancement of capacity building for an environmental emergency early-warning system and whole-process risk control is required, especially in the field of hardware, software and the training of personnel; the risk control and management mechanisms for enterprises should be established and optimized; the enactment and revision of laws, policies, technical standards, and guidelines should be further enhanced, particularly those concerned with the safe disposal of solid waste, industrial contaminated sites, and agricultural soil that is suffering from various forms of contamination.

More training sessions should be organized to assist the environmental protection staff at local level in mastering the necessary techniques and expertise for management. The risk prevention and response capacity should also be enhanced through a platform construction for environmental emergency command, a logistics plan for optimizing emergency supplies, and the appointing of think tanks to consider the various options available for dealing with emergencies.

Emphasizing risk communication

Risk communication includes the promotion of environmental information disclosure; the timely publication of environmental information by local governments and enterprises; the communication of policies related to environmental management, such as the environmental emergency plans; the improvement of public participation and self aid, and the mutual aid capacity of the public during environmental risk control and management actions, and environmental emergency response cases; the triggering of public participation in environmental supervision as well as in setting up public information hotlines and internet platforms; taking public complaints and reports seriously; actively responding to and investigating reported issues and questions.

Promoting fundamental research on environmental health and ecological risk assessment

Research objectives related to risk assessment include setting up a theoretical system for human health risk assessment, technical approaches and guidelines, as well as a manual of key parameters. This system should reflect the actual conditions in China and can be widely applied to fields relevant to environmental risk control. Research should also include the exploration of indicators and methodologies for ecological risk assessment, and the environmental risk assessment of regular pollutants with a focus on the environmental health exposure risks related to polluting substances, such as $PM_{2.5}$, blue-green algae, PCFs, PFOS, PBDEs, PAHs, and dioxin. Research should be conducted on establishing and supporting a comprehensive environmental risk identification and management supporting system, including pollution cause analysis, source analysis, contribution analysis, emergency plans, damage compensation.

Conclusion

China's administrative procedures for managing and controlling environmental emergency accidents should be further enhanced and optimized; risk control and management capacity and environmental emergency response ability should be improved in order to halt the trend towards the increasingly detrimental impacts of environmental emergency accidents on society and the environment. One crucial aspect, in the context of efforts to lower environmental emergency risks to an acceptable level, is to resolve the political and technical issues related to accumulated environmental risk as well as to incorporate the concept of environmental risk management into environmental supervision measures in order to gradually change the current management system, which relies heavily on political approaches for the prevention of environmental risks. For a new environmental management system based on legislation, technology, economic instruments, and public participation, a transparent environmental risk liability system has to be implemented that involves enterprises, governments and the general public.

References

HYYSDZ. Huanjing yingji yu shigu diaocha zhongxin (Center of Environmental Emergency and Accident Investigation), 2010. *Zhongguo tufa huanjing shijian huibian (2006–2010) (Collection of Chinese Emergent Environmental Accidents (2006–2010))*, Beijing.

State Environmental Protection Administration (SEPA) Guojia huanjing baohu zong ju huanjing jiancha ju, 2006. *Emergency Response Handbook for Environmental Accidents (Huanjing ying ji xiang ying shiyong shouce)*, Beijing: China Environmental Science Press (Zhongguo huanjing kexue chuban she).

ZHTN – *Zhongguo Huanjing Tongji Nianbao* (Chinese Environmental Statistical Yearbook) 2001–2015, Beijing: Zhongguo Huanjing Kexue Chubanshe (Environmental Science Publishing House).

ZTN – *Zhongguo Tongji Nianjian* (Chinese Statistical Yearbook), 2015, Beijing: Zhongguo Tongji Chubanshe (China Statistics Press).

PART III

Policy instruments and enforcement

14

POLLUTION LAW ENFORCEMENT IN CHINA

Understanding national and regional variation

Benjamin van Rooij, Zhu Qiaoqiao, Li Na,
Wang Qiliang and Zhang Xuehua

Introduction

Since 1978, China has gradually built an increasingly comprehensive body of laws and regulations to prevent and control industrial pollution. Such laws, if well implemented, could well help curb the country's immense negative economic and health effects of its air, water, solid waste, noise and ocean pollution (Van Rooij 2006b). In practice, enforcement, executed either by so-called environmental protection bureaus (EPBs) or local governments has not been optimal. There is widespread recognition in the existing literature that enforcement of pollution law in China has been challenging (i.e. Ma and Ortolano 2000; Van Rooij 2002; Van Rooij 2006a; Tilt 2007; Lo et al. 2009; Van Rooij and Lo 2010; He et al. 2012; Lo et al. 2012; Ran 2013; Kostka 2013; Kostka and Mol 2013; He et al. 2014). Most studies portray an array of structural problems that undermine enforcement in practice (for an overview see Van Rooij and Lo 2010). These include a lack of regulatory independence originating in the de facto decentralized structure, lack of enforcement capacity with administrative agencies lacking the money, staff, technical skills and equipment to match the complexity and scale of the pollution violations, resistance by polluting firms, lack of central level commitment and successful incentive structures.

Pollution law enforcement in China is highly dynamic. To gain a fuller understanding of China's environmental enforcement challenges it is vital to acknowledge that there is variation in enforcement both over time and in different localities. Some recent studies have, for instance, shown that there is an overall trend towards more and stricter enforcement (cf. Lo et al. 2009; He et al. 2014; Zhan et al. 2014). Moreover, these studies show that stricter and more frequent enforcement has not necessarily been translated in more compliance (cf. He et al. 2014; Zhan et al. 2014).

This chapter discusses the temporal and regional variation of pollution law enforcement in China. The remainder of this chapter will first discuss variation in enforcement over time, then discuss geographical variation, and be completed with probable explanations of the observed variation.

National enforcement trends

Table 14.1 provides an overview of the national total frequency of sanctions against polluting firms EPBs have issued throughout the country for each year. The first row covers what are recorded as administrative sanctions. These are the sanctions issued by EPBs and chiefly consist of fines. The first row clearly shows that between 1999 and 2013 there has been a steady rise, with some peaks and some short-term declines.

The second and third rows concern the level of fines, which were published between 2001 and 2006. What we see is that both the national overall level of fines issued for pollution, as well as the average fine per case have risen dramatically. Overall fines have gone up from 333.8 million RMB in 2001 to 1,255.4 million RMB in 2006. And the average fine per case has gone from 4,685 RMB to 13,586 RMB in 2006.

The fourth row concerns forced relocations and closures. This category concerns polluting firms that have relocated, suspended production temporarily and closed down. They have done so after decisions from local governments, and not the EPBs. Moreover, these decisions are not always sanction decisions for pollution, but may also concern decisions based on economic

Table 14.1 Development of administrative sanctions, fines, fines per case, and relocations and closures of polluting firms in China 1999–2013

Year	1999	2000	2001	2002	2003	2004	2005	2006
Number of Administrative Sanctions	53,101	55,209	71,089	100,103	92,818	80,079	93,265	92,404
Fines (10,000 RMB) 2015 price level	NA	NA	33,308	41,981	46,007	62,324	84,799	125,540
Fine Per Case (RMB)2015 prices	NA	NA	4,685	4,194	4,957	7,783	9,092	13,586
Number of Relocations and Closures	9,175	19,498	6,574	8,184	11,499	13,348	10,777	10,030

Year (continued)	2007	2008	2009	2010	2011	2012	2013
Number of Administrative Sanctions	101,325	89,820	73,719	112,025	119,333	117,308	139,059
Fines (10,000 RMB) 2015 price level	NA	NA	NA	NA	NA	NA	NA
Fine Per Case (RMB) 2015 prices	NA	NA	NA	NA	NA	NA	NA
Number of Relocations and Closures	25,733	22,488	NA	NA	NA	NA	NA

Source: China's Annual Environmental Statistic Yearbooks (1999–2013) (SEPA 2000–2008; MEP 2009–2014).

policy considerations. From the overall number it is impossible to distil ratios between pollution sanctions and economic decisions nor between closures and relocations. The data are important though as these concern the strongest form of governmental interventions, whether for economic or environmental reasons, in the operation of polluting firms. The table shows that there is a clear rise in the frequency of such relocations and closures from 9,175 in 1999 to 22,488 in 2008 (the last year this type of data was published). So for all three data points on enforcement we see a trend that is similar to the existing survey and case study based literature, showing stronger enforcement (He et al. 2014; Zhan et al. 2014).

The overall growth in enforcement is hopeful. We do not know yet, however, whether it already is helping to reduce pollution. We conducted statistical testing to understand whether the growth in enforcement affects pollution. To do so, we conducted fixed-effect regressions with pollution as the dependent variable and with the province fixed effect. We should note that at this point we have only had access to pollution data contained in the 'Annual Statistics Reports on Environment in China'. We have developed a measure of pollution from six main pollution indicators covering industrial air, water, and solid waste pollution in these reports.[1] These are all governmental data that may well contain a bias towards underreporting pollution. This bias may, however, be similar over time and regionally, and as such we use the data here to understand variation in pollution, not what the state of affairs in pollution actually is at any given moment and place. We investigated separately the effect of the frequency of administrative sanctions, the fine amount and the frequency of relocations and closures, controlling for the three major types of GDP output (agriculture, industry and service). We include both the current year value of enforcement variables and the one-year lagged value of those variables in the regressions to investigate the causal relation between enforcement and pollution.

The results are mixed. On the one hand we see that lagged relocations and closures significantly reduce pollution, and the frequency of sanctions is linked to reduced pollution but less significantly. On the other hand, neither current nor lagged amount of fines can predict pollution. Our calculations based on these regressions further show that administrative sanctions and forced relocations or closures can only predict a small amount of the variation in the pollution within the sample of data. Administrative sanction frequency predicts 4.9 per cent and forced relocations and closure frequency 5.8 per cent in the variation of pollution. Overall GDP development, our data show, is a much stronger predictor of pollution variation. Higher industrial output is positively correlated with more pollution while higher agricultural and service output are negatively correlated with pollution.

As such, we can conclude that the strong growth of enforcement has some, but still minor impact on pollution. A very plausible reason for this is that the strength of most administrative sanctions simply remains too weak. The absolute level of fines has remained very low, at least until 2006, the last year for which we have data, at about 13,000 RMB.

Regional trends

Given China's size and the large regional differences it is no surprise that there is a large amount of variation between the different regions in China in how pollution law is enforced. Governmental data about environmental law enforcement allow us a unique view into regional variation. The data set covers all provinces in China and allows us to understand both the frequency of sanctions, the average fine per case and the amount of relocations and closures. In order to make meaningful comparison we do not compare absolute frequencies of sanctions and forced relocations and closures, but rather their ratio related to six main water, solid waste and

Table 14.2 Fixed effect regression with pollution as dependent variable and GDP output and enforcement as independent variables using data from each province from the following years: administrative sanctions (1999–2011), average fines per case (2001–2006) and forced relocations and closures of polluting firms (1999–2008)

Dependent Variable: Pollution

Variables	(1) Prov FE	(2) Prov FE	(3) Prov FE	(4) Prov FE
Agriculture Output	−0.138***	−0.137***	−0.00434	−0.0970***
	(0.0253)	(0.0251)	(0.0411)	(0.0278)
Industrial Output	0.0177**	0.0171**	0.0107	0.0195**
	(0.00689)	(0.00667)	(0.0107)	(0.00756)
Service Output	−0.0143**	−0.0102	−0.0102	−0.0176**
	(0.00671)	(0.00654)	(0.0133)	(0.00831)
Administrative Sanctions		−0.00187		
		(0.00180)		
Lag Administrative Sanctions		−0.00342*		
		(0.00199)		
Fine Amount			−7.64e-05	
			(0.00238)	
Lag Fine Amount			−0.00117	
			(0.00430)	
Relocations and Closures				−0.00197
				(0.00925)
Lag Relocations and Closures				−0.0253***
				(0.00958)
Constant	279.2***	282.7***	202.6***	273.4***
	(11.70)	(13.64)	(20.02)	(13.25)
Observations	372	332	151	265
Adjusted R-squared	0.804	0.832	0.960	0.884
Province FE	YES	YES	YES	YES

Standard errors in parentheses
*** $p<0.01$, ** $p<0.05$, * $p<0.1$

Source: Annual Statistic Reports on the Environment in China (1999–2011) (SEPA 2000–2008; MEP 2009–2012).

air pollutants. This allows us to compare how much enforcement there has been relative to how bad local pollution is. For fines this is not necessary as we can study the average fine per case, by dividing the total fines by the number of administrative sanction cases. To get a first picture

Table 14.3 Regional variation in sanction/pollution (1999–2011), average fines per case (2001–2006) and forced relocations and closures of polluting firms (1999–2008)

Region	Sanctions/ Pollution	Average Fine	Relocations and Closures/Pollution
Central	9.90	5,972	2.40
City	31.22	12,851	2.65
Coastal	33.30	10,961	4.60
Northeastern	43.20	3,423	1.59
Western	5.91	5,465	1.35
Average	24.71	7,734	2.52

Source: Annual Statistic Reports on the Environment in China (1999–2011) (SEPA 2000–2008; MEP 2009–2012).

of regional variation, we have clustered the provincial-level data into five regions: coastal provinces (Guangdong, Fujian, Zhejiang, Jiangsu, and Shandong), central provinces (Hebei, Henan, Hubei, Hunan, Anhui, Shanxi, Jiangxi), province level municipalities (Beijing, Shanghai, Tianjin, Chongqing), Northeast (Jilin, Heilongjiang, and Liaoning) and Western (Ningxia, Inner Mongolia, Xinjiang, Yunnan, Guizhou, Sichuan, Guangxi, Shaanxi, Gansu). Qinghai, Tibet and Hainan were not used in the data here because they have such limited industrial development and therefore are outliers. Table 14.3 outlines the data.

The data show large variation. We see that the largest frequency of sanctions (over the total period from 1999–2011) (in relation to pollution) is in provincial level municipalities, coastal, and especially north-eastern regions. Central and western China are clear outliers in having far fewer sanctions (in relation to pollution). Municipal and coastal areas have the highest average fines (over the period of 2001–2006), while Western and Central China, and especially north-eastern China have fines lower than average. In terms of closures and forced relocations municipalities and especially coastal regions score above average with central and especially western and north-eastern scoring well below average. As such an overall picture emerges of uneven enforcement. In richer regions of the coastal provinces or municipalities we see more frequent as well as more stringent enforcement in terms of fines and relocations and closures. In western and central China enforcement is less frequent and less stringent. Finally, in north-eastern China we have an interesting combination of frequent yet non-stringent enforcement. Such uneven enforcement complements our picture of overall enforcement trends. We should qualify the trend towards stricter enforcement even further, namely that while that trend happened, there was an unbalance with stricter and more frequent enforcement in coastal and city-level provinces, and weaker enforcement elsewhere. Together with the fact that enforcement largely does not match pollution development and industrial development, this can explain why the trend towards stronger enforcement found in other studies need not translate into more effective results in terms of compliance and pollution control.

Changes in central-level policy

To understand the overall trend towards stricter enforcement, central-level policy changes are key factors. Since the late 1990s central-level politicians have increasingly shown more commitment to strengthen pollution enforcement.

Table 14.4 Number of EPB staff 1999–2013

Year	1999	2000	2001	2002	2003	2004	2005	2006
Number of EPB Staff	121,049	131,092	143,766	154,233	156,542	160,246	166,774	170,290

Year (continued)	2007	2008	2009	2010	2011	2012	2013
Number of EPB Staff	176,988	183,555	188,991	193,911	201,161	205,334	212,048

Source: China's Annual Environmental Statistic Yearbooks (1999–2013) (SEPA 2000–2008; MEP 2009–2014).

A first central-level influence potentially affecting local-level law enforcement are legislative changes. Legislation since the early 2000s has strengthened law enforcement options by installing higher sanction limits, and with the new *Environmental Protection Law* of 2014 even creating unlimited per-day fines for ongoing violations. National legal changes since the early 2000s have also decreased discretion about sanctions, most importantly by introducing minimum fine levels in the *Air Pollution Prevention and Control Law* (2000) and the *Environmental Impact Assessment Law* (2002). These changes may be at play in seeing fines go up; however, they have limited relation to the rise in frequency of sanctions and the increase in forced relocations and closures.

Since at least the early 2000s, we also see increased central-level political commitment for environmental protection. Such commitment most importantly comes in the form of central-level payment for local pollution reduction measures, which are paid to local governments through transfer payments. Of the total expenditure on sub-national-level pollution reduction measures, which include the costs of monitoring and enforcement, about 51 per cent is paid through such central transfers to the local level. The budget for such central-level expenditures has risen from 0.73 per cent of GDP during the 8th Five-Year Plan (FYP) (1992–2005), to 0.93 per cent of GDP during the 9th FYP (1996–2000), to 1.2 per cent of GDP during the 10th FYP (2001–2006) to 1.35 per cent of GDP during the 11th FYP,[2] (2007–2011) to 1.4 per cent of GDP during the 12th FYP (2012–2016).[3] For enforcement the most important influence such central-level budget can have is to increase availability of enforcement equipment, including vehicles, and also growth of EPB enforcement staff.

Indeed, as Table 14.4 shows, the yearbook data we have used here show a rapid increase of EPB staff over this period. To understand the effect of the increase of staff on pollution, we have conducted further statistical testing, analysing how staff, when controlled for pollution, GDP growth and complaints predict variation in enforcement intensity. By enforcement intensity we mean the amount of enforcement related to pollution. We use this measure to allow for comparing enforcement for different provinces.

The regressions, reported in Table 14.5 opposite, show that once controlling for pollution, GDP growth and complaints, adding staff itself does not significantly predict a higher frequency of administrative sanctions, nor a higher level of fines. The staff increases do predict significantly a higher level of relocations and closures. For administrative sanctions, which we know consist chiefly of fines, simply adding staff thus does not affect enforcement. The decision to compel a firm to move or close has been under the jurisdiction of the local government and not the local EPB.[4] So maybe what is at play there is not simply a larger number of staff, but rather a local government supporting environmental protection that is willing to allow its well-staffed EPBs do a good job in preparing and executing decisions to close or move polluting firms. Thus, we

Table 14.5 Fixed-effect regression with three enforcement measures as dependent variables and non-industrial GDP, per capita income, staff, letters, visits as independent variables using data from each province from the following years: administrative sanctions (1999–2011), average fines per case (2001–2006) and forced relocations and closures of polluting firms (1999–2008)

Dependent Variable: Enforcement intensity (enforcement/pollution)

Variable	(1) Sanctions	(2) Fine Amount	(3) Relocations and Closures
Percentage Non-Industrial GDP	150.9★★★	112.8★	13.08★
	(42.04)	(68.01)	(7.048)
Per Capita Income	0.000978★★★	0.00173★★★	8.23e-05★
	(0.000259)	(0.000427)	(4.51e-05)
staff	0.00179	0.00263	0.000618★★★
	(0.00132)	(0.00188)	(0.000186)
letters	0.000255★★	0.000523★★★	2.05e-06
	(0.000104)	(0.000126)	(1.37e-05)
visits	−0.00108	−0.000717	−7.70e-05
	(0.000962)	(0.000829)	(0.000123)
Constant	−96.77★★★	−92.06★★	−10.11★★
	(25.33)	(42.86)	(4.345)
Observations	336	183	272
Adjusted R-squared	0.564	0.719	0.387
Year FE and Province FE	YES	YES	YES

Standard errors in parentheses
★★★ p<0.01, ★★ p<0.05, ★ p<0.1

Source: Annual Statistic Reports on the Environment in China (1999–2011) (SEPA 2000–2008; MEP 2009–2012).

may speculate that enforcement is not simply a matter of staff, but depends also on the willingness to use such staff to engage in enforcement. We shall look at this in more detail when discussing the influence of local government below.

The central level also influences enforcement practice through its nationally organized enforcement campaigns. Since 1996, it has continually organized politically driven rounds of concentrated and prioritized enforcement. In these campaigns centrally defined priorities are to be enforced at the local level. Such campaigns receive high levels of central support often from the State Council and multiple ministries supporting the weaker environmental authorities. The first campaign, for instance, focused on closing down small heavily polluting industries with outdated technology. This resulted in the closing down of over 60,000 such enterprises in the course of three months (Van Rooij 2002). In 2000 a national multi-year campaign ended that forced companies to update their environmental technology to meet key standards or else be forced to close down (Van Rooij 2002). This campaign may well explain the peak in forced relocation and closures that occurred in 2000 (see Table 14.1). Ever since then there have been annual national campaigns to enforce pollution law and a so-called campaign enforcement style has developed (Van Rooij 2014). Maybe these ongoing campaigns have each year spurred the frequency of sanctions, the severity of fines and forced relocations and closures to create the trend that we know. Campaigns have had a positive effect in overcoming local protectionism for the duration of the campaign, generating public participation, and allowing for nationwide experimentation with locally adopted enforcement methods (Van Rooij 2006b, 2016). On the downside, the campaigns have had more trouble generating long-term effects, and because of their ad hoc nature disrupt the development of routine enforcement, at times breach due process and undermine the consistency and procedural justice necessary to create sustainable compliance (Van Rooij 2006b, 2016). Also the campaigns do nothing to change either the central local conflicts of interest that exist between national environmental law and local jobs, income and relationships, nor the de facto power local governments still have.

Since 2006, the central government has also sought to enhance environmental governance by changing incentive structures for local leaders. With the 11th FYP (2006–2011), the central government introduced mandatory targets for emission reductions such as 10 per cent reduction of sulphur dioxide and chemical oxygen demand emissions (Lo and Tang 2006). The 11th FYP also shifted the burden of responsibility to meet environmental targets from regulatory agency leaders to the most powerful local level and even industry leaders (Wang 2013). As such local leaders including mayors, governors, county magistrates and even state-owned enterprise leadership were made personally accountable to meeting these targets (for an overview see Wang 2013). These mandatory targets were further expanded since the 12th FYP (2011–2015), adding reductions in nitrogen oxide and ammonia nitrogen to the target systems. In his analysis of the implementation of the 11th FYP targets, Alex Wang (2013) found that there was substantial environmental investment leading to a reported 14.13 per cent drop in SO_2 emissions by 2010 below the 2005 level. Although he concluded that the targets had an uneven impact on enforcement, creating a 'significant degree of shutdowns' of badly performing outdated firms, enforcement had limited contribution to overall reported pollution reductions. A key problem in using indicators to enhance local-level enforcement is how to verify reported actions and pollution reductions, especially in a context where both firms and local environmental regulators have been concealing and doctoring data (Lin 2013; Wang 2013; Plambeck and Taylor 2015). These new targets may be linked to a spike in 2007 relocations and closures concurring with the start of the introduction of the new hard environmental targets. However, by 2008 we see a strong drop in closure, probably due to the global financial crisis that started to unfold. The data on administrative sanctions show a similar story with a small peak in 2007 when the targets were just introduced, followed by a severe drop in 2008 and 2009 as the crisis unfolded, after which there was a very high peak in sanctions in 2010 coinciding with former premier Wen Jiabao issuing a strong message towards meeting the 11th FYP pollution targets (Wang 2013).

Central-level influences thus offer some explanation for the trends, but they do not explain the full trends though. We saw that none of the central-level influences can be clearly linked to the changes over time. More importantly, central-level influences do not explain the immense regional variation that we found.

Variation in local government commitment

Local governments play a key role in pollution law enforcement. They provide the bulk of the funding for EPBs, and they also have the largest influence on leadership appointments. First of all, as we saw above, the most stringent power of enforcement, ordering closure of highly polluting plants, has been vested directly with the local government.[5] Second, the local governments have a direct influence on EPBs, as the local government pays most of the budget and has the strongest say in leadership appointments (Sinkule and Ortolano 1995; Bachner 1996; Jahiel 1998; Yao 1999; Ma and Ortolano 2000; Van Rooij 2006b). Third, EPB leaders have the strongest ties with local government officials and therefore are most susceptible to undue influence while making final decisions on the most important and invasive sanctions. The result has been a situation where the local government can refrain itself or keep its EPB from strongly enforcing the law against important local enterprises who either serve as large sources of tax revenue, are under their ownership, provide employment or are in one or another way connected to local leaders (Ma and Ortolano 2000; Zhang 2008).

There has been variation in the commitment local governments have had on environmental protection. Some local governments[6] have become more committed to the environment, investing more in environmental protection and providing stronger support for local EPBs. The prominent examples are 'State Environmental Protection Model Cities' such as the coastal cities of Dalian, Zhuhai and Xiamen, whose governments boast strong environmental reputations matched with environmental spending and support. Even traditionally pro-growth cities such as Guangzhou, Wuhan and Chengdu have become more environmentally friendly, increasing their spending on environmental protection (Lo and Fryxell 2005; Lo et al. 2006) and introducing pro-environment rhetoric in their general policy plans.

At the same time there continue to be local governments who protect local industry from strong environmental enforcement (e.g. Sinkule and Ortolano 1995; Jahiel 1997; Tang et al. 1997; Jahiel 1998; Ma and Ortolano 2000; Swanson et al. 2001; Van Rooij 2002; Zhang 2002; Tang et al. 2003; Economy 2004; Van Rooij and Lo 2010; He et al. 2012, He et al. 2014; Lorentzen et al. 2014). Lo and Fryxell have, for instance, empirically shown through systematic surveys of enforcement agents that local governments affect enforcement effectiveness (2005). Van Rooij's local-level fieldwork carried out between 2000 and 2004 showed that local-level EPBs in south-western China generally will only seek 33 per cent of fines they are allowed to issue, not wanting to upset local industry. Zhang's research in Hubei province similarly shows that levy reductions were widespread, significant, and systematic at the country level by 2006 (Zhang 2008). Kostka (2013) shows that local leaders appoint EPB directors that will act at the behest of the overall local interest rather than on the more narrow environmental interest. Lorentzen et al. show that cities with large industrial firms have lagged even simply in implementing environmental transparency rules, especially those with highly polluting firms (Lorentzen et al. 2014). Another study by He et al. (2014) shows that even rural enterprises are protected and that 'parallel (economic) interests of and intricate ties and collaboration between the local government and local industry management enabled the companies to continue business as usual' (p. 166).

Our data show the variation of such local governments. On the one hand we have the coastal provinces and the city-level provinces where there is a stronger commitment towards environmental protection. In these provinces we see more administrative cases, higher fines and more forced relocations and closures. It seems here there may be more support for environmental protection and maybe less local protectionism. In the less-developed central and western provinces we see clearly lower frequencies of sanctions, lower fines and fewer forced relocations and closures. As such, what we have here reflects differences in developmental levels, something we found also in an earlier study linking per capita provincial-level GDP to the average fine per case (Van Rooij and Lo 2010). The Northeast is a mixed case where we see high frequencies yet low fine levels and below-average relocations and closures. As such the Northeast might have governments that make a show of numbers rather than stronger enforcement. Of course, all of this is comparing the regions to each other. As we have seen, generally speaking, enforcement does not match pollution nor industrial development, and it seems clear that local governments and their EPBs take good care not to hurt their economic development.

To understand the linkage between enforcement and local-level income levels we can look at the statistical test we did in Table 14.5, predicting variation in enforcement. There we can see that when controlling for non-industrial GDP, staff and complaints, per capita income predicts variation in enforcement for all three forms of enforcement, most significantly for administrative sanctions and the amount of fine, and more marginally so for relocations and closures. In simpler terms the higher the local income, the more likely that there will be more sanctions, higher fines and more relocations and closures. Regional differences in enforcement are, as such, related to the level of income in such provinces.

Moreover, the same regression analysis shows that the structure of the local economy is an important predictor of enforcement. The more non-industrial output there is in the agricultural and service sectors, the more and stronger enforcement is. This is in line with earlier case study research that showed that homogeneous industrial sources of local income will more easily thwart strong local-level law enforcement (Van Rooij 2006b).

Community pressure

Variation should be understood beyond the confines of the state. Increasingly citizens have started to play a role in pollution regulation. They have done so in part simply responding to the ever-worrying levels of pollution, developing an awareness both of their grievances and the necessity for action to get compensation (Van Rooij 2012). The governmental data set allows us to understand the development of one form of community involvement by providing data about the number of pollution-related complaint petitions citizens have submitted to the authorities. We have data covering the period 1999–2006 and from 2008–2010. In 2007 and from 2011 onwards a different data accounting method was used and therefore data cannot be directly compared with other years. Table 14.6 sketches the development of such complaints petitions.

The first row in the table shows that over time there has been a rapid rise of complaints letters and visits from 268,592 in 1999 to 735,756 by 2010. The rise has been continual in each year. The second row shows that complaints have also risen rapidly when divided by the amount of pollution.

In the correlation analysis we ran to prepare for our regressions, we found that complaints, as in both letters and visits to the office, correlate with both the frequency of administrative punishment, the amount of fines, fine per case, as well as closures and relocations. As reported in Table 14.5, regression analysis shows, however, that when we control for pollution, staff and industrial output, overall complaints have only a limited predictive effect of enforcement. Only written letters affect the frequency of administrative sanctions and the height of fines, with more letters leading to more sanctions and higher fines. We do not find any significant effect

Table 14.6 Number of environmental complaints (letters and visits), total complaints per main six types of pollutants 1999–2010

Year	1999	2000	2001	2002	2003	2004	2005	2006	2007	2008	2009	2010
Number of Complaints	268,592	309,800	450,287	526,166	611,016	682,744	696,491	687,409	NA	748,989	738,306	735,756
Complaints/Pol.	192.8	240.1	379.8	468.8	579.7	663.3	644.8	688.3	NA	950.5	1011.7	1080.2

Source: China's Annual Environmental Statistic Yearbooks (1999–2010) (SEPA 2000–2008; MEP 2009–2011).

however of complaints, whether written or in person, on the frequency of administrative sanctions or closures and relocations. Thus the rise in citizen complaints is not having much effect on the enforcement that seems to be most effective in reducing pollution, relocations and closures.

We can also look at regional variation in complaints. Table 14.7 captures such variation by comparing the total amount of complaints in relation to pollution across different regions (column 1).

This clearly shows that city and coastal regions get many more complaints than other regions in China. Central and western China are clearly the lowest, with the Northeast a little below average. This well matches the regional variation we saw in frequency and stringency of sanctions. What we also see from this table is that there is variation in the extent to which a complaint is likely to generate a sanction, with this being far less likely in western and central China.

All in all, we see that complaints have a mixed and varied effect on enforcement. These data should be understood through the existing literature on complaints and enforcement, showing a complex relationship between enforcement and community pressure.[7] On the one hand we see that communities have been able to support weak EPBs who are pressed for resources and local government support. In the 1990s for instance the Guangzhou EPB was able to get better governmental support through the pressure of local citizen complaints (Lo and Leung 2000). Also we know that complaints play a vital role for EPBs to detect violations, especially for those enforcement bureaus that mainly use a reactive enforcement strategy, where they carry out inspections following citizen complaints. Such reactive enforcement was a way to deal with the overwhelming gap between industrial growth and lagging numbers of inspectors and inspection equipment. Some EPBs have even experimented with rewarding successful citizen complaints (Van Rooij 2006a; Zhang 2010).

Public pressure does not always occur and requires certain conditions. We know it chiefly occurs for the most visible problems, not the most severe forms of pollution. Such relatively trivial problems like noise and smoke may derail EPBs' scarce resources away from the largest pollution risks (Yang and Zhang 2013). Moreover, there is a clear link between citizen complaints and income levels (Van Rooij and Lo 2010). Futhermore, income dependency on pollution matters (Van Rooij 2006b). Apart from these economic conditions, citizens face a range of legal, political and social obstacles that prevent them from playing an active role to support enforcement officials. Such obstacles include a lack of information and awareness, a lack of expert support and advice, and direct opposition by local governments and enterprises (Van Rooij 2010).

Table 14.7 Regional variation in total complaints/pollution, and total complaints/sanction

Region	Complaints/Pollution	Complaints/Sanction
Central	47.08	0.36
City	225.36	0.16
Coastal	208.57	0.17
Northeast	116.39	0.15
West	45.55	0.33
Average	128.59	0.23

Source: Annual Statistic Reports on the Environment in China (1999–2011) (SEPA 2000–2008; MEP 2009–2012).

Conclusion

China's environmental challenges require effective enforcement of national legislation at the local level. There has been variation over time and place in how environmental law is enforced. We clearly see an increase in the frequency of all sanctions, a higher level of fines and an increase in the strongest sanctions of forcing companies to relocate or close down. At the same time, we find that not all aspects of such increased enforcement help reduce the amount of pollution as recorded in the governmental reports we have used here. Even when they do, with forced relocations and closures, the explanatory power in explaining the pollution variation is rather small. Also, we see that enforcement has been uneven with clearly more frequent and stricter enforcement in richer coastal and municipal provinces.

All in all, the chapter has several broader implications for environmental governance in China. It shows first of all that China's environmental enforcement challenges are dynamic and different over time and place. It is vital to recognize this to better target analysis to warn against overly simplistic generalization that does not fit conditions as they occur in particular times and places. Moreover, we may well learn how to improve enforcement by looking more closely at places where better enforcement has developed. Here especially, the data point to more focus on understanding relocations and closures, as these seem to have the most effect.

Second, the chapter shows that there is a range of influences, including central-level policies, local government responses and the level of community activism. The data show that despite the high rhetoric of national plans and extra investment, national level influences have not been able to lift enforcement to strongly help reduce pollution. Moreover, central level influences have not yet been able to overcome the immense regional enforcement disparities.

Third, this chapter should be a warning that a potential split may be occurring where the richer coastal and municipal areas will benefit from better enforcement while allowing them to enjoy products and income from less developed regions with weaker pollution enforcement. The question is whether what we see here already is a real split that will become long term, or that the poorer provinces will gain better enforcement as soon as they become richer. One could have two views of such split enforcement. One is a utilitarian view that maybe pollution is moving from richer but also more densely populated areas towards the hinterland where fewer people are directly affected. A second view would be one of environmental justice, questioning whether poorer people should suffer more from pollution, producing products consumed in richer areas.

Notes

1 This composite was developed by adding up the following pollution types: 100 million tons of industrial wastewater, 10,000 tons of total amount of industrial COD, 10,000 tons of total amount of industrial SO_2, 10,000 tons of total amount of soot, 10,000 tons of industrial dust and 10,000 tons of industrial solid waste.
2 http://english.mep.gov.cn/down_load/Documents/200803/P020080306440313293094.pdf (accessed 14 December 2016).
3 http://english.mep.gov.cn/News_service/infocus/201202/t20120207_223194.htm (accessed 14 December 2016).
4 See article 39 of the 1989 EPL, as well as articles 49 and 50 of the 2000 Air Pollution Prevention and Control Law, and articles 49, 50, 51 and 52 of the 1996 Water Pollution Prevention and Control Law.
5 See article 39 of the 1989 EPL, as well as articles 49 and 50 of the 2000 Air Pollution Prevention and Control Law, and articles 49, 50, 51 and 52 of the 1996 Water Pollution Prevention and Control Law.

6   This paragraph draws on Van Rooij's earlier work (see Van Rooij, B. and Lo, C. H. W. 2010. A Fragile Convergence, Understanding Variation in the Enforcement of China's Industrial Pollution Law. *Law & Policy*, 32, 14–37).
7   This and the next two paragraphs draw on Van Rooij's earlier work (see ibid.).

References

Bachner, B., 1996. Regulating Pollution in the People's Republic of China: An Analysis of the Enforcement of Environmental Law. *Colorado Journal of International Law and Policy*, 7, 372–408.

Economy, E. C., 2004. *The River Runs Black, The Environmental Challenge to China's Future*. Ithaca, NY, Cornell University Press.

He G., Lu Y., Mol, A. P. and Beckers, T., 2012. Changes and Challenges: China's Environmental Management in Transition. *Environmental Development*, 3, 25–38.

——— Zhang L., Mol, A. P., Wang T. and Lu Y., 2014. Why Small and Medium Chemical Companies Continue to Pose Severe Environmental Risks in Rural China. *Environmental Pollution*, 185, 158–167.

Jahiel, A. R., 1997. The Contradictory Impact of Reform on Environmental Protection in China. *China Quarterly*, 149, 81–103.

——— 1998. The Organization of Environmental Protection in China. *China Quarterly*, 156, 757–787.

Kostka, G., 2013. Environmental Protection Bureau Leadership at the Provincial Level in China: Examining Diverging Career Backgrounds and Appointment Patterns. *Journal of Environmental Policy & Planning*, 15, 41–63.

——— and Mol, A. P., 2013. Implementation and Participation in China's Local Environmental Politics: Challenges and Innovations. *Journal of Environmental Policy & Planning*, 15, 3–16.

Lin L., 2013. Enforcement of Pollution Levies in China. *Journal of Public Economics*, 98, 32–43.

Lo C. W. H. and Fryxell, G. E., 2005. Governmental and Societal Support for Environmental Enforcement in China: An Empirical Study of Guangzhou. *Journal of Development Studies*, 41, 558–588.

——— and Leung S. W., 2000. Environmental Agency and Public Opinion in Guangzhou: The Limits of a Popular Approach to Environmental Governance. *China Quarterly*, 677–704.

——— and Tang S.-Y., 2006. Institutional Reform, Economic Changes and Local Environmental Management in China. *Environmental Politics*, 15, 190–210.

——— Fryxell, G. E. and Wong W. W.-H., 2006. Effective Regulations with Little Effect? The Antecedents of the Perceptions of Environmental Officials on Enforcement Effectiveness in China. *Environmental Management*, 38, 388–410.

——— Fryxell, G. E. and Van Rooij, B., 2009. Changes in Regulatory Enforcement Styles Among Environmental Enforcement Officials in China. *Environment and Planning A*, 41, 2706–2723.

——— Fryxell, G. E., Van Rooij, B. and Wang W., 2012. Decentered Authoritarian Regulation: Social and Political Influences on Environmental Law Enforcement in Guangzhou City, China. *Regulation & Governance* (Under Review).

Lorentzen, P., Landry, P. and Yasuda, J., 2014. Undermining Authoritarian Innovation: The Power of China's Industrial Giants. *The Journal of Politics*, 76, 182–194.

Ma X. and Ortolano, L., 2000. *Environmental Regulation in China, Institutions, Enforcement, and Compliance*. Landham, Rowman & Littlefield Publishing Group.

Ministry of Environmental Protection, PRC, 2009. *Zhongguo Huanjing Tongji Nianbao 2008*. Beijing: China Environmental Science Press.

——— 2010. *Zhongguo Huanjing Tongji Nianbao 2009*. Beijing: China Environmental Science Press.

——— 2011. *Zhongguo Huanjing Tongji Nianbao 2010*. Beijing: China Environmental Science Press.

——— 2012. *Zhongguo Huanjing Tongji Nianbao 2011*. Beijing: China Environmental Science Press.

——— 2013. *Zhongguo Huanjing Tongji Nianbao 2012*. Beijing: China Environmental Science Press.

——— 2014. *Zhongguo Huanjing Tongji Nianbao 2013*. Beijing: China Environmental Science Press.

Plambeck, E. L. and Taylor, T. A., 2015. Supplier Evasion of a Buyer's Audit: Implications for Motivating Supplier Social and Environmental Responsibility. *Manufacturing & Service Operations Management*, 18 (2), 184–197.

Ran, R., 2013. Perverse Incentive Structure and Policy Implementation Gap in China's Local Environmental Politics. *Journal of Environmental Policy & Planning*, 15, 17–39.

Sinkule, J. B. and Ortolano, L., 1995. *Implementing Environmental Policy in China*, Westport, Praeger.

State Environmental Protection Agency (SEPA). *Zhongguo Huanjing Tongji Nianbao 1998 (China Environmental Statistical Report 1998)*. chin ed. Beijing: SEPA, 1999.

—— 1999. *Zhongguo Huanjing Tongji Nianbao 1998 (China Environmental Statistical Report 1998)*. Beijing: SEPA.

—— 2000. *Zhongguo Huanjing Tongji Nianbao 1999 (China Environmental Statistical Report 1999)*. Beijing: SEPA.

—— 2001. *Zhongguo Huanjing Tongji Nianbao 2000 (China Environment Statistical Report 2000)*. Beijing: SEPA.

—— 2002. *Zhongguo Huanjing Tongji Nianbao 2001 (China Environment Statistical Report 2001)*. Beijing: SEPA.

—— 2003. *Zhongguo Huanjing Tongji Nianbao 2002 (China Environment Statistical Report 2002)*. Beijing: SEPA.

—— 2004. *Zhongguo Huanjing Tongji Nianbao 2003 (China Environment Statistical Report 2003)*. Beijing: SEPA.

—— 2005. *Zhongguo Huanjing Tongji Nianbao 2004 (China Environment Statistical Report 2004)*. Beijing: Zhongguo Huanjing Kexue Chubanshe.

—— 2006. *Zhongguo Huanjing Tongji Nianbao 2005 (China Environment Statistical Report 2005)*. Beijing: Zhongguo Huanjing Kexue Chubanshe.

—— 2007. *Zhongguo Huanjing Tongji Nianbao 2006 (China Environment Statistical Report 2006)*. Beijing: Zhongguo Huanjing Kexue Chubanshe.

—— 2008. *Zhongguo Huanjing Tongji Nianbao 2007 (China Environment Statistical Report 2007)*. Beijing: Zhongguo Huanjing Kexue Chubanshe.

Swanson, K. E., Kuhn, R. G. and Xu W., 2001. Environmental Policy Implementation in Rural China: A Case Study of Yuhang, Zhejiang. *Environmental Management*, 27, 481–91.

Tang S.-Y., Lo C. W. H., Cheung K.-C. and Lo J. M.-K., 1997. Institutional Constraints on Environmental Management in Urban China: Environmental Impact Assessment in Guangzhou and Shanghai. *China Quarterly*, 152, 863–874.

——, Lo C. W. H. and Fryxell, G. E., 2003. Enforcement Styles, Organizational Commitment, and Enforcement Effectiveness: An Empirical Study of Local Environmental Protection Officials in Urban China. *Environment and Planning*, 35, 75–94.

Tilt, B., 2007. The Political Ecology of Pollution Enforcement in China: A Case from Sichuan's Rural Industrial Sector. *The China Quarterly*, 192, 915–932.

Van Rooij, B., 2002. Implementing Chinese Environmental Law through Enforcement, the *Shiwu Xiao* and *Shuangge Dabiao* Campaigns. In: Chen J., Li Y. and Otto, J. M. (eds.) *The Implementation of Law in the People's Republic of China*. The Hague: Kluwer Law International, 149–178.

——, 2006a. Implementation of Chinese Environmental Law: Regular Enforcement and Political Campaigns. *Development and Change*, 37, 57–74.

——, 2006b. *Regulating Land and Pollution in China, Lawmaking, Compliance, and Enforcement; Theory and Cases*, Leiden, Leiden University Press.

——, 2010. The People vs. Pollution: Understanding Citizen Action against Pollution in China. *The Journal of Contemporary China*, 19, (63), 55–77.

——, 2012. The People's Regulation, Citizens and Implementation of Law in China. *Columbia Journal of Asian Law*, 25, 116–180.

——, 2016. Van Rooij, Benjamin. The Campaign Enforcement Style: Chinese Practice in Context and Comparison. In *Comparative Law and Regulation: Understanding the Global Regulatory Process*, edited by Francesca Bignami and David Zaring, 217–237. London: Edward Elgar.

—— and Lo, C. H. W., 2010. A Fragile Convergence, Understanding Variation in the Enforcement of China's Industrial Pollution Law. *Law & Policy*, 32, 14–37.

Wang A., 2013. The Search for Sustainable Legitimacy: Environmental Law and Bureaucracy in China. *Harvard Environmental Law Review*, 37, 367–440.

Yang T. and Zhang X., 2013. Public Participation in Environmental Enforcement . . . with Chinese Characteristics?: A Comparative Assessment of China's Environmental Complaint Mechanism. *Georgetown International Environmental Law Review*, 24, 325–366.

Yao S., 1999. *Huanjing Xingzheng Zhifa zhong Cunzaide Wenti he Duice* (On the Problems and Countermeasures in Administrative Enforcement of Environmental Law). *Environmental Protection*, 7, 14–15.

Zhan X., Lo C. W.-H. and Tang, S.-Y., 2014. Contextual Changes and Environmental Policy Implementation: A Longitudinal Study of Street-Level Bureaucrats in Guangzhou, China. *Journal of Public Administration Research and Theory*, 24, 1005–1035.

Zhang L., 2002. *Ecologizing Industrialization in Chinese Small Towns*. PhD thesis, Wageningen University.

Zhang X., 2008. Enforcing Environmental Regulations in Hubei Province, China: Agencies, Citizens, and Courts. PhD dissertation, Stanford University.

——, 2010. Green Bounty Hunters: Engaging Chinese Citizens in Local Environmental Enforcement. *China Environment Series*, 2010–2011, 137–153.

15

CHINA'S POLICIES ON GREENING FINANCIAL INSTITUTIONS

Assessment and outlook

Arthur P.J. Mol

Introduction

Environmental protection and sustainability have a complex relationship with finances and financial institutions. Financial institutions such as banks, pension funds and insurance companies, are increasingly seen as of vital importance for reaching environmental and sustainability goals. Initially, and at least till the early 1990s, the availability of finances and the functioning of financial institutions were considered to contribute significantly to unsustainable practices. Through their investment and loan practices, banks and other financial institutions were seen as major drivers behind economic growth and as such major contributors to natural resource depletion and environmental pollution. From the 1990s onwards, the sustainability perspective of financial institutions and the availability of finance has diversified. On the waves of ecological modernization (Spaargaren and Mol 1992) financial institutions were also considered as potentially major institutions, actors and instruments in greening investments, industrial development, and infrastructures. And lifting restrictions on finance was no longer one-to-one related to increasing pollution and resource extraction, but also to greening technological development and capitalization of green transitions (e.g. Scholtens 2006; Perez 2008; Yuxiang and Chen 2011, 95–97; UNEP 2014). Also, there was more and more recognition that public finance alone would never be able to free the finances needed to turn economies and societies green, as major investments will be needed in industrial transformations, new infrastructure, retro-fitting existing buildings, zero-carbon development and the like (Shen et al. 2013). This more positive role of financial institutions for the sustainability agenda started to gain prominence in the scholarly literature in the early 1990s, first especially with respect to international institutions such as the World Bank and its International Financial Corporation, other regional development banks, and the International Monetary Fund (IMF) (Perez 2008). These financial institutions decided – under considerable pressure from NGOs and some states – to integrate ecological considerations and later even conditionality into mainstream lending policies and practices. Following these development banks and international financial institutions, private banks also, starting with the larger ones from OECD countries with international operations, began to subject lending to some form of voluntary environmental regulation. The UNEP Finance Initiative, established in the 1990s, was the first to try to provide a global normative framework for the incorporation of environmental considerations into the business practices of public and private financial institutions. During all these initiatives and related debates it became clear that there were still many teething troubles and conflicting goals, which come along with sustainability roles for finance. The ambivalences of finance, financial instruments and financial institutions for the sustainability agenda made the design and implementation of the former three of key importance, and thus subject of research and politics.

Only recently have these discussions and initiatives started to have an impact within emerging economies (China, Brazil, India, South Africa) and even developing economies, where lately so-called south-originating green finance from public and private sources is rapidly emerging (Zadek and Flynn 2013). This chapter focuses on China, the largest provider of south-originating green finance and housing also the world's second largest lender for green projects (the China Development Bank).

Basically, close and more 'constructive' interactions of financial institutions and environmental protection can work two ways. Firstly, financial institutions such as banks, insurance companies, investment funds and pension funds can include environmental criteria, instruments, conditionality and performance goals in their functioning. This can be referred to as the greening of financial institutions. Secondly, environmental protection and policy can make use of financial institutions, mechanisms, and rationalities to obtain their environmental objectives in a better, more effective and/or more efficient manner. Examples are the marketization and financialization of conservation and environment through, among other options, the instalment of carbon (Spaargaren and Mol 2013), conservation (Sullivan 2013) and fisheries credits (Riel et al. 2015). In this mode, the environment is financialized rather than finances ecologized.

This chapter analyses how and to what extent China greens its financial institutions and practices in contributing to China's goals and objectives of a sustainable economy and society. Hence, we will not include the financialization of the environment in China, for instance through the emerging carbon markets in China (Environomist 2014). China is of special interest, not just because it is a major economy but also it has a particular relation between the state/political system and the financial market deviating from western OECD countries. Moreover, because its financial sector has often been accused of a preference for financing highly polluting and destructive projects and companies domestically and abroad (Worldwatch Institute 2008, 188–189). China has shown to be fast and creative in designing and implementing (be it not always to the extent desirable by environmental advocates) new and innovative institutions in coping with its huge and increasing environmental problems (Mol and Carter 2006; He et al. 2012). To what extent and how is China greening its financial institutions, and where do we find major differences with how OECD countries use and adapt their financial institutions for environmental goals?

The chapter starts with an analysis of China's financial system and how it relates to the environment. Subsequently, the policies on green credit provisioning, greening the stock market and greening insurances are reviewed, to finish with an assessment on the need for further improvements in greening China's financial institutions.

China's financial system and environment

Before reviewing the different initiatives, policies and practices of greening China's financial system and institutions, it is essential to provide an introduction into the nature and development of China's financial system and its relation to state agencies, because it is still fundamentally different from the equivalents in western market economies.

Financial sector in China

Until the 1970s, before the open-door policy in China started, state-owned enterprises were mainly financed through interest-free budgetary grants and retained profits. In the 1980s the state-owned enterprises and later also the various forms of private enterprises came to rely on bank loans, and in 1992 30 per cent of their total investment was financed through bank loans. The financial reform in 1993 furthered the importance of bank loans for enterprise investment, especially through the establishment of state-owned commercial banks (Cull and Xu 2005). China's financial system has been strongly controlled by state agencies until at least the mid 1990s and still faces more state control than Western equivalents. Only since then has the liberalization of the financial sector and its institutions started to take shape, for instance through the re-establishment/instalment of the Shanghai and Shenzhen stock markets (1990), the growing number of banks (now 3,800; see Figure 15.1) and their credit facilities, and the growing possibilities of private investments and the creation of private financial entities such as community banks and financial intermediaries.

The Chinese capital markets were established in the early 1990s but have developed strongly. By the end of 2011 2,342 companies were listed in the two Chinese stock markets of Shanghai and Shenzhen, with a total market capital of US$3.3 trillion. Three major market tiers exist: the Main Board tailored at large well-established state-owned and private companies; the SME Board as a financing channel for small and medium-sized companies; and the China Next Board for start-up innovative companies. Two types of stocks are traded: A shares basically available for domestic investors and B shares available to domestic and foreign investors. The government controls stock market-listed companies in three ways. First as owner/shareholder of State-Owned Companies (still some 50 per cent of the listed companies in heavy polluting sectors in 2011) through corporate governance. Second, shareholders are controlled and

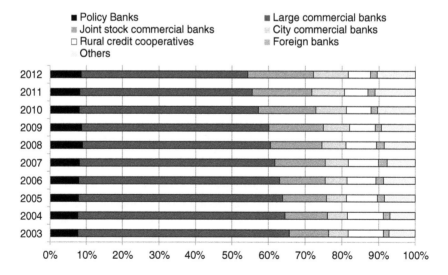

Figure 15.1 Market share (by assets) of China's banking institutions (2003–2012) (CBRC, 2013)[i]

[i] In 2012 there were three policy banks (China Development Bank, Export-Import Bank, Agricultural Development Bank of China), five large commercial banks (Bank of China, Industrial and Commercial Bank of China, China Communication Bank, China Construction Bank, China Agricultural Bank), 12 joint stock commercial banks, 144 city commercial banks, 1,927 rural credit cooperatives, 42 foreign banks and 1,641 other banking institutions.

monitored by the State-owned Assets Supervision and Administration Commission (SASAC). Third, the China Securities Regulatory Commission and its local securities regulatory bureaus oversee and govern the stock markets (Shanghai Stock Exchange [SSE] and Shenzhen Stock Exchange [SZSE]) and listed companies through the securities regulatory policies.

Chinese banks have also raised their profile and influence internationally. Three Chinese banks are among the top five globally by market capitalization. Several banks are also listed on the Hong Kong or Shanghai Stock Exchange, and several are buying stakes in foreign international banks. The number of foreign banks active in China is also increasing although they made up less than 2 per cent of the assets of all banks in China in 2012 (CBRC 2013). Increasingly Chinese banks also finance investments abroad, in almost all countries.

History of greening financial institutions

Sustainable finance or greening finance is widely known in the international financial community and is mostly – but not always – implemented on a voluntary basis by financial institutions such as banks, pension funds, insurance companies and investment funds. In China, however, green finance is to a significant extent a creation of the government, and its implementation has specific combinations of command-and-control regulation and Chinese versions of soft or voluntary policies. Although, as is so often the case with new policies in China, introducing green finance policy and practices in China builds upon experiences from other countries, it definitely has a specific Chinese twist.

Compared to other countries, greening financial institutions in China is strongly a governmental affair. Not only were in 2012 public expenditures and investments on environmental protection and conservation more than a factor of five larger than private finances of, for instance, renewable energy (the largest green sector for private investment and credits; Zadek and Zhang 2014, 12). Also the green investments and credits of financial institutions are strongly driven by national policies, guidelines, assessment systems and targets. In the developed OECD economies finance is coming from marginally regulated commercial banks and from private equity, venture capital and hedge funds. Hence, greening the financial systems in these OECD countries is much more strongly driven by market, shareholder and stakeholder pressures (Wagemans et al. 2014) and the functioning of voluntary measures, private standards, international principles for responsible investment and rating systems (Perez 2008; UNEP 2014), and less so by governments. In OECD countries, governments play at best an indirect role in governing the greening of finances, for instance through transparency and reporting requirements of banking activities.

Li and Hu (2014) distinguish four phases in the inclusion of environmental objectives and conditionality in China's main financial institutions. The first phase started in the early 1980s, when the first policy proposal was developed by the State Council (SC[1981]27) on applying environmental impact assessment approval as a precondition for loans by state-owned banks for major construction works. The second phase started in 1995 and further developed the greening of credit provisioning, culminating in the 2007 Green Credit Policy. In 2001 a third phase started when policies were developed for greening the emerging stock markets. In the fourth phase policies and practices expanded towards the insurance market, when the Ministry of Environmental Protection (MEP) and the China Insurance Regulatory Commission (CIRC) jointly released in 2007 the pilot phase of the environmental pollution liability insurance system (Feng et al. 2014a, 2014b). Regardless of these four phases, it is widely acknowledged that 2007 was of key importance for the breakthrough of green finance policies. The greening of finance and financial institutions has not unwound in isolation but is part of a much broader package of policies to intertwine economic and environmental objectives and measures. Greening tax policies, green government procurement, environmental compensation programmes, greening trade and financialization of the environment are all part of this turn (see e.g. Aizawa and Yang 2010). These come together with a stronger collaboration between China's financial and economic policy-making authorities with the MEP and its lower environmental authorities, often instigated by the latter rather than the former.

International embeddedness

The development of green finance and the greening of the financial sector in China cannot be understood in isolation, but is part of an international process. In developing new green finance policies and practices, Chinese institutions have to some extent cooperated with international financial institutions, such as the International Finance Corporation (through a Memorandum of Understanding (MoU) with Exim Bank, through risk-sharing facilities and through agreements on energy efficiency projects), the United National Environment Programme–Finance Initiative (UNEP 2014),[1] the OECD and the World Bank (Matisoff and Chan 2008, 14ff) as well as with other international banks (e.g. through the Equator Principles, UN Global Compact, and Carbon Disclosure Project; Bai et al. 2014). Western NGOs acknowledge the uniqueness of this: 'China is the only country we've seen that has issued a banking regulation to govern its environmental and social impacts for overseas investments, and deserves some credit for going above and beyond in that sense.'[2]

Hence, the greening of the Chinese financial sector is of relevance beyond its borders, for instance through the export profile of China and the global supply chains Chinese companies are part of. Global relevance is also clear through the financing of increasing outward investment of Chinese companies by Chinese banks (see Mol 2011). Green credit policies are also applicable to foreign investments, and in February 2013 the Ministry of Commerce and MEP jointly released the Guidelines for Environmental Protection in Foreign Investment and Cooperation. But these guidelines are far from always applied (Green Watershed 2013). International NGOs find their way in filing complaints at Chinese banks and the China Banking Regulatory Commission (CBRC) for not abiding by the green credit policies (see below) when providing credit for unsustainable foreign investments, for instance on large-scale copper mining in Amazonian Ecuador.

There has been some debate whether national actions on greening the financial system will have negative consequences for the competitive position of national financial sectors, but there is little evidence of that. Rather we witness lately a new race between leading financial institutions in green innovation of their business, because of the rapid growth of green sector investments and because of a positive correlation (suggested by some, e.g. Simpson and Kohers, 2002) between environmental and financial performance of banks.

Greening credit provisioning

In China greening credit provisioning by banks for investments in industries and large-scale infrastructural projects started in 1995 with policies of The People's Bank of China (PBOC[1995]24) and the State Environmental Administration (SEPA[1995]105), but these policies to include environmental conditions in credit provisioning were poorly operationalized and implemented. In 2007 the MEP, the CBRC and the People's Bank of China introduced the Green Credit Policy (*Opinions on the Implementation of Environmental Policies and Regulations to Prevent Credit Risks*), calling on Chinese banks to withhold credit to enterprises that heavily pollute the environment or showed inefficient consumption of energy and natural resources, and to extend credit to environmental projects on preferential terms. In 2012 CBRC issued *Green Credit Guidelines* as a more elaborated framework for green lending by improving the rules and examination indicators system for green credit, for investigating the loan status of enterprises violating the regulations on environmental protection, and for issuing warning signals to relevant banks. It also strengthened the accountability of the boards of directors and senior management staff of financial institutions.[3] The three main elements of the Green Credit Policy are restricting credit to polluting companies, installing environmental risk assessment as part of the loan process, and advancing credits for green projects.

According to the Green Credit Policy banks are required to promote green concepts and identify, assess, monitor, control and mitigate environmental and social risks of borrowers and loans. A WWF (2013) survey among 12 larger banks and a Green Watershed (2013) investigation on 16 major banks showed that most banks have adopted and applied sustainability principles, policies, guidelines and measures for their credit business. Following that policy, especially the larger Chinese banks have further strengthened their processes on environmental compliance review in approving loans.[4] The environmental standards have been made more stringent, the ceiling of credit volume for which approval is necessary has been lowered, and the principle of 'one ballot veto' has been applied more often.[5] Also restrictions of credit provisioning to 'high pollution, high energy consumption and industries in excess of capacity' is developed as policy by most banks, among others through strict approval procedures, admission control, loan quotas and loan-withdrawal measures. Among others, the MEP established a black list of companies that do not meet environmental standards and which could thus not borrow money.[6] The China Agricultural Bank rejected 792 request for loans (valued US$1.95 billion) for not fulfilling environmental standards in 2010. Especially dual high (*liang gao*) projects and industries (high polluting and energy intensive) have been the target of loan restrictions.[7]

Still, overall the implementation of the *Guidelines* in restricting credit has been weak, because of lack of capacity within banks on environmental assessment, poor reward and punishment, and strong pressure from local governments to provide loans (particularly on local commercial banks and rural credit cooperatives). For example, despite its poor environmental record, Zijin Mining Group received loans from several large Chinese banks (e.g. Exim Bank, Agricultural Bank of China, Bank of China, Industrial and Commercial Bank of China) (Wang and Bernell 2013). While almost all banks report a declining trend, several banks have continued to invest heavily in 'high pollution, high energy-consumption and industries in excess of capacity', such as Bank of China, ICBC and China Merchants Bank (Green Watershed 2013, 26).

The second element of the Green Credit Policy is related to environmental risk assessment. Credit risk is the risk of an economic loss when the lender is unable to fulfil its contractual obligation. Environmental risks may influence credit risks, and environmental credit risk management has increasingly emerged internationally as banks aim to minimize their risks from lending (Perez 2008). Environmental credit risk assessment is also a vital part of China's Green Credit Policy, especially elaborated in the *Guidelines*. One of the key issues for credit risk assessments is information collection by banks[8] and information sharing between the MEP and its EPBs and the banks through the PBOC credit report system. The PBOC database is fed with standardized enterprise environmental information from EPBs and contained in 2009 over 40,000 environmental violations and compliance of enterprises. An international comparison among 120 banks, from 10 Asian-Pacific countries, including 17 Chinese banks representing 70 per cent of total assets of Chinese banks, proved that China is in the middle category of countries whose banks include systematic environmental credit risk management (Hu and Li 2015). Whereas in countries like the US and Canada liabilities were the main drivers for banks to install advanced levels of environmental credit risk management, in China it was mainly governmental policies on installing environmental risk assessment before approving loans. Several Chinese banks have developed their own internal systems, policies, procedures, databases, tools and/or teams for environmental risk assessment in their processes of approving and reviewing loans (see Green Watershed 2013; WWF 2013). The Industrial and Commercial Bank of China has developed a systematic nine-category Environmental Information Labelling System, categorizing borrowers on the basis of their environmental profile, and applying it to the large majority of their clients, suggesting some kind of due diligence to these clients beyond what governmental regulations require (Matisoff and Chan 2008, 19). The Bank of Communication uses three large categories (red, yellow and green) and seven small categories to classify the environmental impact of the clients and projects, and the Industrial Bank adopted the international Equator Principles.[9] However, Zhang et al. (2011) found out that about half of the banks in Jiangsu province did not apply any environmental risk assessment. From a 2012 survey among the top 50 banks in China on environmental risk management, only one received the highest rating, 42 per cent received the lowest of the five grades, meaning they had only superficially adopted environmental risk management measures, while 18 per cent provided no data whatsoever (Policy Research Center for Environment and Economy 2013). Hence, setting and implementing detailed guidelines for supervising company environmental risk performance, and thus implementing Green Credit Policy, proves difficult for many banks.

China has especially advanced in providing credit for projects and companies that plan environmental and renewable energy activities, the so-called green sector.[10] Banks have developed special funds for environmental projects (e.g. Industrial Bank, Beijing Bank), new green financial products (e.g. Bank of China, Industrial Bank China, China Everbright Bank), cooperated with international and foreign institutions (e.g. Huaxia Bank, China Merchants Bank), and/or supported green projects in high-risk sectors (e.g. ICBC, Shanghai Bank). Surveys show that almost all banks participated in this credit provisioning for the green sector and projects. Loans given to the green sector have exponentially grown (up to RMB 6.14 trillion in 2012), and also the percentage of bank loans to the green sector has expanded.[11] All signs and projections point at further major investment in China's green sector up till 2020. The government is also developing new instruments to increase the amount of private capital needed to materialize its plans for greening the real economy, such as its 2013 announcement to develop a green bonds market (Kidney and Oliver 2014). Often, with respect to current green sector credits it remains difficult to obtain detailed information on the exact investment targets, the clients who are given these green credits and the environmental performance obtained through these green credits (Yu 2010; Green Watershed 2013). Data and sector categorization on green sector credits are not harmonized, data are not always published, and reliability of published data on investments in green projects cannot be checked.

The information collected to implement this Green Credit Policy, as well as the outcomes of credit decisions following environmental assessments, are only to some extent made transparent, to play a further role among wider constituencies, such as the media, other company stake- and shareholders and other governmental authorities. Commercial banks are also increasingly pushed (among others by Bank of China, but also by stock market listed disclosure policies) to develop corporate social responsibility policies. Most major banks follow Global Reporting Initiative (GRI) Sustainability Reporting Guidelines in compiling their corporate social responsibility reports, and allow third party verification. But few banks have established and implemented systematic information disclosure mechanisms. Good news easily finds its way to the media, but other information meets 'commercial confidentiality' limitations in disclosure. Banks have not really opened up to the wider public, but this might change now that criticism is increasing of loaning practices, both domestically and internationally. NGOs such as Green Watershed, Banktrack, Greenpeace and WWF are starting to watch the green credit performance of Chinese banks.

Greening stock markets

While banks are still the main source of new investments in China (with estimates of up to 80 per cent of investment credit coming from banks), increasingly other sources are emerging, among which is the stock market. Hence, the second main policy for greening the financial system is Green Securities, aiming at limiting capital expansion of polluting firms through the stock market, both through initial public offerings and through refinancing of existing firms. A first system of environmental examination and approval (EEA) for initial public offering (IPO) and refinancing operations was installed in 2001 by SEPA (SEPA[2001]156; SEPA[2003]101)). This policy was further developed and strengthened through the Green Securities Policy, launched in 2008 by the MEP and the China Securities Regulatory Commission (CSRC) (which oversees the stock markets in China). These policies aim at restricting capital expansion in environmentally unfriendly enterprises by making it harder for polluting enterprises to raise capital through the stock market. Green security policies mainly use three instruments: EEA for IPO and refinancing; environmental disclosure of listed firms by the firms; and third party environmental performance evaluation.

The system of EEA requires a standardized compulsory environmental review on IPOs and refinancing in 14 pollution-intensive industrial sectors at national and provincial levels, as listed by the MEP.[12] Companies have to submit to the MEP a technical report (following guidelines) showing the applicant's environmental performance over the past three years, as well as a consent paper of the provincial EPB after the EPB performed an audit. Companies that fail an initial review face prohibition of raising funds through the stock market unless required remedy or treatment measures are completed within the deadline set by the MEP. The MEP informs the CSRC of the final decision. For the various steps in an EEA procedure for IPOs or refinancing, criteria have been developed and established, but these are often not very specific or unambiguous, leaving much room for interpretation and politics. While initially, in 2007 and 2008, quite a number of listed companies failed the initial review, in 2011 only two out of 50 companies failed an initial review while some others were delayed in the procedure (Li and Hu 2014). It is unclear whether this is related to improved practices of applicants or poor implementation of the Green Securities Policy.

Secondly, the CSRC and SEPA, through the *Measures on Information Disclosure for Listed Companies* (CSRC[2007]40) and the SEPA policies on green securities, require that those who issue or sponsor securities disclose whether environmental criteria of enterprises or projects are met, both during issuance of securities and periodically.[13] Currently, most listed companies falling under the 14 high-polluting industrial sectors fulfil periodic reporting requirements in their annual report or through a specific corporate social responsibility report. In examining all 502 highly polluting companies listed on the Shanghai and Shenzhen Stock Exchanges, Shen and Li (2010) found that in 2009 94 per cent of these companies reported environmental information, while others found lower percentages of around 60 per cent (Li and Guo 2011; Wang and Bernell 2013). Regardless of the quantity differences, all studies found that the quality and completeness of these environmental disclosures of stock market-listed companies were rather poor.[14] Due to the absence of clear, consistent and specific guidelines (Zhong et al. 2011; Kuo et al. 2012; Noronha et al. 2013; Wang and Bernell 2013, 344–346) environmental information disclosure fails in objectivity, preciseness and hard data, timeliness and completeness, and often negative environmental information is deliberately left out of reporting. Overall, companies listed at the SSE did quantitatively and qualitatively better in reporting than those listed at Shenzhen Stock Exchange (SZSE), which might be caused by the difference between mandatory (SSE) versus voluntary (SZSE) environmental disclosure guidelines.[15] This poor performance is caused by: (i) the soft regulatory path that has followed the initial mandatory policies (e.g. the still draft 2010 *Guide on listed companies environmental information disclosure*); (ii) the different interests of regulators (e.g. the SASAC and CSRC versus MEP) which hamper coordination and harmonization in green securities decision making, information sharing, implementation and sanctioning;[16] and (iii) the strong economic interests (in terms of taxes, employment, economic performance) that local authorities have in protecting listed companies located in their jurisdiction.

Thirdly, environmental performance evaluation of all stock market-listed companies has been mentioned in the Green Securities Policy, regardless of whether these companies are aiming for IPO or refinancing and regardless of the sector the companies are part of. This comes close to the use of sustainability indexes by some of the stock exchanges in OECD countries (e.g. Dow Jones Sustainability Index). Listed companies would be placed on a red list (best performing) and black list (poor performing). However, a shortage of reliable and relevant data and information and the lack of specific guidelines, have hampered progress in these kinds of evaluations. Also, and in contrast to the sustainability indexes in other countries, such evaluations have not been made public until today, nor have policy measures been related to performance outcomes. Only the Chinese Academy for Environmental Planning did a pilot examination among 161 companies, with 10 companies placed on the red list and 40 on the black list (as cited by Li and Hu 2014).

The Green Securities Policy has also been discovered by NGOs. Increasingly we see environmental NGOs becoming involved in the environmental examination process, by noticing MEP and EPBs regarding incorrect environmental statements in the company prospectus that is issued for initial public offering or refinancing, or by appealing against a positive decision of MEP on IPO/refinancing (which has to be made public). Six international/Chinese NGOs did that for the first time regarding Gold East Paper in 2008/2009, with little success. But since then other NGOs were more successful in correcting review outcomes or MEP decisions, such as on Sinopec in 2010 (irregularities at 26 subordinate enterprises), on Camel batteries (Hubei) in 2011 and on Beingmate (baby formula; Zhejiang and Heilongjiang) in 2011. These NGOs often accuse companies of violations of the 2010 *Administrative Measures on Information Disclosure of Listed Companies*, of violations of the *Rules Governing the Listing of Stocks on Shanghai Stock Exchange* (1998, revised in 2008) on correct information in prospectuses, or of a past record of environmental misbehaviour.

Compared to government funding and banks, the stock market is of relatively minor importance (<15 per cent) for investments in the green sector over the past years (Shen et al. 2013). However, public equity markets are significantly more important than venture capital and private equity.

Environmental pollution liability insurance

To further manage and control increasing environmental risks, new marked-based approaches in environmental management are being experimented with and implemented in China. Environmental Pollution Liability Insurance, in short pollution insurance, is one of these new marked-based approaches recently introduced in China's still predominantly command-and-control environmental management system. This follows the 1995 *UNEP Statement of*

Environmental Commitment by the Insurance Industry, which reads in article 2.1 'We will reinforce the attention given to environmental risks in our core activities. These activities include risk management, loss prevention, product design, claims handling and asset management'.[17] Most scholars see three strong advantages to pollution insurance as an environmental regulative tool (Richardson 2002; Freeman and Kunreuther 2003; PRCEE 2011; Feng et al. 2014a). First, pollution insurance ensures that victims of pollution can be compensated – even in cases of company bankruptcy – without reliance on government compensation funds. Second, pollution insurance mitigates environmental risks in that it rewards, through lower premiums, polluters who invest in risk reduction and pollution prevention measures. Third, as an insurance tool, pollution insurance spreads the risks and costs of environmental pollution of one company over a group of polluters, to protect individual – insured – companies from bankruptcy and to protect banks and other credit institutions from major financial risks.

Pollution insurance was developed in the late 1960s in especially the USA, France and Germany (Richardson 2002; Bie and Fan 2007). In the 1980s/1990s it spread from the major industrialized countries to emerging economies such as India and China. China's 1982 Marine Environmental Protection Law and China's 1983 Environmental Protection Regulations on the Offshore Oil Exploration and Exploitation included already provisions on oil pollution liability insurance for ships (Chen 2006). Further pollution insurance trial applications, beyond ships and offshore activities, started in the early 1990s, but only in 2006 the Chinese government decided to strongly promote more systematically environmental insurances for polluting companies, especially through its 2007 *Guidelines on Environmental Pollution Liability Insurance*. Hence, pollution insurance for companies in China developed in three stages (Feng et al. 2014a): the fragmented application stage (1991), the pilot application at national scale stage (2006), and the nationwide mandatory application stage (2011), each coming with their own trial programmes and policy documents. It is expected that a comprehensive nationwide pollution insurance programme will be implemented in not too long (MEP and IRC 2007).

The Chinese government defines pollution insurance as the insurance related to the compensation for the loss of third parties caused by environmental pollution accidents. Pollution insurance is jointly regulated by the MEP and the Insurance Regulation Committee (IRC) at national level, and Environmental Protection Bureaus and Insurance Supervision Bureaus (ISBs) at the provincial level. Environmental authorities can compel polluters to buy pollution insurance, and IRC/ISBs overlook the insurance market and insurance companies and 'encourage' the latter to develop pollution insurance products. Third parties, such as insurance brokers and insurance assessors, are still very much in development. Victims, individuals, communities or organizations negatively affected by pollution accidents, can claim compensation from companies, which should reduce the claims for compensation put to governmental authorities.

In 2012, 14 cities and provinces had launched trial application of pollution insurance. More than 10 insurance companies had entered the pollution insurance market in China by 2010, the leading ones being PICC, Pingan and Huatai. But the demand for pollution insurances, the number of companies having pollution insurance, and the number of cases where money has been paid to companies and/or victims following pollution accidents have been minimal. Several reasons are behind this slow dissemination of pollution insurance: poor knowledge of polluting companies on pollution insurance, (too) high premiums (also due to poor risk assessments and low number of participants), maximum coverage limit, limitation to only accidental pollution (and not gradual pollution), and the fact that limited costs are involved when pollution accidents happen due to poor enforcement and limited success of victim complaints, which do not push companies towards insurances (Liu and Chik 2012; Feng et al. 2014a).

In those cities or provinces where authorities made pollution insurance compulsory for specified (heavily polluting or high-risk) industrial sectors, the pollution market did develop into a more mature market, with more insurance companies, more insurance products and more companies buying insurances. Hunan province is a typical frontrunner case of establishing compulsory environmental insurance, strongly backed by provincial policies. By the end of 2012 around 600 industrial companies were involved in pollution insurance with a total premium of over 20 million RMB. Up till early 2014, there were 54 pollution insurance compensation cases in Hunan, and 4.812 million RMB has been paid to victims for industrial environmental damage. When high-level risk industries could voluntarily decide whether to buy insurance for ecological compensation and restoration at private insurance companies, the numbers of companies buying pollution insurance remained low (Feng et al. 2014b).

But the Chinese central government seems determined to continue with pollution insurance, both to limit financial risks of companies and banking institutions due to poor environmental performance, and to increase market incentives for polluting companies to limit environmental risks. Hence, in 2013 a new national scheme for compulsory environmental liability insurance was announced by the MEP and the China Insurance Regulatory Commission. Companies that fail to purchase environmental liability insurance may face loss of funds or withheld approval from the MEP. The MEP is also authorized to share information on environmental insurances with banks as a means to rate clients for credit provisioning. To further strengthen pollution insurance and provide it with a legal basis, which it lacked until recently, pollution insurance was included in the 2014 revision of the Environmental Protection Law, in article 52 (Zhang et al. 2015).

Still, overall pollution insurance is very much in development. Polluting companies have little knowledge of and demand for these kinds of insurance products, insurance companies find it difficult to develop these insurance products and set a competitive price to develop a large market demand, victims are unaware of pollution insurance in demanding compensation, banks do not request pollution insurance as a condition for loans, and local authorities have not fully backed national environmental insurance policies with operationalizations and implementation.

Conclusion

Over the past decade, China has made significant progress in greening its financial institutions, arguably beyond what many OECD countries have achieved. In contrast to OECD countries, greening finance in China is strongly triggered, articulated, regulated and enforced by governmental authorities. Also in comparison with many countries, China's green finance policies are less voluntary and more mandatory. Both financial authorities and environmental authorities – and often jointly – have contributed to issuing regulations and guidelines that environmentally condition financial practices with respect to credit provisioning, stock markets and company insurances. NGOs, shareholders, business associations and environmental victims, among others, have been involved only marginally up till now.

Given this accelerated development in launching ideas, guidelines and regulations on greening financial institutions and practices over a period of only a decade, it should not surprise us that implementation and enforcement is often falling short. Lack of capacity, knowledge, priority and operational instructions and guidelines result in shortcomings in implementing the greening of finances and financial institutions. We should not be too worried about that, as greening finances is a learning, capacity-building and institutionalization process that needs time. Throughout the past decade we can clearly identify major advances and improvements in the three main greening policies on credit, securities and insurance, for instance in moving from trial to full policies, in geographical spreading, in widening sectoral inclusion, and in moving from voluntary guidelines to mandatory policies.

But several structural biases have limited the effectiveness of these policies, and need to be repaired in order to prepare green financing for the future. First, most of China's policies on greening finances are focused on restrictive measures on polluting firms, rather than stimulating and supportive measures on enhancing green sector investments. Finances for, for instance, energy efficiency is still difficult to obtain. And green credit is still not seen as core business for banks, and even seen as a more risky business than credits for mainstream polluting companies.

Second, most of the effort in greening finances is directed at the large-scale enterprises that use public equity or bank loans. Many of these companies are state-owned enterprises or have close relations with state authorities. Policies and measures on greening finances miss to a major extent small and medium-sized enterprises, which produce 60 per cent of the country's GDP. Together, these SMEs are both important as polluters and important as contributors to China's green sector. These companies are mostly not listed on the two stock exchanges, are not included in credit histories and environmental documentation of environmental authorities, and hence have less easy access to credit. Moreover, private capital investment and venture capital for all types of companies are outside the scope of greening finances policies of the state (Shen et al. 2013; Bai et al. 2014, 116).

Third, regardless of the many recent initiatives on enhancing environmental information disclosure, China's financial system witnesses a major lack of disclosure and transparency, and a lack of third party verification of available information. So far, no bank has established a real public information disclosure system on lending, and no bank in its CSR report has achieved comprehensive and neutral information disclosure. In particular, banks are not open to lending when sensitive sectors are concerned (dams, nuclear power, known polluters such as paraxylene [PX] companies) or when lenders prove to have become major – accidental – polluters (Green Watershed 2013; Bai et al. 2014, 116). This lack of transparency reduces the much-needed involvement of wider constituencies in greening finances, such as shareholders, the media, NGOs and the wider public.

Finally, with Chinese capital moving abroad, greening finance should also address internationally operating Chinese firms and credit provisioning by Chinese banks for operations abroad. It will not be sufficient for internationally operating Chinese firms and banks to behave according to local policies and requirements. Global (voluntary) standards are an instrument in that, but so is China's domestic policy of green credit and green securities. Here too, there is still a world to win.

Notes

1 In 2014 six financial institutions (all banks) from China were member of UNEP-FI: Bank of Taizhou, China Development Bank, China Merchants Bank, Industrial Bank, Longjiang Bank and Ping An Bank.
2 Katharine Lu, spokesperson of Friends of the Earth USA, as quoted in: Hill, D. (2014), Chinese banks ignore pleas of Ecuador mining campaigners, *Chinadialogue* 12 May 2014 (https://chinadialogue.net/article/show/single/en/6966-Chinese-banks-ignore-pleas-of-Ecuador-mining-campaigners, accessed 3 December 2016).
3 And also their performance evaluation sometimes includes sustainability criteria, although the impact on income is often not large (WWF 2013, 9).
4 Matisoff and Chan (2008, 34) claim that smaller banks are often leading in signing up to sustainability principles such as the Equator Principles or to have CSR. This is often also related to the higher level of flexibility in adopting these innovations, and the desire to profile the smaller banks vis-à-vis the larger national ones.

5 In such a 'one ballot veto' system a borrower's environmental performance is the decisive factor in considering a loan. The idea is that banks will deny lending to enterprises with environmental violations and suspend loans to companies and projects that face restrictions by industrial policy.

6 Initially, in 2007, only 38 companies were put on the black list.

7 See WWF (2013, 40–41) for examples of companies that have been refused credit due to environmental risks.

8 Banks use environmental risk information from governmental agencies (MEP, CBRC, PBOC), clients, existing bank knowledge, public information from the Internet, third party due diligence, and external assessment tools, but hardly from external environmental rating agencies and site visits (WWF 2013, 16). Banks sometimes also use post-credit regular and ad hoc monitoring of clients, e.g. through EPB lists of violations and on-the-spot inspections.

9 Several banks have made various innovations: ICBC (Industrial and Commercial Bank of China) introduced 'CM 2002 System of Enterprise Environmental Protection Information', China Merchants Bank developed a 'Risk Quantification Technology' and 'Early Warning and Joint Action between Head Office and Local Branch', China Construction Bank introduced 'credit business risk monitoring system', China CITIC Bank specified principles for credit provisioning to key sectors, China Everbright Bank had a system of 'three identifications', and China Construction Bank claims to have a system of real-time monitoring and guiding (Green Watershed, 2013).

10 *China Sustainable Finance Newsletter* no. 18 (2013, 3)

11 Besides government financing, green credit, public equity markets (Shanghai and Shenzhen Stock Exchanges – see below) and international loans, a relatively small amount of private equity financing and venture capital has been invested in the green sector (Shen et al. 2013; Criscuolo and Menon 2014).

12 These industries are thermal power, steel and iron, cement, aluminium, coal, metallurgy, building materials, mining, chemicals, oil, pharmaceuticals, light industries, textiles and leather. Around 31 per cent of the ±1,500 listed companies of the SSE and SZSE were from these sectors in 2010 (Wang and Bernell 2013).

13 This falls in a wider policy in China for mandatory environmental information disclosure of companies and state agencies, most broadly regulated through the 2008 *Environmental Information Disclosure Decree* (Mol et al. 2011) and recently confirmed in the 2014 revision of the *Environmental Protection Law* (Zhang et al. 2015). It also corresponds with wider international developments.

14 Xu et al. (2012) found that disclosing environmental violation events of stock-listed Chinese companies had a much lower reduction of market value than with western companies.

15 See Noronha et al. (2013). In 2014 a SSE Listed Companies' Information Disclosure Consultation Committee was established, with tasks in assessing companies' information disclosure and evaluating the guidelines (*China Sustainable Finance Newsletter*, no. 21 (2014, 3).

16 Wang lists the differences and inconsistencies between the *Instructing Opinions on How to Enhance Environmental Protection Monitoring and Management of Listed Companies (2008)*, the *Guidelines on Environmental Information Disclosure of Listed Companies on Shanghai Stock Exchange* (Shanghai Stock Exchange 2008); and *Guide on Listed Companies' Environmental Information Disclosure (Draft) (2010)*.

17 This statement was merged in 2011 with *UNEP Statement by Financial Institutions on the Environment & Sustainable Development* into a single *UNEP Statement of Commitment by Financial Institutions on Sustainable Development*, signed by >200 financial institutions worldwide.

References

Aizawa, M. and Yang C., 2010. Green credit, green stimulus, green revolution? China's mobilization of banks for environmental clean-up, *Journal of Environment & Development,* 34 (1/2), 389–401.

Bai Y., Faure M. and Liu J., 2014. The role of China's banking sector in providing green finance, *Duke Environmental Law & Policy Forum,* 24, 89–140.

Bie T., and Fan X., 2007. Huanjing wuran zeren baoxian zhidu guoji bijiao yanjiu (Comparative study on the international environmental pollution liability insurance systems), *Insurance Studies,* 8, 89–92.

CBRC (China Banking Regulatory Commission) 2013. *2012 Annual Report,* Beijing: CBRC.

Chen P. 2006. A study on the types of liability of the insurer for oil pollution and that of the party liable. In: M.G. Faure and J. Hu (eds), *Prevention and Compensation of Marine Pollution Damage. Recent Developments in Europe, China and the US,* Alphen a/d Rijn: Kluwer, pp. 241–262.

Criscuolo, C. and Menon, C., 2014. *Environmental Policies and Risk Finance in the Green Sector*, Paris: OECD (OECD Science, Technology and Industry Working Papers 2014/01).

Cull, R. and Xu L.C., 2005. Institutions, ownership, and finance: the determinants of profit investment among Chinese firms, *Journal of Financial Economics*, 77, 117–146.

Environomist, 2014, *China Carbon Market Research Report 2014*, Beijing: Environomist.

Feng Y., Mol, A.P.J., Lu Y.L., van Koppen, C.S.A. and He G.Z., 2014a. The development of environmental pollution liability insurance in China: in need of strong government backing, *Ambio*, 43 (5), 687–702.

Feng Y., Mol, A.P.J., Lu Y., He G.Z. and van Koppen, C.S.A., 2014b. Environmental pollution liability insurance in China: compulsory or voluntary? *Journal of Cleaner Production*, 70, 211–219.

Freeman, P.K. and Kunreuther, H., 2003. Managing environmental risks through insurance. In: H. Folmer and Tietenberg, T. (eds.), *International Yearbook of Environmental and Resource Economics*, Glos.: Edward Elgar, 159–189.

Green Watershed, 2013. *Green Credit Footprint of Chinese Banks (2008–2012) – Executive Summary*, Kunming: Green Watershed.

Hill, D., 2014. Chinese Banks ignore pleas of Ecuador mining campaigners, *Chinadialogue* 12 May 2014 https://chinadialogue.net/article/show/single/en/6966-Chinese-banks-ignore-pleas-of-Ecuador-mining-campaigners (accessed 3 December 2016).

Hu M. and Li W., 2015. A comparative study on environmental credit risk management of banks in the Asia-Pacific region, *Business Strategy and the Environment*, 24 (3), 159–174.

Kidney, S. and Oliver, P., 2014. *Greening China's Financial Markets. Growing Green Bonds Market in China: reducing costs and increasing capacity for green investment while promoting greater transparency and stability in financial markets*, Winnipeg: IISD.

Kuo, L., Yeh, C.C. and Yu, H.C., 2012. Disclosure of Corporate Social Responsibility and Environmental Management: Evidence from China, *Corporate Social Responsibility and Environmental Management* 19, 273–287.

Li Z. and Guo R., 2011. Shangshi gongsi huanjing xinxi pilu de xianzhuang yu wenti fenxi: Yi shihua hangye wei yangben (An analysis of the status quo and problems of environmental disclosure by listed companies: A sample of petrochemical industries), *Communication of Finance and Accounting*, 15, 70–72.

Li W. and Hu M., 2014. An overview of the environmental finance policies in China: retrofitting an integrated mechanism for environmental management, *Frontiers of Environmental Sciences and Engineering*, 8 (3), 316–328.

Liu C., and Chik A.R.B., 2012. Reasons for insufficient demand of environmental liability insurance in China: A case study of Baoding, Hebei Province. *Asian Social Science*, 8, 201–204.

Matisoff, A. and Chan M., 2008. *The Green Evolution. Environmental Policies and Practice in China's Banking Sector*, Nijmegen: Friends of the Earth-US/Banktrack.

MEP and IRC. 2007. The guidelines on environmental pollution liability insurance. Beijing: MEP.

Mol, A.P.J., 2011. China's ascent and Africa's environment, *Global Environmental Change*, 21 (3), 785–794.

Mol, A.P.J. and Carter, N.T., 2006. China's environmental governance in transition, *Environmental Politics*, 15 (2), 149–170.

Mol, A.P.J., He G.Z. and Zhang L., 2011, Information disclosure as environmental risk management: developments in China, *Journal of Current Chinese Affairs*, 40 (3), 163–192.

Noronha, C., Tou, S., Cynthia, M.I. and Guan, J.J., 2013. Corporate social responsibility reporting in China: an overview and comparison with major trends, *Corporate Social Responsibility and Environmental Management*, 20, 29–42.

Perez, O., 2008. The new universe of green finance: from self-regulation to multi-polar governance. In: O. Dilling, Herberg, M. and Winter, G. (Eds.), *Responsible Business: Self-Governance and Law in Transnational Economic Transactions*, Oxford: Hart Publishing, pp. 151–180.

Policy Research Centre for Environment and Economy (PRCEE), 2011. *The Development Report of Environmental Pollution Liability Insurance in China*, Beijing: PRCEE/MEP.

Richardson, B.J., 2002. Mandating environmental liability insurance, *Duke Environmental Law and Policy Forum* 12, 293–329.

Riel, M.C. van, Bush, S.R., van Zwieten, P.A.M. and Mol, A.P.J., 2015. Understanding fisheries credit systems: potentials and pitfalls of managing catch efficiency, *Fish and Fisheries*, 16 (3), 453–470.

Scholtens, B. 2006. Finance as a driver of corporate social responsibility, *Journal of Business Ethics* 68, 19–33.

Shen, B., Wang, M., Li, J., Li, L. Price, L. and Zeng, L., 2013. China's approaches to financing sustainable development: policies, practices, and issues, *WIREs Energy and Environment*, 2, 178–198.

Shen H. and Li Y., 2010. Woguo zhongwuran hangye shangshi gongsi huanjing xinxi pilu xiangzhuang fenxi (An analysis of the status quo of environmental information disclosure by the listed companies in heavily polluting industries), *Securities Market Herald*, 6, 51–57.

Simpson, G. and Kohers, T., 2002. The link between corporate social and financial performance: evidence from the banking industry, *Journal of Business Ethics*, 35 (2), 97–109.

Spaargaren, G. and Mol, A.P.J., 1992. Sociology, environment and modernity: ecological modernization as a theory of social change, *Society and Natural Resources*, 5 (5), 325–345.

Spaargaren, G. and Mol, A.P.J., 2013. Carbon flows, carbon markets and low-carbon lifestyles, *Environmental Politics*, 22 (1), 174–193.

Sullivan, S., 2013. Banking nature? The spectacular financialisation of environmental conservation, *Antipode*, 45 (1), 198–217.

The Worldwatch Institute, 2008. *2008 State of the World. Innovations for a Sustainable Economy*, Washington D.C.: The Worldwatch Institute.

UNEP, 2014. *Aligning the Financial System with Sustainable Development*, Geneva: UNEP.

Wagemans, F.A.J., van Koppen, C.S.A. and Mol, A.P.J., 2014. The effectiveness of socially responsible investment, *Journal of Integrative Environmental Sciences*, 10 (3/4), 235–252.

Wang, H. and Bernell, D., 2013. Environmental disclosure in China: an examination of the Green Securities Policy, *The Journal of Environmental Development* 22, 339–369.

WWF (in collaboration with CBRC and PWC), 2013. *The Sustainable Performance of Chinese Banking and International Financial Institutions. Comparative Study*, Beijing: WWF.

Xu X.D., Zeng S.X. and Tam C.M., 2012. Stock market's reaction to disclosure of environmental violations: evidence from China, *Journal of Business Ethics*, 107, 227–237.

Yu X.G., 2010. *Environmental Record of Chinese Banks*, Kunming: The Green Watershed.

Yuxiang K. and Chen Z., 2011. Financial development and environmental performance: evidence from China, *Environment and Development Economics* 16 (1), 93–111.

Zadek, S. and Flynn, C., 2013. *South-Originating Green Finance. Exploring Its Potential*, Geneva: Geneva International Financial Dialogue.

Zadek, S. and Zhang, C., 2014. *Greening China's Financial System. An Initial Exploration*, Winnipeg: IISD.

Zhang B., Yang Y. and Bi J., 2011. Tracking the implementation of Green Credit Policy in China: top-down perspective and bottom-up reform, *Journal of Environmental Management* 92 (4), 1321–1327.

Zhang L., He G. and Mol, A.P.J., 2015. China's new Environmental Protection Law: a game changer? *Environmental Development* 13, 1–3.

Zhong H., Zhang W. and Zhang E., 2011. *Annual Report on Non-Financial Information Disclosure of Chinese Listed Companies (2011)*, Beijing: Social Sciences Academic Press.

16

ORCHESTRATED ENVIRONMENTAL MIGRATION IN WESTERN CHINA

Jarmila Ptackova

Introduction

Environmental migration is a term that describes the movement of population due to a radical change in climatic circumstances. As the result of a gradual or sudden change in the environment, living conditions become unsuitable and people are forced to leave their original homeland. This type of migration can either be a long-term experience or only a temporary measure. Within many countries a certain degree of assistance on the part of the state is offered to the affected people in order to help them overcome the loss of their land and, in cases of natural disaster, perhaps also their property (see also Gemenne et al. 2014). In China, the term environmental migration has been used to describe the movement of population affected, for example, by earthquakes, but has also been used within the context of gradual environmental changes affecting the homelands of people. In pastoral areas, environmental migration began as part of the process of transforming the grasslands affected in some areas by increasing desertification and erosion. In the 1990s some Chinese newspapers published articles about 'ecological migrants', who had to leave their homes near the headwaters of the Yellow River because the grasslands had become severely degraded (Du and Zhang 2014). The soil in Maduo County in Qinghai province, where the Yellow River originates, is relatively sandy and receptive to erosion, for example when the climate becomes drier. In the neighbouring area of Dari County, by way of contrast, it was the inappropriate management of land initiated as part of the land reform movement that had been implemented since the 1950s that had led to the overuse and, subsequently, to the significant degradation of the pastureland. Currently, especially in the pastoral context, environmental migration in China is no longer a term used to describe only the temporary and occasional migration necessitated by urgent environmental reasons. Instead, since the turn of the century, it has become a huge state-controlled programme of massive relocation inspired by environmental, socioeconomic, and internal political reasons. In contrast to the description of environmental migration as being caused as the result of the acute unsuitability of the natural conditions, a situation in which the state steps in to assist people after they have been forced to leave their place of origin, in China it is now the state which declares certain areas to be unsuitable for living, thus actively initiating the migration of the local population. It is this latter type of population movement, which results from the Chinese state-induced environmental migration strategy, that will be addressed in this chapter.

Jarmila Ptackova

Controlled migration as a means of development

In China, the year 2000 marks the start of a new development strategy targeting the regions in the west (*Xibu da kaifa*). The major general goals of this strategy are socioeconomic improvement, environmental protection and the strengthening of political control in peripheral areas. In pastoral areas of western China large-scale orchestrated migration, i.e. the relocation of the population, has been the result of these three objectives. The various contexts requiring or enabling the controlled migration of population have resulted in a variety of policy projects and labels by which the relocation process is being realized. Individual projects tend to differ in relation to their core aims, the means of implementation, implementation methods and implementation outcomes. Therefore, when speaking about the mass relocation of populations in China, we need to be aware of the variety of the implemented projects. In many cases, current environmental migration activities in China are linked to a project referred to as *shengtai yimin*, which in western literature is identified as 'ecological migration', 'ecological resettlement' or 'environmental resettlement' (Zha et al. 2013). The large-scale implementation of this project began in 2003.[1]

Environmental migration, when used as a general term, may also include other environmentally motivated projects which encourage the process of relocation in pastoral areas, such as *tuimu huancao* (converting pasturelands into grasslands) or *tuimu huanlin* (converting pasturelands into forests),[2] which in areas labelled as being severely degraded determine the need for the relocation of people (*banqian jinmu*). Environmental motivation factors may also be present in other types of project, such as those focusing on the sedentarization of pastoralists, largely for socioeconomic reasons, and projects aimed at establishing a reduced dependence on animal husbandry, such as *youmumin dingju* (nomadic settlement) (Foggin and Phillips 2013).

In the context of the three major aims of the development strategy, we can distinguish projects that are intended to serve national interests and those projects that have been established in order to respond to local challenges. Among the projects serving national level interests, for example, are the large infrastructure projects, such as the building of large water reservoirs, railways and airports, urban and industrial areas, natural resources exploitation sites, etc. These projects require the relocation of the population in order to make space for the new construction projects. The affected people have no other choice than to follow the orders of the state. Relocation executed in order to provide a solution to local needs has a slightly different concept and is often, at least in theory, a voluntary act. Internal political objectives aimed at better controlling the population by concentrating them in settlements naturally belong to the category of projects aimed at serving national level interests. Political control is, however, not mentioned as one of the reasons for relocation in the available documents. Officially therefore, (socio-)economic improvement and environmental protection are the major driving forces behind the mass relocation of people in pastoral areas of China. The nature protection elements of environmental migration projects in China are often designed to serve national environmental protection interests as they impact on the whole country. For example, in Qinghai province, natural protection interests are predominantly focused on the headwaters of large rivers, which are important resources not only for eastern China but also for neighbouring countries in South East Asia. In Inner Mongolia, the environmental policy is intended to counteract land erosion and desertification, which are the main causes of sandstorms that affect the population in cities further to the east, such as Beijing or Shanghai (Cao et al. 2015). At the same time, environmental migration should help to meet the local objective of improving the grasslands ecosystem, thus providing more fodder for the livestock of the pastoralists.

Often, the projects target more than one objective and serve both environmental as well as socioeconomic purposes. *Shengtai yimin*, as the major project linked to environmental migration, is one such multipurpose project. It aims to move people into urban areas in order to enable them to gain access to improved infrastructure and alternative income opportunities. At the same time, the intention is that it should release pressure on the land by resettling people and removing livestock, thus enabling a faster restoration of the overused ecosystem.

The socioeconomic context of environmental migration

Foggin and Phillips (2013) present an overview of the major projects associated with the main implementation sectors of the current development policy, namely: poverty alleviation, community health, basic education, environmental protection and broad development approaches. The *tuimu huancao*, *shengtai yimin* and *youmumin dingju* projects thus fall into the environmental protection sector, even though the agendas of *shengtai yimin* and *youmumin dingju* identify the socioeconomic motive of helping to alleviate the poor livelihood conditions and poor lifestyles on the grasslands of the pastoral population, as clearly outweighing other considerations (Ptackova 2010, 2011). In contrast, the National Development and Reform Commission (NDRC) report on *yidi fupin banqian* (relocation to alleviate poverty) programme presents projects which target poverty alleviation, including those which also address a clear environmental objective, such as the *jingjin fengsha shengtai yimin* (the ecological resettlement of sandstorm origin areas endangering Beijing and Tianjin) or *sanxi yimin* ('Sanxi' resettlement) (NDRC 2008), targeting the Gansu regions of Hexi and Dingxi and the Ningxia region of Xihaigu, which have suffered severe droughts.

It is often difficult to make a clear division between the social and ecological aspects of relocation projects as they are of course interrelated due to the dependency of the rural population on the land and primary resources. This concept of linkage between poverty and the environment was also globally accepted in 2012 (Foggin 2014).

In addition, the different levels of interest mentioned above need to be taken into account. Thus, for example, environmental migration projects aim to address the national objective of ecological restoration and at the same time are promoted as a potential solution to local socioeconomic problems. In environmental terms, the presence of human and domestic livestock and their associated activities within the fragile ecosystems of the pasturelands officially counts, although without any specific evidence (Yeh et al. 2015), as one of the most serious causes of environmental destruction, thus necessitating a reduction in their numbers. The existence of a weak and degraded ecosystem often implies poor living standards for the local population, evidenced in low levels of land productivity, and inhabitants in such regions are often eligible for support through the policy of poverty alleviation. This often results in the two major approaches, i.e. the protection of the environment from further deterioration and poverty relief, being combined within a single project. The interrelationship between ecology and the economy, indicating the relationship between an underdeveloped economy and a poor environment, is a substantial consideration when addressing the economic development of China's west (Wang 2007). It is also stated as an explanation for the complex and far-reaching impact of the development strategy.

Yan and Fei (2009) present statistical data showing that the majority, namely 73 per cent, of poverty-stricken counties are located in western China, in ecologically fragile zones. The internal structure of these zones is described as being unstable in terms of their functioning ecosystem, thus being sensitive to external disturbances, as well as having a reduced capacity to support human socioeconomic activities. The majority of such ecologically fragile zones are situated in western China and this correlates with the regions inhabited by ethnic minorities.

The attempt to stimulate economic growth in western Chinese regions in order to counterbalance the growing socioeconomic gap between the east and the west also represents a major national objective of the current development policy. Relocation projects, among them the *shengtai yimin*, were defined by the development strategy as being one of the crucial means of alleviating poverty in rural areas. The NDRC states that during the 11th Five-Year Plan (2006–2010) 1.627 million people were relocated in order to alleviate poverty in the countryside (NDRC 2012). During the 12th Five-Year Plan (2011–2015), another 3.94 million poverty-stricken people were relocated with a total investment of over 23 billion RMB. According to the State Council (SC) in the current 13th Five-Year Plan (2016–2020) poverty alleviation is still an important part of the policy agenda (State Council 2015).

Relocation has been used as a strategy for addressing the challenges associated with poverty-stricken regions in China since the 1980s. Residents from locations affected by serious land degradation were resettled in Ningxia Hui Autonomous Region, Gansu province and later also in Yunnan, Guizhou and Inner Mongolia (Du 2006). After the year 2000, the development strategy adopted the relocation concept and implemented it on an even larger scale (Du 2006) in the thirteen provinces in western China targeted by the new policy. In 2002, the term *shengtai yimin* was adopted as an official name for this kind of socioeconomically driven relocation initiative and was included in the policy of the central government.

Executing environmental migration

Institutional responsibilities for different environmental and poverty alleviation projects are divided between different government institutions. This influences decisions about project categorization, identifying them as either environmental or socioeconomic. The provincial Development and Reform Commission (DRC) focuses predominantly on poverty alleviation in degraded pastoral areas through the process of relocation. It administers the *shengtai yimin* project and, therefore, provides its socioeconomic background. The Forestry Department and Agriculture and Animal Husbandry Department target the natural protection of grasslands through reducing or banning pastoral activities. The *tuimu huancao* is one of the projects of the Agriculture and Animal Husbandry Department. Although in theory the policy agendas of relocation projects differ from each other, in practice they often intermingle. This can lead to ambiguity about the local project definition and also about the actual dimension of the projects focusing on environmental migration. A summary of all the relocation projects implemented in different parts of China results in the identification of huge numbers of participants. By 2010, according to official statistics, 7.7 million people had been relocated from poverty-stricken regions with scarce natural resources brought about by difficult environmental conditions (Li and Wang 2013). Because of the overlapping implementation process, along with the lack of sufficient information about project execution, it is difficult to distinguish between controlled environmental migration aimed at addressing natural conditions, and poverty relief migration projects targeting the well-being of the people. The respective departments in charge at different administration levels present their own data, often summarizing different kinds of relocation, migration or sedentarization. Moreover, the figures estimated in the theoretical executive plan and the official reports often differ significantly from the implementation success on-site. The data provided by Chinese statistics and national reports should, therefore, be handled with care and also the figures stated in this contribution should be used for orientation only.

Environmental conditions leading to the relocation process

Environmental changes that have caused the erosion of arid land and grasslands, leading to an increase in the frequency of sand and dust storms, as well as the siltation of rivers and the general reduction in the amount of economically usable land, has led to a strengthening of environmental protection initiatives and the implementation of environmentally related projects, especially since the year 2000. The regions in the north-west and west of the country are the most badly affected by land deterioration. Reports from the period between 2003 and 2014 state that the level of land degradation in China is approximately 3 to 3.5 million square kilometres (Berry 2003; Yan and Fei 2009; Patton 2014). The grasslands in China are spread over an area of almost 4 million square kilometres, accounting for about 42 per cent of China's territory (Yeh et al. 2015). In 1998 about 34 per cent of the grasslands were declared by the Ministry of Agriculture to be degraded (Berry 2003) and by 2006 more than half of it had been severely damaged, with about 90 per cent of the grasslands traditionally suitable for animal husbandry having been affected by desertification (Yan and Fei 2009).

There are several explanations for the rapid degradation of the grasslands ecosystem during the past two decades. Official Chinese sources usually identify overgrazing and an enormous increase in the rodent population as the major reasons for the deterioration of the fragile ecosystem (Zhao 2007). However, there are additional factors, which have had an impact on the local environment, such as climate change and large policy interventions on the part of the state into the established process of grasslands management. Most probably, it is the co-occurrence of all these factors that have caused extreme levels of deterioration in relation to the grasslands. According to Du and Zhang (2014), the environmental degradation process had already begun by the 1970s. Due to rising temperatures, increases in precipitation and reduced evaporation, the permafrost layer became thinner and the periods of cold weather shorter. Over the years, climate change, in combination with increased human activities on the high plateau such as extensive farming and herding and gold mining, has led to massive disruptions in the environment. An additional important factor related to the changes has been land management policy. In fact, increases in livestock numbers and animal husbandry production had been promoted previously by the various land reform policies, which had also been implemented in the grasslands areas of western China from the 1950s (see, for example, Goldstein 1996). Other kinds of land reform, such as the allocation of individual pastures through the household responsibility system, which led to the fencing off of individual grassland plots, significantly limited the flexibility of pastoralism, thus promoting overgrazing in areas with large herds.

The new development policy for western China, responding to the degradation of the grasslands ecosystem and introducing restrictions on animal husbandry, has resulted in massive environmental migration. New nature preservation zones and parks were established to demonstrate the national commitment to environmental protection. There are now over 2,500 national nature reserves in China, covering more than 15 per cent of state territory (see Foggin 2014 or Yeh et al. 2015). Particularly within their boundaries, extensive environmental protection measures, including initiated environmental migration, have been implemented.

Shengtai yimin in the Three Rivers' Headwaters Nature Reserve

The upper reaches of the Yangtze and Yellow rivers, as well as regions affected by soil degradation and desertification in China's north and northwest, are the 'hot spots' of environmental migration (Stojanov and Novosak 2006). The largest Chinese environmental protection area, the Three Rivers' Headwaters Nature Reserve (Sanjiangyuan ziran baohu qu), which covers all of the southern half of Qinghai province, is one of the major implementation areas of the *shengtai yimin* project (Wanma 2013). Established in 2000 by the State Forestry Administration and the Government of Qinghai province, the nature reserve gained national status in 2003 (Foggin 2005; Gong 2006). The reserve aims to protect the 318,100 square kilometres catchment area of the headwaters of three of the major Chinese rivers originating in Qinghai province, the Yangtze River, the Yellow River and the Lancang (Mekong) River.

For administrative reasons, Qinghai province has included entire counties in the protection area, even though their territories overlap only partly with the catchment area of the three rivers. As a result, the total protection area was enlarged to 394,500 square kilometres and now includes the Tibetan autonomous prefectures of Yushu, Guoluo, Hainan and Huangnan, as well as the Tangula township of Haixi Mongol and the Tibetan autonomous prefectures (see Figure 16.1). By 2013, the total population of this area amounted to 669,100, of whom 525,300 were engaged in agriculture and animal husbandry (Wanma 2013).

Because of its status as a national nature protection zone, the area of the Three Rivers' Headwaters became eligible for additional funds for environmental protection, which also enable the implementation of large-scale environmental migration projects.

In the Three Rivers' Headwaters Nature Reserve, the implementation of *shengtai yimin* started in 2003. Between 2004 and 2010 a total of 7.5 billion RMB was allocated to the relocation of the population and ecological restoration projects. These included environmentally oriented projects focusing on reducing the levels of animal husbandry and farmlands, as well as the restoration of grasslands and forests, the restoration of deteriorated lands, the poisoning of rodents etc. Among additional projects initiated in response to changes in the environment, but strongly following socioeconomic objectives, were projects aimed at the construction of small settlements and drinking water supply networks (Chen 2007). Between 2004 and 2010, 4.9 billion RMB was invested in environmental protection-oriented projects, while 2.2 billion RMB was allocated for socioeconomic projects, with a further 400 million RMB being invested in geo-engineering projects such as artificial rain creation and the provision of scientific support and environmental monitoring. After 2008 the Chinese government provided an additional 2.5 billion RMB to support all the above-mentioned projects (Du and Zhang 2014; see also NDRC 2013).

In relation to environmental migration, the Three Rivers' Headwaters Nature Reserve has witnessed the partial implementation of *shengtai yimin*, in combination with the *tuimu huancao* project. In addition to the targeted relocation of over 50,000 people, there has been a reduction in livestock numbers by 3,184,000 sheep units.[3] Following relocation, grazing on the original grasslands is either totally banned or is only permissible in cases of seasonal or rotatory grazing for a temporary period of ten years (Du and Zhang 2014). The *shengtai yimin* project is subject to state planning, thus promoting the nationwide objective of environmental protection, as well as the local objective of improving the lives of individual households. Although individual participation in the project is promoted as being voluntary, the relocation quotas serving the achievement of national objectives of development have to be fulfilled. Therefore, the targeted people are strongly encouraged to participate, which serves to create the impression of a certain degree of involuntary relocation (Yeh 2009) or even 'non-voluntary migration' (Du and Zhang 2014). In the Three Rivers' Headwaters Nature Reserve, the implementation of *shengtai yimin* environmental migration resulted in the construction of 86 new settlements (Meng 2012) with a total number of 10,733 Tibetan households comprising 55,773 people being relocated from the core zones of the nature protection area (Wanma 2013; Zha 2014. See Du and Zhang 2014 for similar figures).

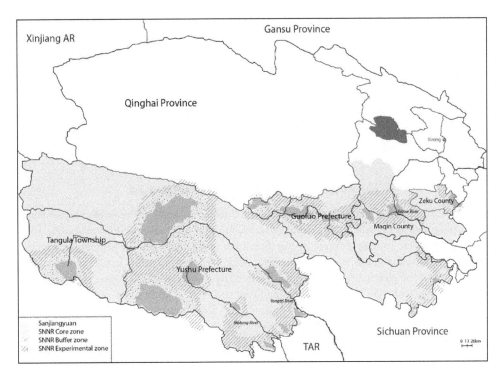

Figure 16.1 Map of Three Rivers' Headwaters National Nature Reserve conservation zones

Cartography: J. Ptackova

The main motivation behind participation in relocation projects is the provision of affiliated subsidies. According to the project agenda of the *shengtai yimin* (see also Chen 2007), the state provides each household with a house of 45 square metres,[4] investing 800 RMB per square metre, an animal shed with a size of 120 square metres, funded at 200 RMB per square metre, and an additional subsidy of 400 RMB per person. Further subsidies are provided depending on the size of the abandoned grasslands. These funds come from the budget of the *tuimu huancao* project, which should provide an annual subsidy to herders for a period of ten years. Households moving to centralized settlements situated in a county or prefecture different from their original location are entitled to receive 8,000 RMB per year for an abandoned pastureland in an area where there is a total grazing ban (Du 2014). Households with shared land-use-right certificates are entitled to an annual subsidy of 6,000 RMB and those without land-use certificates receive 3,000 RMB per year. Starting from 2006, the resettled households were able to obtain a further 1,000–2,000 RMB in annual fuel subsidy and from 2009 onwards an additional allowance for elderly people over 55 and children under 16 years of age (Du and Zhang 2014).

After moving from the grasslands to the new settlements, relocated herders need to become more dependent on alternative sources of income. According to the *shengtai yimin* agenda, resettled households are encouraged to experiment with new animal breeds, i.e. those which require less space and produce more milk. In addition, vegetables planted in greenhouses are seen as a means of providing food for people and a source of income through the sale of the surplus yields.

A slightly different picture emerges when we compare the theoretical information with the actual situation on-site. State initiated relocation is primarily financed by government sources. In general, costs are shared between the central government and the local authorities. However, affected people are often required to pay a small contribution, as stipulated by the executive organs. Since 2003, households participating in *shengtai yimin* are also eligible for financial subsidies provided by the government. These subsidies are intended to support the households during the settling-in period in the new location. Prior to this, compensation was not part of the relocation programme budget and only some projects, i.e. those targeting the poorest households, were able to provide a degree of financial help (Yan and Fei 2009).

The outcomes of environmental migration

During the first years of their implementation it was difficult to assess the impact of environmental migration projects, i.e. whether the results in relation to the affected people and the concerned environment were actually positive or negative. One of the main reasons behind the ongoing uncertainty were the delays in implementation. Many settlements were actually built later than scheduled and the planned service facilities intended to complement the houses and settlement sites were often installed and built with significant delays or were omitted completely during the project-realization phase. There were also large discrepancies in actual implementation depending on the location. From another perspective, many households, which had been selected for resettlement took the final step later than planned. This was not only as a result of the construction delays, but also due to the lack of project information presented to the people, which often caused uncertainty in relation to the available livelihood options in the new village.

The social, cultural and even long-term political impact of the state-encouraged relocation process on the targeted population is something that will only be apparent after one or even two generations. However, now, more than ten years after the launch of projects such as *shengtai yimin*, we can summarize the impact so far and the trends indicated by available data and recorded experiences.

In theory, the goal of the *shengtai yimin* project was to improve the economic situation of the population by encouraging the shift from an environmentally impacted and low-producing grasslands context to a situation based on cash-oriented opportunities. The improvement of the economic situation was expected to result in higher living standards. New permanent homes, sited closer to urban settings, were intended as a means of further upgrading the living conditions of affected households. This concept of economic improvement was built on the presumption that the relocated households would be able to become engaged in alternative employment activities, connected predominantly with the secondary or tertiary industrial sector. In reality, however, for the majority of relocated people, it turned out to be extremely difficult to find alternative sources of income and become settled in the new environment. There is a simple explanation for this. Among the main challenges for the former pastoralists has been the lack of education and insufficient experience in occupations other than animal husbandry. Moreover, the new settlements in rural areas or attached to small townships lack the industrial infrastructure to offer any kind of stable employment opportunities for the resettled population. The private business-activity alternative has often been difficult to realize because of the lack of funds, the lack of competence in the Chinese language, limited management skills, as well as, in most cases, the lack of social connections, which are essential in enabling settlers to establish and maintain private enterprises. For small businesses, such as shops selling small utility items and refreshments, or small restaurants, there is heavy competition and a limited number of potential customers in the settlements and small towns. In reality, the main employment option is temporary engagement as a construction worker or seasonal employee gathering caterpillar fungus (*Ophiocordyceps sinensis*) (for more details see, for example, Gruschke 2012). This type of work provides some degree of income, but does not provide the kind of sustainable livelihood associated with animal husbandry.

The lack of information about project conditions and duration has led to a rather passive attitude on the part of many involved households since they moved into the settlements. According to the data collected[5] among my informants, mainly from the area of the Three Rivers' Headwaters protection zone, many people believed that the relocation was only temporary; they did not realize that giving up livestock and pastures was a pre-condition of involvement in the project. Moreover, they had no information about the amount and duration of state subsidies. Some people thought that the policy might soon change again and reverse the previous directives. A further difficulty in achieving improved living conditions after relocation has been the increased daily expenses incurred as part of urban life in the new villages. For the majority of the relocated people it has become difficult to achieve even the previous standard of living they enjoyed on the grasslands. These and other shortcomings have been observed by numerous researchers in relation to relocation projects that have been implemented in different areas of China (see Stojanov and Novosak 2006; Foggin 2008, 2011; Meng 2012; Zhang 2012; Fang 2013; Du 2014; or Zha 2014), and is also confirmed by my own field research (Ptackova, under review).

In their study, Foggin and Phillips (2013) summarize the so far predominantly negative outcomes of the *shengtai yimin* project. In none of the fields defined by them as the four pillars of sustainability, i.e. economy, environment, society and culture, has the realization of *shengtai yimin* resulted in positive outcomes. Concerning the impact on the local economy they describe *shengtai yimin* as a form of urbanization, with the potential for inducing long-term unemployment. The social aspect, including health, education, hope and equity is described as having the potential for creating long-lasting negative consequences, including a loss of hope, poor health, inadequate vocational training and employment, increasing disparities etc. In relation to culture, it represents a loss of cultural patterns, community structure and support systems etc. If we consider only the environmental issues, Foggin and Phillips (2013) see more room for debate, describing *shengtai yimin* not as harmful, but rather as unnecessary for the long-term sustainable utilisation and conservation of grasslands ecosystems. Other studies disagree with this point (see Du 2014; Urgenson et al. 2014). They regard the aspects of *shengtai yimin* that require pastoralists to remove their livestock from the pastures and leave the grasslands as having a potentially negative impact on the grasslands ecosystem, given the interdependence that exists between the livestock herds grazing and fertilizing the land.

The mentioned challenges for project implementation, as well as the increasing critique from both scientists and, also on the part of local government representatives, have probably contributed to the decision to end the implementation of the *shengtai yimin*. According to a member of the Qinghai Nationalities Cultural Committee, the project ended in Qinghai in 2010 (personal interview, May 2015). The subsidies, however, are still being paid to the original project participants. Thus, it is difficult to confirm the statement about the abolition of the *shengtai yimin*. In 2015, for example, officials from the lower administrative levels in Qinghai province were still unsure about the duration of the *shengtai yimin* and whether or not its implementation was still continuing. Moreover, even though in Qinghai the *shengtai yimin* project might have been terminated, it is clear that the state-controlled type of environmental migration initiatives, relocating and placing large number of people in settlements, continues.

Yidi fupin banqian (alleviating poverty through relocation)

In the programme of the 11th Five-Year Plan (2006–2010) the *yidi fupin banqian* project (alleviating poverty through relocation) was labelled as an important part of the poverty-alleviation process since its aim was to raise people out of poverty and improve their living standards. The objective of this programme is the relocation of people living in regions with a marginally sustainable environment. In addition to poverty alleviation, improvements in environmental conditions are an explicit goal of this project. Formally, *yidi fupin banqian* was approved by the State Council as an experimental project in 2001, targeting 1.22 million people during the first five years (NDRC 2008). The project was especially targeted at the poverty-stricken rural areas of China's west, the nationally classified poor counties. According to the official figures, since the 1980s the poverty rate has been declining[6] and the government declared its ambitious goal as being to provide improved living conditions for all the remaining poor people by the year 2020. There are, however, different indicators that can be used to classify poverty (see also endnote 6) and the data provided by different government reports is often conflicting. For example, in 2005 the NDRC calculated that there were over 10 million poor people inhabiting ecologically fragile areas in mountain regions, deserts, high loess plateaus or similar inhospitable regions. The 12th Five-Year Plan for *yidi fupin banqian* is based on exactly the same poverty-stricken population figure although it was claimed that the number of poor people had decreased during the previous five years (NDRC 2012). The fluctuation in the poverty figures could also have been influenced by the dramatic increase in basic living expenses, especially in rural areas, after the introduction of development measures and following adjustments to the poverty baseline. In the 12th Five-Year Plan relocation projects were again defined as the key measure aimed at helping to improve the living conditions of poor people in such harsh areas. During the 11th Five-Year Plan 1.5 million people were therefore scheduled to move as part of the *yidi fupin banqian* project (NDRC 2008). The 12th Five-Year Plan even states that this goal was exceeded, with a total of 1.6 million people being relocated during the previous five years. Between 2011 and 2015 the relocation schedule targeted an even larger number of people, amounting to around 2.4 million (NDRC 2012). Again, according to a report from 2015, the actual number of relocations was higher and amounted to over 3.9 million affected people (Central Government 2015). Implemented in the name of poverty alleviation, this project had a budget, which included a subsidy of up to 6,000 RMB per relocated person (NDRC 2012). When we add on the costs for constructing the settlement homes and attached infrastructure facilities, such as roads, water and energy networks and buildings for public services, etc. (see, for example, NDRC 2013) the investment amounts to an enormous sum. Between 2006 and 2010 the Central Government spent 7.6 billion RMB (NDRC 2012) and during the following five years more than 100 billion RMB was invested into the *yidi fupin banqian* project alone (Central Government 2015).

The general description of the *yidi fupin banqian* project, the relocation plans and the description of benefits is in a striking conformity with the *shengtai yimin* project. If we look closer at the 11th Five-Year Plan for the *yidi fupin banqian* project, it states that this project is also called *shengtai yimin* (NDRC 2008). This might suggest that even if in Qinghai province the *shengtai yimin* has officially ended, the same project still continues under the different label of *yidi fupin banqian*, which would support the statement by a member of the Qinghai Nationalities Cultural Committee that in Qinghai the *shengtai yimin* was replaced by the *yidi fupin banqian* project, launched by the NDRC (personal interview, May 2015). This assumption seems to be further supported through the figures stated in the reports on the economic and social development of Qinghai, which reveal a radical increase in the number of households targeted through the *yidi fupin banqian* project both before and after 2010. In 2009, only about 7,600 people (almost 1,600 households) were relocated from the eastern areas of Qinghai (NDRC 2010). In 2012, 40 out of a total of 46 counties in the province were declared to be poor and the number of relocated people increased to 60,000 (14,000 households). An additional 135,000 households were targeted through further sedentarization projects in Qinghai, including the *youmumin dingju*, during the same year (NDRC 2013).

Although we find many indicators, it is difficult to find written confirmation of the transformation of *shengtai yimin* into *yidi fupin banqian*. The changing of project labels is not an uncommon practice among the policy executing bureaus, especially in cases where the results do not correspond with the designated aims.

Conclusion

The meaning of the term environmental migration has seen a number of changes within the context of the current Chinese policy aimed at developing the west of the country. Initially, it described the gradual shift from a place stricken by hostile natural conditions, which rendered it unsuitable for sustaining life. Currently, it has adopted more of a general meaning, describing a state-orchestrated mass-relocation initiative involving the rural population and aimed at the socioeconomic restructuring of grasslands communities. The environmental aspect continues to be partly included, almost as a sort of precautionary measure. People no longer move solely because survival is impossible in a particular place; however, their movement should provide an opportunity for the ecosystem to restore itself. The environmental migration initiative does not just target the population in areas of increased grasslands degradation. Instead, the state projects are designed to cover pastoral society as a whole. Sedentarization is seen as a process that will speed up developments in the way of life of the pastoralists, providing improvements in their living standards and easing their access to modern infrastructure and education facilities. There is no single type of project that targets the sedentarization of the pastoral population. Instead, there are various kinds of housing projects, promoting either the agenda of environmental protection or poverty alleviation, all of which are being implemented simultaneously and with a degree of overlap.

As well as the ecological and socioeconomic objectives, there might also be an additional motivation behind large-scale sedentarization initiatives. For example, the centralization of new settlers, who in many cases belong to China's ethnic minorities, within settlements situated near urban centres, makes it easier to reach them and enables the state to enhance its capacity to control the population. The change to urban lifestyles and new livelihoods might also be seen as a means of promoting their integration within the majority Chinese population, or even resulting in the eventual elimination of ethnic minority groups (Yeh 2009). This could lead to a decrease in political unrest based on cultural differences. The centres of such unrest are predominantly in western China, in areas inhabited by ethnic minorities. The majority of these areas have simultaneously been labelled as economically and socially problematic, as well as environmentally fragile, and are the major targets of the migration policy aimed at sedentarization.

As far as outcomes are concerned, the sedentarization projects appear to suffer from a number of severe limitations and contradictions. The *shengtai yimin* project, with its concept of serving both environmental protection and poverty alleviation challenges, stands as a good example. In realizing its aim of solving the issue of poverty, this project should be targeting households which cannot make a living, due to the poor conditions of the environment on which they depend. However, simply moving poor pastoralists away from their traditional grasslands does not always lead to the expected rehabilitation of the environment. Such households often possess only a small number of livestock, or even none, and therefore their relocation does not have a decisive impact on grazing. Richer households, which are still able to make a living out of animal husbandry, do not have sufficient motivation to exchange their established livelihoods for a house in a settlement and a low-level subsidy for a limited period of time. In many cases, encouraging rich households with large herds to leave the grasslands and move into settlements actually results in their impoverishment (see Stojanov and Novosak 2006 or Yeh 2009). The officials responsible for implementing these initiatives seem to be fully aware of these challenges. They prefer to tolerate the situation where rich households remain on the grasslands as their move would negatively impact the regional GDP (Meng 2012). Moreover, relocating self-sufficient or wealthy households would fail to realize the general aim of the *shengtai yimin*, i.e. to help reduce levels of poverty.

From an environmental point of view, the banning of long-established lifestyles that are closely tied to the local environment, such as animal husbandry, is more likely to have a negative impact on a fragile and specific high-plateau ecosystem, because of its interdependence with regular human or livestock activity.

The final and long-term impact of state-encouraged environmentally or socioeconomically motivated migration will only be obvious after one or two generations. Only then will it be possible to assess the impact of the pastoral depopulation strategy. However, even now, after almost fifteen years of its implementation, there should at least be some obvious signs that the strategy of orchestrated migration is meeting its environmental or socioeconomic objectives. This is an extremely sensitive and costly undertaking, and if there are still no clear signs that the promoted positive outcomes are being achieved, it would suggest a need for a fundamental review of the whole approach and its implementation strategy.

Notes

1 For details on the *shengtai yimin* project see, for example, Du 2014; Su 2009; Foggin 2008, 2011; or Ptackova 2010.
2 For details on the *tuimu huancao* project see, for example, Yeh 2005 or Ptackova 2010. See also Stein and Hartmann chapter 11 this volume.
3 Emily Yeh (2013) states a total figure of 100,000 pastoralists being earmarked for relocation in the Three Rivers' Headwaters area.
4 In many areas the house size is set at 60 square metres (see Ptackova 2015).
5 Data presented in this contribution are based on research conducted predominantly within the area of the Three Rivers' Headwaters. Data were collected during several field trips between 2007 and 2015, mainly through semi-structured qualitative interviews with over 100 pastoralist households, as well as with local officials in charge of the implementation of development projects.
6 The figures stating the number of poor people differ in various documents. According to the official figures, there were still an estimated 23,650,000 poor people in China after the completion of the 10th Five-Year Plan. (According to the 12th Five-Year Plan, in 2005, there were 64,320,000 poor people and in 2010, 26,880,000 people.) In the available governmental reports, such as those used in this contribution, it is common to not explain which classification measures have been used to label certain areas as poor.

References

Berry, L., 2003. *Land degradation in China: Its extent and impact*. World Bank.
Cao S., Li S., Ma H. and Sun Y., 2015. Escaping the Resource Curse in China. *Ambio* 44(1), 1–6.
Central Government of the People's Republic of China, 2015. *'Shisan wu' Wo guo yidi fupin banqian pinkun qunzhong 394 wan ren* ('13th Five-Years-Plan' China resettles 3.94 million impoverished people). http://www.gov.cn/xinwen/2015-10/16/content_2948383.htm. Accessed 13 December 2016.

Chen G., 2007. *Sanjiangyuan ziran baohu qu shengtai baohu yu jianshe* (Ecological preservation and constructions in the Sanjiangyuan nature preservation area). Qinghai renmin chubanshe. Xining.

Du F., 2006. Grain for Green and Poverty Alleviation. The Policy and Practice of Ecological Migration in China. *Horizons* 9(2), 45–77.

Du F., 2014. *Sanjianyuan shengtai yimin yanjiu* (Ecologic Resettlement in the Sanjinagyuan of Qinghai). Zhongguo shehui kexue chubanshe. Beijing.

Du F. and Zhang S., 2014. *Xibu caoyuan xumuye jingji zhuanxing yanjiu* (Economic transition of Pastoralism in Western China). Zhishi chanquan chubanshe. Beijing.

Fang Y., 2013. Managing the Three-Rivers' Headwater Region, China: From Ecological Engineering to Social Engineering. *Ambio* 42, 566–576.

Foggin, J. M., 2005. Promoting Biodiversity Conservation and Community Development in the Sanjiangyuan Region. *Plateau Perspectives*. www.plateauperspectives.org. Accessed 13 December 2016.

Foggin, J. M., 2008. Depopulating the Tibetan Grasslands: National Policies and Perspectives for the Future of Tibetan Herders in Qinghai Province, China. *Mountain Research and Development* 28(1), 26–31.

Foggin, J. M., 2011. Rethinking 'Ecological Migration' and the Value of Cultural Continuity: A Response to Wang, Song, and Hu. *Ambio* 40, 100–101.

Foggin, J. M., 2014. Managing Shared Natural Heritages: Towards More Participatory Models of Protected Area Management in Western China. *Journal of International Wildlife Law and Policy* 17, 130–151.

Foggin, J. M. and Phillips, J., 2013. Horizontal Policy Analysis: A Tool to Promote Sustainable Livelihoods Development; with Implications for Ecological Resettlement and Other Major Development Programs in the Tibetan Plateau Region. In: Kolås, A. and Zhaluo, eds. 2013. *Pastoralism in Contemporary China: Policy and Practice*. Social Science Academic Press. Beijing, 3–30.

Gemenne, F., Brücker, P. and Ionesco, D., 2014. *The State of Environmental Migration 2014*. International Organisation for Migration.

Goldstein, M., 1996. *Nomads of Golok: A Report*. www.case.edu/affil/tibet/booksAndPapers. Restricted access with registration.

Gong B., 2006. *Jiangheyuan huanbao shiji xing* (Environmental protection of the sources of the Yangtze and Yellow Rivers in the new century), vol. II (2001–2005). Qinghai sheng jianghe yuan huanbao xing lingdao xiaozu. Xining.

Gruschke, A., 2012. *Nomadische Ressourcennutzung und Existenzsicherung im Umbruch. Die osttibetische Region Yushu (Qinghai, VR China)*. Reichert. Wiesbaden.

Li P. and Wang X., 2013. *Ecological Migration, Development and Transformation. A Study of Migration and Poverty Reduction in Ningxia*. Springer. Heidelberg.

Meng X., 2012. Migrants Selectivity and the Effects on Environmental-Induced Migration Project in Sanjiangyuan Area in China. *Sociology Study* 2(3), 159–172.

NDRC, 2008. *Yidi fupin banqian shiyiwu guihua*. http://www.sdpc.gov.cn/fzgggz/fzgh/ghwb/115zxgh/200804/P02008040 7603189621311.pdf (no longer available).

NDRC, 2010. *Qinghai sheng 2009 nian guomin jingji he shehui fazhan jihua zhixing qingkuang yu 2010 nian jihua caoan de baogao*. http://www.qhfgw.gow.cn/ghjh/ndjh/201002/t20100202_429452.shtml. Accessed 24 February 2015.

NDRC, 2012. *Yidi fupin banqian shierwu guihua* (The 12th Five-Year Plan for Alleviating poverty through relocation). http://www.ahpc.gov.cn/upload/xxnr/1002320133 229380.pdf. Accessed 12 April 2015.

NDRC, 2013. Qinghai sheng 2012 nian guomin jingji he shehui fazhan jihua zhixing qingkuang yu 2013 nian jihua caoan de baogao. http://www.qhfgw.gow.cn/ghjh/ndjh/ 201302/t20130206_431755.shtml. Accessed 24 February 2015 (no longer available).

Patton, D., 2014. More than 40 percent of China's arable land degraded: Xinhua. *Reuters*. http://www.reuters.com/article/us-china-soil-idUSKBN0IO0Y720141104. Accessed 13 December 2016.

Ptackova, J., 2010. The Sedentarization Process in Tibetan Nomadic Areas of Qinghai, China. In: *Mongolo-Tibetica Pragensia*. Charles University Press. Prague, 156–180.

Ptackova, J., 2011. Sedentarisation of Tibetan Nomads in China: Implementation of the *Nomadic Settlement Project* in the Tibetan Amdo Area; Qinghai and Sichuan Provinces. In: *Pastoralism – Research, Policy and Practice*. Springer Open, 1:4. http://www.pastoralismjournal.com/content/1/1/4 (accessed 13 December 2016).

Ptackova, J., 2015. Hor – A Sedentarisation Success for Tibetan Pastoralists in Qinghai? *Nomadic Peoples* 19(2), 69–88.

Ptackova, J., under review. Developing land and peoples. University of Washington Press, Seattle.

State Council (SC), 2015. 'Shierwu' woguo yidi fupin banqian pinkun qunzhong 394 wan ren. http://www.gov.cn/xinwen/2015-0/16/content_2948383.htm. Accessed 30 March 2016 (no longer available).

Stojanov, R. and Novosak, J., 2006. Environmental Migration in China. *Geographica* 39, 65–82.

Su F., 2009. *Anduo Zangzu Muqu Shehui Wenhua Bianqian Yanjiu.* China Minzu University Press. Beijing.

Urgenson, L., Schmidt, A., Combs, J., Harrell, S., Hinckley, T., Yang Q., Ma Z., Li Y., Lü H., MacIver, A., 2014. Traditional Livelihoods, Conservation and Meadow Ecology in Jiuzhaigou National Park, Sichuan, China. *Human Ecology* 42, 481–491.

Wang S., 2007. *Xibu da kaifa de lüsi jingji daolu*: Jingji guanli chubanshe. Beijing.

Wanma, L., 2013. Shengtai yimin yu xinshiqi muqu minzu gongzuo diaoyan baogao. *Qinghai gaoyuan yanjiu* 2.

Yan T., and Fei G., 2009. Environmentally Induced Migration in West China *Morocco: XXVI International Population Conference.*

Yeh, E., 2005. Green Governmentality and Pastoralism in Western China: 'Converting Pastures to Grasslands'. *Nomadic Peoples* 9(1), 9–29.

Yeh, E., 2009. Greening Western China: A Critical View. *Geoforum* 40, 884–894.

Yeh, E., 2013. *Taming Tibet*, Cornell University Press. London.

Yeh, E., O'Brian, J., Ye J., 2015. *Rural Politics in Contemporary China.* Routledge. New York.

Zha L., Kolås Å., and Hao S., 2013. *Dangshi zhongguo youmuye.* Social Sciences Academic Press. Beijing.

Zha L., 2014. Sanjiangyuan diqu shengtai yimin de jingji shehui fengxian fenxi. *Tibetan Plateau Forum* 3, 1–10.

Zhang Q., 2012. The Dilemma of Conserving Rangeland by Means of Development: Exploring Ecological Resettlement in a Pastoral Township of Inner Mongolia. *Nomadic Peoples* 16(1), 88–115.

Zhao X., 2007. Gaohan muqu shengtai yimin, mumin dingju de diaocha yu sikao - yi Gannan muqu weili. *Chinese Journal of Grassland* 29(2), 94–101.

17

PUBLIC PARTICIPATION IN ENVIRONMENTAL IMPACT ASSESSMENT IN CHINA

From regulation to practice[1]

Mariachiara Alberton

Legislative background

It was in October 2002 with the adoption of the *Environmental Impact Assessment Law of the People's Republic of China*[2] that the public participation in environmental impact assessment (EIA) was specifically introduced (for an overview see, for example, Moorman et al. 2007; Ning et al. 1988; Tang et al. 2005; Li 1999; Wang et al. 2003; Wu et al. 2011). Before this law was issued, only construction projects required the EIA and involved, in theoretical terms, public participation. The EIA Law includes now the EIA and the strategic environmental assessment (SEA) for governmental plans for land use and regional development, as well as plans for industry, agriculture, energy, transportation, urban development, tourism and natural resource development. However, not all projects and plans involve public participation. According to articles 7, 11, 16 and 21 in case of construction projects with an expected great impact on the local environment or in case of special plans concerning projects in industry, agriculture, pasturage, forestry, energy, water conservancy, communication, urban construction, tourism and exploration of natural resources (hereafter '*special plans*') likely to produce an adverse environmental impact and directly relating to the environmental rights and interests of the public, public participation is prescribed. Of these regulations only projects are exempted that are defined as state secret or backbone of national economy such as energy projects. If a construction project is perceived to have a mild environmental impact it shall require the preparation of an environmental impact report (EIR), or the completion and submission of an EIA registration form only if the environmental impact is very small (projects of smaller size). Public participation is not required.

The Ministry of Environmental Protection (MEP) is charged with the overall responsibility for coordination and supervision of EIA at the national level; EPBs conduct EIAs at the provincial, county, and municipal levels. Four project types require MEP approval: (1) projects involving state secrets or nuclear facilities; (2) cross-boundary projects involving two or more provinces; (3) projects that are likely to produce cross-boundary pollution, the impacts of which cannot be agreed to by the different provinces; and (4) projects valued at or over a certain sum.

EIA procedures typically involve a phase of investigation design or scoping, a phase of evaluation of existing environmental quality, a phase of prediction of potential environmental impacts, and a phase of assessment and analysis of the environmental impacts. The results of the EIA investigation are compiled in an EIR, which is used as the basis for decision-making by environmental protection departments.

While previous laws prescribed only some general principles, the EIA Law provides some provisions on public participation in EIA. To this end, article 5 states that the public, besides work units and experts, are encouraged to participate in EIA in appropriate ways. In addition, article 11 prescribes that in case of '*special plan*' projects that are expected to cause adverse environmental impacts and involve environmental rights and interest of the public, the drafting organ shall hold meetings or hearings or solicit opinions on the EIA report in other forms from the public and take into consideration those opinions by including explanations in the report. Thus, initially the form of public participation was broadly delineated, the only requirement being that some opportunity is to be made available prior to the completion of a draft EIR. There is no indication of how or when environmental rights and interests of the public are implicated.

According to article 11 the participation requirement for EIR is only limited in conditions where secrecy is required by State stipulations. The EIA Law places an additional requirement on the entity drafting such reports to consider all opinions of the relevant departments, experts and the public on the draft report, and to include their reasons for accepting or rejecting the opinions in the report submitted for approval.

As the mentioned provisions on public participation were quite broad and vague, the former State Environmental Protection Administration (SEPA), now MEP, issued in 2006 the '*Provisional Measures of Public Participation in Environmental Impact Assessment*'[3] with the aim of detailing the public participation system in EIA (Yang 2008) . They define the principles of this system, the rights and obligations of its main participating bodies, the specific range of its solicited opinions, the information disclosure requirements at each stage, and the specific modes and timing etc. of public opinion surveys (Mol et al. 2011). These Measures constitute an effort to fill in the gap between the law and practice concerning public participation in Chinese EIA.

They are formulated to promote and standardize public participation in environmental impact assessment according to public environmental information and provisions on strengthening the social supervision of laws and legal documents, such as the *Environmental Impact Assessment Law of the People's Republic of China*, the *Administrative License Law of the People's Republic of China*, and the *Implementation Guidelines on Comprehensively Promote Administration according to Law* and *Decision of the State Council on Implementing the Scientific Outlook on Development to Strengthen Environmental Protection*.

According to the 2006 Measures, public participation consists of the following four phases:

1 *First public announcement* (art. 8): Seven days after appointment of the organization to undertake the EIA activities (usually an EIA agency) the project owner shall issue a public announcement to inform the public regarding the project covering the following information: name and summary of the construction project; name and contact information of the construction unit; name and contact information of EIA agency; procedures and main missions of EIA agency; modes to solicit the public opinions; main approaches for the public comments.

2 *Second public announcement* (art. 9–10–11). Before submitting the EIR to the MEP or EPB, the project owner or the appointed EIA agency shall issue a public announcement to report the EIA findings and conclusions including:

- brief information on the construction project;
- summary on the potential impacts of construction projects on the environment;
- main points of actions and measures to prevent or mitigate the adverse environmental impact;
- main points of the EIA conclusions from the EIR;
- duration of the EIR available to the public;
- range and main matters of soliciting the public opinions;
- specific means to solicit the public opinion;
- timeframe for soliciting the public opinions.

The announcement period should not be less than 10 days. The information may be released through announcement in the local public media, or printed freely and distributed through other convenient means. The brief EIR may be posted at designated places, included in a special webpage, provided as link on the public websites or special websites, or other media easily available to the public.

3   *Collection of public comments* (art. 12–13–14). After the information announcement is released and the brief EIR is posted publicly, the construction unit or its EIA agency openly solicits the public comments through, for instance, public or expert consultation, a symposium, a workshop or a public hearing. The public consultation can be conducted by means such as a survey. In case the forms of a symposium or a workshop are chosen, the construction unit or the EIA agency shall inform the public at least 7 days prior to the event. For a public hearing the public must be informed at least 10 days prior to the event.

All citizens, legal entities or representatives from organizations that will be affected by the project should be included in the public consultation.

4   *Review of public opinions* (art. 16-17-18). The construction unit or the EIA agency and the responsible authority file the collected raw data for future reference. They should consider the public opinions and include in the EIR the explanations on whether the public opinions have been adopted or not. The responsible authority can organize an expert advisory panel to review such explanations on the adoptions in the EIR, judging its rationality and proposing the relevant recommendations. In the event that the opinion of the public is not adopted and no explanations are provided by the construction unit or its EIA agency, or their statements are irrelevant, the public can address the responsible authority or the court.

In case public opinion collection reveals strong public opposition to the project the responsible Environmental Protection Department for approval can again carry out public consultations by conducting public surveys, expert surveys, technical review meetings, public hearing meetings, etc.

Since 2006, on the basis of these *Measures*, the standing committees of local people congresses, the local people's governments and their competent administrative departments of environmental protection in China have added some special clauses or sections on public participation in EIA in the local regulations (Wang 2012). Those enacted by the province of Shandong will be described in the following sections.

More recently, the revised text of the *Environmental Protection Law* (EPL) – adopted by the Standing Committee of the National People's Congress on 24 April 2014 – became effective on 1 January 2015. The new EPL includes a new chapter entitled 'Information Disclosure and Public Participation' addressing the role of civil society in environmental protection (Yang 2014). Chapter 5 requires disclosure and publication of pollutant emission information to become available to the public by companies and governments – except those considered a state

Mariachiara Alberton

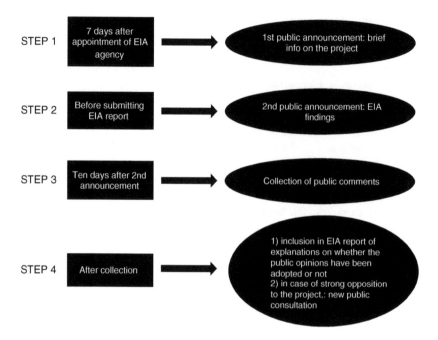

Figure 17.1 Public participation steps in EIA

Source: Author.

secret (Zhang et al. 2015). A significant advance is the inclusion of environmental information disclosure and public participation rights in environmental impact assessment procedures, completed with a set of provisions on liability, access to justice, penalties and remedies. According to articles 53–54 of the EPL, the public, defined as citizens, legal persons and other organizations, have the right of access to environmental information. On the other side, the competent environmental protection administrations shall disclose environmental information, improve public participation procedures, and facilitate and supervise public participation. In particular, the competent department of environmental protection administration at all levels (national, provincial and county level) is in charge of releasing environmental quality, monitoring data of key pollutant sources, environmental administrative permits, environmental administrative punishments, the collection and use of pollutant discharge fees, etc.

In addition, with specific reference to the EIA procedure, the project owner of a construction project is required to explain relevant situations to the potentially affected public when preparing the EIR, and solicit public opinion. Besides, the competent department that is responsible for the examination and approval of EIA documents for the construction project is prescribed to make public the full text of the EIR upon receipt.

A major novelty is the introduction of article 44, which, for the first time, provides a legal principle for the so-called 'Environmental Impact Assessment Restriction Targeting Regions' (EIARTR) (Zhu et al. 2015). This strategy has been developed by the MEP since 2007 to cope with the problem of ambient environmental quality exceeding ambient environmental standards in a specific region. According to the new provision, for regions that fail to fulfil the total emission control quota or achieve the environmental quality targets assigned by the State, environmental departments shall suspend the EIA approval for their new construction projects that may cause the increase of the total key pollutants emission in the region. That means that construction of new or expanding of existing economic activities cannot start as no EIA will be handed out. No need to say that the real impact of EIARTR will depend on how implementing regulations and measures will be further formulated and detailed (for instance through revising the current EIA Law), as well as on the will of competent departments.

Main implementation problems and gaps

Broad public involvement in China's EIA process has been limited so far. The main weaknesses are reflected in both the legislative and institutional system and in the implementation phase and praxis (see, for example, Enserink and Koppenjan 2007; Zhao 2010; Li et al. 2012: Chi et al. 2014; Chen et al. 2015). These gaps may be grouped as follows:

- *Public education and awareness.* The lack of awareness and education about the EIA process constitutes in practice a serious barrier to public participation. The results of on-site investigations show that the socio-economic settings in which the local communities are embedded are relevant. Although knowledge of the EIA objectives, participation rules and the responsibilities of various authorities, as well as the intensity of involvement in different forms of participation, vary significantly across communities located in different contexts (urban/rural, central/peripheral), in general they are quite weak.
- *Access to information.* In general, access to environmental information is often insufficient or even blocked. Governments at all levels are not very transparent with the content and scope of environmental information. The limited environmental information flowing out of local governments and companies deprives citizens of proper knowledge about their surroundings and thus prevents them from taking part in policymaking for and supervision of the environment. Thus, people have little confidence in the information released by local governments. In EIA the project-related environmental information is partly disclosed as prescribed by the law; however it is often scarce, incomplete, not adequate or too simplified; in addition most of the relevant information is not accessible. In fact, despite Chinese relevant laws and regulations detail the obligations and ways of environmental information disclosure in the EIA, in practice the environmental protection departments, construction units or EIA agencies tend to monopolize, conceal and in some cases even falsely report environmental information. Without detailed scope prescription, the disclosed information is generally limited to the project overview, environmental impacts, countermeasures for preventing or reducing an environmental impact, key points of an EIA conclusion and so on, and does not include the description of conditions, reasons and contents for a construction project or plan decision, the comparison and selection reasons of alternative measures for reducing or eliminating major adverse impact and so on. Therefore, the public is challenged when trying to understand the real impacts of the project at stake and the resulting public participation is far from being effective.
- *The right to participate.* In China, the EIA applies only to construction projects and special plans, with the exception of guidance plans; comprehensive plans, environmental legislation and environmental policymaking are also excluded. Therefore, the right of the public to participate in decision-making processes is still quite limited.
- *Stage in the process at which public participation is undertaken.* Public participation in EIA in China occurs only after the draft EIA document has been finalized, as it is prescribed before the draft EIA report of a plan or construction project is submitted for examination and approval. The public is not involved in the work for the preparation of an EIA report. The public participates in the EIA after the contents of an EIA report is almost determined, thus

public involvement risks to be ineffective, since, by that point, the institutional and economic incentives for EIA approval are probably overwhelming. On the contrary, the public should have an opportunity to provide feedback on a project or plan early enough in the drafting of the EIA document so that they may contribute to the formation of the ultimate conclusions about the environmental impacts that form the substance of the draft EIA document.

- *Definition of public concerned.* Public participation is limited and unrepresentative. The public concerned is selected by EIA agencies or project constructors and includes individuals and groups only directly related to the environmental impact of the relevant project or plan, and excludes those indirectly related or those focusing on the project or plan for public interests (i.e. environmental associations and non-governmental organizations). 'Groups' refer to sets of residents in an impacted area or their representatives, and the selection criteria are quite restrictive, e.g. percentage of population, distance from the EIA site, registration, etc.
- *Time frames for public participation.* The timeframes for public participation (i.e. announcement, submission of opinions, etc.) are too short, particularly for those in remote areas. In addition, EIA agencies or project developers in practice tend to even shorten these time frames to avoid an effective participation of concerned public.
- *Modes of participation.* According to Chinese regulations, public participation in EIA is organized through public hearings, seminars, workshops, interviews, questionnaires and expert consultations. However, because there are no legal provisions indicating which methods should be adopted in each stage and circumstances, usually the most cost-effective method, i.e. questionnaires, is employed for public participation. However, this form of involvement hampers proactive participation and discourages citizens from contributing to the process in a meaningful way. The scope of the questionnaires is very general and only provides some specific questions that cannot reflect the real concerns of people. Thus, the results of the questionnaires are not significant nor representative of public opinion.
- *Accountability and transparency.* In practice, the opinions and suggestions from the public are just to be filed and treated as the attachments of an EIA report for the authority's reference, with no relevant implication on EIA results. In general, the project constructors', the EIA agencies' and the competent environmental administrations' behaviour is not accountable as they hold no responsibility for failures to comply with prescribed procedures. The new EPL has already introduced important novelties to this regard, as the transparency of the decision-making processes and the possibility to check and challenge the different steps and decisions taken are crucial not only for guaranteeing formal accountability of the EIA procedure, but first and foremost for strengthening citizens' trust in institutions and their motivation to participate.

The case of Shandong

Some provinces have regulated public involvement in EIA by issuing local provisions. Guangdong, Zhejiang and Shandong have prescribed the identification and selection requirements and methods for public participation and defined the nature, range, proportion, and number of people to be considered as 'public'. The Shandong Provincial Environmental Protection Bureau, in particular, adopted in May 2012 the '*Notification of strengthening the project EIA public participation supervision*', aiming at clarifying critical issues and avoiding the risk of a solely formal public participation. According to these provisions, the implementation main body for public participation is the construction unit or its entrusted EIA agencies. They are not allowed to entrust any third party to carry out public participation. When conducting the public investigation, the construction unit or the EIA agency must ensure the representativeness and coverage of the public questionnaire, and investigate all residents or units one by one within the impacted area. Public participation must deal with the following information: awareness of construction projects, recognition of impact on the air and water quality, acoustic level, environmental impact of solid waste, measures to prevent and control environmental risks, necessity of project construction, agreement (or not) with project constructor. The construction unit or the EIA agency must document the public opinions in the EIA report; for public opinions opposing the projects, explanations must be provided. If a project is opposed by more than 20 per cent of the public, the provincial environmental protection department must hold a public discussion meeting or technical review meeting to gather further public opinion.

The project constructor and EIA agency are responsible for the quality, authenticity and results of the chapter about public participation. In the event that they do not undertake the necessary responsibilities or practise fraud during the public participation work, their responsibility must be investigated and reported. The EIA agency must be stopped from continuing its EIA work, and in case of serious circumstances, the MEP is requested to lower the qualification of the EIA agency or revoke its qualification certificate.

The above-described measures have been adopted to solve the following problems which resulted in petition and complaints occurred in recent years in the Province of Shandong (Xie et al. 2014):

- *Insufficient information disclosure.* In practice, although most environmental departments and EIA agencies considered the information disclosed adequate, it was oversimplified and meaningless. In most cases, EIA-related information was monopolized, by omitting relevant information and providing only formal data, thus causing loss of public trust in governmental bodies.
- *Public inclusion.* As required by the law, public should include citizen, legal person or other organization affected by the construction projects. In spite of that, in real cases some construction units and EIA agencies issued questionnaires randomly, avoiding the involvement of major public affected by the project.
- *Time frame.* As practice demonstrated, several EIA procedures were initiated after the project started, thus public participation was included only as a symbolic exercise. In addition, the local government departments adopted a negative attitude toward public participation and considered it as a mere formality.
- *Modes of participation.* The public participates in EIA mainly through questionnaires. This modality of dialogue with environmental protection bureaus, construction units or EIA organizations is too simple to satisfy the public needs for the environmental public interest.

The case of Yunnan

In Yunnan specific guidelines on public participation have not been approved yet, therefore the national rules and guidelines apply. Major problems in the implementation experience (Chen et al. 2014) of public participation in the EIA relate to:

- *Information release.* The specific environmental sensitive and relevant information concerning the project is usually not released by the competent authority, project proponent and EIA agencies. The information about public participation procedure is uni-directional and in the form of announcements and notifications without reference to the investment scale, technological level, or pollution level or to the scope of the project. It is hard for the interested parties to acquire the project information that they should receive.

- *The public.* The definition of public participants is not clear. It is not prescribed that the public should be those benefiting from or affected by the project. The proportion of each group of participants is not regulated and the minimum number of samples that should be collected is not specified.
- *Time frame.* The time frame for collecting opinions from the public is delayed and in any case is too short, especially for those people living in remote areas of Yunnan. Often only when a project is listed in government planning or it has to be implemented, does the public come to know about its existence. The public does not participate in the project discussion and EIA procedure as the time frame for the acceptance of opinions on the project is too short, thus the opinions collected are not complete or sufficient, and a considerable proportion of the interested parties' opinions are omitted.
- *Modes of participation and accountability.* The main form of participation, i.e. questionnaires, is mostly carried out by the construction unit or the EIA agency. The public opinion survey is mostly restricted to general requirements, and the scientific approach, justice, reliability and effectiveness of questionnaires are often questioned by the public. The contents of most surveys are too simple. Moreover, some questions are designed to avoid the important and critical aspects and dwell on the trivial. With reference to hearings, in most cases experts are hired by the proponents of the project, thus they cannot offer objective and independent opinions about the project.

Recommendations and concluding remarks

In China in general, and in the specific provincial cases considered, growing acknowledgement of the importance of EIA as a tool for promoting sustainability, transparency and participation of the public in decision-making has pushed the legislators, as well as local authorities and practitioners, to identify procedures and methods for guaranteeing earlier, more open, and more determinant public involvement. However, this analysis reveals the existence of some gaps and weaknesses still affecting current legislation and rules. Accordingly, some amendments are hereby recommended:

- The *EIA Law* should be revised in accordance with the new *Environmental Protection Law* by clearly defining the responsibilities and obligations of project units, EIA agencies and environmental protection bureaus, in order to improve public participation in terms of transparency and accountability.
- It should be clarified what exactly environmental information is (e.g. a list), what kind of environmental information should be published, and what kind of information should be given upon specific request and the time frame for such disclosure. Sanctions should be determined for authorities not providing requested information in the time frame established by law. Without such provisions it will not in practice be possible to obtain information. Moreover, information is mostly published on the websites of relevant environmental protection agencies and daily papers of relevant provinces and cities. However, few citizens consult environmental protection agencies' websites, while provincial and municipal daily papers cannot be considered public media since they are not available at newsstands. Thus, law amendments should include the publication of information in local daily papers, evening papers or the city news with the largest distribution readership or on popular local portal websites or community websites.

- Public participation should be shifted to an earlier stage, when all the options are still open and to be discussed. Moreover, the time frame for the submission of public opinion is too short (7–20 days) – particularly for those in remote areas. Thus, it is suggested to extend the time frame to a suitable period to allow expression of interest of all parties (Zhang et al. 2012).
- The EIA approach can be defined as exclusive, i.e. it defines the area of impact of a project, the directly and indirectly impacted population, the NGOs that can be involved, etc. It is suggested that EIA adopts an inclusive approach, with no restrictions on the distance or on directly/indirectly impacted population and on registered NGOs.
- The law states that the public participates in EIA by means of symposiums, workshops and hearings. However, according to this law, the decision on ways to organize public participation lies with the construction unit or its EIA agency. It is suggested to require explicitly that the construction unit or its EIA agency organizes public participation by means of symposiums, workshops and hearings instead of employing questionnaires, at least for projects having a relevant environmental impact.

Bearing in mind that the EIA process not only concerns the normative framework but also comprises practices that can be developed differently in different territorial contexts, even if based on the same or similar legislative and administrative grounds, an effort has to be made to improve national and provincial experiences and practices that have consolidated over time. In fact, regulations alone are not enough if they are not enforced and followed by a favourable implementing environment, i.e. public authorities and project developers, civil society organizations and society at large. This is the lesson learned in recent Chinese experiences like those of Yunnan and Shandong. Therefore, obviously, regulations should be clear and detailed, comprising all key elements listed, but the attitude of the public authorities, project developers and EIA agencies applying them is crucial, as practices make the difference.

In particular, the nature of the public involved by project units and EIA agencies plays an extremely important role: the inclusion of several stakeholders (i.e. directly or indirectly affected communities living around the project site, interest groups, non-governmental organizations), strongly influences the effectiveness of public participation. Similarly, different forms of participation provide for different degrees of power and impact that stakeholders can exercise on decisions taken as a result of the procedure. As revealed by the in-depth analysis, some passive modes of participation give the least power to those who are participating, while the techniques for active participation allow for greater influence. In fact, means such as questionnaires give less space for proactive participation and discourage citizens from contributing when compared to more complex forms of interactive participation like public hearings, roundtables, debates, workshops. As far as timing is concerned, as experience shows, participation should be conducted as early as possible, e.g. during the scoping stage, rather than when an EIA report is prepared, since only at a preliminary stage is the contribution of the public feasible and useful. However, adequate timing alone does not guarantee meaningful participation if, for example, the information necessary for making comments is scarce or not accessible. Moreover, the transparency of decisions and the possibility to contest them is crucial not only for guaranteeing formal accountability of the procedure, but first and foremost for strengthening citizens' trust in institutions and their motivation to participate. Thus, another important acknowledgement emerging from the analysis is that these key factors for public participation need to be considered and guaranteed jointly with the 'ex ante' and 'ex post' environmental procedural rights: the rights of access to information and of access to justice. These two rights are conditions – as the Convention on Access to Information, Public

Participation in Decision-making and Access to Justice in Environmental Matters signed on 25 June 1998 in the Danish city Aarhus underlines – for effective public participation, as participation is based on the information provided and enforcement of the law.

Notes

1   This chapter is mainly based on the results of the Project '*Regulating and promoting public participation in EIA in selected pilot provinces and municipalities*', funded by the European Union through the *EU–China Environmental Governance Programme (EGP)* and carried out in 2013–2014 to improve the quality, transparency and effectiveness of procedures for public participation in Environmental Impact Assessment (EIA) in China.
2   Promulgated by Standing Committee National People's Congress, 28 October 2002, in force 1 September 2003.
3   Promulgated by State Environmental Protection Administration, 24 February 2006, in force 18 March 2006.

References

Chen M. Qian X and Zhang L., 2015. Public participation in environmental management in China: status quo and mode innovation. *Environmental Management*, 55, 523–535.

Chen Y., Yang Z. and Yang L., 2014. Public participation in EIA in China – the case of Yunnan. In: Alberton, M., ed., 2014. *Public Participation in Environmental Decision-Making in the EU and in China. The Case of Environmental Impact Assessment,* Baden-Baden: NOMOS, 107–116.

Chi C.S.F., Xu J. and Xue L., 2014. Public participation in environmental impact assessment for public projects: a case of non-participation. *Journal of Environmental Planning and Management* 57 (9), 1422–1440.

Enserink B. and Koppenjan J., 2007. Public participation in China: sustainable urbanization and governance. *Management of Environmental Quality: An International Journal,* 18 (4), 459–474.

Li T., 1999. Discussion on measures and mechanism of public participation in environmental impact assessment. *Research of Environmental Sciences* 12, 2, 36–39.

Li T.H.Y., Ng S.T. and Skitmore, M., 2012. Public participation in infrastructure and construction projects in China: from an EIA-based to a whole cycle process. *Habitat International* 36 (1), 47–56.

Mol A.P.J., He G.Z. and Zhang L., 2011. Information disclosure as environmental risk management: developments in China. *Journal of Current Chinese Affairs* 40 (3), 163–192.

Moorman, J. L. and Zhang G., 2007. Promoting and strengthening public participation in China's environmental impact assessment process: comparing China's EIA Law and U.S. *NEPA Vermont Journal of Environmental Law* 8, 281–335.

Ning D., Wang H. and Whitney J., 1988. Environmental impact assessment in China: present practice and future developments. *Environmental Impact Assessment Review* 8, 85–95.

Tang S.-Y., Tang C.P. and Lo C.W.H., 2005. *Journal of Development Studies* 41 (1), 1–32.

Wang Y., Morgan, R. and Cashmore, M., 2003. Environmental impact assessment of projects in the People's Republic of China: new law, old problems. *Environmental Impact Assessment Review* 23 (5), 543–579.

Wang Y., 2012. Public participation in EIA, SEA and environmental planning (China). EGP study 2, 1–36.

Wu J., Chang I-S., Bina, O., Lam, K. and Xu H., 2011. Strategic environmental assessment implementation in China: five year review and prospects. *Environmental Impact Assessment Review* 31, 77–84.

Xie G., Shi H., Lu J. and Cai Y., 2014. Public participation in EIA in China – the case of Shadong. In: Alberton, M., ed. 2014. *Public Participation in Environmental Decision-Making in the EU and in China. The Case of Environmental Impact Assessment,* Baden-Baden: NOMOS, 97–106.

Yang, S., 2008. Public participation in the Chinese Environmental Impact Assessment (EIA) system. *Journal of Environmental Assessment Policy and Management* 10 (1), 91–113.

Yang T., 2014. The 2014 revisions of China's Environmental Protection Law (http://cgd.swissre.com/global_dialogue/topics/Environmental_liability/The_2014_Revisions_of_Chinas_Environmental_Protection_Law.html) (Accessed 18 February 2015).

Zhang L., He G. and Mol, A.P.J., 2015. China's new Environmental Protection Law: a game changer? *Environmental Development* 13: 1–3 (http://dx.doi.org/10.1016/j.envdev.2014.10.001) (Accessed 26 September 2015).

Zhang Y., Liu X., Yu Y., Bian G., Li Y. and Long Y., 2012. Challenge of public participation in China's EIA practice *IAIA12 conference proceedings* (http://conferences.iaia.org/2012/pdf/uploadpapers/Final papers review process/Zhang, Yuhuan. Challenge of Public Participation in China's EIA Practice.pdf) (Accessed 3 December 2016).

Zhao Y., 2010. Public participation in China's EIA regime: rhetoric or reality? *Journal of Environmental Law* 22 (1), 89–123.

Zhu X., Zhang L., Ran R., and Mol, A.P.J., 2015. Regional restrictions on EIA approval in China: the legitimacy of environmental authoritarianism. *Journal of Cleaner Production* 92, 100–108.

18

ACCESS TO ENVIRONMENTAL INFORMATION IN CHINA

Transparency, participation and the role of media

Sam Geall

Introduction

Access to information refers to the right of citizens to access public information held by the state. In environmental governance it is closely related to the idea of public participation: the ways in which individuals are consulted before a decision is made. It is also closely related to issues of media freedom, civil society and the public sphere. The first time public participation in environmental decision-making was codified in an international agreement was in Principle 10 of the Rio Declaration, agreed at the United Nations Conference on Environment and Development in 1992. The signatories of this declaration included China, and it provides a good set of working definitions for the terms in this chapter. It states:

> Environmental issues are best handled with participation of all concerned citizens, at the relevant level. At the national level, each individual shall have appropriate access to information concerning the environment that is held by public authorities, including information on hazardous material and activities in their communities, and the opportunity to participate in decision-making processes. States shall facilitate and encourage public awareness and participation by making information widely available. Effective access to judicial and administrative proceedings, including redress and remedy, shall be provided.
>
> *(UNEP 1992)*

This principle therefore directly links access to environmental information (transparency) to opportunities for public participation and to access to justice or redress.

The *Guidelines for the Development of National Legislation on Access to Information, Public Participation and Access to Justice in Environmental Matters* (the 'Bali Guidelines'), adopted in 2010 by the governing body of United Nations Environment Programme, which includes China, set out basic implementation guidelines for Principle 10 (UNEP 2010). These represent the international consensus on transparency and public participation in environmental matters. More than 90 countries, including China, have since adopted laws or regulations that provide for access to information and public participation in environmental matters.

As this chapter shows, the statements, policy documents, laws and regulations around open government in China often seem ambitious in scope. Perhaps surprisingly so, in light of the characteristic opacity of China's authoritarian governance structures and its extensive online and offline censorship apparatus. The legislation, therefore, raises a number of questions that I will address. How did such policy experiments evolve, and how do they compare with past approaches in China? How well have they been implemented to date, what barriers exist and what are their prospects for future development or improvement? The chapter starts, however, by exploring the stated principles, before it addresses these additional questions by way of historical and contextual illustration.

In China, the main laws that provide for public participation in environmental decision-making are the *Environmental Impact Assessment (EIA) Law* (2002), the *Administrative Licensing Law* (2003), the Ministry of Environmental Protection's *Interim Measures on Public Participation in the EIA Process* (2006) and the revised *Environmental Protection Law* (2014), which led to 2015's *Measures for Public Participation in Environmental Protection (Trial)*. Article 53 of China's *Environmental Protection Law* states:

> Citizens, legal persons and other organizations shall have the right to obtain environmental information, participate and supervise the activities of environment protection in accordance with the law. The competent environmental protection administrations of the people's governments at various levels and other departments with environmental supervision responsibilities shall disclose environmental information pursuant to the law, improve public participation procedures, and facilitate citizens, legal persons and other organizations to participate in, and supervise, environmental protection work.
>
> *(Environmental Protection Law 2014)*

Open government information has also been incorporated into Chinese law. The Chinese Academy of Social Sciences (CASS) established a specific research institute on open government information laws in 1999. In 2003, Guangzhou piloted open government information reforms (Ker 2015). In 2006, the CASS institute submitted China's first draft regulations on open government information to the State Council, and the *Open Government Information Regulations of the People's Republic of China* (OGIR) came into effect in May 2008. The *Measures on Open Environmental Information*, the first specific decree based on the OGIR, entered into force at the same time.

The *Measures* require not only environmental authorities but also enterprises to disclose environmental information, both proactively and in response to information requests from citizens. They also stipulate that environmental protection departments should disclose government environmental information on their own initiative: in the words of the OGIR, 'by means of government websites, government gazettes, press conferences, as well as through newspapers and other publications, radio, television and other methods that make it convenient for the public to be informed' (State Council 2008).

The government mandates the disclosure of certain types of environmental information from industry, including emergency plans for sudden environmental pollution accidents, and discharge information if polluters have exceeded national or regional pollution limits. The *Measures* specify that government environmental information should be made available to the public within 20 working days; responses to information requests from citizens should be answered within 15 working days; and major polluters must disclose and report emissions data within 30 days. Article 1 of the OGIR states that the purpose of the regulations is to ensure that citizens, legal persons and other organisations obtain government information in accordance with the law, enhance transparency of the work of government, promote administration in accordance with the law, and bring into full play the role of government information in serving the people's production and livelihood and their economic and social activities.

(State Council 2008)

In theory, at least, this article suggests protection for civil-society activists and concerned citizens practising oversight of environmental matters – and it should enable journalists, operating in a more open and pluralistic information environment to inform the public about environmental hazards or controversies. Furthermore, access to information is promoted at the highest levels. In 2013, Premier Li Keqiang said that fighting official corruption in China could be achieved through a more open 'sunshine government' (*zhengfu yangguang*). 'Power must be exercised in the sunshine', said former President Hu Jintao in 2007, 'to ensure that it is exercised correctly' (Buckley and Blanchard 2007).

Some of China's most recent high-level environmental commitments mention access to environmental information. The April 2015 state policy document, *Central Document Number 12: Opinions of the Central Committee of the Communist Party of China and the State Council on Further Promoting the Development of Ecological Civilization*, which purports to signal a central government effort to achieve wide-ranging environmental governance reforms, supports active public participation in ecological civilization (Geall and Ely 2015). This document refers specifically to: accurate and timely environmental information disclosure; the expansion of the scope of this transparency; guaranteeing the public right to know; safeguarding the environmental rights and interests of the public; and improving the systems of whistle-blowing, public hearings and public environmental interest litigation. It also promises that ecological civilization 'will expand public participation in the initiation, implementation and post-assessment of construction projects in an orderly manner' and that it will 'guide all types of social organizations [...] to pursue healthy and orderly development and give play to the role of non-governmental organisations (NGOs) and volunteers' (State Council 2015).

Historical perspectives

Throughout the Mao era, the state controlled all access to information, environmental or otherwise, and severely constricted participation. Environmental catastrophes occurred without being reported in the national media, such as the most lethal dam failure in world history, which occurred in Henan province in central China in August 1975. The Banqiao Reservoir Dam collapsed after being hit by a typhoon, triggering the failure of a second dam and a cascade of destruction. The death toll remained a state secret until 2005. Records now state that 26,000 people died from flooding and a further 145,000 people died in the epidemic disease and famine that followed (Geall 2013: 21).

Government information about the environment during that period, especially from 1949 until 1972, reflected prevailing political discourses about nature, as promoted by the Chinese Communist Party (CPC) under Chairman Mao Zedong, including 'utopian urgency' and 'dogmatic uniformity', as they were aptly characterized by Shapiro (2001: 4). Media reports represented nature as a battlefield, one on which the effectiveness of collective, ideologically motivated and militaristic mobilization could be demonstrated – and near-boundless abundance could be unlocked. Political repression strongly curtailed any participation or attempt to access or challenge government information about the environment. For example, during the

'Hundred Flowers' movement, a moment of purported liberalization in 1956 that was followed by the brutal crackdown of the Anti-Rightist Movement, discussions occurred among water experts regarding the risks and potential merits of the proposed Three Gorges Dam on the Yangtze River and the Sanmenxia Dam on the Yellow River, these ended swiftly with the purge of dam critics Li Rui and Huang Wanli in 1959 (Shapiro 2001: 63; McDonald 2004).

In 1972, China saw a first turning point in environmental attitudes, thanks not only to domestic pressures – a red tide (a toxic algal bloom) in coastal waters near Dalian, in north-eastern China, caused a huge die-off of shellfish and, separately, fish sold in Beijing were found to have high levels of toxic chemicals in their flesh (Muldavin 2000: 252) – but also the PRC's participation that year in the influential Conference on the Human Environment, held in Stockholm (Edmonds 2011: 15–16). In 1973, Beijing played host to the first national conference on environmental protection (Muldavin 2008: 253) and China founded its first environmental publication, *Environmental Protection* (*Huanjing Baohu*), with the writer and official Guo Morou (who had been severely persecuted during the first phase of the Cultural Revolution) providing the calligraphy on the masthead (CCICED 2013).

Such official environmental campaigns remained highly top-down in nature, and in the early Reform Era there was little progress on official transparency. However, media gradually became more pluralistic, increasing the range of environmental information available to the public, and there was progress on public participation in environmental matters – including through letters of complaint and petitions to the environmental authorities.

Until the 1990s all Chinese newspapers remained subsidized by the government, either as official publications of the Party or specialized papers affiliated to mass organizations (Akhavan-Majid 2004). However, following the authorization of advertising in newspapers in 1979, non-party papers started to gain in importance. Some local papers became major national players, often reporting about anywhere except their home province, putting them out of reach of local government censorship. Government-run newspapers spawned so-called 'child' papers to turn a profit. Media outlets multiplied rapidly and – crucially – they increasingly competed for audiences by covering issues of public concern. In 1978, China had 186 newspapers and 930 magazines. By 2014 (the latest figures available), China had 1,912 newspapers and 9,966 magazines (National Bureau of Statistics of China 2015).

Environmental reporting grew to become an important and dynamic part of this media landscape (Geall 2012). The emergence of China's 'green public sphere' (Calhoun and Yang 2007) reflected a shift in popular discourses around the environment, which, in contrast to Mao's 'war against nature', emphasized the fragility of the environment and the need for its protection. Coverage of green issues in Chinese newspapers grew steadily through the 1990s and accelerated through the following decade. Yang (2010) studied key words related to the environment and found remarkable increases: the word 'pollution', for example, rose in frequency in the same database of Chinese newspapers from around 21,000 instances in 2000, to more than 82,000 in 2007.

Many accounts (Sun and Zhao 2008; Zhan 2011) have stressed the role of environmental NGOs in this emerging sphere; and others have noted (Geall 2013: 17) that many of China's important first generation of environmentalists – such as Ma Jun, of the Institute of Public and Environmental Affairs (IPE), (see below p. 000) and Wang Yongchen, of Green Earth Volunteers – started as investigative journalists, operating in this more open media sphere. Ho and Edmonds (2008) defined this permitted sphere of NGO activity in environmental governance as 'embedded activism', where the government was restrictive, but also selectively conducive to voluntary action in order to aid local enforcement of environmental regulations, particularly through public participation processes.

For example, in 2004, the suspension of a proposed cascade of dams on the Nu River, in south-western China, came after a public outcry by a then unprecedented coalition of journalists, environmentalists, officials, local and regional NGOs (Boyd 2013: 61–66). In 2005, the influential vice-minister of the State Environmental Protection Administration (SEPA, now the Ministry of Environmental Protection, MEP), Pan Yue, also a former journalist, launched a 'storm' of suspensions of around 30 industrial projects that had dodged their environmental impact assessments (EIAs), forcing the companies to secure approvals before resuming construction. In 2005, Pan also deployed EIA-related laws to force China's first public hearing on the environment – an instrument SEPA attempted to deploy frequently in this period – after a public outcry about a potentially damaging renovation plan for the lakes of the Old Summer Palace Park (*Yuanmingyuan*), an important cultural site in the capital. This, a conflict that started with a report in the state newspaper *People's Daily* that was then covered in the increasingly influential Guangzhou-based newspaper *Southern Weekend*, targeted plastic sheeting laid, without approvals and consultation, to prevent seepage into a local lake, after opponents charged that it would damage plant and animal species and deplete groundwater levels (Ansfield 2013: 141–142).

Much of the plastic sheeting remains, but during this period, the environmental authorities trialled various methods of public participation, which principally included: public hearings (also see p. 000 below), surveys, expert consultations and seminars. The MEP's *Measures for Public Participation in Environmental Protection (Trial)* from 2015 lists: 'questionnaires, symposia, workshops and hearings' and adds that 'the general public can submit their opinions and suggestions through phone calls, letters, Internet and social media platforms' (MEP 2015). But no detailed, standardized instructions for the conduct of hearings, nor the selection of public representatives to participate in hearings, have been produced (CCICED 2013; see also Alberton chapter 17 this volume).

The first decade of the century also saw the introduction of Hotline 12369, operated by the MEP, which aimed at public supervision of environmental regulations through telephone tip-offs about pollution incidents. However, a survey conducted in 2005 showed that fewer than 20 per cent of those questioned knew that it existed. In June 2013, the hotline received a total of 149 complaints from the public, suggesting awareness of the hotline remained low (CCICED 2013).

Moving online

More recent initiatives, incorporating Internet communication and particularly social media, continued to build on this approach. China has around 642 million Internet users, according to the International Telecommunications Union. Mobile Internet users stand at 527 million, and 83.4 per cent of China's 'netizens' access the web via a mobile device, which in 2014 for the first time exceeded the number of people who access the web via PC (80.9 per cent) (Millward 2015a). Furthermore, the distinction between online platforms and media has blurred. Three large portals, Sina, Netease and Tencent, dominate the online news ecosystem; all of these have 'public interest' (*gongyi*) channels, which cover environmental issues.

Beyond government websites, big portals and established media outlets, however, social media now means that news and opinions can be shared among the public more than ever before – and the environment has become a key issue of concern. Social media have become important and trusted news channels in themselves – and have had a significant influence on the evolution of environmental activism and opinion in China (Sullivan and Xie 2009). Some smaller and more independent media producers, including NGOs and public intellectuals, can thrive and set the agenda in this new ecosystem – and breakout investigative reports, like 2015's *Under the Dome* (an online documentary about air pollution, financed and presented by Chai Jing, a prominent former state television reporter from China Central Television, CCTV) are good examples.

Today, media control, often described officially as 'guidance of public opinion', is still a significant force, affecting official and unofficial outlets alike. Alongside the well-known, sophisticated censorship tools of the 'Great Firewall', including website blocking, keyword filtering and localized disconnection, the government uses direct pressure on editors, publishers and individual users to shape online news coverage. Until 2013, China's Twitter-like micro-blogging service Sina Weibo was immensely popular – and it still boasts some 212 million monthly active users (Millward 2015b) – but it was brought to heel after a concerted government campaign against users and particularly its so-called 'Big Vs' (verified account holders with millions of followers), who were seen to wield too much power. That year a new interpretation of libel and defamation laws was introduced to criminalize online speech, with users spreading 'rumours' viewed by 5,000 or forwarded by 500 users facing possible prosecution or jail time.

However, the political conversations on social media are still lively, even if they sometimes resemble a cat-and-mouse game between 'netizens' and authorities. Journalists find numerous tips and leads online, and users find ingenious methods to work around censorship, using humorous and sometimes elaborate code words, images and substitutions of sensitive characters. For example, when in 2012, after the residents of Shifang, in Sichuan province, protested against the proposed construction of a copper refinery, a photograph of a baton-wielding police officer chasing student demonstrators was wittily re-imagined and circulated online. Liu Bo – the police officer's name had been identified through crowd sourcing, also known as the 'human flesh search engine' (*renrou sousuo*) – now ran after the famous hurdler Liu Xiang, and charged into the background of Edvard Munch's painting 'The Scream' (Geall 2013).

Today, WeChat and Weibo are used not only by environmental journalists and activists to disseminate news and ideas, but also by government, which has experimented with greater online transparency of environmental information. These efforts, which often also aim at gauging public opinion on environmental issues for planning purposes – but also to the neutralizing of information seen as sensitive or socially destabilizing, through the control of 'rumours' or disinformation – point to a new governance arrangement that MacKinnon (2012) has described as 'networked authoritarianism'.

For example, in an effort to create a communications platform between the government and the public that was effective in the new media context, the Chongqing Environmental Protection Bureau started a series of micro-blog accounts, one for each of the municipality's 40 districts, intended as platforms for faster information dissemination, greater transparency and improved responsiveness to public opinion and citizen complaints. Environmental Protection Bureau (EPB) employees were given specialized training on how to use and coordinate micro-blogging effectively, which focused on increasing public trust as well as responding to environmental incidents when they occurred. These accounts are used for releasing air quality information, tips on more environmentally responsible behaviour and practical advice. When environmental emergencies occur, the accounts are supposed to be used to give citizens accurate information about the risks and hazards faster than traditional media, thus quickly helping to dispel rumours. The official Xinhua news agency has praised the accounts as a model for helping to avoid social unrest (CCICED 2013).

Online platforms have also been used for the publication of environmental laws and regulations, and in a more bottom-up fashion, activists and entrepreneurs have used websites and mobile apps to disseminate air quality and other key environmental information.

Implementation

As with much regulation in China, the existence of legislation on transparency and participation – much of which, on the books, looks to be in line with international norms – doesn't mean that it is being effectively, consistently or accurately enforced. Given the complexity of the implementation challenges – and the dynamism of China's rapidly changing society and economy over the past decade – it is therefore advisable not only to look at the legislation, but also to explore some of the varied attempts at its implementation as a way to illustrate the progress of public participation in Chinese environmental affairs. This has been documented in media reports and secondary literature; here I note some of these cases with attention to the ways in which different actors and institutions over the past decade have negotiated access to information and public participation rules, challenging and shaping the implementation of these rules in the process.

Xiamen's 'strolls' (2007)

In 2007, China experienced an event that would later seem paradigmatic of a new form of environmental contention: the country's first major urban protest in response to anticipated pollution and associated questions about transparency and participation. In Xiamen, in the south-eastern province of Fujian, a series of protests led to the shelving of a proposed plant manufacturing paraxylene (PX), a petrochemical. Ansfield (2013) has provided the most comprehensive account of this event, which laid bare the emergent role of new media and mobile technologies in this movement.

The protests started when a conflict over the development of the city's Haicang district spilled into the open: the area had concurrently been planned as a residential zone, with a building boom spurred by a city government-controlled investment group, and as an industrial zone, slated for a long-delayed petrochemical plant, which some charged with flouting safety regulations that should prevent it being sited near residents. Many of the earliest opponents of the PX project were newly socially mobile residents of the area, who had arrived from poorer provinces.

Local online residents' forums filled with discussions about the emissions of an existing chemical plant operated by the same owner; property owners started writing letters about the proposed plant to the district government, the mayor's office and the local EPB. However, they received no response and, crucially, residents expressed concern that they could not find the EIA that had granted the project passage. In effect, the conflict pitted a newly constructed form of middle-class, urban citizenship – where residents demanded a stake in local planning decisions and the implementation of often ignored rules around transparency and participation in the planning process – against traditional, opaque forms of top-down decision-making.

Two elements helped to catalyse the protest. The first was a chemist at Xiamen University, Zhao Yufen, who in 2007 submitted a critical proposal to the China People's Political Consultative Conference (CPPCC), questioning the process by which the PX project passed its original EIA and bringing attention to the fact it had not been released to the public. Then, a mysterious mobile-phone message, forwarded thousands of times, called on city residents to 'stroll' against the project, which, it said, would be like 'an atomic time bomb that has been released on Xiamen Island'.

The resulting demonstrations – which involved thousands of people from many communities across the city – lasted two days, and were tentatively supported by liberal-leaning media outlets like *Southern Weekend* and reported live by bloggers from around the country, some of whom travelled to Xiamen just to cover the strolls. These eventually forced officials to freeze construction pending a new EIA process. Again SEPA vice-minister Pan Yue took the lead and organized for a strategic environmental assessment and even a televised public hearing, which resulted in the plant being relocated down the coast to Zhangzhou.

Sometimes described as a victory for civil society, the Xiamen protests are perhaps better understood as setting the tone for a phase of environmental contention in China characterized by low public trust and frequent challenges to the perceived lack of transparency and proper implementation of participation in planning procedures. This phase continues today: similar protests are staged against PX plants (for example, in Dalian in 2011, Ningbo in 2012, Kunming in 2013, Maoming in 2014 and Shanghai in 2015), as the chemical became something of a signifier for wider concerns about regulation and planning, despite its relative obscurity elsewhere. Incineration and other large infrastructure projects have also raised public concern, typically characterized as 'not-in-my-backyard' or NIMBY movements. Pan Yue later said that the Xiamen PX project had not, in fact, been 'a victory of people's opinion', as some had cast it, 'but manifested a systematic problem. It shows the demands of the middle class on the environment. It shows the relationship between environmental assessment, the middle class and the environment' (Ansfield 2013: 143).

Cover-up in the Bohai Gulf (2011)

In June 2011, users of the then popular micro-blogging service Sina Weibo read this short post: 'Two wells at a Bohai oil field have been leaking for two days. I hope the leaks are controlled and pollution prevented.' Censors worked fast to delete the original post, but it spread even faster. It was likely written by a whistle-blower at China National Offshore Oil Corp (CNOOC), the state-owned Chinese company that formed half of a joint venture with ConocoPhillips at an oilfield in the Bohai Sea, off China's north-eastern coast. It turned out to have been correct. In the end, the size of the oil sheen officially reached about 2,500 barrels, polluting around 4,250 square kilometres of sea. However, the State Oceanic Administration did not confirm the leak until an entire month later (Geall 2011).

As oil and drilling fluid spilled into the water, a public controversy began to swell about the lack of transparency, only a year after another pipeline explosion in the Yellow Sea had caused the country's worst ever oil leak. Fishermen in Hebei province blamed the spill for the deaths of massive numbers of scallops. After that lone micro-blogger sounded the alarm, Chinese environmental activists and journalists started to ask questions, but CNOOC and China's State Oceanic Administration (SOA) remained tight-lipped. (It later turned out that the micro-blog referred to an accident that had happened on 17 June, but another leak had also occurred on 4 June, and neither the SOA nor the company had made this information public.)

But the pressure continued to build. The *Southern Weekend* journalist Feng Jie arrived on the scene of the Bohai spill on 30 June 2011, long before the SOA had confirmed the accident. Feng found confirmation from insiders at the organization and became the first to publish in print what many on social media suspected. She then followed the story closely for the next six months. When a number of media reports pointed the finger at the US company ConocoPhillips, one half of the joint venture that ran the oil platform, she suggested that Chinese state-owned company CNOOC was shirking responsibility – and that the government regulators were not doing their job. Significantly, she seemed to earn the trust of the regulators and was able to interview key SOA officials before other journalists. Feng had previously worked at the *China Economic Herald*, a heavyweight financial newspaper managed by the country's top economic planner, the NDRC. There, she developed the deep contacts and the know-how that would later help her. Feng reportedly went so far as to barge into an SOA department head's office. 'My editor's always asking which key people I've interviewed or what facts I've got,' she told the Beijing-based journalist Liu Yuan (Liu 2012).

Then on 12 July another leak occurred at a different CNOOC oilfield in the Bohai Sea. But this time the response was different: the SOA announced the small leak – and the next day ordered the company to cease operations and to make data about it available to the public – the first time a Chinese government department has requested an information disclosure of this kind. For data-focused green activists like Ma Jun – a former investigative journalist, author of the seminal 1999 book *China's Water Crisis* and founder of Beijing-based NGO the Institute for Public and Environmental Affairs (IPE) – this was a breakthrough for transparency in China. It was, Ma wrote at the time, 'the first time a government department has urged a polluting company to disclose information on an incident of this kind'. It meant, that 'finally, the publication of environmental information has moved from being a public and media desire to a government requirement' (Ma 2011).

IPE has, in fact, been one of the more important actors in China to push the principle of environmental transparency up the public agenda. Using publicly available information, IPE has compiled online maps of air and water pollution levels across China, organized consumer campaigns, and even jointly run regular compliance evaluations to see which cities and provinces have the most open (and closed) information systems. These regular assessments, known as the Pollution Information and Transparency Index (PITI), provide a valuable resource for tracking the progress of environmental transparency in China. Overall, the scores on these indices have shown greater progress in richer regions, such as the Pearl River Delta. However, the most polluted cities in poorer provinces such as Henan, tend to perform the most poorly. There is also great variation between different types of information, with 'complex and sensitive' information, such as EIAs, being some of the most difficult to obtain (Ker 2015).

Airpocalypse now (2011)

As mentioned above, China's flagship transparency legislation – the *Open Government Information Regulations* (OGIR, State Council 2008), and the *Measures* that operationalized them for environmental information – is crafted much in line with similar legislation in other countries, requiring both proactive government disclosure and in response to requests from citizens. It is generally on the proactive side of the *Measures* that there has been the most effective implementation (Article 19 2010). Municipal EPB websites, for example, tend to disclose various categories of environmental information. Significantly, an online 'storm' of citizen complaints on micro-blogs led to an increase in the scope of this proactive disclosure in early 2012.

In late 2011, an unusually polluted few weeks in Beijing had seen aeroplanes grounded and roads closed as thick smog obscured all but the lowest of buildings. The focus of anxiety among concerned, networked citizens in northern Chinese cities became not only the smog, but also what was seen as secrecy in the official reporting of it. Every year since 1998, when public reporting of air quality began, the Beijing government had increased the total number of annual 'blue sky days'. This was a measure based on the city's air pollution index, but it was a measure that did not match people's visual observations of deteriorating air quality. Nor did it take into account airborne concentrations of $PM_{2.5}$, that were being collected and shared hourly not by the government EPBs but by the US Embassy on their Twitter micro-blogging account @ beijingair (Boyd 2013: 41–42).

One revealing comparison between the US Embassy and official statistics was produced by Steven Q. Andrews, an independent scholar and consultant (Andrews 2011), who looked at

$PM_{2.5}$ and other data, and concluded that the city authorities had artificially deflated air pollution statistics by adding new stations further out, in cleaner suburbs. Consequently, an online 'storm' of citizen complaints on micro-blogs called for the release of real-time information about airborne concentrations of $PM_{2.5}$. An online poll started by the well-known property developer Pan Shiyi saw tens of thousands call for the government to release more accurate measurements: calls which that were heard, when in January 2012, Beijing trialled the release of $PM_{2.5}$ data, scaling up the effort later in the year.

Significantly, the government not only acknowledged, but championed the role of public pressure in the campaign, with state news agency Xinhua praising the 'stirring campaign' and the 'satisfying response' from policymakers (Xinhua 2012), which did lead to an increase in information disclosure, with Beijing and some 73 other cities starting to release the data automatically. Later that number expanded to cover 179 cities, with real-time data from 15,000 enterprises. In 2013, these efforts were codified in a series of regulations. Some, such as the *Measures for Self-Monitoring and Information Disclosure with Key Enterprises in China (Trial Implementation)* aimed at improving real-time data releases by enterprises. Others, *the Guide to Governmental Information Disclosure of Environmental Impact Assessments for Construction Projects (Trial)*, focused on the EIA process. Significantly, another set of regulations, first piloted in Tianjin in north-eastern China and included in the *Measures for the Hazardous Chemical Management and Registry*, have focused on the establishment of a pollution release and transfer registry (PRTR) system. This system, which exists in the European Union and is similar to the US Toxics Release Inventory (TRI) system, would create an accessible database of all the potentially hazardous materials enterprises release into the environment.

These moves towards the expansion of data transparency, and particularly the use of continuous emissions monitoring, have also aligned with China's increasingly ambitious climate policies – in particular, with the requirements for establishing its seven pilot emissions trading schemes, launched in 2011, and international pressure to establish robust systems for 'monitoring, reporting and verification' (MRV), regarding the country's pledges to the UN Framework Convention on Climate Change (UNFCCC) (Hsu et al. 2015).

Information requests

However, beyond this progress on proactive disclosure, compliance evaluations, such as that by Article 19 (2010), Zhang et al. (2010) and the PITI (IPE 2009, 2013), have found that EPBs are poor by comparison in their responses to requests for information from the public. The Article 19 report's author, Amy Sim, told me in 2011: 'A lot of officials interpret [the regulations]: as long as it's not within the 17 types of proactive disclosure, they will not disclose.' More sensitive environmental information is difficult to obtain. Speaking at a seminar in 2011, Wang Canfa, director of Beijing's Centre for Legal Assistance to Pollution Victims, claimed that: 'Although the regulations list 17 types of information that should be disclosed and only one short clause on exemptions, that one short clause has become a catch-all'. His reference here was to Article 8, the exemption clause in the national regulations regarding national security and social stability, which also applies to the environmental decree (Geall 2011).

Open information legislation across the world contains similar exemptions, and the extent to which governments rely upon these can give a good indication of their commitment to their own openness policies. However, the evidence from my own interviews and from evaluations such as Sim's (Article 19 2010) and others' (cf. Zhang et al. 2010) suggests that in China the situation is more complicated: since, although refusals from Chinese government agencies to release information are frequent, such justifications based on the Article 8 exemptions were not cited as much as other explanations that, in fact, had no legal basis whatsoever. The grounds for rejection, Sim found, were generally 'not very clear': many officials replied that the information was simply 'inconvenient to disclose' or that it was 'liable to be sensationalised by the media'.

In 2011, a campaigner opposed to waste incineration projects in the Beijing suburbs told me that his requests had been refused on the grounds that the relevant documents had been lost by an intern in the EPB office. This suggests the problems with the OGIR expose a lack of capacity, training and perhaps also with the specificity of enforcement provisions in the regulations, as well as a pervasive bureaucratic culture of secrecy at a local level, rather than what might be imagined as a conventionally authoritarian response to citizens' requests.

Chinese journalists have taken an active interest in the poor implementation of transparency rules. In 2009, it became headline news in the country when two journalists from Xinhua were stopped from photographing documents listing pollution violators, information that the authorities are supposed to disclose, at a provincial government meeting in Heilongjiang province, north-eastern China.[1] When an official told them the information was 'confidential' and the media had already had 'enough' information about pollution, the reporters walked out of the meeting in protest – a gesture that earned them widespread sympathy from Chinese media commentators. In early 2009, *Southern Weekend* published on its website an EIA, obtained using open government information laws, which approved the construction of a controversial petrochemical plant in Fujian province. But such cases are still rare. Despite their interest in the implementation of the regulations, most Chinese journalists have not made much use of the legislation itself. Surprisingly few Chinese journalists that I have interviewed in my research (cf. Geall 2014) are aware that open information laws exist, and very few have used them as reporting tools. The culture of investigative reporting that exists in China has grown in a context where information is shared unofficially, and there is little trust in the efficacy of such government-sanctioned measures.

Most of the pressure for greater disclosure has come from NGOs. Friends of Nature (FON), for example, campaigned for the government to disclose information about boundary changes at a protected area for rare and endangered fish species ('The Upper Yangtze Rare and Endemic Fish Nature Reserve') on the Yangtze River, decisions which helped to make way for the Xiaonanhai Dam project near the city of Chongqing, in south-west China. Campaigners feared the changes could mean extinction for these endangered species, particularly the Yangtze sturgeon, a so-called 'living fossil' that has survived since the era of the dinosaurs. Using open government information laws, FON requested a copy of the government's on-site investigation report and the declaration of the boundary change, which included an impact assessment. The Ministry of Agriculture initially refused these on the grounds that 'procedural' data was not covered by transparency legislation. A campaigner from FON told me at the time: 'This is like a "Catch-22" situation for the public who wish to supervise and participate in the government's decision-making.' His meaning was: if the government isn't willing to disclose how its decisions are made, and if its procedures aren't being correctly followed, it's difficult to see how freedom of information can be used to hold the government to account at any time other than after the event. In a rare piece of good news, it seems this campaign was a success. A letter from the Ministry of Environmental Protection in 2015, which approved another dam on the river, stated that the Xiaonanhai Dam should be banned, as the 'project will lead to major changes to the water environment and water ecology as well as the land ecology, causing [an] irreversible impact' (Hornby 2015).

Conclusion

This chapter has illustrated that China's environmental laws and regulations, and even its top leadership, make frequent reference to greater access to environmental information and its link to improved public participation. The broad trend over time has also been towards greater transparency, especially in the areas of proactive and real-time environmental information disclosure. However, much of this is owed to the growth of an increasingly pluralized, commercial and diverse media sphere, including in online media, as well as the growth of environmental NGOs, civil society and an increasingly connected and informed middle class. Many local authorities, often in the most polluted areas of the country, have lagged in their implementation of transparency and participation rules. A pervasive culture of secrecy remains at many levels of government, and environmental incidents are still routinely covered up; certain forms of information, such as soil pollution data, remain difficult to obtain (He 2014). This has been challenged by the public at various points – and a number of critical junctures over the past decade have led to breakthroughs in transparency. For example, in Kunming in 2013, in Yunnan in south-west China, a conflict over the citing of a PX plant ended with a commitment to greater transparency, particularly online (Hu and Guo 2013). The municipal government in Jiaxing, in Zhejiang province, also has promoted itself as a pilot city for enhanced environmental transparency (Wang 2014).

In a context of low public trust around a range of environmental risks and uncertainties, from the planning of urban petrochemical plants to food safety, it is clear that one potential government response has been to expand the scope of transparency in order to increase structured participation, avoid conflict and thus improve policy implementation. However, such examples stand in contrast to prevailing political approaches, which continue to restrict media that would make use of greater access to environmental information. In a context of not only restrictive censorship but also increasing scrutiny of civil-society groups, particularly those with foreign funding or engaged in advocacy (Duchâtel and Kratz 2015), it is likely that transparency and participation will continue to be fraught and contested areas of legislation. The implementation of such principles is therefore likely to be an important indicator of the Chinese government's wider commitment to political reform.

Note

1 It was also this province that was most affected in 2005, when a series of explosions at a petrochemical plant created an 80-kilometre-long toxic slick in the Songhua River. The State Environmental Protection Administration, the predecessor of the MEP, only admitted the serious pollution of the river ten days after the explosion and one day after water was cut off in the provincial capital of Harbin.

References

Akhavan-Majid, R., 2004. 'Mass Media Reform in China', *Gazette,* 66 (6), 553–565.

Andrews, Q., 2011. 'Beijing's Hazardous Blue Sky', *chinadialogue,* 5 December. Available at: https://www.chinadialogue.net/article/show/single/en/4661-Beijing-s-hazardous-blue-sky (accessed 24 December 2015).

Ansfield, J., 2013. 'Alchemy of a Protest: The Case of Xiamen PX' in: Geall, S., ed., *China and the Environment: The Green Revolution.* London: Zed Books, 136–202.

Article 19, 2010. *Access to Environmental Information in China: Evaluation of Local Compliance.* (London: Article 19).

Boyd, O., 2013. 'The Birth of Chinese Environmentalism: Key Campaigns' in: Geall, S., ed., *China and the Environment: The Green Revolution.* London: Zed Books, 40–95.

Buckley, C. and Blanchard, B., 2007. 'China's Hu Says Communist Party Must Stay in Charge' *Reuters*, October 15. Available at: http://www.reuters.com/article/us-china-party-idUSPEK28373420071015 (accessed 4 April 2016).

Calhoun, G. and Yang G., 2007. 'Media, Civil Society, and the Rise of a Green Public Sphere in China', *China Information* 21, 211–236.

China Council on International Cooperation on Environment and Development (CCICED), 2013. 'Media and Public Participation Policies on Promoting China's Green Development'. Available at: https://www.chinadialogue.net/reports/6808-Media-and-Public-Participation-Policies-on-Promoting-China-s-Green-Development/en (accessed 24 December 2015).

Duchâtel, M. and Kratz, A., 2015. 'China: Waging "Lawfare" on NGOs', European Council on Foreign Relations. Available at: http://www.ecfr.eu/publications/summary/china_waging_lawfare_on_ngos5022 (accessed 24 December 2015).

Edmonds, R. L., 2011. 'The Evolution of Environmental Policy in the People's Republic of China', *Journal of Current Chinese Affairs*, 40 (3), 13–35.

Environmental Protection Law of the People's Republic of China, 2014. Unofficial translation by the EU–China Environmental Governance Programme. Available at: https://www.chinadialogue.net/Environmental-Protection-Law-2014-eversion.pdf (accessed 4 April 2016).

Geall, S., 2011. 'Data Trap', *Index on Censorship* 40 (4), 48–58.

Geall, S., 2012. 'Media Coverage of the Environment' in: Geall, S. et al. (eds)., *Berkshire Encyclopedia of Sustainability: China, India, and East and Southeast Asia: Assessing Sustainability*. Great Barrington, MA: Berkshire Publishing, 242–245.

Geall, S., 2013. 'China's Environmental Journalists: A Rainbow Confusion' in: Geall, S., ed. *China and the Environment: The Green Revolution*. London: Zed Books, 15–39.

Geall, S. 2014. *Changing Political Climates: Chinese Environmental Journalism and Sustainable Development.* PhD Dissertation, University of Manchester.

Geall, S. and Ely, A., 2015. *Innovation for Sustainability in a Changing China: Exploring Narratives and Pathways*, STEPS Working Paper 86, Brighton: STEPS Centre.

He G., 2014. 'Special Report: The Victims Of China's Soil Pollution Crisis', *chinadialogue*, 30 June. Available at: https://www.chinadialogue.net/article/show/single/en/7073-Special-report-The-victims-of-China-s-soil-pollution-crisis (accessed 24 December 2015).

Ho, P. and Edmonds, R. L., 2008, *China's Embedded Activism: Opportunities and Constraints of a Social Movement*. Oxford: Routledge.

Hornby, L., 2015. 'China Blocks $4bn Xiaonanhai Dam Development', *Financial Times*, 8 April. Available at: https://next.ft.com/content/a7ab9b40-ddd5-11e4-9d29-00144feab7de (accessed 24 December 2015).

Hsu A., Moffat, A. and Xu K. 2015. 'Data Transparency: New Dynamic at COP-21 in Paris', *ChinaFAQs*, 22 December. Available at: http://www.chinafaqs.org/blog-posts/data-transparency-new-dynamic-cop-21-paris (accessed 24 December 2015).

Hu Y. and Guo A., 2014. 'Communication Essential for Yunnan Chemical Project', *China Daily*. Available at: http://usa.chinadaily.com.cn/china/2013-05/18/content_16508480.htm (accessed 24 December 2015).

Institute of Public and Environmental Affairs (IPE), 2009. 'Pollution Information and Transparency Index'. Available at: http://wwwen.ipe.org.cn/reports/Reports.aspx?cid=18336&year=0&key= (accessed 13 December 2016).

Institute of Public and Environmental Affairs (IPE), 2013. 'Pollution Information and Transparency Index'. Available at: http://wwwen.ipe.org.cn/reports/Reports.aspx?cid=18336&year=0&key= (accessed 13 December 2016).

Ker, M., 2015. 'Getting Down to Business: Deepening Environmental Transparency in China'. *Solutions*, 4(5), 40–50.

Liu Y., 2012. 'Delving Behind the Headlines', *chinadialogue*, April 12. Available at: https://www.chinadialogue.net/article/show/single/en/4868-Delving-behind-the-headlines (accessed 24 December 2015).

Ma J., 2011. 'Transparency Test in the Bohai Sea', *chinadialogue*, July 20. Available at: https://www.chinadialogue.net/article/show/single/en/4418-Transparency-test-in-the-Bohai-Sea (accessed 24 December 2015).

MacKinnon, R., 2012. *The Consent of the Networked*. New York: Basic Books.

McDonald, H., 2004. 'One Dam Mistake After Another Leaves $4.4bn Bill', *Sydney Morning Herald*, May 22. Available at: http://www.smh.com.au/articles/2004/05/21/1085120121829.html (accessed 4 April 2016).

Millward, S., 2015a. 'The Latest Numbers on Web, Mobile, and Social Media in China in Early 2015', *Tech in Asia*, January 21. Available at: https://www.techinasia.com/china-web-mobile-data-start-2015 (accessed 24 December 2015).

Millward, S., 2015b. 'Weibo Hits 212M Monthly Active Users, Most Now on Mobile', *Tech in Asia*, 19 August. Available at: https://www.techinasia.com/weibo-212-million-active-users (accessed 24 December 2015).

Ministry of Environmental Protection, 2015. *Measures for Public Participation in Environmental Protection (Trial)* Unofficial translation by the EU–China Environmental Governance Programme. Available at: http://www.ecegp.com/files/2/Measures%20for%20Public%20Participation%20in%20 Environmental%20Protection%20%28Trial%29%202015.pdf (accessed 5 April 2016).

Muldavin, J., 2000. 'The Paradoxes of Environmental Policy and Resource Management in Reform-Era China', *Economic Geography,* 76 (3), 244–271.

Muldavin, J., 2008. 'The Politics of Transition: Critical Political Ecology, Classical Economics, and Ecological Modernization Theory in China' in: Cox, K. R., Low, M.; Robinson, J., eds., *The Political Geography Handbook*. London: Sage, 247–262.

National Bureau of Statistics of China, 2015. *China Statistical Yearbook 2015.*

Shapiro, J., 2001. *Mao's War against Nature.* Cambridge: Cambridge University Press.

State Council 2008. *Regulations of the People's Republic of China on Open Government Information.*

State Council 2015. *Central Document Number 12: Opinions of the Central Committee of the Communist Party of China and the State Council on Further Promoting the Development of Ecological Civilization.*

Sullivan, J. and Xei L., 2009. 'Environmental Activism, Social Networks and the Internet', *The China Quarterly* 198, 422–432.

Sun Y. and Zhao. D., 2008. 'Environmental Campaigns' in: O'Brien, K.J., ed., *Popular Protest in China.* Cambridge, MA: Harvard University Press, 144–163.

United Nations Environment Programme (UNEP) 1992. *Rio Declaration on Environment and Development.* Available at: http://www.unep.org/documents.multilingual/default.asp?documentid=78&articleid= 1163 (accessed 24 December 2015).

United Nations Environment Programme (UNEP), 2010. *Guidelines for the Development of National Legislation on Access to Information, Public Participation and Access to Justice in Environmental Matters.* Available at: http://www.unep.org/civil-society/Portals/24105/documents/Guidelines/GUIDELINES_TO_ACCESS_ TO_ENV_INFO_2.pdf (accessed 24 December 2015).

Wang K., 2014. 'The "Jiaxing Model" and the "Polder Model": A Comparative Study on Public Participation in Environmental Governance in Jiaxing and The Hague', International Association on Social Quality, The Hague/Amsterdam, November 15. Available at: http://www.socialquality.org/ wp-content/uploads/2015/02/Final-Report-Kai-Wang-IASQ-25-November-2014.pdf (accessed 24 December 2015).

Xinhua, 2012. 'PM$_{2.5}$ in Air Quality Standards, Positive Response to Net Campaign', *People's Daily*, 1 March. Available at: http://en.people.cn/90882/7744434.html (accessed 5 April 2016).

Yang G., 2010. 'Brokering environment and health in China: Issue entrepreneurs of the public sphere', *Journal of Contemporary China* 19 (63), 101–119.

Zhan J., 2011. 'Environmental Journalism in China', in: Shirk, S., ed., *Changing Media, Changing China.* Oxford: Oxford University Press, 115–127.

Zhang, L., Mol, A.P.L., He G. and Lu Y., 2010. 'An implementation assessment of China's Environmental Information Disclosure Decree', *Journal of Environmental Sciences* 22 (10), 1649–1656.

PART IV

Related policy fields – conflicts and synergies

19

ENVIRONMENT AND ENERGY POLICY

Background and main challenges

Andreas Oberheitmann and Paul Hugo Suding

Any economic activity, indeed every human activity, is associated with the use of energy services such as heat, light, power and others, which are predominantly produced from fossil fuels, though often indirectly via electricity. Increasing energy services is important to drive economic development and increase economic welfare of a country. However, the combustion of fossil fuels also entails negative environmental side effects such as local pollution, including emissions of particles, soot and sulphur dioxide (SO_2) from incomplete combustion of coal with high sulphur content, emissions of carbon dioxide (CO_2) and other global greenhouse gases (GHGs). Achieving economic development and accelerating the growth of gross domestic product (GDP) increases the demand for energy services so that, if energy efficiency remains poor and the share of non-fossil energy remains low, even more high-emitting fuel is used, which results in a vicious circle, if, for example, cleaning up exhaust gases needs more energy.

Against this background, China faces three major challenges for environmental and energy policy in the twenty-first century:

- economic growth and rapid urbanization;
- energy security;
- vulnerability to environmental pollution and negative impacts of climate change.

China's environmental policy has to cope with these challenges in order to balance the requirements of economic development and welfare on the one side and the negative environmental effects and public interest on the other side. The objective of this chapter is to provide an overview of the background and institutional arrangements as well as an analysis of the main drivers for environment and energy policy in China. Detailed analysis of selected energy-related aspects of environmental policies and measures are covered by other chapters of this handbook, including air pollution (by Ahlers and Hansen, chapter 7), climate change and carbon governance (by Heggelund and Nadin, chapter 8), green energy innovation (by Lewis, chapter 20) and low carbon urban development (by Liu and Wang, chapter 21).

In view of the main challenges, this chapter is structured as follows. After introducing the current and persistent main challenges, the first section briefly recalls the evolution of the energy resources, the policies and institutional arrangements and main actors for Chinese environmental and energy policy since the turn of the century. The next section analyses the main challenges and drivers of China's environmental and energy policy in the twenty-first century, i.e. economic growth and rapid urbanization, as well as China's vulnerability to the adverse impacts of climate change and its contribution to their global mitigation. The third section provides an overview of the synergies of energy security and climate change policies and shows the interdependencies between different energy and environmental policy measures. The final section gives an outlook into the future of China's environmental and energy policy.

Recent evolutions of environmental and energy policy in China

Fundamental reconciliation challenges of energy and environmental policies

China's overall energy policy priority is to provide secure and sufficient, appropriate and affordable energy for its economic and social development. Since energy supply is mainly based on fossil fuel, economic growth is associated with energy related emissions of carbon dioxide (CO_2) and other gases, which are released during combustion in energy transformation and consumption. This is the core of the principal reconciliation challenge between energy and environmental policy. Economic growth and well-being requires energy services, customarily gained from fossil fuels. The increase of fossil fuel-based energy consumption leads to an increase in emissions of the greenhouse gas CO_2 as well as airborne pollutants such as sulphur dioxide (SO_2), nitrogen oxides (NO_x) and particulate matters (PM_{10}, $PM_{2.5}$).

Increasing urbanization in China exacerbates the challenge since it accentuates the concentration of spot emissions of these gases as well as emission levels in urban environments. China's energy policy challenge to reconcile growth and environment is further complicated by the energy security objective, which is very high on the energy policy agenda. China is still following the paradigm of a reliance on domestic resources to the utmost possible extent, which leads to many and various domestic energy supply activities with environmental impacts.

In addition, China faces an upcoming challenge from vulnerability to the adverse impacts of climate change. Many large cities located in coastal regions are facing rising sea levels and the risk of floods or extreme weather events such as typhoons. For the energy sector, in view of the important hydropower capacities and cooling water requirements of thermal power, changes in the water regime are of great concern.

Energy resources and energy security concerns

In China, energy security concerns are traditionally addressed by a concept of self-sufficiency in energy, which, in times of high consumption growth and in light of future high demand, is complemented by imports. Climate change mitigation adds further requirements and modifies the energy security policy.

From a resources point of view, China has favourable conditions for a secure energy supply. It is the only country in East Asia with significant fossil fuel reserves. With 17.8 per cent of the world's hard coal reserves (Table 19.1), China's deposits are the second largest in the world after the US (31.9 per cent; BGR 2015). With 52.1 per cent, China is now the largest coal producer in the world; far ahead of the US (11.7 per cent; BGR 2015). Although China also has its own lignite, crude, natural gas and uranium deposits,[1] the domestic oil reserves especially have already not been able to satisfy the growing demand with domestic production for 20 years. The country has been a net importer of crude oil since 1996, and of crude oil and petroleum products since 1993. In 2014, China's domestic crude oil production accounted for

Table 19.1 Comparison of energy reserves, production, imports and consumption in China and the world (2014)

	Reserves	Production	Imports	Consumption	Static availability
China					
Hard coal (Mt)	124,059	3,725	291	4,010	31
Lignite (Mt)	7,555	145	0	145	52
Crude oil (Mt)	2,514	211	308	518	5
Natural gas (bn. m³)	3,459	133	58	185	19
Uranium (kt U)	94	2	5	6	15
World					
Hard coal (Mt)	698,660	7,153	1,343	7,151	98
Lignite (Mt)	285,964	1,023	0	1,024	279
Crude oil (Mt)	218,864	4,271	2,109	4,305	51
Natural gas (bn. m³)	197,841	3,484	1,014	3,483	57
Uranium (kt U)	1,213	56		66	18
World share China (%)					
Hard coal	17.8	52.1	21.7	56.1	–
Lignite	2.6	14.2	–	14.2	–
Crude oil	1.1	5.0	14.6	12.0	–
Natural gas	1.7	3.8	5.8	5.3	–
Uranium	7.7	2.7	6.9	9.6	–

Source: BGR 2015.

211.4 million tons (5 per cent of total world production), while actual oil consumption amounted to 518 million tons (equal to 12.0 per cent of total world demand) (BGR 2015; BP 2015).

In 2014, the difference between domestic consumption and China's own production (net-import share) was already 59.5 per cent. The so-called 'depletion mid-point' for conventional oil or 'peak-oil' is likely to be achieved within the next 10 to 15 years followed by a successive decline in domestic production. Thus, a long-term increase of the import quota up to a value of almost 100 per cent can be expected in the future, if consumption is at least constant (Oberheitmann 2008).

Looking at the static availability of China's fossil energy reserves in 2014 (Table 19.1), i.e. domestic reserves divided by the respective consumption in that year, even hard coal would only last for another 31 years until 2045. The respective forecast for lignite is 52 years, but this energy source only plays a minor role in primary energy supply in China (about 4 per cent of total coal consumption in China). Based on current consumption patterns, domestic crude oil reserves would only be able to serve demand until 2019, although shale oil recovery might help expand availability for a couple of years. The static availability of natural gas and uranium is only 19 and 15 years respectively, but domestic demand is expected to further increase in the future as these respectively low-carbon and non-carbon energy sources are promoted in China as clean energies. Hence, static domestic availability of natural gas may quickly decrease within the years ahead, although shale gas recovery, if introduced, may fend off the decrease for some years. China has started to import coal and contracted natural gas imports.

In addition to fossil energy resources, China has abundant renewable energy resources. Hydropower potentials have been tapped already to a high degree. Wind energy resources are very significant and are rapidly developed. Solar radiation is very high in some parts of the country and sufficient in others. Falling cost in particular for photovoltaic technology transforms the resources increasingly to a technically and economically proven reserve. The fact that ideal conditions for developing renewable energy resources are rather found in the western remoter areas far away from the economic and densely populated centres in the east causes transportation bottlenecks. This is a common problem for China's energy supply, not only for the electricity sector.

In 2011, China surpassed the United States and became the world's leading producer of electric power (EIA 2015). Most of the electricity is generated with coal (63 per cent), followed by hydropower (22 per cent), wind energy (6 per cent) and natural gas (5 per cent). Oil, solar and biomass together account for 4 per cent of total power generation (EIA 2015). Power generation is still the largest coal consumer in China having considerable negative implications both on local and regional emissions such as sulphur dioxide (SO_2) and other pollutants (see below) as well as global carbon dioxide (CO_2) emissions. Transboundary SO_2 emissions are not only negatively affecting the environment in China (e.g. with acid rain), but also its neighbouring countries such as Korea and Japan.

Pivots and concepts of reconciling energy and environmental objectives

To control growing atmospheric emissions, China has introduced government programmes to decommission old high-emitting plants and to introduce end-of-pipe cleaning technologies for new plants and existing plants that have many more service years projected. These programmes have been implemented since the turn of the century and included the closure of many small-size old coal power plants and also the coal-fired small district thermal plants in urban areas of northern China. At first, the government used a command and control approach, which simply targeted in particular state-owned assets. The programme became part of development planning and Five-Year Plans, and supported the upgrading of larger units of coal power plants with higher efficiency, electric particle precipitators, DENOX equipment for de-nitrification and flue gas desulphurization plants. For desulphurization, however, the government experimented with a cap and trade approach within the eastern China region. Later, the polluter pays principle was introduced with emission ceilings in combination with polluter fees (Song et al. 2009). Emission standards for power plants, which have been in effect since 2003, became stricter in 2014 (WRI 2012).

The policy had mixed success. To supply electricity to a fast-growing demand, however, the generation companies expanded very rapidly coal power capacities and operations. During 2000–2005, the period when fossil power generation doubled from approximately 1,000 to 2,000 TWh, SO_2, NO_x and PM (particulate matter) emissions of coal-fired power plants increased by 1.5, 1.7 and 1.2 times respectively (Zhao et al. 2008). From 2005 to 2010, when fossil power generation grew again by approximately 1,000 TWh, the SO_2 and PM emissions were reduced whereas NO_x emission were stable from 2007 (Wang and Hao 2012) .

In order to address the double challenge of energy security and environmental protection, China made energy efficiency a top priority in 2004 in a special programme (NDRC 2004). This was a wide-ranging programme with an overall quantitative conservation objective in 2020 and targets for end-use sectors, principle products and services. It was a meticulous command and control programme with little economic incentive (Suding 2005).

Another pivotal policy, which is supposed to help with both energy security and emission mitigation, is the government support for non-fossil energy. In addition to the construction of large hydro dams and nuclear power stations, which are contested for other than air emission concerns, renewable energy is promoted. After the extremely successful expansion of solar heating since around 2000, which replaces electricity use and its emission-intensive generation, wind power has made a rapid expansion and solar power is on the rise. Due to slower electricity demand growth and more non-fossil generation i.e. hydropower, other renewable energies and nuclear power, the sector's coal use was reduced and CO_2 emission growth was halted in 2015 (Energy Post 2016).

Institutional rearrangements of energy and environmental policy

Since the turn of the twenty-first century, the energy sector has been included in the development of the 'socialist market economy', which has continuously unfolded. Planned allocation had been replaced by price allocation as principal allocation scheme in the economy. The respective operational decisions were based on price signals and market opportunities rather than on plan fulfilment, as were investment decisions by privately owned companies, which were increasingly dominant in services, commerce and light industry commodity production. State ownership was, however, retained for basic industries including the energy sector. The State-Owned Assets Supervision and Administration Commission (SASAC) was created in 2003 and is tasked with supervising the management of state-owned enterprises (SOE). There was a tendency to organize competition in more sectors, and even SOEs were forced to compete among themselves, with private or foreign owned companies. This became also a concept in parts of the energy sector (Suding 2005).

In 2003, the former State Development Planning Commission (SDPC) was renamed the National Development and Reform Commission (NDRC) while the former State Economic and Trade Commission (SETC) was dissolved, which only a few years earlier had incorporated the former subsector ministries, namely the Ministry for Electric Power as well as the competences for the oil and coal sector (Yang 2006). NDRC became a major player to introduce reforms in the energy sector. In the same year the National Energy Bureau was created under the NDRC reporting to the Chinese State Council, which has broad administrative and planning control over energy in the Chinese economy. The State Electricity Regulatory Commission (SERC) was also created the same year, which completed an entirely new institutional set-up.

In 2008, the National Energy Administration (NEA) was established but lacked power to carry out its tasks because the energy sector management was spread between various agencies. Finally, the National Energy Commission (NEC) was established in 2010 to coordinate the overall energy policies. NEC includes 23 members from other agencies such as environment, finance, central bank, NDRC and coordinates energy matters across all departments.

Interestingly, the NDRC did not situate the competence for energy efficiency with the Energy Bureau nor with and NEA, but rather with the Department of Resource Conservation and Environmental Protection. This indicates the perception that energy efficiency is: a) largely a task outside the energy supply sector; and b) associated with the solution of environmental issues.

Already before the turn of the century, the operative organizations of the energy sector (namely State Power and the oil companies) had gained some autonomy, when the various industry ministries were incorporated into SETC. The next step coincided with the rearrangement of SETC and SDPC to NDRC and the SASAC. Later on the vertically integrated State Power Corporation which had become extremely strong, was partly disintegrated into two regional grid companies and horizontally separated into five state-owned generation companies, which received all the assets except very large dams and were supposed to operate in the whole territory. These 'big five' companies generate currently nearly 50 per cent of

China's electricity. Much of the remainder is generated by locally-owned enterprises or by independent power producers, often in partnership with privately listed arms of the state-owned companies (EIA 2015). The SERC is fundamentally important also for the enforcement of environmental policy.

Whereas the institutional development of the traditionally strong energy sector went through a process of separation between energy supply, operative functions from supervision and policy functions, the institutions of Chinese environmental policy were created almost from scratch. Only in 1998, the National Environmental Agency was upgraded to the State Environmental Protection Administration (SEPA). Ten years later SEPA was finally elevated to ministry level (MEP). The relative delay of the institutionalization of environmental protections might be relative to the importance of energy and environmental policy, but the upgrading may also indicate a growing sense of the significance of environmental issues.

In 2005, the designated national authority for the Clean Development Mechanism (CDM) in China was installed under the NDRC, and later a Department of Climate Change was created within NDRC, which put NDRC firmly in the driving seat of China's climate policy.

An important feature of the Chinese administrative system is the 'double bind' of vertical and horizontal chains of instruction and/or reporting. Vertically, the departments of executive powers and – with particular strength – the departments under DRC, are represented on all levels of government, from central to provincial, municipal, and even to county and township levels. This includes assignment of officials. At the same time, department heads on each level report (horizontally) to the respective level government. In addition, there is a reward system for leading officials oriented towards a set of given goals. Thus vertical instruction needs to square with horizontal reporting.

This system also applies to SOEs, in particular the electricity sector, with a hierarchy of affiliates from the central to the local level utility. At the turn of the century, the power sector was still vertically integrated from generation to distribution. In 2002, power generation was separated and split in several SOEs, whereas the grid system remained integrated in two regionally delimitated SOEs. In addition, the hierarchical single-party system mirrored the vertical line of instruction and the reward system of the administration

Thus, there is an extremely powerful institutional framework to implement and enforce policies from top down. Nonetheless, there is also a risk of conflict, in particular when the priorities of a local government are in conflict with objectives of the central department. Typically, the local governments used to be very keen on their cities being top performers in economic growth, whereas the national sector departments needed success in their specific area of competence, i.e. the energy or environment departments, in attaining their objective indicators. In order to provide more weight in decentralized decisions, the indicator systems for evaluation of provincial and local officers were modified to include energy efficiency or pollution control targets. Apparently, the 'fragmented authoritarianism', which scholars had diagnosed already during the early stages of economic reform (Lieberthal 1992) was or may be still at work.

With the increasing numbers of private enterprises, local governments lost direct control, and saw their powers reduced. Administrative instruction did not work to reach objectives any more. Some found new ways to implement their objectives and to reap rewards, which bore the risk that 'public authority and assets are extensively traded by state agents for self-defined purposes' (Lin 2001).

With economic reforms, some tools of the planning traditions continued to be used in energy policy although with a modified purpose. Long-term energy forecasting had become a tool for supporting decisions rather than a rigid planning framework. Five-Year-Plans continued to be prepared and adopted on all levels and departments as a tool for coherent general programming across departments, but not as a rigid allocation framework.

Special transitory programmes were drawn up to deal with specific issues, such as energy inefficiency. These latter programmes were, however, still characterized by the spirit of command and control, rather than using indirect incentive policies. Typically, a programme had a number of important pilot projects financed by the state, i.e. public investment.

An organizational specialty of the reform process was the 'leading group' by representatives of the concerned departments and sectors, which was formed in order to study and design a reform in a specific subsector, in which the state deemed to need reform. Nonetheless, policies or specific measures may also originate from other bodies than the executive arm of government. Subcommittees of the legislature bodies would take the initiative to propose new pieces of legal framework, as happened in the case of the renewable energy legislation, and work year round in order to submit them to the People's Congress (NPC) once a year. In some cases, the reform design was tested first in a limited region and/or with non-legislative measures before becoming codified in a law. The classical Chinese approach 'crossing the river by feeling the stones' was applied also in the energy sector.

All these idiosyncrasies of Chinese policy making and implementation have had and continue to have consequences for the success of energy policy.

Current and future main challenges and drivers for environmental and energy policy in the twenty-first century

Urbanization, economic growth and impacts on climate change

In 30 years of reform policies, China witnessed an urbanization of unprecedented pace. It took 120 years in the UK, 40 years in the US, 30 years in Japan, but only 22 years in China to increase the urbanization rate from 20 per cent to 40 per cent (Oberheitmann and Ruan 2012). Currently, more than half of China's 1.4 billion people (2014: 53.7 per cent) live in urban areas; this corresponds to the world average. According to the National New-type Urbanization Plan (2014–2020), by 2020, the urbanization rate is expected to reach 60 per cent (Xinhua Net 2014). It is further expected that the trend to urbanization will continue over the next 30 years. At present already

- 85 per cent of Chinese GDP is generated in cities.
- 90 per cent of the Chinese service industry is located in cities.
- 75 per cent of the total Chinese energy use is consumed in cities.

Cities highlight a variety of environmental problems such as large, concentrated resources consumption and impacts on ecological systems (Stern 2006). And cities are becoming increasingly vulnerable to the impacts of climate change, for example to extreme weather events such as heatwaves, typhoons and floods (IPCC 2014). Faced by these pressures, a low-carbon economy and the development of low-carbon cities is vital for China. In the scientific discourse on climate and energy policy, the so-called Kaya identity (Kaya 1990) is used to describe the most important determinants of CO_2 emissions. These determinants are population, per capita GDP, primary energy intensity of GDP and the CO_2 intensity of primary energy supply.

In 2013, average per capita income in China was 2,747 per cent higher compared to 1965. The population grew by 92 per cent in the same time period and thus had a much lower effect on the growth of CO_2 emissions in China. The growth of the emissions is reduced through:

- a reduction of the energy intensity of GDP or by increasing energy efficiency of generating GDP in the various economic sectors, e.g. in industry (APEC 2011) or in the building sector (Oberheitmann 2011); and
- by reducing the CO_2 intensity of primary energy supply, i.e. by fuel substitution in favour of lower-carbon primary energy sources (natural gas and petroleum) and the increased use of zero-carbon renewable energy sources (hydropower, wind energy, solar energy, nuclear energy etc.).

Between 1965 and 2010, the energy intensity of GDP decreased by 60 per cent but the CO_2 intensity of primary energy consumption by only 11 per cent. Hence, the impact of energy efficiency gains in transformation and energy end use is much more prevalent than the changes in energy mix. This phenomenon is evident not only at the aggregate national level, but also at the level of cities (Oberheitmann 2012).

These factors have a significant impact. Comparing the development of the GDP, primary energy consumption and CO_2 emissions in China in the past 50 years (Figure 19.1), a decoupling of economic development (measured by GDP), energy consumption and related environmental impact (measured by absolute CO_2 emissions) can be seen since about 1990.

Interestingly, econometric tests using the Granger causality approach (Granger 1969; Sims 1972; Granger 1988) show that economic development only since the beginning of economic reform in China in 1978 has a significant explanatory effect on primary energy consumption and associated CO_2 emissions (Oberheitmann and Frondel 2006). Until 1978, China, being a 100 per cent planned economy, the explanation direction was the other way around, i.e. energy consumption was able to explain economic growth.

The decoupling of environmental pollution and economic development is a phenomenon that is visible both in the comparison of different countries in one respective year and in a certain country over time. In environmental economics, this hypothesis, building upon the work of Kuznets (1955) for economic growth and income inequality, is described by the so-called 'Environmental Kuznets Curve'. The hypothesis of this inverted U-shaped curve is that in a given country, the negative environmental impacts of increasing development first increase, but from a certain value of per capita income and increasing environmental awareness decrease (Grossman and Krueger 1991; Grossman and Krueger 1995). For China, this hypothesis so

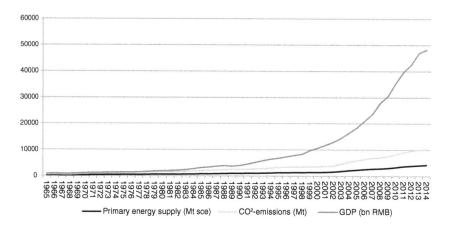

Figure 19.1   Development of GDP, primary energy supply and CO_2 emissions in China 1965–2014 (BP 2015, State Statistical Bureau 2015, authors' calculations)

far can only be demonstrated in the rising part of the Environmental Kuznets Curve; the need for the reduction of emissions per capita income is apparently not yet reached (Oberheitmann and Li 2008).

Hence, in order to improve environmental and economic conditions in China, cities are becoming increasingly important. Apart from climate change-related challenges, increasing coal combustion in particular is leading to local emissions such as particulate matters and acid rain.

Climate change impact and vulnerability

In China, the impact of climate change is visible. Compared to the average for 1961–1990, since the 1980s, surface temperatures have significantly increased. China, especially the northern part, including Beijing, Tianjin, the provinces of Hebei, Henan, Shandong, Shanxi, Anhui Province and parts of Inner Mongolia, is increasingly vulnerable to the adverse effects of climate change, such as water scarcity (only 500 cubic metres per capita are available every year) (Zhou 2008), which also affects the cooling of power plants, the water balance of hydropower plants and more recently the fracking for shale oil and gas. Climate change leads to a higher probability of floods in southern China as well as the coasts of the East and South China Sea. On the Tibetan Plateau, climate change led to a change in river flows and melting of glaciers (Lai 2009; Tiezzi 2014; Heggelund and Nadin chapter 8 this volume).

Synergies of energy security, environmental protection and climate change policies

In China, energy security, environmental protection and climate change mitigation must be seen in a close political relationship. Against the background of a tradition of self-sufficiency in energy, which is still a key concept to increase security, and in view of an increasingly precarious resource situation, environmental protection and climate change mitigation policy in China have become new elements of energy security policy (Oberheitmann 2009). To put it in a nutshell: saving 1 ton of CO_2 by increasing energy efficiency or fuel substitution in favour of low-carbon (natural gas and mineral oil) or carbon-free energy sources (renewables and nuclear energy) saves 360 kg of coal, 325 kg of crude oil or 460 cubic metres of natural gas. Thus, climate change mitigation policy helps to mitigate the following prevailing energy security issues.

About two-thirds (65.2 per cent in 2014) of China's primary energy is coal (BP 2015). Coal industry in China traditionally has been fragmented among large state-owned coal mines, local state-owned coal mines, and thousands of town and village coal mines. The top state-owned coal companies and main players on the coal market are Shenhua Group and China National Coal Group, which produce about half of the country's coal. Local state-owned companies account for about 20 per cent, and small town mines for 30 per cent of total coal output in China (EIA 2015). The predominant energy security issue related to coal in China is not availability but transport. Coal still accounts for more than 50 per cent of the total freight volume by rail in China. There have been repeated transport shortages of coal in China due to missing or poor transport routes (Transport policy net 2014). Since 60 per cent of the coal is not washed due to the lack of water in many coalfields, a considerable part of coal transport is energetically unusable rock (SDS Ventures 2013). The saving of coal by climate change mitigation policies and measures including introducing clean coal technologies (highly efficient super-critical and ultra-supercritical power generation units with up to 20 per cent less emissions compared to conventional thermal power plants, demonstration projects for carbon capture and storage etc.) and related regulations, such as the *Thermal Power Plant Emission Standards* (2012), can make a valuable contribution to increasing energy security improvement and greenhouse gas emission reduction as well as cleaner coal combustion with lower dust emissions. Since 2007, the share of coal in total primary energy supply is slowly decreasing. This has a positive impact on the average carbon intensity of primary energy supply.

In contrast to coal, the availability of mineral oil, which in 2014 accounted for 17.8 per cent of primary energy supply in China (BP 2014), is perceived as an energy security problem in view of the self-sufficiency paradigm. In particular, the volatility in the international crude oil markets is considered negative for the competitiveness of the domestic industry. Again, crude oil savings through climate protection activities, such as the increase of fuel efficiency in cars for environmental reasons, also reduce the perceived energy security challenge of rising crude oil imports. Against this background, in 2013, the Chinese government announced their intention to reduce the average fuel consumption of passenger cars to 6.9 litres per 100 kilometres by 2015 and 5.0 litres/100 km by 2020 (Richard 2013). As fuel demand is price inelastic, falling oil prices have little effect on private transport demand. Short term, they might reduce the pressure to increase fuel efficiency.

On another line of increasing energy security, since 2008 China's national oil companies (CNPC, Sinopec and CNOOC) have rapidly expanded their purchases of international oil and natural gas assets through direct acquisitions of equity and financial loans in exchange for oil supplies, in order to secure more oil and gas supplies, to make long-term commercial investments and to gain technical expertise in more challenging oil and natural gas ventures (EIA 2015). The Middle East remains the largest source of China's crude oil imports, although African countries, particularly Angola, have begun contributing more to China's imports in the past decade. As part of China's energy-supply security policy, the country's national oil companies are attempting to diversify supply sources in various regions through overseas investments in upstream oil projects and long-term contracts. Chinese companies are participating in upstream activities in 42 countries, and half of the overseas oil production stems from the Middle East and Africa.

Similar to coal, for natural gas, which accounted for 6.2 per cent of total primary energy supply in China in 2013, transport is a limiting factor (BP 2015). Since the construction of the West–East pipeline, this problem is largely under control. Over the past four years, China has also increased imports of natural gas via international pipelines as gas production from Central Asia and Myanmar grew and gas infrastructure in the region improved (EIA 2015). Hence, currently, domestic sources can largely meet demand.

Since the Chinese government promotes fuel substitution from coal to natural gas, the demand for clean-energy gas increases. Therefore, it is only a matter of time until the transport and then also the availability problem becomes virulent again. Environmental policy amplifies the energy security problem as the use of natural gas tends to be largely based on local pollution control (reduction of particulate matters such as $PM_{2.5}$) and climate change mitigation policy consideration (Oberheitmann 2009). Hence, the use of gas will further increase, and bottlenecks may even quickly re-occur. In order to improve the framework conditions for the gas transport sector, in February 2014, NDRC introduced *The Management Measures of Natural Gas Infrastructure Construction and Operation*, effective from 1 April 2014. The aims of these measures are to 'regulate the construction and operation of natural gas infrastructure, encourage different types of investment into the natural gas infrastructure market and to further liberalize the market by promoting fair competition' (King and Wood Mallisons 2014).

The highly controversial, from an environmental point of view, exploitation of shale gas is also discussed as an option in China. Even though China's shale gas industry has huge growth potential, currently it is still in its early stages. Developers and regulators are still working through many challenges. Most of China's proven shale gas resources are in the Sichuan and

Tarim basins in the southern and western regions, and in the northern and north-eastern basins (EIA 2015). Currently, due to low oil prices, shale oil extraction is not economically viable. In addition, water shortages are a huge challenge, for example in Xinjiang.

Similar to oil, main actors in the natural gas sector are CNPC, Sinopec and CNOOC. Growth in natural gas demand in recent years, particularly in the urban coastal areas, has led China to become the world's third-largest liquefied natural gas (LNG) importer after Japan and South Korea since China built its first re-gasification terminal, Dapeng LNG, in 2006 (EIA 2015).

As for electricity, the current energy security problem nowadays lies less with availability of generation supply capacity, but more with transportation (grid stability, congestion). China's energy security and low-carbon strategy builds as well on nuclear power, but ambitious plans have been scaled down after the Fukushima nuclear disaster in 2011 (World Nuclear Association 2014). By increasing variable renewable energy capacities, especially for wind and solar energy (144 GW and 44 GW, respectively, installed by the end of 2015; REN21 2016), the diverging non-dispatchable production and power consumption patterns over time and geography are becoming a challenge for transmission, in particular balancing demand and guaranteeing grid stability in the short term and assuring coverage of load profile in the long run. Currently, the electricity generation in wind power plants highly concentrated in north-west China encounters technical challenges and regulatory obstacles.

Here again, climate protection clashes with energy security issues as the additional construction of renewable energy is largely motivated by climate policy. China's government is pushing for regional diversification and chronological divergence of renewable energy resources by supporting utility-scale solar power and recently also consumer-scale solar PV. China is forecasted to have an installed onshore and offshore wind capacity of approximately 230 GW by 2020 and a solar PV power capacity of 100 GW (IRENA 2014). The solution of these issues, however, in combination with smart grids (Brunekreeft et al. 2015) presents also a huge business opportunity (Yuan et al. 2014).

Although, since the economic reforms in the last century, the Chinese economy's overall trend of energy and carbon efficiency is improving, the specific policies of energy efficiency have rarely met their targets on time. In subsectors like housing, where many new non-government actors were required to implement the required measures, the classical command and control approach did not work, as long as the prices and the incentive structures were not in line. In addition, reward structures of the local authorities did not include rewards for efficiency and environmental protection. Incentives were added to policies and reward structures changed only at the end of the first decade of 2000. With respect to renewable energy, the developments were entirely different. The growth of renewable energy until the end of 2014 (wind power capacity of 96 GW) was much faster than it was announced and planned by NDRC in 2005 (30 GW for 2020). The driving forces are again on the local and provincial level, in this case producing over-achievement. Local businesses and authorities see renewables as an opportunity for the development of their area. Hot spots of wind and solar energy generation coincide with provinces where the respective industries are blossoming. Nonetheless, some energy policy measures and climate mitigation measures, including the programme on energy efficiency in existing buildings, the introduction of CDM and others, were effective in using the classical concept of vertical integration.

Summary and outlook to the future

This chapter has provided an insight into the background and institutional arrangements as well as an analysis of the main drivers for China's environmental and energy policy. China faces three major challenges of environmental and energy policy in the twenty-first century: economic growth and increasing urbanization, vulnerability to the adverse impacts of climate change, and energy security issues. Energy and environmental policy has to cope with these issues. Currently, China is still in the dilemma of economic growth-related energy requirements and the resulting growth of global greenhouse gas emissions and local pollutants. Currently, China's urbanization rate is about 50 per cent, increasing urbanization in China (forecast at 60 per cent in 2020; Ying 2010) will lead both to growing concentration of spot emissions of these gases from cities and to an increasing emission of local pollutants in urban environments. In 2007, China surpassed the United States as the largest contributor to CO_2 emissions. In 2014, about 67 per cent of the worldwide CO_2 emission growth in the preceding ten years was accumulated on China's account (BP 2015). With increasing urbanization, large cities, especially those in coastal regions are increasingly vulnerable to the adverse impacts of climate change. Economic growth also increases energy security challenges for China, especially as the country is still trying to rely on domestic resources as much as possible.

Currently, China is the world's largest investor in renewable energies (REN21 2016). However, besides hydropower, other renewable energies still only account for approximately 3 per cent of total final energy supply within a total of 11.1 per cent of non-fossil energies. China has the target to increase this share to 20 per cent by 2020 (REN21 2016). Thus, on a global scale, China's intentions to use its opportunities to significantly contribute to climate change mitigation now and in the future are still due to the country's currently still low labour costs for the production of clean technology, especially of cheap renewable energy sources such as solar power.

Energy security policy and environmental policy, especially climate protection, are going hand in hand, as saving energy through energy efficiency improvements for energy security reasons is directly linked to the reduction of local pollutants and the emissions of global GHGs such as CO_2. For the foreseeable future, China will still be in the dilemma of economic growth and environmental pollution. This raises the question of when the emissions per capita will cease increasing along with growing per capita income as assumed in the Environmental Kuznets Curve hypothesis. In terms of international responsibilities and related actions, the difference for China compared to developed countries, however, is the rapid increase of economic growth-related emissions in China. Future climate problems can only be solved together with China because China's share of world greenhouse gas emissions will continue to grow.

Keeping global warming within the 2°C target by 2050 is still subject to the implementation of the Paris agreement of 2015 (becoming effective in 2020) and proposals of the international climate change community for a post-Kyoto climate protection regime. For example, in a post-Kyoto approach based on cumulative per capita CO_2 emission rights, including (Oberheitmann 2010) or excluding (WBGU 2009) the historical emissions of the individual states before 1990, China would only have until about 2025 to stabilize the growth of their CO_2 emissions. Against this background, the emission peak by 2030 envisaged by the Chinese government in the INDC to UNFCCC seems to be too late to be able to stabilize global warming to 2°C by 2050. If, however, the current reduction of coal intensity of primary energy supply and the reduction of economic growth in China persists, there might be a realistic chance to reach the peak even before 2030 and thus have a chance to limit CO_2 emissions before it is too late.

Note

1   2.6 per cent of the world reserves of lignite, 1.1 per cent of the world reserves of oil, 1.7 per cent of the world reserves of natural gas and 7.7 per cent of the world reserves of uranium (BGR 2015).

References

APEC, 2011. *Economy Update – China: China Industrial Energy Efficiency Programs and Projects Update.* Submitted by: China. 37th Expert Group on Energy Efficiency and Conservation Meeting Washington, D.C., United States 28 February–2 March 2011.

BGR (Bundesanstalt für Geowissenschaften und Rohstoffe), 2015. *Energiestudie 2015: Reserven, Ressourcen und Verfügbarkeit von Energierohstoffen* (19). Hanover, Germany: BGR.

BP, 2014. *BP Statistical Review of World Energy June 2014.* Available at http://www.bp.com/statisticalreview (accessed 11 December 2016).

BP, 2015. *BP Statistical Review of World Energy June 2015.* Available at https://www.bp.com/content/dam/bp/pdf/energy-economics/statistical-review-2015/bp-statistical-review-of-world-energy-2015-full-report.pdf (accessed 11 December 2016).

Brunekreeft, G.; Luhmann, T.; Menz, T.; Müller, S.U. and Recknagel, P. 2015. China's way from conventional power grids towards smart grids, in *Regulatory Pathways for Smart Grid Development in China*, pp. 19–43. Berlin: Springer Vieweg.

EIA (Energy Information Administration), 2015. *China – International energy data and analysis.* http://www.eia.gov/beta/international/analysis.cfm?iso=CHN (accessed 20 December 2016).

Energy Post, 2016. China's electricity mix: changing so fast that CO_2 emissions may have peaked. Available at http://energypost.eu/chinas-electricity-mix-changing-fast-co2-emissions-may-peaked/ (accessed 11 December 2016).

Granger, C.W.J., 1969. Investigating causal relations by econometrics models and cross spectral models. *Econometrica* 37, 424–438.

Granger, C.W.J., 1988. Some recent developments in a concept of causality. *Journal of Econometrics* 39, 199–211.

Grossmann, G.M. and Krueger, A.B., 1991. Environmental impacts of a North American free trade arrangement. National Bureau of Economic Research Working Paper No. 3914. Cambridge, MA: NBER.

Grossmann, G.M. and Krueger, A.B., 1995. Economic growth and the Environment. *Quarterly Journal of Economics* 110 (2), 352–377.

IPCC, 2014. Climate Change 2014: Synthesis Report. Contribution of Working Groups I, II and III to the Fifth Assessment Report of the Intergovernmental Panel on Climate Change [Core Writing Team, Pachauri, R.K and Meyer, L. (eds.)]. Geneva, Switzerland: IPCC.

IRENA, 2014. Renewable energy prospects: China, REmap 2030 analysis. Abu Dhabi: IRENA. Available at http://irena.org/remap/IRENA_REmap_China_report_2014.pdf (accessed 11 December 2016).

Kaya, Y., 1990. Impact of carbon dioxide emission control on GNP growth: interpretation of proposed scenarios. Paper presented at the IPCC Energy and Industry Subgroup, Response Strategies Working Group. Paris: Mimeo.

King and Wood Mallisons, 2014. China further liberalizes the natural gas infrastructure market—the management measures of natural gas infrastructure construction and operation took effect as of April 1, 2014. In China Law Insight – Energy and Resource. http://www.chinalawinsight.com/2014/05/articles/energy-resource/china-further-liberalizes-the-natural-gas-infrastructure-market-the-management-measures-of-natural-gas-infrastructure-construction-and-operation-took-effect-as-of-april-1-2014/ (accessed: 11 December 2016).

Kuznets, S.S., 1955. Economic growth and income inequality. *American Economic Review* 45 (1), 1–28.

Lai E., 2009. Climate change impacts on China environment: biophysical impacts. China Environmental Health Project Research Brief, February 2009. Washington, DC: Mimeo.

Lieberthal, K.G., 1992. Introduction. The 'fragmented authoritarianism' model and its limitations. In Lieberthal, K.G.; Lampton D.M. (eds), *Bureaucracy, Politics, and Decision Making in Post-Mao China.* Berkeley: University of California Press.

Lin Y.M., 2001. *Between Politics and Markets Firms: Competition and Institutional Change in Post-Mao China.* Cambridge, UK and New York: Cambridge University Press.

National Development and Reform Commission (NDRC), 2004. Medium- and long-term energy conservation plan (Unofficial translation: Mimeo). Beijing: NDRC.

Oberheitmann, A., 2008. Ökonomische Modernisierung in Ostasien im Spannungsfeld der Umwelt- und Energiesicherheitspolitik. In Maull, H. W.; Wagener, M. (eds), *Prekäre Macht, fragiler Wohlstand? Globalisierung und Politik in Ostasien* pp, 83–110. Baden-Baden: Nomos.

Oberheitmann, A., 2009. *China's Energy Security Strategy and the Regional Environment – Assessment of Economic Growth and its Environmental Impact Applying a Dynamic Welfare Optimisation Approach.* Saarbrücken: VDM-Verlag.

Oberheitmann, A., 2010. A new post-Kyoto climate regime based on per capita cumulative emissions rights – rationale, architecture and quantitative assessment of the implication for the CO_2-emissions from China, India and the Annex-I countries by 2050. *Mitigation and Adaptation Strategies for Global Change* 15 (2), 137–168.

Oberheitmann, A., 2011. CO_2-emission reduction in China's residential building sector and contribution to the national climate change mitigation targets in 2020. *Mitigation and Adaptation Strategies for Global Change.* Springer. DOI: 10.1007s11027-011-9343-5.

Oberheitmann, A., 2012. Development of a Low Carbon Economy in Wuxi City. *American Journal of Climate Change* 1 (2), 64–103.

Oberheitmann, A. and Frondel, M., 2006. The dark side of China's increasing economic prosperity: will energy consumption and global emissions rise drastically? Bleischwitz, R.; Budzinski, O. (eds.) *Environmental Economics – Institutions, Competition, Rationality. INFER Annual Conference 2004, Wuppertal, Germany,* pp. 207–224. Berlin: VWF.

Oberheitmann, A. and Li, Y., 2008. Main factors of decoupling China's energy related emissions from its economic growth – Where is China on the Environmental Kuznets Curve? *Asien* 1, 7–23.

Oberheitmann, A. and Ruan, X., 2012. Low carbon city planning in China. In Urban, F.; and Nordensvard, J. (eds), *Low Carbon Development: Key Issues* pp.270–283. London: Earthscan, Routledge.

REN21, 2016. *Renewables 2016 Global Status Report,* Paris. Available at http://www.ren21.net/status-of-renewables/global-status-report/ (accessed 11 December 2016).

Richard, M.G., 2013. China increases 2020 fuel economy standard to 47 MPG. *Treehugger,* 26 March. Available at http://www.treehugger.com/cars/china-increases-2020-fuel-economy-standard-47-mpg.html (accessed: 11 December 2016).

SDS Ventures, 2013. Greening the Chinese coal sector: business opportunities for the Netherlands. Beijing: Mimeo.

Song H., Cosbey, A. and Savage M., 2009. China's electrical power sector, environmental protection and sustainable trade, International Institute for Sustainable Development, December 2009; Available at https://www.iisd.org/sites/default/files/publications/china_power_sector_sd.pdf (accessed 11 December 2016).

Sims, C.A., 1972. Money, income and causality. *American Economic Review* 62, 540–552.

State Statistical Bureau, 2015. *China Statistical Yearbook.* Beijing: China Statistics Press.

Stern, N.S., 2006. Review of the economics of climate change. Available at http://webarchive.nationalarchives.gov.uk/ (accessed 17 November 2014).

Suding, P., 2005. Using all energy sources and efficiency to keep people's dream of prosperity alive. In World Energy Council 2005. *China's Energy Supply: Many Paths – One Goal* pp. 9–41. Berlin: WEC.

Tiezzi, S., 2014. In China, climate change is already here. *The Diplomat,* 14 August. Available at http://thediplomat.com/2014/08/in-china-climate-change-is-already-here/ (accessed 11 December 2016).

Transport policy net, 2014. China: Light-duty: Emissions. Available at http://transportpolicy.net/index.php?title=China:_Light-duty:_Emissions (accessed 11 December 2016).

WBGU – German Advisory Council on Climate Change, 2009. Solving the climate dilemma – the budget approach. Berlin: Mimeo.

World Nuclear Association, 2014. Nuclear power in China (updated December 2014). Available at http://www.world-nuclear.org/info/country-profiles/countries-a-f/china--nuclear-power/ (accessed 11 December 2016).

Wang, S. and Hao J., 2012. Emissions of air pollutants from power plants in China, Powerpoint Presentation. Tsinghua University, 9 October 2012.

WRI, 2012. China adopts world-class pollutant emission standards for coal power plants (June 2012). World Resources Institute. Available at http://www.chinafaqs.org/files/chinainfo/China%20FAQs%20Emission%20Standards%20v1.4_0.pdf (accessed 11 December 2016).

Xinhua Net, 2014. China unveils landmark urbanization plan. Available at: http://news.xinhuanet.com/english/china/2014-03/16/c_133190495.htm (accessed 28 April 2016).

Yang, H., 2006. Overview of the Chinese electricity industry and its current issues. Cambridge Working Papers in Economics. Available at http://econpapers.repec.org/paper/camcamdae/0617.htm (accessed 11 December 2016).

Yuan J., Shen J., Pan L. and Zhao C., 2014. Smart grids in China. *Renewable & Sustainable Energy Reviews* 37 (9), 896–906.

Ying C., 2010. Overview of the 30 years of China's urbanisation (in Chinese). Available at http://www.chinacity.org.cn/cstj/csfz30/53369.html (accessed 19 November 2015).

Zhou Y., 2008. Vulnerability and adaptation to climate change in North China: the water sector in Tianjin. Research unit Sustainability and Global Change, Hamburg University and Centre for Marine and Atmospheric Science. Hamburg, Germany: Mimeo.

Zhao Y., Wang S., Duan L., Lei Y., Cao P. and Hao J., 2008. Primary air pollutant emissions of coal-fired power plants in China: Current status and future prediction. *Atmospheric Environment* 42 (36), 8442–8452.

20

GREEN ENERGY INNOVATION IN CHINA

Joanna I. Lewis

Introduction

China's green innovation strategy has propelled its clean energy sector to be among the largest in the world. As a latecomer to the clean energy innovation field, cooperation with many of the countries that have expertise in specific clean energy technologies has been a very important way for Chinese firms to enter this sector. These technology transfers to China from overseas firms have led in many cases to fruitful cooperation, and occasionally to tense relationships over intellectual property. This rise has also launched international trade battles with its biggest green technology competitors.

China's ability to leapfrog to cleaner energy technologies will be determined in part by its ability to become an innovator and global leader in the development of these technologies that it so critically needs. Its entry into these sectors also has important implications for the ability of these technologies to diffuse globally. For example, China's entry into the manufacturing of wind and solar technologies has led to significant cost reductions and increased learning globally.

This chapter examines China's national green innovation strategy, particularly as relates to the development of two of its leading clean energy technology sectors: the wind and solar power industries. It begins by examining China's national energy sector trends during the 12th and 13th Five-Year Plan (FYP) periods, including the drivers of China's national energy policy strategy, and the role of different energy sources and sectors driving energy consumption. It then turns to an examination of the increasingly important role that clean energy is playing in China's domestic energy innovation agenda in recent years, including key research and development (R&D) programmes and institutions involved in promoting innovation in the sector. The chapter then evaluates the factors that led to the successful development of China's wind and solar power sectors, followed by a review of the trade and intellectual property tensions that its clean energy dominance has created. It concludes with a discussion of the outlook for continued green energy innovation, including potential challenges and opportunities China faces in the coming years.

Energy in the 12th and 13th Five-Year Plan periods

China's science and technology (S&T) priorities in the energy sector have changed over time with evolving domestic energy needs. The decade that preceded the 12th FYP period (from 2000–2010) brought new challenges to the relationship among energy consumption, emissions, and economic growth in China. From 2002–2005, two decades of declining energy intensity reversed, with energy growth surpassing economic growth. This reversal has had dramatic implications for energy security and greenhouse gas emissions growth trends in China during the latter part of the last decade. By 2007 China's CO_2 emissions were up 8 per cent from the previous year, making China the largest national emitter in the world. By 2010 China became the world's largest energy consumer and producer, and was emitting almost 50 per cent more CO_2 annually than the United States and over 100 per cent more than the European Union.

Increasing concerns among China's leadership about national energy security also shape China's domestic energy policy agenda. China became a net importer of petroleum products in 1993 and is now the world's largest oil importer, and second-largest consumer of oil behind the United States. China's long-term energy security is dependent not only on having sufficient supplies of energy to sustain its very high rate of economic growth but also on being able to manage the growth in energy demand without causing intolerable environmental damage. China's increase in energy-related pollution in the past few years has been driven primarily by industrial energy use, fuelled by an increased percentage of coal in the overall energy mix. Industry consumes about 70 per cent of China's energy, and China's industrial base supplies much of the world. As a result, China's current environmental challenges are fuelled in part by the global demand for its products.

As a result, China's 12th and 13th FYPs (2011–2020) aim to promote the service industries because of their higher value-added to the economy, as well as for the potential energy saving and environmental quality benefits associated with a shift away from heavy manufacturing. To facilitate this industrial shift, the government explicitly identified a new set of high-value strategic industries in the 12th FYP as essential to the future of the Chinese economy. Many low-carbon energy industries were targeted for government support, including the nuclear, solar, wind and biomass energy technology industries, as well as hybrid and electric vehicles, and energy savings and environmental protection technology industries (Government of the People's Republic of China [PRC] 2010; Government of the People's Republic of China 2011). These 'strategic and emerging' industries are being promoted to replace the 'old' strategic industries such as coal and telecom, often referred to as China's pillar industries, which are heavily state-owned and have long benefited from government support. Over 70 per cent of SOE assets and profits are concentrated in the 'old' strategic industries.

The 12th FYP also included a target to increase non-fossil energy sources (including hydro, nuclear and renewable energy) to 11.4 per cent of total energy use up from about 8.3 per cent in 2010, which was achieved; the target has been increased to 15 per cent by 2020 in the 13th FYP (People.com.cn 2011; Seligsohn and Hsu 2016). Other relevant 13th FYP clean energy targets include 200 GW of wind power and 100 GW of solar by 2020, along with the other targets listed in Table 20.1. The 12th FYP solar target for 2015 was increased several times; the previous target was 15 GW, which had just months before been increased from an earlier target of 5 GW. In 2015, China added more than 15 GW of new solar capacity bringing it to 43 GW total and surpassing Germany as the world's largest solar power market (Martin 2016).

China's carbon intensity targets have been a cornerstone of the country's climate policy and the pledges made to the UNFCCC, first in Copenhagen in 2009 and then in Paris in 2016. China's 12th and 13th FYP targets were designed to help the country meet its Copenhagen

Table 20.1 Clean energy targets in China's 12th and 13th FYP

Target type	12th FYP target (2010–2015)	Actual level achieved by 2015	13th FYP target (2016–2020)
Hydro power	260 GW	319 GW	350 GW
Wind power	100 GW	129 GW	200 GW
Solar power	35 GW	43 GW	100 GW (150 GW)
Nuclear	40 GW	26 GW	58 GW
Carbon intensity	17% ↓ from 2010	20% ↓ from 2010	18% ↓ from 2015
Energy intensity	16% ↓ from 2010	18.2 % ↓ from 2010	15% ↓ from 2015
Non-fossil share of primary energy	11.4%	12%	15%

Source: Government of the People's Republic of China 2011; Su 2010; National Climate Strategy Center 2014; NDRC 2014; Seligsohn and Hsu 2016.

target, which is to reduce carbon dioxide emissions per unit of GDP by 40–45 per cent by 2020 compared to 2005 levels (Su 2010). China's nationally determined contribution (NDC) submitted in advance of the Paris Agreement extends its carbon intensity targets to 2030, with a 60–65 per cent reduction from 2005 levels. China's pledges under the Paris Agreement also include an aim to achieve the peaking of CO_2 emissions around 2030, 'making best efforts to peak early', and extend the non-fossil energy target to a 20 per cent share by 2030, reaching into the next two FYP periods (NDRC, Department of Climate Change 2015).

Despite increasing carbon emissions and a continued reliance on coal, recent policies to promote clean energy in China and slow fossil energy demand appear to be working. Even as China's electricity system has added 80–90 GW every year for the past decade, the share of non-fossil energy in these new additions is growing. In 2013, new non-fossil energy capacity additions, including renewables, nuclear and hydro, surpassed thermal installations for the first time. It is also increasingly becoming clear that coal consumption peaked that year (Evans 2015), and as of 2016 has not yet gone back up.

Clean energy in China's innovation agenda

The concept of a 'low-carbon economy' began taking hold in China over the last decade. Some would trace the origins of China's low-carbon strategy to the emergence of what was called the 'scientific viewpoint of development', developed in the Central Economic Work Conference in December 2004 (Zang 2009). In the past, economic growth was based on high-volume consumption of energy and raw materials, causing heavy pollution, low output and low efficiency, whereas this growth mode would be based on conservation, science and technology (People's Daily Online 2004a; People's Daily Online 2004b).

Since economic reforms began in China in 1978, innovation performance in Chinese energy industries has been strengthened. The political and economic reforms that have most likely influenced the innovation system include the decentralization of decision making and resource allocation, the encouragement of competition between firms, the increased competition for labour and for jobs, the greater diversity within organizations and less functional specialization, and the increased public R&D funding for basic research (Lewis 2013).

By 1993 more than half of China's large state-owned enterprises had established technical development centres aimed at improving production efficiency as well as increasing product quality and marketability. Innovation performance has been shown to be strongest in those industries that have experienced the most institutional transformation and increased market competition in the post-reform period, while industries that have maintained the pre-reform characteristics of central control and weak intellectual property protection have demonstrated less innovative activity (Karplus 2007). China's SOEs still dominate much of the energy sector, and industrial R&D investments remain comparatively weak as technology investments continue to be predominantly determined and financed by the central government.

The 2000s were a crucial time for building institutional, scientific, and technical capacity in clean energy within China. Clean energy industries are now central to the government's push for a stronger, innovation-based economy, and the target of numerous domestic programmes in the 12th Five-Year Plan. Having recently become a global leader in the manufacturing of many core clean energy technologies, China has seen increases in both public and private R&D spending across clean energy fields. Since 2013 it has led the world in new renewable energy investments, surpassing the United States and the European Union, and in 2015 its annual investment reached US$102.9 billion, as illustrated in Figure 20.1.

The 13th FYP period so far has seen a major overhaul of China's national S&T support system, which has become a targeted sector for broader government reforms. Plans for reform include centralization of S&T funding authority that had previously been spread across multiple actors and government ministries with little coordination. The new model proposes reorganizing S&T support and integrating all existing programmes into five new overarching categories for S&T support (NSF Beijing Office 2016). This means China's cornerstone R&D programmes, including the '973 National Basic Research Program' named for its establishment in March of 1997, and the '863 National High-Tech Program' named for its establishment in March 1986, will no longer exist in their current form. A key element of the new model is a coordinated focus on key projects of particular national importance, with various stages of R&D support targeting specific technologies and industries. Specific green energy industries, including electric or new energy vehicles, are one such targeted industry under the new S&T support model.

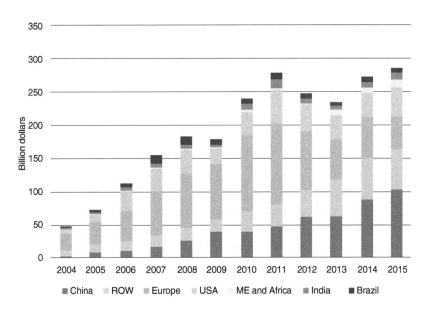

Figure 20.1 Annual renewable energy investments by country or region

Notes: ROW = Rest of world; ME = Middle East
Source: Chart created using data published in Frankfurt School–UNEP/BNEF Centre 2016.

As China continues to make the transition to a market economy, its national innovation system will continue to evolve as well, particularly as innovative activity is further rewarded in the marketplace. Although innovative activity was not as valued in China under a centrally planned government system, there is a clear trend towards increased private sector investment in R&D, and in private sector innovative activity, as well as an increase in patents being granted to enterprises. Many studies have pointed to unclear property rights and intellectual property protection, as well as weak patent law and contract law, as major remaining barriers to innovation in China, although these areas are evolving rapidly as well.

Renewable energy industry development

China's policies to promote renewable energy have always included mandates and incentives to support the development of domestic technologies and industries. While some elements of these industrial policies – like requirements for using locally manufactured materials – are unduly protectionist, the policies aimed at promoting domestic renewable energy deployment are less controversial and in many cases modelled after similar policies first used in other countries.

China's promotion of renewable energy was kick-started with the passage of the *Renewable Energy Law of the People's Republic of China* that became effective on 1 January 2006 (National People's Congress 2005). The *Renewable Energy Law* created a framework for regulating renewable energy and was hailed at the time as a breakthrough in the development of renewable energy in China. It created four mechanisms to promote the growth of China's renewable energy supply: (1) a national renewable energy target; (2) a mandatory connection and purchase policy; (3) a feed-in tariff system; and (4) a cost-sharing mechanism, including a special fund for renewable energy development (Schuman 2010). Several additional regulations were issued to implement the goals established in the *Renewable Energy Law*, including pricing measures that established a surcharge on electricity rates to help pay for the cost of renewable electricity, plus revenue allocation measures to help equalize the costs of generating renewable electricity among provinces. In December 2009, amendments to the *Renewable Energy Law* were passed, further strengthening the process through which renewable electricity projects are connected to the grid and dispatched efficiently (National People's Congress Standing Committee 2009). They also addressed some of the issues related to interprovincial equity in bearing the cost of renewable energy development.

Since the passage of the *Renewable Energy Law*, numerous policies and regulations have followed that aim to support key renewable energy technology industries. While framework policies set the national stage for the promotion of renewable energy and pricing policies promoted its deployment, another set of policies aimed at promoting the technology transfer and then the localization of renewable energy technology. Of the 'non-hydro' renewables, wind and solar have been particularly successful in China in the last decade. China's solar technology sector was developed almost entirely for export, while China's wind power sector was developed almost entirely for domestic use. As a result, the energy and industrial policies targeting these sectors has differed. The story behind the development of China's wind and solar technology industries is briefly summarized below.

Wind power

A late adopter of wind power technology, China has quickly risen to become the largest wind power market in the world, and Chinese firms are now among the leading manufacturers of wind turbine technology globally. By the end of 2015, China had constructed 145 GW of wind power, more than all the EU countries combined, and almost twice as many as the second-largest installer of wind power capacity, the United States (GWEC 2016). Wind energy generated accounted for 3.3 per cent of China's total electricity generation in 2015, up from 2.8 per cent in 2014 (REN21 2016).

China has pursued the development of a domestic wind turbine industry almost from the very beginning of its development of wind power (Lewis 2013). China's development of indigenous wind technology capabilities was aligned with its broader domestic innovation strategy to move away from reliance on foreign technologies and build up local manufacturing capacity in strategic sectors. Renewable energy has long been identified as a strategic sector for the country, and, if anything, it has become even more critical given recent initiatives to reduce the country's reliance on coal given concerns about climate change and air pollution.

China's wind power industry has benefited from various forms of government policy support; some policies have specifically targeted industrial development for the wind power industry, while others have indirectly supported industrial development by establishing a local market for wind power. While framework policies set the national stage for the promotion of renewable energy and pricing policies promoted its deployment, another set of policies aimed at promoting the technology transfer and then the localization of wind power technology (Lewis 2016a). Trade policies have also been used in a variety of ways over time to try to encourage different modes of local manufacturing and industry development.

Consistent policy support specifically targeting Chinese firms has led to the emergence of a Chinese wind technology manufacturing industry built upon foreign technology transfers. European and American wind turbine manufacturers were demonstrating their technology in China as early as the mid-1980s. These demonstrations created opportunities for learning, led to local partnerships, and eventually to technology transfers from these overseas companies to local Chinese companies, whether in the form of intellectual property, skilled personnel, or other informal means of knowledge transfer (Lewis 2013). The mid-1990s saw the establishment of the first Sino-foreign joint ventures in wind turbine manufacturing, and the first Chinese-owned wind turbine manufacturers were established in the late 1990s. By the mid-2000s, many new Chinese manufacturers had entered the Chinese market, and today Goldwind, the most successful wind company in the world in terms of global market share, hails from China (Shankleman 2016). While Chinese firms still lag in novel and frontier innovations in this sector, they are producing world-class technology that has dominated within the Chinese market and is increasingly being sold outside the Chinese market.

Today, the biggest challenge facing China's wind sector is integration: making sure the wind power being produced by China's wind farms is absorbed by the grid and consumed. In 2015, 15 per cent of China's wind generated electricity was curtailed, a record high. Curtailment leads to major losses for wind farm operators, and from an environmental perspective leads to wasted pollution-free electricity (Lewis 2016b). Addressing wind curtailment has been the focus of several policies introduced by the government in 2015, including regulations requiring grid operators to give renewable power sources priority access to the grid. The location of China's wind resources leads to difficulties in transmitting China's wind power to population centres, and many completed wind farms sit idle while they wait for the construction of long-distance transmission capacity.

Solar power

China's global dominance in solar power utilization is quite recent, while its dominance in manufacturing is not. Most of the past decade saw China increase its solar panel manufacturing primarily for export to wealthier countries, and very low levels of solar power utilization domestically. The global financial crisis was a turning point in China's solar industry, leading the government to introduce many domestic stimulus policies that benefited China's struggling solar industry. As a result, by 2015 China had become the top country for installed solar capacity, adding 15.2 GW to reach a total of almost 44 GW, and overtaking long-time leader Germany (REN21 2016).

China's innovation model in the solar technology sector has been somewhat similar to the wind sector, in that most Chinese companies have purchased some form of production technology from companies located in countries that were earlier innovators in the solar industry. As the production lines moved to China, PV manufacturers gradually adapted them to local conditions, for example if less expensive inputs were available. It is notable that technology licensing has not played a major role in the Chinese adoption of solar manufacturing technology, since this has been the primary source of technology acquisition in the Chinese wind power industry (La Tour et al. 2011; Lewis 2013).

Since a major part of the PV manufacturing process includes 'know-how' as opposed to just technology hardware, access to skilled employees has been a major asset to Chinese companies. One study estimates that over 60 per cent of the leadership (CEOs and board members) of Chinese solar companies studied or worked abroad (La Tour et al. 2011). Know-how is particularly important in the silicon purification process and in the latter stages of the PV supply chain: namely system integration and installation. These stages – technically outside of the manufacturing supply chain – also tend to be the most expensive components of the supply chain since they are the most labour intensive. While many of the manufacturing processes can be automated, system integration and installations still must be done manually by skilled workers (Morin 2012). By 2016, domestic competition has become steep, and as a result many Chinese PV companies are expanding into emerging markets, building manufacturing plants overseas and even acquiring foreign companies to aid with this expansion (Liu 2016).

Chinese government policy support for solar PV goes back to the 6th FYP (1981–1985), and has appeared in every plan since. Most of China's early policy support for solar was for off-grid, decentralized applications. For example, China's Brightness Program, implemented in 1996, was the first major programme to promote rural electrification through off-grid solar, targeting 20 million people through 2010 (National Renewable Energy Laboratory 2004). This changed in the late 2000s with the introduction of the Golden Sun Demonstration Program announced by the Ministry of Finance, Ministry of Science and Technology, and the National Energy Administration. The programme established a subsidy for grid-connected solar PV equal to 50 per cent of the investment cost, and for off-grid PV of 70 per cent of the investment cost. Overall the programme targeted over 600 MW of PV to be installed across the country by 2012, with a minimum of 20 MW in each province. Then in 2011, the first national feed-in tariff policy for solar photovoltaics was announced, providing a subsidy to encourage the deployment of solar energy within China (NDRC Pricing Department 2011). While the majority of China's solar policies in recent years have targeted support for large-scale solar manufacturing deployment, this is actually starting to change as a result of recent integration challenges, seeing China return to its original solar strategy of promoting decentralized applications.

As with wind, China's primary challenge for its solar industry is integration. But unlike with wind, solar can work very well as a distributed source of power. As a result, recent Chinese government policies have targeted increasing the use of distributed solar and building-integrated PV so that the electricity is consumed at the point of generation and not transmitted over long distances.

Green innovation and protectionism

China is playing an increasingly significant role in the manufacturing of renewable energy and other advanced energy technologies. The manufacturing scale it brings to these industries, as well as its comparatively low-cost inputs to the manufacturing process, may contribute to cost reductions in these technologies. However, with its rapid entry into these sectors, China has put pressure on its competitors, and as a result has become the target of several international trade disputes with the US, EU and others (Lewis 2014).

While several factors contributed to the rise of many new wind turbine manufacturers in China, the implication of their rise has been added competition for the foreign firms operating within the Chinese market. As China's wind market has risen to become the largest in the world over the past few years, China's home-grown wind turbine manufacturers have been able to capture the majority of Chinese market share, increasing competitive tensions between foreign and Chinese firms. Industrial policies that foster protectionism that have been widely used in China's wind sector certainly have been a factor in China's success. For example, local content requirements (LCRs) aiming to encourage the domestic development of wind technology have been widely used for well over a decade (Lewis 2013).

While far rarer than claims of protectionism, there have been some claims of blatant theft of intellectual property from Chinese wind firms. A recent high-profile intellectual property (IP) dispute between an American and a Chinese wind company has elevated concerns of some US clean energy firms looking to cooperate with Chinese firms. The US firm, American Superconductor (AMSC), entered the Chinese market through its partnership with Sinovel, then a leading Chinese wind turbine manufacturer. The two companies engaged in the joint R&D of several new wind turbine models. What in the fall of 2009 AMSC characterized as a successful partnership began to sour publicly by April 2011, when a company press release updating investors on fourth-quarter financial results stated that Sinovel had 'refused to accept shipments of 1.5 MW and 3 MW wind turbine core electrical components and spare parts' that it had previously agreed to purchase, and that it has also failed 'to pay AMSC for certain contracted shipments made in fiscal year 2010' (AMSC 2011). Then in June 2011, while servicing wind turbines in China, AMSC engineers discovered that Sinovel was utilizing a version of AMSC's low-voltage ride through (LVRT) software in a wind turbine in China which AMSC had not sold or licensed to Sinovel (Beyer 2013). This discovery led to legal proceedings in both China and the US court systems. AMSC claimed that Sinovel paid an AMSC systems integrator in Austria for source code and software that Sinovel used to upgrade hundreds of its wind turbines in order to meet proposed Chinese grid codes.

More so than its wind industry, China's solar industry has become notorious for its role in global trade disputes. In August 2009, two major German producers of PV cells, SolarWorld AG and Conergy, filed a complaint with both the German government and European Union authorities complaining about subsidization of the Chinese PV industry and requesting that an anti-dumping investigation of Chinese PV exports be initiated. The German companies pointed to the Golden Sun Program and the Solar Rooftops Program, which provide direct subsidies to panel deployment in China. This complaint marked the beginning of a multi-year solar trade battle with China that continues today. The United States got involved in 2010, and by 2012 the US government had placed duties on Chinese solar imports. While China and the EU were able to resolve the majority of their solar trade dispute bilaterally, the US and China have continued to go back and forth on levels of sanctions, and reduced duties were imposed by the US in 2015, and World Trade Organization (WTO) deliberations continue (Wesoff 2015; WTO 2016).

Conclusions

China's green innovation strategy has simultaneously propelled its clean energy sector to be among the largest in the world, while also launching international trade battles with its biggest green technology competitors. As a latecomer to the clean energy innovation field, cooperation with many of the countries that have expertise in specific clean energy technologies has been a very important way for Chinese firms to enter this sector. The examples of the wind and solar sector demonstrate how China has been able to become a global technological leader in a relatively short amount of time through directed energy and industrial policies supporting the strategic development of these industries both domestically and overseas.

China's innovation priorities in the energy sector have changed over time with changing domestic energy needs. As clean energy technologies have been prioritized during the 12th FYP period, both as a strategic industrial policy, as well as for environmental reasons, China has emerged as a global leader in these industries in terms of investment and deployment. But it is becoming increasingly clear that large investments cannot solve China's growing pains with renewable energy. Current issues with curtailment and integration point to a complex political economy surrounding powerful industries with vested interests in maintaining coal's dominance. Persistent protectionism in these competitive global industries has given some of its clean energy companies a tarnished global reputation, hurting the ability of other companies to expand into markets outside of China.

China's continued ability to leapfrog to cleaner energy technologies will be determined by its ability to become an innovator and global leader in the development of the technologies that it so critically needs. There is no doubt China can become a leader in developing the green energy industries of this century. It will be far more challenging, however, for China to transform to a truly low-carbon economy. A centrally led green innovation strategy can only take the country so far. Ultimately, difficult decisions will need to be made by China's leadership about how to deal with powerful energy and industrial producers, how to increase enforcement of environmental regulations and reduce corruption, and how to improve the business environment to encourage rather than discourage international collaborations.

References

American Superconductor (AMSC), 2011. AMSC issues update regarding its anticipated fourth quarter and fiscal year 2010 financial results. Available at: http://files.shareholder.com/downloads/AMSC/34 17528077x0x536822/2199f389-7a0e-4f8d-8da2-bbd1a8b33198/AMSC_News_2011_4_5_General. pdf (accessed 12 December 2016).

Beyer, J.K., 2013. AMSC/Sinovel industrial espionage thriller takes a procedural detour, threatening U.S. criminal prosecution | Lexology. *Lexology*. Available at: http://www.lexology.com/library/detail. aspx?g=c06d91c6-1d63-4fb0-a1a7-d803bf90ef60 (accessed 24 June 2014).

Evans, S., 2015. IEA: China might have passed 'peak coal' in 2013. *Carbon Brief*. Available at: https:// www.carbonbrief.org/iea-china-might-have-passed-peak-coal-in-2013 (accessed 26 July 2016).

Frankfurt School-UNEP/BNEF Centre, 2016. Global trends in renewable energy investment 2016. Available at: Frankfurt School – UNEP Collaborating Centre for Climate & Sustainable Energy Finance. http://fs-unep-centre.org/publications/global-trends-renewable-energy-investment-2016 (accessed 12 December 2016).

Global Wind Energy Council (GWEC), 2016. *Global Wind Report 2015*, GWEC. Available at: http:// www.gwec.net/publications/global-wind-report-2/ (accessed 26 July 2016).

Government of the People's Republic of China (PRC), 2010. Guowuyuan guanyu Jiakuai Peiyu he Fazhan Zhanlve Xingxinxing Chanye de Jueding: Guofa 2010, 32 hao (State Council Decision on Accelerating the Development of the Strategic Emerging Industries, Document No. 32). Available at: http://www.gov.cn/zwgk/2010-10/18/content_1724848.htm (accessed 12 December 2016).

Government of the People's Republic of China, 2011. Zhonghua Renmin Gongheguo Jingji he Shehui Fazhan di Shierwu Nian Guihua gangyao (12th Five-Year Plan for National Economic and Social Development of the People's Republic of China). Available at: http://news.xinhuanet.com/politics/2011-03/16/c_121193916.htm (accessed 1 June 2012).

Karplus, V.J., 2007. *Innovation in China's Energy Sector*, Program on Energy and Sustainable Development, Center for Environmental Science and Policy, Stanford University.

La Tour, A. de; Glachant, M.; Meniere, Y., 2011. Innovation and international technology transfer: the case of the China photovoltaic industry, *Energy Policy*, (39)2, 761–770.

Lewis, J.I., 2013. *Green Innovation in China: China's wind power industry and the global transition to a low-carbon economy*. New York: Columbia University Press.

Lewis, J.I., 2014. The rise of renewable energy protectionism: emerging trade conflicts and implications for low carbon development. *Global Environmental Politics*, 14(4), 10–35.

Lewis, J.I., 2016a. The development of China's wind power technology sector: characterizing national policy support, technology acquisition and technological learning. In Y. Zhou, W. Lazonick, & Y. Sun, eds. *China as an Innovation Nation*. Oxford, UK: Oxford University Press.

Lewis, J.I., 2016b. Wind energy in China: Getting more from wind farms. *Nature Energy*, 1(6), 16076. doi: 10.1038/nenergy.2016.76.

Liu Y., 2016. Developing trends in China's solar PV industry for 2016. Available at: http://www.renewableenergyworld.com/articles/2016/03/developing-trends-in-china-s-pv-industry-for-2016.html (accessed 26 July 2016).

Martin, R., 2016. China is on an epic solar power binge. *MIT Technology Review*. Available at: https://www.technologyreview.com/s/601093/china-is-on-an-epic-solar-power-binge/ (accessed 26 July 2016).

Morin, William G. 2012. Solar PV and US-China Trade. Paper presented at the GW Solar Symposium 2012, April 12, George Washington University. Available at: http://www.slideshare.net/gwsolar/william-morin-gw-solar-symposium-2012 (accessed 21 December 2016).

National Climate Strategy Center, 2014. Comments on Sino–US Joint declaration on climate change. *China National Climate Strategy Center*. Available at: http://www.ncsc.org.cn/article/yxcg/yjgd/201411/20141100001254.shtml (accessed 26 July 2016).

National Development and Reform Commission (NDRC), 2014. National climate change plan (2014–2020). *National Development and Reform Commission*. Available at: http://www.sdpc.gov.cn/zcfb/zcfbtz/201411/t20141104_642612.html (accessed 26 July 2016).

National Development and Reform Commission (NDRC) Department of Climate Change, 2015. China's nationally determined contribution. Available at: http://www4.unfccc.int/ndcregistry/PublishedDocuments/China%20First/China's%20First%20NDC%20Submission.pdf (accessed 21 December 2016).

National Development and Reform Commission (NDRC) Pricing Department, 2011. NDRC notice on improving solar PV electricity pricing policy (No. 1594) (in Chinese). *National Development and Reform Commission*.

National People's Congress, 2005. *The Renewable Energy Law of the People's Republic of China*.

National People's Congress Standing Committee, 2009. China renewable energy law decision. Available at: http://www.npc.gov.cn/englishnpc/Law/2011-02/16/content_1620764.htm (accessed 21 December 2016).

National Renewable Energy Laboratory, 2004. Renewable energy in China: Brightness Rural Electrification Program. Available at: http://www.nrel.gov/docs/fy04osti/35790.pdf (accessed 12 December 2016).

National Science Foundation (NSF) Beijing Office, 2016. China announces major reform of competitive S&T funding. *NSF.gov*. Available at: http://www.nsf.gov/od/oise/beijing/perspectives/china_reforms_st_funding.jsp (accessed 26 July 2016).

People.com.cn, 2011. Zhang Guobao: ' Shierwu' mo Lizheng Feihuashi Nengyuan Zhan yici Nengyuan Bizhong 11.4 percent ('Twelfth Five' push to non-fossil energy to account for 11.4 percent share of primary energy) *people.com.cn*. Available at: http://energy.people.com.cn/GB/13670716.html (accessed 12 December 2016).

People's Daily Online, 2004a. China sets energy, resources saving as one of key economic targets. *People's Daily Online*. Available at: http://english.peopledaily.com.cn/200412/06/eng20041206_166239.html (Accessed 12 December 2016).

People's Daily Online, 2004b. Put into effect scientific viewpoint of development in an all-round way. *People's Daily Online.* Available at: http://english.peopledaily.com.cn/200412/14/eng20041214_167332.html (accessed 12 December 2016).

REN21, 2016. *Renewables 2016 Global Status Report*, Paris: REN21 Secretariat. Available at: http://www.ren21.net/status-of-renewables/global-status-report/ (accessed 12 December 2016).

Schuman, S., 2010. *Improving China's Existing Renewable Energy Legal Framework: Lessons from the International and Domestic Experience*, Natural Resources Defense Council (NRDC).

Seligsohn, D. and Hsu A., 2016. How China's 13th Five-Year Plan addresses energy and the environment. *ChinaFile.* Available at: https://www.chinafile.com/reporting-opinion/environment/how-chinas-13th-five-year-plan-addresses-energy-and-environment (accessed 26 July 2016).

Shankleman, J., 2016. China's Goldwind knocks GE from top wind market spot. *Bloomberg.com.* Available at: http://www.bloomberg.com/news/articles/2016-02-22/china-s-goldwind-knocks-ge-from-top-spot-in-global-wind-market (accessed 26 July 2016).

Su W., 2010. Letter from China on autonomous domestic mitigation actions submitted to Appendix II of the Copenhagen Accord. Available at: http://unfccc.int/files/meetings/cop_15/copenhagen_accord/application/pdf/chinacphaccord_app2.pdf (accessed 12 December 2016).

Wesoff, E., 2015. A setback for Solarworld and a trade case win for Chinese solar manufacturers. Available at: https://www.greentechmedia.com/articles/read/A-Setback-for-SolarWorld-and-a-Trade-Case-Win-for-Chinese-Solar-Manufacture (accessed 26 July 2016).

World Trade Organization (WTO), 2016. Dispute DS437: United States – countervailing duty measures on certain products from China. Available at: https://www.wto.org/english/tratop_e/dispu_e/cases_e/ds437_e.htm (accessed 26 July 2016).

Zang, D., 2009. Green from above: climate change, new developmental strategy, and regulatory choice in China. *Texas International Law Journal*, 45, 201–232.

21

LOW-CARBON URBAN DEVELOPMENT IN CHINA

Policy and practices

Liu Wenling and Wang Can

Introduction

Cities are major contributors of greenhouse gas emissions (GHG); more than 70 per cent of global GHG emissions come from cities (Khanna et al. 2014). Due to high population agglomeration, cities are also particularly vulnerable to climate impacts. China already has the highest number and largest size of cities in its history, and in recent decades these cities have been causing severe environmental problems. Among the ten most polluted cities in the world, seven are Chinese cities (Zhang and Crooks 2012). China's rapid urbanization has created mass migration from rural areas to urban centres. This migration comes with energy- and climate-related challenges (Wang et al. 2014). Urban energy use is estimated to be three times higher than that of rural areas (excluding non-commercial energy consumption) (Liu et al. 2013). The increasing demand for energy and other resources, as well as the high emissions in urban China, have become a great challenge for the entire world, forcing researchers to rethink the way that they understand urban development.

Low-carbon development has become the common goal of major cities worldwide. Low-carbon urban development, and particularly low-carbon cities, is also receiving growing attention from the Chinese government. Recognizing the importance of cities in mitigating future energy and CO_2 emissions growth, the Chinese government launched a demonstration programme of five low-carbon pilot provinces and eight pilot cities in 2010, and expanded the programme to 28 cities and one province in 2012. China has become a vast living laboratory for low-carbon urban development experiments. This chapter reviews the use and development of low-carbon city-related concepts, discusses domestic research progress, gives an overview of the policies and practices of low-carbon urban development thus far, and discusses low-carbon urban development and new urbanization in China. This overview provides an explanation of Chinese low-carbon city construction and helps policy makers and researchers understand the emphasis and trends of low-carbon urban development.

Concepts development and research progress

Development of low-carbon urban concepts in China

China started taking action for environmental protection in the early 1970s. At that time, the focus was mainly on pollution monitoring and end-of-pipe solutions (Zhang and Wen 2008). The United Nations Conference on Environment and Development in Rio de Janeiro in 1992 was a turning point in China's urban development and national environmental strategy (Liu et al. 2014). China set its own Agenda 21 to promote sustainable development of both the economy and the society. Concepts such as green city, garden city and national environmental protection model city were promoted and began to spread. At the turn of the century, the environmental situation continued to deteriorate. Meanwhile, increasing domestic and international pressure relating to climate change and energy conservation forced China to take further steps to establish national sustainable development strategies. As the centres of population, industry, transport and infrastructure, cities receive more attention and are emphasized as the first priority in actions and strategies on climate change. This has led to the emergence of concepts such as eco-cities, low-carbon cities and low-carbon eco-cities.

The concept of eco-cities started from the idea of applying ecological principles to city planning. In 1995, the concept of eco-communities was first officially proposed in the *Guidelines for Building National Eco-Demonstration Communities (1996–2050)* issued by the State Environmental Protection Administration (now Ministry of Environment Protection [MEP]). Later, the concept of eco-county, eco-city, eco-province and related ideas were successively proposed and a number of laws, regulations, plans, actions and guidelines were issued and implemented (Zhang and Wen 2008). The goal of building eco-demonstration communities is to protect and rebuild the eco-environment, improve the traditional resource-dependent development model and achieve higher economic development at a lower resource and environment cost. As summarized by Zhou et al. (2012), the eco-city and related concepts emphasize the well-being of citizens and society through integrated urban planning and management that harnesses the benefits of ecological systems and protects and nurtures assets for future generations.

In 2003, the UK government issued an Energy White Paper titled 'Our Energy Future – Creating a Low Carbon Economy' (DTI 2003). This paper was the first to propose the concept of a low-carbon economy and initiated an international discussion. Since then, related concepts, such as 'low-carbon development', 'low-carbon lifestyle', 'low-carbon city' and 'low-carbon town', have been proposed as methods to cope with global climate change challenges caused by increasing carbon emissions from human activities. Due to their enormous contributions to national carbon emissions, cities were particularly emphasized as a cause for concern in China in the context of the 'low carbon' campaign. In 2007 the World Wide Fund for Nature (WWF) launched a project called 'Low Carbon City Initiatives' in China to explore low-carbon development methods in China's urban areas (The Climate Group 2010). In 2010, the National Development and Reform Commission (NDRC) launched a national low-carbon province and low-carbon city experimental project for five provinces (Guangdong, Liaoning, Hubei, Shanxi and Yunnan) and eight cities (Tianjin, Chongqing, Shenzhen, Xiamen, Hangzhou, Nanchang, Guiyang and Baoding). The programme targets the climate change challenges that cities may be confronted with, and experiments with strategies to decouple economic growth from growth of fossil fuel use by shifting towards consumption characterized by energy efficiency, renewable energy and green transportation (Zhou et al. 2012).

In 2007, the 17th National Congress of the Chinese Communist Party promoted the idea of 'eco-civilization', which was not a new concept but was the first time that it was included in the Party's political report in China. Since then, an eco-civilization campaign has started in China. This is the context in which the concept of low-carbon eco-cities emerged. It is literally a combination of the pre-existing concepts of 'low-carbon city' and 'eco-city', and highlights two core issues of 'eco-civilization'; energy efficiency and environmental protection. As stated in Zhou et al. (2012), the idea of a low-carbon eco-city combines both concepts by featuring energy-saving and environmentally friendly cities that symbolize low energy consumption and low environmental impact (e.g. low pollution and low carbon emissions).

The progress of research on Chinese low-carbon urban development

Although the notion of low-carbon urban development is fairly new, studies on this topic have increased dramatically in recent years. Literature has looked at various aspects of low-carbon urban development.

There have been many attempts to define the concept of a low-carbon city (see for example Liu et al. 2009; Liu and Wang 2010; Li et al. 2012; Yang and Li 2013). Although low-carbon city has been defined in a variety of different ways, the concept of a low-carbon city in China is closely connected with a low-carbon economy. The core idea is to integrate the concepts of a low-carbon economy and a low-carbon society into the development of cities, and propose development goals that emphasize an economic development model with the transition of production, consumption, and lifestyle.

Several studies have been looking into the evaluation methodologies of low-carbon cities. Because there is no comparable benchmark for all countries, this exercise has to be done locally. Price et al. (2013) present and test a methodology for the development of a low-carbon indicator system at the provincial and city level in China, and provide initial results for an end-use, low-carbon indicator system. Lin et al. (2014) use Xiamen as a case study and integrate city-level carbon intensity targets into a low-carbon city indicator system through a decomposition method. Shen and Zhou (2014) examine and compare the effectiveness of nine existing indicator systems introduced in China. An eco- and low-carbon indicator tool for evaluating cities (ELITE cities) was developed by researchers at the Lawrence Berkeley National Laboratory in 2012 to evaluate cities' performance by comparing them against benchmark performance goals as well as ranking them against other cities in China; Zhou et al. (2015) explain the general framework of the ELITE cities tool, the methods by which the indicators and indicator benchmarks were established, and a detailed guide on tool applications. The Institute for Urban and Environmental Studies at the Chinese Academy of Social Science has worked on the development of a low-carbon city indicator system for many years. Their publication *Reconstruction of China Low-Carbon City Evaluation Indicator System* provides a methodological guide for the application of this indicator system (IUES 2013).

City planning is another aspect that has been receiving great attention in academic research related to low-carbon (eco-)cities. The Chinese Society for Urban Studies began analysing the idea of a low-carbon eco-city very early. In their book *China's Low Carbon Eco-city Development Strategy*, they discuss the policy, technology and institutional capacity necessary for low-carbon eco-city development (CSUS 2009), as well as a framework for an evaluation indicator system for low-carbon eco-city planning. In addition, an annual report *China's Low Carbon Eco-city Development Report* has been published since 2010 (CSUS 2010–2014), which summarizes the achievements of low-carbon eco-city development in China and provides instructions and case studies. Gu (2013) provides a systematic framework and examples for low-carbon city planning. Cao and Li (2011) take the new eco-city of Tianjin as an example to explore practical experiences with low-carbon eco-city planning ideas and development strategies. Liu et al.

(2014) propose the use of metabolic thinking and eco-cycle models derived from the discipline of industrial ecology to support urban planners in developing more sustainable and resource-efficient urban pathways.

Other studies focus on models, methods or pathways of low-carbon city development. For example, Chen and Lu (2010) discuss the framework, development routes and vision for a low-carbon city, using Shanghai as a case study. Li et al. (2012) propose the definition of a Chinese low-carbon town and the main approaches to developing Chinese low-carbon towns through a system analysis in a Chinese context. Qin (2013) elucidates the theoretical basis of low-carbon city research and introduces models and methods for low-carbon city studies. Chen and Zhu (2013) carry out a quantitative and empirical analysis of carbon emissions in the process of Shanghai's development and seek out the conflicts of interest and other issues involved in order to determine the overall strategic objectives for building, industry (production) and transportation in the future. Lehmann (2013) compares two case studies and draws lessons from a German case for Chinese urbanization, in terms of urban design of new sub-centres to ensure a delivery of economic, social and environmentally sustainable outcomes. Yu (2014) explores the low-carbon eco-city initiatives in China and critically analyses the problems existing in the development of such an environmentally friendly development model.

Some scholars have paid special attention to the institutional construction, policy support and governance issues in the development of low-carbon cities. For instance, Dhakal (2010) explores efficient governance for mitigating greenhouse gas emissions from cities. Lo (2014) looks at the issue of poor implementation of Chinese low-carbon policies. Wang and Chang (2014) examine the development of policy instruments that support low-carbon governance in China. Khanna et al. (2014) review the historical development of and context for low-carbon urban development in China and present an ex-ante comparative assessment of the low-carbon development plans and supporting measures formulated for each of China's eight pilot low-carbon cities.

Policy implementation and practices

Pilot low-carbon (eco-)city initiatives

Since 2009, in order to promote the development of a low-carbon economy in China, government departments have either independently or jointly taken action to formulate relevant urban planning or other related supporting policies. As summarized in Table 21.1, these actions have resulted in a number of pilot projects, referring to low-carbon city, district, town and industrial demonstration parks. The pilot low-carbon (eco-)city initiatives have led to nationwide action. Besides the pilot projects launched by the MEP, NDRC and the Ministry of Housing and Urban–Rural Development (MOHURD), the Ministry of Finance and the Ministry of Industry and Information also united with other departments to provide fiscal and technological support for the implementation of low-carbon pilots (WRI 2014).

As early as 2003, the MEP initiated a programme to establish eco-counties, eco-cities and eco-regions within China, and issued the guideline *Indicators for National Ecological County, Municipality and Province (trial)* on 13 December 2003. By July 2011, 38 cities had been labelled 'ecological city (county)' under the MEP's guideline and assessment, including cities in Jiangsu, Zhejiang, Shandong, Guangdong, Sichuan, Anhui, Shaanxi, Liaoning provinces and the municipalities of Shanghai, Beijing and Tianjin.

The pilot low-carbon cities programme started from 2007, when the WWF launched a project called 'Low Carbon City Initiatives in China'. Shanghai and Baoding became the first

Table 21.1 Low-carbon actions and planning issued by the Chinese government

Government Departments	Time	Actions or planning	Contents
MEP	2009/04	'COOL CHINA-2009 national low carbon action pilot project'	Advocating low-carbon lifestyles; 11 pilot cities selected: Tianjin, Shanghai, Xian, Yinchuan, Nanjing, Changzhou, Suzhou, Guangzhou, Xiamen, Shenyang and Chongqing
	2009/12	'Enhancing the development of low carbon economy in the national eco-industrial demonstration parks'	Requiring the prioritization of the development of a low-carbon economy in the process of building and developing national eco-industrial demonstration parks nationwide
MOHURD	2010/01	'Cooperation framework agreement' signed by MOHURD and Shenzhen Government	Shenzhen became the first state low-carbon eco-city, striving to develop green transport and green buildings, promoting the transition of Shenzhen to a more sustainable development process
	2011/06	'Management measures of declaration for MOHURD low carbon eco-city (town)'	Standardization of MOHURD low-carbon eco-city (town) criteria; six cities were selected in context of a China–US cooperation pilot low-carbon eco-cities, including Hefei, Langfang, Rizhao, Weifang, Hebi and Jiyuan
	2011/09	'Evaluation indicators on green low carbon small towns' issued by MOHURD and NDRC	Standardization of the selection and evaluation criteria for green low-carbon small towns
	2013/03	'"The 12th Five-Year Plan" development planning on green building and green eco-urban district'	During the 12th FYP period, selecting 100 cities to plan and build their new built urban districts following green eco-urban district standards
NDRC	2010/07	'Low carbon economy pilot project'	Launching low carbon economy pilots in five provinces and eight cities
	2011/10	'Carbon emission trading pilot'	Seven provinces and cities selected as carbon emission trading pilot areas, including Beijing, Tianjin, Shanghai, Chongqing, Guangdong, Hubei and Shijiazhuang
	2012/11	'The second low carbon economy pilots'	The low-carbon economy pilots were extended to 29 more cities and additional provinces, including Beijing, Shanghai, Hainan, etc.
	2014/03	'Low carbon community pilot project'	Establishing low-carbon community pilots in cities at the prefecture level and above; planning to build 1,000 low-carbon communities by the end of the 12th FYP

pilot cities in China. Domestically, the NDRC initiated a low-carbon pilot province and city programme in July 2010, as the first batch of five provinces and eight cities across the country were chosen as pilot regions. This programme was expanded to 28 more cities (districts) and Hainan province in 2012. As listed in Table 21.2, in addition to six pilot low-carbon provinces, there are 36 pilot low-carbon cities and one district. The majority are megacities or large cities. The two batches of low-carbon pilots were implemented in 24 provinces, with the population accounting for 18.5 per cent of the national population and the GDP accounting for about 33 per cent of the national GDP (based on 2011 statistical data).

In addition to domestic government programmes, many organizations and research institutions have partnered with government and other stakeholders to explore the planning and best practices of low-carbon cities in China (The Climate Group 2010). Besides the WWF project mentioned above, in 2007, the Rockefeller Brothers Fund started to support a study in order to develop a low-carbon economy roadmap for Guangdong province and Hong Kong. In 2008, the United Nations Development Programme, the Government of Norway and the European Union jointly launched a project to support Chinese provincial climate change programmes and projects. The United Kingdom Strategic Programme Fund (SPF) provided support to Jilin City, Nanchang, Chongqing and Guangdong province in their low-carbon city development, research and planning. With support from the Energy Foundation's China Sustainable Energy Program, Tsinghua University conducted preliminary studies on developing a low-carbon strategy for Suzhou and Shandong province. In 2010, the Sino-Swiss Low Carbon Cities Project was launched, and Yinchuan, Beijing Dongcheng District, Dezhou and Meishan were selected as pilot cities, with emphasis on city management, low-carbon economy, transportation and green buildings (Khanna et al. 2014).

According to nationwide surveys undertaken by the Chinese Society of Urban Studies, by 2012, around 97 per cent of prefectural cities (374 prefectural cities in total), including sub-provincial cities and metropolises under the direct jurisdiction of the State Council, had announced or started eco-city or low-carbon city or low-carbon eco-city as their development strategy (Yu 2014).

Table 21.2 Low-carbon pilot provinces and cities in China

Batches	Pilot provinces and cities	Types	Population standard
The first batch	Guangdong, Liaoning, Hubei, Shanxi, Yunnan;	Provinces	–
	Tianjin, Chongqing, Shenzhen, Hangzhou, Nanchang, Baoding;	Megacity	Over 5 million
	Xiamen, Guiyang	Large city	1–5 million
The second batch	Beijing, Shanghai, Shijiazhuang, Suzhou, Ningbo, Wenzhou, Ganzhou, Qingdao, Wuhan, Guanzhou, Zunyi, Kunming; and Hainan (province)	Megacity	Over 5 million
	Qinhuangdao, Jincheng, Hulunbeier, Jinlin, Huanan, Zhenjiang, Chizhou, Nanping, Jingdezhen, Jiyuan, Guilin, Guangyuan, Yanan, Wulumuqi;	Large city	1–5 million
	Daxinganling District, Jinchang	Small city	Less than 500 thousand

Note: The taxonomy of cities refers to Qi (2014).

Distinctive examples of pilot, low-carbon (eco-)cities

Over the years more and more low-carbon (eco-)cities have been established. Among these are some that have developed distinctive characteristics in integrated planning making, target setting and/or selecting a unique focus on city construction. This section introduces three examples of pilot cities with special features.

Shenzhen low-carbon eco-city

Shenzhen is located in the southern part of China, bordering Hong Kong. It has benefited from China's economic reform and was selected as the country's first special economic zone in 1979. Since then, Shenzhen has undergone tremendous changes. It is already one of the largest cities in China and plays a particularly significant role in the Pearl River Delta. However, the intensive urbanization process in recent years has caused many environmental and social problems. The shortage of land, energy constraints and a growing population are putting increasing pressure on the city and threatening the city's future development (Liu et al. 2014).

In 2010, the Shenzhen government and MOHURD signed a framework contract to establish Shenzhen as China's first national level low-carbon eco-demonstration city. According to the jointly agreed programme, the demonstration project will focus on exploring the transformation of the city development model and low-carbon eco-city planning under southern climate conditions. The contract also emphasizes that the construction of Shenzhen's low-carbon eco-city should be low cost, replicable and sustainable.

The eco-demonstration city programme stresses the importance of building a city that is economically sustainable, socially harmonious and environmentally friendly. The overall aim is to develop Shenzhen as a world-class, low-carbon eco-demonstration city that plays an important and demonstrative role in China. The target is to create an intensive and compact city development model which significantly improves the ecological environment, increases resource efficiency and maintains a low level of carbon dioxide emissions. In a proposed quantitative indicator system, a strong focus is laid on the construction of infrastructure related to traffic, green belt, water and waste management. In addition, the programme highlights the development of designated low-carbon, eco-city demonstration districts within the city. Finally, Shenzhen city also plans to develop a low-carbon eco-city indicator system that can be used as a model at the local level in China.

Zhenjiang emission peak target

The peak target is a mechanism or method which forces the transformation of development patterns by promoting an accelerated decline of total GHG emissions. The NDRC has required the second batch of pilot, low-carbon cities to conduct a preliminary calculation and estimate the year in which their GHG emissions would peak. Zhenjiang, an industrial city of 3 million inhabitants in Jiangsu province is the first pilot low-carbon city that has proposed a GHG emissions peak target. According to a business-as-usual scenario, taking into consideration population, GDP, industrial structure and energy structure, Zhenjiang city would reach its carbon emission peak around 2039. Zhenjiang now proposes to realize the peak target in advance, in 2019, by implementing stricter mitigation measures and industrial restructuring.

Zhenjiang is one of the pilot low-carbon cities located in eastern China. With relatively advanced economic development and experiences of low-carbon development, it has served as a demonstration for other similar cities. Following the example of Zhenjiang several other pilot low-carbon cities in eastern China have recently announced peak targets. Suzhou (2020), Huaian (2025), Ningbo (2015) and Wenzhou (2019) are examples of cities that have set their GHG emissions peak targets (Qi 2014).

Hangzhou 'coal free district'

Hangzhou is a city surrounded by misty hills on all but one side, with a sloping terrain stretching from the south-west to the north-east, while south-west winds prevail in summer and north-west winds prevail in winter. Such a terrain and wind condition is adverse to the diffusion of atmospheric pollutants and thus it is easy to form ash haze weather in Hangzhou. In addition, historically the city industrial enterprises relied on coal for production, which led to serious air pollution.

In May 2013, the Hangzhou government issued *Implementation Schemes for Establishing 'a Coal Free District' in Hangzhou*. This is an ambient, environmentally integrated renovation programme, aiming to improve the city's atmospheric environment and speed up energy conservation and emission reduction in Hangzhou. According to this programme, it is required to implement measures such as closing down, relocating and renovating coal-fired equipment, as well as developing the main city zone into a 'a coal free district' before the end of 2013, and creating an entire 'coal free' city by 2015 (for Hangzhou's air pollution policy also see Ahlers and Hansen chapter 7 this volume).

In order to achieve the target, the city government has implemented strict, total control of regional coal consumption and severely regulates energy evaluation and approval processes. Within the 'coal free district', all newly built, extended and rebuilt projects are not allowed to use coal or other high-pollution fuels. Group heating for industrial parks must be implemented at the district or county level, and installing coal boilers on their own is forbidden. The city government is closing and renovating current coal-fired boilers of power enterprises. In the main city zone, there are 55 enterprises that need to demolish, close down, move or renovate their boilers. Meanwhile, the city has closed down or renovated all coal boilers used for enterprises engaged in crop farming and breeding. The city government has also enacted specific fiscal subsidy policy to support phasing out and renovating boilers and assist those enterprises that implement clean energy renovation.

Strategy of low-carbon (eco-)city development and new urbanization in China

Building low-carbon cities as an inevitable choice for new urbanization in China

China is currently undergoing rapid urbanization, which is leading to the aggregation of industries and populations and has the potential to bring new sources of economic growth. However, Chinese cities have a large volume and fast growth of energy consumption and carbon emissions, so the transition from rural to urban will inevitably accelerate energy consumption and aggravate increasingly serious ecological and environmental problems. Facing the serious constraint of resources and the challenges of environmental pollution and tackling climate change, the resource-dependent development pattern is difficult to sustain in China. Therefore, urbanization in China should avoid following the high-carbon development model based on excessive consumption of fossil fuels that developed countries have often followed.

The 18th National Congress of the Chinese Communist Party has emphasized the importance of ecological civilization and proposed the ideas of green development, circular economy and low-carbon development. The constitution of an ecological civilization calls for the transition of both production mode and lifestyle, and advocates patterns of green and low-carbon development. Low-carbon development has therefore become a significant characteristic and tendency of the urbanization process. Establishing low-carbon cities and following a low-carbon urbanization path are important areas and key points for promoting ecological civilization and realizing low-carbon development. Low-carbon urbanization requires a shift in development patterns and the construction of low-carbon industrial systems. Other key measures of constructing low-carbon cities include introducing low-carbon infrastructure and consumption modes.

A long way to go for low-carbon urban development in China

Nationwide the development of low-carbon cities is now in full swing. However, the journey is still long towards achieving true, low-carbon urban development in China. Taking two groups of pilot low-carbon cities (36 cities) as research objects, Song et al. (2015) evaluated the carbon-emission levels of these cities. Compared to their research, during the 11th Five-Year Plan (2006–2010) the average carbon emissions per unit GDP of pilot low-carbon cities were 3.22 tons CO_2 per 10,000 RMB, and therefore higher than the national average of 3.06 tons CO_2 per 10,000 RMB. The average per-capita emissions of pilot low-carbon cities were 9.96 tons CO_2, much higher than the national average of 5.96 tons per person. The carbon emissions per person in these pilot cities are still much higher than those of some major cities in the world, for example Paris, Copenhagen, Tokyo, London, Berlin, San Francisco or New York (Qi 2014, 110; Wang and Zheng 2013). Overall, the pilot low-carbon cities in China are facing great pressure to reduce their carbon emissions and need to explore a pathway to reduce energy consumption and carbon emissions, while at the same time ensuring reasonable economic growth.

Rapid expansion of low-carbon city pilots has also brought problems in the implementation process of those initiatives and policies. According to Khanna et al. (2014), due to the absence of explicit definitions for low-carbon cities and the multitude of parallel programmes, complexity, confusion and overlap in the development of low-carbon cities have emerged. The implementation gap still exists between national goals and local plans; local economic interests are often still favoured. These problems have no doubt weakened the effectiveness of low-carbon pilot implementation. Rapid urbanization is causing great challenges for the pilot cities. The limitation of policy instruments at the local level is also an underlying reason for the low efficiency of local governments in low-carbon pilot exploration. In particular, the public involvement is weak, and there is less engagement of market mechanisms compared with regulations and administrative measures (Wang et al. 2013).

Conclusion

Recognizing the importance of cities in mitigating future energy and CO_2 emissions growth, the Chinese government has launched several demonstration programmes for low-carbon (eco-)city development. The top-down institutional and policy design has successfully promoted the progress of low-carbon city construction. Several governmental departments have independently or jointly taken action to facilitate these pilot and demonstration programmes. Exploration and practice of low-carbon pilot (eco-)cities spread over the whole country, and experiences of some distinctive local examples have provided an effective demonstration for other similar cities. However, problems still exist. For instance, there is still a big gap between national plans and local action, since local economic interests are still favoured. The launch of several domestic eco- and low-carbon city programmes by different government and international institutions has also resulted in some overlap and confusing standards. Exploring a pathway to reduce energy consumption and carbon emissions, while at the same time ensuring reasonable economic growth, is a critical challenge for low-carbon pilot cities. Rapid urbanization is aggravating China's serious ecological and environmental problems. It is of utmost importance that the country explores a low-carbon urbanization path. Establishing low-carbon cities has been vital for promoting ecological civilization construction and has also become an inevitable choice for new urbanization in China.

Acknowledgement

This work was supported through the National Natural Science Foundation of China under the projects No.71403141 and No.71521002.

References

Cao S. and Li C., 2011.The exploration of concepts and methods for low-carbon eco-city planning. *Procedia Environmental Sciences*, 5, 199–207.

Chen F. and Zhu D., 2013. Theoretical research on low-carbon city and empirical study of Shanghai. *Habitat International*, 37, 33–42.

Chen W. Z. and Lu Y., 2010. *Ditan chengshi fazhan de kuang jia lu jing yu yuanjing: yi Shanghai wei li* (The framework, routes and visions for a low-carbon city: a case study of Shanghai), Beijing, China: The Science Press.

CSUS (Chinese Society for Urban Studies), 2009. *Zhongguo ditan shengtai chengshi fazhan zhanlue* (China's low carbon eco-city development strategy), Beijing, China: China City Press.

CSUS (Chinese Society for Urban Studies), 2010–2014. *Zhongguo ditan shengtai chengshi fazhan baogao* (China's low carbon eco-city development report), Beijing, China: China Building Industry Press.

Dhakal, S., 2010. GHG emissions from urbanization and opportunities for urban carbon mitigation. *Current Opinion in Environmental Sustainability*, 2(4), 277–283.

DTI (Department of Trade and Industry), 2003. Energy White Paper: Creating a Low Carbon Economy. London: DTI.

Gu C. L., 2013. *Qihou Bianhua yu ditan chengshi guihua* (Climate change and low carbon city planning), Hunan, China: Southeast University Press.

IUES (Institute for Urban and Environmental Studies), Chinese Academy of Social Science, 2013. *Chong Gou Zhongguo ditan chengshi pingjia zhibiao tixi* (Reconstruction of China low-carbon city evaluation indicator system), Beijing, China: Social Science Academic Press.

Khanna, N.; Fridley, D. and Hong L., 2014. China's pilot low-carbon city initiative: A comparative assessment of national goals and local plans. *Sustainable Cities and Society*, 12, 110–121.

Lehmann, S., 2013. Low-to-no carbon city: Lessons from western urban projects for the rapid transformation of Shanghai. *Habitat International*, 37, 61–69.

Li Z., Chang S., Ma L., Liu P., Zhao L. and Yao Q., 2012. The development of low-carbon towns in China: Concepts and practices. *Energy*, 47(1), 590–599.

Lin J.; Jacoby, J.; Cui S.; Liu Y. and Lin T., 2014. A model for developing a target integrated low carbon city indicator system: The case of Xiamen, China. *Ecological Indicators*, 40, 51–57.

Liu H.; Zhou G.; Wennersten, R. and Frostell, B., 2014. Analysis of sustainable urban development approaches in China. *Habitat International*, 41, 24–32.

Liu, W.; Spaargaren, G.; Heerink, N.; Mol, A. P. J. and Wang, C., 2013. Energy consumption practices of rural households in north China: Basic characteristics and potential for low carbon development. *Energy Policy*, 55, 128–138.

Liu W. and Wang C., 2010. Zhongguo ditan chengshi fazhan shijian yu fazhan moshi (Practice and patterns of low carbon city development). *China Population, Resources and Environment*, 20(4), 17–22.

Liu Z.; Dai Y.; Dong C. and Ye Q., 2009. Di Tan Cheng Shi Li Nian yu Guo Ji Jing Yan. (Low carbon city: Concepts, international practice and implications for China). *Urban Studies*, (6), 1–7.

Lo K., 2014. China's low-carbon city initiatives: The implementation gap and the limits of the target responsibility system. *Habitat International*, 42, 236–244.

Price, L.; Zhou N.; Fridley, D.; Ohshita, S.; Lu H.; Zheng N. and Fino-Chen C., 2013. Development of a low-carbon indicator system for China. *Habitat International*, 37, 4–21.

Qi Y., 2014. *Zhongguo ditan fazhan baogao.* (Annual review of low carbon development in China), Beijing, China: Social Science Academic Press.

Qin Y. Z., 2013. Studies on low carbon city: Models and methods, Beijing, China: Science Press.

Shen L. and Zhou J. (2014) Examining the effectiveness of indicators for guiding sustainable urbanization in China. *Habitat International*, 44, 111–120.

Song Q.J.; Wang Y.F. and Qi Y., 2015. *Zhongguo ditan shidian chengshi de tan paifang xianzhuang.*(Study on present status of carbon emissions in China's low carbon pilot cities). *China Population Resources and Environment*, 25(1), 78–82.

The Climate Group, (2010). Low carbon cities – an international perspective. London: The Climate Group.

Wang C.; Lin J.; Cai W. and Zhang Z., 2013. Policies and practices of low carbon city development in China. *Energy & Environment*, 24(7/8), 1347–1372.

Wang C.; Lin J.; Cai W. and Liao H., 2014. China's carbon mitigation strategies: Enough? *Energy Policy*, 73, 47–56.

Wang N. and Chang Y.-C., 2014. The development of policy instruments in supporting low-carbon governance in China. *Renewable and Sustainable Energy Reviews*, 35, 126–135.

Wang W.G. and Zheng G.G., 2013. Ying dui qihou bianhua baogao 2013: Ju jiao ditan chengzhenghua. (Annual report on actions to address climate change [2013]: focus on low carbon urbanization), Beijing, China: Social Science Academic Press.

World Resources Institute (WRI), 2014. Low carbon planning for Chinese cities: A manual for policy makers. Working report.

Yang L. and Li Y., 2013. Low-carbon city in China. *Sustainable Cities and Society*, 9, 62–66.

Yu L., 2014. Low carbon eco-city: New approach for Chinese urbanization. *Habitat International*, 44, 102–110.

Zhang K. and Wen Z., 2008. Review and challenges of policies of environmental protection and sustainable development in China. *Journal of Environmental Management*, 88(4), 1249–1261.

Zhang Q. and Crooks, R., 2012. Towards an environmentally sustainable future country environmental analysis of the People's Republic of China: Asian Development Bank.

Zhou N.; He G. and Williams, C., 2012. China's development of low carbon eco-cities and associated indivator systems. LBNL Report 5873E. Berkeley: Lawrence Berkeley National Laboratory.

Zhou N.; He G.; Williams, C. and Fridley, D., 2015. ELITE cities: A low-carbon eco-city evaluation tool for China. *Ecological Indicators*, 48, 448–456.

22

MUNICIPAL SOLID WASTE MANAGEMENT

Thomas R. Johnson

Introduction

In 2014, the world's biggest waste-to-energy (WTE) incinerator began to operate on the site of a deserted lime quarry in the Mengtougou District of Beijing (Li 2014). The Lujiashan incinerator, which can handle 3,000 tons of waste per day, was completed in just two years – lightning speed for a project of this nature. Local officials claimed that the facility was an eco-friendly solution to Beijing's mounting waste problem. They highlighted in particular the incinerator's capacity to generate 420 million kilowatt hours of power per annum, the equivalent of 140,000 tons of standard coal (Li 2014). Yet others remained sceptical. Outspoken incineration critic and retired China Academy of Sciences researcher Zhao Zhangyuan criticized the project's expedited approval process – the 80 approvals required for the project to go ahead were obtained in three months, a process that would normally take several years (Zhao 2011; Li 2014). Others expressed concern that the plant's official name – the '*Beijing Capital Steel Biomass Power Project*' – was indicative of officials' attempts to mislead a public that was becoming increasingly concerned about the construction of incinerators within close proximity to their homes (Meng 2011).

The Lujiashan incinerator highlights many issues related to municipal solid waste (MSW) management in contemporary China. The first is the sheer scale of the country's waste challenge. Despite successfully decoupling MSW generation from economic growth (OECD 2007), overall quantities of waste continue to grow.[1] China overtook the United States in 2004 to become the world's biggest generator of waste, and the World Bank predicts it will generate twice the amount of MSW produced in the US by 2030 (Hoornweg and Bhada-Tata 2012). China's per capita MSW generation of 1.02 kg/day is low compared with most OECD countries, yet this gap is predicted to narrow (Hoornweg and Bhada-Tata 2012).

Urbanization, population growth, and growing affluence are the main drivers behind the dramatic increase of MSW in China (World Bank 2005, 5). In 1979, the official urban population stood at 185 million, or 19 per cent of the total population. By 2013, the official urban population had risen to 731 million people, or 53.7 per cent of the population. Moreover, these figures exclude the 245 million people who currently make up China's 'floating population' (National Bureau of Statistics of China 2014). According to the World Bank, urban dwellers produce between two and three times more garbage per capita than their rural counterparts (World Bank 2005, 5). Economic reforms transformed consumption patterns and public perceptions of waste (Gerth 2010). Whereas people became accustomed to 'standing in line, rationing, and scarcity' during the Mao years (Yu 2014), there is now an abundance of goods available for Chinese consumers. Organic waste still forms the bulk of China's urban waste stream, but materials such as plastics and paper are on the increase (World Bank 2005).

Second, the Lujiashan incinerator shows how China is in the process of establishing a new 'waste regime', defined as 'the production, representation, and politics of waste' (Gille 2007), to deal with growing quantities of MSW. Despite official support for moving China up the 'waste hierarchy' (see Figure 22.1) towards more sustainable solutions such as waste reduction and reuse, Chinese cities have concentrated on developing 'end-of-pipe' solutions including landfill and, more recently, a massive expansion of waste incinerators (Johnson 2013a).

Waste collection and treatment levels have improved significantly. In 1984, Chinese cities collected only 5 million tons of MSW (Su et al. 2014, 103). By 2013, the reported figure exceeded 172 million tons (National Bureau of Statistics of China 2014). Yet despite this significant increase, waste treatment infrastructure has not kept pace with the unprecedentedly rapid spike in waste generation. In cities such as Beijing, state-of-the-art waste treatment facilities exist alongside (and sometimes in competition with) a huge informal sector that scavenges value from waste, and which continues to thrive despite serious environmental and public health concerns (Kirby and Lora-Wainwright 2015).

A closer examination of the Lujiashan case reveals a third characteristic of waste management in China – its growing contentiousness. Local governments across the country have faced strong public opposition to waste infrastructure, and some issues (especially waste incineration) have been openly debated online and in the media (Johnson 2014). Whilst some protests resemble the classic 'not-in-my-backyard' problem, they cannot be separated from genuine public concern about officials' ability and motivation to effectively regulate waste treatment facilities, which, like Lujiashan, are often pushed through with minimal attention to procedural details (Johnson 2014). Against this backdrop, the decision to build a huge facility in a relatively remote part of the city on a plot of land owned by the Beijing Capital Steel Company was partly motivated by the desire to circumvent public opposition, which had already undermined several waste incinerators slated for construction in the city's suburbs (Johnson 2013b; Li 2014).

This chapter provides an overview of recent developments concerning China's MSW situation. The next section provides an overview of the legislative and administrative framework for waste management. This chapter then examines recent shifts in waste treatment techniques,

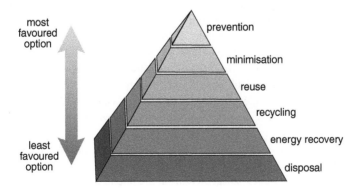

most favoured option

least favoured option

prevention

minimisation

reuse

recycling

energy recovery

disposal

Figure 22.1   The waste hierarchy

in particular the transition from landfill to incineration. It then focuses on some of the environmental impacts of the country's waste challenge by looking at the regulation of landfills and incinerators, before concluding.

Waste governance in China

Municipal solid waste can be defined as 'waste originating in urban areas from residential, commercial, institutional, and municipal services sources' (Su et al. 2014, 95). It includes everyday garbage such as kitchen waste (which makes up over half of China's MSW stream), paper, plastics, glass, metal and items such as batteries and discarded household appliances (Su et al. 2014). It does not include industrial waste, most of which is handled by industries themselves (World Bank 2005, 8).

China's legislative framework for handling waste is relatively highly developed. The main piece of legislation for addressing MSW is the *Law on Prevention and Control of Environmental Pollution by Solid Waste* (1995, amended 2004) (National People's Congress 2004). It sets out the main principles guiding MSW management in China, including the need to reduce the volume and hazardousness of MSW. Whereas the 1995 version of the law limited producer responsibility to waste stemming from the production process, the 2004 amended version extended this to take consumption and disposal of goods into account (Chen et al. 2010). It therefore established extended producer responsibility (EPR) as a key principle underpinning MSW management. In a similar vein, the 2002 *Law on Promotion of Cleaner Production* (amended in 2012) stipulates that manufacturers must reduce waste throughout the manufacturing process (World Bank 2005, 16), and the 2008 *Circular Economy Promotion Law of the People's Republic of China* establishes the principle of the '3 Rs' – reduce, reuse, and recycle – in the production process (National People's Congress 2008).

Responsibility for MSW management cuts across several ministries and various levels of government. The Ministry of Environmental Protection (MEP) and its subordinate units, Environmental Protection Bureaus (EPBs), are responsible for regulating pollution from waste treatment facilities and for environmental impact assessment approval. The Ministry of Housing and Urban–rural Development (MOHURD) at the central level, and departments of urban environmental hygiene at the local levels, are responsible for cleaning up, collecting, storing, transporting and treating waste (including provision of MSW treatment infrastructure) (National People's Congress 2004). The Ministry of Commerce oversees recycling.

Under China's decentralized administrative system, local governments are primarily responsible for day-to-day waste management. MSW management – which globally is often the biggest budgetary expense for local governments (Hoornweg and Bhada-Tata 2012) – is a serious financial burden to local governments in China (Zhang et al. 2010). Public investment in waste treatment has lagged behind investment in other environmental issues (OECD 2007). As a result, the Asian Development Bank (2009) estimates that almost half of China's MSW is untreated and disposed of in unsuitable landfills on the edges of cities. This, however, masks the considerable inter- and intra-regional variation in financial capacity for waste treatment. For example, in 2006 the city of Dalian was able to spend 4.5 times the national average on waste treatment (Chen et al. 2010).

The funding problem has been overcome to an extent by private (including overseas) investment into waste management facilities (OECD 2007). This is part of a conscious strategy to transfer responsibility for waste management from the public to the private sector in order to improve MSW treatment (Chen et al. 2010). Several policies have been promulgated to this effect, including establishing a legal basis for waste charging in 2002 (Chen et al. 2010) and, more recently, the provision of generous subsidies for waste-to-energy incinerators. According to Su et al. (2014, 108), private companies and public–private joint ventures own between 30 and 40 per cent of waste treatment facilities in China.

Waste collection and treatment

MSW collection and treatment started in earnest in the 1980s. At that time, less than 2 per cent of MSW was properly treated and disposed of (Su et al. 2014). Before the mid-1980s, most of Shanghai's MSW was being used as organic fertilizer in adjacent fields, a practice that became less feasible as the proportion of inorganic materials in the waste stream increased (Su et al. 2014, 102). As Figure 22.2 shows, MSW treatment capacity has increased substantially. According to one estimate, 86 per cent of MSW is collected, and of that 76 per cent is disposed of safely (Tian et al. 2013, 148). However, it is recognized that further improvement is needed. Speaking in 2011, the then Premier Wen Jiabao noted that rapid urbanization, growing consumption and a dearth of adequate waste treatment infrastructure was seriously affecting the urban environment and undermining social stability (China Waste Information Network n.d., b). To address this, the 12th Five-Year Plan (FYP) (2011–2015) set the ambitious goal of increasing MSW treatment capacity by 580,000 tons per day, to 871,000 tons per day, by 2015. Meeting this target will be tough – by 2013, daily MSW treatment capacity had yet to exceed 500,000 tons (see Figure 22.2).

Figure 22.2 does not include scavenged waste, which is not included in official statistics, and estimates of which vary significantly. According to one 2001 study, it represents between 8 and 10 per cent of MSW in China (Wang and Nie 2001, 251), whereas a 2014 study estimated that at least one-third of MSW was scavenged (Su et al. 2014, 103).

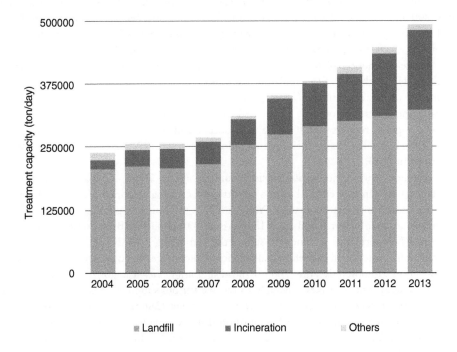

Figure 22.2   Municipal solid waste treatment, 2004–2013

End-of-pipe solutions: landfill and incineration

Landfill and incineration are the main MSW treatment methods, and reliance on these two technologies is set to increase in the foreseeable future. Although China's first waste-to-energy incinerator was built at Qingshuihe in Shenzhen as early as 1988, other jurisdictions were slow to follow suit. Most local governments favoured landfill, which was seen as a relatively easy and inexpensive way to dispose of MSW. In 2004, an average of 205,889 tons of waste were sent to landfill every day. By 2013 this had risen to 322,783 tons per day. Chinese cities remain heavily reliant on landfill, and the number of landfill facilities is set to increase during the 12th FYP (Su et al. 2014, 107).

Although landfill remains the dominant MSW treatment method, the percentage of waste sent to landfill declined from 86 per cent in 2004 to just over 65 per cent in 2013, with waste incineration taking up the slack (see Figure 22.2). Compared with landfill, incineration requires far less space, and waste can be burnt indefinitely. Yet toxic ash (which can be anything between 5 and 50 per cent of pre-burn volume) still needs to be disposed of, and incinerator emissions can be harmful to public health if not properly regulated (Denault 2012). Critics also argue that incineration discourages waste reduction, reuse and recycling (Denault 2012). Despite these concerns, WTE incinerators are being constructed across China, with some commentators comparing their rapid emergence to a waste incineration 'Great Leap Forward' (Johnson 2013a).

By the end of 2004, China only had 54 municipal waste incinerators with a combined capacity of 16,907 tons per day, with each incinerator averaging 313 tons per day. By 2013 it had 166 incinerators with a combined capacity of 158,488 tons per day, representing an almost tenfold increase in waste incineration capacity in under a decade (National Bureau of Statistics of China 2014). On average, each incinerator was burning close to 1,000 tons per day. It was expected that China would have over 300 incinerators with a combined daily capacity of 300,000 tons by the end of the 12th FYP. In other words China constructed almost 200 incinerators during the plan period. To put this into perspective, Elizabeth Royte noted in a book published in 2005 that, whilst the United States had not constructed any incinerators since 1996, 'other nations are more gung-ho. [Worldwide] since 1996, 165 WTE [waste-to-energy] plants have either been built or are under construction' (Royte 2005, 81). The 12th FYP also stipulated that waste incineration should account for at least 35 per cent of waste treatment capacity nationally, and at least 48 per cent in the Eastern Seaboard. Incineration should be prioritized over landfill in 'eastern regions, economically developed regions, regions with scarce land resources, and cities with large populations' (12th FYP).[2] China met the waste incineration ratio target, with 32 per cent of treated MSW incinerated in 2013.

In common with other post-socialist countries (Gille 2004), China's promotion of incineration has been viewed as a business opportunity, creating an unprecedented 'golden age' for domestic and overseas companies (Yang 2012). One estimate put the market value of incineration at 26.6 billion RMB in 2015 and over 43 billion RMB by 2020 (China Waste Information Network, n.d., a). Since the start of the 11th FYP (2006–2010) the Chinese central government has issued a raft of preferential policies to encourage the construction and operation of incinerators. Importantly, the 2005 *Renewable Energy Law* categorized incineration as renewable energy, which makes it eligible to receive various subsidies.[3] Examples include the 2006 *Management Scheme on Renewable Electricity Tariff and Cost-Sharing*, promulgated by the National Development and Reform Commission (NDRC), which gave incinerator operators 0.25 RMB per kilowatt-hour (kWh) of electricity generated. In March 2012, the NDRC raised this to 0.65 RMB per kWh.

As well as receiving subsidies for electric power generation, incinerator companies earn money for every ton of waste burnt. The Chinese authorities favour a 'build–operate–transfer' (BOT) approach to waste incinerators. Under this system, after construction is completed, waste incinerator companies are given the right to operate the incinerator for a set period of time, usually between 20 and 30 years. The incinerator then reverts back to public ownership.

Composting

Composting refers to 'the decomposition and stabilization of the organic fraction of MSW carried out by a microbial community under controlled, aerobic conditions' (Vergara 2012, 137). In common with most countries, composting (*duifei*) remains limited in China (Vergara 2012).[4] There are ten composting sites across the country with a combined capacity of just 5,480 tons per day (less than double the daily capacity of the Lujiashan incinerator) (Tian et al. 2013). Composting is not economically attractive due to the difficulties associated with separating out compostable waste (mainly kitchen waste), and because of the availability of cheaper synthetic alternatives (Tian et al. 2013). In addition, the quality of compost is often low due to insufficient sorting prior to composting (World Bank 2005, 27).

Recycling

The OECD claims that, with the exception of paper and cardboard, recycling rates in China are relatively low compared with OECD countries (OECD 2007). However, informal recycling is not accounted for in official statistics, and estimates of its size vary significantly. According to the World Bank, 2.5 million people work in the informal waste sorting and recycling sector, which is almost double the 1.3 million people estimated to work in the formal urban waste collection system (World Bank 2005, 25). Indeed, waste scavenging can be a lucrative business. Illegal dumps, such as the estimated 500 or so that form Beijing's 'Seventh Ring', operate outside of the formal waste management system (Liu 2011; Watts 2010).[5] China's informal recycling sector comprises approximately 60,000 small-scale family-run recycling businesses (Minter 2013). Until a government crackdown in 2011, one-third of these were located in just one place – Hebei Province's Wen'an County (Minter 2013).

The precarious nature of China's informal recycling sector has resulted in calls to legalize and properly regulate it (OECD 2007). An attempt is under way to consolidate and modernize the industry. For example, a huge 455-acre recycling park, which will eventually process one million tons of plastic per year, is being constructed in Qingyuan, Guangdong Province (Sun 2014b). Such facilities present themselves as environmentally friendly alternatives to the informal recycling sector, which is often portrayed as dirty and backwards. To quote the person in charge of the Qingyuan project, 'These new recycling parks will ensure the recyclers are equipped with technology, management skills, and environmental protection' (Sun 2014b). However, it remains to be seen whether scaling up the recycling sector will genuinely lead to a greener and more efficient industry.

China imports a huge quantity of waste for recycling. One reason is that materials such as scrap metals are in high demand from China's manufacturing sector (Minter 2013). For example, it is estimated that scrap copper imports provide the feedstock for one-third of the country's copper production (Davis 2015). In 1997, China imported US$194 million of scrap and secondary materials from the United States (World Bank 2005, 26). By 2002 this had reached US$1.2 billion (World Bank 2005, 26), and in 2010 China imported over US$10 billion of scrap metal and paper from the US (Plumer 2013). China is the world's biggest importers of waste plastics. In 2013 it imported 7.9 million tons, most of which was recycled by companies located in the Eastern Seaboard (Sun 2014a).

In February 2013, China announced a crackdown on poorly sorted or contaminated waste imports through its 'Green Fence' policy. This meant that any shipment of substandard waste would be rejected at Chinese ports. During the first six months of operation, 800,000 tons of recyclable waste and scrap were rejected, and 247 companies had their import licences suspended (Earley 2013). Overall, however, the impact on volumes of imported waste has been limited (Miller 2014; Sun 2014). One consequence of this policy has been to increase the role played by South East Asian countries in washing and sorting waste before shipping it to China – increasingly, via Hong Kong, where waste shipments can be consolidated before entering the Mainland (Miller 2014).

Regulating waste treatment facilities

MSW and its treatment have potentially important environmental implications. Tian and colleagues state that

> hazardous air pollutants and greenhouse gases discharged from waste disposal and treatment processes have become one of the new significant emerging air pollution problems in China and received great concerns about their adverse effects on surrounding ambient air quality and public health.
>
> *(Tian et al. 2013, 152)*

China has enacted numerous technical standards to regulate waste management facilities. Landfills are subject to requirements set out in the *Pollution Control Standard for MSW Landfills* (2008). However, over the years many landfills have been poorly operated and resulted in serious health problems for local communities. In 2004, Nie and colleagues found that only 10–30 per cent of landfills met national standards (Nie et al. 2004), whilst the OECD claimed that less than 10 per cent of waste was being disposed of in landfills that conform to technical standards based on OECD countries (OECD 2007). Zhang et al. (2010, 1629) state that, 'only newly developed landfills (e.g., in Shenzhen, Guangzhou) are considered to be operating at anywhere near internationally accepted standards'. China recovers approximately 20 per cent of its landfill gases, compared with an estimated 60 per cent in western countries (Tian et al. 2013, 147). In addition, the high moisture content of Chinese MSW – which is due to kitchen waste comprising around 60 per cent of household garbage (Zhang et al. 2010) – increases the amount of leachate at landfills (World Bank 2005).

Chinese cities must deal with the legacy of previous MSW policies, particularly in relation to simple waste dumps that pose a serious threat to groundwater quality. It is estimated that there are over 5,000 such brownfield sites in cities exceeding one million residents that require cleanup (World Bank 2005). The municipality of Chongqing has 50 such sites alone (World Bank 2005, 31).

Critics of waste incineration have long expressed concern about toxic incinerator emissions. Environmental concerns were cited as the main reason why no new incinerators were constructed in the United States between 1995 and 2006 (Denault 2012). Technology has improved however, and proponents stress that incinerators are safe provided they are properly regulated (Rootes 2009). In contrast, opponents raise questions about how incinerators are operated, and claim that some local authorities do not install state-of-the-art filters, which can be more expensive than the rest of the facility.

In common with other countries, Chinese regulatory standards for waste incinerators have become stricter over time (Rootes 2009). The main standard for controlling waste incinerator emissions is the *Pollution Control Standard for Municipal Waste Incineration (GB 18485-2001)*, which was updated in 2014 *(GB18485-2014)*. The 2014 version introduced stricter standards for a variety of pollutants including lead, mercury and sulphur dioxide. It also tightened the standard for dioxin emissions. The 2004 *Research Strategy for Controlling and Reducing China's Dioxin-Type Persistent Organic Pollutants* lists waste incineration as one of the country's six major dioxin-emitting industries, and public concern about the impact of living next to incinerators has often been expressed in terms of fears about dioxin pollution and its impact on public health (Johnson 2013a). The standard for dioxin emissions in the 2001 version was set at 1.0 nanogram of toxic equivalent per cubic metre (ngTEQ/m^3), or ten times laxer than the European Union standard of 0.1 ngTEQ/m^3 (contained in *EU2000/76/EC*). The 2014 version adopted the EU standard, meaning a tenfold increase in stringency. Incinerators built before 2014 were required to apply the new standard after 2016.

Chinese laws and regulations do not stipulate an overall maximum acceptable concentration level of dioxins – they only target individual sources of dioxins. However, in 2008 the MEP, NDRC and National Energy Administration issued the *Notice Regarding the Strengthening of Environmental Impact Assessment Management Work for Electricity Generation from Biomass Projects*. This Notice asks EIA units to consult the Japanese standard for overall dioxin concentrations when evaluating potential incinerator sites. The Japanese standard, which was passed in 1999, sets a maximum of 0.6 pgTEQ/m^3 for airborne dioxin emissions. Other countries have stricter standards – for example, Canada sets the limit at 0.1 pgTEQ/m^3 (Mao 2011).

Measuring dioxins is expensive and technically demanding, and there are only six organizations capable of measuring and analysing dioxins in the entire country (Zhao et al. 2011, 88). Some government departments have openly admitted that they lack the capacity to measure dioxins. For example, when a group of NGO activists wrote to the Sichuan Provincial EPB to request the disclosure of a list of companies that emit significant amounts of dioxins, the reply read as follows: 'because Sichuan is in the relatively underdeveloped western region, our technology and equipment for monitoring dioxins is not up to standard. We are therefore temporarily unable to provide a list of major dioxin-emitting companies' (on file with author).

Due to limited transparency, it is difficult to determine the performance of incinerators in China, especially when it comes to emissions of dioxins. In 2012, several environmental NGOs filed information disclosure requests with EPBs overseeing all of China's 122 operational incinerators. Information on dioxin emissions was only provided in relation to ten incinerators. According to this data, all of these incinerators were in compliance with national dioxin emission standards, although half exceeded the much stricter EU standards. Activists frequently cite a 2009 article in the journal *Chemosphere*. This article examined dioxin emissions from 19 incinerators. It found that 13 emitted dioxins in excess of the EU standard of 0.1 ngTEQ/m^3, and three incinerators failed to meet the national standard of 1.0 ngTEQ/m^3.

The high moisture content of China's MSW reduces the efficiency of incineration, including by limiting the amount of energy that can be generated. As a result, coal is often combined with waste before burning. National standards limit the proportion of coal that can be added to WTE incinerators to 20 per cent, but in some cases coal accounts for as much as 70 per cent of incinerated materials (Balkan 2012).

Conclusion

When it comes to waste management, China has come a long way in a short period. It has increased its waste treatment capacity considerably, which is just as well given the huge scale of the country's MSW challenge (Hoornweg and Bhada-Tata 2012). As Gille's study of waste politics in socialist Hungary highlights, it would be wrong to assume a teleological transition towards a better system for handling waste (Gille 2007). China exhibits significant regional variation in waste treatment capacity and infrastructure, and many challenges remain (Chen et al. 2010).

Despite enshrining principles regarding waste reduction, reuse, and recycling in various pieces of legislation, the Chinese authorities have focused overwhelmingly on 'end-of-pipe' solutions. Many of these facilities are lagging behind international standards. In 2007 an OECD report stated that, 'modern waste management practices such as separate collection, use of landfill gas and incineration with energy recovery are still the *exception rather than the rule in China*' (OECD 2007, 131, italics in the original). There have been some improvements, including a concerted effort to promote waste incineration – however, even this has proved controversial due to concerns about cost, and environmental and public health impact, which are believed to vary hugely between different facilities (Balkan 2012). Limited transparency has added fuel to public concern that incinerators, like landfills before them, are often poorly regulated, and scholars have advocated increasing transparency and public participation in order to build trust with local communities affected by waste infrastructure (Che et al. 2013).

Chinese environmentalists hope that more attempts can be made to move China up the waste hierarchy through greater reduction, reuse and recycling of MSW. In particular, they have advocated better source separation prior to disposal. Various pilot projects have been attempted, including one implemented in eight major cities that began in 2000. However, results were disappointing, with poor performance blamed on various factors including vague legislation, bureaucratic fragmentation, limited facilities for waste sorting, and limited public involvement (Tai et al. 2011; World Bank 2013). Raising public awareness about MSW issues is an important element of a more holistic waste management system. Confrontations over waste infrastructure, most notably during the 2009 anti-incinerator campaign in Panyu, Guangzhou, have sometimes evolved into broader discussions about how to deal with the waste problem, including the role of individual citizens (Johnson 2014). Arguably, however, much more needs to be done to push Chinese cities higher up the waste treatment hierarchy.

Notes

1 Statistics on waste should be taken with more than a pinch of salt (Gille 2007). Most official data in China refers to waste collected instead of waste generated (World Bank 2005, 6). Waste categorization sometimes varies between different cities (World Bank 2005, 8).
2 Chinese small- and medium-sized cities also have a number of small-scale incinerators that typically burn about 100 tons of waste per day. Local governments finance most of these facilities, and their safety levels are unreliable. There are also many small-scale incinerators in rural areas, which burn around 2–20 tons of waste per day, and which do not use any pollution reduction technology.
3 Similar provisions also apply in the United States and European Union (Denault 2012).
4 According to Vergara (2012, 139), composting rates are highly variable, ranging from 1 per cent in the United Kingdom to 9 per cent in the United States and 22 per cent in the Netherlands.
5 The other six rings refer to Beijing's six ring roads. As Su et al. (2014, 96) note, MSW services in most cities are concentrated in central areas and do not extend to the suburbs or rural fringes.

References

Asian Development Bank, 2009. ADB supports clean waste-to-energy project in the PRC. News Release. Retrieved from https://www.adb.org/news/adb-supports-clean-waste-energy-project-prc (accessed 12 December 2016).

Balkan, E., 2012. Dirty truth about China's incinerators. *Chinadialogue*, 4 July. Retrieved from https://www.chinadialogue.net/article/show/single/en/5024-Dirty-truth-about-China-s-incinerators (accessed 17 June 2015).

Che Y.; Yang K.; Jin Y.; Zhang W.; Shang Z. and Tai J., 2013. Residents' concerns and attitudes toward a municipal solid waste landfill: integrating a questionnaire survey and GIS techniques. *Environmental Monitoring and Assessment*, *185*(12), 10001–10013. Retrieved from http://link.springer.com/article/10.1007/s10661-013-3308-y/fulltext.html (accessed 4 December 2016).

Chen X.; Geng Y. and Fujita T., 2010. An overview of municipal solid waste management in China. *Waste Management*, *30*(4), 716–724. Retrieved from http://www.sciencedirect.com/science/article/pii/S0956053X09004590 (accessed 4 December 2016).

China Waste Information Network (n.d., a). Newsletter No. 2. Retrieved from http://www.waste-cwin.org/node/36 (accessed 4 December 2016).

China Waste Information Network (n.d., b). Newsletter No. 4. Retrieved from http://www.waste-cwin.org/node/34 (accessed 4 December 2016).

Davis, A., 2015. Copper imports seen supporting prices. *Bloomberg Business*, 23 January. Retrieved from http://www.bloomberg.com/news/articles/2015-01-23/china-s-tumbling-scrap-copper-imports-seen-supporting-prices (accessed 4 December 2016).

Denault, J.-F., 2012. Incinerator construction trends. In C. A. Zimring & W. L. Rathje (eds), *Encyclopedia of Consumption and Waste: The Social Science of Garbage*. Thousand Oaks, CA: Sage, 408–409.

Earley, K., 2013. Could China's 'green fence' prompt a global recycling revolution? *The Guardian*, 27 August. Retrieved from http://www.theguardian.com/sustainable-business/china-green-fence-global-recycling-innovation (accessed 4 December 2016).

Gerth, K., 2010. *As China Goes, so Goes the World: How Chinese Consumers Are Transforming Everything*. New York: Hill and Wang.

Gille, Z., 2004. Europeanising Hungarian waste policies: progress or regression? *Environmental Politics* *13*(1), 114–134. Retrieved from http://www.tandfonline.com/doi/pdf/10.1080/0964401041000168 5164 (accessed 4 December 2016).

Gille, Z., 2007. *From the Cult of Waste to the Trash Heap of History: The Politics of Waste in Socialist and Postsocialist Hungary*. Bloomington, IN: Indiana University Press. Retrieved from http://www.loc.gov/catdir/toc/ecip0620/2006026312.html (accessed 4 December 2016).

Hoornweg, D.; Bhada-Tata, P., 2012. *What a Waste: A Global Review of Solid Waste Management. Urban Development Series; Knowledge Papers No. 15*. Washington DC: The World Bank.

Johnson, T., 2013a. The health factor in anti-waste incinerator campaigns in Beijing and Guangzhou. *The China Quarterly*, *214*, 356–375. Retrieved from http://journals.cambridge.org/abstract_S0305741013000660 (accessed 4 December 2016).

Johnson, T., 2013b. The politics of waste incineration in Beijing: the limits of a top-down approach? *Journal of Environmental Policy & Planning*, *15*(1), 109–128. Retrieved from http://www.tandfonline.com/doi/abs/10.1080/1523908X.2012.752183 (accessed 4 December 2016).

Johnson, T. R., 2014. Regulatory dynamism of environmental mobilization in urban China. *Regulation & Governance*. doi: 10.1111/rego.12068.

Kirby, P. W., and Lora-Wainwright, A., 2015. Exporting harm, scavenging value: transnational circuits of e-waste between Japan, China and beyond. *Area*. doi: 10.1111/area.12169.

Li Y., 2014. Laying garbage to waste. *China Daily USA*, 7 October. Retrieved from http://usa.chinadaily.com.cn/epaper/2014-10/07/content_18702261.htm (accessed 4 December 2016).

Liu J., 2011. Mounting trash emergency encircles Beijing. *Time*, 20 July. Retrieved from http://content.time.com/time/world/article/0,8599,2083990,00.html (accessed 4 December 2016).

Meng D., 2011. Laji fenshao, yuanhe 'mingxiu zhandao, andu chencang.' 'Liulitun' zhong qijian, 'Lujiashan' ji shangma (Why is waste incineration akin to 'mending the road in the light, entering into secret liaison in the dark?' 'Liulitun' is finally abandoned, 'Lujiashan' in a rush to begin). *Southern Weekend*, 25 February. Retrieved from http://www.infzm.com/content/55573 (accessed 4 December 2016).

Thomas R. Johnson

Miller, K., 2014. Green fence boon for China, group says. *Plastics News*, 14 November. Retrieved from http://www.plasticsnews.com/article/20141114/NEWS/141119952/green-fence-boon-for-china-group-says (accessed 4 December 2016).

Minter, A., 2013. *Junkyard Planet: Travels in the Billion-dollar Trash Trade*. New York: Bloomsbury Press.

National Bureau of Statistics of China, 2014. *China Statistical Yearbook 2014*. Beijing: China Statistics Press.

National People's Congress, 2004. *Law of the People's Republic of China on the Prevention and Control of Environmental Pollution by Solid Waste (Revised)*. Retrieved from http://www.chinalaw.gov.cn (accessed 4 December 2016).

National People's Congress, 2008. *Circular Economy Promotion Law of the People's Republic of China*. Retrieved from http://www.chinalaw.gov.cn (accessed 4 December 2016).

Nie Y.; Li T.; Yan G.; Wang Y.; Ma X., 2004. An optimal model and its application for the management of municipal solid waste from regional small cities in China. *Journal of the Air & Waste Management Association*, *54*(2), 191–199. Retrieved from http://www.tandfonline.com/doi/pdf/10.1080/10473289.2004.10470894 (accessed 4 December 2016).

OECD, 2007. *OECD Environmental Performance Reviews: China*. Paris: OECD.

Plumer, B., 2013. China doesn't even want to buy our garbage anymore. *The Washington Post*, 9 May. Retrieved from http://www.washingtonpost.com/blogs/wonkblog/wp/2013/05/09/chinas-crackdown-on-trash-could-make-it-harder-for-u-s-cities-to-recycle/ (accessed 4 December 2016).

Rootes, C., 2009. Environmental movements, waste and waste infrastructure: an introduction. *Environmental Politics*, *18*(6), 817–834. Retrieved from http://www.tandfonline.com/doi/full/10.1080/09644010903345587 (accessed 4 December 2016).

Royte, E., 2005. *Garbage Land: On the Secret Trail of Trash*. New York: Little, Brown. Retrieved from http://www.loc.gov/catdir/toc/ecip052/2004024732.html (accessed 4 December 2016).

Su L.; Huang S.; Niu D.; Chai X.; Nie Y. and Zhao Y., 2014. Municipal solid waste management in China. In Pariatamby, A. and Tanaka M., eds, *Municipal Solid Waste Management in Asia and the Pacific Islands: Challenges and Strategic Solutions*. Singapore: Springer, 95–112.

Sun, N. Y., 2014a. China quells waste imports, recycling still continues to grow. *Plastics News*, 20 May. Retrieved from http://www.plasticsnews.com/article/20140520/NEWS/140529999/china-quells-waste-imports-recycling-still-continues-to-grow (accessed 4 December 2016).

Sun, N. Y., 2014b. China's largest compounder shaking up the recycling industry. *Plastics News*, 19 May. Retrieved from http://www.plasticsnews.com/article/20140519/NEWS/140519918/chinas-largest-compounder-shaking-up-the-recycling-industry (accessed 4 December 2016).

Tai J.; Zhang W.; Che Y. and Feng D., 2011. Municipal solid waste source-separated collection in China: a comparative analysis. *Waste Management*, *31*(8), 1673–1682. Retrieved from http://www.sciencedirect.com/science/article/pii/S0956053X11001589 (accessed 12 December 2016).

Tian H.; Gao J.; Hao J.; Lu L.; Zhu C. and Qiu P., 2013. Atmospheric pollution problems and control proposals associated with solid waste management in China: a review. *Journal of Hazardous Materials*, *252*, 142–154. Retrieved from http://www.sciencedirect.com/science/article/pii/S0304389413001222 (accessed 4 December 2016).

Vergara, S. E., 2012. Composting. In Zimring, C. A. and Rathje, W. L., eds, *Encyclopedia of Consumption and Waste: The Social Science of Garbage*. Thousand Oaks, CA: Sage, 137–139.

Wang H.; Nie Y., 2001. Municipal solid waste characteristics and management in China. *Journal of the Air & Waste Management Association*, *51*(2), 250–263. Retrieved from http://tandfonline.com/doi/abs/10.1080/10473289.2001.10464266 (accessed 4 December 2016).

Watts, J., 2010. Beijing to sweeten stench of rubbish crisis with giant deodorant guns. *The Guardian*, 26 March. Retrieved from https://www.theguardian.com/environment/2010/mar/26/beijing-rubbish-deodorant (accessed 12 December 2016).

World Bank, 2005. *Waste Management in China: Issues and Recommendations*, Urban Development Working Papers, East Asia Infrastructure Department, Working Paper No. 9.

World Bank, 2013. China: 3 million to benefit from improved solid waste management in city of Ningbo. Press Release, 31 May. Retrieved from http://www.worldbank.org/en/news/press-release/2013/05/31/china-3-million-to-benefit-from-improved-solid-waste-management-in-city-of-ningbo (accessed 4 December 2016).

Yang C., 2012. Chengshi shenghuo laji guanli: Zhengyi zhong qianxing (Municipal domestic waste management: moving forwards in the middle of dispute). In: Yang, D., ed., *Zhongguo Huanjing Fazhan Baogao (2012) (Annual Report on China's Environmental Development (2012))*. Beijing: Social Sciences Academic Press (China), 124–134.

Yu L., 2014. *Consumption in China: How China's New Consumer Ideology is Shaping the Nation.* Cambridge, UK: Polity Press.

Zhang D. Q.; Tan S. K. and Gersberg, R. M., 2010. Municipal solid waste management in China: status, problems and challenges. *Journal of Environmental Management,* *91*(8), 1623–1633. Retrieved from http://www.sciencedirect.com/science/article/pii/S0301479710000848 (accessed 4 December 2016).

Zhao Z., 2011. Duobi gongzhong gao fenshao zhe, hai neng daibiao renmin liyi ma? (Can those who do incineration whilst avoiding the public still represent the people's interests?) *China Waste Information Network Newsletter,* 1, 10–11. Retrieved from http://www.waste-cwin.org/sites/default/files/zhong_guo_la_ji_xin_xi_gong_zuo_wang_luo_ji_kan_zhong__0.pdf (accessed 9 June 2015).

23

DEALING WITH DISCARDED E-DEVICES

Yvan Schulz and Benjamin Steuer[1]

Introduction

The issue of discarded electrical and electronic devices (DEDs) has been closely associated with China for over a decade. In the early 2000s, a group of (mostly American) NGOs released a report (Puckett et al. 2002) accompanied by a documentary in which they revealed how consumer electronics discarded in regions such as North America or Western Europe ended up in poor regions of Asia, where they were dismantled and processed by unskilled migrant workers using basic technologies. The report and documentary stressed the pollution caused by such 'primitive' recycling operations and its harmful impact on local populations. They referred in particular to the town of Guiyu (贵屿), located in Guangdong Province, that soon became infamous as the epitome of environmental harm resulting from technological progress and consumerism.

Since then, the issue of 'e-waste' has been framed in remarkably consistent ways in China, at least if we look at laws and regulations, academic conferences and publications, policy papers, corporate documents, and media reports. By and large, the story goes like this:

The E-waste story

E-waste is imported through illegal channels as well as generated within China. The country must deal with ever-growing volumes since consumption of household appliances and electronics is on the rise and products have limited lifetimes. E-waste is made up of various types of materials, many of which are recyclable and some of which even have a high economic or strategic value. Therefore, it can, and should, serve as a source of natural resources. However, recycling as practised by small workshops leads to the release of organic pollutants and heavy metals, in other words toxic substances that cause serious environmental and health damage. Moreover, the so-called informal sector only manages to recover a small portion of the materials it processes. Thus, for the sake of both pollution control and higher resource efficiency, e-waste management and treatment should be entrusted to corporations, who are in a better position to conduct proper recycling than the

> informal sector, since they are capable of investing in state-of-the-art technologies that comply with international standards. Not only that, but corporations also show more concern for environmental protection, whereas individual entrepreneurs and privately owned small companies are only motivated by profit.

This dominant discourse (rendered here in an ideal-typical way) highlights certain moments in DEDs' lifecycles while obscuring others, favours certain economic actors while discrediting others, and promotes certain techniques while ignoring others. It justifies the necessity and appropriateness of the 'formal recycling system' (*zhenggui huishou zhidu*) that has been set up by the central government in response to 'the e-waste problem'.

The present chapter provides a description, analysis and critique of this system. Briefly put, we observe a focus on materials recovery and industry scaling-up, and claim that it is correlative with the disregard of: (1) the multitude of economic actors – collectively referred to as the 'informal sector' – that already deal with DEDs and, in most cases, have been doing so for a long time; (2) DEDs' specific material characteristics and the concrete politics of value that determine their fate; (3) reuse practices and their potential benefits. As we shall see, these three aspects are closely linked to one another.

Chinese state authorities made their first attempts at controlling flows of DEDs in 2000. However, a fully fledged regulatory system came into force in the late 2000s and early 2010s and is just starting to produce tangible results. Scientific and government experts readily acknowledge the slow pace of change in this field and the 'formal system's' lack of effectiveness. Some of them blame it on a weak implementation of the law – an argument often heard when it comes to environmental policy in China. By contrast, we regard policy design as most problematic. The 'formal system' rests on a programmatic approach to development and a tendency to look abroad for inspiration (see Tong and Yan 2013) that do little to solve the issues emerging on the ground, in specific situations and configurations that have a strong local character.

Policy outline

This section describes the regulatory system China has come up with in order to deal with DEDs.

Focusing on imports

China's first efforts at regulating the management of DEDs date back to the late 1990s and were aimed at imports. According to some estimations, approximately 70 per cent of all DEDs generated in high-income countries (14–35 million tons) were imported into China up until 2004 (Yu et al. 2010, 991)[2] and chiefly handled by small, unregistered businesses. To counter these flows, the central government banned the import of twelve categories of obsolete products in 2000[3] (SEPA 2000), including television sets, refrigerators, air conditioners, microwave ovens and computers. The restriction was progressively extended and reached fifty-five categories in 2008 (SEPA 2008). However, these measures have done little to curtail imports (Chung and Zhang 2011, 2639). In 2014, Chinese customs discovered for instance that, 72,000 tons of banned DEDs originating from Japan had successfully made their way into China in 2013 (Global Times 2014).

It must also be noted that the ban on imports does not apply to second-hand, functional goods or categories of products that 'can be used as raw materials', which includes waste wires and cables, waste electrical motors and other electrical scrap (Yang et al. 2008, 1591 and AQSIQ 2012). Some actors take advantage of these 'legal loopholes' (Chi et al. 2011, 734) and falsely declare their goods in order to facilitate border crossing. In 2013, the government adopted an allegedly tougher stance by launching a crackdown operation named Green Fence. Assessing its repercussions on the trade in DEDs is not an easy task: officials claim the operation was a success, whereas feedback from traders suggests that smuggling still takes place on a large scale.[4]

Managing domestic DEDs

In parallel to regulating imports, the central government also set up a system to address the issue of domestically generated DEDs. Three of this system's characteristics can be highlighted upfront:

1   High-level, general laws such as the *Cleaner Production Promotion Law* or CPPL (NPC 2002/2012) and the *Circular Economy Promotion Law* or CEPL (NPC 2008) apply to DEDs.
2   Key laws dealing directly with DEDs, known as the *China Waste Electrical and Electronic Equipment* (*WEEE*) (State Council 2009) and the *Restriction of Hazardous Substances* (*RoHS*) (MIIT 2006) Directives, emulate similar European regulations (EU 2003a and 2003b).
3   Experience gained through pilot projects throughout the 2000s played a key role in shaping the current regulatory system.

With regard to the first characteristic, the CPPL and the CEPL are key industrial policy documents that appeared in recent five-year plans. The CPPL does not mention DEDs explicitly but states that the treatment of discarded products must be pollution-free and environmentally friendly. The CEPL includes five articles on DEDs (no. 19, 38, 39, 51 and 56) that address issues such as toxicity, recycling and refurbishment. On the whole, however, both laws remain vague as to how DEDs are to be dealt with.

The second characteristic reveals that Chinese authorities relied on legal transplants while devising their own 'formal system of e-waste management'. Their models were always countries with a longer history of industrialization, that can be described as belonging to the first world (Schulz 2015).

Experimenting through pilot projects

As for the third characteristic, it shows that the central government adopted a double strategy consisting of issuing laws and regulations directly at the national level and, at the same time, conducting pilot projects at the local level. The first batch of pilot projects was launched in Beijing and Tianjin in 2000 and 2001, respectively, and a second batch followed in Zhejiang (2004) and Qingdao (2005). The legal framework for these projects stressed the importance of proper treatment but did not specify how they were to be realized. Local governments left the door open for experimentation with technologies and business models. The main aim was to observe how collection and dismantling operations would evolve at the local level so as to subsequently develop national DEDs recycling standards. Many projects took the shape of so-called public–private partnerships. According to most experts, pilot projects were effective in producing the necessary know-how (Chung and Zhang 2011; Hicks et al. 2005; Qu et al. 2013, 177). However, the experience revealed that small and unregistered businesses represented a challenge for the establishment of a formal recycling sector. In Hangzhou, for instance, the pilot project failed to collect sufficient amounts of DEDs because it did not make use of pre-existing collection networks set up by these businesses. Out of the expected 800,000 units per year, only 200,000 were collected and treated within two years (Yu et al. 2010, 994; Zhejiang Trade Net 2005). Similarly, the Qingdao project never achieved the targeted 600,000 units, as its collection system was mainly stationary and ignored non-registered collectors. Haier, the main private company involved in this project, backed away from the plan to set up a collection and treatment centre when it realized that volumes would be too small. The Beijing and Tianjin pilot projects seem to have faced similar difficulties (Computer World 2010).

Drawing lessons from these local projects (Zhou and Xu 2012), the central government introduced a second type of pilot project, this time at the national level. Referred to as the 'old for new' take-back scheme (OfN or *yi jiu huan xin*), this project was conducted in nine areas of China from 2009 to 2011. The main idea was to redirect flows of DEDs away from non-registered collectors by influencing consumer behaviour: owners of DEDs were offered a 10 per cent rebate on the purchase of a new device if they turned in an old one at a designated collection point or directly at a retail store. In order to enable companies involved in the OfN scheme (i.e. retailers, collectors and processors) to compete with non-registered actors – who bought DEDs at high prices – the government supported them with a state subsidy. The funds came from both the central (80 per cent) and the local levels (20 per cent) (Zhong 2010, 51–2) and were meant to allow these companies to offer better prices to consumers (Wang et al. 2013, 36).

The OfN scheme was first and foremost an economic instrument, not marked by environmental considerations. It served not only to provide support to licensed recycling companies, but also to boost domestic consumption and thereby compensate for a weakening demand on China's export markets (Wang et al. 2013, 34). The government issued guidelines that included, among others, requirements on collection (see MOF et al. 2009, art. 16–20). However, licensed recycling plants eventually relied on unregistered actors for access to devices – and they did so at least until 2015, since 85–100 per cent of their input was supplied by self-employed individuals and families running small businesses (Steuer et al. 2015).

The current system

China's pilot projects led the way for the current regulatory system, which is based on: (1) a central legal text, namely the *China WEEE directive* (State Council 2009); and (2) a financing mechanism drawing on the principle of extended producer responsibility (EPR). The *China WEEE directive* was adopted in 2009 and became effective in 2011. It is modelled on an earlier text adopted by the European Union (EU 2003a; Zhou and Xu 2012, 4714), however, the former only applies to a limited number of appliances, namely television sets, washing machines, air conditioners, refrigerators and personal computers (*siji yinao*), whereas the latter covers practically all kinds of DEDs found on the market. At the time of writing (June 2015), there were plans to extend the Chinese catalogue to a total of thirteen categories of products by March 2016.

China's national fund for the recycling of DEDs began to be implemented in 2012. It can be described as an EPR system to the extent that companies selling electrical and electronic devices ('producers') are required to pay a recycling fee on each device sold on the Chinese market. However, it should be distinguished from other national EPR systems (European ones, for instance), because producers in China are not required to organize DEDs collection and recycling in autonomous ways. The collected fees are transferred to a national fund that the

Chinese government uses to allocate subsidies to selected recyclers. The latter must comply with mandatory standards and procedures in order to obtain or retain their licence. At the time of writing (June 2015), a total of 106 recycling companies were enjoying funding and this number was expected to increase to 126 in coming years, according to the Ministry of Environmental Protection (Hu 2015). The government's main objective with this financing mechanism was to increase the scale and upgrade the technology of the DEDs recycling industry.

The development process of the most recent Chinese regulation on domestic DEDs management owes much to a pattern often encountered in the PRC (Heilmann 2008), namely experimentation at the local level followed by consolidation at the national level. Basically, the system is now centred on two principles (see State Council 2009, art. 5 and 34): (1) 'concentration of treatment' (*jizhong chuli*): small-scale facilities are supposed to make way for large-scale ones; and (2) 'multi-channel collection' (*duo qudao huishou*): licensed companies are free to supply their DEDs from any source.

Towards a stabilization of the legal system

Since the beginning of pilot projects and up until the end of the OfN scheme an increasing number of laws were adopted in this field. Each major regulation was followed by several minor implementation measures. This process seems to have ended with the issuance of the WEEE Directive. Since then, regulatory activity has declined (see below, Figure 23.1), which leads to the assumption that the system will undergo only minor changes in the near future.

Policy outcomes

This section discusses some of the results achieved in the implementation of the policies highlighted above as well as some of the obstacles encountered along the way.

The creation of a regulatory system

The main result achieved by the Chinese government in the field of DEDs management is arguably the construction of a comprehensive regulatory framework. As the previous section made clear, China has plenty of laws, decrees and measures that tackle DEDs' afterlife. This conveys the impression that the country is well equipped to deal with the issue, much like those it takes as models (i.e. Japan, Germany, Taiwan, etc.) – and Chinese officials use this favourable comparison to stress China's progress towards modernization (Schulz 2015).

However, shortcomings become evident when we look beyond official documents and discourse. For instance, the high frequency at which legal texts were adopted in China up until the China WEEE Directive, i.e. one piece of legislation every year or two, betrays their limited impact. Also, the Chinese government is often credited with setting up and implementing a genuine EPR system, which comes across as a major achievement given the complexity of such systems. But actually, EPR has only been realized to a limited extent in China. Policymakers initially discussed the possibility to require producers to take back their own devices and organize the latters' 'end of life' themselves, but eventually settled for the sole payment of a tax for recycling (Tong and Yan 2013, 200). This meant ignoring the initial idea behind the EPR principle, namely to encourage producers to improve the design of their products so as to facilitate recycling and better distribute the corresponding costs – it must be noted, however, that most EPR systems worldwide have failed to achieve this objective. Some producers claim

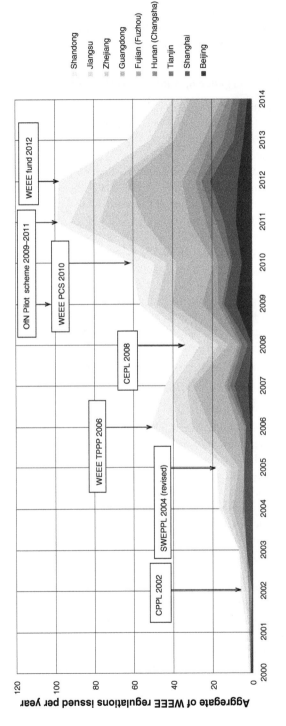

Figure 23.1 Regulatory development of DEDs management[1]

[1] Abbreviations are as follows: Solid Waste Environmental Pollution Prevention Law (SWEPPL), Cleaner Production Promotion Law (CPPL), Circular Economy Promotion Law (CEPL), WEEE Technical Pollution Prevention Policy (WEEE TPPP) and WEEE Pollution Control Standard (WEEE PCS).

they would have been better incentivized if given more leeway. In an interview in 2014, a representative of a multinational company importing electronics into China acknowledged that his company was trying to opt out of China's EPR system, which he described as opaque and largely ineffective.[5] He also argued that larger volumes of DEDs would be recycled if the industry was allowed to organize recycling in an autonomous way.

The emergence of a new recycling sector

Another major achievement that Chinese state authorities can be credited with is the creation of an industrial sub-sector made up of more than one hundred companies that operate recycling plants throughout the country – albeit exclusively in large urban centres – deal specifically with DEDs and are subject to state monitoring. The OfN was instrumental in kick-starting this sector (Wang et al. 2013, 36). Volumes of treated DEDs dropped after it ended in 2011, but are coming back up again according to official figures (CHEARI 2015, 6). Optimism, however, is tempered by the facts that licensed companies: (1) survive chiefly thanks to the subsidy they receive from the state-managed fund for recycling (REWIN 2015) – a situation referred to as 'feeding on the subsidy' (*chi butie*); (2) still suffer from a short supply; and (3) manage to lay their hands only on certain types of products. In 2013, no less than 3.3 billion RMB (approx. US$531 million) went into guaranteeing the competitiveness of these companies, yet they managed to collect only 39.87 million devices (compared to a total annual capacity of more than 100 million) and 94 per cent (in weight) of these devices were cathode-ray tube (CRT) television sets (CHEARI 2014). In other words, these plants require massive external funding, run below their full capacity and have an unbalanced product mix. It should also be noted that, at the time of writing, some of them had slowed down their production lines in reaction to delayed subsidy payments, which are themselves due to the recycling fund's deficit. Finally, since the introduction of the subsidy market prices for DEDs have gone up, raising DEDs management's overall costs.

The most difficult aspect of Chinese 'e-waste' policies to assess is arguably the government's alleged crackdown to 'suppress' so-called 'illegal activities', such as environmental pollution and smuggling. Repressive measures orchestrated by state authorities enjoy a wide publicity, especially in the media,[6] but this hardly compensates for the dearth of data on these activities. Indeed, their scale and nature remain subject to much speculation and imprecise or even erroneous claims (see Lepawsky et al. 2015). Some of the measures taken by state authorities at the local and central levels undoubtedly made business more difficult for the small enterprises that have been involved in the trade or transformation of DEDs during the last decades. Lora-Wainwright (2015) claims for instance, that recyclers in Guiyu suffer from a 'gradual and uneven disconnection' from China's flourishing economy. According to her, they are victims of a 'discourse of formalization' that portrays them as 'outcasts', 'no longer vehicles of development but obstacles to it'. On the other hand, places like Guiyu have been recycling DEDs at least until 2015 despite having been declared hotspots of clandestine and harmful activities long ago.

This apparent contradiction owes a lot to state authorities' stance towards 'small workshops' (*xiao zuofang*), which alternates between repression and deliberate ignorance. Local governments tend to wait until public attention and concern on the issue of pollution peak – triggering orders from above – before launching crackdowns, soil remediation programmes, or other kinds of measures likely to prove that they are taking action (see Kirby and Lora-Wainwright 2015). Meanwhile, they avoid interfering with small-scale dismantlers and processors' business. In townships that are heavily involved in DEDs recycling, like Guiyu or Longtang (龙塘), local governments have little incentive to restrain this industry. It generates considerable wealth and benefits them more or less directly (see Minter 2013, 192). At times, their interests may be at odds with those of higher administrative levels and their stance may jeopardize the latter's plans, but that need not necessarily be the case. Adam Minter argued for instance, that the main reason why recycling activities in Guiyu were still taking place in 2012, despite the bad press they had been attracting for a decade, was that authorities in Beijing had tacitly decided to let them go on, at least temporarily (Lamb 2012).

Environmental Protection Bureaus (EPB)'s lack of resources also hampers the success of repressive measures ordered against the so-called 'informal sector' of DEDs recycling. It prevents them from monitoring the whole range of recycling facilities that engage in this type of activity and requires them instead to focus more on licensed (large) plants.

Finally, small enterprises often manage to counter repressive measures by diverting goods through new routes and relocating facilities to remote areas. In the case of electronics, for instance, the Pearl River Delta likely remains a major area of entry at present, and Guiyu a major processing centre, but evidence suggests that shipments are now making their way into China through other ports (e.g. Dalian[7]) and to other rural regions (e.g. Jiangxi[8]) as well.

Shortcomings in policy design

The majority of institutional experts in China view the 'formal system of e-waste management' as an appropriate tool for dealing with DEDs in an effective and environmentally friendly way. They take for granted that solutions designed by developed countries are also applicable *mutatis mutandis* in China (Schulz 2015). For instance, Li Jinhui, a prominent figure who acts as counsellor to the Chinese government, recently appealed for technology transfers from rich countries to China during an international conference on electronics recycling in Asia (Li 2014). According to the dominant discourse within academic, government and media circles, China is on the right path and only needs time to progressively implement the measures adopted thus far.

In this section, we challenge such an assumption and argue that slow progress and lack of efficacy should rather be attributed to inappropriate policy design. Chinese regulations actually ignore essential aspects of DEDs recycling. Below, we make this clear by analysing three interconnected and problematic issues.

Excluding small enterprises

Because they are tailor-made for corporations operating capital-intensive facilities, China's e-waste policies all but leave out small businesses and individual entrepreneurs. For the latter, participating in the 'formal system of e-waste management' is extremely difficult, if not impossible. It requires investments that are beyond their means and skills that they never had the opportunity to develop. This system currently relies on self-employed individuals and family businesses for the collection, accumulation and delivery of DEDs, but it does not acknowledge these actors and their role. As a result, the latter are deprived of legitimacy, security and support. Furthermore, corporations' efforts to bypass these middlemen and source DEDs directly from consumers, for instance by deploying 'big data',[9] trigger favourable and enthusiastic responses from state authorities (see, e.g. Zha 2015) – though they have yet to prove effective.

The exclusion of small enterprises is even more pronounced in the field of dismantling and processing. Wilful ignorance and repression are hardly compatible with collaborative work between recyclers operating small facilities and state authorities, and thus stand in the way of improvements. While some managers claim that they would be willing to upgrade their facilities, better protect their workers, reduce their environmental impact or transition into other industrial sectors, it is hard to see how they could do so without any form of state recognition.

In brief, no significant effort is made in China to include small enterprises in what would be a truly comprehensive regulatory system. Things rather unfold as if these actors were doomed. But there are good reasons to doubt they will vanish soon. China's contemporary economic growth relies on a lively private sector, in which small enterprises' innovativeness, flexibility and efficiency still play a major role. Large corporations may have grown strong in and around first-tier and second-tier cities, but development in third-tier and fourth-tier cities, as well as in the countryside, still relies largely on small and medium enterprises (Naughton 2007). Thus far, the process of replacing small enterprises involved in DEDs recycling by bigger ones has proven slow and cumbersome, and as of June 2015 there were no signs of acceleration.

Moreover, excluding small enterprises runs counter to recommendations found in the literature on waste management in developing and emerging countries (e.g. Benson et al. 2014). Several authors contend that the 'informal sector' of recycling should be 'integrated' into the 'management system' for DEDs (Chi et al. 2011; Wang et al. 2012; ILO China 2013). Its characteristics, size and role should be taken into consideration at the level of policy design. Failure to do so, these authors warn, can result in delayed and incomplete implementation. From a social welfare perspective, it is worth noting that in China great numbers of people make a living by engaging with DEDs in more or less unregulated ways. The question of what professional activity these people could, would or should turn to if deprived of their current source of income is crucial – and yet barely touched upon in China (for an exception, see ILO China 2013).

Approaching DEDs as waste

China's policy on 'e-waste management' – much like those of countries it takes as models – is based on a conception of these objects as a form of waste and a source of secondary raw materials. This is reflected in the wide use scientific researchers, government officials, environmental activists and similar institutional experts make of concepts such as 'solid waste management' (*guti feiwu guanli*), 'urban mining' (*chengshi kuangchan*) and 'resource renewal' (*zaisheng ziyuan*). Their approach dominates in public discourse and passes for obvious, but its limitations become manifest as soon as we take a close look at what actually happens to DEDs and why.

Many of electrical and electronic devices' characteristics distinguish them from other types of objects and substances commonly qualified as waste. First, they are technologically complex products whose design and manufacture require considerable know-how, advanced equipment and intricate industrial networks. This affects their value at any given time in their lifecycle. Average prices of new devices may be dropping, but refrigerators, television sets and mobile phones still count among the most valuable objects found in households, at least in China.

Second, DEDs remain in use for a relatively long period of time – notwithstanding the accelerating pace at which they become obsolete – at least compared to disposable crockery, left-over food or effluent. In this regard, they rather resemble garments, vehicles or furniture, i.e. consumer goods that, when discarded by their first owners, are more often referred to as 'second-hand' than 'waste'.

Third, owners often dispose of their devices before the latter become unusable. Opportunities thus arise for direct resale and reuse, activities that take place on a large scale in China. Markets selling second-hand DEDs abound and are powered by fast-paced economic growth, uneven wealth distribution and impressive demographics. Many people, for instance, make a living by collecting DEDs in rich urban centres and selling them to peripheral and poorer areas (Minter 2013, 27; Schulz 2015).

Fourth, most types of DEDs, when defunct, can still be repaired, refurbished or repurposed, or even exploited as a stock of spare parts and components (Schulz 2016). In China, the job of transforming DEDs or their constituent parts so as to extend their lifetime requires more and more expertise while yielding less and less profit. Nevertheless, it remains a vibrant sector, as the presence of specialized repair shops in most neighbourhoods indicates. Fifth, DEDs are routinely portrayed as a dangerous form of waste, much like medical or nuclear waste. Direct contact with DEDs, however, does not inevitably lead to health and environmental damage. As long as these devices are in use or stocked properly they remain relatively innocuous. They only release toxic substances when cracked open, burnt or shredded. Accordingly, they do not represent a danger in themselves, but rather a substrate for potentially dangerous actions.

All of the above characteristics affect DEDs' fate. Chinese street pedlars and self-employed collectors, for instance, prefer used DEDs to other kinds of stuff they manage to obtain. When advertising their services, they always start by mentioning that they buy back television sets, refrigerators, washing machines, air conditioners, and so on. These used products allow them to achieve better profit margins than old newspapers, empty plastic bottles or rusty window frames. Admittedly, DEDs' attractiveness owes much to the fact that they contain copper, the most valuable material found (in significant quantities) in municipal solid waste. However, as a rule of thumb, devices are worth more than their constituent materials if one manages to preserve or restore their functionality (Yang et al. 2008). Independent collectors are fully aware of this and avoid dismantling devices that are functional and in demand. Instead, they employ a diversified strategy, which allows them to squeeze much value out of each device.

To approach DEDs as a form of waste arguably makes more sense in the context of developed countries than in emerging countries such as China – and a fortiori in developing countries. Chinese owners who discard DEDs, in particular, are used to selling their devices, not giving them away for free or throwing them in rubbish bins, contrary to their counterparts from rich, industrialized countries. Therefore, DEDs rarely end up in landfills or incinerators in China. The large-scale wasting of functioning devices that takes place in developed countries and preoccupies experts can hardly be observed in China. Even when they enter the waste stream, DEDs leave it much sooner than other forms of waste, for they are, to a great extent, either recycled or reused.

Nevertheless, China's current regulatory system remains oblivious to DEDs' potential for reuse (Steuer 2016). It treats them as mere bundles of raw materials and promotes a single technique for dealing with them, namely destruction and extraction. The recycling subsidy is allocated on the basis of how many devices undergo dismantling, crushing and sorting. Thus, licensed companies are incentivized not to salvage and resell any of them, even if they are still in good condition. This affects licensed companies' competitiveness and provides a good explanation for the difficulties they have in securing goods – one that competes with the routine statement that they face higher operating costs as a result of their adherence to rules and standards. Furthermore, promoting destruction contravenes the principle of the 'waste hierarchy' (also known as the 3Rs doctrine), according to which reduction and reuse should be preferred to recycling (StEP 2009).

Rediscovering reuse?

It is undeniable that DEDs are reused on a large scale in China, and yet current policies all but ignore this phenomenon. State authorities have been promoting remanufacturing[10] in official documents for over a decade now, but that has not led to the adoption of specific regulation thus far (Tan et al. 2014). Besides, remanufacturing is practised exclusively by producers and their partners, who represent a minority in China's large repair and refurbishing sector, and only on recent models. Therefore, encouraging and monitoring it does not amount to promoting reuse in general.

This situation seems to contrast with that of certain developed countries, where attempts have been made recently to acknowledge the positive role of repair and reuse. In the 2012 recast of the EU's WEEE Directive, for instance, reuse apparently plays an important role (EU 2012).[11] Given these dispositions' low threshold and vague formulation, however, they are unlikely to have any significant positive repercussion on the environment. Spain was the first country to transpose them in its own legislation and, tellingly, it did so chiefly in order to create jobs and contend with economic slowdown.[12]

That the rediscovery of reuse owes more to economic interests than to environmental concerns is even more obvious in multinational corporations' efforts to switch from a business model based on sales to one centred on leasing. In parts of the world where DEDs are seldom being repaired, major brands producing electronic and electrical equipment now seek to take back and recondition their devices themselves in order to sell them again, thereby increasing their profit (on Apple, see Minter 2013, 250ff.). Thus far, they have been remarkably unambitious in this area in China, but some of them are starting to take on the 'informal sector'[13] and seriously contend for the reuse market.

These cases make clear that governmental and corporate interest in, and support for, reuse practices rely on an appropriate economic context. But such a context is largely lacking in today's China, where electronics and home appliances account for a considerable part of the country's total manufacturing output (itself responsible for 45 per cent of the gross domestic product in 2012[14]). In 2014, this sector also contributed almost a quarter of China's total exports.[15] In recent years, the central government has been stimulating domestic consumption in order to boost China's economy, make it less dependent upon exports, and create a wide enough consumer base for national brands to evolve into global market leaders.[16] Reuse is hardly compatible with such a strategy, since it extends the lifetime of devices, thereby making the purchase of new ones unnecessary. This may not impact sales in affluent urban centres, where people can afford to buy brand new and costly models, but it make a big difference in peripheral areas, for example in the countryside, where every yuan counts and retailing chains have not yet established stores.[17]

Conclusion

Our main aim in this chapter was to expose the programmatic character of China's 'e-waste management' policies. The question of how to deal with DEDs raises a series of issues such as pollution prevention, resource efficiency, occupational health, economic justice, and the digital divide. These issues take centre stage in public discourse on 'e-waste', they are what the phenomenon is known for globally – and understandably so since they arise out of real situations. However, it seems that the policies and regulations China has come up with as a way to 'manage e-waste' owe more to other factors – the same claim could certainly be made, to a certain extent, with regard to other countries. Some of these factors deserve a special mention, e.g. Chinese state authorities' efforts to: enhance their legitimacy through fast-paced economic growth and ever-greater material comfort; concentrate and better control industrial forces; upgrade and upscale domestic manufacturing; assert territorial sovereignty; compare with 'developed' countries.

Even environmental protection, which supposedly acts as a guiding principle in policy-making, plays an ambiguous role. On the one hand, China's 'formal system' requires the establishment of mechanisms to avoid and control pollution caused by DEDs recycling. On the other hand, it promotes the complete destruction of old devices and the parallel consumption of new ones, which accelerates and expands material cycles, thereby aggravating pollution.

In sum, in order to understand decisions taken by Chinese state authorities in the field of 'e-waste management', one needs not so much to take into account the concrete challenges posed by DEDs on the ground in terms of environmental protection, but rather the path Chinese leaders have embarked on and the plans and aspirations they have for their country.

Notes

1 Yvan Schulz's and Benjamin Steuer's research was funded by, respectively, the Swiss National Science Foundation (project nr. 100013_149559) and Switch Asia (Project REWIN, DCI-ASIE/2011/263-084).
2 Like many other sources, this one relies on figures that are themselves rough estimations, which is highly problematic (see Lepawsky et al. 2015).
3 Dates for legal texts are those of their issuance, not implementation.
4 Personal communication with DEDs traders, Guangzhou, May 2015.
5 Shanghai, November 2014.
6 See, e.g., http://www.legaldaily.com.cn/index/content/2014-02/24/content_5302644.htm?node=6139 (accessed 26 June 2015).
7 See http://www.legaldaily.com.cn/gallery/content/2014-02/24/content_5301614.htm?node=8171# (accessed 26 June 2015).
8 See http://www.jxnews.com.cn/jxrb/system/2012/07/19/012046706.shtml (accessed 26 June 2015).
9 See, e.g., Baidu's web-based 'Collecting Station'. http://www.cn.undp.org/content/china/en/home/mdgoverview (accessed 26 June 2015).
10 Remanufacturing consists in restoring products to an 'as new' condition and selling them with a warranty matching that of freshly manufactured ones.
11 See, however, http://www.techweekeurope.co.uk/workspace/eus-new-weee-directive-fails-on-reuse-says-computer-aid-55782 (accessed 26 June 2015).
12 See http://www.recyclinginternational.com/recycling-news/8584/research-and-legislation/europe/spanish-law-targets-reuse-optimisation (accessed 26 June 2015).
13 See http://www.scmp.com/tech/enterprises/article/1773449/foxconn-website-overwhelmed-first-day-sales-recycled-apple-iphones (accessed 26 June 2015).
14 See http://www.reuters.com/article/2014/07/07/us-china-economy-gdp-idUSKBN0FC08920140707 (accessed 26 June 2015).
15 See http://www.worldstopexports.com/chinas-top-10-exports/1952 (accessed 26 June 2015).
16 See http://www.displaybank.com/_jpn/share/press_view.html?id=234397& (accessed 26 June 2015).
17 Unsurprisingly, the central government had a policy of supporting sales of electronics and household appliances in rural areas for several years. See House Appliances Go to the Countryside, *jiadian xiaxiang*, http://rural.cheaa.com (accessed 26 June 2015).

References

AQSIQ (General Administration of Quality Supervision, Inspection and Quarantine), 2012. *Guanyu gongbu jinkou keyong zuo yuanliao de guti feiwu guowai gonghuoshang youxiao zhuce dengji zige de gonggao (di 128 hao)* [Announcement on releasing the valid registration qualifications for overseas suppliers importing solid waste that can be used as raw materials (no. 128)].

Benson, E.; Best, S.; del Pozo-Vergnes, E.; Garside, B.; Mohammed, E.Y.; Panhuysen, S.; Piras, G.; Vorley, B.; Walnycki, A. and Wilson E., 2014. *Informal and green? The forgotten voice in the transition to a green economy*, London: International Institute for Environment and Development (IIED). Available at: <http://pubs.iied.org/pdfs/16566IIED.pdf> (accessed 26 June 2015).

CHEARI (China Household Electrical Appliances Research Institute), 2015. *Zhongguo feiqi dianqi dianzi chanpin huishou chuli ji zonghe liyong – hangye baipishu 2014*. (White paper on WEEE recycling industry in China 2014).

—— 2014. *Zhongguo feiqi dianqi dianzi chanpin huishou chuli ji zonghe liyong – hangye baipishu 2013*. White paper on WEEE recycling industry in China 2013.

Chi X.; Streicher-Porte, M.; Wang Y.L.M. and Reuter, A.M., 2011. Informal electronic waste recycling: a sector review with special focus on China. *Waste Management*, 31, 731–742.

Chung S. and Zhang C., 2011. An evaluation of legislative measures on electrical and electronic waste in the People's Republic of China. *Waste Management*, 31, 2638–2646.

Computer World, 2010. *'Polanwang' ao chutou* (Scavenger kings endure hardships). Available at: <http://blog.sina.com.cn/s/blog_62ac24a70100itfj.html> (accessed 10 December 2016).

EU (European Union), 2003a. *Directive (2002/96/EC) on waste electrical and electronic equipment* [EU WEEE Directive]. Available at: <http://eur-lex.europa.eu/legal-content/EN/TXT/HTML/?uri=CELEX: 32002L0096&from=EN> (accessed 26 June 2015).

—— 2003b. *Directive (2002/95/EC) on the restriction of the use of certain hazardous substances in electrical and electronic equipment* [EU RoHS Directive]. Available at: <http://eur-lex.europa.eu/legal-content/EN/ TXT/HTML/?uri=CELEX:32002L0095&from=EN> (accessed 26 June 2015).

—— 2012. *Directive (2012/19/EU) on waste electrical and electronic equipment* [recast of the EU WEEE Directive]. Available at: <http://eur-lex.europa.eu/legal-content/EN/TXT/HTML/?uri=CELEX: 32012L0019&from=EN> (accessed 26 June 2015).

Global Times, 2014. Police bust 'e-trash' smugglers, seize 72,000 tons of goods. *Global Times* [online], 26 February. Available at: <http://www.globaltimes.cn/content/844788.shtml> (accessed 26 June 2015).

Heilmann, S., 2008. From local experiments to national policy: the origins of China's distinctive policy process. *The China Journal*, 59, 1–30.

Hicks, C.; Dietmar, R. and Eugster, M., 2005. The recycling and disposal of electrical and electronic waste in China: legislative and market responses. *Environmental Impact Assessment Review*, 25, 459– 471.

Hu H., 2015. [No title]. (Personal communication, Beijing, May 2015).

ILO China (International Labour Organization, Coordinating Office for China and Mongolia), 2013. *The labour, human health and environment of the e-waste management sector in China*. Available at: <http:// apgreenjobs.ilo.org/resources/the-labour-human-health-and-environmental-dimensions-of-e-waste-management-in-china/> (accessed 26 June 2015).

Kirby, P.W. and Lora-Wainwright, A., 2015. Exporting harm, scavenging value: transnational circuits of e-waste between Japan, China and beyond. *Area*, 47(1), 40–47.

Lamb, L., 2012. 'Should we be sending our e-waste to China? Adam Minter thinks so'. *TCL* [online], 2 October. Retrieved from: <http://tlc.howstuffworks.com/family/should-we-send-e-waste-china-adam-minter-interview.htm> (accessed 26 June 2015, no longer available).

Lepawsky, J.; Goldstein, J. and Schulz, Y., 2015. Criminal negligence? [blog post] *Discard Studies*. Available at: <http://discardstudies.com/2015/06/24/criminal-negligence/> (accessed 26 June 2015).

Li J., 2014. The demand and transfer mechanism of technology & equipment of e-waste recycling in Asia. In: WRF (World Recycling Forum), *Electronics Recycling Asia*, Singapore, 12–14 November 2014.

Lora-Wainwright, A., 2015. The trouble of connection: e-waste in China between state regulation, development regimes and global capitalism. In Ferguson J., ed. *The anthropology of disconnection: the political ecology of post-industrial regimes*. Oxford, Berghahn [no page].

MIIT (Ministry of Industy and Information Technology), 2006. *Dianzi xinxi chanpin wuran kongzhi guanli banfa (di 39 hao)* (Measures for administration of the pollution control of electronic information products (no. 39), referred to as the China restriction of hazardous substances directive or China RoHS directive). Available at: <http://www.gov.cn/ziliao/flfg/2006-03/06/content_219447.htm> (accessed 12 December 2016).

Minter, A., 2013. *Junkyard planet: travels in the billion-dollar trash trade*. London, Bloomsbury.

MOF (Ministry of Finances), MOFCOM (Ministry of Commerce), NDRC (National Development and Reform Commission), MIIT (Ministry of Industry and Information Technology), MEP (Ministry of Environmental Protection), SAIC (State Administration for Industry and Commerce), AQSIQ (General Administration of Quality Supervision, Inspection and Quarantine), 2009. *Guanyu yinfa jiadian yi jiu huan xin shishi banfa de tongzhi* (Notice on the measure for the implementation of the old for new scheme). Available at: <http://www.gov.cn/zwgk/2009-07/02/content_1355598.htm> (accessed 12 December 2016).

Naughton, B., 2007. *The Chinese economy: transitions and growth*, Cambridge, MIT Press.

NPC (National People's Congress), 2002 [revised in 2012]. *Zhongguo qingjie shengchan cujinfa* (The China cleaner production promotion law). Available at: <http://www.gov.cn/flfg/2012-03/01/ content_2079732.htm> (accessed 26 June 2015).

—— 2008. *Zhongguo xunhuan jingji cujinfa* (The China Circular Economy Promotion Law). Available at: <http://www.gov.cn/flfg/2008-08/29/content_1084355.htm> (accessed 26 June 2015).

Puckett, J. et al., 2002. *Exporting harm: the high-tech trashing of Asia*, Basel, Action Network (BAN) and Silicon Valley Toxics Coalition (SVTC).

Qu Y.; Zhu Q.; Sarkis, J.; Geng Y. and Zhong Y. 2013. A review of developing an e-wastes collection system in Dalian, China. *Journal of Cleaner Production* 52, 176–184.

REWIN, 2015. Internal project report [unpublished], Vienna, February 2015.

Schulz Y., 2015. Towards a new waste regime? Critical reflections on China's shifting market for high-tech discards. *China Perspective*, 3, 43–50.

Schulz, Y., 2016. 'Fin de vie' et renaissance clandestine: le sort des écrans plats en Chine du sud. *Techniques & Culture*, 65–6, 158–161.

SEPA (State Environmental Protection Administration [now MEP]), 2008. *Dianzi feiwu wuran huanjing fangzhi guanli* (Administrative measure on pollution prevention of waste electrical and electronic equipment). Available at: <http://ewasteguide.info/files/MeasurePollutionPreventionofWEEE_(SEPA)_(Chinese)_2.pdf> (accessed 26 June 2015).

SEPA (State Environmental Protection Administration [now MEP]), 2000. *Guanyu jinkou di qi lei feiwu youguan wenti de tongzhi* (Notice on problems of importing wastes of the seventh category).

State Council, 2009. *Feiqi dianqi dianzi chanpin chuli guanli tiaoli (di 551 hao)* (Ordinance (no. 551) on the administration of the recovery and disposal of waste electronic and electrical products, referred to as the China Waste Electrical and Electronic Equipment Directive or China WEEE Directive). Available at: <www.gov.cn/zwgk/2009-03/04/content_1250419.htm> (accessed 26 June 2015).

StEP (Solving the E-Waste Problem), 2009. *One global understanding of re-use – common definitions*, Bonn, Solving the E-Waste Problem (StEP). Available at: <http://www.step-initiative.org/World_Step_One_Global_Understanding_of_Re-Use_Common_Definitions.html> (accessed 26 June 2015).

Steuer, B., 2016. What institutional dynamics guide waste electrical and electronic equipment refurbishment and reuse in urban China? *Recycling*, 1(2), 286–310.

Steuer, B.; Ramusch, R.; Salhofer, S.; Staudner, M., 2015. Report on existing collection systems for WEEE from households with focus on formal and informal systems. REWIN Project report 2015. More information at: <http://www.rewin-china.net> (accessed 8 September 2016).

Tan Q.; Zeng X.; Ijomah, W.L.; Zheng L. and Li J., 2014. Status of end-of-life electronic product remanufacturing in China. *Journal of Industrial Ecology*, 18(4), 577–587.

Tong X. and Yan L., 2013. From legal transplants to sustainable transition: extended producer responsibility in Chinese waste electrical and electronic equipment management. *Journal of Industrial Ecology*, 17(2), 199–212.

Wang F.; Huisman, J., Meskers, C.E.; Schluep, M.; Stevels, A. and Hagelüken, C., 2012. The best-of-2-worlds philosophy: developing local dismantling and global infrastructure network for sustainable e-waste treatment in emerging economies. *Waste Management*, 32(11), 2134–2146.

Wang F.; Kuehr, R.; Ahlquist, D. and Li J., 2013. *WEEE in China: a country report*, Institute for Sustainability and Peace (ISP), United Nations University (UNU). Available at: <http://collections.unu.edu/eserv/UNU:1624/ewaste-in-china.pdf> (accessed 12 December 2016).

Yang J.; Lu B. and Xu C., 2008. WEEE flow and mitigating measures in China. *Waste Management*, 28, 1589–1597.

Yu J.; Williams, E.; Ju M. and Shao C., 2010. Managing WEEE in China: policies, pilot projects and alternative approaches. *Resources Conservation and Recycling*, 54, 991–999.

Zha P., 2015. Shanghai WEEE recycling management practice. In: CHEARI (China Household Electrical Appliances Research Institute) et al. *International Conference on WEEE & Used Battery Management and EPR Principle* Shanghai, 20–22 May 2015.

Zhejiang Trade Net, 2005. 'Dadi huanbao' de fannao – huanbao shiye youdai shehui lijie (The trouble with the 'environmental protection of the earth' – Society still needs to understand the ideal of environmental protection). Available at: <http://biz.zjol.com.cn/05biz/system/2005/06/29/006146804.shtml> (accessed 26 June 2015).

Zhong W., 2010. Zhongguo feiqi dianqi dianzi chanpin huishou chuli jincheng ji fazhi jianshe (Advances in China's WEEE collection and treatment process and legislative institutional build-up). *Zhengce chuanzao yanjiu*, 3, 41–56.

Zhou L. and Xu Z., 2012. Response to waste electrical and electronic equipments in China: legislation, recycling system, and advanced integrated process. *Environmental Science Technology*, 46, 4713–4724.

PART V

China's environmental policy in the international context

24

ENVIRONMENT AND TRADE

Hu Tao and Song Peng

Introduction

Widely regarded as an economic miracle, export expansion has driven China's economic growth (Rodrik 2006; Duan et al. 2012). With exports growing faster than the gross domestic product (GDP), the share of exports within China's GDP increased from 6.6 per cent in 1978 to 22.6 per cent in 2014 (World Bank 2015). China's international trade has soared rapidly since China's reform and opening up to the world, and especially since China's accession to the World Trade Organization (WTO). During the period from 2001 to 2014, China's exports and imports increased by 7.8 times and 7.1 times, respectively. The total volume of exports increased from US$266 billion in 2001 to US$2,342 billion in 2014, with an average annual growth rate of 18 per cent (See Figure 24.1).

The rapid growth in China's exports boosted China's trade surplus and foreign exchange reserve. In 2001, the trade surplus was only US$22.5 billion, but in 2008 it increased to US$300 billion. Even in 2009, after the severe impact of the global financial crisis on international trade, the surplus was still more than US$190 billion. By the end of 2010, China's foreign exchange reserves amounted to over US$2.85 trillion, and according to the People's Bank of China, the reserves amounted to US$3 trillion by the end of March 2011. China's high foreign exchange reserves are essential, not only for maintaining the stability of the RMB exchange rate, but also for the financial stability and the entire economy of China.

Since joining the WTO, China has achieved rapid growth in trade volumes, but China's emissions have also increased dramatically. The magnitude of the export and trade surpluses in monetary value has created a large 'deficit' in resources and the environment. China's greenhouse gas (GHG) emissions now rank no.1 in the world with over 6 billion tons of CO_2, SO_2 emissions have peaked at 25 million tons, and other emissions, such as NO_x, PM, COD, etc., have also increased rapidly. A substantial share of these emissions is associated with the production of goods for export. Li and Zhang (2004), Chen et al. (2005) and Zhu (2007) carried out empirical analyses on this issue in the Chinese context. Vennemo et al. (2007) investigated the environmental impacts of China's WTO accession. Peters et al. (2007) found that 25 per cent of China's emissions were embodied in exports in 1997 and 32 per cent in 2002. Peters and Hertwich (2008) estimated that 24 per cent of China's CO_2 emissions were embodied in exports

331

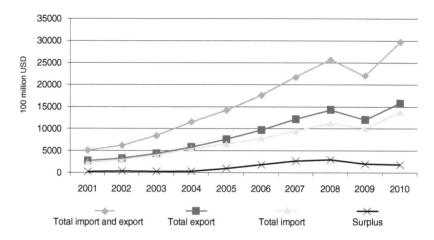

Figure 24.1 General conditions of China's imports and exports during 2001–2010

Source: Ministry of Commerce of the People's Republic of China (MOFCOM) 2015.

in 2001. Weber et al. (2008) argued that, in 2005, around one-third of China's emissions were due to the production of goods for export, and that this proportion had increased from 12 per cent in 1987. Xu et al. (2009) investigated the energy and air emissions embodied in China–U.S. trade and demonstrated that the embodied energy accounted for approximately between 12 and 17 per cent of China's energy consumption, and the embodied CO_2 represented approximately 8–12 per cent of China's CO_2 emissions. SO_2 and NO_x emissions embodied in eastbound trade accounted for 1,015 per cent and 8–12 per cent of China's total emissions, respectively. For the period between 1997 and 2007, Yan and Yang (2010) estimated that 10–26 per cent of China's annual CO_2 emissions were produced by manufacturing goods for export. Ren et al. (2014) demonstrated that the embodied carbon emissions of China's international trade accounted for approximately 30 per cent of the country's industrial carbon emissions.

The potentially serious – and detrimental – impact of China's trade liberalization on the environment led to environmental protection and sustainable development being taken into account in the formulation of China's policies which have evolved accordingly, from GDP-oriented development towards a scientific approach to development, from a grey/black economy model towards green economy transformation, and from an export-oriented trade policy towards a balanced trade policy. In this chapter, we investigate the green trade policies of China by drawing on studies of the environmental effects of China's international trade. Since China is entering a 'post-fast development era' (more often referred to as a 'new normal' development era) characterized by deceleration and structural adjustments, such a study has important policy implications due to the increasing demand for adjustments to be made to China's exports and greening China's trade policies.

This chapter is structured as follows: the first section estimates the domestic environmental impacts of China's trade. This is followed by a case study on the environmental impacts of China's trade on the lower Mekong countries. The next section constructs the structure of the green trade policy framework of China, providing directions for the transition to a green trade system. The final section discusses the emerging issues and offers some concluding remarks.

Environmental impacts on China of China's trade

Ex-post EIA on China's WTO accession

Many international studies have been undertaken on impact assessment, including sustainability impact assessment (SIA), environmental impact assessment (EIA), and regional trade agreement (RTA), etc. For an EIA on trade, the ex-post EIA on NAFTA serves as a good reference for this ex-post EIA on China's WTO accession. The environmental measurement of the balance of trade is a useful approach for assessing the impact of trade on the environment, and the earlier case of the ex-ante EIA on the China–Japan–South Korea Free Trade Agreement (C-J-K FTA) proved that this method is highly effective.

At present, most of the measurements of trade balance refer only to trade value, and pay scant attention to the cost in terms of resources and effects on the environment. The Trade Expert Group of the Ministry of Environmental Protection (MEP) examined the measurement of the balance of trade from the perspective of resources and the environment (Hu 2008b). During the process of production and consumption, goods and services consume resources and emit pollution; these resources and emissions can be described as being embedded in the product and can thus be described as virtual pollutants, such as virtual water, virtual SO_2 and virtual CO_2. We can measure the impacts on the environment through the pollutants embedded in the traded goods.

From the point of flow side, we define the export of virtual pollutants as negative and the import of virtual pollutants as positive. When the sum of these is greater than zero, there is an environmental trade surplus and a trade deficit. We can also assess this with respect to the stock: if the trade leads to improvements in the resources and the environment, we describe this as the environmental surplus, and vice visa.

Using the CE3-GEM (China Energy–Economy–Environmental General Equilibrium Model) and China's Input-Output tables from 2002, 2005 and 2007, we assessed the trade impacts on SO_2, CO_2, COD and energy consumption after China's accession to the WTO (Hu 2008b).

Results

In the last decade, China had a trade surplus in terms of monetary value, but a trade deficit in terms of environmental indicators, reflecting the fact that when goods are exported to other countries, the pollution remains in China.

Net export contributions to SO_2 emissions by virtual pollutants

With regard to the impacts of trade on SO_2 emissions during the period from 2002 to 2007, although the average annual growth rates of virtual SO_2 emissions due to exports and net exports were lower when compared with the growth rates of the total volume of exports and total net export value, they were still 10 per cent higher than those of the total SO_2 emissions, which indicates the important impact of exports on China's SO_2 emissions. SO_2 emissions increased annually before 2005, but as a result of the stricter emission control policies introduced during the 11th Five-Year Plan (2006–2010), the total SO_2 emissions as well as virtual SO_2 embedded in exports began to decrease after 2005.

As shown in Figure 24.2, the export ratio and net export of virtual pollutants in relation to the total SO_2 emissions increased rapidly from 2002 to 2005, and then declined by a small

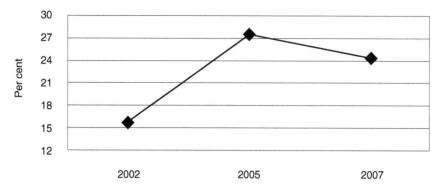

Figure 24.2 2002–2007 proportions of virtual SO$_2$ emissions driven by net export

Source: Hu 2011.

margin, accounting for nearly 50 per cent and 20 per cent respectively by the end of 2007. The export of virtual pollutants has become one of the most important influencing factors in SO$_2$ emissions, constituting over 20 per cent of the total volume of these emissions.

Net export contributions to CO$_2$ emissions by virtual pollutants

In recent years, China has witnessed a high growth rate in CO$_2$ emissions, with an average annual growth rate of about 12.5 per cent between 2002 and 2007. The growth rates of the virtual CO$_2$ emissions contributed by exports and net exports were higher than those of the total CO$_2$ emissions by 9–12 per cent, indicating that export goods are more carbon intensive than other goods.

Similarly to SO$_2$ emissions, in 2005, the virtual CO$_2$ emissions linked with exports were higher than those in 2002 and in 2007. Furthermore, the CO$_2$ emissions linked with exports and net exports in proportion to the total CO$_2$ emissions increased significantly between 2002 to 2005, and edged down in 2007. However, even by the end of 2007, the CO$_2$ emissions contributed by the export trade accounted for more than 65 per cent of the total emissions, while the virtual CO$_2$ percentage of emissions linked with net exports accounted for nearly one-third (see Figure 24.3). Exports have become a major source of CO$_2$ emissions. In 2007,

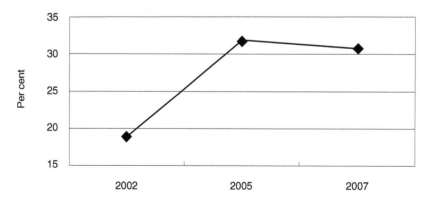

Figure 24.3 2002–2007 proportions of virtual CO$_2$ emissions driven by net export

Source: Hu 2011.

assuming a carbon price of US$10/t, the CO_2 emissions contributed by net exports were equivalent to US$17.1 billion of economic losses.

Net export contributions to COD emissions by virtual pollutants

A similar trade-linked impact is found in China's virtual COD emissions between 2002 and 2007. The average annual growth rates of COD emissions related to exports and net exports were lower than those of the total export and net export values, but considerably higher than the growth rates in China's domestic COD emissions. This shows that although the COD intensity of exported goods was decreasing, the export sector still played a vital role in China's COD emissions. Before 2005, the virtual COD emissions related to export and net export gradually increased, but due to the policies aimed at enhancing energy efficiency and emission reduction during the 11th Five-Year Plan (FYP) (2006–2010) period, the virtual COD emissions of net export began to decline after 2005.

The emissions of the export sector in proportion to total domestic COD emissions increased steadily between 2002 and 2005, and then began to decrease. By the end of 2007, COD emissions from the export trade still accounted for 40 per cent of domestic COD emissions. In contrast, the ratio of virtual COD emissions contributed by net exports increased more slowly, and remained stable at around 20 per cent after 2005 (see Figure 24.4).

All in all, the virtual pollutant emissions driven by exports, including virtual SO_2, CO_2 and COD, increased substantially between 2002 and 2005, and decreased after 2005. This shows clearly that the emission control policies of the 11th FYP have already achieved remarkable results.

Forecast for 2010–2030

If the current trends in economic development and technological progress as well as in emission control policies continue, China's virtual energy consumption and the pollutants generated by trade will gradually decrease, but will not achieve a balance until 2030 (although the COD emissions-related trade will still have some deficits even then, see Figure 24.5).

At the end of the 12th FYP (2010–2015), the contribution of trade to pollutant emissions and energy consumption experienced a decline due to a trading downturn, but still remained at

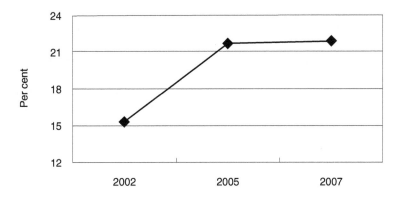

Figure 24.4 2002–2007 proportions of virtual COD emissions driven by net exporting

Source: Hu 2011.

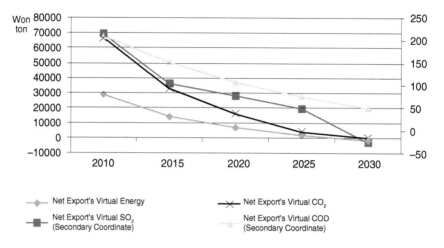

Figure 24.5 2010–2030 virtual pollutants emissions driven by net export

Source: Hu 2011.

a very high level. Net exports calculated in million tons of coal equivalent (tce) amounted to 403 for energy consumption, 3.8 for SO_2, 4 for COD and 962 for CO_2 emissions. Now China has entered the 'new normal' period, and given the predictions of a decline in exports, virtual emissions embedded in net exports are expected to decrease during the 13th FYP (2016–2020), even if no further stringent emissions control policies are implemented. However, the 13th FYP period will still witness great environmental deficits. The net export of emissions will decrease and calculated in million tce, energy consumption is forecast to reach 268; SO_2 2.5; COD 2.1; and 641 for CO_2 emissions.

Possible reasons

Adverse structure of trade

The adverse structure of trade places great pressure on China's environmental trade balance. It consists of the following three aspects: firstly, too many resource-intensive and pollution-intensive products are exported. The greater part of China's exports consists of textiles, leather products, chemical products, cement, iron and steel, which are all high pollution-intensive and resource-intensive industries. Secondly, most of the exports are low value-added products. In the international divisions of industry, China is at the lower level of the industry chain. More than 55 per cent of China's total exports and 90 per cent of the high technology exports come from the processing trade. Thirdly, the export trade in goods as well as the growth rate in this sector is far greater than that in the export of services. Between 1997 and 2003, the export trade in goods increased by about 30 per cent on average, while the export trade in services only increased by 11 per cent.

Low efficiency of exports

China's exports, including goods and service products, have high levels of average energy consumption and pollution intensity. For most exports, the pollution intensity per product in

China is higher than that found in developed countries. Taking textiles, for example, in China, 3.5 tons of water and 55 kilograms of coal are usually consumed to produce 100 metres of cotton, with emissions amounting to 3.3 tons of wastewater, 2 kilograms of COD and 0.6 kilograms of BOD. In contrast, in developed economies, the production of 100 metres of cotton consumes less than 1 ton of water with emissions amounting to less than 0.5 ton of wastewater and almost no COD and BOD.

Large scale and rapid growth in trade

The total value of China's exports is not only large in scale, but also has an exponentially high growth rate. This high growth rate, of 20 per cent to 30 per cent per year, greatly promotes the development of related industries, especially industries with high emissions and energy consumption. According to an assessment carried out by the Development Research Centre of the State Council of China, during the 10th FYP period (2001–2005), the structure and scale of the export trade contributed 20 per cent and 5 per cent to China's total SO_2 emissions respectively, while SO_2 emissions abated by production efficiency represented minus 5 per cent of the total emissions.

Mitigation measures

In order to mitigate the impacts of trade on environmental pollution, a strategic approach to green trade transformation is urgently needed. In line with the principle of internalizing environmental costs in China, green trade policy instruments will mainly concentrate on exports and can be classified according to the levels of production, the companies involved, the business sector and the macro economy.

Case study: environmental impacts of China's trade on lower Mekong countries

The Mekong River basin covers China, Cambodia, Lao People's Democratic Republic (Lao PDR), Myanmar, Thailand and Vietnam. China is situated in the upper Mekong River (in Chinese: Lancang Jiang). The remaining countries are situated in the lower Mekong River basin. Cambodia, Laos, Myanmar, Thailand and Vietnam are referred to as the lower Mekong basin countries or the lower Mekong countries.

The China-ASEAN Free Trade Agreement (CAFTA) was developed during the last decade. At present, CAFTA is the largest free trade area in terms of population and the third largest in terms of nominal GDP.

Mekong countries' trade with China

With the exception of Lao PDR in 2010 and 2011, the Mekong countries are net goods importers from China. This means that they have a trade deficit with China. The value of net goods imports increased from about US$3 billion in 2003 to US$27 billion in 2011. The total value of the goods trade from China increased from US$33 billion in 2003 to US$200 billion in 2011, an increase of almost 500 per cent. The share of trade from China increased from 16 per cent to 30 per cent of the total volume of the goods trade and in these countries (for details, see Figure 24.6, Figure 24.7).

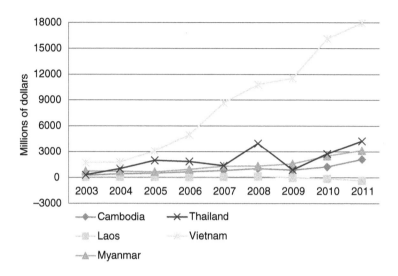

Figure 24.6 Mekong countries' net goods trade with China 2003–2011

Source: Cao and Hu 2014.

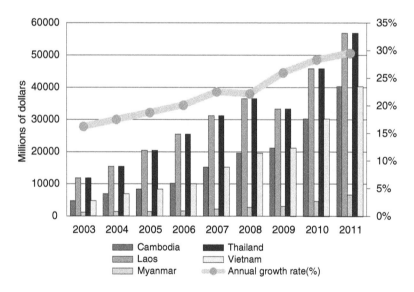

Figure 24.7 Mekong countries' total amount of goods trade with China 2003–2011

Source: Cao and Hu 2014.

Results

The approach for assessing the emissions derived from trade was introduced by Cao and Hu (2014). We assumed that the production structure was similar to the imported goods structure, and that the per-unit of GDP emission of CO_2 was the same as that of trade. If one country's import value was greater than its export value, it meant that the country had the status of net import and could decrease its CO_2 emissions by reducing production, while export goods had virtual CO_2 emissions. We considered that the positive net goods import value meant that minus CO_2 emissions were produced, while the negative net import value meant that a positive amount of CO_2 emissions were produced.

In order to use the CO_2 emissions factor (kg per US$ of GDP), we transferred the current price annually into the base year price by means of the GDP deflator.

The CO_2 emissions balance by China's trade in Mekong countries is summarized below.

From Table 24.1, we concluded that the CO_2 emissions by net goods imports were negative, since the value of net goods imports from China was positive. This means that trade with China had a positive effect on the reduction of CO_2 emissions in the Mekong countries. Specifically, the absolute value of virtual CO_2 emissions by net goods imports from China experienced an annual increase between 2003 and 2008, in addition to an increasing trend in the share of total domestic emissions. However, this trend fluctuated between 2009 and 2011 by approximately 4 per cent.

Mitigation measures

There is no doubt that trade can contribute to economic development, especially in developing countries. The flow of goods and services from one country to another is encouraged, making use of countries' comparative advantages and satisfying the world's needs. However, trade is like a double-edged sword: used to good effect, it can help to develop the economy and improve living standards; used inappropriately, however, or without constraint, then it can in fact damage countries' economic, environmental and social development. Governments at central and local levels are now tightening up the regulations on environmental protection. Several large factories have been forced to close down due to non-compliance with rules and regulations. In order to gain more positive environmental effects from trade, the implementation of green trade policies and regional cooperation on sustainable development are essential. We suggest that China's trade policies should be 'greened' by continuing to adopt the advantageous features and avoiding the shortcomings.

Table 24.1 CO_2 emissions by China's trade in Mekong countries (kt)

	Cambodia	Laos	Myanmar	Thailand	Vietnam	Total	Share of total domestic emissions
2003	−174.72	−43.72	−679.94	−522.6	−3139.94	−4560.92	−1.35%
2004	−265.29	−38.77	−789.37	−1704.96	−3554.98	−6353.37	−1.65%
2005	−283.34	−34.02	−787.1	−3097.88	−5391.93	−9594.27	−2.41%
2006	−348.58	−26.53	−846.54	−2724.07	−5990.71	−9936.43	−2.58%
2007	−405.94	−27.47	−794.76	−1788	−11999.17	−15015.34	−3.69%
2008	−480.74	−33.96	−446.92	−4970.18	−13209.42	−19141.22	−4.44%
2009	−359.39	−0.59	−387.65	−1098.17	−14037.12	−15882.92	−3.68%
2010	−421.22	22.31	−428.57	−2994.84	−13988.16	−17810.48	−4.32%
2011	−692.28	57.64	−	−4361.32	−11316.31	−16312.27	−4.06%

Source: Author's calculations.

Green trade policy of China

The concept of national green trade policy is new. China is the only country in the world which applies exporting tariff for environmental protection purposes. Such policies are of great importance for international trade development and the reduction of environmental impacts. If China succeeds in finding a way to green its trade policy, this could serve as a highly significant reference model.

Green trade policy framework

Based on our previous work on trade and environment, we suggest that China's green trade policy could be structured on four levels: the product (goods and services), the company, the sector and the macro-economy level. In addition, at these individual levels, policies contained within the specific policy measures are implemented, such as export tariffs, market access and green investment targeting the potential environmental requirements, resources and environmental means. The relationship between the policies and the specific measures at the different levels is summarized in the following matrix (Table 24.2).

Based on the green trade policy matrix shown in Table 24.2, a framework for China's green trade policy can be constructed as follows (Figure 24.8), taking fully into consideration the policy levels, categories and specific measures.

At each level there are four categories: encouraged, allowed, restricted and prohibited. For example, at the company level, 'encouraged' companies refers to enterprises which produce in

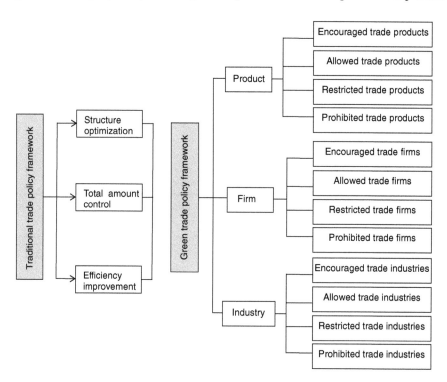

Figure 24.8 Framework for China's green trade policy

Source: Hu 2008a.

Table 24.2 Matrix of green trade policies

Levels	Measures	Restricted and Encouraged			Prohibited	Allowed
		Tariff/Subsidy	Non-tariff	Investment	Laws and regulations	Without the government intervention
Export	Product	Export tariffs/tax rebates/subsidies for environmental/resource goods	export encouragement for goods with environmental labels; Export quotas for heavy polluting goods and resources; Export permit; EIA on sensitive products		Ban on exports	
	Company	Export tax rebates/subsidies; Export credits	Green list/blacklist management; Environmental audit			
	Industry Sector	Industry duty free/subsidy	Industrial environmental standards; Quotas and permits	Guidelines for China's OFDI		
Import	Product	Import tariffs/tax exemption/subsidy for environmental/resource goods	Import quotas and permits for environmentally friendly goods		Ban on imports, especially the MEAs related regulations	
	Company	Import tax rebate/subsidy; Import credit	Environmental qualification review for import firms	Guidelines for foreign investment		
	Industry Sector	Import tax exemption for specific industry	Industrial environmental standards; Quotas and permits			

Source: Author's compilation.

accordance with environmental standards and requirements, and have received environmental management system certification as, for example, 'green' companies or as 'national friendship enterprises'. Half of all the companies in the world have been awarded ISO14000 certificates. These policies have a positive impact on foreign trade and should be encouraged. One example here is the 'green name list' of environmentally friendly enterprises, which was introduced in 2010.

The terms 'restricted' and 'prohibited' are used to refer to enterprises with serious pollution problems. These companies, if ordered to 'close, stop, merge and transfer' according to the environmental law, should have their permits and foreign trade operating rights cancelled. A 'black name list' should be set up to enable the sharing of information among the MEP, MOFCOM, Ministry of Finance (MOF) and National Development and Reform Commission (NDRC) in order to restrict the export of products, subsidies and investments for these companies.

The majority of companies belong to the category 'allowed'. For this group, the main target is to encourage them to reach the level of 'encouraged' companies by adjusting import and export tariffs, guiding investment and export orientation, and strengthening the environmental awareness of the staff.

Export tariffs

Export tariffs on products that are highly polluting, as well as energy and resource intensive, can be categorized as China's main green trade policy. In 2007, export tariffs were levied on 142 products for reasons linked with pollution, energy and resource intensity. Similarly, to mitigate domestic environmental pressure, the cutting and cancellation of export tax rebates for products that are highly polluting, energy and resource intensive was implemented in 2004. For example, in 2007, the export tax rebates on 553 products were cancelled and those on a further 2,268 products were reduced by MOF.[1] Although some minor adjustments were made in the export tax rebate (ETR) policy after 2010, the ETR rates did not change significantly. The provision of ETR refers to refunding the value-added business, and the payment of special consumption taxes on export goods to encourage a nation's export trade (Mah 2007). In the WTO, ETR embodies the spirit of non-discriminatory fair trade and is therefore regarded as a non-prohibited subsidy.

In China, export tariffs are mainly levied on products that are highly polluting, and energy and resource intensive, such as coal, coke, crude oil, petroleum products, crude steel, iron alloy, aluminium, copper and rare earth elements.[2] These tariffs helped to reduce exports of polluting, energy and resource-intensive products, which in turn helped to adjust the trade structure and reduced the consumption of resources and energy. In the last decade, export tariffs contributed to relieving the pressure on the environment to some extent.

However, China's export tariff system is still in need of further optimization. In the short term, the ETRs should be cancelled and export tariffs should be levied on products derived from iron and steel, and steel alloys, among others. In the long term, the ETRs for products derived from leather, paper, chemical rubber and plastic, textiles, clothing, other minerals, iron and non-alloy steel, stainless steel and other base metals should be eliminated completely, and export tariffs should be levied on these products to further enhance the environmental performance of China's export tariff system.

Green trade transition

China is now building more environmental considerations into its trade policies, with the aim of changing the traditional grey/black trade model to green. Green trade transition can help

China to reduce the trade deficit in terms of environmental costs towards sustainable development. From the framework of green trade policy highlighted above, the tariff and non-tariff instruments should be implemented at each of the four different levels, i.e. the product, company, sector and macro-economy levels. To ensure this and to accomplish the green trade transition, the following measures are recommended.

- Green the customs nomenclature of import and export products, and reclassify products from the perspective of environmental protection.
- Make extensive use of export tariff as a way of promoting green trade policy transition.
- Implement favourable policies, such as preferential taxes, for eco-label products, and encourage their export.
- Adopt the import substitution policy to achieve a trade balance and to promote energy saving and emissions reduction.
- Raise the environmental requirements for FDI access, and guide the OFDI activities of investors outside China.
- Restrict trade policies for importing waste; guard against the environmental risks posed by the waste trade.
- Improve the RMB exchange rate moderately, to accelerate green trade transition.

Discussion and Conclusion

China and the world

Since acceding to the World Trade Organization (WTO) in 2001, China has experienced a particularly strong growth in trade volume. In 2001, the total volume of exports and the trade surplus were US$266 billion and US$22.5 billion, respectively. By 2012, the total volume of exports and the trade surplus amounted to US$2,048 billion and US$230 billion, respectively. China's ranking in exports has increased steadily. Since 2009, China has been the largest exporter and the second largest importer in the world, with a total annual trade value of nearly US$3 trillion.

However, the magnitude of the export and trade surpluses in terms of monetary value has created a large 'deficit' in terms of resources and the environment (Kirkpatrick and Scrieciu 2008; George 2010), which means that China exports products but consumes natural resources and produces pollution at home (Liu and Diamond 2005). According to our previous estimations, the virtual SO_2, CO_2, and COD emissions embodied in China's 2007 net exports corresponded to 24.4 per cent, 30.8 per cent, and 21.8 per cent respectively of the national total of SO_2, CO_2, and COD emissions. The results of the analysis of the emissions in China's trade with lower Mekong countries also reflect the fact that when goods are exported to other countries, the pollution remains in China. China is currently the world leader in emissions of greenhouse gases. The CO_2 emissions have now exceeded the combined amounts of the USA and the EU, accounting for about 29 per cent of global emissions. Other emissions have also increased rapidly, and China, in recent years, has also become the leader in emissions of SO_2, NO_2 and PM.

Confronted with such severe environmental pressure both domestically and globally, China is now rethinking its traditional trade policies. The previous export-oriented trade policy is gradually being diluted by the emergence of a balance in trade and green trade. What will be the outcome? China is lurching between accelerating trade-related environmental damage and accelerating trade-related environmental protection. During the last two decades, China created an economic miracle. We hope that, during the next two decades, China will be able to create an environmental miracle and set a prime example for other nations to achieve both economic and environmental sustainability. China's transition from a traditional trade model to a green model is ongoing. The outcome will affect not only China, but the entire world.

Global governance

Currently, the WTO and United Nations Conference on Trade and Development (UNCTAD) serve as two huge global trade governance systems. In addition, there are many RTAs and bilateral free trade agreements (FTAs) that play essential roles in governing trade partners and trade activities. For global environmental governance, the United Nations Environment Programme (UNEP) is the main organization with more than 100 multilateral environmental agreements (MEAs).

However, when global trade meets environmental problems, the global governance system usually fails, because the global trade governance system and the global environmental governance system lack coherence and coordination. In reality, the Marrakesh Decision on Trade and Environment has brought environment and sustainable development issues into the sphere of WTO work. The WTO Committee on Trade and Environment (CTE) was established with the aim of making trade and environmental policies mutually supportive, but little progress has yet been made in CTE negotiations.

During the past two centuries, global pollution has been transferred along with global industrialization processes from Europe to North America to Japan to the Four Asian Tigers and finally to the mainland of China. The degree of environmental pollution and degradation has increased ever since, due to the failure of the global environmental governance system. Recently, China has announced a 'One Belt, One Road' (OBOR) strategy, which might accelerate global pollution transfers from China to other countries along the OBOR route. In the future, therefore, global governance related to the environment should undoubtedly be strengthened.

In this current study, by quantifying the embodied GHG and pollutant emissions in China's trade between 2002 and 2007, we found that the huge trade volume has contributed heavily to environmental deterioration by exporting goods but leaving pollution in the country of origin. This study also analysed the environmental impacts of China's trade with the lower Mekong countries, which indicated that CO_2 emissions in this region deriving from China's trade have decreased in recent years. Although we did our utmost to optimize the process of the analysis, this study also has some shortcomings. First of all, other major aspects of trade liberalization, such as reductions in barriers to foreign investment, protection of intellectual property rights, securing market access and cooperation in dispute settlements, were not taken into consideration. Second, the role played by the composition effect, which is linked with trade structure transition and might provide more evidence about green trade policies, has not been discussed. Finally, studying the environmental impact of China's trade on China and the lower Mekong countries alone is not enough. China's trade has an impact on the entire world through changes in trade patterns, and further studies will need to be carried out in this field in the near future.

Exports, investment and consumption are the troika of China's economic development. This research focused on an environmental assessment of China's international trade and the results indicate that the effects of environmental deterioration are not as drastic as earlier studies have claimed. China should continue to push for trade liberalization in the future and, at the same time, reduce the adverse effect on the environment by implementing a green trade policy, while optimizing the export and import structures to achieve green trade transition.

Notes

1 Ministry of Finance and the State Administration of Taxation (2007, Document No. 90): 'Notification on the adjustment of export tax rebates of some commodities'.
2 China lost the trade dispute of quota and export restrictions on Rare Earth Tungsten and Molybdenum, which means quota and such export restrictions will be prohibited for China in the future.

References

Cao C.M. and Hu T., 2014. Study to quantify the environmental impacts derived from China's foreign investment and trade in the greater Mekong sub-region. *Environment and Sustainable Development*, 1, 77–80.
Chen J.Y., Liu W., Hu Y., 2005. China's foreign trade, environmental protection and economic sustainable development. *Asia-Pacific Economic Review*, 74–77.
Duan Y.W.; Yang C.H.; Zhu K.F.; Chen X.K., 2012. Does the domestic value added induced by China's exports really belong to China? *China & World Economy*, 20, 83–102.
George, C., 2010. *The truth about trade: the real impact of liberalization*. Zed Books, London & New York.
Hu T., 2008a. Build green trade system and release resource and environmental pressure of China. *Chinese Journal of Population Resources and Environment*, 18 (2), 200–203.
Hu T., 2008b. Analysis on the resources and environmental deficit in China's foreign trade. *Chinese Journal of Population, Resources and Environment*, 18 (2), 204–207.
Hu T., 2011. Environmental implications of China's accession to WTO. *Proceedings of China: One Decade after WTO*. ICTSD, Geneva
Kirkpatrick, C. and Scrieciu, S., 2008. Is trade liberalization bad for the environment? A review of the economic evidence. *Journal of Environmental Planning and Management*, 51, 497–510.
Li X.X. and Zhang T., 2004. An empirical analysis on China's environmental impacts of export growth: case study on CO_2 emissions. *International Trade Journal*, 7, 9–12.
Liu J.G. and Diamond, J., 2005. China's environment in a globalizing world. *Nature*, 435, 1179–1186.
Mah, J.S., 2007. The effect of duty drawback on export promotion: the case of Korea. *Journal of Asian Economics*, 18, 967–973.
Ministry of Commerce of the People's Republic of China (MOFCOM), 2015. Annual statistic data for China's trade. http://data.mofcom.gov.cn/channel/includes/list.shtml?channel=mysj&visit=A
Ministry of Finance and the State Administration of Taxation, 2007. Document No. 90 'Notification on the adjustment of export tax rebates of some commodities'.
Peters, G.P.; Christopher, L.; Weber, D.G.; Klaus, H., 2007. China's growing CO_2 emissions: a race between increasing consumption and efficiency gains. *Environmental Science & Technology*, 41, 5939–5944.
Peters, G.P. and Hertwich, E.G., 2008. CO_2 embodied in international trade with implications for global climate policy. *Environmental Science & Technology*, 42, 1401–1407.
Ren S.; Yuan B.; Ma X.; Chen X., 2014. The impact of international trade on China's industrial carbon emissions since its entry into WTO. *Energy Policy*, 69, 624–634.
Rodrik, D., 2006. What's so special about China's exports? *China & World Economy*, 14, 1–19.
Vennemo, H.; Aunan, K.; He J.W.; Hu T.; Li S.T.; Rypdzal, K., 2007. Environmental impacts of China's WTO-accession. *Ecological Economics*, 64, 893–911.
Weber, C.L.; Peters, G.P.; Guan, D.; Hubacek, K., 2008. The contribution of Chinese exports to climate change. *Energy Policy*, 36, 3572–3577.
World Bank, 2015. World Development Indicators 2015. http://data.worldbank.org/products/wdi (accessed 14 December 2016).
Xu M.; Allenby, B.; Chen W., 2009. Energy and air emissions embodied in China–U.S. trade: eastbound assessment using adjusted bilateral trade data. *Environmental Science & Technology*, 43, 3378–3384.
Yan Y. and Yang L., 2010. China's foreign trade and climate change: a case study of CO_2 emissions. *Energy Policy*, 8, 350–356.
Zhu Q.R., 2007. Empirical analysis on the relationship between export and industrial pollution and controlling in China. *World Economy Study*, 47–51.

25

CHINA'S POLICY FRAMEWORKS FOR SUSTAINABLE CONSUMPTION AND PRODUCTION SYSTEMS

Patrick Schroeder

Introduction: greening value chains through SCP

After more than 30 years of rapid economic growth, China's economy has become closely integrated into global value chains: raw materials for China's manufacturing industries are sourced from across the world, consumption of goods produced in China is taking place in Europe and the United States and waste materials such as plastics, paper or e-waste are recycled in China.

There are no national environmental laws or multilateral environmental agreements (MEA) which specifically regulate the flow of resources in global value chains in their entire length and complexity. National policies can at best address one or two stages of these complex multi-actor chains, which take place within the country's territorial boundaries. The international framework which aims to address environmental challenges across value chains in a systematic way is the 10-Year Framework Plan (10 YFP) on Sustainable Consumption and Production (SCP), which was agreed upon by the heads of state during the 2012 Rio+20 conference in Brazil. The activities under this programme, coordinated by the United Nations Environment Programme, and more generally the concept and approaches of SCP, are increasingly having influence on China's environmental policy development and value chains.

The greening of China's value chains has started through implementation of SCP policies and multi-stakeholder initiatives on different levels. The policies that are considered most relevant include those which set the standards and specifications for products, either for domestic use or export, international standards such as ISO certification, labelling and certification schemes, and circular economy practices. International environmental cooperation increasingly includes private sector stakeholders, not only governments. Large multinationals manufacturing in China have been under pressure from their customers to provide safe and greener products. Likewise have Chinese urban consumer demands increased and pressure leading Chinese companies. Local governments are tasked with a number of challenging responsibilities including the implementation and enforcement of national laws and regulations and green public procurement practices to lead by example, but which not always favour local manufactures (see Figure 25.1).

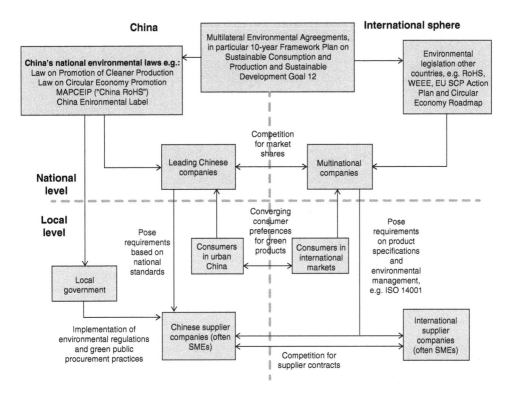

Figure 25.1 Domestic and international actors and dynamics for greening China's value chains

There is no standard definition of green value chain management. While in principle there is a difference, the term is in practice also conflated with green supply chain management. As in this chapter we focus on the Chinese context, we adopt the definition given by the China Council on International Cooperation and Development (CCICED) in their report on green supply chain management (see Figure 25.2).

> The concept is based on the life cycle of goods and services, considering all stages when considering the impact on the environment. For an enterprise this means not only to take its own processes into account, but also the sourcing of raw materials, transport, the consumption phase of the products, as well as the recycling of the wastes at the end of life stage.
>
> *(CCICED 2011)*

The CCICED has also emphasized the importance of green supply chain management to address potential trade barriers based on environmental issues. To further promote 'Made in China' products in the international market, deepening green supply chain management is recommended by the CCICED. 'A fully realized green supply chain management program would be beneficial not only for China to reduce environmental impacts and energy consumption domestically, but also to avoid the economic risks arising from green barriers to international trade' (CCICED 2011, 386). While there currently is little evidence to suggest that strengthening environmental regulations deteriorates international competitiveness, but rather environmental legislation induces innovation in clean technologies, impacts on

Patrick Schroeder

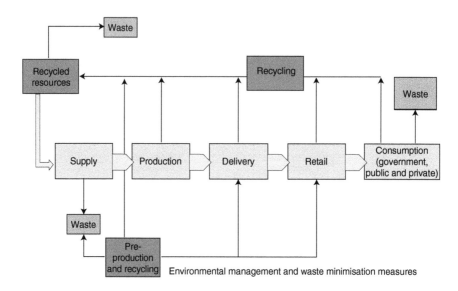

Figure 25.2 China's green supply chain management system (adapted from CCICED, 2011)

competitiveness could increase in the future if efforts to control pollution diverge significantly across countries (Dechezleprêtre and Sato 2014). Therefore, CCICED's recommendation to implement green supply chain management practices is an important step to competitiveness of Chinese industries and avoid trade conflicts arising from environmental legislations.

In this chapter, the framework of SCP which is based on the life cycle concept, is applied as an analytical framework to examine the relationship of environmental and industrial policies relating to China's value chains, including both production and consumption stages, upstream and downstream. By using the SCP approach, it is possible to understand the connections between various stages of production and consumption. Furthermore, it enables identifying the interaction between China's domestic and international actors and policy development. For the production side, this chapter will discuss and analyse the interplay between green value chain management practices of large multinationals and local Chinese supplier companies. In addition, it will show how some environmental policies of other countries, in particular the EU Restriction of Hazardous Substances (RoHS) and Registration, Evaluation, Authorisation and Restriction of Chemicals (REACH) regulations have influenced China's environmental policies. China's *Circular Economy Law* is discussed as a promising element for future cooperation for greening industry and innovation. For the consumption side, the chapter discusses a number of approaches, which are being implemented in China, including eco-labelling and consumer information systems, green government procurement and education and awareness-raising campaigns for sustainable lifestyles. As these policies are also tied to environmental and social issues which have not yet been tackled by industrialized countries, the chapter argues that there will be increasing cooperation and exchanges on these common challenges in the future.

Cleaner Production Law: controlling industrial pollution from manufacturing in China

Policies and laws targeting unsustainable practices during the production stages through 'end-of-pipe' solutions have generally been the first environmental policies to be designed and

348

implemented by governments, including China. Industry has been the largest source of pollution in China and industrial activities that occur 'upstream' of value chains have been a major cause of water, air and soil contamination, and environmental degradation in China over the last decades. The effectiveness of China's environmental laws and policies targeting industry, when it comes to implementation on local levels, have in many cases been suboptimal. Significant challenges continue to exist to improve, on a large scale, the environmental performance of China's industries (Mol and Liu 2005). For instance, small and medium-sized enterprises (SMEs) located in rural areas, including township and village enterprises (TVEs) and private rural companies, have been the main source of water pollution in many parts of China, where monitoring and enforcement of environmental policies is difficult (Wang et al. 2008). A number of laws have been enacted to address the issue of industrial pollution occurring during the production phase, in particular China's *Cleaner Production Promotion Law*, enacted in 2002 to promote cleaner production, ban the use of certain toxic and hazardous materials and increase the efficiency of the utilization rate of resources, thereby reduce and avoid the generation of pollutants, protect and improve local environments, ensure the health of citizens and promote the sustainable development of the economy and society. The *Cleaner Production Law* for the first time made clear what cleaner production is and included specific articles on incentives, legal liabilities and awards (Mol and Liu 2005). However, several years after the enactment of the law, factors such as the difficulty in mainstreaming cleaner production in industries, limited institutional resources as well as constraints in financial and technical resources of SMEs still hindered the widespread adoption of cleaner production. In addition, due to local disparities, different regional approaches for its implementation of the law have evolved (Hicks and Dietmar 2007). According to Shi et al. (2008), the top three barriers to adoption of cleaner production practices by Chinese SMEs were found to be: (a) lack of economic incentive policies; (b) lax environmental enforcement; and (c) high initial capital cost. One main recommendation by Shi et al. (2008) has been that current governmental policy should give higher priority to lessening those barriers relating to external policy and financial barriers rather than internal technical and managerial barriers. According to Mol and Liu (2005), the enactment of the law also showed the growing attention of China to environmental and cleaner production industrial policies in the outside world. International experts and Official Development Assistance funds were not only at the foundation projects with cleaner production in the 1990s; also the making of the law itself has been heavily influenced by experiences in other countries. In the decade following the introduction of the *Cleaner Production Promotion Law* the cooperation intensified, in particular with China's major trading partners such as the European Union, Japan and the US.

The influence of EU environmental legislation

A number of foreign environmental legislations and policies, especially of those countries that receive Chinese exports, have via international supply chains influence on Chinese SCP policies and the behaviour of Chinese enterprises. The following section discusses the influence of European green industrial policies on the environmental performance of China's industry. It looks in particular at the European Union's legislation restricting the use of hazardous substances in electrical and electronic equipment (RoHS Directive), *Waste of Electrical and Electronic Equipment (WEEE Directive)* and the *Registration, Evaluation, Authorisation and Restriction of Chemicals (REACH)* regulation.

The EU legislation restricting the use of hazardous substances in electrical and electronic equipment (RoHS Directive 2002/95/EC) and waste of electrical and electronic equipment (WEEE Directive 2002/96/EC) both entered into force in February 2003. These schemes aim to increase the recycling rates of WEEE and/or re-use and require heavy metals such as lead, mercury, cadmium, and hexavalent chromium and flame retardants such as polybrominated biphenyls (PBB) or polybrominated diphenyl ethers (PBDE) to be substituted by safer alternatives (European Commission 2015a). Both directives are highly relevant for greening value chains in the electronics sector as they consider several stages of the value chain including the production phase of electronic equipment, which often takes place in China, the consumption or use phase of electronics in Europe, and the end-of-life and recycling stage, which then, despite restrictions of international shipments of e-waste through the Basel Convention, in turn occurs again in China (see also Schulz and Steuer chapter 23 this volume).

Cooperation between the EU and China on environmental policies and regulations for cleaner production has been an important element of the bilateral relationship. The link between environmental policies and economic and trade cooperation becomes clear when looking at the RoHS regulation. The specifications of this policy have had far-reaching influence on electrical appliance manufacturers worldwide, especially in China, as many actors of the electronics industry supply chain consisting of electrical items manufacturers, distributors, as well as contractors are based in China. Electrical appliance manufacturers seeking market shares in the EU have to sustain higher costs arising from this 'green barrier'. They also need to advance their production technologies and enhance product quality including extension of product life, the reduction and substitution of hazardous substances and the continuous greening of production lines (CCICED 2011). In particular, supply chain management, raw material testing and cost implications appear to be key challenges for China's companies in addressing issues surrounding the directives. Until 2006, little evidence was found to suggest that these directives had effectively driven China's electrical equipment manufacturers towards systematic eco-design (Yu et al. 2006). As electronic equipment accounted for 24.4 per cent of China's exports in 2014 at a value of more US$570 billion (Workman 2015), it is very likely that more companies, especially those in the electronic sector aiming to build international brands, have moved towards advanced cleaner production practices and eco-design principles. Otherwise this growth in exports of electronics would not have been possible.

On policy level, the European RoHS has influenced the development of the *Measures for the Administration on Pollution Control of Electronic Information Products* (MAPCEIP), also known under the name of China RoHS, which was issued by China's Ministry of Industry and Information Technology (MIIT) in 2006. This regulation has been enforced in China since 1 March 2007, an update was issued in 2010. The MAPCEIP regulates only the products sold in the market of Mainland China. While it remains a politically sensitive issue to indicate specifically that China is 'following' a foreign environmental law or industrial policy, there is little doubt that European RoHS developments have influenced the lawmakers behind China RoHS and the China RoHS 2 update (Ferris and Zhang 2010). The products exported from China to other countries are not impacted by the MAPCEIP, for products exported to the European Union RoHS is applicable. Even if the two have some similarities and the MAPCEIP deals with the same six hazardous substances as the European RoHS, MAPCEIP is different from the European RoHS. The scope of the first version was limited to the category of Electronic Information Products (EIPs). In the updated version from 2010, all electrical and electronic products are included, 'electronic and electrical products' defined as 'devices and accessory devices with working electrical voltages of less than 1500 volts direct current and 1000 volts alternating current' (China RoHS 2, proposed Article 3(1)).

Similarly, the so-called *China WEEE Directive (Management Regulations on the Recycling and Disposal of Waste Electronic and Electrical Products)* was introduced in January 2011. It covers five major items of discarded household appliances for mandatory recycling, including televisions, computers, refrigerators, washing machines and air conditioners. These five items form the current scope of the regulation, representing a significant percentage by volume and weight of the total WEEE produced in China. It specifies the responsibilities of a wide range of WEEE value chain actors, such as the manufacturers, importers, distributors and repair shops (Zhang 2011).

The *Registration, Evaluation, Authorisation and Restriction of Chemicals (REACH)* is a 2006 European Union regulation which controls chemicals management by the private sector. It too has influenced China's laws and policies relating to chemicals management. According to Bergkamp (2013), there are a number of chemical regulatory programmes in China, which have been influenced to some degree by REACH, including the *Regulation on Environmental Management of New Chemical Substances* (or *'New' Chemicals Regulation*, effective from 15 October 2010) for which the Ministry of Environmental Protection is the lead regulatory authority. Chinese policymakers are closely monitoring the influence and development of REACH and actively engage in the promotion of it to the private sector, in particular to the companies that produce for export to Europe. Beginning in 2008, the General Administration of Quality Supervision, Inspection and Quarantine (AQSIQ) and the Standardization Administration of China (SAC) have started officially assisting Chinese chemical exporters to comply with new technical standards in China.

Green supply chain management of China's leading companies and multinational firms

The regulations and policies described above are by no means the only drivers and pressures for improving environmental performance of companies. As mentioned above, the influence of global industry players on value chains is highly relevant and described in more detail in this section.

A study by Zhu, Cordeiro, and Sarkis (2012) shows that international institutional pressures on Chinese firms, by being integrated in global value chains, have positive impact on adoption of three important proactive corporate environmental practices and routines by Chinese firms – ISO 14001, TQEM (total quality environmental management), and eco-auditing. Interestingly, the study also finds that this relationship is greater than that arising from corresponding normative, coercive, and mimetic internal domestic pressures. There is a close link between knowledge and awareness of environmental policies and the implementation of green supply chain management (GSCM) practices by industry actors. Statistical analyses by Zhu et al. (2015a) have shown that leading Chinese companies with high awareness of both international and domestic environmental legislations are motivated to implement eco-design practices. There is increasing evidence that China's leading companies – those that are responding to the government's call to become global leading brands – care about their reputation and have fostered a public image in China's domestic marketplace to build and protect their brands (Hart et al. 2015). Environmental performance is becoming an increasingly important element of brand building. China's leading companies are therefore progressively making efforts to green their supply chains. This is not only considered an issue of environmental compliance, but seen as a strategy to improve competitiveness. An example is Huawei, one of China's leading information and communication technology (ICT) companies with global reach. According to the company's sustainability report, Huawei uses eco-design principles based on product life-cycle information to reduce environmental impacts. Huawei has established an internal green product certification process, and in 2013, as the first ICT company, received the TÜV Rheinland Green Product Mark certificate for its intelligent switch products. In 2013, Huawei released the Huawei Substance List V4.0, in which the number of restricted substances was 35, and the number of reported substances was as high as 90 (Huawei 2013).

Furthermore, good customer–supplier relationships are of importance to successfully implement green supply chain measures among Chinese companies. According to Luo et al. (2015), the relationship between supply chain partners, especially when an innovation is being introduced, has an important influence on the implementation of GSCM in Chinese firms. Therefore, Chinese manufacturers who are planning to implement GSCM with their supply chain partners first approach those with whom they have close relationships, in most cases their immediate suppliers. To enhance their relationships with partners further upstream, it becomes necessary to extend these relationships. There is a parallel role of *guanxi* building in GSCM and environmental policy implementation, in particular on local levels. Such informal relationships, which reflect a Chinese cultural predisposition to harmony and consensus-building among key actors, play according to Hills (1998) a central role in determining how environmental policies are implemented, and how stringently regulations are enforced at the local level.

According to Zhu et al. (2012), domestic government regulation and pressure from customers and competitors alone might be insufficient to spur the adoption of environmental management routines such as ISO 14001 by Chinese firms. There is some evidence that international pressures in the form of market forces are more effective in moving Chinese manufacturers than environmental policies placed on them by domestic regulations. Positive effects of international parenting or partnering on the adoption of proactive corporate environmental practices and routines can be observed. An example of a multinational company engaged in GSCM with Chinese firms is Walmart. Its sustainable value chains programme is focused primarily on products such as electronics, textiles or seafood. Walmart notably also has a special value chain specifically focusing on China, since 50,000 of Walmart's approximately 60,000 suppliers are based in China (Denend and Plambeck 2007). The initiative was launched in 2008 by former Walmart Vice Chairman and CEO Mike Duke's announcement that the company would improve the energy efficiency of its top 200 China-based suppliers by 20 per cent by 2012 (Schuchard 2010). The rules took effect in January 2009. Suppliers who would not comply with the new regulations were threatened to be excluded from Walmart's supply chain. According to Walmart, since 2008 the implementation in its China facilities has already resulted in a 20 per cent reduction of energy use in 210 factories, along with a US$279 million cut in energy costs. In its most recent initiative, Walmart is inviting 70 per cent of its suppliers in China as part of an energy efficiency programme before the end of 2017. The initiative not only involves suppliers, but also Walmart's large retail stores in China. Refrigerator retrofits were undertaken at 250 stores, which replaced existing doors with glass ones and installed LED lighting to improve energy efficiency (Clancy 2014).

Closing the loop: China's *Circular Economy Promotion Law*

The circular economy (CE) as a concept is based on cradle-to-cradle and life-cycle principles and goes beyond simple pollution control and cleaner production measures. It encourages manufacturers to design products and systems in such a way that they can be returned and the materials recycled, reused or remanufactured. The benefits are enhanced resource productivity by using less raw materials in longer and integrated product life-cycle loops, reflecting the awareness that the current linear 'take, make, dispose' economic model which relies on large quantities of cheap, easily accessible materials and energy is reaching its physical limits (Ellen MacArthur Foundation 2015). For instance, regarding water management in factories, CE practices encourage recycling during manufacturing, cleaning of wastewater to a high standard and returning it to the local sources. For materials used to manufacture products, the least dangerous chemicals for humans and the environment are used and sound chemical management is implemented through collection and safe recycling practices. Finally, CE aims to avoid waste through eco-design concepts and principles of industrial symbiosis, by which factories' waste products can be used as resources by other industrial facilities. In China, the concept of CE was first proposed by academics, researchers and practitioners in the field of eco-industrial development in the late 1990s, introducing practices from industrialized countries in Europe, the US and Japan. The first CE support policies were formally issued in 2002 by the central government as a new development strategy aimed to support environmental protection, pollution prevention and sustainable development. Several policies were issued to promote the uptake of CE practices by industry over the years, leading to a comprehensive *Circular Economy Promotion Law* in 2009 (Mathews and Tan 2011). An overview of related CE policies is provided in Table 25.1. In addition to these policies specifically referring to circular economy, several other non-environmental policies are also relevant, including tax regulation for resource utilization and waste disposal.

The *Circular Economy Promotion Law* is an important piece of environmental legislation that has not received sufficient attention in the past. Wu et al. (2014) analysed the effectiveness and impact of CE policy and practices for the period of the 11th Five-Year Plan (2006–2010) and found that the CE policies have been quite effective and contributed to improving resource efficiency. The study also revealed that average resource efficiency in the east of China is higher than in the central and western areas. According to Wu et al. (2014), future CE development in China will require stronger implementation of policies and better coordination among them. Local governments should be stimulated to be actively involved in CE development, and CE policy needs to be comprehensively assessed in view of regional differences. This confirms previous findings by Xue et al. (2010), who identified that the main barriers for CE development are the weakness of public awareness and lack of financial support. Implementation of environmental policies, including the *Circular Economy Promotion Law*, relies to a large degree on the awareness of local officials. In regions where officials have a higher awareness and are strong drivers for change, the actual enforcement performance is much better. The gap between policy-making and practical action was considered a serious problem, therefore; according to Xue et al. (2010), the most effective method to push CE development would be to execute compulsory regulations for industry.

Table 25.1 Evolution of China's circular economy policies

Year	Name of policy document	Relevant institution
2003	On Accelerating the Development of Circular Economy	SEPA
2005	On Accelerating the Development of Circular Economy	State Council
2007	Notice on Evaluation Index System for Circular Economy Development	NDRC, SEPA, National Bureau of Statistics
2009	Circular Economy Promotion Law	National People's Congress
2010	Guidelines for the Preparation of Circular Economy Development Plan	NDRC
2012	Twelfth Five-Year Plan for Circular Economy Development	State Council

Source: Based on Wu et al. 2014.

One element of the government's efforts of promoting CE practices is closely related to eco-industrial parks (EIPs) that have been promoted as instruments for achieving sustainable industrial development. EIPs are expected to implement practices of CE such as industrial symbiosis to enhance eco-efficiency. Yet, Zhu et al. (2015b) state in their study on the external and internal barriers for EIP development in 51 Chinese industrial parks that only in a few EIPs successful operational implementation has been realized. Problems especially occur if former standard industrial parks are transformed into EIPs only at a later stage. Industrial park senior-manager perspectives on barriers and hardships show that technological development and capacity building are the most pressing issues that need to be addressed. Zhu et al. (2015b) conclude that cooperation in developing technological solutions for EIPs seems to be a major thrust that should be pursued by EIP stakeholders.

Other challenges that impede the successful implementation of the *Cleaner Production Law* in China, as identified by Su et al. (2013) based on their study of three pilot cities, Beijing, Shanghai and Tianjin, are lack of reliable information, shortage of advanced technology, poor enforceability of legislation, weak economic incentives, poor leadership and management, and lack of public awareness. Su et al. (2013) also note that the 12th Five-Year Plan (2011–2015) put forward the implementation of the CE to a deeper and wider extent in China than before. The Chinese government has realized that the CE presents a unique opportunity to introduce a new economic model, which takes into account the systemic goals of resource efficiency, energy conservation and waste reduction. However, the question is whether this trend of improvements can be sustained, or whether the country reverts to old practices and standards, considering the complexity, diversity and great regional discrepancy of this economy. In order to adopt the CE as a future economic model, immense efforts are required to perfect the existing measures as well as to deploy a wider range of policies to overcome these challenges. Su et al. (2013) recommend policies based on international best practices, including economic measures, for example pricing reforms and preferential tax policies, insurance for liability resulting from environmental damage, a cap-and-trade system, and environmental labelling systems.

The barriers for China's CE share some commonalities with those identified by the EU Circular Economy Roadmap (European Commission 2015b), including market failures such as weak price signals due to lack of internalization of externalities, split incentives for actors across the value chain, lack of information for investors or consumers, but also governance and regulatory failures. For the EU some of the problems have been linked to deficiencies in EU legislation, e.g. ineffective or insufficiently developed policy tools, unaddressed implementation gaps and lack of coherence between policy instruments and lack of harmonized standards. Interestingly, in the EU the term circular economy had previously not been used in any environmental or industrial policy document. Only in December 2015 was a comprehensive circular economy strategy published. Future cooperation programmes and policy dialogues with China on this topic can be expected.

Consumer information and product labelling policies

Moving from the production stage to the retail and consumption stages of value chains, product certification systems and labels are important elements of environmental policies to provide information to consumers, thereby addressing environmental impacts resulting from consumption choices and activities. China has implemented a range of policies and regulations aiming to build up transparent and reliable product information systems to inform consumers to make greener choices.

The *China Environmental Label* (*zhong guo huan jing biao zhi*) was initiated in 1993 by the State Environmental Protection Agency, now the Ministry of Environmental Protection (MEP), and the Ministry of Finance (MOF). The MEP develops and updates the label's technical requirements, certification procedures and implementation rules. Certification is carried out by China Environmental United Certification Center (CEC), which was established by the MEP in 2003. The label sets environmental standards for construction materials, textiles, vehicles, cosmetics, electronics and packaging. As of 2012, more than 1,800 companies and 40,000 products have been certified with the China Environmental Label. Sales of certified products amounted to about RMB 200 billion per year (China's Preparatory Committee for the United Nations Conference on Sustainable Development 2012). In 2010, the MEP launched a low-carbon product certification based on the framework of the China Environmental Label. The China environmental labelling programme consists of two types, based on criteria for ISO 14020 and ISO14024. Type I labelling applies to products in the scope of existing technical standards issued by the MEP. For products without existing standards, applicants can apply for type II labelling, where self-declaration is verified by CEC.

The *China Energy Conservation Certification* (*zhong guo jie neng ren zheng*), which was developed by China Energy Conservation Programme (CECP) is another important label. Initiated in 1998 by the NDRC and China Quality Certification Center (CQC), it is the main voluntary certification programme aiming to save energy and reduce emissions by encouraging manufacturers to produce more resource efficient products and supporting consumers to make more sustainable purchase decisions. Certification includes factory examination based on ISO9002, product tests, re-examination and inspection. The products covered by this certification are home appliances, lighting, office equipment and industrial equipment. In 2005 another energy efficiency-related label, the *China Energy Label* (CEL) (*zhong guo neng xiao biao shi*), an energy consumption label for products in China, similar to the EU energy label, was introduced. For manufacturers of specified electronic devices it is obligatory to attach a CEL label to their goods to inform China-based consumers about the products' energy efficiency performance. The label shows the products' energy efficiency class on a scale from 1–5 and provides additional information regarding their energy consumption. The 'Catalogue of Products to Implement Energy-Efficiency Labelling' and the 'Rules for Implementing Relevant Product Labels' stipulate which products require CEL certification and which minimum energy efficiency class they need to pass. Applications for the label have to be filled in at the China Energy Label Center (CELC), the main authority for classification of the China Energy Label. In order to obtain the label manufacturers have to file an application with CELC, get their product tested, and after concession of the label have it registered with CELC. The label is mandatory for both domestic manufactured products as well as for imported products. A study about the trust and awareness of consumers in Liaoning province regarding the CEL (Feng et al. 2010) highlighted some serious concerns about the energy efficiency labelling and product identification programme. Only 35 per cent of the respondents believed that the energy efficiency labels accurately described how the products would perform, and 25 per cent said they did not care about the label at all when selecting products. While these numbers are not necessarily representative and consumer awareness might have increased in recent years, some of the explanations given by respondents are probably relevant for understanding the implementation gaps in sustainable consumption. For example, some respondents stated that they have low trust in product information systems as they believe that there are systematic sources of error, i.e. incorrect information provided by manufacturers and mismanagement of the programme, and incompetent supervision of the labelling process by official institutions.

The China Environmental Label and the China Energy Conservation Certification play also an important role for China's sustainable public procurement (SPP), which is discussed in the following section.

Leading by example: sustainable government procurement

Sustainable consumption behaviour of the public sector, SPP, is not only an important environmental policy, but also plays a symbolic role in social learning. The public sector can take the lead in promoting sustainable consumption among society and raise public awareness for this issue. SPP can also have a positive impact on industry as it gives a strong signal to the market which types of products are preferred by public institutions. Strong leadership by governments independently or within public–private partnerships can help drive other businesses and consumers to follow suit. According to the Marrakech Task Force on Sustainable Consumption and Production, sustainable public procurement has been defined as

> A process whereby organisations meet their needs for goods, services, works and utilities in a way that achieves value for money on a whole life basis in terms of generating benefits not only to the organization, but also to society and the economy, whilst minimizing damage to the environment.
>
> *(UNEP, n.d.)*

The United Nations 10 YFP officially launched the SPP programme on 1 April 2014, which at the time of writing has been joined by 81 organizations. China's Environmental Development Center of Ministry of Environmental Protection (EDC) is a member of the SPP's Multi-Stakeholder Advisory Committee (UNEP 2015).

In China, since 2003 the *Government Procurement Law* regulates the scope of public procurement. It is necessary to highlight that in China a clear distinction is made between government procurement (*zheng fu cai gou*) and public procurement (*gong gong cai gou*). The former refers exclusively to central and local government bodies, while the latter also encompasses other public bodies, agencies and state-owned enterprises (SOEs) and the like (Denjean et al. 2015). It is also important to note that there is still no SPP law in China and there is no clear official definition of sustainable procurement. Two related SPP practices are simultaneously implemented: the first one is the policy for energy conservation procurement which is based on a two-page announcement issued by the State Council in 2007; the second one is the policy for procurement of products with the China Environmental Label, based on a two-page announcement issued by the MOF and MEP in 2006. Both announcements only provide the general principles for procurement (Hu and Yi 2014).

Energy efficiency criteria were first included in government procurement practices. These energy efficiency measures were mainly driven by energy security concerns in the early 2000s; environmental and climate change concerns became important only at a later stage. After six years' voluntary implementation, the current system of government procurement of energy conservation products (ECPs) was formally enacted in December 2004 with the *Circular on Opinion on Implementing Government Procurement of ECPs*, which was jointly issued by MOF and NDRC (2004). The *Circular* indicates that energy-saving products should have priority in procurement bidding by government agencies. In addition, the *Circular on Establishing System of Compulsory Government Procurement of ECPs*, issued by the State Council in 2007, requires authorities to compile a transparent list of relevant ECPs. The *Circular* stipulates that

Table 25.2 Summary of main points for government procurement regarding ECPs

Products procurement list	Bi-annually updated, last updated version is the 16th as of December 2014
Online information available at	www.ccgp.gov.cn/qyycp/jnhb/jnhbqd/jnqd/
Criteria/Standard	
	China Energy Conservation Mark
Certification authority	CQC
Relevant ministries	MOF, NDRC, AQSIQ
Related policy documents	Implementation Opinions on Government Procurement of Energy-Saving Products (jointly issued by the Ministry of Finance and National Development and Reform Commission in 2004) Circular on Establishing System of Compulsory Government Procurement of Energy Conservation Products (issued by State Council in 2007)

Source: Based on Hu and Yi 2014; Denjean et al. 2015.

energy-saving products must be certified by the central government's authorized certification agencies and must have a verifiable energy-saving effect.

The *Recommendations on the Implementation of Environment Labelling Products (ELPs) in Government Procurement*, jointly issued by the MOF and MEP in 2006, are a policy document that promotes the China Environmental Label as a standard for procurement practices of national and local administrations.

Table 25.3 Summary of main points for government procurement regarding ELPs

Product procurement list	Initiated in 1993, bi-annually updated, last updated version is the 14th as of December 2014, includes 91 product categories
Information available at	www.ccgp.gov.cn/qyycp/jnhb/jnhbqd/hbqd/
Criteria/Standard	China Environmental Label (CEL)

Certification authority	China Environmental United Certification Center, CEUCC
Relevant ministries	MEP and MOF
Related policy document	Recommendations on the Implementation of Environment Labeling Products (ELPs) in Government Procurement (issued by MOF and MEP in 2006).

Source: Based on Hu and Yi 2014; Denjean et al. 2015.

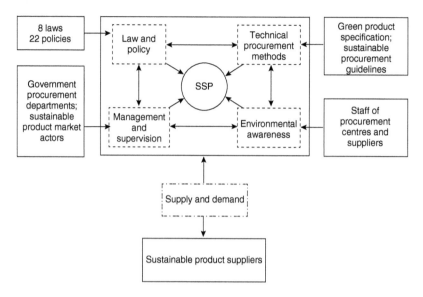

Figure 25.3 Structure of the sustainable public procurement system in China (adapted from Denjean et al. 2015)

The effects of China's SPP efforts are significant. Since 2006, when the country launched its approach to SPP, billions of RMB worth of certified environmentally friendly goods have entered the Chinese market. At the same time, a number of challenges persist and the implementation of SPP in China is still suboptimal, which limits the potential of SPP to contribute to greening the market. This includes a complicated government procurement hierarchy, which creates confusion about green procurement among stakeholders. From central to local procurement, there are four to five different levels of agencies involved in the day-to-day implementation of procurement (Hu and Yi 2014). Another challenge is to provide capacity building to local procurement officials, for instance on life-cycle cost calculation methods (Geng and Doberstein 2008). Currently, almost all procurement decisions are based on actual purchase costs, not on life-cycle assessment of costs, and therefore do not take into account the advantages of energy-efficient products (Cao et al. 2010).

The existing SPP policies and practices are ready for a thorough review and update. There have been no major changes in SPP policies since 2007. Even the compulsory product categories have remained the same during the last seven years. As noted above, there is no sustainable procurement law in China and there is no clear official definition of SPP, therefore the legal framework is still incomplete. At the time of writing, there was no indication of when a fully fledged law on SPP would be enacted in China.

Looking downstream the value chain: sustainable consumption and lifestyles

China is becoming a major consumption hub and the growth of Chinese consumerism reflects increasing prosperity, rising incomes and growing demand. Lifestyles and consumption patterns of China's urban upper- and middle-class consumers and those of consumers in industrialized countries are increasingly converging. Chinese urban consumers have higher expectations about the quality of the products available in the Chinese market, increasingly expecting safe and healthy green products. Green consumption preferences on behalf of consumers can be a strong driver to increase the number and quality of green products in the market.

Green consumption can only be effective if consumers have strong preferences for green products. One question for consumers is how to identify green products in the market. The issue of lack of trust of Chinese consumers in environmental product information systems and labels has been mentioned above. Another issue is the willingness to pay more for green products. Li et al. (2014) surveyed more than 3,000 consumers in the cities of Beijing, Shanghai, Wuhan and Shenzhen between 2009 and 2013. The results show that almost 84 per cent of consumers surveyed were willing to pay some premium for green products out of environmental considerations and concerns about their health. Of these about 12 per cent were willing to pay a premium of 10–30 per cent, another 25 per cent were willing to pay 5–10 per cent more for green products. In another survey carried out by Hart et al. (2015), albeit carried out on a smaller scale with 210 participants, more than 73 per cent of consumers taking part in the survey stated they were willing to pay more for green products, of these 6 per cent would pay more than 10 per cent. Consumers who were married, with children and owning their own house were most willing to pay a premium.

Chinese consumers are also increasingly powerful actors when it comes to information and transparency. Communication and transparent information provision has been a weakness of most Chinese companies. Using social media apps such as 'weixin', Chinese consumers rapidly now exchange information about harmful products and polluting companies, even if this information is not reported by the official state-run media (Hart et al. 2015). Consumer oriented policies are gaining importance as unsustainable consumption patterns are becoming an increasingly potent factor creating negative impacts on the environment. Classic examples of such policies are demand-side measures to reduce the use of private passenger vehicles in cities to reduce urban air pollution and reduce energy consumption in buildings. The Chinese government has recognized the issue of unsustainable consumption patterns, which needs to be addressed by appropriate policy measures. In 2013, the China Council on International Cooperation on Environment and Development (CCIDED) initiated a task force on the topic of sustainable consumption and green development. The task force's report (CCICED 2013) states that sustainable consumption has been on the Chinese policy agenda as early as China's Agenda 21 and that a number of policies aim at promoting sustainable consumption. However, a systematic policy approach that strongly pushes for sustainable consumption could not be identified. Such a policy approach would include an overarching framework and perhaps a national action plan. So far, China's sustainable consumption policies demonstrate that, to date, the Chinese government has been primarily using financial incentives to encourage the consumption of more energy-efficient products. The main government body for these policies has not been the MEP, but the Ministry of Finance. An overview of relevant policies is provided in Table 25.4.

Several initiatives and new policy developments for sustainable consumption are under way. For instance, the CCICED initiated a pilot project on the design and introduction of sustainable consumption indicators for municipal policies. New green consumption policies can be expected to be linked with urbanization-related policies, municipal waste management, information-based product policies, setting advanced green standards for goods and services and closing the gap between urban and rural lifestyles.

Table 25.4 Recent policies for promotion of energy-efficient products

Name of policy document	Issued/enacted by	Year
Notice on adjusting the financial subsidy policy for energy-saving air-conditioners	MoF	2010
Notice on further implementing demonstration and promotion of energy-saving and new energy automobiles	MoF	2011
Implementation rules for promotion of high-efficiency and energy-saving flat-screen TV	MoF	2012
Implementation rules for promotion of high-efficiency and energy-saving refrigerators	MoF	2012
Implementation rules for the promotion of high-efficiency and energy-saving electric washing machines	MoF	2012
Implementation rules for promotion of high-efficiency and energy-saving water heaters	MoF	2012

Source: CCICED 2013.

Summary and conclusions

In this chapter we have taken a value-chain perspective to show how China's environmental policies for the promotion of sustainable production and consumption patterns have evolved since the 1990s. On the production side, industrial policies for pollution prevention, such as the *Cleaner Production Promotion Law*, which aim mainly at end-of-pipe solutions for industry, are comprehensive. Regarding eco-design of products and elimination of hazardous substances, we have shown that Chinese policies have largely followed EU legislation, in particular RoHS and REACH Directives. In addition to policy, China's emerging global brands and multinational companies manufacturing in China have influence on SMEs' environmental performance through green supply chain management practices.

The life cycle-based approaches of CE and industrial symbiosis are promoted through the *Circular Economy Promotion Law* and are being tested in China's eco-industrial parks with mixed results. However, the wider application of these principles encounters a wide range of barriers, including lack of awareness among local officials and need for technology cooperation. In terms of required policies, CE experts have suggested economic instruments such as tax incentives and resource pricing reforms.

Regarding policies for the consumption side, the chapter discussed China's Environmental Label and China Energy Conservation Mark. A large number of products in the Chinese market already carry these labels, but to be effective as consumer information tools, the credibility of these certifications and trust in the labels need to be enhanced among Chinese consumers. The labels are also relevant for China's sustainable public procurement system, which is so far not being guided by a systematic and comprehensive policy framework. Finally, we discussed policies targeting unsustainable consumption patterns of China's emerging consumer class. As for government procurement, no comprehensive policy framework has so far been developed. Policies so far focus on financial subsidies for energy-efficient products. As the consumption patterns and lifestyle of China are converging with those of industrialized countries, which are also still in the process of identifying the right policies, cooperation in this area is very timely. Specific cooperation opportunities exist in the context of the 10 YFP on Sustainable Consumption and Production.

References

Bergkamp, L., 2013. *The European Union REACH Regulation for Chemicals: Law and Practice.* Oxford University Press, Oxford.

Cao F.; Yan Y. and Zhou F., 2010. Towards sustainable public procurement in China: policy and regulatory framework, current developments and the case for consolidated green public procurement code. Retrieved 26 July 2015 from: http://www.ippa.org/IPPC4/Proceedings/07GreenProcurement/Paper7-7.pdf

CCICED, 2011. Practices and innovation of green supply chain. CCICED Annual General Meeting 2011. Retrieved 13 December 2016 from: http://www.cciced.net/cciceden/POLICY/rr/prr/2011/201205/P020160810466195337216.pdf

CCICED, 2013. Task force summary report on sustainable consumption and green development. Annual General Meeting 2013. Retrieved 13 December 2016 from: http://www.cciced.net/cciceden/POLICY/rr/prr/2013/201412/P020160810466225060920.pdf

China's Preparatory Committee for the United Nations Conference on Sustainable Development, 2012. China's national report on sustainable development, Beijing. Retrieved 13 December 2016 from: www.china-un.org/eng/zt/sdreng/P020120608816288649663.pdf

Clancy, H., 2014. Walmart extends energy efficiency focus to Chinese suppliers. Forbes, 29 August 2014. Retrieved 26 July 2015 from: http://www.forbes.com/sites/heatherclancy/2014/08/29/walmart-extends-energy-efficiency-focus-to-chinese-suppliers/

Dechezleprêtre, A. and Sato, M., 2014. The impacts of environmental regulations on competitiveness. Policy brief, November 2014. Grantham Research Institute on Climate Change and the Environment and Global Green Growth Institute.

Denend, L.; Plambeck, E. L., 2007. Wal-Mart's Sustainability Strategy. Case study, Graduate School of Business, Stanford University, Stanford, CA OIT-71.

Denjean, B.; Dion, J.; Huo L.; Liebert, T., 2015. Green public procurement in China: quantifying the benefits. IISD Discussion Paper.

Ellen MacArthur Foundation, 2015. Delivering the circular economy: a toolkit for policymakers. June 2015.

European Commission, 2015a. Recast of the RoHS Directive. Retrieved 18 July 2015 from: http://ec.europa.eu/environment/waste/rohs_eee/index_en.htm

European Commission, 2015b. Circular economy roadmap. April 2015. Retrieved 26 July 2015 from: http://ec.europa.eu/smart-regulation/impact/planned_ia/docs/2015_env_065_env+_032_circular_economy_en.pdf

Feng D.; Sovacool, B. and Vu, K., 2010. The barriers to energy efficiency in China: assessing household electricity savings and consumer behavior in Liaoning province. *Energy Policy,* 38 (2010), 1202–1209.

Ferris, R. J. and Zhang H., 2010. China 'RoHS 2' and implications for the electrical and electronic products industry. Holland and Knight LLP. 5 August 2010. Retrieved 19 July 2015 from: http://www.lexology.com/library/detail.aspx?g=ed0b96f1-a08b-422c-88fc-4de0de95a225

Geng Y. and Doberstein, B., 2008. Greening government procurement in developing countries: building capacity in China. *Journal of Environmental Management,* 88 (4), 932–938.

Hart, C.; Ma Z.; Ying J. and Zhu J., 2015. Corporate strategy and competitive advantage in China's war on pollution: pursuing the new Chinese consumer. China Carbon Forum and Renmin University. Retrieved 5 December 2016 from: http://www.chinacarbon.info/wp-content/uploads/2015/06/Corporate-Strategy-in-Chinas-War-on-Pollution-English.pdf

Hicks, C. and Dietmar, R., 2007. Improving cleaner production through the application of environmental management tools in China. *Journal of Cleaner Production,* 15 (5), 395–408.

Hills, P., 1998. Environmental regulation and the industrial sector in China: the role of informal relationships in policy implementation. *Business Strategy and the Environment,* 05, 7(2), 53–70. Retrieved 20 June 2015 from: http://www.researchgate.net/publication/229911314_Environmental_regulation_and_the_industrial_sector_in_China_the_role_of_informal_relationships_in_policy_implementation

Hu B. and Yi S., 2014. Status report of China's green government procurement. Top10 China Report. Retrieved from (no longer available): http://www.sustainable-procurement.org/fileadmin/template/scripts/sp_resources/_tools/put_file. php?uid=ce35fa4b

Huawei, 2013. Reducing the Environmental Impact. Huawei Sustainability Report 2013. Retrieved 5 December 2016 from: http://www.huawei.com/ilink/ru/download/HW_U_355539

Li Y.; Lu Y.; Liu L. and Zhang X., 2014. The gap between the consumers' willingness to pay for green products and their premium in Chinese representative cities. Beijing, China 15–16 November 2014. SCORAI Workshop on Sustainable Consumption Research in China.

Luo J.; Chong A.; Ngai E. and Liu M., 2015. Green supply chain collaboration implementation in China: the mediating role of guanxi. *Journal of Transportation Research* Part E, 71C, 98–110.

Mathews, J. and Tan H. 2011. Progress toward a circular economy in China: the drivers (and inhibitors) of eco-industrial initiative. *Journal of Industrial Ecology*, 15 (3), 435–457.

MOF and NDRC. 2004. *Circular on Opinion for Implementing Government Procurement of ECPs*. Ministry of Finance of the People's Republic of China & National Development and Reform Commission.

Mol, A. and Liu Y., 2005. Institutionalising cleaner production in China: the Cleaner Production Promotion Law. *International Journal of Environment and Sustainable Development*, 4 (3), 227–245.

Schuchard, R. 2010. Five lessons from Walmart's supply chain work in China. *GreenBiz*, 21 April 2010. Retrieved 13 December 2016 from: https://www.greenbiz.com/blog/2010/04/21/learning-walmarts-supply-chain-work-china

Shi H.; Peng S.Z.; Liu Y. and Zhong P., 2008. Barriers to the implementation of cleaner production in Chinese SMEs: government, industry and expert stakeholders' perspectives. *Journal of Cleaner Production*, 16, 842–852.

Su B.; Heshmati A.; Geng Y.; Yu X., 2013. A review of the circular economy in China: moving from rhetoric to implementation. *Journal of Cleaner Production* 42, 215–227.

UNEP website, no date. What is Sustainable Public Procurement? United Nations Environment Programme. Retrieved 12 May 2016 from: http://www.unep.org/resourceefficiency/Consumption/SustainableProcurement/WhatisSustainablePublicProcurement/tabid/101245/Default.aspx

UNEP, 2015. 10 YFP SPP Programme Partners List. 12 June 2015. Retrieved 15 January 2016 from: http://www.unep.org/10yfp/Portals/50150/10YFP%20SPP%20Programme%20Partners.pdf

Wang M.; Webber, M.; Finlayson, B.; Barnett, J., 2008. Rural industries and water pollution in China. *Journal of Environmental Management*, 86, 648–659.

Workman, D., 2015. China's Top 10 Exports. WTEx, July 16, 2015. Retrieved 12 December 2015 from: http://www.worldstopexports.com/chinas-top-10-exports/1952

Wu H.; Shi Y.; Xia Q.; Zhu W., 2014. Effectiveness of the policy of circular economy in China: a DEA-based analysis for the period of 11th five-year-plan. *Resources, Conservation and Recycling*, 83, 163–175.

Xue B.; Chen X.; Geng Y.; Guo X.; Lu C.; Zhang Z. and Lu C., 2010. Survey of officials' awareness on circular economy development in China: based on municipal and county level. *Resources, Conservation and Recycling*, 54, 1296–1302.

Yu J.; Welford, R. and Hills, P., 2006. Industry responses to EU WEEE and ROHS Directives: perspectives from China. *Corporate Social Responsibility and Environmental Management*, 13 (5), 286–299.

Zhang H., 2011. Analysis of the 'China WEEE Directive': Characteristics, breakthroughs and challenges of the new WEEE legislation in China. Master's thesis in Environmental Sciences, Lund University. Retrieved 1 February 2016 from: https://lup.lub.lu.se/luur/download?func=downloadFile&recordOId=2202304&fileOId=2202306

Zhu Q.; Cordeiro, J. and Sarkis, J., 2012. International and domestic pressures and responses of Chinese firms to greening. *Ecological Economics*, 12 (83), 144–153.

Zhu Q.; Qu Y.; Geng Y.; Fujita T., 2015a. A comparison of regulatory awareness and green supply chain management practices among Chinese and Japanese manufacturers. *Business Strategy and the Environment*. http://onlinelibrary.wiley.com/doi/10.1002/bse.1888/abstract (accessed 5 December 2016).

Zhu Q.; Geng Y.; Sarkis, J.; Lai K.-H., 2015b. Barriers to promoting eco-industrial parks development in China: perspectives from senior officials at national industrial parks. *Journal of Industrial Ecology*, 19 (3), 457–467.

26

CHINA–EU RELATIONS AND PATTERNS OF INTERACTIONS ON EMISSION TRADING[1]

Olivia Gippner

Introduction

The European Union and its member states have for years tried to influence and shape the international climate change agenda. China, as the biggest country and since 2006 also as the biggest emitter of greenhouse gas emissions, has been the core target of engagement and lobbying by other countries. Taking the European Union and its policies on emissions trading, the chapter follows the emission trading system (ETS) policy process from agenda-setting to policy adoption in China. It therefore fits in with the bigger research on when and how climate policies are adopted in China and what role one specific actor, the European Union, as a global leader on climate change, can play.

'This is a landmark step China has made in building a domestic carbon emission trading market,' commented Xie Zhenhua, former Vice Director of China's National Development and Reform Commission (NDRC), the top economic planning agency, on 16 August 2012 (Xinhua 2012). He was referring to the launch of the Shanghai emissions trading scheme, one of seven schemes that were approved by his agency in November 2011. ETS through allocation of emissions certificates to heavy polluters are part of the market-based measures advocated by the international climate change regime to lower overall carbon emissions in a cost-effective way. If implemented nationwide in 2017, the Chinese ETS will be the biggest in the world.

The case study of developing ETS was one of the core project areas the EU carried out with China, and targeted the building of Chinese capacity in developing regulatory approaches and establishing ETS as a strategy to combat climate change. Do external actors such as the European Union influence bureaucratic dynamics surrounding policy adoption? And how?

European–Chinese initiatives on emissions trading started in 2006 and were the first to consistently accompany the Chinese development towards emissions trading. The Ministry of Finance (MOF) and NDRC as core stakeholders took centre stage on how to reduce emissions. There were two main positions advocated – while the NDRC was supporting the ETS, the MOF strongly advocated a carbon tax. Each actor preferred the policy alternative that would allow it to retain control. In 2011 and 2013 the NDRC and State Council approved emissions trading, while the MOF had to content itself with advocating for the introduction of a carbon tax at a later stage. Thus, in the process of policy adoption, from agenda-setting, through research and development, to adoption as a national strategy, the NDRC has so far prevailed in pushing through its policy preferences. This case study looks at the domestic actor constellations, and the role of external actors in the adoption of the policy.

In this chapter I will first carry out a policy analysis of ETS and its main alternative, a carbon tax, as policies combating climate change and fulfilling criteria of Chinese national interests. The chapter will then follow the process towards policy adoption and revisit the active and passive initiatives by representatives of the European Union to engage with China and to influence ETS introduction. Thus I follow the causal mechanism from agenda-setting, to turf acquisition, and finally turf consolidation. The research is based upon secondary and primary data from 60 interviews carried out in the EU and China from 2012–2015. The chapter concludes with a comparison with other countries that were actively supporting the introduction of ETS in China.

Background on emissions trading

The first introduction of ETS as a policy instrument to combat climate change was the US sulphur dioxide emissions trading programme implemented in 1992. In contrast to the US, the EU at that time had a more sceptical attitude to market instruments addressing climate change (Victor 2000, 5). After the signing of the Kyoto Protocol the attitude towards emissions trading within the EU and its member states started changing and several member states, such as Denmark, the UK, the Netherlands, Ireland and Sweden, started preparations for domestic trading systems. The following policy formulation proceeded quickly: in December 2002 the EU's environmental ministers decided on rules for a trading scheme (European Council 2002) and in October 2003 the EU directive 2003/87/EC establishing a scheme for greenhouse gas emission allowance trading within the EU entered into force (European Council 2003). In the current third phase of ETS introduction (2013–2020) emissions allowances are auctioned and there is a single EU-wide cap covering 45 per cent of all emissions in the European Union.

The history of emissions trading in China started ten years later. In November 2011, NDRC officially approved a list of pilot emissions trading schemes, which were established in five cities (Beijing, Tianjin, Shanghai, Chongqing and Shenzhen) and two provinces (Guangdong and Hubei). They are planned to be scaled up nationally during the 13th Five-Year Plan from 2016–2020. Most of the systems are based on the EU ETS and EU-style introduction, with two preparatory phases including free allocations until a fully fledged carbon market is established in the third phase. From early discussions on emissions trading NDRC was in constant contact with the European Commission's DG Climate, carrying out capacity-building activities. For the Chinese emissions trading pilots, the 15th China–EU summit in September 2012 signalled a turning point.

> Both parties agreed to intensify international collaboration and to 'deepen policy dialogue and pragmatic cooperation on tackling climate change' (Council of the European Union 2012, 7), notably in the areas of sustainable urbanization and emissions trading, with the EU pledging to provide €25 million in financial assistance and know-how to a set of pilot projects in China.
>
> *(Belis and Schunz 2013, 196)*

Considering these parallel developments, a diffusion of policies from the EU to China seems to be a compelling explanation. The Chinese adoption of emissions trading is all the more surprising as the EU has been experiencing a severe carbon-credit crisis, exposing the shortcomings of the approach and making it less attractive for China.

Policy analysis and bureaucratic politics: carbon tax v. emissions trading

Taking a step back, the two main options globally discussed today in order to reduce fossil fuel use are emissions trading, also called cap-and-trade system, and carbon taxes. A cap-and-trade system imposes limitations on fossil fuel use and requires the biggest producers of greenhouse gas emissions, such as coal power plants and industries, to buy so-called 'carbon credits' which allow pollution and can be traded on carbon markets. The logic is that with this system, industries that can reduce emissions in the cheapest way can sell their permits to other industries, thus creating an efficient reduction of overall carbon emissions. The second option, a carbon tax, is levied on the consumption of greenhouse gas-producing materials, mostly fossil fuels. 'Proponents of both methods say the economic hardship created by higher energy prices could be offset by rebates to taxpayers' (Yale Environment 360 2009).

CO_2 taxes and tradable allowances or permits yield several similar results: they reduce emissions by assigning a price to emissions, ultimately achieving an overall reduction at the lowest cost. Both can be administered to fossil fuel producers or to emitters and consumers in large industries (Parry and Pizer 2007, 80). Parry and Pizer do not find a clear advantage of one policy approach over the other, but both policy options are clearly less expensive than traditional regulation, such as source-specific emissions standards.[2]

> Supporters of cap-and-trade argue that it has two main strengths. It sets a steadily declining ceiling on carbon emissions, and, by creating a market that rewards companies for slashing CO_2 [...] it uses the free enterprise system to wean the country off fossil fuels and onto renewable energy. Proponents of a carbon tax say their plan has one overriding benefit: Its simplicity.
>
> *(Yale Environment 360 2009)*

The two policy alternatives differ in their certainty on emissions reductions, prices, and the availability of revenue for the government. Concerning implementation of ETS, compliance will be difficult in China, due to the lack of a market economy and the existence of powerful state-owned companies in energy-intensive sectors. Similar to the EU ETS, current Chinese pilot projects have over-allocated emissions allowances. Thus, considering the EU experience and the practice in the current emissions trading pilots, a carbon tax would have been a more appropriate tool, given the overall goal of reducing emissions. This view was further supported by several of the interviewees.[3]

The policy process towards introduction of the seven Chinese ETS pilots

Policy development towards carbon trading mainly occurred at the beginning of the twenty-first century. While there were several examples of using market mechanisms to reduce sulphur dioxide emissions in China at the beginning of the 1990s, in 2008 several municipalities took up voluntary carbon trading. In 2011 NDRC officially endorsed carbon trading by approving regional carbon-trading pilots and declared it one of the priorities for the 12th Five-Year Plan.

Table 26.1 Development of Chinese policy on emissions trading (dependent variable)

Year	Policy Document
2002	*Measures for the Administration of SO$_2$ Emissions trading (a trial version)*, Taiyuan City government, Shanxi Province, 2002 The first pilot domestic sulphur dioxide trading system was created in 2002 (Shin 2012).
2008	Voluntary Trading Schemes, Shanghai Environment Energy Exchange, the Beijing Environment Exchange and the Tianjin Climate Exchange
2010/2011	Fifth plenary session, the 17th CPC Central Committee, October 2011, and 12th Five Year Plan (2011–2015), NDRC, March 2011 Chapter 21, section 1 provides guidance to 'gradually establish a carbon emissions trading system'. In a 2012 White Paper climate change was further prioritized within the 12th Five Year Plan.
November 2011	Approval of Pilot Emissions Schemes by NDRC: five cities (Beijing, Tianjin, Shanghai, Chongqing and Shenzhen) and two provinces (Guangdong and Hubei): upon implementation these pilots are expected to make China the world's second-largest trader of emissions.
2012–2016	Testing Phase, all pilots start operation by 2014
2017–2020	Planned: Improvement Phase, commencement of national carbon trade system
2020	Planned: Full Trading

Analytical framework and process tracing

The overview of ETS development above demonstrates the steps in implementation and political challenges that led to the adoption of ETS pilots and plans for a national system. As will be detailed further below, a special role in the process fell towards bureaucratic politics between core ministries in the Chinese decision-making structure. The larger research by the author on the interaction between domestic bureaucratic actors and the European Union developed a causal mechanism, expecting policy adoption to result when the bureaucratic actor that is empowered by an EU-inspired and advocated policy succeeds vis-à-vis other actors in a bureaucratic power struggle (Gippner 2015). In the case of ETS, NDRC was advocating an emissions trading system, while the Ministry of Finance's interests would have been met by the introduction of a carbon tax. Considering that both actors have crucial influence on ETS policy-making, but are endowed with different responsibilities but also relative power (NDRC being primarily tasked with policy planning), *ex ante* the mechanism would have only expected ETS adoption, if NDRC was able to emerge as the strongest bureaucratic actor on the issue (allocation of control and resources). Connecting this mechanism to the question of a European role, the ETS case study promises to yield insights into the kind of promotion activities the EU has carried out and which channels have proven to be consequential.

Agenda-setting: interaction between the EU and Chinese counterparts

From the beginning of the debate about emissions trading, the European Union was in direct interaction with the NDRC. In January 2010 the Climate Group, an international low-carbon advocacy group with an office in China, published a study on the prospects of carbon trading in China. It mentioned a workshop co-hosted by the European Commission and the NDRC on sharing European experiences, as 'positive signs of China's movement towards establishing a carbon trading' (The Climate Group 2010). The European Union fulfilled two roles, first as an example for the biggest existing ETS (a passive, indirect role), and second as an active promoter of ETS adoption through capacity-building projects (an active, direct role).

Passive EU: the European emissions trading system

When NDRC announced the pilot cap-and-trade system to be launched across the country in January 2012, the EU ETS was a key source of lessons, as 'only Europe offers a precedent of comparable size' (Tu and Livingston 2012). The EU ETS in 2012–2015 proved to be a government failure, suffering from low carbon prices and resistance by the larger member states to extend the system to its biggest polluting industries. An expert interviewed for this study confirmed:

> The EU ETS is seen as a role model but not for imitation, as the Chinese are very aware of the shortcomings of the ETS (price falls and over allocation of certificates in the initial phase). In fact other systems, such as the [previous] Australian one, seem to be more appealing, since it is more flexible [...and] more sustainable in terms of financing and sovereignty.[4]

More often than not, however, the European ETS was seen as an important source of experiences, based on its size and partial integration of energy networks[5] and its unique position within the world, for instance integrating even carbon credits from the Clean Development Mechanism (CDM).[6] It was perceived that 'China should work with the EU, Denmark, Germany, and the UK, because China doesn't have experience in emissions trading'.[7]

There are several areas, where the EU and China can cooperate or face common challenges. Torney and Biedenkopf see clear opportunities, such as on measurement reporting and verification (MRV), where EU capacity-building efforts could support and provide an impetus for changes in the Chinese system so as to help ensuring the design and adoption of an efficient system (Torney and Biedenkopf 2015). On the other hand, domestic conditions hinder cooperation, 'for example the great extent of state-control of the economy', which means that power prices are politically controlled, which hindered the maturation of previous experiences with SO_2 trading (Tao and Mah 2009, 186). Furthermore, China's draft climate law proposes both emissions trading and a carbon tax. 'On these aspects, a Chinese ETS will have its own characteristics and differ from the EU' (Torney and Biedenkopf 2015, 38).

Active EU: capacity building

The EU has interacted with China on emissions trading in two ways: by explicit capacity building (trainings, summer schools, delegation visits) for the establishment of an ETS and through CDM.

> As well as enabling European companies to purchase Chinese CERs through the linking of the CDM and EU-ETS, the EU and member states have also participated directly in the CDM through government purchases of CERs, and through provision of capacity building for the CDM in China.
>
> *(Torney and Biedenkopf 2015, 34)*

The EU–China Clean Development Mechanism Facilitation Project was launched in June 2007 until January 2010 under the 2005 framework of the Partnership on Climate Change, with €2.8 million in funding provided by the European Commission (EuropeAid 2010).

ETS discussions between the NDRC and the European Commission started in May 2010, when the NDRC's Xie Zhenhua and EU Commissioner Heedegard met at a monthly video conference. They decided on a cooperation based on capacity-building projects, and in July the Climate Group, the NDRC and the EU Director General for Climate, Jos Delbeke, organized a workshop on the design and implementation of ETS. In October 2010 another workshop and a fully funded ICAP[8] summer school on allocation mechanisms and monitoring followed. Since 2010 there has been a bilateral cooperation project on tenders and assessments to bid. In July 2013 €5 million were allocated on a three-year project on capacity building and to explain the EU ETS experience on assessment and modelling. There was a lack of expertise on how to implement an ETS in China, and thus efforts by the European Union were welcomed by the participating actors, in particular the NDRC and academic institutions.[9] As a member of the European Commission stated, 'our role is to support the Chinese experts, but it is not up to us what they actually implement in terms of infrastructure, MRV and stakeholder involvement'.[10]

There are many examples for the kind of actions that built the capacity of Chinese policy-makers on emissions trading. Besides the EU, individual EU member states, in particular Germany and the UK, as well as Norway, Italy and international actors like the World Bank engage in cooperation with different Chinese actors and regions on emissions trading (Torney and Biedenkopf 2015, 34).[11] The World Bank Partnership for Market Readiness gave €8 million to China to develop a registry. The diversity among EU member states' energy and GDP profiles is considered to provide helpful examples to China in dealing with its diverse provinces' needs.[12] A member of the European Commission explains that Chinese actors in these cooperation projects prefer to focus on the trading aspect and less on compliance. Thus there is also distribution of which country to consult on which issue. Inter-ministerial meetings occur with Germany and the UK on a technical level, Italy (for CDM), and France (limited). EU DG Climate Action supports the CDM informally.[13]

> Chinese delegations visited Europe to meet with EU and Member State experts (mainly from Germany and the UK) on emissions trading. These delegations came from the pilot projects of Shanghai, Beijing and Guangdong. [...] Visits were organised on the request of the Chinese visitors. The British Consulate financed the Guangdong delegation. The Shanghai delegation was financed by the German agency on international cooperation GIZ and the Beijing delegation was self-financed.
>
> *(Torney and Biedenkopf 2015, 34)*

A particularly strong engagement on a member state-level took place under UK-funded projects.

Since its creation in 2003, the UK's Strategic Programme Fund (SPF) had China as a focus country and involved cooperation with a variety of actors. As part of its fifth policy area under the SPF the UK works with government think tanks and other organizations including institutes under the State Council, the NDRC; the MEP and the MOF. Within this policy area it explores both a 'green tax' and building 'institutional capacity to implement market-based approaches' (UK Foreign and Commonwealth Office 2013, 6). Eleven interviewees specifically mentioned the UK as one of the most active actors in emissions trading capacity building. As one interviewee explains:

> The biggest cooperation was probably the 'EU–China interdependence Report' by Chatham House (The Royal Institute of International Affairs 2007). So compared to

other countries there is much more funding for projects on climate change action through the UK. In the first three years they assessed Chinese needs on low-carbon city and ETS.[14]

In summary, the European Union and its member states stood out as the most consistent external actors to cooperate with Chinese authorities and researchers on emissions trading. Besides these positive examples of EU capacity building, in 2012 the attempt to extend EU ETS to the international aviation sector failed. It demonstrated once more that the EU has no coercive instruments vis-à-vis China (this particular case will be dealt with in more detail below).

Since 2012 EU–China capacity building has increased in areas such as data management, especially sensitive data. As China still does not allow international experts on MRV, the EU sees training domestic experts as the basis for emissions trading, to acquire the relevant baseline 'numbers'.[15] In the area of emissions trading a data basis is an important precondition for cooperation projects. As a German diplomat expressed:

> How can we do a workshop without data? [...] On financing mechanisms and market mechanisms such as CDM and ETS, China says we cannot introduce new systems every few years, which would mean new experts. It is difficult to introduce new systems on all levels in China. From their perspective first it's CDM then ETS and then another system?[16]

Thus, the ETS was not the only policy the EU could have promoted, as its own implementation was not a mere success story – and yet Chinese policy-makers decided to adopt ETS policies. The following sections will delve deeper into answering some of the open questions – why was the interest so much bigger in emissions trading? What other dynamics besides the EU's capacity building affected the speedy development of the ETS policy process in China?

Carbon tax v. emissions trading

From 2006 on, the Chinese frame towards climate change moved away from a focus on historical responsibilities by the developed countries, to the vulnerability to climate change in China itself (Gippner 2014). In the following years the agenda was set on addressing climate change and reducing overall emissions and a quest for policy solutions began. Studies on appropriate taxation levels were carried out (Wang et al. 2009). 'A 2009 study on carbon taxes conducted by the Research Institute for Fiscal Science, the research unit of the finance ministry, projected that the introduction of carbon tax could decrease inflation without gravely impacting on growth' (Lin 2013). By 2010 the Ministry had already prepared the necessary legislation had it not been for the high inflation in the Chinese economy in the latter part of 2010 (Lin 2013). 'MOF experts suggested levying a carbon tax in 2012 at 10 yuan per tonne of carbon dioxide, as well as recommended increasing the tax to 50 yuan per tonne by 2020' (Hou 2013). In 2010 a task force comprising members of the MOF and NDRC explored the requirements of a carbon tax system. While concluding that a carbon tax would lead to energy price increases and worsen inflationary trends, the taskforce's report recommended the introduction of a tax by 2011 (Daily News 2010).

Meanwhile the NDRC and its think tanks carried out feasibility studies for emissions trading and engaged in policy learning in other countries, most notably the European Union, which had one of the few functioning emissions trading systems at the time.

In 2011 the State Council and the NDRC issued official notices endorsing emissions trading pilot systems. NDRC in the following time established itself as the most competent actor on

ETS, for instance by furthering its portfolio on international cooperation. At this point 'the narrative had changed, in the beginning modeling was all about energy security, health. In 2010 it was on co-benefits'.[17] In the following year the pilot locations were decided and the respective features of pilot systems prepared. The NDRC increased its interaction with external actors, including NGOs, such as Greenpeace, WRI, Climate Group, Nature Conservancy, Green River, and Ecofys. Ecofys took a leading role on NGO activities on ETS in China.[18] Bilaterally, the EU started to organize study tours for Chinese counterparts to Brussels and to other countries, such as Germany.

External shock: extension of ETS aviation

In spring 2011 the European Union announced that it planned to extend its requirement for airlines to buy carbon credits within the EU ETS to non-European airlines flying to and out of EU airports. The reaction was outrage from most non-European countries, including the US, China, Russia, India and several Middle Eastern countries. In the Chinese media the issue was widely discussed and interpreted as interference in the country's sovereignty. The government concurred with this interpretation, as Ma Tao, the Chinese representative at the International Civil Aviation Organization confirmed: 'China opposes such unilateral actions firmly [...a better approach would be] to strive for agreement or consensus through multilateral consultation and negotiations' (Xinhua 2011). A second point of criticism brought forward was that extension broke with the principle of common but differentiated responsibilities under the UNFCCC (Alberola and Solier 2012, 16; Scott and Rajamani 2012, 473). As one interviewee explained,

> presently the EU is simply too aggressive in its approach. This becomes obvious in the EU ETS. The EU pushed through with the system, making everyone unhappy, which is a very bad strategy, as it will not work. The UNFCCC process really needs compromise from all sides. The ETS dispute is not over, in fact, it has been the biggest thing this year.[19]

Interestingly, there was also support of the EU's extension policy, most notably by NGOs and think tanks. Besides communication there is also a lack of capacity to deal with the issue of EU ETS extension: 'The number of people working on the EU in Beijing is very small. I believe that capacity has to be built. Only very few people are actually capable of explaining the issue.'[20] Often the EU ETS was mistakenly likened to a tax.[21] Besides the lack of capacity on the Chinese side 'the EU had clearly failed to prepare the Chinese partners and to explain the measures. Only after the public outcry did they look for the interaction, and the DG Climate came to Beijing.'[22] The debate became very public.

> Around the Chinese New Year, the debate on this issue painted a very bad picture of the EU. In a way this issue rallied the media, the general public and businesses based on a very nationalistic sentiment, which actually reduced flexibility for the Chinese government to deal with this issue. The rejection of a subsequent Airbus bidding, was then often seen as a retaliation.[23]

The opposition manifested as diplomatic and commercial pressure as well as legal action in the case of the US. Interestingly, however, the Chinese government, while prohibiting its airlines to take part in the system, on 6 February 2012, also proposed a policy of improving energy efficiency and collecting a domestic passenger tax. In this way, given the European Commission approves the measure as equivalent to participation in the EU ETS, the Chinese government would actually comply with the European directive. On 12 November 2012 the European Commission suspended the extension, officially due to progress being made in negotiations on a global emissions deal on aviation, suggesting the proposal successfully pressured other countries (European Commission 2012a, b). A member of the NDRC's Energy Research Institute, however, explained, 'there is a big picture strategy towards 2030. I supported the ETS airline extension and I did a speech in front of the China aviation authority and the NDRC.'[24]

While it is true that extension of the EU ETS Aviation scheme preceded the introduction of the Chinese emissions trading pilots, a direct influence on the pilots cannot be proven. The reception on the side of the Chinese government was decidedly negative. China took an even stronger stand than other countries against the issue, threatening a trade war. This case demonstrated that the EU cannot act coercively and that it would rapidly create suspicion towards an underlying imperialist attitude.

Thus, close cooperation continued after calming of the airline extension scandal. As a representative of the European Commission explained,

> in 2013 the debate became more technical. In order to avoid failure, the Chinese government has been engaging in a lot of testing. In the ETS Outreach we do a lot of technical work. It benefits to talk strategy, so we do the same thing, where we try to convince the others to reduce their emissions. If we had more money we would do more publicity.[25]

Adoption of the emissions trading – piloting stage

With the launch of the ETS pilots, the plan for emissions trading is well under way (Duan et al. 2014; Zhang et al. 2014). The seven planned pilots draw on various experiences of emissions trading, and are mostly based 'on the Australian, EU and Californian examples'.[26] For instance,

> Shenzhen has drawn lessons from trading systems all over the world, such as allowance allocation and information systems from EU-ETS, market risk control from the Californian market, emissions reduction of buildings from Tokyo, and setting a floor price from the Australian market. Meanwhile, Shenzhen also shows its innovation in design, such as introducing the game mechanism during allowance allocation process.
>
> *(Climate Bridge 2013)*

Other actors interested in developing ETS in China and alternative explanations

The European Union was not the only actor informing the Chinese debate on emissions trading. Most likely influencers are other countries who have been implementing ETS (see Table 26.2), as well as the United Nations, where similar market-based mechanisms have been a particular focus and used in the shape of the CDM. There are alternatives in terms of policy approaches and external actors involved. The various policy approaches have been dealt with in the policy analysis of the two main competing policy alternatives above.

The US has contributed to the development of the concept of emissions trading through its earliest experiment of SO_2 trading under the 1990 Clean Air Act Amendments to address the problem of acid rain (Chan et al. 2012, 419). The United States Environmental Defense Fund (US EDF), the United States Environmental Protection Agency (US EPA), Resources for

Table 26.2 Selected emissions targets and timelines

	Timetable	Target	Coverage
EU	2005–2020	20% below 1990 levels by 2020	11,500 Installations, 40% of Total Emissions
Alberta	2007–present	Annual intensity reduction of 12% below baseline	All industrial facilities
New Zealand	2008–2020	10–20% below 1990 levels by 2020	Forestry (2008). Energy Fuels and Industrial (2010). Waste and Synthetic GHGs (2013)
RGGI (states and provinces in the Northeastern United States and Eastern Canada regions)	2009–2018	10% below 2014 levels by 2018	Power Sector
California	2013–2020	Reach 1990 levels by 2020	Energy Industrial Sources (2013). Oil and gas (2015). Reaches 85% of Total Emissions.
Australia	2013–2020	5% below 2000 levels by 2020 (Higher targets conditional on global agreement)	Energy, industrial process, commercial transport. 60% of Total Emissions

Source: IETA 2013.

In addition India, Québec, Kazakhstan, Switzerland, Tokyo and Korea have introduced their own emissions trading systems.

the Future (RFF) and the Asian Development Bank (ADB) raised awareness, provided finance and technological know-how to Chinese representatives in the central and local governments.

> One of the monumental events was that Mr. Xie Zhenhua, the SEPA director, and Ms Carol Brown, the administrator of US EPA signed the 'Agreement on Cooperative Feasibility Study in Application of Market Mechanism in Reducing SO2 Emission in China' during Premier Zhu Rongji's visit to the United States in April 1999.
>
> *(Shin 2012, 924–925)*

While the US was active in promoting the idea of emissions trading in the case of SO_2, it did not take a prominent role on emissions trading of other greenhouse gases.

At the state level, ten north-eastern states (Regional Greenhouse Gas Initiative) and California have introduced their own emissions trading scheme. Other options are existing ETS in Canada, Australia, as well as immediate neighbours, including Japan and South Korea, who have themselves embarked on ETS policies in their countries. All these actors carried out projects with China and provided financial support. Canada and Australia were particularly active, but there was also financial support from Japan, the United States and South Korea; South Korea having adopted its own emissions trading system for implementation in 2015 (Environmental Defense Fund and IETA 2013, 1). Nevertheless, the European Union stands out in its involvement with Chinese decision-makers on emissions trading.

Is the ETS a European idea?

In the US emissions trading is only a loose idea of the EPA and only at the policy level. Regardless of the current backloading questions, the ETS as an idea that makes basic common sense. The fact that the EU is doing it is not the reason, but it makes it easier, provides certainty, templates of existing legislation and saves time. We have no illusion, for instance Korea introduced a different system, there was no EU involvement.[27]

From the very beginning, the EU Commission was involved and cooperated with its Chinese counterpart NDRC. As a participant to several capacity-building measures explained, the EU was particular, as it 'continued' support. He continues to say that the 'EU is the most active supporter of Chinese ETS. There is a changing benefit from the EU climate attitude – on the level of researchers and policy makers, which is typical for the Chinese decision-making process.'[28]

This brings us to the counterfactual of EU influence. Would the ETS have been adopted without Europe's passive or active involvement? Looking at the failure of the SO$_2$ trading system at the beginning of the 2000s this question has to be negated. Domestic emissions trading does not have a good track record in China. Secondly, the CDM which has been a success story in China is based on the EU ETS market, and the credits gained through the CDM are traded on the EU market. Thirdly, without the active capacity building by the EU, a different timeline and slower implementation in China can be expected. The lack of domestic capacity on many of the technical issues was pointed out particularly by the Chinese interviewees.

Conclusion

This case study followed the process of policy adoption of ETS regulation, from agenda-setting, through policy analysis, to adoption as a national strategy and pilot study. Most notably MOF (for now) lost the 'emissions reductions turf' to NDRC, when the State Council endorsed it as a national strategy. There are several lessons to be drawn from this case study: the role of individual leaders, the role of the EU as an 'early mover' and the dominance of the NDRC as a key decision-making body before the MOF or the MEP.

Notes

1 This research would not have been possible without the financial and institutional support from the NFG Research Group 'Asian Perceptions of the EU' at Freie Universität Berlin. The author is particularly grateful to May-Britt Stumbaum and Miranda Schreurs for their support and helpful feedback, as well as to Lena Schaffer who provided very useful comments on an earlier version of this chapter and the research that underpins it. The chapter has benefited from interviews with many policymakers and representatives of business, NGOs, and academia in the EU and China in the period 2012–2015. The author is grateful to all of those who helped with the preparation of this research, but since anonymity was promised in most cases, their help cannot be acknowledged individually.

2 Source-specific emissions standards '(1) generally fail to trade low-cost reductions off against high-cost reductions, (2) tend to provide overlapping incentives for reductions from some types of sources while excluding others, and (3) often fail to provide proper incentives for conservation', (Parry and Pizer 2007, 86). An example for such a standard is the emission standard on Ethylene Oxide Sterilizers and aerators as part of clean air regulation, which prescribes the amount and control efficiencies used in each facility.

3 Interview, Carnegie-Tsinghua Center for Global Policy, Beijing, 12/07/2012.

4 Interview, Chinese Association for NGO Cooperation, Beijing, 05/05/2012.

5 Interview, Carnegie-Tsinghua Center for Global Policy, Beijing, 12/07/2012.

6 Interview, Tsinghua University, Beijing, 20/07/2012.

7 Interview, Carnegie-Tsinghua Center for Global Policy, Beijing, 12/07/2012.
8 International Carbon Action Partnership (ICAP), an intergovernmental partnership by countries establishing carbon market systems.
9 Interview, World Resources Institute, Beijing, 08/08/2012; Interview, Renmin University, Beijing, 23/07/2012; Interview, Chinese Delegation to the UNFCCC, Bonn, 06/06/2013; amongst others.
10 Interview, European Commission, Brussels, 02/05/2013.
11 Interview, European Commission, Brussels, 02/05/2013.
12 Interview, European Commission, Brussels, 02/05/2013.
13 Interview, European Commission, Brussels, 02/05/2013.
14 Interview, Energy Research Institute, Beijing, 15/08/2012.
15 Measurement Reporting and Verification, first and foremost refers to measurement of greenhouse gas emissions. Only by measuring actual emissions of plants can the suitable amount of carbon credits be purchased for offsetting. There are efforts to standardize MRV procedures internationally to allow for comparison. China currently is using national MRV standards.
16 Interview, German Embassy, Beijing, 04/09/2012.
17 Interview, European Commission, Brussels, 02/05/2013.
18 Interview, German Embassy, Beijing, 04/09/2012.
19 Interview, National Resource Defense Council, Beijing, 08/05/2012.
20 Interview, Carnegie-Tsinghua Center for Global Policy, Beijing, 23/04/2012.
21 Interview, Carnegie-Tsinghua Center for Global Policy, Beijing, 23/04/2012; and Interview, China Association for NGO Cooperation, Beijing, 05/05/2012.
22 Interview, China Association for NGO Cooperation, Beijing, 05/05/2012.
23 Interview, Carnegie-Tsinghua Center for Global Policy, Beijing, 23/04/2012.
24 Interview, Energy Research Institute, Beijing, 15/08/2012.
25 Interview, European Commission, Brussels, 02/05/2013.
26 Interview, Energy Research Institute, Beijing, 15/08/2012.
27 Interview, European Commission, Brussels, 02/05/2013.
28 Interview, Energy Research Institute, Beijing 15/08/2012.

References

Alberola, E. and Solier, B., 2012. Including International Aviation in the European Emissions Trading Scheme: A First Step Towards a Global Scheme? *CDC Climat Research Climate Report,* (34).
Belis, D. and Schunz, S., 2013. China and the European Union: Emerging Partners in Global Climate Governance? *Environmental Practice,* 15 (03), 190–200. doi: doi:10.1017/S1466046613000276.
Chan G.; Stavins, R.; Stowe, R. and Sweeney, R., 2012. The SO$_2$ Allowance-Trading System and the Clean Air Act Amendments of 1990: Reflections on 20 Years of Policy Innovation. *National Tax Journal,* 65, 419–452.
Climate Bridge, 2013. Shenzhen Launches China's First Carbon Trading Scheme: First 8 Transactions completed. http://climatebridge.com/2013/06/shenzhen-launches-china%E2%80%99s-first-carbon-trading-scheme-%E2%80%93-first-8-transactions-completed/ (Accessed 14 February 2014, no longer available).
Council of the European Union, 2012. Joint Press Communiqué. 15th EU-China Summit: Towards a Stronger EU-China Comprehensive Strategic Partnership. Brussels.
Daily News, 2010. Expert Group: Implementation of a Carbon Tax Earliest Possible from Next Year (Kètí zǔ zhuānjiā: tàn shuì zuì kuài míngnián shíshī, Daily News. http://www.gesep.com/News/Show_2_199611.html (Accessed 21 February 2014).
Duan, M.; Pang T. and Zhang X., 2014. Review of Carbon Emission Trading Pilots in China. *Energy & Environment,* 25 (3/4), 527–549.
Environmental Defense Fund and IETA, 2013. South Korea – The World's Carbon Markets: A Case Study Guide to Emissions Trading. https://www.edf.org/sites/default/files/South-Korea-ETS-Case-Study-March-2014.pdf (Accessed 11 December 2016).
EuropeAid, 2010. EU-China CDM Facilitation Project. http://eeas.europa.eu/delegations/china/documents/projects/1_eu-china_cdm_facilitation_project_fiche.pdf (Accessed 9 February 2014).

European Commission, 2012a. Decision of the European Parliament and of the Council Derogating Temporarily from Directive 2003/87/EC of the European Parliament and of the Council Establishing a Scheme for Greenhouse Gas Emission Allowance Trading within the Community. Strasbourg.

European Commission, 2012b. Stopping the Clock of ETS and Aviation Emissions Following Last Week's International Civil Aviation Organisation (ICAO) Council. Edited by DG Clima. Brussels.

European Council, 2002. 2473rd Council Meeting. Environment (9 December). Brussels, European Commission.

European Council, 2003. Directive 2003/87/EC of the European Parliament and of the Council of 13 October 2003. Establishing a Scheme for Greenhouse Gas Emission Allowance Trading Within the Community and Amending Council Directive 96/61/EC. *Official Journal of the European Union* 25 (25 October), 32–48.

Gippner, O., 2014. Framing it Right: China-EU Relations and Patterns of Interaction on Climate Change. *Chinese Journal of Urban and Environmental Studies,* 2 (1), 1–22.

Gippner, O., 2015. *Chinese Climate Policy and the Role of The European Union: A Bureaucratic Politics Approach to Understanding Changing Climate Policy during the Hu-Wen Leadership (2003–2013).* PhD thesis, Department of Political and Social Sciences, Freie Universität Berlin.

Hou Q., 2013. China to Introduce Carbon Tax: Official. Xinhua. http://news.xinhuanet.com/english/china/2013-02/19/c_132178898.htm. (Accessed 14 February 2014).

Lin L., 2013. China to Introduce Carbon Tax Scheme when Inflation Falls. chinadialogue.net https://www.chinadialogue.net/article/show/single/en/6193-China-to-introduce-carbon-tax-scheme-when-inflation-falls (Accessed 14 February 2014).

Parry, I.W.H. and Pizer, W.A., 2007. Emissions Trading versus CO$_2$ Taxes versus Standards. *Resources for the Future: Issue Brief CPF* (5).

Scott, J. and Rajamani, L., 2012. EU Climate Change Unilateralism. *European Journal of International Law,* 23 (2), 469–494. doi: 10.1093/ejil/chs020.

Shin S., 2012. China's Failure of Policy Innovation: The Case of Sulphur Dioxide Emission Trading. *Environmental Politics,* 22 (6), 918–934. doi: 10.1080/09644016.2012.712792.

Tao, J., and D. N. y Mah., 2009. Between Market and State: Dilemmas of Environmental Governance in China's Sulphur Dioxide Emission Trading System. *Environment and Planning C: Government and Policy,* 27 (1), 175–188.

The Climate Group, 2010. Prospects for Carbon Trading in China. http://www.theclimategroup.org/_assets/files/Prospects-for-Carbon-Trading-in-China.pdf (Accessed 9 February 2014).

The Royal Institute of International Affairs, 2007. Changing Climates: Interdependencies on Energy and Climate Security for China and Europe. http://www.chathamhouse.org/sites/default/files/public/Research/Energy,%20Environment%20and%20Development/1107climate.pdf (Accessed 14 February 2014).

Torney, D. and Biedenkopf, K., 2015. Cooperation on Greenhouse Gas Emissions Trading in EU-China Climate Diplomacy. In Reuter, E. and Jing M. (eds.), 2015. *China-EU: Green Cooperation,* Singapore: World Scientific Publishing, 21–38.

Tu, K., and Livingston, L., 2012. Carbon Trade Lessons from the EU. carnegieendowment.org/2012/04/12/carbon-trade-lessons-from-the-eu/a7td (Accessed 12 July 2012).

UK Foreign and Commonwealth Office, 2013. Partners in Low Carbon, High Growth Development https://gov.uk/government/uploads/system/uploads/attachment_data/file/259637/20131119_SPF_case_studies_Publication_ENG.pdf (Accessed 14 February 2014).

Victor, D., 2000. *The Collapse of the Kyoto Protocol and the Struggle to Slow Global Warming.* Princeton: Princeton University Press.

Wang J.; Yan G.; Jiang K.; Liu L.; Yang J.; Ge C., 2009. The Study on China's Carbon Tax Policy to Mitigate Climate Change. *China Environmental Science,* 29 (1), 101–105.

Xinhua, 2011. UN Aviation Body Opposes EU Emission Trading Scheme Extension. Climate Change Infonet. http://en.ccchina.gov.cn/Detail.aspx?newsId=37901&TId=97 (Accessed 9 November 2013).

Xinhua, 2012. Shanghai launches carbon emission rights trading scheme. http://www.china.org.cn/business/2012-08/17/content_26262656.htm (Accessed 14 December 2016).

Yale Environment 360, 2009. Putting a Price on Carbon: An Emissions Cap or a Tax? http://e360.yale.edu/feature/putting_a_price_on_carbon_an_emissions_cap_or_a_tax/2148/. (Accessed 3 November 2013).

Zhang, D.; Karplus V.; Cassisa C. and Zhang X., 2014. Emissions Trading in China: Progress and Prospects. *Energy Policy,* 75, 9–16.

INDEX

Page numbers in *italic* refer to figures. Page numbers in **bold** refer to tables. Page numbers with n after them refer to note numbers.

carbon dioxide (CO$_2$) 61, 85, 265, 266, 268, 282, 297
carbon intensity 6, 87, 99, 100, 107, 274, 281, 282, 293
carbon market 99, 100, 106, 209, 364, 365
carbon sequestration 155
carbon tax 12, 363–74
carbon trading 50, 365, 366; pilots 365; voluntary 365
caterpillar fungus (*Ophiocordyceps sinensis*) 231
CDM *see* Clean Development Mechanism
censorship 54, 249, 251, 253, 259
Centre for Legal Assistance to Pollution Victims (CLAP) 79
certified emission reduction (CER)106
Chai Jing 6, 56, 84, 253
Chang Jiang 75 *see also* Yangtze
Chengdu 55, 201
China Banking Regulatory Commission (CBRC) 212
China Council on International Cooperation and Development (CCICED) 5, 62, 64, 347
China Development Bank 209
China Energy Conservation Certification 355–6
China Energy Conservation Program (CECP) 355
China Environmental Label 12, 355–7
China Environmental United Certification Center (CEC) 355, 357
China Quality Certification Center 255
Chinadialogue (www.chinadialogue.net) 54
Chinese Academy for Environmental Planning 216
Chongqing 104, 182, 183, 197, 253, 258, 292, **295**, 296, 308, 364, **366**
circular economy (CE) 5, 58, 60–1, 346, 347, 352–4
Circular Economy Promotion Law (CEPL) 5, 60–1, 63, 304, 316, 347, 348, 352–4, 360
Clean Development Mechanism (CDM) 106, 130, 270, 275, 367, 368, 369, 373
cleaner production 349–52
Cleaner Production Promotion Law (CPL) 304, 316, 319, 347–9, 354, 360
climate change 2, 3, 6, 29, 41, 50, 58–62, 97–107, 144, 152, 155, 162, 227, 265, 266, 273, 292, 356, 363, 364, 366–7, 369; and air pollution 84–93, 285; energy 273–6, 292; urbanisation 271, 298
Climate Law: draft 101

CO$_2$ 2, 266, 268, 273, 276, 299, 331, 333; emission 2, 10, 84, 85, 100, 102, 106, 108n15, 265–6, 269, 271–2, 276, 281–2, 291, 299, 331–2, 334–45; intensity 271–2; tax 365
coal 6, 9, 58, 71, 83–6; **88**, 90, 93n2, 99–101, 108n2, 108n6, 163, 165, 220n12, 265–9, **267**, 273–4, 276, 281–2, 285, 288, 298, 309, 337, 342; combustion 84; consumption 84, 298; industry 10, 39; washing 86
coal equivalent 309, 336
coal-fired: boiler **88**, 298; power plant 18, 39, 50, 83, 90, 177, 365
Coal Law 21, **21**
COD 42, **75,** 77, 79, 204n1, 331, 333, 335–7, 343
command and control 72, 80, 91, 268, 271, 275; instruments 33; mechanism 91, 106; methods 32; regulation 211
compliance 21, 32, 39, 42, 74, 78, 79, 186, 193, 197, 200, 213, 256, 257, 309, 351, 365, 368; non- 33, 40, 61, 74, 339
composting 307, 310n4
consumer 12, 50, 52, 256, 303, 314, 317, 321, 322, 324, 346, *347*, 354, 355, 358–9; awareness 355; behaviour 317; information 348, 354, 359
contaminated sites 183, **184**, 187, 188
Convention on International Trade in Endangered Species (CITES) 52
Copenhagen Accord 100
corporate social responsibility 214; report 215
cradle-to-cradle 352
Cultural Revolution 19, 83, 132, 150, 251

Dalian 50, 170, **176**, 178, 183, 201, 251, 255, 304, 321
Dazhai 149–50
deforestation 64, 132, 147, 151
Deng Xiaoping 83, 140n3, 150
desertification 7, 18, 64, 116, 144, 151–2, **153**, 156n3, 223, 224, 227
dioxin 11, 170, 189, 309
Disability Adjusted Life Years (DALYs) 167
discarded electrical and electronic devices (DED) 11, 314–25 *see also* e-waste
Dow Jones Sustainability Index 216
dragon-head enterprises 123
drinking water 48, 49, 115, 167, **176**, 177, 228
drought 6, 71, 97, 147, 148, 151–2, 156n1, 225
dryland 7, 144–56; degradation 150–1
dust storm 7, 144, 152, 156n1, 227

For Product Safety Concerns and Information please contact our EU
representative GPSR@taylorandfrancis.com
Taylor & Francis Verlag GmbH, Kaufingerstraße 24, 80331 München, Germany

www.ingramcontent.com/pod-product-compliance
Ingram Content Group UK Ltd.
Pitfield, Milton Keynes, MK11 3LW, UK
UKHW050951280425
457818UK00033B/826